# HOLY ENEMIES

# OF FREEDOM

How Martin Luther Unleashed the Beast of Anti-Semitism

SECOND FULLY REVISED EDITION

A.J. Deus

MISSING ELEMENT
Publications

Holy Enemies of Freedom
How Martin Luther Unleashed the Beast of Anti-Semitism
SECOND FULLY REVISED EDITION
Copyright © 2024 by A.J. Deus

Missing Element books may be ordered through booksellers or by contacting the publisher at www.missingelement.media.

Because of the dynamic nature of the Internet, any web addresses or links contained in this book may have changed since publication and may no longer be valid.

**ISBN: 978-1-9995270-9-9 (paperback)**

Library of Congress Control Number: 2024904316

To future generations…

*My friend, it is not a question of what you know or what you wish to know, but of what you ought to know, what you are obliged to know.*

*— Martin Luther —*

*You wish to know my experiences while disentangling truth lost in the medley of sects and divergencies of thought, and how I have dared to climb from the low levels of traditional belief to the topmost summit of assurance [...]*

*Each sect, it is true, believes itself in possession of the truth and of salvation, 'each party,' as the Qur'an saith, 'rejoices in its own creed;' but as the chief of the apostles, whose word is always truthful, has told us, 'My people will be divided into more than seventy sects, of whom only one will be saved.' This prediction, like all others of the Prophet, must be fulfilled.*

*– Imam Ghazali, twelfth century[1] –*

[1]   Imam Ghazali, *Deliverance from Error and Attachment to the Lord of Might and Majesty*, Introduction (1109), from Charles F. Horne, ed., *The Sacred Books and Early Literature of the East* (Parke, Austin & Lipscomb, 1917) Vol. VI 99 -133.

## Table of Contents

### Introduction: Juden-Sow

Imagine that those speaking against Jews were heroes. Here is what one such man had to say:

*** 

*[The Jews] boast of being the noblest, yes, the only noble people on earth. In comparison with them and in their eyes, we Goyim [non-Jewish] are not human; in fact we hardly deserve to be considered poor worms by them. For we are not of that high and noble blood, lineage, birth, and descent. [...]*

*They live among us, enjoy our shield and protection, they use our country and our highways, our markets and streets. Meanwhile our princes and rulers sit there and snore with mouths hanging open and permit the Jews to take, steal, and rob from their open money bags and treasures whatever they want. [...]*

*Why, their Talmud and their rabbis record that it is no sin for a Jew to kill a Gentile, but it is only a sin for him to kill a brother Israelite. Nor is it a sin for a Jew to break his oath to a Gentile. [...] they cannot treat us too harshly or commit sin against us, for they are the lords of the world and we are their servants, yes, their cattle [...].*

*What shall we Christians do with this rejected and condemned people, the Jews?*

*First, to set fire to their synagogues or schools [...]*

*Second, I advise that their houses also be razed and destroyed. [...]*

*Third, I advise that all their prayer books [...] be taken from them.*

*Fourth, I advise that their rabbis be forbidden to teach henceforth on pain of loss of life and limb [...].*

*Fifth, I advise that safe-conduct on the highways be abolished completely for the Jews. [...]*

*Sixth, I advise that usury be prohibited to them, and that all cash and treasure of silver and gold be taken from them and put aside for safekeeping [...].*

*If they wish to apply Moses' law again, they must first return to the land of Canaan [Israel] [...].*

*Seventh, I recommend putting a flail, an ax, a hoe, a spade, a distaff, or a spindle into the hands of young, strong Jews and Jewesses and letting them earn their bread in the sweat of their brow, as was imposed on the children of Adam.[2] [...] No, one*

---

[2]  This refers to the punishment from God for having eaten from the forbidden tree in Genesis 3:17-3:19 (NIV).

*should toss out these lazy rogues by the seat of their pants.*

*[...] compute with them how much their usury has extorted from us, divide this amicably, but then eject them forever from the country. [...]*
*Therefore, in any case, away with them! [...]*[3]

\*\*\*

Such hate speech is outlawed in many countries today. An exception exists where diatribes like this continue to be tolerated: in places of worship, where sacred texts are being read that are protected by freedom of religion. How do I know? The author is Martin Luther,[4] who was the founding father of the Protestant Reformation, 'the Reformer'.

Even those who are otherwise well acquainted with history might be surprised to find Martin Luther cited in the foundation of Adolf Hitler's anti-Jewish thought framework.[5] In *'Mein Kampf,'* the Führer admired Luther as a great reformer.[6] The rebellious theologian became a role model for Nazis. Long before Hitler was democratically elected, he had published how he would fight against perceived Jewish manipulation of Germany's democracy. Parroting the Reformer, the German leader insisted that Jews were determined to wipe out humanity for their own gain. Hitler was standing with the will of God to fight against them.[7]

The Führer – a monster – thought that he was saving the world from destruction by Jews. Hitler's accusations against them echoed their historic predecessors: Jews engaged in treachery, infiltration, and financial enslavement. He pointed out that Jews had already bankrupted the Bavarians and the Prussians through their financial machinations.[8]

His answer was National Socialism and anti-Semitism.[9]

This reasoning creates an inconvenient bond between the Holocaust, during which six million Jews lost their lives, and the Protestant churches. The Lutheran agenda was for centuries set against Jews and other religious groups.

Hitler mirrored Luther. Luther foreshadowed Hitler.

---

[3] Martin Luther, *On the Jews and their Lies,* part XI (1543), translated by Martin Bertram (Fortress Press & Augsburg Fortress, 1971).

[4] Martin Luther, 10 November 1483 – 18 February 1546.

[5] Johannes Wallmann, The Reception of Luther's Writings on the Jews from the Reformation to the End of the 19th Century, n.s. 1 (Lutheran Quarterly, Spring 1987) 1:72-97.

[6] Adolf Hitler, Mein Kampf, official Nazi translation by James Murphy (Hurst and Blacket, 1939) Chapter VIII.

[7] Ibid.

[8] Ibid., Chapter VII.

[9] Ibid.

Germans did not elect Hitler **despite** his well-known hatred of Jews. With the support of Protestants, they elected him **because** his policy promised their destruction, the same fate fervently preached by their founder and from the pulpits of Protestant churches. It was part of the political package-deal that German Protestants then embraced. Documentary footage of the rise of Hitler shows in chilling brutality how the masses saluted the alienation of their hated Jewish contemporaries. The age-old tactic that the Führer employed was to dehumanize Jews while lifting his nation above all: Germany first.

The German race was to be set above all others.

Hitler had learned from history. Executions of the *public enemy* were conducted in secret. Atrocities took place far away from scrutiny. This was meant to prevent a backlash to the otherwise effective propaganda machinery.

Compassion would have thwarted Hitler's plans. It eventually did.

Since some Western nations are in the process of tearing down safeguards against passions of organized religion, this book embarks in answering a simple question about the Holocaust:

Why?

These accusations echo through the millennia. Meanwhile, nobody appears to be interested in basic questions whether any of this hatred was based on factual historical trauma that might have been inflicted by Jewish leaders.

The reasons for the Holocaust or for hatred of Jews cannot be explained in simple terms, but Martin Luther's era provides valuable insights into the mechanisms at play.

Through the Reformer's soul we can see into the abyss.

In all fairness, Lutheran sects today are typically embarrassed by their founder's anti-Semitic teachings. The living memory of the Holocaust compels them to emphasize a message of charity, peace, and love. This was not always the case, however, and Luther's sermons and books were widely used until the Second World War. Many of them contained anti-Semitic statements, even though they typically relied on the Bible.

They will be used again.

But Luther is not the only culprit.

The Protestant Reformation in the sixteenth century sparked a radical break from the authority of the Catholic papacy in Rome. The tragic legacy of the conflicts between the two churches is 500 years of religious wars that cost millions of lives. In between the fronts, one holocaust after another took place.

Distrust between Catholics, Protestants, and Jews endures today.

The inter-Christian conflicts since Luther's era devastated half the world. They were about differences in religious dogma and rituals that are so minute that they cannot easily be extracted from the Bible, which is almost identical for both Catholics and Protestants. The exceptions are a couple of books that exert negative influence on the economic motivation of Catholics but do not otherwise merit discussion here.

It is little wonder that sectarian wartimes also brought forth a series of civilization-shattering famines and diseases that indiscriminately decimated populations. History has shown that these are part of the devastating collateral damage inflicted on weakened populations. Through the effects of warfare, people succumb to the silent violence of hunger and vermin.

As time progressed, the advancement of humanism and secularism entered the conflicts in an attempt to liberate societies from the grip of organized religion. The churches were then not hesitant to inject their disciples' blood into the struggle for freedom from religion to hold on to their tyrannical rule.

They were enemies of freedom.

The centuries were filled with external conflicts as well, markedly those connected to the madness of missionizing and colonizing distant lands around the world. The human toll is mind-boggling. Savages needed to be enlightened with the teachings of Christ.

Sectarian fights were extended under the guiding hand of missionaries into the new territories in America. In fact, religious violence forms the very foundation of (religious) liberties in the Constitution of the United States.

A geographical demarcation line at the intersection of Muslim and Christian civilizations has moved little in a thousand years. The consequence were never-ending beheadings between disciples of the two great Abrahamic religions. Still today, devout Christians hate Muslims and devout Muslims hate Christians. Jews hate both. Both hate Jews. They view one another as infidels. At least, the two successor-religions have some fundamental differences over problems such as whether Jesus, the founder of Christianity, was a divinity or whether Muhammad, the founder of Islam, can be accepted as a prophet. These issues are earth-shattering. Literally. Only prophets are acceptable as recipients of divine inspiration. And popes. Or supreme imams. Or high priests.

The internal sectarian flexibility was always enormous. The external stubbornness remains without bounds.

The 'other' side can be witnessed today. The fire between Sunnis and Shi'ites in the Middle East has refused to burn out. It may take another few centuries to do that.

What was the role of the Jewish leadership in all this fighting?

To be sure, there are black sheep within every nation and ethnicity. But it is unique that Jews are looked at collectively as some sort of menace. Modern Muslims find it easier to hate them by the existence of the state of Israel alone. In addition, Jews are singled out by the Koran as one of the groups that deserves the deadly wrath of followers of Islam. But, to use one of the politically incorrect stereotypes about Jews, if anything, they are an industrious and intelligent people. Except for extremist Ultra-Orthodox zealots, most of them work hard and strive for social and economic advancement. In particular in America, they are so well integrated that many Jews have to communicate Jewishness to *not* blend in perfectly.

There must be more to it. We will have a close look at the zealous machinations of Ultra-Orthodox Jewry. It is a hotbed of hatred and is a source of some of the worst anti-Semitic tropes – tropes that turn out to be supported by undisputable evidence.

Neither Christians nor Muslims had a nation of Israel to hate before the twentieth century. Or so, we thought. Jews were dispersed and formed their busy minority communities all over the world. Yet, they were often segregated from non-Jewish populations. That created easy targets for hatred. We will open this Pandora's Box.

Could Christians hate Jews for having killed Jesus? The question itself is offensive. Because they did not. Romans did. At least according to the Christian Gospels. Some may have wanted to hang the one Jew responsible for betraying Jesus Christ. However, convicting entire communities collectively for any specific crime is outrageous by any measure. In particular, when it was committed 2,000 years ago.

Further, that one Jew, Judas, was among the first twelve followers of Jesus. Technically, Judas was already a former Jew. Among the first Christians. In addition, the betrayal of Jesus is part of prophecy. Without its fulfillment, there is no salvation – and no Christianity.

The argument is circular. The accusation of having killed Jesus is an expression of already simmering hatred rather than a biblical 'fact-based' rejection of Jews. However, according to the Gospels, Jews acted like a lynch mob, shouting for the crucifixion of Jesus Christ. They proclaimed, *'let his blood be on us and on our children!*[10] This is an expedient escape hatch for extremists. It justifies hatred for all generations to come. In his last writings, Luther made a heart-wrenching remark that the responsibility has come to find them.[11]

History disagrees even with the basics of the alleged murder and the successive crucifixion or resurrection of Jesus Christ. Muslims say that Jesus is still alive, like their Mahdi, their own kind of savior who lives on. The two are just hidden away, waiting for their moment – undead, so to speak. It may be true that Muslims entered the theater of religious history 600 years after Jesus. Yet, they relied on traditions that are just as old as those used by the Catholic Church. Instead, Christianity and Islam pretend to have lived through sharply differing religious world histories, even though both evolved as enemies in the same cultural environment. However, only one can be true.

I know. Yours.

Moreover, Jewish biblical texts form the foundation of Christianity. They are like the cornerstone upon which a house is built. Except for some minor deviations that are irrelevant for the layman, the base is the same. It has worked both ways. Large Jewish groups have embraced Jesus Christ as the Messiah as well as sections of the Christian scripture.[12] The Koran does this as well.

One foundation. Different floors. Same house.

On the other hand, the Bible contains self-portrayals of the Israelites as a hated nation from the moment Hebrews stepped into the biblical story. There must have been deep-seated cultural trauma already at the beginning of this tale. The questions are by whom was it inflicted and why? This self-representation as a reviled group serves as an unfortunate binding mechanism for the Jewish people. It compels them to stick together against everybody else. However, this line of thought has not been advocated for hating Jews.

There is one exception: the argument that the god of the Israelites abandoned the Jews 2,300 years ago. He despised them for their disobedience. This claim is one of the preferred spins for Christian-Jewish animosities that have frequently re-emerged. But again, it rationalizes negative attitudes that were already present. It is not the deeper cause for hating Jews.

---

[10]  Matthew 27:22-27:26 (NIV).
[11]  Martin Luther, Vom Schem Hamphoras and the Lineage of Christ (Wittenberg, 1543) 19.
[12]  In particular The Gospel of Matthew.

To answer this question – why? – I will guide you through Luther's intellectual evolution. I am not going to present a lineup of the usual religious terrorists-turned-folk-heroes – *martyrs*, as they are called in all Judaic sects. In its place, I will put the spotlight on the religious leadership itself.

Martin Luther's story provides insight into a mechanism that has been repeated many times through the ages. It takes place in one of the darkest eras of our past. Accordingly, I discuss the events along the evidence of the historical record.

Considering the difficult topic, one important point needs to be clarified upfront: now as then, every human being is equipped with extraordinary gifts of intellect and reason. No man can exonerate himself from the responsibility of injuring or killing another human being, except for self-defense. Religious madness has nothing to do with defense. The survival of humanity lies in global cooperation, not in the democratization of nuclear weaponry or in religious urges for bloody revenge.

Religious leaders understand the world through the Bible, the Gospels, the Koran, or whichever scripture or role models they follow. Therefore, we need to get into their heads. In order to drill down to the heart of religious hatred and violence against Jews, we will need to look at scripture itself.

It provides a looking glass into the future.

In educating ourselves about the sources of anti-Semitism, moderns need to understand the essence of the underlying beliefs as understood in Luther's time. The evidence leaves no room to overlook his calls to violence and to robbing his followers of all their freedoms.

While this book investigates Luther's path to anti-Semitism, the contemporary interactions between leaders of organized religions and their sects and also with nobility are made visible. Through this contextual mutual involvement, the causes of anti-Semitism and other religious hatred surface in unprecedented ways. Without full understanding, humanity is unable to recognize that yet another holocaust is approaching.

We remain incapacitated to prevent the next wave of religious terrorists.

The three Judaic religions present themselves in the public eye as being peaceful, loving, reconciliatory, and charitable. It may be viewed as unfair to single out religious violence over political brutalities. Indeed, the world has plenty of poke marks from fatal political events that were frequently self-inflicted. They were a factor even before the first signs of Judaism. However, there is a crucial difference between political follies and religious passions.

The former are temporary and typically heal within a couple of generations, even though some of these have risen to near-religious creeds.

As a contrast to organized religions, the atrocities committed by Stalin's atheist communist regime in Russia are just one of countless examples of grandiose leadership gone rogue. However, Communism also resembles a quasi-religion with an indoctrinated, faithful following. Nationalism falls into the same class. We need only consult a map that depicts income levels to realize that there is a relationship between religiosity and systemic poverty. The correlation to economic and intellectual mass poverty – one of the most effective forms of religious and quasi-religious violence – in South America, Africa, Asia, as well as the Middle East is obvious to the naked eye.

Communist China, I need to emphasize in this context, has grown richer not through its own success, but rather with the help of a worldwide development effort through free trade. This concerted effort of humanity has been hugely successful, brought over a billion people out of extreme poverty, and constitutes the modern foundation of global welfare. Now, ignorant leaders have forgotten how we got here and lash back at our planet's most significant peaceful achievement in history instead of eliminating loopholes of abuse and sending aggressors back into the dark age.

The difference with violence through organized religion is its longevity and its permanent hierarchy that continues to subvert the internal bond and peace of entire civilizations. Christianity has been in charge since the fall of the Roman Empire; Islam since the fall of the Persian Empire. Unless humans understand its causes and effects, religious violence will bring suffering to generations for thousands of years into the future, as it has for thousands of years in the past. Not a single century has gone by without atrocities by any of the three Judaic religions that have been orchestrated from the highest authorities, despite their claims to the contrary. Once their deadly long-term gameplan is transparently understood, they might be able to focus on their positive characteristics and leave aspirations to power at all costs behind.

In Luther's story, we will see how religious leaders pulled the strings, notwithstanding attempts to attribute all responsibility to the political class. That class was installed and controlled by the religious leadership. Non-conformists were habitually terminated.

In the spotlight, the shadows of spiritual leaders' crimes are long enough for us to recognize the gravity of the disease: Without checks and balances, man relies on faith and force alone.

Indeed, minute details in creeds about matters beyond the understanding of ordinary people have created the religious division between East and West today. Can you tell the difference in how Islam views Jesus compared to Christianity? If you can explain how the two religions relate the Word of God to Jesus' humanity, you might count yourself among experts. The point is that no person in their right mind goes about killing other people over such issues as whether the divinity of its leaders rests on a spirit or on the leader itself. Instead, the divination of emperors, kings, or religious bosses was customary throughout history. Even though we see bloodshed over changes in royal succession, it is hardly conceivable that the choice of their oppressor, or the question of divination could have been taken by common folks of the past as a justification for ramming pitchforks into their neighbors' chests.

There were ringleaders who stood behind the scenes without getting blood on their hands.

These guiding hands are at the center of our interest in answering this most pressing question of our time – why?

There is a tangible difference between secular and religious violence. Indeed, quite frequently, secular violence has found its roots in holding back religious aggression. In its very core, the secular fight for freedom is a fight against the tyrannies of organized religion and despots. The enjoyment of religious freedoms is the happy consequence for the faithful.

It is self-evident and confirmed by a large body of data that secular social organization has outdone theocracies in wisdom, welfare, social advancement, and wealth – if we manage to continue nurturing the delicate balance needed to maintain this success.

In contrast, systemic intellectual and economic poverty was the norm for social organization under the yoke of religion for thousands of years. For eternity, they have been praying for the destruction of the entire world to bring about a religious renewal. Those who disagree will need to wait just a few pages more until the evidence starts pouring in.

Some will criticize the approach here as an oversimplification of complex issues and will claim that it jeopardizes peace efforts. Quite the contrary. It is a matter of perspective: addressing the issue head-on through the leadership renders the complexities rather clear and straightforward. The bosses are in command. There is no excuse for the originators of the violence.

As a researcher, it may help that I have been taught in a Franciscan Catholic convent.[13] Admittedly, I may have been an apocalyptic nightmare for the Capuchin monks. Why? Why, and why again.

This Franciscan monastic order was established in Luther's time. Originally, Capuchins were not allowed to touch money, had to live in extreme austerity and survive exclusively from begging. They were to go bare-footed and to preach among the underprivileged.

They missionized poverty upon the poor!

The vast majority of religious people and of those free from religion on this planet are repulsed by violence. I will demonstrate that the peaceful majority is irrelevant. The commands for the feet to march come from the head.

A cautious approach is sought out here for the scriptural foundations. The educated reader must refuse to either selectively look the other way or to see something where there is nothing.

The bone holds plenty of beef for common men to get a taste of the juice.

The topic is uncomfortable and bears the risk of attracting hatred from every direction. But not to have an honest conversation about this defining problem of humanity is disingenuous, even self-destructive.

In organized religion, only *one* Truth can be true. There cannot be a competition in Truths or compromises with half the Truth. The one who owns the Truth must defend *against* all untruths and not cooperate *with* these untruths. After all, only the religious disciples with the *correct* Truth will find *salvation*.

Organized religion did not spread because of silent prayer. Inter-sectarian violence acted as the billboards of the time, forcing otherwise peaceful populations to take sides. Usually, leaders would make those decisions for entire communities.

Martin Luther had this to say:

> For there are other beliefs which the world calls faith. The Jews, the Turks [Muslims], the Papists [Catholics], claim they also believe in God who created heaven and earth. That such belief is not the true faith, however, is proved by the fact of its ineffectiveness. It does not contend and overcome, and it permits the believer to remain as he is, in his natural birth and under the power of the devil and sin.
>
> But the faith which believes Jesus is the Son of God is the true, triumphant sort. It

---

*is an invincible power wrought in the hearts of Christians by the Holy Spirit. It is a sure knowledge that does not gaze and vacillate hither and thither according to its own thoughts. It apprehends God in Christ the Son sent from heaven, through whom God reveals his will and his love and transfers us from sin to grace, from death to a new and eternal life; a refuge and trust that relies not upon its own merit or worthiness, but upon Christ the Son of God, and in his might and power battles against the world and the devil. Therefore, the Christian faith is not the cold, ineffective, empty, lifeless conception which Papists and others imagine it to be; no, it is a living, active power, ever followed by victories and other appropriate fruits. Where such fruits are lacking, faith and the new birth are not there.*[14]

Luther agrees – except when it concerns his own Truth. Call to mind, when Luther wrote this, he represented a new 'religion,' one that had just broken away from the Catholic Church. His words are particularly troublesome, because the experts who could tell how the Word of God relates to Jesus in Islam and in Christianity are now in trouble: how on earth does the Protestant Church preach the Truth about the Son of God while the Catholic Church does not? The same claims about the Truth can be found in the scriptures of both, Jews and Muslims. These are just different Truths.

Each of them is worth dying for?

A quick note to diligent students is opportune: No artificial intelligence has been deployed anywhere in the research and creation process of this book. It is perhaps one of the last such works that rely entirely on the limited intellect of human beings. Since artificial intelligence relies on quantity, the window of opportunity to find underlying causes to the historic progression may very well soon close, and the narrative of tradition may become eternally petrified through the overwhelming power of this technology.

The narrative is simplified for popular language and reduced to the most important events. *Primary* evidence constitutes the guiding principle of this book's storyline. There is plenty to talk about where there is no dispute, and where there is, I will make the reader aware of it. This second edition is much more advanced with *facts* that have been found and incorporated since the first edition was published. While the big picture has become clear, students need to take particular care when quoting non-consensus material.

Do not turn a rock if you fear snakes hiding underneath.

---

[14]   Martin Luther, Sermons, Sunday After Easter, ca. 1536, translated by John Nicholas Lenker.

Deep historical discoveries are dependent on sound methodology. First, post-apocalyptic prophecy offers insights into our past and future. Second, a string of messiahs or saviors in their historical context reveals biblical patterns. Third, only leadership and power structures matter. Individuals and beliefs are mere tools for power. Fourth, it is better to be proven wrong in assuming deception than to fall for one. This includes our own historical environment. Now that we have that sorted out, lastly, sticking as hard as possible to properly vetted and *contemporary* primary evidence.

My preference is to always provide in-page primary evidence in the footnotes. However, the tremendous number of sources and their associated copyright costs would render this book unattainable.

When it comes to history as well as many other issues of life, final truths have come too easy. Any finding must remain subject to continued scrutiny, criticism, and evolution. Evidence, opinions, and judgement in any one issue remain in flux, including what is laid out in this book.

The Catholic Church, the Protestant Church, and Islam were masterfully persecuting Jews. It is impossible to investigate the root-causes of anti-Semitism without these religious organizations coming under the wheels of inconvenient evidence or without making errors. Focus on the big picture, not on petty details.

By all means, I appreciate issues being addressed with me.

History is not what we wish it to be. It is what it is.

For future students embarking on a journey into the depths of any historical era, I recommend beginning with the original (!) text of Benjamin of Tudela's eye-opening account of Baghdad. By comprehending the power structures at play, one gains fresh insights into our collective past. For those who harbor doubts about the narrative presented here, I encourage them to set this book aside momentarily, delve into Tudela's passage, and then seamlessly continue their exploration of this saga.[15]

I have no qualm with any believer and ask those with religious sensitivities to keep this in mind.

I ask for tolerance for my intolerance of intolerance.

Now, we embark on finding answers.

Why?

---

[15] The passage and its consequences are summarized in the chapter The Iron Rod on pages 178-180.

# I: COMPASSION

### *In the Ghetto*

1492.

After Ottoman-Turkish Muslims conquered Constantinople,[16] modern day Istanbul, the traditional transportation route for goods through the Silk Road to Europe became too dangerous. In the quest to find an alternative trade route from Europe to India and China, a potential course around the Cape of Good Hope of South Africa was found by the Portuguese.

Based on a proposal by an astronomer[17] from the Italian city-state of Florence, Christopher Columbus and his brother were determined to attempt a crossing of the Atlantic Ocean to reach the Indies. But because Portuguese authorities thought that sailing around Africa might be easier, they rejected the brothers' ambitions. Neither England nor the Italian city-states of Genoa and Venice showed interest. A feasibility study by the Catholic Monarchs of Spain[18] concluded that the Columbus brothers significantly underestimated the distance to the Indies and advised against supporting such an exploration.

The breakthrough for Columbus came in April 1492. Against the opposition of the top functionary of the Catholic Church in Spain, Christoph Columbus finally received the blessing of the Spanish monarchs to prepare for his journey from Spain across the Atlantic Ocean.

One man – stubborn beyond the reason of conformity – would come to beat all odds that were stacked against him. This one man's perseverance to achieve the impossible, as thumbed down by learned men of the time, marks the dawn of unbelievable discoveries on unknown continents that brought new opportunities to European white Christian men. His errors in sound judgement, his underestimation of risks, or his willingness to lose his life did not matter. The accomplishment of his vision would come to speak for itself, even though he missed it by the margin of a full continent plus another ocean. An era of exploration began that led to the migration of streams of white settlers into the American continents. An escape route for religiously persecuted families

---

[16]    The conquest of Constantinople was conducted by Mehmed II in 1453, commonly known as Mehmed the Conqueror, ruler of the Ottoman Empire 1444 – 1446 and 1451 – 1481.

[17]    Paolo dal Pozzo Toscanelli, 1397 – 1482, was an astronomer who presented his idea to the Portuguese King Alfonso V in 1474 that ships could sail westwards to reach the Indies.

[18]    Isabella I of Castile and Ferdinand II of Aragon. Isabella I was Queen of Castile 1474 – 1504. Ferdinand II of Aragon was King of Castile and Léon 1475 – 1504 and King of Aragon 1479 – 1516.

opened. At the same time, a road to hell for non-white people was paved. The period symbolizes the seed of the free world and the establishment of the United States of America, the land of the free.

It did not come easy.

A month before entering into an agreement with Columbus, the Catholic monarchs of Spain issued the Alhambra Decree, ordering the expulsion of all practicing Jews from Spain within four months. Jews in Spain had previously prospered for centuries under Muslim rulers. However, with the re-conquest of the Iberian Peninsula (the Spanish Reconquista) under the leadership of the Catholic Church, forced conversions became the norm. Involuntarily converted Jews were known by the demeaning term *Marranos* – literally *sows* – and force-converted Muslims were called *Alpujarras* after their core region. The decree accused Jews of subverting the Catholic Church with covert Jewish practices and of attempting to convert Marranos back to Judaism.[19] Now that the Spanish Reconquista came to a close, Jews were given three choices: convert to Christianity with conviction, leave, or face *'summary execution.'*[20]

Saying it like that sounds almost as though nothing else should be expected from the Catholic Church other than getting rid of all Jews who refused to convert. Our judgment needs to patiently wait for the evidence.

As for Martin Luther's path to radical anti-Semitism, it was a pan-European practice of the Catholic Church to collectively dehumanize Jews and to brand them as sows. Anti-Semitism was part of the cultural Zeitgeist, which was under the control of the Catholic Church.

The man behind the decree was the Catholic Cardinal Cisneros.[21] Cardinals are the second highest ranked officials in the Catholic Church, second only to the pope. Their assembly, the College of Cardinals, primarily elects the pope from its own ranks and advises him in all matters of church business.

At this time, Cisneros was not yet a cardinal. But the barbaric Alhambra Decree followed immediately after he became the Spanish Queen's Catholic confessor.[22] This was the religious *'counselor'* in state and private affairs to the queen – the man who pulled the strings of royal puppets.

At the time, the Vatican retained the sole right to nominate royals.

---

[19]  Isabella I of Castile and Ferdinand II of Aragon, Alhambra Decree, March 31, 1492.

[20]  Ibid.

[21]  Francisco Jiménez de Cisneros, 1436 – 1517, became Cardinal and Grand Inquisitor for Castile and León in 1507.

[22]  Daniel Eisenberg, Cisneros y la quema de los manuscritos granadinos (Journal of Hispanic Philology, 16, 1992) 107-124.

The Catholic Church was in control of the culture, including its anti-Semitism.

With this power behind him, Cisneros arranged the royal marriage in Spain between Isabella of Castile and Ferdinand of Aragon.

His predecessor had also been confessor to the queen. This was the Grand Inquisitor Tomás de Torquemada[23] – the hammer of heretics – whose family appears to have been Jewish *conversos*. Torquemada was a radical zealot who managed the growth of the Spanish Inquisition from one tribunal to an entire network of 'Holy Offices.' Inquisitors were part of the religious police that had been deployed by the Catholic Church all over Europe to persecute crimes of thought and imagination – heresies, which deviated from the ideas that the Catholic Church approved of. The role of inquisitors can be envisioned today by looking at the religious police in Saudi Arabia, only much worse. It was state sponsored terrorism by the Papal States of the Catholic Church. Under Torquemada's direction, Spain was to be cleansed of all heresy. This targeted Muslims, Jews, and non-Catholic Christians.

He was the boss of the Spanish Inquisition when a twelve-year-old daughter of a shoemaker, Ines of Herrera, was burned for announcing Elijah as the forerunner of the Jewish Messiah.

According to the court records of the Inquisition, she announced that the Jews would return to the Promised Land. There, they would find all they needed.[24] The souls of those who had been burned by Torquemada were now living there in abundance and glory.[25] The 'clarity' – the Holy Spirit – started to reveal visions to her in the fall of 1499, and she was arrested by the Inquisition in the coming spring.

Similar stories occurred in Chillon, about 100 miles north of Herrera, and Valencia, further to the north-east. In Chillon, a peasant girl by the name of Maria made trips to heaven, announcing that the conversos should return to Judaism to be carried off to the Promised Land. In Valencia, one Miguel Vives was himself reincarnated as Moses.[26]

---

23   Tomás de Torquemada, 1420 – 1498
24   Mary E. Giles, ed. Women in the Inquisition: Spain and the New World (JHU Press, Copyright © 1998, reprinted with permission of Johns Hopkins University Press) 143, 46-50.
25   John E. Longhurst, Luther's Ghost in Spain (1517 – 1546) (Coronado Press, 1964) 86.
26   Ibid., 87-88.

Jews had gone undercover, keeping the knowledge of the Talmud alive in the remotest regions of Spain. This was evidenced in the thorough biblical knowledge that was apparent in Ines' prophecies.[27] Even today, the Talmud continues to be the primary source of Jewish learning.

Previously force-converted Jews believed that their redemption would begin on March 9, 1500. That day, *'the conversos will leave behind all their businesses [and their jewelry], and the old Christians will quarrel and kill each other in the fight to possess them.*[28] The superstitious looked for heavenly signs – a comet, for example – that are typically associated with messianic hopes.

Many children of conversos joined the movement,[29] playing, singing, and dancing.[30] Indeed, passive aggression can include playing, singing, and dancing. Some of them had been led to believe that a deceased parent or someone close to them would rise from the dead if they fasted. And fast they did.

Girls as young as nine or ten were tried by the Inquisition for having followed Ines' lead. Many were handed over to a faithful Christian family for reeducation. That was the best case. The idea was to brainwash the brainwashed. In the worst case, children, girls and boys, were sentenced to life in prison or to be burned at the stake. At Herrera, Chillon, and Valencia, the Inquisition put an efficient end to it all.

This Torquemada had no moral compass.

This is the reward for parents when they raise fundamentalist children: they never make it out of imaginary role plays. The father of Ines of Herrera had managed the silly scheme. He should have been tried for child abuse and conspiracy in his daughter's assassination.

These children were dangerous, all right, brought up to become the terrorists of their time – or perhaps freedom fighters, freedom dancers, perhaps.

Ines' father had no moral compass.

As Grand Inquisitor, Torquemada was the national leader of an army of exterminators. Soon thereafter, Cisneros became Grand Inquisitor himself. He was now the boss of Catholic thought control.

Just wait for what was in store from this barbarian.

---

[27] Giles, 1999, 46 and 48.
[28] Ibid., 48.
[29] Ibid., 49.
[30] Ibid., 50.

Also involved in the engineering of the royal wedding was the Sephardi Jew, Rabbi Abraham Senior,[31] a banker and member of the most important tax farming dynasty for the Crown of Castile. Tax farming was widely used in feudal Europe and in the Ottoman Empire of Martin Luther's time. The idea of the Catholic Church was to stabilize revenue streams in the absence of a bureaucracy – illiterate as Christians were. They leased out entire provinces to individuals who then raked in tremendous profits by extorting taxes from the population by the principle of whim. That was not Senior's only source for cash flow. He also supplied provisions to the royal army. He was a weapons dealer. And he was treasurer of the Holy Brotherhood, a militia that policed the towns under its influence. It ensured that the income streams continued flowing.

This man had his bed made.

Senior was also the chief rabbi of Castile – the crown rabbi.

We will learn more about this function of the crown rabbi. For now, we can compare him with the role of a prime minister in a royal governmental organization. One with dictatorial powers.

In his function as crown rabbi, he was involved in the permission for Christoph Columbus' voyage. One of Senior's sons[32] appears to have been aboard Columbus' second voyage.

This son would become Constable of the Indies.

Rabbi Senior chose to convert to Catholicism upon the execution of the Alhambra Decree. He retained his privileges with a new, Catholic identity, chosen after his godfather (!), King Ferdinand, himself of marrano heritage.[33] Senior morphed from the loftiest Jewish ranks to Spanish Catholic nobility.

Jewish royalty in Spain?

That is easy to answer with a question: in a sea of illiteracy, Jews were the only group that was not only highly educated but globally organized in a tight-knit and loyal network, the Diaspora. How could there not be Jewish royalty anywhere this feudal system of oppression was in place?

Senior was transfused from officially being of the blood of sows to blue blood. His Catholic name was now Coronel.

---

[31] Rabbi Abraham Seneor, aka Senior, 1412 – 1493. He converted to Catholicism in 1492 and was renamed to Ferran, Fernan, or Fernando Perez Coronel, aka Fernando Coronel Nunez or Perez Nunez Coronel. Coronel had been an extinct noble lineage.

[32] Pedro Fernandez Coronel.

[33] Eliyahu ben Elqana Capsali (c1490-c1555), Seder Eliyahu Zuta (Hebrew University, Jerusalem, 1975) Chapter 58 in volume I, p. 182-184.

His 'house' in Segovia tells a jaw-dropping story of income inequality and of the immense riches that could be amassed through tax farming and profiteering from every business activity under the sun. While Christians were commanded to live in intellectual and economical poverty and serfdom, emperors would have felt right at home in the neo-noble's not-so-humble dwelling.

The forced conversions of Jews amounted to a massive brain gain for the otherwise uneducated Christians. Without being able to read, write, or compute, the latter were largely unable to manage the financial affairs of a tax farming operation. At the same time, Christianity invited itself to be subverted through this process.

Jews were – and still are – a religiously and economically ambitious people. It may have been their intention to continue their ritual adherence in secret. Who could blame them? Since there was no freedom of conscience under the yoke of the Catholic Church, they were repeatedly charged for doing so and were dragged in front of the Inquisition's courts for religious show trials.

And convicted to burn at the stake.

Many conversos ended up in top positions in the Catholic Church. Even in the ranks of the Inquisition. For example, Senior's brother was secretary to none other than Cardinal Cisneros, the Grand Inquisitor. This makes no sense for someone who was just force-converted. Perhaps we are dealing here with ulterior motives. I lack the understanding how the persecuted could have turned into the persecutor. The simple answer may be that there was just too much money at stake for a tax farmer to stick with the 'wrong' religion. But why become killers? For show? Or were they indifferent to those against whom the habitual killings were carried out? Was it perhaps shameless vanity? Were they already killers before their conversion in the name of extorting taxes?

Staying close to the winners at the time – the Inquisition – was probably an economically shrewd choice. I would not be surprised to find Jewish converts on the throne of the papacy in Rome or on more thrones of European royalty than just in Spain. Advances in genetics will bring about a sea-change in our understanding of how Jewish and Muslim brain-gain penetrated Europe's elite.

Rabbi Abraham Senior had a close friend:  Isaac Abrabanel,[34] an even more important Jew.

---

[34]  Isaac ben Judah Abrabanel, aka Abravanel, Abarbanel, Avravanel, Barbernell, or Barbanel, 1437–1508.

His name alone bears a heavy burden. It literally means high priest of God: 'Ab' (father); 'Rabban' (priest); 'El' (of God). This renders him among the highest Babylonian Rabbinic authorities. His family identified itself as direct successors of King David. This is the royal originator of the tribe that is believed to be entitled to bring forth a messiah, the savior who is to come to snatch Israel from its owners.

In the late thirteenth century, one of Abrabanel's ancestors[35] had become a treasurer and tax farmer for the Spanish crown of Castille. In his role as top rabbi, he also financed wars.[36] He eventually fled to Portugal and 'reverted back' to Judaism. In his absence, Abrabanel's family retained high positions in Spain. One was royal treasurer in Andalusia and later comptroller in Castille.[37]

Like Senior who had turned into Coronel, Abrabanel was among those who were in charge of raising tax revenues for Portugal and the Catholic Church. Similar to his ancestor, he had risen into this position through the rewards of financing wars. This Jewish career in high finance was not the exception. It was repeated throughout European history and territories.[38]

Indeed, for hundreds of years, every Christian and Muslim community in the Iberian Peninsula was managed by an 'arrabi'. That was a Jewish functionary of the crown. An outpost of royal authority.[39] These 'arrabis' oversaw the royal administration. And the courthouses. And tax collection. And trade. Banking. Distinct from spiritual rabbis, the crown rabbi presided over the 'arrabis' and sat at the table of kings, almost like a parallel throne. He reported to the king and oversaw the kingdom's audits of their own corruption![40] Such positions over subservient populations are attested for centuries in Castile, Aragon, and Navarre. We are told that this was rare during the Golden Age of Jewish Culture in Spain. It was the norm. We find one Samuel ibn Naghrillah, the Prince, tax

---

[35] Don Judah Abravanel was treasurer and tax collector for King Sancho IV of Castile (1284–95) and King Ferdinand IV of Castile (1295–1312).

[36] The siege of Algeciras.

[37] Samuel of Seville aka Juan Sánchez (de Sevilla).

[38] For example Yahia Ben Yahi III – the Nasi – aka Jahia Negro Ibn Ya'isch, Yahya Ha-Nasi, Yahya Ibn Yaish or Dom Yahia 'o Negro', died 1185. King Afonso I of Portugal made Yahia Ben Yahi III tax collector and confirmed him as the first Chief-Rabbi of Portugal. His grandson, Joseph Ben Yahia, aka Jose Ibn-Yahya, still profited from this position.
Another example is the Benveniste family tree, also with the title Nasi. They first appeared in the French city of Narbonne in the eleventh century. They would be found as tax farmers in the Provence, France, Barcelona, Aragon, and Castile.

[39] Jonathan Ray, Jewish Communal Organization and Authority, The Sephardic Frontier: The Reconquista and the Jewish Community in Medieval Iberia (Cornell University Press, 2006) 124–128.

[40] Cardozo de Bethencourt, J Leite de Vasconcellos (ed.), Inscriptions Hébraïques du Portugal [Hebrew Inscriptions of Portugal] (Museu Ethnográphico Português, 1903) 8 (2): 37.

collector and vizier of Granada's ruler. And elsewhere. Portugal followed their model of punitive administration by Jewish overlords.

Where else was this in play?

We can find it at various times in France and Germany as well. Even in the provinces of the early Roman Empire and beyond into deep history. Above all, the latest research demonstrates that handing Jewish leaders and their functionaries an all-encompassing monopoly over the Islamic administration was the standard form of state organization for hundreds of years since the beginnings of Islam.[41] I will share more details about it as the story progresses.

Saying that the riches of these high-flyers provoked considerable resentment by those at the bottom of the food chain would be putting it prudently. The injustice was obvious in particular for the illiterate and penniless, meaning the entire population with the exception of the top one percent of the noble strata.

Can you understand that the Jewish administrative system would sooner or later be overthrown?

Abrabanel was not only the successor to David – the king of the world in waiting – but also the treasurer of the King of Portugal.

This was an important man; so important, indeed, that he had to flee from Portugal to Toledo in Spain when the Portuguese King died. His co-conspirator was executed. In his new home of his ancestors in Spain, he rose to again become a tax farmer for Queen Isabella of Castile. Together with Rabbi Abraham Senior, he also was supplier of provisions for the royal army. Another arms dealer. He helped to send Columbus abroad.

Abrabanel, had three sons: Samuel, Joseph, and Judah Abrabanel Leone Ebreo – the Hebrew Lion. The latter happened to become the personal doctor of the royal family.

How did his clan and Senior's become so intermingled with Portuguese and Spanish royalty?

Christian or Muslim subjects glorify poverty, obey the priesthood, and do not lend money against interest. Less than one percent could read or write.

This is not so with Judaism.

With universal literacy, the learned Jewish minority was sought after for the upper echelons on the courts of kings, emperors, and popes.

Isaac Abrabanel chose not to convert.

---

[41]  A.J. Deus, *Iran's Poisoned Qibla Arrows* (2024) available at academia.edu.

In the wake of the Alhambra Decree, he and his family had to flee for Naples, Italy, where Jews still found protection for a short period. There, again, he became a 'financial advisor' to the King of Naples. When this royal family had to flee to Messina in Sicily, Abrabanel was among them.

Given the loss of Abrabanel's and the Jewish people's homes and easy fortunes, it is little wonder that he advocated the Coming of the Jewish Messiah. His messianic works incorporated Christian interpretations and were consequently widely used in Jewish and Christian scholarship alike. The books focused mainly on salvation, meaning the redemption of Israel, and the return of the Jewish people to Jerusalem. When this time came, the dead would be resurrected, the Temple would be rebuilt, and God would again sanctify the people of Israel, Abrabanel predicted, meaning putting them back above all others. Finally, the entire world would come to accept Judaism under the rule of a king of the Jews. He prophesied the arrival of the Messiah in the year 5263 AM (Anno Mundi, calculated from God's Creation of the universe). The Messianic Age was to commence with the fall of Rome, which he predicted to occur in 1531,[42] a year chosen not by chance but by the anticipated passing of Halley's Comet.

It appears as though Abrabanel predicted himself as the Messiah, the King of the Jews.

It would not be difficult for Christians to understand this his prophecies as an intention by Jews to subvert Rome and to bring about its collapse. That Christians would take a violent stand against such provocation could be expected. On the other hand, Jews could not have understood the prediction in any other way than being obliged to subvert Rome politically and economically.

Without Rome's fall, the Messianic Age could not begin.

After short stays in Greece and southern Italy,[43] Abrabanel finally settled in Venice in 1503, which happened to fall together with the prophecy of the arrival of the Messiah in the year 5263 AM. There, he made a name of himself as a negotiator for a commercial treaty between Venice and Portugal. He would die in Venice five years later.

Before we engage in compassion about this man's endless flight from place to place, we should review the evidence as it rolls in. If this is a messiah, then the function of this rabbi is one of deception. This man is literally the Deceiver. To deceive us is his and his successor buddies' job.

---

[42]   Julius H. Greenstone, The Messiah Idea in Jewish History (Jewish Publication Society, 1906) 189.
[43]   Corfu and Monopoli.

He was not fleeing. He was forming a global alliance against Christianity.

The only thing between him and success was death.

Abrabanel's burial place in Padua was next to Mahari Minz.[44] The latter died in the same year. His full name was Judah ben Eliezer ha-Levi Minz, a German immigrant and then the most prominent Italian rabbi. His name identifies him as the leader of the Palestinian Rabbinic creed. These two were members of a Sanhedrin substitute, which was a council with the authority to approve messianic missions. These men were among a few select who were holding command over the worldwide Jewry. One of his granddaughters would come to be known as a descendant of King David.[45]

We will hear more about Abrabanel shortly.

I need to come back to the Grand Inquisitor Cardinal Cisneros for just a moment longer.

Legend has it that this guy was such a radical ascetic that he doubled his fasts and slept on the bare floor of his cell in the convent. Nevertheless, he would become regent of Spain – twice – a position that was second in command after the king.

He was the man of Catholic royalty standing behind the veil.

This is the same position that was before held by the crown rabbi whose brother was now Cisneros' secretary.

This cocktail may be difficult to grasp: the messianic spirit must rise from Abrabanel's tomb to descend onto his firstborn. His brother was likely already secretary of the second in command (crown rabbi Abrabanel), and he simply continued his job under Cisnero. Better yet, one from the Jewish messianic linage sat at Cardinal Cisnero's dinner table.

A few years after the Alhambra Decree, the grand Cisneros commanded the Franciscan Order's members to become celibate. As a consequence of his enforcement, 400 monks and friars fled with their concubines to Africa and converted to Islam.

I will discuss the issue of celibacy a little later. For now, let us understand it as a concept that rests on the misogynist idea that any contact with women defiles men and deprives them of salvation. This is why monks did not marry.

---

[44] Judah ben Eliezer ha-Levi Minz, ca. 1405 – 1508.
[45] Albert Montefiore Hyamson, A History of the Jews in England (1908) 182.

Regardless of the imagined consequences, they had plenty of sex with their concubines, partners out of wedlock. However, for most of these monks, we do not need to imagine a whorehouse with revolving doors. Because marriage was not allowed for monks, they formed their relationships outside of the bond of Catholic Canon Law. They were similar to modern common law couples. But there were others, those who would turn into sexual predators. And they would not fail to make it into the news of the historical record.

Cisneros also guided the brutal suppression of the First Rebellion of the Alpujarras. It arose after he ordered forced mass conversions of Granada's Muslims and the burning of all their Arabic manuscripts.[46] He had overruled a less violent approach to conversion by the archbishop in charge.[47] The latter was dragged before the court of Cisneros' Inquisition for having been the bastard son of a Jewess.

After Cisneros was through with applying his style of conversion, in his own words, there were no longer non-Christians left in the city of Granada and all mosques were converted to churches.[48] This cardinal in the top rank of the Catholic Church was out of control. We can feel the pride that the cardinal expressed for having conducted a successful ethnic cleansing operation. Such over-confidence can typically be found in extremists of faith who believe that they are doing the 'right thing' in the name of God. The people of Granada could choose to convert, to leave, or to die. What Cisneros unleashed was just another holocaust among many.

Sent by the Vatican in Rome,[49] this man was a terminator. Could the pope in Rome have stopped Cisneros? Of course.

He did not.

It was not an accident that Cisneros arrived in this position. He was a born inquisitor. In his early twenties, he became an advocate for the Catholic Church in the Vatican. There, his inquisitorial successes already attracted the attention of the pope so much that he was sent back to Spain with a papal *benefice*. This is an endowment of a territory to those who ensure submission to the Catholic Church and transfer the church revenues to the Vatican.

---

[46]  Eisenberg, 1992, 107-124.
[47]  Archbishop of Granada Hernando de Talavera, 1428 – 1507, was a monk of the Order of Saint Jerome.
[48]  Cardinal Cisneros in William Hughes, Western Civilization: The Earliest Civilization Through the Reformation (McGraw-Hill, 1993) 152.
[49]  Pope Innocent VIII, 1484 – 1492, Pope Alexander VI, 1492 – 1503, Pope Pius III, 1503, and Pope Julius II, 1503 – 1513.

So, like Abrabanel, Cisneros was a tax farmer? Both in Toledo? We do not have the evidence, but Abrabanel's flight and demise appear legendary. So are Cisneros' 'humble' beginnings. How did he get through law school at a time when 99% of Christians were illiterate? Did Abrabanel convert to become Cisneros just like Senior became Coronel?

For now, I have nothing to go by, but we better be on high alert. A deceiver is roaming the landscape.

Nevertheless, Cisneros provides us with insight how crown rabbis and their arrabi hordes would have treated the populations under their feet.

Holders of benefices were typically also the military rulers of their areas. These people were called *nobles*. In the realm of the Catholic Church, the feudal system was in total control over Europe's land holdings. So was the creation and confirmation of nobles. Or dragging them to the scaffold.

Cisneros' mission was to cure souls for money. Souls who needed the cure were not in line with the official doctrines and beliefs of the Catholic Church. Jews and Muslims were first in his line of fire. But also Christians of competing sects. A cut from the cash flow was for himself. He was set for life. Everybody else was stuck in dung – and dependent on Cisneros' *charity*, as they called the breadcrumbs that were thrown back at the cheated population – those who survived the ordeal.

This guy was a radical thoroughbred, trained and deployed by the pope of the Catholic Church – who must have failed to order a background check on this psychopath.

History is full of irony, and this is one of these incredible coincidences. Cisneros' deadline for Jews to leave or die fell within one week of Columbus' first voyage. The start of the journey that would lead to one of humanity's greatest accomplishments fell together with one of man's darkest hours.

Jews were forced to depart penniless, prohibited from bringing *'gold or silver or minted money'* [50] on their journey to nowhere. It would take Spain 500 years to acknowledge the *'shameful events in the country's past.'* [51] The Catholic Church never did.

---

[50] Alhambra Decree, 1492.
[51] Sephardic Jews eager to apply for Spanish citizenship, Washington Post, February 17, 2014.

It also left us in the dark about the abusive system that Jewish leaders had maintained for so long. A few years later, Jews would also be expelled from Portugal. For better understanding, we will have a closer look at the ethnic cleansing in that place.

Through the intervention of the chief rabbi of Turkey, Moses Capsali,[52] the Ottoman Navy sent a relief mission to Jewish refugees. Muslims were ordered to welcome the new arrivals as citizens of the Ottoman domain. Anyone who abused a Jew would be punished with death. The Ottoman ruler knew that it was prudent to appreciate the economic value of Jews.[53] However, this created friction with Muslims who had learned from the Koran and the Hadiths, their religious traditions, how to hate and mistreat Jews.

During the next two decades, Spanish Jews in Turkey became an important factor in an enormous expansion of Sunni Ottoman rule. Essentially, Ottoman-Turks came to swallow the competing Muslim nations in the Middle East, except for Persia (Iran). With the surrender of the Mamluk Sultanate, Egypt, the eastern part of modern-day Libya, the eastern coastal area of the Red Sea down to Mecca, and the Levant up to modern-day Turkey were soon joined to the empire. Because the expanding Portuguese Empire aimed at controlling the trade routes to India, it was necessary for Muslims to prepare for the defense of Mecca, Islam's holiest place.

Out of the concerns about a rising Christian world power, Mecca fell to the Ottomans without a shot being fired.[54]

In the face of Portuguese Christian aggression and with the help of Jews, the next Ottoman-Turkish leader became the first *caliph* over the entire Sunni Muslim world. This happened against the will of Shia Islam, the remaining Muslim main competitor, which was centered in Persia (Iran).

The Catholic Church and its subservient rulers across Europe were horrified by the news of Ottoman-Turkish expansion.

Rabbi Capsali was in extraordinarily good standing with Ottoman rulers. He held a seat next to the grand mufti of Islam, its highest leader in religious 'law.' Capsali's couch next to the leader needs to be called *'Throne of David,'* a parallel throne next to the sultan as commanded by the Koran.[55] Not unlike the crown

---

[52]  Moses b. Elijah Capsali, 1420–1495.

[53]  Isidore Singer, Cyrus Adler, The Jewish Encyclopedia: a descriptive record of the history, religion, literature, and customs of the Jewish people from the earliest times to the present day, Vol.2, (Funk and Wagnalls, 1912) 460.

[54]  Philip Mansel, Constantinople: City of the World's Desire, 1453–1924 (St. Martin's Griffin, 1998).

[55]  Koran 38:26 (Rodwell).

rabbi in Spain, Capsali was responsible for the Jewish system of administration in the Ottoman realm.

Unfortunately, Capsali's leading Rabbinic successors at the Ottoman court fall into obscurity despite the fact that their positions would be important to Luther's story. Not to worry, though, there is plenty of smoke for us to see through.

Capsali seems to have played a role in the capture of Constantinople (Istanbul) by Ottoman-Turks, where he had been chief Rabbi of the then-Christian city.

The fall of Constantinople marked the end of the Byzantine Empire. The city was then the capital of the last fragment of the ancient Roman Empire. Symbolically, Ottoman-Turks had conquered Rome. This had tremendous biblical and koranic consequences. For all three – Christians, Muslims, and Jews – it was understood as a warning that the End of the World was near.

When Constantinople was under siege, the Byzantine Emperor had managed too late to submit to the conditions for assistance by the Catholic Church. The age-old enmity between the two Christian churches in Greece and Rome was suicidal. A Greek priest would *'not approach an altar upon which a Latin priest has celebrated the sacred mystery unless he has first provided for repeated ablutions of the altar.*[56] It was a disgusting public demonstration of sectarian hatred.

The pope preferred to have a Christian empire go up in flames rather than sending his forces to the city's defense, unless the Orthodox churches submitted to the Vatican.

This tells us quite a bit about how the Catholic Church may have been able to rise to become the dominant force in Europe. Through granting or refusing assistance in warfare, the pope could have managed to slowly encroach over entire continents. He would win either way. In entering an alliance, he could play Catholic Monopoly. In rejecting it, he could parade the love of Christianity.

Sword or word, the Catholic Church had figured out how to bring about totalitarian control over its regional leaders and their subjects.

Another destination that welcomed Sephardi Jews was Amsterdam. The city became a New Jerusalem from where they would lead reform movements.

---

[56] Libellus, 664-665 in Kenneth M. Setton, The Papacy and the Levant, Volume III (The American Philosophical Society, 1984) 147.

Many Jews also found a home in the Berber Kingdom of Tlemcen, which was situated south of Spain on the North African coastal areas, stretching from modern day Algiers to Morocco under the little known Zayyanid dynasty. This clan ruled the Berber Kingdom between the middle of the thirteenth and the middle of the sixteenth centuries. Under the advice of a Jewish viceroy,[57] Tlemcen welcomed Jews and Muslims fleeing from Spain.

The capital city Tlemcen lies about 50 km inland, approximately halfway between modern day Algiers and Tangier, which is situated near the Strait of Gibraltar. It was regarded by Jews as the Jerusalem of the West[58] and was also the main trading place in the central Maghreb (North Africa, west of Egypt), as well as its intellectual center. There, Jews found respect as a protected minority.

For a while.

Around the turn of the sixteenth century, the Kingdom of Tlemcen's Muslim religious authority, the fanatic Al-Maghili,[59] targeted Jews with an outpour of hatred. Apparently, Jews were associated with the Muslim ruling class, and they were too successful in their gold trade.

Indeed, the caravan routes carrying African gold and merchant goods through the Sahara to Europe passed through Tlemcen. Of course, they were associated with the ruling class. The Koran instructs its rulers so. And they were too successful with gold *because* of their close association with the ruling class. Those who managed the administration and taxed people, land, and trade enjoyed a de facto monopoly.

It was a not so noble cartel.

The arrangement between the Rabbinic leadership and royalty was not unusual. We have already seen a similarly high level of Jewish involvement in Spain, Portugal, and Turkey.

With the appearance of Al-Maghili, the Jewish administrative system was overthrown. The Muslim leader had previously converted the ruling class to Islam and was now engaged in eliminating his Jewish competition.

He thought that Jews subverted the royals.

Was it not he who just subverted the royals with fundamentalist Islam?

---

[57]  The viceroy's name was Abraham.
[58]  John Hunwick, Jews of a Saharan Oasis: The Elimination of the Tamantit Community (Wiener, Copyright © 2007, reprinted by permission of Wiener).
[59]  Muhammad ibn Abd al-Karim al-Maghili, ca.1440 – ca. 1505.

Thinking of it, the ruling dynasty should have been Muslims long before. What did they convert from?

Al-Maghili made it legal to kill Jews and to plunder their property.[60] Their synagogue in the capital city Tlemcen was destroyed. Henceforth, Jews were humiliated, beaten, deported, thrown out of their homes, and wanted nowhere that Al-Maghili's preachers showed their enlightened faces.

Within just a few years, the kingdom was transformed from being a welcoming home for the feudal Jewish administrative system of oppression to triggering a holocaust.

Tlemcen was in chaos.

The Catholic Church under the personal command of Cardinal Cisneros, the radical Spanish Grand Inquisitor, took advantage of the situation and captured the kingdom's north-western trading city of Oran shortly thereafter.[61]

At around the same time as the Tlemcen expulsion and for a few years prior to that, Jews in Germany were ousted from the area of Nuremberg where they had enjoyed a similarly lofty status. While many Sephardi Jews were rescued by Ottoman-Turks, a significant number of German Ashkenazy Jews seem to have found a home in northern Italy, in particular Milan, which was then under the protectorate of the Kingdom of France.[62]

Venice.

The elegant city in the Adriatic lagoon, is famous for its canals and romantic gondolas, for good Italian food on summer evenings, and for strolls among its treasures of architecture and art. Tightly aligned with the now-defunct Byzantine Empire in Constantinople (Istanbul), the Republic of Venice had been a tremendously successful naval and trading power. During the previous few centuries, it had become the richest place in Europe. It boasted over 3,000 ships under the banner of the winged lion and over 30,000 sailors. However, for the last fifty years since the Muslim Ottoman-Turks had conquered Constantinople, Venice was in trouble. From that time on, the city state started to lose its eastern Mediterranean territories to the Ottomans. The opening of the sea route to India around the Cape of Good Hope in South Africa in 1499[63] put a final spell on Venice's commercial fortunes. Through its successful gamble, Portugal had a

---

[60] Ibn Askar (ca. 1575), in Bat Ye'or, *The Decline of Eastern Christianity under Islam* (Associated University Presses, Copyright © 1996, reprinted by permission of Associated University Presses) 360-361, the brackets () are part of the text in Bat Ye'or.

[61] The sack of Oran took place in 1509.

[62] Among the expelled was Elia Levita who will come to play a role in this story.

[63] The explorer was the Portugese Vasco da Gama, c. 1460s – 1524

huge first-mover advantage that led to its rise as a world superpower. Venice failed to keep up with the race to colonize the New World after Christoph Columbus discovered America for the Spanish crown.

At this junction, the Republic of Venice was attempting to reform its churches and submit the clergy of the Catholic Church to secular tribunals, disregarding the 'jurisdiction' of the papacy.

In 1509, Venice suffered a total defeat against the armies of the Papal States under the personal command of the pope. The city recanted its aspirations to freedom from the Catholic Church by the force of blood dripping from the holy spear.

The word *ghetto* was coined here, in the romantic lagoon. The Venetian Ghetto is claimed to have been the first of its kind. This is not so. One had already existed in Cracow, Poland a few years earlier, and another 300 years earlier in Constantinople,[64] but they did not know that it was supposed to be called a 'ghetto.' The idea of keeping Jews away from Christians was already established at the Third Lateran Council of the Catholic Church in 1179. If historians were to dig deeper, they would probably find them even a thousand years before that.

Having said that, we could not even imagine what the origin of the 'ghetto' was. We will learn that it was entirely different than we thought. For now, we must not envision Jews living among Christians and being driven into the Jewish quarter by force. Their homes were there all along.

On March 29, 1516, Doge Leonardo Loredan decreed the total segregation of Jews in the Venice Ghetto. They now had to wear a sign of identification, and the rates at the city's pawnshops were regulated.

The Doge was like an elected president of the city's governing Council of Ten, which was responsible to the Great Council of the Republic of Venice. The council was constituted by the nobles of the town. They were all Christians, of course. Under the deadly patronage of the Catholic Church.

Christian soldiers guarded the Jewish quarter, which was now called 'ghetto'. The gates were closed between six in the evening and noon on the next day.

Yet, in this microcosm, where one should expect universal solidarity, competing sectarian synagogues dominate religiously zealous Jewish bands. There were Germans with the Ashkenazi rite, Portuguese and Spaniards with the Spanish rite, Palestinian Jews with the Sephardic rite (which is an older

---

[64]    The Itinerary of Benjamin of Tudela (1171) 23-24.

Spanish rite), and Italians with the Italian rite. Each group had its own synagogue.

This little world shows how organized religion binds ethnic groups together and keeps them inside their tragic segregation – even behind walls with armed guards.

Worse, Jews would see their debasement as the fulfillment of prophecy that had warned them of unbearable consequences should they fail to obey their god's commands.[65] This would only strengthen their resolve in suffering.

So, history tells us that the Doge Jews in the first ghetto that bore the name, but it does not help us understand why he ordered the segregation at that precise juncture. Could it have been that the Catholic Church insisted on an ethnic cleansing operation similar to the one executed earlier in Spain? Could they have been in control of the administration in Venice, too? The engagement of the Catholic Church against Jews in a similar context was not limited to Germany, Spain, and Sicily. After all, the Venice Ghetto had something systemic and permanent about it, rather than isolated and random.

In any case, Martin Luther could not have had anything to do with the Venice Ghetto. His reform movement had not yet become active.

A little over a decade earlier, Jewish communities in Europe had been in uproar over 'the year of penance'. A German Jew by the name of Asher Lemmlein had appeared in Istria, which is a peninsula not far to the east of Venice by the Adriatic Sea. He claimed to be the forerunner of the Jewish Messiah who was to appear in Palestine during Passover in the next year.

Then as well as now, Passover is the most important Jewish holiday. It glorifies how their god sent plague after plague over Egypt's population, culminating in a godly killing spree. The god of the Israelites would *pass over* the houses, which secretly bore a Hebrew mark[66] – the one that is symbolically attached to virtually every doorpost in modern Jewish households. All the firstborn in Egypt, both human and animal, were stricken dead.[67]

Passover plainly celebrates the murdering of all Egyptian firstborn children by the god of the Israelites.

The excuse for the divine monstrosity is that Jews were held in slavery by the pharaoh.

---

[65]   Leviticus 26:16, Leviticus 26:20, Leviticus 26:22, Leviticus 26:25-26:26, Leviticus 26:29-26:30, Leviticus 26:32-26:33, Leviticus 26:36-26:37.

[66]   Exodus 12:7.

[67]   Exodus 12:12.

The tragedy of the Passover disaster is that it was not necessary. The god of the Israelites had personally made the Egyptian monarch, the pharaoh, forbid the Israelites' departure from Egypt.[68] This god would have had the power to soften the opposing leader and to simply plant its spirit into the ruler's mind in order to let them leave. Instead, the divinity intended to impress with its power to terrorize an entire nation.

Terror for show.

The point of the story is that the readers are supposed to be scared into submission to the omnipotent powers of this god.

The killing of firstborn Egyptians never actually happened. It is mere myth.[69] Archaeology has not been able to bring forth a single piece of evidence of over 600,000 fighting Israelite men[70] in ancient Egypt. Not even of one man. For this reason, most histories of Israel do not include this part of Israel's foundation myth, called the Exodus.

Regardless, Jews continue to celebrate the rampage of their god as if it was the greatest real event in the history of Judaism.

It is an overt display of hatred against mankind.

Besides, the word 'slavery' serves to trigger compassion. It means that they were 'slaving' in Egypt to maintain an oppressive administrative system.[71]

Lemmlein's prophecy came with the condition that all Jews had to spend six months in repentance and be charitable. Jews believe that they can bring about their redemption through 'hard,' outwardly 'work' of faithful behavior.

Hence, the forerunner found a sizable Jewish and Christian following in Italy, Germany, and Austria, but especially around Venice.[72] Like lunatics, they prayed and fasted in preparation of the coming of the Messiah.

However, Lemmlein appears to have vanished after having pronounced himself King of the Jews.[73] Since there are no further sources, it is unclear whether the loss of the forerunner mattered for the event of the Messiah to show up in Jerusalem. Yet, it appears that the messianic aspirations could be

---

[68]  Exodus 11:9–10.

[69]  For foundation myths see Kenton L. Sparks, Genre Criticism, in, Thomas B. Dozeman, Methods for Exodus (Cambridge University Press, 2010) 73.

[70]  Exodus 12:37–12:38 and Numbers 1:46.

[71]  Talmud - Mas. Kiddushin 70b.

[72]  Greenstone, 1906, 190.

[73]  Harris Lenowitz, the Jewish Messiahs (Oxford, Copyright © 1998, reproduced with permission of Oxford University Press through PLSClear) 100.

understandable in context of their earlier expulsion from Spain, Germany, and Tlemcen, among others.

The homeless were in search of a home.

An anti-Semitic polemicist, Johannes Pfefferkorn,[74] a convert from Judaism to Dominican Catholicism, was offended by the faith in Lemmlein. He mocked Jews for not having had a king since Jesus Christ and for having lost the Temple in Jerusalem a long time ago. Pfefferkorn ridiculed them for having hoped for the destruction of all churches in Christendom and for being brought up in a fiery pillar together with a cloud when they would return to the Promised Land.[75]

Nothing of that sort has happened – yet.

Briefly, the arrival of the Messiah is the most important event in all Judaic religions, signifying the redemption of Israel and a return of the Jewish people to Jerusalem.

After each historical holocaust, we can find apologetic Rabbinic voices that claim that the messianic mission is irrelevant to Judaism. But this does not hold water. The messianic chain of events can be summed up with the End of the World, culminating in the conquest of the Promised Land. Judaism, Christianity, and Islam merely distinguish themselves as armed adversaries to the same end. They work toward their final war for world supremacy on the battlefield at Armageddon.

ISIS dared its Western and Jewish adversaries to show up at that very place. Modern Ultra-Orthodox Jews work hard toward this goal. Ask any Christian, and you will find them in the comfortable territory of an alternate reality.

In other words, Lemmlein's skull could have been clubbed in a dark alley, and it would not have led to the slightest deviation from the historic trajectory. I say this not only because you will find clarity by meeting a number of these messiahs, but also for the reason that Lemmlein was encouraged by the prominent Portuguese Jewish leader – who had before been expelled from Spain – Abrabanel.

Since Jewish leaders habitually use different names for individual languages, we cannot figure out how Lemmlein fits it. By design, this custom disjoints historical events from the leadership.

After the fact, rabbis claimed that they had feared that a figure like him could rise. Instead, it was part of their calculation.

---

[74] Johannes (Josef) Pfefferkorn, 1469–1523.
[75] Johann Pfefferkorn, (the Jew-Glass) der Judenspiegel (1507) transl. A.J. Deus.

Lemmlein had retold Abrabanel's story of the arrival of the Messiah in 1503 and the beginning of the Messianic Age in 1531. This was a forerunner, one who made the announcements for the coming messiah and the successive redemption of Israel.

When the Doge came to shut the gates to the ghetto a few years later, the successor of Abrabanel was the 'Rabbi of Venice,' again, the highest Jewish authority in Europe. Lemmlein appears to have merely been a cleverly placed messenger, rather than a Jewish individual that has gone rogue.

If Abrabanel was a deceiver, then the Rabbi of Venice was a deceiver.

When put into the context with the broad Jewish involvement with royalty and with the messianic aspirations, the anti-Semitic actions in Tlemcen and Venice as well as all across Europe appear reactionary, almost as though executed in self-defense. There is no excuse for collective punishment of an ethnic group. But as inconvenient as it may be, we must embark on this journey to better understand the causes and effects of religious hatred and violence, in particular when it comes to anti-Semitism.

Pfefferkorn's booklet had nothing flattering to say. Jews ridiculed Jesus Christ in a blasphemous manner, calling him a seducer of the people, hung, or born from an unclean union.[76] The churches, they called shithouses.[77] They had special prayers against Christians. One of them went as follows:

> *There is no hope for the baptized, and all infidels will soon be gone and all the enemies of your people Israel will be suppressed and destroyed. This will happen soon.*

As the pamphlet goes, these words were prayed *'every day three times with great devotion'* and while being obliged to stand. Likewise, they prayed for the *'Roman Empire, that it may be broken up and destroyed.'* Another prayer sounds even less friendly:

> *May God destroy the thoughts and counsel of our enemies with death, sword, starvation, plague, and other scourges, and may it happen for our sake.*

Who are the enemies?

We all are.

Why?

For not being Jewish.

---

[76] Erika Rummel, The Case Against Johann Reuchlin (University of Toronto, Copyright © 2002, reprinted by permission of University of Toronto Press) 54.

[77] Ibid., 55.

Then Pfefferkorn set out to describe how Jews were plotting *'how to uproot the power and might of Christians and destroy them.'* Since they are not able to accomplish this, the author continues, *'they use usury and other kinds of deception.'* The way they went about their lending business was hinted at earlier in the regulation of pawnshops in Venice: lend little against something worth exponentially much more. Jewish shops always won, even more when the client could not pay back a loan or when it involved stolen goods.

In order to protect their businesses and get ahead, Jews were *'allowed to swear a Jewish oath,'* even if it was false, Pfefferkorn said. The Jewish Oath of Treachery. Like that, they could disown almost anyone they pleased even if they robbed them personally. This is how Jews *'usually prevail in court and quite rarely lose their case.'*[78] Luther would come to agree that with Jews, bearing false witness *'was quite a common and ordinary matter.'*[79]

Is this even possible? The answers lie in monopolized judiciaries, administrations that are responsible for permits, and tax systems that would favor their own. We see this mechanism at play in modern day Palestinian territories that are controlled by Israel. The legal system simply disowns the natives. We must wonder just how widespread such practices of hatred against mankind might persist among Jews whom we consider our friends today? If you are being greeted with *'Seind wilkum'*, you might not perceive that anything is wrong. The supposedly benign corruption of *'Seid wilkum'* (be welcome) to *'Seind wilkum'* is not as welcoming as it might seem. It means *'Devil, be welcome.'*[80]

Some of the rules in the book of Deuteronomy, for example, encourage deceitfulness, indeed. We will later see how a treachery would lead to the inheritance of a nation.

But the Bible is peppered with stories where Jew betrayed Jew. For example, a Jewish mother and one of her sons lied to the patriarchal father in order to get their way.[81] Late in the son's life, the deceiver himself was betrayed by his sons.[82] Even the god of the Israelites, who has the power to simply impose his will, at times engaged in ridiculous treacheries, testing subjects for a dare, sending disasters just to impress, and on and on.

---

[78] Ibid., 60.
[79] Martin Luther, The Large Catechism, Second Edition (1529) WA 30 I,125-238.
[80] Rummel, 2002, 56.
[81] Genesis 27:20.
[82] Genesis 37:31-37:33.

Such fables teach believers in the Bible that anything goes if it serves the purpose of getting ahead of others. Treachery, deceit, fraud, betrayal, lying, stealing, killing, even the termination of entire nations of other races is tolerable — even commanded by God — as long as it serves the organized religion of Judaism.

Not surprisingly, the accusations are not accidental oddities but a disturbing motif that constantly re-emerged throughout Jewish history. It rose to historical prominence with financial empires that were based on usury.

This readiness to betray the trust of others to get ahead is taught to children in modern-day Jewish schools through the Bible as a cultural and ethical foundation. It works against the basic human instinct of relying on mutual trust.

But if treachery is to be assumed, then a potential cycle of violence is created once it turns out that trust is not merited – not even among family members.

Currently, we do not seem to be aware in what kind of danger our oblivious civilization is. We need to find ways to regulate these packs of wolves dressed in sheepskin and to stop these leaders – first and foremost – from teaching such nonsense to children.

It is child abuse to infiltrate cradles with hatred.

Thus closes Pfefferkorn his pamphlet, *'the Enemy of Jews:'*

> *[…] as long as the Jews live freely, it is not possible to avoid such evil. For it would not be enough for them to abandon usury and go on living in great wealth. Rather, one should oblige them to do all kinds of lowly work, such as keeping the streets clean or sweeping chimneys or, similarly, sweeping latrines and collecting dog droppings, etc. And, in the meantime, one must not, as I have sometimes said, leave them the false book of the Talmud, but take it from them, and leave them nothing except the text of the Bible.*[83]

We will see that Martin Luther fitted right in.

---

[83]  Rummel, 2002, 62.

## The Vatican's Banker

October 31, 1517 marks the start of the Protestant Reformation. The date when Luther nailed his 95 Theses to the door of the All Saints' Church in Wittenberg, Germany falls, within a fortnight or so, a full year and a half after the gates at Venice were first closed on Jews. This opening act is free of anti-Semitism. Atrocities against Jews were instead committed in Cracow, Poland, and in Berlin, Germany, during the preceding decade. But there is no mention of Jews and no hint at animosities between the Reformer and them.

In the absence of anti-Semitism, why did Luther want to break ranks with the Catholic Church?

Luther's intent was to return the Catholic Church to a purer and poorer form of faith. He criticized the customs of selling forgiveness of sins to the destitute and the selling of indulgences, a practice that had recently been applied to the dead as a new way to generate revenue for the church.[84] However, Luther was more concerned about the use of the money from indulgences rather than the indulgences themselves. He approved of these.[85]

In its search for revenues, the Catholic Church created fictional forms of money. It partly paid for its soldiers with indulgences, the forgiveness of all their sins. They needed only to serve long enough under arms or die on the battlefield as martyrs. Payments for indulgences would free the dead's soul from purgatory. This is an imaginary place of infernal suffering. There, the sins of the deceased are cleansed in order for their souls to achieve the holiness necessary to ascend to heaven. This is the place where paradise is located.

For example, an encyclical by one of the popes of our story encouraged holy war in Africa by promising everlasting felicity in the Kingdom of Heaven for those who participated.[86] To be clear, remission of sin was to come through the shedding of infidels' blood. Better yet, the dead on the front were frequently Catholics on both sides.

Such was the level of superstition in the Christian civilization.

Those who think that religion is limited to questions about a god may be surprised that their view might be simplistic. Organized religion comes in a variation of sectarian package deals.

It is complicated and expensive.

---

[84] The practice of applying the sale of indulgences to the dead was established by Pope Sixtus IV (1471–1484), see James Patrick, Renaissance and Reformation (Cavendish, 2007) 1231.

[85] Martin Luther, Letter to Christoph Scheurl, March 5, 1518.

[86] Raynaldus, ad ann. 1505, no. 5, vol. XX. P. 21, in Setton, 1984, 38.

Luther intended to enforce the Gospels' concept of poverty and modesty and bring the church back to its good old days. In his focus was the lack of openness of the church and its reluctance to put its treasures to good use for the needy.[87] Luther condemned the Catholic Church for its secrecy and whim. It was a corrupt religious organization, he thought.

He criticized the opulence of the pope's entourage and the bishoprics, which were swimming in riches.

In addition, the pope had initiated a lavish building project for the new church of Saint Peter in Rome. Luther said that the papacy should pay for the construction out of its pocket, rather than extorting its cost from the disadvantaged.[88]

Indeed, a Jewish chronicle noted that the pope went as far as having earrings stripped off women and girls to pay for the extravaganza.[89]

Perhaps the strongest point was Luther's assault on papal authority, which was enforced through the terror of the Inquisition.[90] Luther's 95 Theses had a lot to do with clerical malpractice in the Catholic Church. According to Luther, faith and the Christian principles of poverty and social rejection should be enforced.

The eighteenth-century historian David Hume claimed that the priesthood had enriched itself through cashing in on the poor.[91] He also alleged that Luther's core motivation was economic. Under the first Medici Pope Leo X,[92] the Catholic Church diverted the task of collecting revenue from the Austin Friars, also called the Order of St. Augustine, to the Dominican Order.[93]

They lost the revenue streams that had fed their Augustinian bellies.

In short, Luther was already an active Austin leader when the river of money dried up.

To understand the circumstances better, the 'Medici' suffix of the then-pope warrants a short detour.

---

[87]   Martin Luther, *95* Theses (1517).

[88]   Ibid.

[89]   Joseph Ha-Cohen aka Rabbi Joseph Ben Joshua Ben Meir, the Sphardi, The Chronicles, Vol. I, translated by C.H.F. Bialloblotzky (Valpy, 1836) 430.

[90]   Luther, *95 Theses,* 1517, 90.

[91]   David Hume, *The History Of England* (M'Creery, 1807) Volume IV, 31.

[92]   Pope Leo X, born Giovanni di Lorenzo de' Medici, was pope 1513 – 1521.

[93]   Hume, 1807, Volume IV, 33-34.

About 200 years earlier, a man by the name of Salvestro de' Medici 'il Chiarissimo' ('The Very Clear') arrived in Florence from an unknown home.[94] This city-state was one of the richest in the Italian Peninsula. Its citizens and business bosses were early political Renaissance activists. Florentine enterprises, merchants, and financiers of the era had their powerful economic networks laid out across Europe. Salvestro's son was Averardo de' Medici. The name of this second known generation is an indication that the family intended to link itself to the legendary Knight Averardo under the French King and emperor of the Holy Roman Empire, Charlemagne.[95]

The Medicis' pro-French attitude showed in their earliest appearance and persisted during Luther's era.

Since it constitutes an important part of the foundation of the sixteenth century Lutheran religious environment, I need to highlight the big picture of this relationship.

Charlemagne's son[96] exempted Jews from laws against usury.

Since their banking monopoly is part of the divine Law of the Bible,[97] there was nothing a Christian or a Muslim could do about it. While similar privileges existed before elsewhere, the Carolingian monopoly opened the doors to financial engineering for cash-strapped governments and warfare. How the tax farming dynasties of the Seniors, Abrabanels, and others we will meet rose to their lofty positions is no mystery.

Rabbinic leaders seem to have had it all figured out for themselves. At the cost of everybody else, they were laughing all the way to the bank. You could hate them and drive them into ghettos, but nothing stopped Jewish leaders from making money.

Tons of it.

---

[94] While the origin of the Medicis is in the dark, another family serves as a template to Florentine's special status of a French-oriented bastion. We hear first in the early eleventh century from a family with vast riches and properties: the feudal Ricasoli Dynasty. […].

[95] Charlemagne, Charles the Great (742 – 814), was Holy Roman Emperor 800 – 814, King of the Lombards from 774, and King of the Franks (the French) from 768.

[96] Louis the Pious, 778 – 840), the Fair, was King of the Franks and co-Emperor with Charlemagne from 813 – 840. He was also King of Aquitaine from 781.

[97] Deuteronomy 23:19-23:20.

For centuries before Luther, Franco-Carolingians had already clashed at Rome with a Spanish flavor of Christianity, which was influenced by Jewish and Muslim rituals. The French version was at the heart of a simpler, Germanic form of Christian rituals.[98]

Averardo de' Medici was not living in poverty. A grand estate outside of Florence — a fortress — was known as 'Gafaggiolo de' Medici' during his lifetime.[99] The fortress had previously belonged to the Republic of Florence.

In plain English: he was already among the super-rich before the Medici Bank even started.

The third member of this dynasty was Giovanni di Bicci de' Medici, founder of the Medici Bank, which would become the largest bank in Europe and its dynasty the wealthiest in Europe. Ultimately, their later royal power found its roots through a marriage arrangement that came to be forged in Luther's time by a Medici pope.

Giovanni di Bicci de' Medici was trained by and worked with a distant cousin, Vieri di Cambio who was a banker in Florence. His name, *Change* or *Exchange* in English, suggests that the Medici cousin di Cambio may have been a Jewish money changer, and that the Medici bankers could have originally been Jews[100] who migrated from France. The mechanism appears similar to Abrabanel's and Senior's.

At the time, the Catholic Church enforced strict usury laws, essentially endorsing the Jewish monopoly for interest-bearing businesses. In the laws' consequence, Christians were not allowed to take interest.

However, in di Cambio's time, the seat of the Catholic Church was not in Rome but in Avignon, in modern southern France.

This era is called '*the Babylonian Captivity of the Papacy,*' because the Vatican was occupied by so-called anti-popes. This latter term is generally understood to refer to illegitimate claimants to the papal throne, but it probably stands for popes of competing sectarian denominations.

The popes in Avignon were supported by the French kings and the Medici.

---

[98] Opposed to Catholics, Arians do not believe that Jesus Christ was both, man and God. God and Jesus were distinct. The Germanic beliefs go back to the fourth century Paulinic Ulfilas Bible. However, the original Arian position is not clearly documented in the historical record.

[99] John Shearman, The Collections of the Younger Branch of the Medici (The Burlington Magazine 117 No. 862, January 1975) 17.

[100] JewischHistory.org.

According to mainstream history, the anti-popes were upheld by Italians.[101]

Before continuing with the Medicis, let me zero in on Cambio's name. When the Catholic Church was talking about usury, it was not only referring to interest on loans. As our modern banks vividly visualize, a banking business dependent on interest revenues alone is like a cake half-baked. Of course, when you pay little or no interest on deposits and take a lot on loans, then you should make a bundle. Should. But there is a little pitfall built in that is often overlooked: risk. If a loan defaults, large amounts are being lost that need to be made up by the small trickle of interest from other loans. A way around it is to ask for collateral to secure loans. We have already heard from Pfefferkorn's accusation against the Jewish pawnshop principle and the respective regulation in Venice. The riches came not from the interest but from the liquidation of assets worth much more than the loan.

The lender had a hidden interest in the failure of the borrower.

However, in government loans, the collateral could be as big as tax farming.

But there is another way to reduce the risk and make more money: lend out money that you do not have. In simple terms, taking and giving out loans depends on the scale of the operation. The bigger the lending business gets in any particular market, the more the bank can lend out money without having it. The loan of one client becomes the deposit of another.

This works best wherever a lender enjoys a monopoly in any given market.

It works even better where deposits are prohibited from receiving interest.

Since there were no regulations in Luther's time, except for the usury laws, the lending business could be driven up infinitely – until the 'bank' collapsed through a bank run. The small depositors lost everything. The bankers always won.

Respectable as they were, they lived in palaces.

But then, there are other banking businesses. The big ones back then engaged in what today would be called investment banking and arbitration, the exchange of currency. In 'investment banking,' the mainly Jewish banks financed wars on both sides and trade voyages, entire ships, complete with crew and all of their merchandise. A single successful venture could enrich them beyond belief. A sunken ship translated into a total loss.

---

[101] This is not always so clear, because sometimes – as the Catholic Church chose – the roles between Avignon and Rome were reversed. These anti-popes were more likely connected to a Spanish sect that has not yet been properly identified.

The trouble with this was that they already needed to be big to play big. Unless they pooled the money of many to the same goal. And that is exactly what they did. In the process, the organizer of the venture eliminated all his risk. Win or lose, money poured in either way.

Which brings us finally back to di Cambio's name that relates to money changing operations. Other than for arbitration in modern banks, I used to think of exchanging money as a sort of small-minded business idea. Change a hundred bucks here and there from one currency to another and make a couple from it. My late father-in-law – a Muslim man who was full of wonders – used to own a money exchange business. Because I never thought of scale, I was in sheer disbelief over how much money the business made with its small operation. In Afghanistan, he told me, moneychangers advertised their services with Euros and Dollars bundled up on transport pallets. Since the local currency was worthless, exchange of hard currency was an essential factor of business. These exchanges made so much money that their owners could literally swim in it. And they never paid a single dollar in taxes. Since many transactions ran off the books, business partners were able to enrich themselves by funneling away a little here and a little more there. Nobody would ever know. Back then, there were no unified currencies as we know them today. The more fractured currencies were, the more money could be made with exchange services.

Money, money, money.

Before founding his own bank, Giovanni di Bicci de' Medici had been promoted to general manager of di Cambio's branch in Rome. In this capacity, the Medici supported the return of the Avignon papacy to the Vatican, developing a deep business relationship with the papal court. At some point, di Cambio's money business broke into three banks. Giovanni took partnership of the one in Rome and eventually moved its headquarters to Florence.

He cashed in when it was finally time for the Avignon popes to move to the Eternal City. Being grateful for his continuing support, his Rome branch was awarded control of the Apostolic Chamber.

As unbelievable as it may seem, Medici took command over the beating heart of the finances of the Catholic Church, its treasury.

Similar to the King of the Jews, Abrabanel, in Portugal and Spain, Giovanni was now treasurer of Europe's largest business, the Catholic Church. It does not appear to have been unusual. At the end of the twelfth century, the treasurer of Pope Alexander III was a descendant of the great Talmudist Rabbi Nathan.

From there on, the Medici Bank expanded and branched out into virtually everything: trade, factories, jewelry, transportation, politics, philanthropy, charity, warfare, and tax farming – the world's most lucrative business, a contract to extort taxes from the poor sheep of the Catholic Church with whatever means it took and to keep a good portion of the proceeds.

This was one ruthless tribe.

The Catholic priesthood insisted on a biblical right to taxation to line its own pockets,[102] and the Medicis lent their hand, axe, knife, and sword as the enforcers of the cash flow. The Medici Bank's success was unstoppable under French-friendly popes, and its stamp would eventually be on – everything.

Giovanni died one of the richest men in one of the richest cities in Europe.

Thanks to the usury laws, the Medici Bank did not even have to pay interest on the tax money that they owed the Vatican.

100 years later, the Vatican in the Medici banking empire still provided for over half of its profits. For a business, that generally constitutes an uncomfortable lump risk. Nevertheless, with their good relations to the Vatican, the political influence of the family grew with their wealth.

Cosimo and Piero di Cosimo de' Medici were de facto rulers of Florence.

The political situation in the Italian Peninsula and the Medici business grew unstable during the time of the next generation with Lorenzo the Magnificent. The latter remains famous today with connoisseurs for his support of two of the great Renaissance artists of the time, Botticelli and Michelangelo.

Lorenzo was 'il primo cittadino d'Italia,' first among Italy's citizens. He was the most prominent and important of all men in the Italian Peninsula. One of his daughters gave birth to *two* sons who later became cardinals, and one of his grand daughters became mother of Pope Leo XI. Another daughter was married to the son of Pope Innocent. One of their sons also became a cardinal.

But Lorenzo could not always enjoy smooth sailing.

---

[102] Sirach 7:30–31.

A Dominican friar by the name of Savonarola[103] turned Florence into a war zone. Under siege by a French army, and instead of submitting to orders from the Catholic Church, the Florentine extremist combined his puritan teachings with armed youth gangs and managed to have the French-friendly Medicis thrown out of their hometown – together with all Jews.[104]

Thenceforth, the Medici family spent the years between 1494 and 1512 in exile. Their business went belly up.

Savonarola promised to become the center of a new imperial power with riches to bless the city like never before.[105] Given Florence's wealth, one might think that was a preposterous thing to say. However, in organized religion, *wealth* is measured by the number of paying believers.

The fanatic was intent on creating a New Jerusalem in Florence. For this to happen – we will learn about the mechanism later – he needed a messiah and he had to hasten the End of the World. If one were to look for a really radical reformer, he was the one. Luther looked like a frightened lamb compared to this guy. Both bedeviled the corrupt clergy of the Catholic Church.

A pattern emerged: New Jerusalem was multiplying.

Savonarola was excommunicated by the pope for his hostile refusal to join the Vatican's fight against the French King. The Catholic Pope at the time was Alexander VI, the Spanish-born Borgia (Borja).[106] Political opponents described the Borgia clan as 'Marranos' – with the unmistaken meaning of *sows* – converts from Judaism.

Alexander VI was now the one under fire by Savonarola.

Things turned sour.

The Florentine populace lost its faith in the holy man.[107] Savonarola ended up hanged and burned in Florence's main square, the awe-inspiringly beautiful Piazza della Signoria.

---

[103] Girolamo Savonarola, 1452 – 1498.

[104] [On December 26, 1595, Savonarola] expelled the Medici and the Jews from Florence. The Jews, who had previously served as the Medici's bankers, were replaced by the Monte di Pieta, a public loan bank. (Jewishhistory.org.il, retrieved September 22, 2017).

[105] Girolamo Savonarola in Donald Weinstein, Savonarola and Florence Prophecy and Patriotism in the Renaissance (Princeton, 1970) 143.

[106] Pope Alexander VI aka Rodrigo de Borja (Borgia), Roderic Llançol i de Borja, Rodrigo Lanzol y de Borja, 1431 – 1503, was pope 1492 – 1503.

[107] Niccolò Machiavelli, The Prince, Concerning New Principalities Which Are Acquired By One's Own Arms And Ability (1532).

Whoever travels to Florence should visit the Convent of San Marco, just a couple of busy blocks north of the cathedral and the city's traffic-free main sights. The preacher had his quarters there from 1482. Looking past the incredible art, Savonarola's and his friar brothers' cells speak an unmistaken language of a place of religious radicalization. Perhaps any convent that can be visited by the public would provide for a similar aha-moment for just how low human life is willing to degrade itself to halt or reverse progress in the name of superstition.

Another Giovanni de' Medici with the suffix *'delle Bande Nere,'* was a son of the most significant woman of the Renaissance, Caterina Sforza, raised humanist at the Sforza court in Milan. Money attracts money. By this time, Caterina's reputation could be summed up in her nickname, *'The Tiger of Forlì.'*

In the chaos of Savonarola's aftermath, the Milanese humanist *'Tiger of Forlì'* ended up in Castel Sant'Angelo, a prison in the Vatican with the name of an angel, in which the Medici wife was incarcerated. Allegedly, she had tried to poison the Borgia Pope Alexander VI.

Martin Luther studied some of Savonarola's writings. He praised him as a martyr. The extremist Savonarola was one of the forerunners of the Protestant Reformation[108] after whom Luther would come to shape his approach to separating from the Catholic Church.

The two Medicis who we are really interested in are Lorenzo's sons Giovanni di Lorenzo and Giulio di Giuliano de' Medici.[109] The former was now himself Pope Leo X, the one in Martin Luther's eye. Through his family connections to previous popes, he had been named a cardinal at the age of sixteen. Sent to Florence by his predecessor, Pope Julius II (della Rovere), with a papal army, he himself came to reinstate Medici rule in the city just before ascending to the papal throne in Rome. Giulio later became Pope Clement VII.

The Medicis were not sucking their thumbs in exile.

They were working hard behind the scenes with a very long-term outlook. The game plan could well have gone wrong. But putting a Medici on the papal throne was a genius strategy. When Giovanni di Lorenzo was made Pope Leo X, he was only thirty-seven years old and was not even yet ordained a priest.

Business can only be merry, one might think.

---

[108] Donald Weinstein, Savonarola: The Rise and Fall of a Renaissance Prophet (Yale, 2011) 360, note 26, drawing on works in German (Nolte) and Italian (Simoncelli and Dall' Aglio).

[109] Because the son of Lorenzo's brother had been murdered, Giulio ended up being adopted by the family patriarch.

After returning to their home base, the Medicis established themselves as the hereditary rulers of Florence.

When Luther talked about corruption in the Catholic Church, it would have been imprudent of him to engage in name-calling. However, there is little doubt that his contemporaries, including the pope, knew exactly what he was talking about.

### Holy Lord of Wars

While the Medicis were important for the flow of hard currency for the Vatican, we need also to understand the internal workings of the Catholic Church. We remember that income had been redirected from Luther's Augustinian Order to the Dominicans.

Under the leadership of the Augustinian Vicar General Egidio Viterbo,[110] the order of the Austin Friars was 'unified' into regular Catholic congregations. This consolidation appears to have been the result of a short-lived pan-European alliance[111] that was forged to get the rebellious Venetians in line.

As a member of the Erfurt Augustinian convent at the time, Luther was opposed to this merger.

Six other Augustinian convents rebelled against the command to submit to the Catholic creed. As a representative of the disobedient friars, Luther had already been in Rome in the fall of 1510. He thought of the Catholic Church as stubborn, butting their way through in an all-or-nothing approach.[112]

The deal fell flat, and many Augustinian convents celebrated their independence. Consequently, there was an inter-Augustinian schism; those for integration and those for 'freedom' from the yoke of the Catholic Church.

That Luther ended up as an Augustinian leader is sort of a surprise.

He did not seem to have found his footing in life. Having started to study law and then switching to philosophy and theology, he lacked orientation. In philosophy, he learned how to reason. It did not satisfy his faith.

---

[110] Egidio Viterbo (Ægidius Viterbensis), aka Giles Antonini, aka Giles of Viterbo, 1472 – 1532, was an Austin Friar, bishop of Viterbo and cardinal of the Catholic Church.

[111] The League of Cambrai.

[112] Martin Luther, On war against Islamic reign of terror (On war against the Turk, 1528) WA 30 II, 107-148.

45

A terrifying moment when lightning struck near him[113] led him to subscribe to life as a hermit in the Augustinian cloister at Erfurt in 1505. It is almost as though he attempted to reconnect with a lost faith and punish himself for his sins.[114]

Lack of purpose is a feature that is frequently found among extremists.

The St. Augustine Monastery in Erfurt reaches back to the late thirteenth century. Its prison-like structures had been built through public donations and the sale of indulgences.[115] Almost 150 hermits resided there with Luther.

In addition to living off donations, they traded in a blue indigo dye that was processed from the woad plant. Erfurt was a medieval center for this color.[116]

For a decade after Luther's arrival, a large library was under construction in the monastery.

Erfurt was the point of no return on Luther's march to radicalization. Surrounded by like-minded monks, the Reformer henceforth focused on the imaginary. He was isolated from reality behind the monastery's walls. His human interactions were limited to admirers of divinities with a singular Augustinian worldview.

Luther was ordained in 1507. The next year, he became a teacher at Wittenberg University.

He rose like a star.

Two years later, he represented the rebellious Austin Friars in Rome, even before he was awarded the title of Doctor of Theology.

By the time of his 95 Theses, he was in charge of eleven monasteries.

He would later come to declare monastic houses as *'nothing more than an estate founded by worldly wisdom for the sake of getting money and revenues.'* Still in his words, *'everything about it is merely external, temporal, perishable pomp.'*[117] He would come to call them *'death traps, the very ramparts of hell.'*[118]

---

[113] Martin Brecht, Martin Luther, translated by James L. Schaaf (Fortress Press, Copyright © 1985–93, reprinted by permission of Fortress Press) 1:48.

[114] James Kittelson, Luther The Reformer (Fortress Publishing, 1986) 79.

[115] Theresia Simon, Die Augustiner-Eremiten im Spätmittelalter: Am Beispiel des Augustinerklosters in Erfurt (AV Akademikerverlag, 2014).

[116] Joan Thirsk, Alternative Agriculture: A History: From the Black Death to the Present Day (Oxford, 1997) 81-82.

[117] Martin Luther, A Sermon on Keeping Children in School (1530), from Luther's Works, Vol. 46 (Fortress, Copyright © 1967, reprinted by permission of Fortress) 213-57.

[118] Ibid.

Indeed, these are places of radicalization. A monk might enter with good intentions. But the inhumane environment could turn him into a monster with a mind full of demons sooner rather than later.

Egidio Viterbo and Martin Luther were arch enemies.

This Viterbo opened the Fifth Lateran Council of the Catholic Church at Rome in 1512. At the start of the Reformation, he already had become cardinal. An Austin friar, or rather the boss thereof, he was by now a fully integrated member of the top leadership of the Catholic Church.

Soon thereafter, Viterbo came to be considered a favored successor to the papal throne.

With this career outlook, it is little wonder that he was willing to sell out his Augustinian friends.

Two issues should help us understand the complex religious context. First, it appears essential to know what was going on in the Fifth Lateran Council. We need to spend some time with it, because it will provide some answers for Luther's later behavior. Secondly, we need to learn what the Austin Friars believed in. There is no better way than to ask St. Augustine himself.

The Fifth Lateran Council was held in sessions over a period of six years and ended a few months before Luther nailed his 95 Theses to the church door at Wittenberg in 1517. However, most of the bishopric outside of the Italian Peninsula or Spain did not, or refused to, attend. This lack of attendance highlights the dire circumstances that the Catholic Church was in.

Luther was only one of the problems to come.

The pope at the time, Julius II,[119] had higher ambitions.

He intended to rid the Catholic domain of feudal kings and, with this move, to ensure the 'independence' of the church from earthly influence. Julius wanted the Catholic Church to rule the world through its clerical network alone. It should be a full-fledged theocracy, rather than the ill-conceived one that it was.

To implement this would neither come easy nor be without resistance and bloodshed.

For hundreds of years, Catholic kings and princes were hanging in a delicate balance with the papacy. Church and nobility fed each other by mutual reinforcement. The Catholic Church created noble overlords preferably from its own ranks. In return, the nobility promised to uphold the power of the church.

---

[119] Pope Julius II was pope of the Catholic Church 1503 – 1513.

This allowed feudal states to emerge and to be maintained under the tyranny of church-allied royals. These were sort of dual governments that lived according to biblical prescriptions.

The papacy played shepherd, and its noble dogs kept the sheep in check and milked taxes for the Vatican.

Following the Bible,[120] noble families typically delegated one of their sons to a clerical career. This acted like an insurance policy for their own privileges within the ecclesiastical inner circle. However, biblical rules are deceptions. The Bible mandates the highest despots to be from the leading Jewish class, the Levites.[121] This safeguards the priestly succession and nobility to remain a closed-knit network.

Ordinary Jewish or Christian families could send their firstborn sons to the monasteries as they wished. The biblical hierarchy was rigged against their ascent into the noble class. They were tricked not only to send their firstborns with no prospects for their livelihoods but also to sustain the system of their own oppression with taxes. The way to break into the caste would have been to become pope. He was the one with the power to give or take away the benefices necessary to ascend to the one percent – nobility. To make oppression perfect, they did not tolerate dissent or violence against the ruling class, even if it concerned one of their staunchest enemies. The offender ended up before the hangman.[122]

The success and riches of the upper class were pre-programmed. They rose to become bishops and cardinals or popes in Rome. The Vatican created and maintained the royals' power and enforced it through the word of their god.

It was an utterly corrupt system of governance.

Martin Luther *opposed* the pope's ideas to limit the power of nobility. He thought that they were responsible for 'protecting' the people and that the church should take care of spiritual questions. Luther wanted to *strengthen* the status of nobility. Because of their difference, Luther called Pope Julius a *'wicked iron-eater'* in reference to his function as a leader in wars and thought of him as *'half devil.'*[123]

The approach of the Reformer rested on right-wing tradition, preservation, and opposition, rather than on innovation.

---

[120] Exodus 22:29–30.
[121] Numbers 3:11.
[122] An example of the mechanism is in Ha-Cohen, Vol. II, transl. Bialloblotzky, 1836, 52.
[123] Luther, On War, 1528, WA 30 II, 107-148.

The geo-political currents can be understood through the election speech of Julius. It may just be gossip, but he is said to having flat-out refused to be in the same room that his Spanish-born predecessor, the Borgia Pope Alexander VI, had lived in.

Julius claimed that Borgia had *'usurped the papal power by the devil's aid.'*

Considering an otherwise inexplicable transfer of Borgia's palace in Rome to the cardinal who was responsible for the election of Pope Alexander VI and also recipient of the vice-chancellorship of the Vatican,[124] Julius might have had a point. His intent was to wipe out Alexander's memory. He wanted his body sent back to Spain,[125] so it is said. Given the support of all corrupt cardinals in the room, including Alexander's nephew, Cardinal Cesare Borgia, and ten other Spanish cardinals, Pope Julius might have thought to say something like it. But he likely did not risk having his life cut short. In contrary and on other occasion, the pope held Alexander VI in *'happy memory.'*[126]

How treacherous the path of a pope was is apparent with Julius' direct predecessor.[127] He lasted for less than a month. For his election, he was too sick to walk and too lame to kneel, according to mainstream history.[128] To play for time, they had elected a member of the walking dead to replace the Borgia Pope Alexander VI – a compromise candidate, so they say.

However, because this papacy was not long enough to cash in, the Spanocchi Bank of Siena was ruined. They had invested in a dead man?

The pope's election was corrupt.

The Italian cities of Florence and Pisa had long been disobedient to the Catholic Church, particularly when the pope was not friendly with the Kingdom of France. Julius deployed the troops of the Papal States in order to rectify their religious spirits through armed intervention.

He was not nicknamed *'The Warrior Pope'* by mere chance.

The pope was a holy lord of wars.

---

[124] Setton, 1978, 434.

[125] Pope Julius II in Nigel Cawthorne, Sex Lives of the Popes (Prion, 1996) 219 [unable to verify the original source].

[126] Archive di Stato di Roma, Introitus et Exitus, Reg. 535, fol. 182, cited by Pastor, Hist. Popes, VI. 224, note, and Geschichte der Päpste, III-2 (repr. 1956) 693, and note 8, in Setton, 1984, 36.

[127] Pope Pius III aka Francesco Todeschini Piccolomini, was pope from September 22, 1503 to October 18, 1503.

[128] Setton, 1984, 4.

Since Pope Julius wanted to rid himself of royalty, the bishoprics of the Kingdom of France had deemed it within their right to withdraw from the Catholic Church. The papal forces had lost decisive battles at Milan, Bologna, and later Ravenna. The French victors organized a general council at Pisa, which amounted to another anti-papal schism. The pope was invited. He refused to attend.

French Christians had their own kind of reformation.

Modern Pisa boasts a medieval city core second to none. Just outside, its massive cathedral and Leaning Tower attract millions of visitors every year. Back then, the city was an utterly unsuitable place for a council, the pope contended. Indeed, *'Pisa had suffered so grievously in a full fourteen years of siege and desolation that there were hardly any houses still left with their walls intact.* [129] In light of the dangers to the bishops and cardinals while travelling to the council, the meetings at Pisa did not take place with the planned crowds. Because of the possibility of assault, the rebellious undertaking was moved from Pisa to Milan and finally to Lyon in France. Thanks to the mutual bickering of the few cardinals in attendance, it amounted to nothing.

Among other non-issues, they decided to suspend the authority of Pope Julius II.[130]

The damage to the papacy was inflicted anyway.

With Pandora's Box already open, the authority of the Vatican was again criticized by Martin Luther. Nevertheless, all sides insisted on profound church reformation and some kind of enforcement of peace among the feudal overlords.

The ulterior goal of pope and clergy was to plan holy war against the Ottoman-Turks to restore the Holy Land and Jerusalem to Christian rule.[131] To this end, they needed to bring the royals to a pan-European peace and war treaty.

In other words, the thinly attended Fifth Lateran Council at Rome was not entirely voluntary, even though the corrupt package-deal for the election of Pope Julius II contained the obligation to call for a council within two years.

---

[129] Ibid., 95.
[130] Ibid., 120.
[131] Pastor, History of the Popes, VI, append., no. 76, pp. 647-48, in Setton, 1984, 51. Also page 75.

The council focused on suppressing the schism with Pisa-Milan, which was under the protectorate of the French king,[132] one of those monarchs on the pope's list to be militarily eliminated. The holy lord of wars did not seem to have taken into account that when God's intermediary shot, the arrows might come back for him. Like the pope, the French king's ambition – he bore the honorary title 'Most Christian King' – was to attain a 'world monarchy.'[133]

Revolt was written all over.

Under guard by armed Knights Hospitaller, Egidio Viterbo, Luther's Austin Friar anti-friend, opened the council by addressing the evils of the church and pleading for its reform. He insisted that men must act in accordance with immutable religion, not religion with men.[134] Calling for peace among the one-percenters, he wanted to shift the focus such that the *arms of our kings be turned upon Mohammed, the common enemy of Christ.*[135]

In almost every religious council in history, the meaning of peace is the same: war against heretics, those who dare to disagree.

We know next to nothing about the discussions during the few sessions that took place. At least, we are in possession of the council's proclamations. Viterbo seems to have been an advocate of concordance (one united doctrine) and church reform. He attempted also to uphold some of the Augustinian principles. This must not have been an easy feat, in particular because his adversaries of the Dominican order were to argue reform from their radically different point of view.

The man on the other side was the Dominican Master-General, Cajetan,[136] master of terror by the Papal States, that is – the Inquisition. Cajetan was the boss of the national grand inquisitors. He would become a saint in which capacity he remains patron of Argentine – and of gamblers and document forgers – Saint Cajetan.

But wait!

I am confusing Saint Cajetan with another by the name of Thomas Cajetan. He had two faces and one mind. It is an artful maneuver. Both lived around the same time, pursued the same professional obsession, and roamed the Vatican at the same time; one disappeared into life in the service of religious *'charity'* – an

---

[132] Louis XII was King of France 1498 – 1515, Duke of Milan 1499 – 1512, and King of Naples 1501 – 1504.
[133] Setton, 1984, 29, 61.
[134] Ibid., 121.
[135] Ibid.
[136] Thomas Cajetan, aka Gaetanus, aka Tommaso de Vio or Thomas de Vio, 1469 – 1534.

euphemism for advertisement, paid for with the money extorted from the poor – while the other appeared at that moment as a papal diplomat; of one we know where he studied and of the other where he worked; one spoke a lot, but nothing is written down, and the other left a pile of works behind, but he spoke of nothing. Some of the works by the one who knew how to write were later *'expunged'* by the University of Sorbonne in Paris. They came to be viewed as heretical.

The term *expunged* is a red flag. It indicates engineering of history to align with wishful thinking. The works have been censored in order to merit the approval of the Catholic Church.

The intention of the council was to restore peace in the Catholic domain and to overthrow heresies and schisms.

The words *peace* and *overthrow* form a poetic pair.

They wanted to organize a campaign to weed out the enemies of their Truth *'so that the mouths of all schismatics and enemies of peace, those howling dogs, may be silenced and Christians may be able to keep themselves unstained from such pernicious and poisonous contagion.'*[137]

Silencing the howling dogs.

This is not some unfortunate misstep. It is part of the written resolution as agreed on at the council.

Poisonous contagion?

In the definition of Cardinal Cajetan, Christians live their lives in the efficacy of the sacraments under the tutelage of a priesthood obedient to the pope, the Supreme Pontiff of the Catholic Church[138] – the equivalent to the Pontifex Maximus of the long-gone Roman Empire – a dictator. The pope's authority is second only to his god's. All citizens owe total submission to him. It was a wholly totalitarian system that was designed around a despot by leveraging the superstitions of the subjected populations. Infidels upset the harmony of the divinely ordained society.

There is no place for them – except for six feet under.

According to this Truth, everyone who does not follow it is among those needing correction.

---

[137] Fifth Lateran Council, Session 2, May 17, 1512.
[138] Setton, 1984, 126-127.

A diabolic plan was being drawn up by the council to restore the only Truth that was *'sure knowledge.'*

Luther soon became the bull's-eye.

Although the pope's intention was to rid the world of feudal overlords, he made a disastrous mistake. He sent none other than Giovanni di Lorenzo de' Medici to wrest the city of Florence back from the enemies of the Catholic Church.

This ended the Medici family's exile and – we know nothing about it – might have spelled the pope's own end. Supposedly, the Medici cardinal was captured by French troops and ended up in the contested city of Milan. There, he is said to have absolved Milanese and Frenchmen and promoted that nobody should work against the church.[139] A cousin of the cardinal, Giulio de' Medici, appears to have been the messenger for the renewed submission of Kingdom of France and the Medicis to the power of the Catholic Pope.

Trust – but whom?

The two, Giovanni di Lorenzo de' Medici and Giulio di Giuliano de' Medici, just so happened later to become popes of the Catholic Church. 'In the last minute,' the Medici cardinal had escaped from French captivity.

The Medicis were no turncoats.

They had been playing on the French team all along.

---

[139]   Ibid., 129.

### Another Reformation

The council prohibited the sale and purchase of church offices. Including the throne of the pope. The practice has been attempted to be rooted out countless times through the centuries. Its varnished technical term is *simony*.

Corruption does not follow laws.

In addition to its enforcement of the Truth, the Catholic Church had a nose for money.

In its regulation against simony, one can find *'intermediaries, brokers, and bankers'* barred from *'making or benefiting from a will.'* The church gave itself the authority to confiscate their property.[140] The council also included secular banking businesses. In these cases, they consented to such property being seized by the 'secular' authorities. Those nobles in bed with the Catholic Church. The disdain of the papacy could bankrupt them in the blink of an eye. The greed of royalty could bust them in an instant.

The power of the Truth was enforced by creating noble dependencies. There was no business without supporting the Catholic Church.

Apologists claim that the resulting disasters were caused by the political situation. With this council, we have the primary evidence that royalty had no choice but to advertise Catholicism. The ringleaders were the heads of the Catholic Church, the pope, his cardinals, and his enforcers from the terror network of the Inquisition. If the nobles did not sufficiently uphold and expand Catholicism or failed to send growing tax revenues to Rome, they lost their feudal privileges through the intervention of the Inquisition.

Could they have rebelled?

Of course – in rags.

Under Luther's leadership, some would soon come to refuse compliance.

However, the Catholic Church did not need Martin Luther to enlighten its leaders about the corruption in its religious organization.

They were fully self-aware.

As it is with warfare, things do not always work out as planned, and a stroke of luck turned the tide on the French front in favor of the papacy. French troops had to withdraw into their trenches at home. Their king had to declare his allegiance to the Vatican.

---

[140] Fifth Lateran Council, Session 5, February 16, 1513.

Now we can see just how corrupt the feudal system was: in advance of the victory, the pope had made a most secret arrangement with the King of England. In it, the latter would not only be granted the title and rights to the Kingdom of France, but in gratitude, the title *'Most Christian King'* would be transferred from the King of France to him.[141] The pope was the Vicar of Christ. The Triple Crown of the Vatican symbolized emperors and kings as his vice-regents.

The pope was in charge, and royal obedience paid off.

At least, it should have.

The French-averse Pope Julius II died around the time of the total defeat of the Francophones – surprise! – and the French-friendly Medici pope, Leo X, started out powerless, so it is said, only to immediately pick up the trail of the ongoing council. The schism with Pisa-Milan was ended. The formerly disobedient clerics had their honors and dignities restored.

They appeared as though they had won the challenge to papal authority.[142]

We know nothing about how Julius found his martyrdom. He died of a fever, so history records, or perhaps of grief. He should have been more careful whose wine he sipped in celebration of his victories.

Having a Medici buoy to the top is an indication that the printed laws did not prevent the progression of worldly realities of corruption. That is how important a pope was for the Medici clan and the other banker families.

The here-portrayed preference of the pope conflicts with mainstream history. Wait for actions to speak for themselves.

What had happened was that the papal alliance basically disintegrated over the spoils of its success against the Kingdom of France. Venice, traditionally not on good terms with the Vatican, quickly rebuilt its relations with the defeated to hold the hated Pope Julius in check.

That the Venetians would jump ship at first opportunity was a given after they had earlier been stabbed into religious submission by the papal troops. Put into this equation the French-friendly Florence as well as Genoa. Things could have turned against the papacy in a heartbeat.

---

[141] Setton, 1984, 124.
[142] Ibid., 150.

Pope Julius was under the protectorate of the Holy Roman Empire and the half-hearted English. But the death knell was the invitation of Spain to battle against the Kingdom of France. It resulted in the re-encroachment of Spanish interests over the Italian Peninsula.

The blood-dripping swords of France had merely been replaced with the blood-soaked daggers of Spain.

Christian blood, that is. On all sides.

Leo's goal now was to enforce peace among the Christian rulers – and then go after the 'enemies' of the Catholic faith.[143] The idea was not universal peace but a unification of Catholic forces against everybody else – still. Simply put, the dream – or rather the nightmare – was ultimately to obliterate all competing Christian sects, Judaism, and finally Islam.

The collective idea in this council was that they could solve the pan-European sectarian differences by deciding – for all others – what was right or wrong.

The council's decisions were written down and distributed as evidence. The paper put the opposition on fire.

Those men had no soul.

The human soul is a marvelous idea, if one considers it to be the spirit of humanity. When we refer to a person's good soul, we do not mean something tangible, much less so something worth fighting over how 'it' should be understood. Back then, beliefs were different, much more deep-seated than they are today, even among the best of Christians. The council insisted on an *immortal* soul. This terminology sought to eliminate all doubts about what 'it' was supposed be.[144] For that, they were willing to condemn anyone who either rejected or doubted its immortality.

The issue was not belief. Their determination to *impose* the Catholic version of faith with terminal love was a crime against humanity. On the other hand, the problem for the church was straightforward: without immortality of the soul – since they must have recognized that the body is given to worms after death – the Gospels' promise for eternal life seemed impossible to fulfill; there would be no resurrection; no salvation. In consequence, there would be no End of the World and, with this, no New Jerusalem.

Without the immortal soul, Christianity was to collapse by the weight of its religious rationale.

---

[143] Fifth Lateran Council, Session 6, April 27, 1513.
[144] Fifth Lateran Council, Session 8, December 19, 1513.

What is the soul?

Is there any evidence to show for this mysterious creature? Any at all? Believe it or not, an eyewitness account reports that the soul of a pope was *'carried to heaven in a fiery globe,'* at midnight.[145] The same witness lists a host of other miracles and armies of souls that went to heaven. Spectacular! The witness was Pope Gregory[146] from the turn of the seventh century.

Given the conflict of interest, he was probably not the most credible of all possible witnesses.

In the absence of tangible evidence, we need to look a little deeper.

In the biblical story of the first humans, the god of the Israelites warned Adam under threat of life not to eat from the tree of knowledge of good and evil. In 'disobedience,' Eve gave Adam fruit to eat from the tree, consequently giving humanity the gift of intellect[147] – soul. Had this act not taken place, humans would be no smarter than chimpanzees. Devoid of understanding, primate apes (the hominid state of Adam and Eve before eating the fruit) could not have been responsible for the disregard of the godly warning.

Eve's deed was the cause of human enlightenment.

Judaic believers are eternally thankful by declaring her noncompliance as the original sin. It is for this 'sin' that all of humanity needs to suffer until a savior comes to our rescue.

Luther said that a woman adopts her husband's name as *'confirmation of the punishment or subjection which the woman incurred through her sin.'*[148] This crime was not committed by Eve alone. Adam went along. And her action was nothing but curiosity. Nevertheless, by the reasoning of all Judaic religions, Eve's guilt was collectively transferred to the next generation of the entire female gender. And the next. Up until today.

The original sin is the eternal justification for treating women as second class.

The merciful, almighty god was tricked by Eve.

The god banished the arch-couple from the Garden of Eden to make sure that humans did not eat from the tree of life also. Eating from it would have enabled humanity to live forever.

---

[145] Gregory the Great, *Dialogues* (ca. 600 AD) IV:VII.

[146] Pope Gregory I was pope of the Catholic Church 590 – 604 AD.

[147] Genesis 3:7-3:12 (NIV).

[148] Luther's Works, Volume I, Lectures on Genesis, Chapters 1-5, Edited by Jaroslav Pelikan, translated by Georg V. Schick (Concordia, Copyright © 1958, reprinted by permission of Concordia) 235.

The god even placed angry angels and a flaming sword in front of the garden in order to block access to the tree.[149] He could simply have commanded them to stay off his property.

After all, he is God.

But in the myth, Adam and Eve were given knowledge, intellect – soul.

Sooner or later, boundless human curiosity posed a threat to the Truth of organized religions of Judaic origin. Targeting the teaching of philosophy at its church-censored universities, the council's argument was that study that lacked *'the flavoring of divine wisdom and the light of revealed truth – sometimes leads to error rather than to the discovery of the Truth.'*[150] The study of philosophy was limited to five years. After this, only those devoted to theology were permitted to continue. The idea was that those would cleanse and heal *'the infected sources of philosophy and poetry.'*[151] They had a religious police academy in mind.

Moderns still rely on church-'cleansed' literature, because all too often, that is all that is left of what was not destroyed in this process.

Expunged.

Some apologists and even respected scholars might like to say that this is just history. We are living in the twenty-first century, after all. But since we have been blessed with Eve's gift of a soul, this position is intellectually lazy.

It is also patently false.

Scripture discourages believers to think on their own.[152] After all, thinking derives from the original sin.

The rejection of curiosity provides for the rule of turning a blind eye to religious abuse and puts sound judgment into the hands of the clergy alone.

Faith requires the unconditional submission to the church's institutions and their leaders, to the synagogues, and to the mosques.

So says the Bible.

Therefore, it must be true.

The real goals are in the symbolism of the Vatican City's coat of arms. On its flags, it depicts the Tiara with the Triple Crown, the symbol of king of kings – world leadership.

---

[149] Genesis 3:22-24 NIV.
[150] Fifth Lateran Council, Session 8, December 19, 1513.
[151] Ibid.
[152] Sirach 3:21–24.

The King of the Jews is the king of the world; the pope of the Catholic Church is the leader of the planet; the Muslim caliph is the supreme boss of the universe. This is not a trivial problem. It defines our time.

It had, has, and will have grave consequences for all of humanity.

We need to carefully consider the evidence at hand.

The violent and hateful content of the Bible as a *'moral compass'* of humanity is perhaps not the best way forward considering those who wish to freely choose not to have anything to do with it.

The next topic in the council was Bohemia, which today is essentially the Czech territory between Germany and Hungary.

Bohemia had long fallen off the Catholic faith through the reformer Jan Hus.[153] He was another forerunner of the Protestant Reformation, providing Martin Luther with a roadmap on how to organize his church 100 years after Hus.

The Hussite Revolution was an era during which the Bohemians withstood five crusades that were organized by the pope to get Hus' followers back under his fatherly control.

In its essence, their shortlist of demands, known as the Four Articles of Prague, sounded similar to Martin Luther's 95 Theses.

The subjects to be considered were *'intended mainly to expose the corruptions of the church, the avarice, extortion, lewdness, and hypocrisy of the clergy.*

> *[...] These are the prohibition of gross public sins whether in laity or clergy;*
>
> *the inconsistency of large revenues and pomp with the simplicity of ministers of Jesus Christ;*
>
> *the freedom of the word of God to be read and preached in all places, 'without any inhibition of either spiritual or earthly power;'*
>
> *and the communion of the body [bread] and blood [wine] of Christ as he ordained [also to disciples].*[154]

---

[153] Jan Hus, 1369–1415.

[154] Ezra Hall Gillett, The life and times of John Huss: Or, The Bohemian reformation of the fifteenth century (Gould and Lincoln, 1864) Band 2, 369. The full articles are on page 442-443.

The revolution ushered in religious resistance along the line of thought of the Four Articles of Prague – until it was finally crushed again by the Catholic Church 100 years after Martin Luther. The conflict left behind tens of thousands of widows, orphans, and mothers who lost their sons.

How do I know that Martin Luther was a product of the Hussite Revolution? His home base Wittenberg is merely 60 miles[155] north of the locations of the border raids by the followers of Jan Hus. The four articles appear as a prototype for Luther's ideas, almost as though he had used the text for his draft for the 95 Theses.

Luther successfully continued what others had long begun.

But we must be aware of the kind of freedom that the Hussites had in mind. They have nothing in common with what modern Westerners take for granted. Instead, their plan was to go back to a more pious time, without economic ambitions, and under the full control of the Hussite Church and the watchful eyes of the Christian community. They wished to remain in the larger body of the Catholic Church, without unnecessary innovations other than going back to the roots of paucity.

Indeed, after the land was ravaged by the Catholic Church, Bohemia suffered for generations under extreme systemic poverty.

They got what they asked for.

And they were among the first to join the Protestant Reformation.

Even though there were some 'democratic' underpinnings in the causes for the Hussite Wars, life in piety and abject poverty was their choice.

The four articles clarify that they were a direct consequence of the teachings of the Gospels, which glorify poverty. Written under the rule of the Roman Empire, the New Testament stokes its followers into passive aggression by refusing to partake in economic or social life – even family life is rejected – other than what is necessary for barebones subsistence. This differentiates itself only little from today's doctrinal impoverishment of the Muslim world, which, given democratic opportunities, votes itself right back into theocracies.

Where the pious rule, *freedom* means piety in the image of their only Truth.

Freedom may bear sharply diverse ideas when uttered from fundamentalist lips.

---

[155]   100 kilometers.

In short: organized religion is an enemy of freedom for the individual and of freedom for all.

That does not mean that religious freedom is not sacrosanct. It is. Everyone is free to believe in ghosts or in rocks turning into meat. But the business of organized religion is *not* to be free any more than other businesses are 'free'.

According to the council under Pope Leo, the power of the *infidels* – a word that we are accustomed to from Muslim hate sermons – had grown remarkably.[156] The council's mission was to bring Bohemia back home to the caring lap of the Holy Father in the Vatican. There were grand words and gestures of peace, but they were conditional either to voluntary submit to Rome or to be converted by the force of arms. To this end, inquisitors were sent to 'negotiate' a deal – with thumbscrews in their luggage.

Their behavior was anti-Renaissance, anti-social, anti-humanitarian, anti-progress, and against the freedom of individuals. This was then a criminal organization, thoroughly dedicated to oppressing or eliminating anyone who stood in the way of its power.

Point in case: the Catholic Church was attempting thought control at a time of great intellectual awakening.

At the same time, Europe was exhausted by war. *'Italy has been almost wiped out by internecine slaughter, cities and territories have been disfigured, partly overturned and partly levelled.'*[157] Instead of Muslims killing Muslims, in Italy, Catholics slaughtered Catholic Christians. Yet, their recipe to fix the disaster was to call for higher Catholic unity in order to fight the enemies of the faith as one force.[158]

With this goal in mind, Pope Leo X issued an ill-fated Papal Bull to the Hungarians to organize a crusade against the Muslim Ottoman-Turks. This external enemy was on the march north up the Balkan toward Hungary, Austria, and Bohemia. While the papal call led to the quick gathering of 40,000 peasant solders, the leading cardinal failed in leadership and supplies.

This Catholic Cardinal had joined the ranks of the super-rich and had tried to bribe himself onto the throne at the Vatican. The Crusade turned into a yearlong civil war of peasant crusaders against Hungarian nobility. They had enough of being brutally exploited by their feudal overlords in the service of the church.

---

[156] Fifth Lateran Council, Session 8, December 19, 1513.
[157] Fifth Lateran Council, Session 9, May 5, 1514.
[158] Ibid.

Many Hungarians were indifferent over whether they would be under the yoke of the Catholic Church or Ottoman Muslims. Moreover, Western Europeans did not think much of Hungarians. The latter's leadership was deeply divided by bitter factional strife. Their German-influenced court party was hated by the people.[159]

National superiority-complexes and aspirations to imperial leadership stood in the way of focused joint operations.

The conflict weakened the kingdom to the point of offering an open door for Ottoman-Turks to march into Europe. Their fights with the Safavids in Persia and the Mamluks in Syria and Egypt prevented them from simply walking through Hungary to Austria.

Despite all this, the pope was opposed to a truce because he viewed a proposed peace as a mere Ottoman prelude to the next opportunity to overrun the weakened kingdom.

He was fantasizing of his own offensive to wipe out the Muslim infidels.[160]

Moreover, when the King of Hungary and Bohemia died,[161] his ten-year-old son came to the throne.[162] In his stead, Pope Leo put a cardinal[163] in charge of ruling Hungary for the next five, critical years of the nation's disintegration.[164] Hungary was soon thereafter annexed by Ottoman-Turks. This same cardinal had failed in the earlier crusade against the Ottomans. At least, he succeeded in amassing a fortune – he was a clerical billionaire of the time.

The Catholic Church was in control of the royal dynasties.

---

[159] Setton, 1984, 235.

[160] Ibid., 163.

[161] Vladislaus II was king of Hungary and Bohemia 1471 – 1516.

[162] Louis II of Hungary was king of Hungary and Bohemia 1516 – 1526. At the age of two, he had been crowned King of Hungary in 1508 and of Bohemia in 1509. As a nine year old, he was adopted by Emperor Maximilian I and married to his granddaughter, Mary of Austria, in 1515.

[163] Cardinal Tamás Bakócz, 1442 – 1521.

[164] Setton, 1984, 158.

### Inclination to Evil from Youth

To stem corruption, the council established moral guidelines for cardinals. While Luther accused the clergy of the Catholic Church of living in splendor, the council sought to force all cardinals into a frugal life of modesty and kindness.[165] This appears to be an odd approach to reforming the Catholic Church. After all, the sender was the head of the Medici dynasty, one of the richest families in Europe.

This idea overlooked human nature, from which even cardinals and popes could not escape. People love comfort. Today, the question is how hard they are willing to work for it. Back then, you were born into comfort.

Or not.

The need for a show of modesty appears to have its origin in a decision from almost a century earlier. For the election of a pope,[166] one-half of all revenues were pledged to flow into the pockets of the cardinals.

You may want to reread this. Half of all church revenues were funneled into the wallets of the one-percenters of the clergy.

This is not to be confused with a massive tax cut for the wealthy. It can get much worse. Instead, they were *subsidizing* the rich who had already enjoyed tax cuts to the point of being exempt. And they were just warming up.

All for one. None for all.

Even though the actual numbers are kept under a shroud of secrecy, we can put this in a modern perspective. For example, among many other countries Germany's government acts as the tax farmers of the Catholic Church today. It transfers almost 10 billion U.S. dollars a year to the Vatican. The budget of the Catholic Church in the United States of America, where it represents a minority religion, is nearly 200 billion U.S. Dollars. The United States government does not act as tax farmers. However, religious schools benefit from education- and construction-funds. Religious organizations can also receive subsidies through businesses that they control. Globally, the Catholic Church owns almost 200 million acres of land[167] that it originally stole from the people. The Vatican alone has a modern annual budget in the vicinity of half a billion U.S. Dollars.

Half of all revenues went to the cardinals.

---

[165] Fifth Lateran Council, Session 9, May 5, 1514.

[166] Pope Eugene IV, aka Gabriele Condulmer, was pope from 1431 to 1447.

[167] Over 700,000 square kilometers.

At least, the council appears to have recognized the storm on the horizon and attempted to address the problem, although amateurishly. They were also obsessed with creating laws about the attire of church staff and house staff of the clergy. They crafted an outward air of modesty. Robes had to be at least ankle-length and of no color other than the permitted uniforms.[168] Multi-colored garments were prohibited at the threat of excommunication and loss of job and decorations.[169]

The council was much more concerned with appearance rather than substance. But it was specifically designed to set the clergy visually apart from diplomats, ambassadors, nobles, royals, and other dignitaries. At that time, showing off the richness of functionaries' dresses was a matter of courtesy at Europe's courts.[170]

Because the church wanted to rid itself of nobility, its dress code was intended to distinguish its members from them.

The church recognized early on that one way to maintain an oppressed religious society is to teach religion to children. Indeed, it is part of the Gospels.[171] An epistle muses that indoctrinating humans from a very young age works best.[172]

In this council, the teaching of religion to children – radicalizing them from an early age – was such a focus. They knew that youth is lost if it cannot be infiltrated early.[173]

The council called it an *'inclination to evil from youth.'*

The Catholic clerics intended to enforce a unified religious message of conformity through the abuse of young minds.

During Luther's time, no formal system of early education existed. Christians and Muslims alike were, if at all, schooled in churches and mosques. For this service, parents had to pay fees to their oppressors. Only a few could afford it, and education depended on wealth and status. Christians and Muslims relied otherwise on their illiterate parents. The few who received an education did so primarily in reading the Gospels and the Koran, respectively. They learned everything they needed to know – about the End of the World.

---

[168] Fifth Lateran Council, Session 9, May 5, 1514.
[169] Ibid.
[170] Setton, 1984, 153.
[171] Ephesians 6:4.
[172] Polycarp, The Epistle of Polycarp to the Philippians (110–140 AD).
[173] Fifth Lateran Council, Session 9, May 5, 1514.

In a perfect cycle of self-enforcement, the successfully conformed students could rise in the bureaucracies and become secretaries or judges, for example.

In contrast, Jews diligently trained their children in their religious duties, boys *and* girls.[174] In the synagogues, of course, and at home. While the Jewish population was universally educated, its general members still did not learn anything useful other than how to obey their religious leaders. But for the Rabbinic leadership, it was easier to identify talent and to train and deploy it for their purposes.

We can see today how narrow-minded communities can emerge that pose an increasing threat to the general population.

An estimated 550,000 Hasidic Jews live in Brooklyn, New York today. Their chances of success for stepping outside of their community into the real world are from minuscule to nil. Members rely on the support of their Hasidic comrades all their lives. They receive no professional education to make a living, so much so that a 2019 state-standardized test in reading and math agreed to be given to more than 1,000 boys by the Central United Talmudical Academy brought forth its gravity:

every! one! failed!

They know nothing but the first five books of the Bible and the rules of their penitentiary. For them, stepping out of Brooklyn is equivalent to travelling to another planet. Even English is alien.

It is true. Change comes about most effectively through children.

New York's uneducated Hasidic community is 'officially' among the poorest in North America. Hasidic schools received US$ 1 billion in government funding in the four years between 2018 and 2021 alone.[175] The government pays Hasidic private schools. This enables the building of powerful voting blocks. The result is a government left powerless to enforce laws that ought to protect children's education. Government funding only starts with the schools; food stamps plus WIC,[176] housing vouchers, Medicaid, and subsidies under Section 8 enable lifelong habits of fundamentalism.

---

[174] Talmud – Mas. Yoma 82a.

[175] Eliza Shapiro, Brian M. Rosenthal, In Hasidic Enclaves, Failing Private Schools Flush With Public Money (New York Times, September 11, 2022).

[176] Women, Infants and Children (WIC) is a federal assistance program of the Food and Nutrition Service (FNS) of the (USDA) for healthcare and nutrition of low-income pregnant women, breastfeeding women, and children under the age of five.

These schools receive funding in exchange of promises to meet the educational standards of the laws.

They will never be met. Fulfilling the promises violates the word of their god.

This organized crime is defrauding the government in the billions. For example, in October 2022, the Central United Talmudical Academy in Williamsburg, Brooklyn entered a deferred prosecution agreement. This is the largest private Hasidic Jewish school in New York State. Among other habitual abuses of various government programs, they were reimbursed for student meals. The school never provided them. As a peculiarity in the American justice system, a stay-out-of-jail card for these criminals cost them just over eight million dollars. It is such a small cost for the business of a criminal organization that they probably budgeted for it. Not that they needed to. They could simply pay the fines from the uninterrupted cash-flow from the government for services that they do not intend to provide.

And thus, the government enables the schemes to continue.

Put that together with North America's highest birth rate in these communities. It is a perfect subversion of democracy itself.

They seem to be at their best in milking public treasuries for children with special needs. Only that some or many do neither need support nor use it or get it. In some of the Hasidic schools, more than half of students are classified as such compared to one fifth across all schools in New York. Here is how it works: an application is made for assisting a child's education for special needs; the application includes 'enhanced' rates that can be as much as five times the standard rate for the 'educator' to speak Yiddish. This closes the circle. The entire cash-flow ends up in a community that is unwilling to even entertain integrating, participating, or contributing to society as a whole.

In New York, about 80% of such requests originate in districts with predominantly Hasidic and Orthodox communities.[177]

They are gaming the system at our expense.

Their behavior is a magnet of hatred.

Yet, those with the courage to raise the issue are branded anti-Semites.

---

[177] All data from Brian M. Rosenthal, How a Windfall of Special Education Funding Benefited Hasidic Schools (New York Times, December 29, 2022).

In order to understand what was going on in the minds of church leaders during the sixteenth century, we can have a look at the activities around the Red Mosque in Islamabad, Pakistan, in our time. The mosque was a school (madrasa) for training children to become mujahedeen to fight with the Taliban. Footage on social media shows how children are taught to memorize the Koran without understanding a word of it.

There are an estimated 40,000 such schools for militants throughout Pakistan. Like slurry, they pump out millions of extremists. Many students of its network joined ISIS. Asked how peace could be found in his country, the imam asserted that the implementation of the Koran and Sharia Law was the only way to peace.

He supported ISIS as an organization, which wanted to implement an Islamic system.[178]

Under the command of the dictator Pervez Musharaf, the Pakistani army attempted to flatten the mosque in 2007. Dressed in a burqa, the leading Imam[179] tried to flee the scene. In the wake of the crisis, neighboring moderate schools had to be closed.

The children ended up being the losers in any case.

How they recruited their disciples is a lesson in the economics of organized religion. Enrolling children in these madrasas is free. There, they learn the Koran – nothing else. On top of free indoctrination, the madrasas provide them with all they need, including food.

The incentive for poor families is obvious.

In particular, those who cannot feed their ever-growing households on wages that can barely support one person. They teach intellectual and economic poverty as the ideal state of laity. How did they pay for the 'social services' – and the guns – that were provided to Pakistani kids?

Alms. From the poor.

Countries with overwhelming religious majorities are among the poorest in the world. Since systemic poverty and trauma[180] fosters religiosity, the vicious cycle is perpetuated by recruiting the youngest into schools of militancy.

---

[178] Azam Khan, No regret over supporting IS, says Lal Masjid [Red Mosque] cleric, Tribune Pakistan, October 20, 2017.

[179] Imam Abdul Aziz, ca *1960 – .

[180] Chris Sibley, and Joseph Bulbulia, Faith after an Earthquake: A Longitudinal Study of Religion and Perceived Health before and after the 2011 Christchurch New Zealand Earthquake." Plos One, 2012.

Who are the major beneficiaries of traumatic experiences, such as violent conflicts or other humanitarian disasters?[181]

War is profitable for weapons dealers – and for organized religion.

Their payoff is enormous: a martyr warrior for a few pieces of bread.

We have already learned how democracy can vote itself into tyranny in the most unexpected ways. A healthy democracy rests on intellectual diversity and tolerance, not on uniformity.[182] It can best be fostered in settings of diversity and merit during the formative years of children.

It is again France that is at the spearheading change. Its administration approved the Charter of Republican Values that includes measures aimed at restricting home-schooling to medical reasons and scrutinizing religious schools. Public funds are limited to those who sign a secular 'charter.'

What else did it take to make the despotic feudal system under the leadership of the Catholic Church work? Anyone who committed blasphemy lost their livelihood.[183] Blasphemy is to show contempt, not only to a deity but also to clergy.

The council noted that this *'has increased beyond measure.'*

The consequences of blasphemy are defined in the Bible in a passage that brought death to a woman who had blasphemed the god of the Israelites.[184] The biblical message includes having to fear one's neighbors, who could watch every move of others and could accuse anyone of blasphemy. This could potentially lead to a death sentence by stoning, even if the accused did nothing wrong. In engaging its followers, the faith built its strength on group dynamics of Stasi-style[185] espionage and reverse-whistle-blowing.

---

Ronald C. Kessler, Sandro Galea, Russell T. Jones and Holly A. Parker, Mental illness and suicidality after Hurricane Katrina, Bulletin of the World Health Organization, 2006.

Jeremy E. Uecker, Religious and Spiritual Responses to 9/11: Evidence from the Add Health Study, Sociological Spectrum, 2008.

[181] Pew Research Center, The Age Gap in Religion Around the World, June 13, 2018. See also Mihai Croicu and Ralph Sundberg, UCDP GED Codebook version 17.2, Department of Peace and Conflict Research, Uppsala University, 2017.)

[182] Diversity is also democracy's weakness because of its poor decision-making and prioritizing processes. Religious or otherwise fundamentalist minority groups can undermine it through their uniform and intolerant stance on issues by sowing division among those outside of their conformist groups. Democracies could be safeguarded with anti-alliance and anti-monopolizing rules that ensure pluralism in legislatives and executives.

[183] Talmud – Mas. Yoma 82a.

[184] Leviticus 24:10ff.

[185] Stasi stands for Staats-Sicherheit and refers to the department of security in the former German Democratic Republic under Erich Honegger, in Eastern Germany. It probably was the most effective

Nobility could buy its way out of trouble. Regular people were imprisoned. Repeat offenders were incarcerated for life or sent to *'the galleys.'*[186] Detainees became rowers on warships. Tens of thousands who either did not recant their faith or were found guilty of blasphemy ended up in the nautical form of medieval concentration camps.

Many of them died in 'service.' Hardly any recanted.

Faith can be quite stubborn, in particular at sword-point.

But here comes the kicker: judges who did *not* take action could be subject to the same penalties. And even that was not all. Those who *did* take action could line their wallets with a third of the fines imposed.[187]

That makes for one heck of an impartial legal system.

The only way to not get sucked into the mill of the judicial and religious machinery was to stay low or go underground.

It was corrupt to its core.

For Luther's sake, there was something worth dying for.

The Christian Gospels are a trough of anti-Semitic blasphemies against Rabbinic Judaism. But when the words flew the other way, it was a different matter. Then the bully suddenly feigned tender feelings for someone not being politically correct.

To be fair, the Koran of the Muslims is a full-blown diatribe against Jews, Christians, and anyone else who fails to convert to Islam. The cursing and blaspheming start with the first sura and hardly ever end until the very last. It starts with asking not to be guided to the path of those who have evoked the anger of their god.[188] The last sura seeks for refuge from the evil whisperer.[189] It literally blasphemes an opponent of Islam.

I will get to their false claim of peace later.

Things have changed. However, blasphemy is still a crime in many Western majority Christian countries today. Austria, Denmark, Germany, Greece, Italy, Poland, and Switzerland are only a few of those.

In the Middle East? Blasphemy is a death trap.

---

and repressive secret police organization in the West. Its agents heavily relied on ordinary citizens to spy on their neighbors.

[186] Fifth Lateran Council, Session 9, May 5, 1514.

[187] Ibid.

[188] Koran 1:5-1:7 (Rodwell).

[189] Koran 114 (Rodwell).

Full-face veils are particularly disturbing because they intentionally create a barrier against human socialization. They disable the female face to play its role in personal interactions. Should we be so impressed by their religious devotion that we at once convert to their inhumane version of theocratic lunacy? The higher moral of having their beat-up women dressed as ghosts walk 5 feet behind their husbands is an appalling display of misogyny. Their display screams hatred against secular values and freedoms for all. Turbans, side-locks, or other religious symbolism, all serve this same purpose: stay away unless you think like me.

It defines bigotry.

The burqa or medieval priestly garments signal an impenetrable spiritual fence that those who think differently must not cross.

Priestly garments are designed to instill fear and respect in their subjects before they merit any of it.

Considering the increasing weaponizing of organized religion and the threat that is perceived through the display of religious symbolism, the European Court of Huan Rights accepts restrictions by employers. In the name of freedom of and from religion and of living and working together in a free and pluralist society, they can keep workplaces and customer areas free of any kind of concealment or religious symbolism.

While this may sound counter-intuitive to freedom at first, a look at the travel norms for foreign women in Saudi Arabia is enlightening. Unless women are met at the airport by a husband, a male relative, or a sponsor, they are not allowed to enter the country. Female travellers are advised to dress conservatively, wear a veil, and cover at least collarbones and knees. Figure hugging dresses are not appreciated. The norms are so effective that every foreigner obliges. In some cities and in business settings, women are bullied into wearing an abaya, a full-length head covering. Gender segregation is held up high: men and women generally socialize in same-sex groups. Women should not be surprised if men refuse to shake hands with them. It is inappropriate for men to touch them. The Mutawwa, the Saudis' religious police, are watching out for cultural violators. As late as 2017, a woman could be arrested if she travelled with a man to whom she was not married or was not a male relative or a sponsor. Likewise, women are often not served in restaurants if they are not appropriately accompanied.

In 2017, the Mutawwa have lost their arresting powers – for now. It is a case study in how governments can put religion on a leash. Afghanistan, Indonesia, Iran, Malaysa, Nigeria, Palestine, and Sudan are other nations who pride themselves of similar theocratic enforcement agencies.

Travellers to Abu Dhabi in the United Arab Emirates may find themselves surprised by a 14-point pamphlet by the Abu Dhabi Tourism Police that instructs them with the city's social norms.

The pamphlet ends with *'Your Safety is Our Concern'.*

In Luther's time, these words could have been nailed to the church doors at St. Peter's in Rome.

Have a safe journey to heaven.

The dark reality will hit home as we proceed.

Where the terror of blasphemy can lead was made clear when in 2016 a poor 15-year-old Pakistani[190] approached his imam.[191] Earlier, the boy had shown his hand in response to a question that he misunderstood to be asking who loved Prophet Muhammad. As soon as he realized his error, the teenager put down his hand, but the imam was screaming at him, *'blasphemer!'* The boy fled in disgrace as others joined the imam in shouting him down and questioning *'Don't you love your prophet?'*

It does not take a religious context for this to be the ultimate nightmare, a traumatic humiliation that would leave deep scars and lifelong anxiety in almost any person.

Since the boy's 'offence' was paramount to a death sentence, he fled in fear of being lynched and later returned to the mosque to beg for forgiveness of his sin – an honest mistake. As a sacrifice, he had cut off his right hand and presented it on a plate.

What followed is even more astonishing. Despite the arrest of the cleric, for the love of Prophet Muhammad, the boy and his family declined to press charges.[192]

This is an environment where parents show pride in their children's religiosity. The more extreme their offspring, the better their reputation.

---

[190] Anwar Ali.

[191] Shabir Ahmad.

[192] Waqar Gillani and Rod Nordland, Boy's Response to Blasphemy Charge Unnerves Many in Pakistan, New York Times, January 18, 2016.

This is what the culture of the Catholic Church in the sixteenth century looked like.

The Koran is outspoken about the consequences of being not in favor of Prophet Muhammad. Those should be slain or crucified, it says, or have their alternate hands and feet cut off.[193] The text leaves some interpretative latitude with other forms of punishments. But the faithful tend to respond with the most stringent rules to humiliation. At the heart of the matter is the loss of good standing in the entire community, the loss of pride and self-worth.

Chatter-boxes have the long memory of an elephant.

Cutting off limbs was also part of the arsenal of terror during the Inquisition. Throughout Christian history, church writers prided themselves on cutting off hands, feet, or noses from their religious dissenters. The cruel tradition can be traced right back to the Gospels. There, Jesus Christ himself said that those who made followers stumble in their faith should be thrown into the sea with millstones around their necks. And if your own hand causes you to doubt, cut it off, he commanded.[194]

Jesus' words are law for Catholic, Protestant, or any other Christian sect.

Jews are not lagging in their cruelty.

A number of nations have already recognized the fallacy. In France, the Burqa has to stay inside the home. In Belgium, people who cover their faces in public places face a $200 fine and up to seven days in jail. In the Netherlands, the Burqa cannot be worn in public places, such as public transport, schools, hospitals, or government buildings. In 2016, Switzerland and Bulgaria prohibited wearing the Burqa in public places.

Belgium and other countries still collect 'taxes' for the Catholic Church. Having replaced the medieval tax farmers, the Belgian annual contribution is to the tune of 400 million Euros. Likewise do Austria, Croatia, Denmark, Finland, Germany, Italy, Sweden, and Switzerland for a multitude of their accepted religious organizations. It is a remnant of feudal lordship over its subjects.

Sorcery merited consequences not unlike blasphemy. It is the use of magic, black arts, witchcraft, wizardry, spells, incantations, and, in the words of the council, *'enchantments, divinations, superstitions and the invoking of demons.*[195] The members of the council regulated superstitions. None of these imaginary things exist in the real world. However, the faithful not only believed in their divinities,

---

[193] Koran 5:33-5:35 (Rodwell).
[194] Mark 9:42-9:48.
[195] Fifth Lateran Council, Session 9, May 5, 1514.

anti-divinities, and the supernatural, they also took demons, witches, and magical tricks for real. They even believed in the power of religious relics from their saints – although they were fakes.

A chip from the True Cross to which Jesus Christ had been nailed was worth a fortune.

This cross had been misplaced for 300 years before it was found by a woman named Helena. She was the mother of Emperor Constantine the Great.[196]

Nobody cared. The souvenir business was booming.

All these imaginary dangers, collectively lumped together with Judaizers and other kinds of heretics were *'subject to excommunication'* – for what the targets cared – and subject to *'rightful'* convictions. These penalties could be inflicted on anybody practicing critical thinking, or just anybody at any time, and in particular those who attracted the attention of the civilian or ecclesiastical authorities by merely being economically successful.

It worked both ways.

Those who believed differently or not at all were socially isolated. Christians were forbidden to interact with them. They were *'to be totally excluded from the company of Christ's faithful and expelled from any position.'*[197] They applied the full force of group pressure. Unlike today, the price for not believing as they did was astronomical and could include job, limb, and life.

Defenseless targets were persecuted by the faith police – the Catholic version of the Mutawwa, Saudi Arabia's religious police – and *'with careful enquiry,'* church-appointed *'judges'* reached their verdicts. *'Careful enquiry'* was conducted through the Inquisition. It translates to testimonies and confessions through torture – expressly sanctioned by the council.[198]

What an incredible collusion where accusers and judges – men of faith – are of the same religious party! Woe to those who got entangled into the wheels of the Catholic Church!

---

[196] Constantine the Great aka Flavius Valerius Aurelius Constantinus Augustus was emperor of the Roman Empire. He was Caesar in the West from 306, Augustus from 309, and sole emperor of the entire empire 324 – 337.

[197] Fifth Lateran Council, Session 9, May 5, 1514.

[198] Fifth Lateran Council, Session 10, May 4, 1515.

Before the council, some persons had long been able to acquire certificates from the Catholic Church that entitled them to a status of *'exempt.'* They paid bribes in order to gain legal immunity. The idea was initially meant to be applied to notaries of the Vatican. As a lucrative source of revenues, the concept of *'exempt'* was expanded to whoever could afford to satisfy the hungry church.

With this council, the category of *'exempt'* was cancelled, and these people were expressively targeted for intimidation. Better yet, the cost of processes against the *'exempt'* was loaded onto the persecuted.[199]

Heads up, you lose. Heads down, you cannot win.

The church went out to *'set examples'* in order to frighten the rest of the dissenters.[200] The sentenced were punished through the arm of the Inquisition *'without any hope of pardon or forgiveness.'* It was a verdict to either rotting for life in a damp cellar of a castle, being forced to labor on the galleys, being chained up and tortured, or being expedited to heaven.

In any case, a 'conviction' would change the outcome only in the timing of the Dark Angel's arrival.

The threat of terror was designed to keep the entire population in obedience.

It is easy to imagine a tribunal by the Taliban in the mountains of Kandahar, Afghanistan. For those guilty of an imaginary crime, stoning is the expected mode of expiry.

Death does not come easy.

These decisions were made at a time of great social awakening – the Renaissance – a time when humanist thought started to radically change art, architecture, politics, science, and literature.

Leonardo da Vinci,[201] the Universal Genius and embodiment of the Renaissance Man was now 63 years old. A decade earlier, he had created the Mona Lisa. The Master was now working on a scientific treatise on anatomy.

Another Renaissance Man, Michelangelo,[202] was busy with the designs for the façade of the Basilica of San Lorenzo in Florence. It had been commissioned by Pope Leo X. For lack of funds, it was never finished.

---

[199] Ibid.
[200] Fifth Lateran Council, Session 10, May 4, 1515.
[201] Leonardo di ser Piero da Vinci, aka Leonardo da Vinci, 1452 – 1519.
[202] Michelangelo di Lodovico Buonarroti Simoni, 1475 – 1564.

While Savonarola had held Florence in his religious zeal, Michelangelo had completed his Pietà, a stunning marble sculpture with Mary grieving over the body of Jesus Christ.

After Savonarola had been executed in Florence, the artist had worked on his Statue of David. It was placed in front of the government palace, the Palazzo Vecchio.

The story of the statue was about the small French-friendly Republic of Florence taking a stand against the Catholic Church, which was then led by the Spanish Borgia Pope Alexander VI. Its unveiling hit a nerve, elevating it to its symbol of Florentine freedom. At the time of the council, Michelangelo had already completed the ceiling of the Sistine Chapel, commissioned by the Holy Lord of Wars, the Rovere Pope Julius II.

The Western world was in a state of arousal from the thousand-year-long oppression through the Christian churches. The art of the period is overwhelmingly beautiful and often paid for by the Catholic Church. It was abused for its propaganda machinery.

The Catholic Church responded with determination to suppress the blossoming humanist ideas, yet again. It was not politics. The leaders of organized religion thought the wisest course was to eliminate those who did not believe in the blessings of their Truth.

Had our ancestors failed to rid themselves of the religious monopoly, it would have perpetuated itself until a few brave men rolled back their sleeves and fought with their lives for change that would eventually benefit all. It took 500 years of wars after Martin Luther to reach our modern freedoms. My grandparents still dedicated their first male child to monastic service. This is how recently these changes have made headway in Western secular societies.

The reason that western religious sects are somewhat less violent today is that their minority positions prevent them from ruling.

## The Monk's Concubine

Priests were supposed to be celibate. They evaded the law of the Catholic Church by living with concubines. Many formed a kind of common law relationship, outside of the 'legality' of the Catholic Church. Celibacy was earlier enforced in Spain through the hardline approach of Grand Inquisitor Cardinal Cisneros.

Cohabiting with concubines was now universally prohibited by the council.[203]

Since this 'new' prohibition of the council has an air of actuality, I would like to briefly address its implications.

The idea of the celibacy is the ultimate humiliation of womanhood. It originates with Eve's achievement of giving soul or intellect to humanity through her non-compliance with the Word of God.

This humiliation went as far as dissolving existing marriages in order for the clergy to stay clear of female temptations.

The book of Revelation explains the reasoning for celibacy and the monastic lifestyle: only those who were not defiled by women would survive the End of the World.[204] Monasteries were also hiding places of the jihadists of the ancient world, Jewish, Christian, or Muslim monk-warriors.

There were many monks and priests, bishops, cardinals and popes who had spent their entire lives in the service of their god. When Judgment Day finally arrived, the girls at their sides prevented them from making it across into their promised utopia alive. It is evidence that they carried a last sprout of humanity. They sacrificed the entire purpose of their lives for the urge to keep their hands on their concubines.

Yet, they held on to the comfort of their clerical jobs.

Today, it is self-evident that you are immediately defiled after touching a woman. As it should be. Certainly when not invited.

Even though the Catholic Church attempted to push its members to extreme self-deprivation, no normal human being can abstain from loving affection without falling into the abyss of madness. Naturally, some entered a monogamous 'common law' relationship, but others became sexual predators.

---

[203] Fifth Lateran Council, Session 9, May 5, 1514.
[204] Revelation 14:3-14:5 and 7:3-7:8.

The problem may go back to changes to celibacy that were introduced toward the end of the fifth century, over a thousand years before this council. In direct opposition to the Bible, priestly celibacy was then extended to lower clerical ranks.[205]

We might think that the overstepping of sexual boundaries by the clergy toward minor boys and girls is a modern occurrence. Instead, celibacy had been cursed from day one. In all fairness, offenses are not limited to those preaching celibacy,[206] but we are talking about a council of the Catholic Church here. We need to understand the ramifications of what is being said.

While the frequent overstepping of such boundaries might find its causes in the position of trust and power that religious clergy enjoys, it almost seems as though celibacy created some sort of attraction for the sick minds of pedophiles. Victims were close by in abundance, gullible children, boys and girls, foster children, orphans, young faithful women who longed to be near a divinity, the poor, the divorced, or widows. The latter two were weak and generally snubbed by religious society. They were ripe to be plucked for sexual exploitation by members of the priesthood who chose to ignore the boundaries of human decency.

Just before Christmas 2017, the 17-volume report of the child sex abuse royal commission in Australia was released. It investigated tens of thousands of cases of child abuse *'in many of the nation's most - trusted institutions, with the problems "so widespread" and "abuse so heinous" it was difficult to comprehend.'*[207] The report arrived at a clear condemnation of celibacy. It was satisfied to conclude *'that there is an elevated risk of child sex abuse where compulsorily celibate male clergy or religious have privileged access to children in certain types of Catholic institutions, including schools, residential institutions and parishes.'* Together with other risk factors, it might have contributed to psychosexual dysfunction.[208] Australia is a nation of majority Christianity, with Catholicism being its largest church.

Let me expand on this problem.

---

[205] Pope Leo I, Letter XIV (446 AD).

[206] For example, the 17 volume report of the child sex abuse royal-commission in Australia sets the Catholic portion to about 62% of the tens of thousands of cases. The report also criticised other religious organizations, including the Anglican Church, Jehovah's Witnesses and Jewish institutions as well as state run organizations. Source: Nicola Berkovic, Sam Buckingham-Jones, Child abuse inquiry report: church and state clash on new laws, The Australian, December 16, 2017.

[207] Nicola Berkovic, Sam Buckingham-Jones, Child abuse inquiry report: church and state clash on new laws, The Australian, December 16, 2017.

[208] Ibid.

Childhood was a sign of purity — guaranteed virginity and its related health, that is. Moreover, the Bible leaves open a loophole for pedophiles to rationalize their actions: while men are instantly defiled by touching women, there are no such consequences for sexual involvement with children.

However, it was not that the Renaissance priests did not know right from wrong. The Jerusalem Talmud, for example, contains an exact definition that childhood ends when adolescence begins.[209] A pamphlet by ISIS – and it was not likely different when this council took place – makes it clear that intercourse is permitted with whomever *'is fit for intercourse.'* If she is not fit, then you can *'enjoy her'* without intercourse.[210] This leaves little room for interpretations other than who is supposed to *'play'* and with whom. With what?

This is the very definition of pedophilia.

Is it outrageous to compare ISIS or the Taliban with the Catholic Church? In Luther's time, girls were placed into arranged marriages among nobility between the ages of nine and twelve, and sometimes even as young as three. In the late nineteenth century, the age of consent in most American states was set to between ten and twelve years of age. These limits were increased to modern cultural norms during the time of the world wars.

But to the horrors of the world, there were as many as 250,000 child marriages recorded between 2000 and 2010 in the United States. Twelve-year-old girls were married in Alaska, Louisiana, and South Carolina.[211] These incredible numbers came into focus when a case in Florida was made public about an 11-year-old girl who was married to a 20-year-old church member who had raped her.[212] Run that by me again?

We cannot excuse this with an apology that this was cultural, back then.

The Catholic Church *was* the culture.

It is contextually similar with Prophet Muhammad. He was fifty-six years old when he raped the nine-year-old Aisha, his wife.[213]

---

[209] Moise Schwab, The Talmud of Jerusalem, Vol. I. Berakhoth (Williams and Norgate, 1886) ch. VII., p. 129.

[210] Questions and Answers on Taking Captives and Slaves (Al-Himma Library, Muharram 1436 [Fall 2014]), provided by MEMRI JTTM.

[211] As of 2018, out of the 50 U.S. states, only Delaware has banned all child marriages and its exceptions. There is no minimum age for marriage in 20 states (Tahirih Justice Center's Forced Marriage Initiative).

[212] Nicholas Kristof, 11 Years Old, a Mom, and Pushed to Marry Her Rapist in Florida, New York Times, May 26, 2017 [the data is from Unchained at Last].

[213] Bukhari, ca. 864 – 870 AD (CMJE and the University of Southern California, 2007-2009), 7:62:64.

The Australian report contains 409 recommendations, among which we can find the introduction of laws that dismiss any existing excuse or privilege relating to religion, breaking the seal of confession, or making celibacy voluntary.

So, when the council spoke of concubines, then it logically included young girls. Perpetrators would never give up their sexual privileges to the freshest and prettiest – boys or girls – to satisfy their appetite. In fact, the treatment of *'concubines'* in this council suggests that the priesthood had viewed this as normal.

Two things were shaped here. First, it emboldened a culture of a veil of silence, where superiors protected their priests, in consequence forming the foundation of our modern chain of scandals that had to be covered up in the name of the said outwardly modesty that was just enacted in this same council. Secondly, it asked those of the priesthood who lived a modest life with a loved one for a cruel sacrifice: not only were they not allowed to marry the woman or girl that they loved, but now they had to toss her into the street altogether.

This alone would have opened the door to many priests switching sides to the Protestant Reformation, where they could get or remain married.

In lack of an alternative, other monks, as I have shown, fled by the hundreds from Cardinal Cisneros' zealotry for the North African Kingdom of Tlemcen. There, they became Muslims. Legalized polygamists. Ahh. That sounds so much more attractive. There is this minor issue that polygamy, too, rests on the premise that women are second class. Cows, actually. But for the monks, Islam sounded like a sex sect. Men could have free sex with underage girls who were caged under the Burqa. Nobody would ever find out.

These decisions to separate from loved ones and to enforce celibacy were so personally detrimental to monks and priests that they alone could have constituted the spark to the Reformation.

Martin Luther merely came to ride a tsunami that had already been in its drawback. After having endured the life of a hermit for years, Martin Luther recognized monastic life as unnatural, and he later abolished it altogether.[214]

---

[214]   Luther, Large Catechism, 1529, WA 30 I,125-238.

### A Word from God

The council also spoke about money. A lot. They made sure that the cash that they collected – like a business, they called it *'revenues'* – could not be touched by civil authorities. If they dared to take coins from the Catholic Church, they lost their privileges and would otherwise be persecuted.[215]

Until now, the church held tough against usury, the lending of money against interest. The credit situation in the Catholic West was worse than it is today in Islamic nations. With the Renaissance, credit organizations sprang up that provided loans for interest. Some operated under the guise of helping the poor by providing micro-loans.

The reason for the rise of these credit organizations is quite simple: since the Carolingian decision in the eighth century, it increasingly became the exclusive domain of Jews and *'other aliens'* who swallowed up the poor by *'the greed of usurers.'*[216]

Now, the Catholic Church went after the wealth of Jews in order to increase its own revenues. In fact, two years later, Pope Leo X pushed it further and strictly prohibited Jews from lending money at interest in the Reggio.[217]

Before the Renaissance, there were few businesses other than the Catholic Church. But divisions within the church eroded its supremacy, not only inside its own hierarchy, but also in governments and economies as a whole. Now, everybody wanted in on it, and the poor – almost everybody – looked for credit to start building their trades.

Even masters of theology were part of the dealings.

Boom times!

The council was clear about its former position: *'Our Lord, according to Luke the evangelist, has bound us by a clear command that we ought not to expect any addition to the capital sum when we grant a loan.'*[218]

Not a little interest was to be added. None, whatsoever. Nothing at all.

We must not forget who the head of this council and of the Catholic Church was – Pope Leo X, born Giovanni di Lorenzo de' Medici, son of the heir of the richest family in Europe and the private bankers of the Catholic Church. One may wonder what the bankers' son would do in the face of soaring credit

---

215 Fifth Lateran Council, Session 9, May 5, 1514.
216 Fifth Lateran Council, Session 10, May 4, 1515.
217 Shlomo Simonsohn, The Apostolic See And The Jews (Pontifical Institute of Mediaeval Studies, 1991) 16, relating to the inhibition, dated November 14, 1516.
218 Fifth Lateran Council, Session 10, May 4, 1515.

business when his family was essentially excluded from the gold rush because of the draconian anti-usury laws.

Can anyone guess what Pope Leo would do?

Leo, the Medici Pope, did receive instructions from on high.

In Leo's dreams, God miraculously inserted his opinions on how to deal with monetary investments contrary to the biblical commands.

Finally: evidence of the direct involvement of God in human affairs!

From then on, the Catholic Church allowed interest and expenses to be added to loans, *'provided that no profit is made therefrom.'* The credit organizations had to be approved by the Catholic Church.[219]

The Medici Bank?

Previously under total prohibition, now *'such a type of lending is meritorious and should be praised and approved.'* This was not a roundabout permission to charge whatever one pleased for loans. But businesses can often shape 'profit' at will. The council opened a giant loophole. It was *almost* a roundabout permission to charge whatever. They just needed to put the bank in a bigger palace, drink more of the best wine, be attended by more servants, and place eight horses in front of the carriage instead of one.

It enabled living without profit – like kings. The business world figured it out rather quickly, and the decision may have acted as an unintended economic kick-starter.

But the papal creativity did not end there. In order to *'help the poor,'* they *wished* for the credit organizations to reduce the cost of credit by charging no more than *'half of the wages'* of the organizations.

If you are not sitting now, then you probably should be.

In return, the Catholic Church spoke of subsidies in the amount of the other half of the wages to the credit organizations.[220]

Add a summer palace, staffed for important credit summits, stage concerts for important clients, and get three new carriages for bodyguards. If you were a banker, you were an important man - women excluded, sorry – and you literally could not go wrong, except with women, of course.

Do not get your hopes up. If you were not already noble and rich, you had no part of the cake other than paying for the folly.

---

[219] Ibid.
[220] Ibid.

Now we know how it was possible that so many awe-inspiring Renaissance palaces went up during that time – probably most not-for-profit. The secret was not-for-profit gangsta' operations that were subsidized by the Catholic Church. These were the same organizations that helped the poor by extorting church taxes from them, if need be, with the swords of knights – idolized Christian robber bands.

To top it off, the council promised to excommunicate anyone who dared to speak up against the new rules of taxing the poor to line the pockets of the super-rich.[221]

Some would call it corporate welfare.

We still applaud our government leaders today when taxes are reduced by a few bucks for the lower and middle classes. 500 years after Martin Luther, we still have not figured out how the people are being duped. Simple: tax the poor a lot; tax the rich a little. Subsidize the rich with money from the poor; tax the poor more. Pay too much for goods and services from the rich; tax the poor just as much so they do not revolt. Such is the nature of tax systems that the little guys pay taxes, while the big shots end up with net profits through their businesses that directly or indirectly provide services to governments or receive subsidies.

We no longer need to wonder how numerous super-rich Renaissance family dynasties made their fortunes: they were all honest and frugal workaholics, exclusively dedicated to the wellbeing of their employees and the poor, their customers.

They had their nests made through the flow of liquidity by extortion and by the super-whammy of having half their wages subsidized.

Did they not know what the consequences of their doings were? They were fools not in how they defrauded the poor but in how they misjudged the mounting pressures by well-informed reform movements from within.

The answers lie in Martin Luther's accusations of corruption.

We have its essence from the source of betraying the poor for a promise of salvation that was impossible to be fulfilled. The accusations were not suspicions, they were bone-dry facts to the best of Luther's knowledge.

The scam has two names: Ponzi-Scheme and organized crime.

Both on a *very – big – scale*.

---

[221] Ibid.

For Jews, their monopoly on credit for interest was at stake. Their very livelihood. Is it possible that many of them converted to Catholicism but remained secret Jews? Is it probable? We have seen one example of a big shot: Rabbi Abraham Senior, the tax farmer – now Coronel, the tax farmer.

I can only speculate, but money constitutes a force all on its own. For them, the new ruling was profound.

Previously, their business and way of making a living was institutionalized.

Now, they were not among the approved.

But they had one advantage: they still held the cash.

It is ironic that a Medici would have such a profound effect on usury and bank financing. This was perhaps the single biggest contributor to the economic awakening at the time. The power of leveraging finances constituted the steppingstone to the Industrial Revolution.

Full abolishment of usury laws for credit organizations came soon thereafter through Luther's contemporary, King Henry VIII[222] of England. He dropped the prohibition of usury altogether and canceled all tax payments to the Catholic Church in Rome. With the English Reformation starting less than two decades from here, a believing Catholic king came to grab the divine power, make himself head of the (new) Church of England and subjugated it to his political power.

The Catholic Clergy – Anglicans from then on – willingly submitted to him and played along. And he took full advantage of the new freedoms: he married six times.

England was on its path to a world power.

Yet, just as Luther was not the first to act on reform, so was Henry not the first to proclaim lordship over the church.

The council complained that princes and nobles throughout Europe were meddling with church affairs, seizing jurisdictions and submitting the local clergy to secular rule.[223] Who can blame them for retaliating against the Vatican's plan to rid itself of nobility?

Since the abolition of usury laws was such an important factor, let me talk about this just a little longer.

---

[222] Henry VIII was King of England 1509 – 1547.
[223] Fifth Lateran Council, Session 10, May 4, 1515.

Martin Luther complained that a new form of usury was invented that was perfectly legal – legit, as crooks would say: buying of income. Of course, as modern Muslim countries vividly demonstrate, the usury laws were evaded in one way or another. But Luther thought that nothing good was invented anymore and that the people have become *'bent upon wealth and honor and luxury, without any limit.'*[224] He alleged that this sort of scheme to buy income *'can scarcely be conducted without violation of the natural law and the Christian law of love.'* Similar to the dangerous effects of *'no-risk'* derivatives today, he observed in his time that *'many cities and principalities'* were sucked dry and ruined *'as no usury could have done.'*[225] Luther thought that the profiteers were penurious blisters who were engaged in a shameless conspiracy for anyone to see and recognize.[226]

Henry's abolition could not have come soon enough.

But when discussing Martin Luther's contribution to the succeeding economic revolution, we possess the evidence that he was hell-bent on enforcing the old usury laws and bringing his church back to dictatorial dominance.

His upcoming movement distinguished itself by opposing changes to the usury laws. He glorified poverty.

As he was an anti-force to extended freedoms for the population, Luther was also a roadblock to the economic and social awakening that lie ahead of society.

---

[224] Martin Luther, On Trading and Usury (1524), translated in Works of Martin Luther (Holman, 1915) Vol. 4.
[225] Ibid.
[226] Ibid.

## Censor Librorum

Through the centuries, as the power of the Catholic Church waned, it eventually came up with the idea of the separation of church from state. The doctrine was as reactionary as this council. Church laws act as parallel laws to secular legal systems. These are maintained just in case an opportunity comes up to seize power again at some point in the future.

What happens to those who do not enforce the superiority of secular laws is in vivid memory with pedophilia cases that rocked the Catholic Church. Obstruction, reassignment, cover-up, and obfuscating the trails of evidence and guilt.

Allegedly, all the way to the top.[227]

The reasoning for the ruling against the power of 'lay people' over church matters found its justification in the idea that *'such actions detract, with disastrous results which must be condemned, not only from the honour of ourself and the apostolic see but also from the peaceful and prosperous condition of churchmen.'*

Yet, we must not forget that Pope Leo was friends with the Kingdom of France and on restrained terms with the emperor of the Holy Roman Empire. The political aim of the religious authority was nothing less than the delegitimization and the subjugation of the emperor himself to the laws of the Catholic Church.

This was not reform. This was cartel talk among despots.

This council was a shameful exhibition of self-interest in the maintenance of the power of the Catholic Church and its complicit clergy. It had no concern for its subjects, who continued unabated to be treated like dairy sheep. They were squeezed out to their last drop.

After all, poverty was to be glorified.

They intended to squeeze some more.

The council insisted on *'ecclesiastical liberty'* in the same sentence wherein everybody else was deprived of all liberty and freedoms. The feelings of the bosses were *'insulted.'* The desire for freedom of the many posed an existential threat to the Catholic Church that needed extinguishing at its roots.

---

[227] Carlo Maria Viganò, Titular Archbishop of Ulpiana, Apostolic Nuncio, TESTIMONY, August, 22, 2018.

But whoever has nothing left to lose has nothing left to give. If a pitchfork is your last possession, the temptation to stick it to your oppressors' chests is near. The worst collateral damage that could result from an impulsive act, this time around, was the unleashing of collective anger and the rise of a hero.

Eventually, the millennia-old bastion had to fall.

Martin Luther's timing fell into an era of collective humanitarian awakening. The acre was already sown; the arguments were already made; the verdict was already in. But the Catholic Church refused to give in to the realities of the time. And ringleaders were willing to take an armed stand against the liberation of mankind from their yoke.

The threat? *'Divine displeasure and the fitting reaction of the apostolic see,'* meaning whatever the Vatican pleased when it came to sentencing an inconvenient target. To add injury to insult, it put the entire nobility into legal limbo.

They knew who they were messing with, but they did not understand the signs of the time.

Many nobles punished the Catholic Church by joining up with Luther.

The Catholic Church had a choice. The decision to fight the realities of the time came at the cost of millions of lives. They could instead have applied Christian love as role models and let the good people go in peace as they freely chose. But that is not what they did.

Not now.

Not during the previous thousand years.

To say that the council did *not at all* think of its subjects is inexact.

When it did so, it only thought about how to keep them in line. One of the council's anxieties was how the Catholic Church could *'bring back to the path of Truth those going astray, and gain them for God.'*

What might they have had in mind? Listen in to the council for a moment:

> *It is certainly possible to obtain without difficulty some learning by reading books. The skill of book-printing has been invented, or rather improved and perfected, with God's assistance, particularly in our time. Without doubt it has brought many benefits to men and women since, at small expense, it is possible to possess a great number of books. These permit minds to devote themselves very readily to scholarly studies. Thus there can easily result, particularly among Catholics, men competent in all kinds of languages; and we desire to see in the Roman church, in good supply, men of this type who are capable of instructing even unbelievers in the holy commandments, and of gathering them for their salvation into the body of the*

*faithful by the teaching of the Christian faith. Complaints from many persons, however, have reached our ears and those of the apostolic see. In fact, some printers have the boldness to print and sell to the public, in different parts of the world, books—some translated into Latin from Greek, Hebrew, Arabic and Chaldean as well as some issued directly in Latin or a vernacular language—containing errors opposed to the faith as well as pernicious views contrary to the Christian religion and to the reputation of prominent persons of rank. The readers are not edified. Indeed, they lapse into very great errors not only in the realm of faith but also in that of life and morals. This has often given rise to various scandals, as experience has taught, and there is daily the fear that even greater scandals are developing.*[228]

They had not seen anything yet. While the Catholic Church appears to have acknowledged the benefits of learning, it needed to make sure that nothing would be learned that could in any way oppose the doctrines or faith of the church.

*[...] our care must be exercised over the printing of books, precisely so that thorns do not grow up with the good seed or poisons become mixed with medicines. It is our desire to provide a suitable remedy for this danger, with the approval of this sacred council, so that the business of book-printing may go ahead with greater satisfaction the more that there is employed in the future, with greater zeal and prudence, a more attentive supervision. We therefore establish and ordain that henceforth, for all future time, no one may dare to print or have printed any book or other writing of whatever kind in Rome or in any other cities and dioceses, without the book or writings having first been closely examined, at Rome by our vicar and the master of the sacred palace, in other cities and dioceses by the bishop or some other person who knows about the printing of books and writings of this kind and who has been delegated to this office by the bishop in question, and also by the inquisitor of heresy for the city or diocese where the said printing is to take place, and unless the books or writings have been approved by a warrant signed in their own hand, which must be given, under pain of excommunication, freely and without delay.*[229]

The council developed a mass-conformation strategy.

No books could be circulated that challenged the Catholic faith.

They were attempting to control the new 'social media' of the time, the recently invented mass-printed books. The consequence of printing unapproved materials was the burning of the books and draconian fines.[230]

---

[228] Fifth Lateran Council, Session 10, May 4, 1515.
[229] Ibid.
[230] Ibid.

Of course, accuser and judge were of the same club.

What did Luther do? Print books. Unapproved by the Catholic Church. Lots of them. For that and the dangers that he put himself in – not for the contents – he deserves our moderns' respect.

We will examine some of Luther's books that have evaded the Inquisition of the Catholic Church.

He was not the only one printing books.

Print shops multiplied across Europe. They brought about a dramatic change in the 'unity' of the old continent. Before the printing press, Europe's nobility was linguistically unified by Latin, the universal language that had been introduced by the Roman Empire. Now, the vernacular languages were *en vogue*. This laid the foundation for the rise of nation states. It had a disruptive effect on papal authority. It set the stage for the slow decline of the power of the church.

At the same time, the council was also troubled by an increasing number of preachers who strayed off the path. They were accused of claiming miracles and committing religious fraud with invented stories.[231] In the words of the church, these preachers were

> *caught up in the enthusiasm of their oratory, they entangle the hearts of their hearers with verbal errors as if with nooses, and while perhaps they wish to appear wise, in their delusion they foolishly tear asunder the sinews of the hoped-for virtue.*[232]

The priests were further blamed for *'invented miracles, new and false prophecies and other frivolities hardly distinguishable from old wives'* tales[233]

It is tragic, but we are speaking about spiritual differences where one imaginary version clashed with the old wives' tales of another version of the same sort of *'delusion,'* as the council called it.

The absurdity of these demands is apparent, in particular within the ranks of the church's priesthood, and even more so because we are in the midst of a period of renewed intellectual curiosity. According to their reasoning, the responsibility of the Catholic Church was to ensure salvation of its subjects. Such practices by non-compliant preachers made the fulfillment of the promise to eternal life impossible.

---

[231] Fifth Lateran Council, Session 11, December 19, 1516.
[232] Ibid.
[233] Ibid.

Again, Martin Luther was not alone. An entire army of preachers had already chosen their own paths of dissent. To control this number of dissidents, the Catholic Church had to deploy its most draconian measures through its terror network, the Inquisition.

Martin Luther's time was a short era when competing to see who could learn more, acquire more and broader knowledge, as attainable at the time, was becoming fashionable. As we moderns show off our gadgets, some started to show off their knowledge and oratory skills in multiple languages.

Instead, the consequences for dissenters in the Catholic Church were straightforward. Choose. Get in line. Or have your memory wiped off the face of the earth.[234]

To make sure that we understand this in its proper context, these were Pope Leo's words of *fostering everywhere the peace and mutual love so much commended by our Redeemer.*[235] This wisdom was directed at the many Catholic priests who acquired a thirst for novel ideas. These were not some Muslims or, heaven forbid, Jews, throwing religious insults at the Vatican.

Finally, we need to grasp the consequences for someone like Martin Luther.

He did not begin with his protest movement before he heard from this council. Yet, the Reformer, as chief dissenter, came to attempt the imposition of the same thought control over his clergy and his subjects. The mainstream reasoning was that the clergy was brainless. Instead, it was awakening, and Luther, as the Catholic Church before him, intended to put them back into their happy slumber of imbecilic doctrinal submission.

The Catholic Church was plotting the eradication of the stain of heresy and criticism. The pope and his cardinals at the council viewed discontent as some sort of a cancer inside the Catholic society.

Luther came to do the same for the Protestants.

When Luther started his Protestant Reformation, he was fully aware of the dangers to his life.

Trying to stand up against this monster of faithful rigidity was like Knight George.

I will come back to this hero when the time is opportune. Let me just say for now that he went out to slaughter an imaginary dragon with his bare hands. It is a version of the tale of David and Goliath.

---

[234] Ibid.
[235] Ibid.

This is illustrative of Luther's upcoming fight against the Catholic Church.

Luther became the dragon slayer.

The council of the dragon had already made the fatal, self-destructive moves that would lead to its collapse in northern Europe. Those priests who remained in the Catholic Church were intellectually apathetic, conforming parrots. Perfectly trained for religious extremism and holy war, unable to critical thinking.

This is why many modern clergymen display that eternally happy gaze of knowing nothing – other than the Truth.

### *Denial of Reality*

The council prohibited the preaching of the coming of the Antichrist or the prediction of a precise Judgment Day.[236] The Antichrist is a demonized figure in prophecies about the End of the World, the beast that needs to be defeated. I will talk about it in more detail. This prohibition is in line with the End of the World scenario that was fashionable in Jewish communities. It had not escaped the attention of the council. They spoke of the Antichrist, while Abrabanel was trying to bring the Christ to life, the Jewish Messiah. Because of that, the council declared them *'liars'* who were responsible for the church's widespread loss of authority.

The devil is in the detail.

Those who predicted the End of the World without setting a time owned the Truth. Those who set a time were deceivers. Even though the difference is clear, there is no variance in fact. It does not matter how faith intended to twist the argument. The marginally different End of the World is still imagination.

The End of the World has not yet happened, and it will not happen – unless humanity brings it upon itself.

While the logic was circular, it is also *'factually'* incorrect.

As part of the Christian New Testament, the book of Revelation sets out a time. It is precise enough to provide for a narrow time frame of a century. Like the pope and his council, the book unveils the intention to inflict violence on those who did not conform. The story ends in the End of the World and its total destruction.

---

[236] Ibid.

An angel seized the dragon, *'bound him for a thousand years,'* and sealed the abyss over it. After a thousand years, the dragon must be freed for a short time.[237] The coming of the second Christ was to happen.[238] After the world was totally destroyed, the latter would rule forever.[239] Only a few 'righteous' survivors would remain. Henceforth, their god was to live among men in Jerusalem.[240]

There it was: the End of the World.

From the point of view of Pope Leo and his sixteenth century brethren, the problem was that the End of the World had already happened 500 years earlier.

Or it should have already happened. But it did not. Obviously.

A thousand years passed. Nothing. Eleven hundred years. Still nothing.

Eventually it dawned on the functionaries of the Catholic Church that the event needed to be postponed *ad infinitum*, indefinitely. But for this, they needed to pick and choose which verses of the New Testament to ignore. So, they invented that not only was the End of the World to be expected in their future, but also that no timing could be set.

The exponents of the Catholic Church may have thought that a little 'Truth'-bending was preferable over allowing the messianic expectations to implode. The faithful were not enlightened enough to recognize that this was essentially a capitulation that their messianic revelation would never come true.

From then on, the Catholic Church mirrored Islam: only God knows.

The End of the World has not happened. It has been postponed many times over the millennia. Every so often, it has failed to occur.

The straw that broke Martin Luther's patience was the attempt of the Catholic Church no longer to tolerate doctrinal differences among its various orders, in particular the order of the Austin Friars.

Since the church was inflexible in adjusting its doctrines of faith, it expected all others to comply. To make sure that they did not simply feign submission, the church tested their 'knowledge' and certified those willing to conform.

Luther failed the exam. By never taking it.

---

[237] Revelation 20:1–3.
[238] Revelation 12:1–5.
[239] Revelation 11:15.
[240] Revelation 21:1–7.

But even if the Austin Friars were fully accepted into the rigidity of the Catholic Church, their standing was hindered by a host of restrictions, essentially turning them into second class priests.[241]

In addition, they had to submit to the authority of the local bishops.[242]

This was a sure-fire way to lose them.

But again, trouble was approaching fast, even before Martin Luther's 95 Theses.

At the mere rumour of the election of a pope, the house of the supposedly elected and the homes of cardinals in the electorate were ransacked and plundered by the Roman *'mob.*[243] Given the big picture of French and Spanish friendly papal factions, the mob had nothing to do with it. However, Rome, it appears, had lost its respect for Catholic institutions. Not only was a portion of the priesthood already angry but somebody stoked the fires on the streets, readying laity to erupt into a full-blown revolution.

The revolution came to be called the Protestant Reformation.

Finally, the nuisance of meeting Muslims with Christian love was addressed at the council.

The portrayed image of modern Christianity, its very core of spreading the message with love, should lead us to believe that its vision can be summed up in a few words: to turn the other cheek.

The scars of history tell otherwise.

The reality is that it would never have gotten anywhere by turning the other cheek.

Europe and the Americas would now be Islamic.

Instead, the historical record shows that the religion advanced with militancy and bloodshed from its earliest days. Almost every Christian city in Europe prides itself on the blood of their militant founding saints, rather than some love-spreading role models of holiness.

If anywhere, the real face of Christianity should be found on the lips of its head, now Pope Leo X: *'Our aim is also to crush the Turks and other infidels standing firm in the eastern and southern regions,*[244] referring to the Balkan and North Africa.

---

[241] Fifth Lateran Council, Session 11, December 19, 1516.
[242] Ibid.
[243] Fifth Lateran Council, Session 12, March 16, 1517.
[244] Ibid.

As a consequence of the Catholic Church's abusive behavior, Pope Leo faced a perfect storm of internal and external disasters. Disobedience within the priestly ranks tore apart its internal fabric – one that was held in place by brute force. The schism that came to be the Protestant Reformation was showing its fractures before it started. The populace was ready to revolt. Ottoman-Turks threatened the supremacy of the Catholic Church over the world and were determined to shred it to pieces.

A time that called for unity was met with disunity. It found its culmination in an attempt to 'reform' the Catholic Church with the arrogance of despots.

The masquerade of finding peace among the Kingdom of France, the Holy Roman Empire, and the Catholic Church was in the pursuit of egomaniacal power and with the intention of eliminating all competing spiritual leaders in Europe and then waging all-out war against the Ottoman-Turks with united European armed forces.

Referring to the *'universal peace between Christian kings and princes'* under a single doctrinal faith, the papal council stated: *'once the matters concerning the praise of God and the exaltation of the aforesaid church have been completed, the holy and most necessary expedition against the enemies of the catholic faith shall take place and a successful triumph over them be accomplished with the aid of the most High.'*[245] Well, the help of their god might not have been enough. The pope doubted that prayers would be the most effective path to victory.

It took a little more than that. To begin with, money.

Lots of it.

In order to prepare the audience for the financial sword to come, the council bragged about its military prowess in the wake of the fall of Constantinople, how it *'crushed'* its opponents' *'fury'* and how it *'avenged'* the *'wounds of Christ.'*[246]

This Christian holy war was paid for through leveraging extra war revenues from poor peasants for three years.

The audience in the council probably understood what was to come: the consequence of any religious or political decision made. It was the cost of the popular disease of not being able to distinguish between essential and wishful; the price to pay for undertakings in the name of the 'good for all' or in the name of a god; summarized in the world's favorite word: tax.

Martin Luther came to spell it out for them.

---

[245]  Fifth Lateran Council, Session 12, March 16, 1517.
[246]  Ibid.

But the council seems to have been blinded by a roundabout denial of reality.

*God himself, who is the supreme light and truth of all things, knows how we never ceased to beg and implore of him, by many prayers and constant appeals, that he would deign of his mercy to influence the Christian flock—which he has entrusted to our care, despite our lack of merits—to enter upon a stable and enduring peace, now that this same flock has been roused by the warmth of mutual charity.[247]*

History is unambiguous about the failure of the attempted 'reforms' in the Catholic Church. It did not turn out as envisioned. The prayers went unheard. The warmth of mutual charity did not rouse the flock of sheep either.

If they were roused, then it was by the cold iron that pierced them in the process of extorting more taxes – alms.

Shortly after the council, Pope Leo uncovered a conspiracy to have him poisoned for not supporting a government change in the city of Siena. Several cardinals were involved. The ringleaders[248] were severely punished. The first was imprisoned and strangulated in his cell at the Vatican's Castel Sant'Angelo; the second died of a sudden cause, suspected of being poisoned; and the third vanished.

The Vicar of Christ was offering the other cheek.

In the wake of the cleanup, Pope Leo appointed thirty-one new cardinals, mostly from powerful Roman nobles and pro-Medici factions.

Just a few months thereafter, the beginning of the end was knocking on the doors, and a few years later, Europe was engulfed in a century dredged in blood over religious dogma.

The collateral damage of irresponsible decisions by the Vatican constituted the End of the World – literally.

---

[247] Ibid.
[248] Cardinal Alfonso Petrucci, Cardinal Bandinello Sauli, and Cardinal Raffaele Riario.

## The City of God

For the previous 300 years, the hermitical Austin Friars were a semi-autonomous order of the Catholic Church. The Dominican Order had been commissioned with executing the task of the Catholic Inquisition — a symbol for an unmatched scale of terrorism over many centuries. This was not 'church-sponsored' terrorism. The Inquisition was organized and executed by the Catholic Church itself. It has been part of its business model and culture for a long time.

The members of the two orders could be distinguished by their woolen robes. The Austin Friars wore all black. The Dominicans dressed in white.

To understand what is going on, we need to look under the robes.

Today, the Augustinians are just another assimilated order of the Catholic Church. We have already seen that a merger between a part of the Austin Friars and the Catholic Church led to the conformation of the former to the latter. But Luther's faction refused. At the turn of the sixteenth century, there were at least 300 Augustinian convents across Western Europe. Not only could Luther rely on a vast network through which his communications could flow, but it was also already under 'reformation' at that time.

In fact, the Austin Friars had just recently founded the University of Wittenberg – Luther's Wittenberg.

I turn to the snake-oil salesman St. Augustine – a converted womanizer. The role model of the Austin Friars. We have access to his extensive library of fifth century works. Unfortunately, it is contaminated with foreign ideas and later additions.[249]

Expunged and inflated.

Yet, what we do have is probably similar to what the Austin Friars believed in at Luther's time.

---

[249] Augustine's reading of the book of Revelation is restricted to book XX, which is in itself curious. A computer analysis reveals that the terms testament, church, or Jesus are each overused in chapters XVII, XVIII, and XX. There is a possibility that the text was inserted into *The City of God* much later. While Augustine is quite focused on the evolution of his argument, book XX is an unusual distraction near the end of his work, and it does not seem to be aware of the arguments in the preceding books. Rather than dealing with the evolution of the big picture, it explores expertly details in an abstract fashion and requires in-depth knowledge of the book of Revelation. Augustine displays precise doctrinal ideas that were fought over only after his death. Distractions into the relationship between church and state (XX) as well as Chalcedonian definitions (IX:15, conflicting in other places) are strong hints at later edits. Unaware of the Book of Revelation, Books XXI and XXII seem to be the end points of *The City of God* rather than of book XX. These final two books do not tie the treatise about the New Haven and the New Earth back into the narrative, which would be natural due to its close relationship.

Augustine's most influential work, *'The City of God,'* was written within thirteen years of the sack of Rome by the then-invading Paulinic Christian Goths (one should say Germanics). His work was specifically meant to guide the spirits of Western Christians. Like Luther, Augustine argued that Christians should be concerned with the spiritual rather than the earthly.

He thought that the divine City of God, the New Jerusalem, was historically in conflict with the material City of Rome for dominance.

It is little wonder that Luther had no problems intellectually compartmentalizing Rome as his enemy. He already had done so before through the mere adherence to the Austin Friars.

Augustine delivered the framework of exceptions for warfare in arguing that the commandment *'thou shalt not kill'* was not violated if his god commanded *'just'* killings through the authority of the church.[250]

At the same time, Augustine laid the intellectual framework for a new kind of tyrannical regime that relied on total control of its pupils, from their thoughts to their activities.

Under the impression of the destruction of Rome in his time, Augustine was convinced that the End of the World had come. Rome, overflowing with dead and sick people, with its infrastructure crumbling, and with filth and rot everywhere, must indeed have felt like the end. From this, he concluded that only total rejection of wealth could save the people from future calamities like the one that was brought upon Rome.[251]

He argued that Christians had been suffering because they were imperfect in the eye of his god.[252] Augustine thought that Christians who had died of famine, were *'rescued from the ills of this life.'* Survivors were made stronger in order to endure longer religious fasts.[253]

These Augustinian ideas lead to collective refusal to aid the ill and injured. It is passive aggression at its best.

Martin Luther was about to repeat the inhumane approach.

The ideal Christian, in Augustine's view, rejected the seeking of all sorts of human glory, had to forgo pleasures, and be dedicated to promoting Christianity. He went as far as rejecting sex with a spouse.[254]

---

[250] Augustine, *The City of God* (354–430 AD), I:21.
[251] Ibid., I:10.
[252] Ibid., I:8.
[253] Ibid., I:10.
[254] Ibid., XI:20.

Augustine made a point of living a chaste life, thinking that sexuality was for procreation only. Sex should be entirely free of desire.

Augustine was a former sex-addict who was now preaching abstinence. While the Paulinic writings allowed marriage for those who could not confine their lust, Augustine condemned it altogether.[255]

This role model of social rejection constituted the foundation of Luther's stern lifestyle. Much like Luther, he had built a circular pyramid of faith without ever touching a single fact.

Jews were blamed for the death of Jesus Christ. Augustine turned the aggression of Jews into sheer murder.[256] This is such a tragic pit that Jewish leaders had dug for their own: the murder of Jesus Christ was merely part of a Jewish messianic story.

It is a classic on how to dig your own grave.

Luther's attitude toward Jews is mirrored in Augustine: life on earth was punishment enough for them. After all, their offence led to the salvation of Christians.[257]

In significant ways, Augustine's books contradict the New Testament, in particular those parts that had already been in the hands of the Goths (Germanics) at his time.[258] While Luther's German ideas rested on Augustine's and the Reformer's opposition to changes in the Catholic Church, the fifth century fundamentalist relied on the Goths' and his enmities with them.

The rapid success of the Reformation appears like a return to what was already there. No new church needed to be organized. Instead, an old one fell into Luther's lap. He became its leader.

Luther's lack of intellectual depth and absent visionary attitudes can be explained with the Reformer's reliance on what he had been indoctrinated with since he had joined the Saint Augustine's Monastery at Erfurt.

But Augustine's book was written a thousand years earlier. How could it have influenced Luther so much? Because Jesus Christ's story is 2,000 and Moses' over 3,000 years old, so we are told. The wheels of organized religion not only turn slowly, they also have eternal momentum.

Now we have a better foundation for grasping the changes to come.

---

255  Ibid., XIV:16.
256  Ibid., XVIII:46.
257  Ibid.
258  This concerns the books of St. Paul.

The Catholic Pope Leo may already have feared that the Austin Friars might not comply as intended in the original arrangement with his papal predecessor. Since we will see some of the differences in Luther's work, I am not going to lay bare the belief system of the Catholic Church here also. It is probably enough to bluntly state that it was incompatible with the Augustinians. Besides, much of their thinking was already revealed through the council of the Catholic Church.

Hume alleged that Luther – the Austin Friar – had been offended by the reorganization of the money flows. This was the motivation for questioning the authority of the Catholic Church.[259] But then, we have seen that Luther was not the first to criticize the Vatican or to question the authority of the pope. Hume thought that the Reformer stood out merely as a function of the recently invented printing press and the revival of learning, rather than being based on Luther's reason.[260]

Luther lacked ingenuity, indeed. But he was at the forefront of the historical trajectory from even before the beginning of the Reformation.

This seems a good place to quickly clean house.

That Luther nailed his 95 Theses to the doors at the church in Wittenberg is a myth – a legend. The Reformer was embedded in the efforts to reform the Catholic Church from within. A few months after the supposed nailing, the Reformer expressed his surprise in a letter that his 95 Theses had been translated and circulated everywhere.

His intention was to submit his propositions to a few learned men for discussion about reforms.

He had earlier sent his 95 Theses to the noble elector and archbishop of Mainz,[261] a passionate collector of holy relics. It was a scholarly refutation of Pope Leo X's plan of extorting more funds for the construction of Saint Peter's Basilica at Rome.[262]

Electors were a group of seven who elected the emperor of the Holy Roman Empire. Among them were at least three Catholic archbishops, from Mainz, Cologne, and Trier.

---

[259] Augustine, *The City of God* (354–430 AD), 35.

[260] Ibid., 37.

[261] Cardinal Albrecht von Brandenburg, 1490 – 1545, was elector, archbishop of Mainz and Magdeburg, and cardinal of the Catholic Church.

[262] Martin Luther, Letter to Albrecht von Brandenburg, October 31, 2017. The 95 Theses were called '*Disputation of Martin Luther on the Power and Efficacy of Indulgences.*'

This corrupt archbishop had purchased his lofty position as a holy man – with Fugger money. We will learn shortly just what that means. The deal of the bribe-loan included the provision that the Fugger Dynasty would be paid through raising the indulgences for Saint Peter's – tax farmers, or rather alms farmers.

The man in charge of the extortion ring was the Saxon Grand Inquisitor.[263] This 'saint' was accused of selling indulgences for sins not yet committed. Luther called him out on his greed and avarice.[264] He was also suspected of perpetrating frauds and embezzlements.

While these claims are discredited by mainstream historians,[265] we should know better: selling indulgences for sins amounts to fraud and embezzlement – committed or not.

*As soon as the gold in the casket rings*

*The rescued soul to heaven springs.*[266]

It may be that this Grand Inquisitor overstepped the doctrine of the Catholic Church a little.[267] However, these gangsters of thought control had a lot of leeway, including making heretics or opponents quietly disappear.

Coins voluntarily fell out of pockets as the laity dangled from the gallows.

Even the *imagination* of inquisitorial affection would have nobility and peasantry comply in terror.

At this point, Luther regretted having authored the 95 Theses.[268]

It almost seems as though he was gradually pushed into his role, beginning with this leak of information that would clog the communications channels and upset the Catholic Church. Puzzlingly, we are told from a trial by the Inquisition in Spain that Luther's proposals for reform were at first widely embraced[269] – until they became grounds for persecutions.

---

[263] Johann Tetzel, 1465 – 1519. He was a Dominican friar. In addition, he was a Grand Inquisitor of Heresy to Poland, and later became the Grand Commissioner for indulgences in Germany

[264] Luther, *95 Theses*, 1517, 28.

[265] Henry George Ganss, Johann Tetzel, in Charles Herbermann, Catholic Encyclopedia, 14 (Appleton, 1912) 539–541.

[266] Ibid., 540.

[267] Ludwig von Pastor, ed. Ralph Francis Kerr, The History of the Popes, from the Close of the Middle Ages, 7 (Kegan Paul, Trench, Trübner, 1908) 347-348.

[268] Luther, Letter to Scheurl, 1518.

[269] From the trial by the Spanish Inquisition against Doctor Juan de Vergara in Longhurst, 1964, 284: At first, when Luther only spoke of the need for reform in the Church ... everybody approved of him. The same persons who now write against him confess in their books that at first they were drawn to him.

Regardless, nothing of this sort can explain why Luther became a fierce Jew-hater. Indeed, his odium *'On the Jews and Their Lies,'* was not written until almost two decades later.

Having said this, I cannot withhold that Luther wrote that *'the greater part of the nation'* had *'to disguise their opinions for fear of the Jews'* in this same letter.[270] Since he placed this in context with the issue of the indulgences, I long failed to understand what the Reformer intended to say. Was it an expression of anxiety about being exposed to ridicule? Or did he fear some sort of retaliation? Was he perhaps referring to the power of Jewish tax farmers who might have collected payments for indulgences? How were they part of this discussion? Was he thinking within the biblically inspired opposition against Jews?

The history of Jews in Regensburg, a free city of the Holy Roman Empire, might provide some context. This Bavarian city lies about 250 miles[271] south of Wittenberg. Its medieval center is today listed as a UNESCO World Heritage Site. In Luther's time, Regensburg was a cultural center of south-eastern Germany. For the previous 500 years, it was also Germany's most important Talmudic hub, a center of Jewish learning.

Regensburg Jews concentrated their economic activities in banking and dealings with precious metals.

After the Fourth Lateran Council of the Catholic Church in the early thirteenth century, the Jewish quarter in Regensburg was walled in. They had to wear special clothing, avoid contact with Christians, and stay off the streets during Easter festivities.

The Regensburg Cathedral of the Catholic Church – as are many churches in Germany – is decorated with a sculpture of a Judensau (Jew sow) with three Jews suckling on a sow's teats. In one of his later anti-Semitic works, the Reformer commented on this portrayal of Jews. Behind the sow stands a rabbi, he said, looking with great effort into the Talmud under the sow, attempting to gain divine wisdom from under the sow's behind.[272]

The church in Luther's Wittenberg was also 'decorated' with a Judensau.

The image of Jews as sows originates with their biblical prohibition to eat pork. Because they viewed pork as unclean, the obscene image of the sow suckling Jews was stuck back onto them. The sow stood as a symbol for everybody else, depicting Jews as parasites – *'Marranos.'* That sow-suckling Jews

---

[270] Luther, Letter to Scheurl, 1518.
[271] 400 kilometers.
[272] Luther, Schem Hamphoras, 1542, 34-35.

served as decoration for churches revealed a deep-seated hatred against them. It had existed long before Luther.

The fourteenth century witnessed waves of violence against Jewish communities in Bavaria and Austria. For a short time, Regensburg acted as a sort of refuge for survivors. Increasing oppression and special taxation led to the impoverishment of the Jewish Regensburg community during the fifteenth century. Finally, Regensburg wiped itself clean of all Jews in 1519, right under Luther's nose. Their synagogue with the entire Jewish quarter was destroyed. Even headstones were stolen from Jewish graveyards. They were incorporated into Christian buildings as symbols of victory against Jews. Consensus suggests that the Anabaptist Christian reform leader[273] had incited Regensburg against Jews.

All of this does not give us an indication of what had happened.

The son of the top Rabbi at the time, Anton Margaritha, laid out reasons why he had turned into an anti-Semite.[274] According to his account, there were two large sects of Jews in Regensburg. Both groups were determined to rule the other.[275] One party insisted on their older 'rights' as citizens, claiming preference to the highest offices in the city's administration.[276]

This was the party of Margaritha's Rabbinic father.

The other party was behind the rich Rabbi Moses,[277] whose family was known as the *'wolves.*[278] They had been late arrivals in Regensburg and aimed at bribing their way into citizens' rights for themselves and usurping the positions of the established Jews.[279] However, the old Jews had a pact with the city not to invite foreign Jews. They intended to prevent sectarian fights and warfare.[280]

They were aware of just how dangerous sectarian divisions were. Accordingly, established Jews attempted to close the doors of Regensburg to Jewish refugees from other places.

---

[273] Balthasar Hübmaier aka Hubmair, Hubmayr, Hubmeier, Huebmör, Hubmör, Friedberger, Pacimontanus, ca. 1480 – 1528.
[274] Anton Margaritha aka Antony, Anthony Antonious, or Antonius Margarita, ca. 1500 – ca. 1550s.
[275] Anton Margaritha, The Whole Jewish Belief / Der Ganz Jüdisch Glaub (Frankfurt, 1544) 108.
[276] Ibid., 109.
[277] This is probably Moses Auerbach (born ca. 1462) who was the court Jew to the bishop of Regensburg from around 1497.
[278] Margaritha, Jewish Belief, 1544.
See Genesis 49:27 (NIV).
[279] Margaritha, Jewish Belief, 1544, 109.
[280] Ibid.

As the story unfolds, Moses, the wolf, went to the city mayor to tell how Jews were mocking him behind his back.[281] The mayor was nicknamed *Haman*, the wolf claimed. This was an enemy of Jews in the biblical book of Esther, who ended up hanged. Margaritha specified that Jews were generally contemptuous toward the authority of their Christian hosts and indeed viewed the major as Haman.[282]

In betrayal of his own, Moses ended up usurping the top Rabbinic position in Regensburg, filling all administrative positions according to his whim.[283]

After that, a letter came to light that unveiled Moses' evil machinations.[284] When the latter and his clan seized the letter, the two parties clashed violently. Had it not been for their violent division, Margaritha clarified, Jews would not have been driven from Regensburg.[285]

Interestingly, a small remnant of the rich Rabbi Moses' family remained near Regensburg.[286] The rest were deported down the Danube River.

We can take the academic consensus as we wish, but looking at only one side of the coin does not help answering the most pressing questions about why Jews were hated and driven from their homes.

Pointing at an Anabaptist Christian villain is willfully misleading.

We need to be careful with potential polemics from Margaritha, and we still have no account about the state of Jews in Regensburg before their expulsion.

However, here, we can see two things that are striking. First, the penetration of Jews in the city's administration puts a spotlight at the inequality between Christians and Jews. These 'administrators' were in a position of power. And they were tax farmers. They attracted Christian hatred not by merely going about their business of praying to their god but by making it their business to prey on impoverished Christians. Second, it was a self-inflicted disaster, even if it may have been embellished by a defector. This story ended in sectarian riots among extremists who did not want to give in. The events may have been *accelerated* by the Anabaptist reform leader Hübmaier, who seized the opportunity of Jewish unrest to drive them out of town.

---

[281]   Ibid., 109-110.
[282]   Ibid., 110.
[283]   Ibid., 110-111.
[284]   Ibid.
[285]   Ibid., 111.
[286]   Joseph of Rosheim, The Historical Writings of Joseph of Rosheim: Leader of Jewry in Early Modern Germany, edited by Chava Fraenke Goldschmidt and Adam Shear, translated by Naomi Schendowich (Brill, 2006).

If such an anarchic clash were to occur in modern New York – and it probably will – they would face deadly force from armed police or the army.

It appears that Martin Luther's *'fear of the Jews'* was embedded in the general spirit of his time. He might have been afraid of retaliation from the government administration, where literate Jews filled important positions. This may have included many judges, if not all.

I will demonstrate later that in other places, Jews led the fiscal, administrative, and judicial authority over Christian subjects – a magnet of hatred. The dominant belief seems to have been that Jews needed either to be converted, by force if necessary, or to leave.

Germany's anti-Semitism simmered in Luther's heart all along.

Nothing could have been done to change the course of history other than a few good men standing up in the face of evil.

However, Hume's assessment of Luther's unimportance underestimates the power of the Sunday masses.

Because the shaken priesthood in Germany needed a guiding hand, Luther distributed his sermons to all with detailed instructions. This was an excellent communications strategy through the exploitation of a new media. Across the Reform areas, the message uniformly promoted a radical break from the Catholic Church, with the pope as the personification of the people's oppressor. For those already angry, their battle-cry found validation inside their holy places of worship from their community authorities, the Austin Friar preachers.

Luther's prominence as the leader of the Reformation is quite simple: He just happened to have been the leader of the Austin Friars at this time, and the leak of the 95 Theses together with his refusal to merge with the Catholic Church put the train of Luther's Reformation in motion.

## Knight George

The Vatican and its bishoprics, the emperor, and nobility were living a feudal life of excess and splendor in an unhealthy interdependence. The ultra-rich top percent relied on extorting taxes and payments for penance from a population that was held in serfdom. The decisions of the council were complemented with unjust civil laws of the Holy Roman Empire. They helped nobility to confiscate virtually all land as they pleased, degrading the peasants to indebted rent-payers.

The establishment protected itself and its economic superiority through its professional armies – also involuntarily paid for by the impoverished peasantry, of course.

The conspiracy against Europe's population was perfect. It was the end-game of income inequality. The ultra-rich never hesitated to grab more – until a revolt tore them down.

This unspeakable treachery is perhaps the reason why this era brought forth not only the new Protestant Church but also a movement that rejected both churches and placed a non-theistic thinking into its focus, centered on humanity and based on reason and ingenuity: a reborn humanism carried over from Antiquity.

It was the Reformation's twin brother, even though the word 'humanism,' which would come to define it, would not be re-invented until a couple of hundred years down the road. Humanism and Secularism played the leading role in the Age of Enlightenment, when reason became the guiding hand for authority.

Such terms as liberty, progress, tolerance, fraternity, constitutional government, and separation of church and state[287] were, by nature, foreign to organized religion in vision and substance.

Tradition is in faith and fear; progress is in courage to change.

At the time, 'reason' had a different meaning. It was embedded in faith. Religion provided for a framework that confined the liberties of 'reason.' *'A person endowed with reason realizes that life in this world is transitory and engages in good deeds and prayer, rather than worldly pleasures.'*[288] During Luther's time, most were unable to break from these boundaries.

That Humanism was important will be challenged by experts. Read on.

---

[287]  Dorinda Outram, Panorama of the Enlightenment (Getty, 2006) 29.

[288]  Mevahib, 82b, 329b, in Kaya Şahin, Empire and Power in the Reign of Süleyman: Narrating the Sixteenth-Century Ottoman World (Cambridge University Press, Kindle Edition, Copyright © 2013, reprinted by permission of Cambridge University Press), 234.

Luther's goal was to bring Christianity back to the Augustinian belief that this world was of no essence; only the eternal life in the next world was of importance. Material and intellectual progress stood in the way of the grand vision of living in poverty, in the image of Jesus Christ. The true enemy of the Catholic Church was not the Antichrist – another imaginary concept that shall be explored in due time – or the Protestant Reformation, but reason. But in an environment of religious thought, reason is hard to come by and to learn.

Superstition was omnipresent.

Let me turn the focus to one of the Achilles heels of the feudal system. Men of power are inclined to hand their might to the next generation of their bloodline. Except for democracies, we seldom see in history that power is voluntarily transferred to the man with the most merit. The rule of thumb for secular as well as spiritual rulers is 'from father to son.' Within a few generations, this leads to fragmentation of the wealth and power of families. To stem the nature of destruction, dynastic bonds were engineered among men in power.

The only direct heir of Emperor Maximilian I, Philip the Handsome,[289] had died a decade earlier. In an arranged family exchange between Spanish and German royals, Philip had before been betrothed to the second daughter of King Ferdinand and Queen Isabella. These were the two Spanish rulers who had signed the Alhambra Decree and sent Christopher Columbus abroad. This marriage between their daughter, Joanna of Castile,[290] and Philip the Handsome led to a rather unexpected Habsburg rule over Spain.

The son of the two was Charles. He was half-Spanish, half-Habsburg. Now, during Luther's rise, this son became the Holy Roman Emperor, Charles V. The engineering of the family bonds worked its miracles as intended.

Likewise, King Francis of France was from two important dynasties. On his father's side, he was bound to the House of Valois, which had held the French throne for the previous 200 years. His mother was in the lineage of the House of Savoy through 'Antipope' Felix V[291] from a century earlier. The latter was the founder of an order of knighthood, the Order of Saint Maurice.

Antipope Felix had been a sword-wielding, lethal knight.

An extremist boss of the order.

It was a knightly robber band that provided the House of Savoy with its power.

---

[289]  Philip the Handsome was Habsburg King of Castile from July – September 1506.

[290]  Joanna of Castile was Queen of Castile and León 1504 – 1555 and Queen of Aragon 1516 – 1555.

[291]  Antipope Felix X aka Amadeus VIII, Duke of Savoy, 1383 – 1451

A private militia.

It is irrelevant here that this antipope's history was expunged. King Francis was descendant from a pope who himself was hell-bent to make sure that his family was immensely enriched and secured through intermarriage. The House of Savoy can be traced back to ecclesiastical origins in the tenth century. The story of its founder tells us in no uncertain terms that the feudal system had not changed in the 500 years before Luther.[292]

Francis I was also related to Charles V to the fourth degree.

The Catholic Church was divided along dynastic fault lines that it had itself created. We will see the continued back and forth of the main factions, pro-French and pro-Habsburg, with Lutheran Germans squeezed in the middle.

Because of the dynastic fragmentations, it was not quite as simple as being an heir to become emperor. How Charles conquered the imperial throne is essential to Luther's story.

In the dynastic game of musical chairs, only one can win.

The German Holy Roman Emperor at the time, the Habsburg Maximilian I,[293] was in notoriously desperate financial straits. In his later years, he had become eccentric. He insisted that his coffin travel along with him.[294] Ongoing war with the Kingdom of France and ambitious political programs put continuous stress on the empire. Charles, his successor, had been born at the turn of the century in Spain but brought up in the Netherlands.

As the French-friendly Medici streak ran low, a German family that supported the Habsburgs had risen to immense power and wealth. They became the most influential bankers and financiers of the time. To make a very long story sweet and short, the Fugger Dynasty essentially bribed Maximilian to choose his grandson, Charles, as the heir to his throne. The reward for the empire was a loan in the amount of almost two years of imperial tax revenues.

The magnitude of this loan is astonishing. If we were to translate this to the modern United States of America, the no-interest-bearing bribe-loan would amount to over six trillion dollars in modern coin.

Of course, a bribe is a bribe and an interest-free loan a loan.

---

[292] Humbert I (ca. 980 – ca. 1048), the Whitehanded, was Count of Savoy.
[293] Maximilian I was King of the Romans 1486 – 1519 and Holy Roman Emperor 1493 – 1519.
[294] Gerhard Benecke, Maximilian I (London, 1982) 10.

Always leaning toward equivalency and prudence, the legend of the bribe is refuted by academic consensus. But since the elector and archbishop of Mainz[295] had before been purchased into office, we can put aspiration and bribe into a context of the mechanism. The reward: protection of the Fugger copper monopoly and the revenues from the persecuted Spanish orders of knights, including the Knights Templar – tax farming.

I leave it at that without forgetting to mention that Charles V also received support from an army.

With his ascent to the imperial throne, Charles became the head of a fractured empire at the age of nineteen.

Bribe, loan, or force, somebody had to come up short.

This man was Frederick the Wise.

He was from an old royal dynasty in Germany, the House of Wettin. Its descendants sat on thrones of Portugal, Bulgaria, Poland, Saxony, Great Britain, and Belgium. The latter two nations have not yet gotten over their admiration of medieval feudalism. The German House of Wettin are the ancestors of the House of Saxe-Coburg (today's ruling monarchs in Belgium) and the House of Windsor (today's royals of Great Britain).

Medieval predators cling to their thrones.

According to consensus, Frederick had been favored by the Medici Pope Leo X for the imperial succession. Yet, this official version defies the historic trajectory of the consistently pro-French Medici Dynasty.

To make the pope's true heart apparent, let me turn to a secret meeting that took place at Bologna a few months after the coronation of King Francis. Allegedly. No notes were taken. Nothing was recorded. Even the pope's historian learned nothing about the content or outcome of that meeting. Gossip had it that the pope promised the imperial throne to the French King and also to elevate him to be emperor of Constantinople in the event of the city's re-conquest. The rumour was supported by contemporary displays of French imperialism at Rome.[296] The crown of Naples was added to the French as a harbour of departure for a crusade against Constantinople. Real actions matched the unconfirmed promises.

The fog of a bigger game is lifting.

---

[295] Cardinal Albrecht von Brandenburg.
[296] Pastor, History of the Popes, VIII, 141-142, in Setton, 1984, 162.

Frederick the Wise resided in a romantic castle with its own church. He was a collector of thousands of authentic religious relics. One in the collection stands out: milk from the Virgin Mary. After Jesus Christ was born a god, they milked Mary and put the liquid in jars to be marvelled at by the rich 1,500 years later.

They were in possession of real evidence from the lineage of the world's most important boy.

That is beside the point.

Frederick the Wise, the loser with the milk jar, was the protector of the one man of our focus: Martin Luther.

The bigger game just turned into a monumental checkerboard with the aspiration of the owner of the jar to own the world.

As Luther's mentor, the Wise encouraged the Reformer to prepare Protestant sermons for all Sundays, in particular for the Easter masses. An imperial subversion through organized religion was shaping up, and the plan was diabolic: risk the lives of thousands of his own people by breaking the bonds with the Catholic Church and the empire in order to insist on imperial privilege. The executioners were the clergy of the Austin Friars, the preachers of St. Augustine, with Luther at their helm.

Christianity was weaponized.

Luther was compromised before he even started.

The loss of the Wise suited Pope Leo's real intentions. But the winner by massive bribe left behind more losers by bribe and conspiracy, not just the Wise. This happens to have been first, the pope himself, and second, the young King Francis of France.

The latter's puppeteers had likewise been paying electors off in order to climb up onto the imperial throne.

We can only guess who might have arranged for Francis' financing. We do not know what was going on behind the scenes. But perhaps the French-friendly name of the Medici clan comes to mind, those who just so happened also to come up short with luck. We do not need to be sorry for them. As the lavish Medici palaces and the castle-projects of the French King show, they were not descending into poverty. But somebody would have to foot the bills of bribes and palaces either way: the people. Who would extort the taxes from them? The Fuggers and the Medicis. Plus somebody in Luther-land who financed Frederick the Wise.

This was one heck of a high-stakes game.

Pope Leo does not seem to have fully understood what stage he was playing on. He did not know how to deal with the defector Luther after a public debate of the 95 Theses had turned awkward.[297] In a Papal Bull, he tried to condemn the preacher for disturbing the peace, unity, and Truth of the Catholic Church.[298] In an offensive display of overconfidence, the church leader thought that Luther's and others' ideas were scandalous, false heresies that would be seductive of simple minds who *'wish to be wiser than they should be.'*[299]

He did not know that he was being outsmarted.

After being kicked by a raging bull, Luther did what every decent rebel would do: he got up, went to the Elster Gate in his beloved Wittenberg, and burnt the Papal Bull. His response to Leo appears to have been measured and to the point.

The pope excommunicated the Reformer[300] based on a draft, which had been prepared by none other than Cardinal Cajetan, the Dominican Master-General of the Inquisition – the two-faced master of terror. Now, this cardinal had become the persecutor of Luther. According to the latter, the pope had written that the Reformer was possessed by the devil and that his mother was a whore and a bathhouse attendant.

Luther's work was destroyed by the Inquisition.[301]

Because being excommunicated is akin to being thrown out of a club, this might be perceived by moderns as no big deal or even a badge of honor. Back then, such a verdict had grave consequences for the superstitious – the entire population of the Old World – whereas Luther was turned into an outcast of the religious community.

Do you remember the boy in Pakistan who cut his hand off to beg for forgiveness for an imaginary offence? This is the kind of feeling that we can imagine the group pressure would have exerted upon Luther. Only much worse. Luther was convicted for offending the Catholic Church by its highest religious authority, Pope Leo himself.

---

[297] Martin Luther's 95 Theses were publicly debated at the Leipzig Debate at Pleissenburg Castle in Leipzig, Germany in the summer of 1519. It was a theological disputation between the first Lutheran bishop, Nikolaus von Amsdorf, the Dominican Johann Eck (defender of papal authority and under Fugger protection), Protestant theologian Andreas Karlstadt, Martin Luther, and the Reformation's intellectual leader, the young Philipp Melanchthon.

[298] Pope Leo X, *Papal Bull* issued June 15, 1520 (Eternal Word Television Network, 1999).

[299] Ibid.

[300] Pope Leo X, Decet Romanum Pontificem (Vatican, January 3, 1521).

[301] Luther, Jews and Their Lies, 1971, part IX.

In plain English, the pope bullied Luther into religious shame with the intention that the target should take his critique back, recant, and perish in silence. In a similar situation, the Pakistani boy could have cut hands, feet, and tongue off. It would not have helped. He would still have been beaten and stoned by his religious community. An insensitive comment could have cost a life in an instant, regardless of its validity.

The pope went even further. He cut a deal with the Holy Roman Emperor Charles V – the one who prevailed over Frederick the Wise and King Francis of France – to turn Luther into a civil outlaw also.

Other than taking up the fight, Luther was not given many options, was he? And take up the fight he did.

However, Luther had another option. The Papal Bull was never delivered to the Reformer. What nobody knew, nobody cared about. The younger brother[302] of Frederick the Wise withheld the document.

Religious organizations revel in embellishing their stories with fictional courage of their leaders. In other words, Luther's burning ceremony is another myth.

It never happened.

Other than the pope, Charles was then the most powerful man in Europe. His domain included the Holy Roman Empire, the Archduchy of Austria, the Kingdom of Spain, the Habsburg Netherlands, the Duchy of Burgundy, and the New World across the Atlantic, which was under discovery since Columbus' first voyage.

But it seems that Charles did not imagine that the pope could dance at two weddings. Inexperienced, the emperor just turned twenty years old now.

In a letter to a friend, Luther addressed *'The Babylonian Captivity of Church Jesus,'* an allusion to the French papacy, which was formerly in Avignon and was now represented by Pope Leo X. He intended to write a book about it, arguing that the Catholic Church lacked authority over its disciples.[303] Luther was also upset about ritual changes that had been undertaken by the council of the Catholic Church.[304]

He was increasingly radicalized in his differences with the Catholic Church.

---

[302] Johann the Steadfast was Elector of Saxony 1525 – 1532.
[303] Martin Luther, The Babylonian Captivity of Church Jesus, letter to Herman Tulich, October 1520, translated by John Nicholas Lenker.
[304] Ibid.

His rapper-style language exposes one enraged fellow.

> *Come hither then, ye popish flatterers, one and all! Fall to and defend yourselves*
> *against the charge of godlessness, tyranny, lese-majesty against the Gospel, and the*
> *crime of slandering your brethren — ye that decry as heretics those who will not be*
> *wise after the vaporings of your own brains, in the face of such patent and potent*
> *words of Scripture. If any are to be called heretics and schismatics, it is not the*
> *Bohemians nor the Greeks, for they take their stand upon the Gospel; but you*
> *Romans are the heretics and godless schismatics, for you presume upon your own*
> *fictions and fly in the face of the clear Scriptures of God. Parry that stroke, if you*
> *can!*[305]

Bohemia served as a role model for Luther on how to break from the Catholic Church.

In the letter, the Reformer also expressed some not-so-subtle racism against French people,[306] which is an age-old tradition among Europeans. Along the religious divides, their nationals love to hate each other. But then again, we can understand the context of the affiliation between Pope Leo and the Kingdom of France. Luther took offense in the fact that the papacy in Rome had been installed by them. By the same token, he expressed pride that the Holy Roman Empire was in German hands.

He was a born Evangelical nationalist supremacist.

But in all of this, we must perhaps be reminded that the fight that was to become the cause of so many lives lost was not about tangibles. Instead, the disputes were about questions of faith, against the veneration of angels in the church, and about how things ought to be understood and organized, based on the proper learning from the Gospels.

However, behind the veil, this new religion was deliberately engineered to create divisions intended to bring power to Frederick the Wise.

Power lies in division. Divide and rule.

Christians took it for real.

We drink the blood of Christ in a ritual re-enactment of Jesus' Last Supper, disciples might object. As Luther might say, it is real bread and real wine, in which Christ's real flesh and real blood are present.[307]

---

[305] Ibid.
[306] Ibid.
[307] Ibid.
Luther, Large Catechism, 1529, WA 30 I,125-238.

Luther agreed that it should not be a big deal for his followers and found a solution for the stringent ritual norms: Christians shall do as they please.[308] In other words, they can demand their right to the cup or not, but the decision is neither with the priesthood nor with the pope: *'Only let them not press us to accept their opinions as articles of faith.'*[309]

Luther was asking for nothing less than freedom from another religion.

Here we finally have something worthy of an armed stance.

But before you reach for the rifle, the 'freedom' that Luther talked about might not share much with freedom as we may understand it today. We will see later that this freedom was not to be extended to his subjects but only to himself and to nobility.

Yet, Luther was upset about petty ritual differences. The rebel did not shy away from declaring the Catholic Church as the Antichrist,[310] the gravest insult that he could think of.

There are some more fundamental questions in his letter that should have been resolved a thousand years earlier. The complexities are avoided here, but they point at a fight over doctrine that has been buried by religious historians under the rubble of the Reformation.

For the curious, three of the questions concern the nature of Jesus Christ (the divine essence is not begotten rather than the Son of God), the birth from Mary (born from Jesus' mother rather than from the Godmother),[311] and the nature of the soul (the soul as the form of the human body). Such positions should not have survived in Western Christianity, since their bastion is the Koran, the holy book for Muslims. They are also old ideas of Eastern Christianity.[312]

If you are willing to risk being grabbed by the throat, try discussing with a modern Christian the possibility that Jesus was not begotten by God. Luther's answer would be, *'even though philosophy cannot grasp this, faith grasps it, and the authority of God's Word is greater than the grasp of our intellect.'*[313]

---

308   Ibid.
309   Ibid.
310   Ibid.
311   Martin Luther, That Jesus Christ was Born a Jew (1523), translated by Walter I. Brandt, in Luther's Works (Fortress, Copyright © 1962, reprinted by permission of Fortress) 205.
312   Eastern Orthodoxy in Syria/Melchites.
313   Luther, Babylonian Captivity.

The allegation of Eastern Christian influence is so far off the beaten path that it would not be printed here, were it not for an independent eyewitness – a well-respected Muslim authority – who alleged that 'Melchite' (i.e. Syrian/Eastern) Christianity was the dominant faith in Europe barely a century before Luther was born.[314]

When and how did the change to the modern Catholic Church take place?[315]

Luther asserted that fundamental changes started to be implemented 300 years before his time.[316]

Luther, the rebel that he was, wanted to turn the clock back and return to his true Christianity, the one that had been taken from his Austin Friars 300 years earlier when they were forced to submit to the Catholic Church, the Melchite Church, or whichever mess it was then.

Faith is persistent, so much so that sectarian division was able to hide under the mantle of the Catholic Church, only to return with a vengeance hundreds of years later.

It is not clear which event Luther referred to. However, it was a time of broad upheaval in the Catholic Church. The goal of a crusade against the French Waldensians (Cathars) was to eradicate '*all signs that the heresy had ever existed: the heretics and the houses in which they had lived were burned, and later generations were forbidden to honor the memory of their heterodox ancestors.*'[317]

The sect of the Waldensians complained then that the Vatican was a den of thieves and that it housed the Antichrist. For the Catholic Church, the baptismal water was no better than river water, they alleged, and the body of Christ did not differ from ordinary bread.[318] We heard the same accusations from Luther. Were rituals and doctrines of the Catholic Church then changed?

The conflicts during that time cost the loss of vast cultural treasures from ancient Rome. And countless lives.

---

[314] Muhammed ibn Khaldun (1332 – 1406 AD), The Muqaddimah (1377 AD), translated by Franz Rosenthal (Princeton University, 1958) Chapter III.31.

[315] The century before Luther's era may provide a framework for this swap. Within a few years after Khaldun's publication, the Melchite power structure collapsed. Solving this problem will enable humanity to better appreciate the divisions that could have sparked the transformation under Luther's feet.

[316] Luther, Babylonian Captivity.

[317] Luc Racaut, Hatred in Print: Catholic Propaganda and Protestant Identity During the French Wars of Religion (Routledge, Copyright © 2017, reprinted by permission of Routledge) VII, The Polemical Use of the Albigensian Crusade, 2.

[318] From Raynaldus, Annales, in S.R. Maitland, tarns, *History of the Albigenses and Waldenses*, (Rivington, 1832) 392-394.

Also, Saint Francis of Assisi[319] founded the Franciscan Order[320] at that time. This saint's nature can be summed up with his loving words: cursing and damning everybody who dared not to listen or not to fulfill his god's commandments.[321] Francis chose for his order to live in absolute poverty and dependent on Christians to give.

Only a decade after the Franciscan Order was established, the fundamentalist Dominican Order[322] was founded by Saint Dominic.[323] These became the masters of the Catholic Inquisition, as they still were during Luther's time. Its task was to eradicate not only heresy but also all evidence that differing thoughts inside the Catholic Church had ever existed.

In its wake, historical records of humanity were destroyed or manipulated.

And then there was the Fourth Lateran Council. Its leaders thought it wise that Jews and Saracens – Muslims – across Christian Europe should be marked with identifying symbols.[324]

During this council, it was expressed why the display of religious symbolism was desirable: because of a lack of differentiation, ordinary Christians entered relationships with non-Christians.

The reasoning went on that Christians were increasingly oppressed by the treachery of Jews through the practice of usury. Indeed, this had been granted to them through the Carolingian banking monopoly. So the argument went that Christians needed to be protected against the cruelty of Jews.[325]

The pattern of history repeats itself.

Something else happened in that period, 300 years before Luther. Over 20,000 Saracens were relocated from Sicily into the heart of Italy, into a town merely 150 miles[326] southeast of the city of Rome.[327]

This was a greater number of new arrivals than the population of most Italian cities. Even Rome was smaller. It must have had a profound impact on the intelligentsia of the Italian Peninsula.

---

[319] Giovanni Francesco di Bernardone 1182 – 1226.
[320] The Franciscans can still be recognized today by their brown robes with a rope around their waists.
[321] Francesco D'Assisi, Gli Scritti, Lettera Prima a Tutti i Fideli (1209.
[322] The Dominicans can still be recognized today by their black mantles over white robes.
[323] Domingo de Guzmán Garcés 1170 – 1221.
[324] Forth Lateran Council, Canon 68, 1215, from H. J. Schroeder, *Disciplinary Decrees of the General Councils: Text, Translation and Commentary* (Herder, 1937) 236-296.
[325] Ibid., Canon 67.
[326] The city of Lucera lies 240 km or about 150 miles south of Rome.
[327] Julie Anne Taylor, *Muslims in Medieval Italy: The Colony at Lucera* (Lexington, 2005) 12.

And on the Catholic Church.

In 1452, Frederick III the Fat,[328] great-grandfather of Charles, was crowned Holy Roman Emperor by the then-pope.[329] He was the first emperor of the House of Habsburg. Fourteen years before, the emperor had entered a deal for his coronation with the Vatican.[330]

Part of the agreement was that the German churches lost their denominational liberties to the Catholic Church.

The German churches had for long questioned the legitimacy of the papacy in Rome and had declared themselves supreme, even over the pope.[331]

While it may have been for the sake of expediency, the Protestant Church itself claims that two churches had existed since apostolic times. Modern researchers think that there remains a connection between the Reformation and French heterodox sects of that time, which maintained their independent parallel hierarchies.[332]

But more relevant to the Protestant prelude, archbishops from the German diocese of Mainz had traditionally viewed themselves as sort of popes north of the Alps.[333]

Even today, Mainz is the only diocese in the world that calls its jurisdiction Holy See.[334]

The disobedience of the Germans shows in the historical record immediately after dealing with the Fat. The pope[335] appointed a German by the name of Adolf[336] to the archbishopric of Mainz. He rampaged the city in 1462. 400 people who refused to submit perished.

The rest of the disobedient survivors were thrown out of town or into jail.

Their property was seized and distributed among those who got in line.

---

[328] Frederick III aka the Fat or the Peaceful, 1415 – 1493.

[329] Pope Nicholas V, aka Tommaso Parentucelli, was pope from 1447 to 1455.

[330] Pope Eugene IV, aka Gabriele Condulmer, was pope from 1431 to 1447.

[331] Council of Constance, fifth session, April 6, 1415.

[332] Michel Jas, Braises cathares: filiation secrete a l'heure de la Réform, in Luc Racaut, The Polemical Use of the Albigensian Crusade During the French Wars of Religion (Oxford, 1999) Vol. 13 No. 3, 261-279.

[333] Primas Germaniae.

[334] Sancta sedes.

[335] Pope Pius II aka Enea Silvio Bartolomeo Piccolomini (1405 – 1464) was pope 1458 – 1464.

[336] Adolf II von Nassau-Wiesbaden-Idstein c. 1423 – 1475.

One might have thought that this sealed the deal for the faithful. Love and peace in Mainz, at last. Twenty years later, a man known as the Dominican Hammer of Witches of the Catholic Inquisition[337] plotted to get Mainz, Cologne, Trier, Salzburg, and Bremen in line.

These were not just any cities. Four of these five had in common that they were still autonomous. Trier's history is spiked with its struggle for independence from the Catholic archbishopric. The first three of these five were also among the seven electorates of the Holy Roman Empire.

The assaults by organized religion were about controlling the throne of the Holy Roman Empire.

Approving of the inquisitorial request, the then-pope[338] signed the bull *Summis Desiderantes*.[339] Witches, male or female, were to be burned, killed or imprisoned, whichever promised to extinguish heresy. The pope acknowledged the reality of their supernatural presence with the force of his pen.

He deployed yet another superstitious layer for his deadly goals.

The German churches refused to cooperate in the papal subversion of the empire – until they chose to subvert the empire for themselves.

Under Luther, the backlash from the unholy pact with Frederick developed into a full earthquake. Erfurt, where Luther's Saint Augustine's Monastery is located, was part of the diocese of Mainz since the eighth century and also of the Electorate of Mainz at the time of the Holy Roman Empire.

Dissent from the Catholic Church was in the blood of the Germans.

It was in Luther's arteries.

Luther was to bring the German Church *back* to the Germans.

One of the reasons that Luther was able to pump out incredible volumes of works was that he did not need to think them through. All he had to do was write down what he was already professionally trained to preach as an Austin Friar.

In contrast, innovation is hard, and it takes time to sort out the details.

The Germans shook off something that had been foreign to them – the Catholic Church – and they may have returned to the folk beliefs that had been preached for centuries throughout the churches of the Austin Friars.

---

[337] The Dominican Inquisitor Heinrich Kramer (c. 1430 – 1505). The 'Hammer of Witches' is the name of his book Malleus Maleficarum, written in 1487.

[338] Pope Innocent VIII aka Giovanni Battista Cybo (1432 – 1492) was pope 1484 – 1492.

[339] Pope Innocent VIII, Papal Bull, Summis desiderantes, 1484.

I must unveil what the letter *'The Babylonian Captivity of Church Jesus'* to Luther's friend contained about Jews. The Reformer was merely concerned with comparative religious and social practices. There is not a hint of hatred against them. Obviously, his mind was in a different sphere, and so far, he was being consistent in demanding religious independence for his church business.

In another letter of the same year, Luther expressed himself without ambivalence that Jews needed to be treated kindly *'for there are future Christians among them.'*[340] He saw in Jews potential converts and wealthy taxpayers, and he thought that the good example of Christians would do the job. He agreed that the *'Servitude of the Jews'* was an absurd proclamation of hatred against Jews.[341]

Was it propaganda?

With the mediation of Frederick the Wise, Luther was granted safe passage to a meeting with Emperor Charles V, the Diet of Worms in 1521. The intent and purpose of the meetup with a pre-arranged backroom deal was that Luther would unsuccessfully defend himself for the works that he had created, including the 95 Theses and *'The Babylonian Captivity of Church Jesus.'*

For three years already, Luther was sued to recant by Cardinal Cajetan, the Dominican Master-General of the Inquisition. The two-faced saint. At the Inquisitor's side was Hieronymus Aleandro.[342]

The latter had just returned from Antwerp.

There, he instigated the public execution of two reform monks.

They were burned alive at the stake.

Aleandro was also a notorious desktop criminal who was involved in 'expunging' texts that were not to the liking of the Catholic Church. He was one of the fiercest opponents of Luther's reform efforts.

Aleandro would soon become the librarian of the Vatican – a professional forger – and later cardinal.

A Franciscan priest was also keenly interested in Luther's progress: Francisco de Quiñones.[343] He had been educated by none other than the Grand Inquisitor Cardinal Cisneros. Nothing good could be expected from his students.

---

[340] Martin Luther, The Magnificat, 1520-21, in the Works of Martin Luther, Phila. Ed., vol. 3, p. 197.

[341] Martin Luther, in Elliot Rosenberg, But Were They Good for the Jews? (Birch Lane, 1997) 65.

[342] Hugh Chisholm, Girolamo [Hieronymus or Jerome] Aleandro or Aleander, 1480 – 1542 was a Venitian who first became librarian of the Vatican since 1519 under Pope Leo X and then cardinal of the Catholic Church in 1536 by Pope Paul III.

[343] Francisco de Quiñones, aka Francisco de los Angeles, 1482 – 1540.

De Quiñones was entrusted with a mission to the Americas by Pope Leo X. He was to share his responsibilities with the confessor[344] of Charles V.

Destruction and death was brought to the indigenous people of the New World.

Due to Charles' confessor's unexpected death, de Quiñones became Commissary General of the Franciscans north of the Alps – Luther-land. A couple of years later, he was promoted to Minister General of the Order. In this function, he became responsible for the Franciscans in Spain, the Spanish Netherlands, and Italy. The prefix of his name, 'de', identifies him as being of 'noble' birth. De Quiñones was an imperial loyalist.

It appears obvious that the Inquisition intended to subvert the Franciscan Order with a leadership loyal to the command of the Grand Inquisitor of the Catholic Church in order to prevent them from defecting.

Cardinal Aleandro and de Quiñones were now Luther's persecutors at the Diet of Worms.

What would you do, if you had come thus far to put half of northern Europe on passion alert?

That is exactly what Luther did:

> *Unless I am convinced by the testimony of the Scriptures or by clear reason (for I do not trust either in the pope or in councils alone, since it is well known that they have often erred and contradicted themselves), I am bound by the Scriptures I have quoted and my conscience is captive to the Word of God. I cannot and will not recant anything, since it is neither safe nor right to go against conscience. May God help me. Amen.*[345]

We must remember that the Wise was standing there and that the rest of the judges over spiritual matters probably did not know about Judas among them.

*'Judas'* is a religious code name that can brand anyone as a sort of double agent, a subversive element who betrays the leader and with it the religious community as a whole. The biblical Judas delivered Jesus Christ to his enemies by identifying the holy man with a welcome kiss.

In the modern political world, a *'Judas'* is someone who habitually pretends to support a cause, while his real agenda is with its opponent or for himself.

---

[344] Charles' confessor at this time was the Friar Jean Glapion.
[345] Brecht, Luther, transl. Schaaf, 1985–93, 1:460.

It was during these meetings that Martin Luther met another of his most important early supporters. Philip I of Hesse the Magnanimous,[346] now only seventeen years of age, was so impressed by the Reformer that he would become one of the earliest Protestant regional rulers.

A gullible teenager – and a primary beneficiary of Luther's success.

To everyone's surprise, Luther disappeared during the fake deliberations and was snatched by a band of robbers in the forest near his hometown Wittenberg.

They brought the Reformer to Wartburg Castle under the name of Knight George.

The masked horsemen were sent by the Wise himself – Luther's protector.

The choice of names with religious fundamentalists is never by accident, and it is worthwhile to look them up when an enemy is tagged with such a designation. A name or a single word can carry deep religious meaning.

Saint George was a legend of a knight. He refused to disavow the Christian religion in the face of persecution. Dragged behind a horse through the streets, he was thereafter venerated as a martyr.

George is the patron saint of many organizations, towns, and countries. He is not the stuff of the imaginary for being of steadfast belief but rather because he killed a dragon, an imaginary dragon, that is. Not a single contemporary historian reported either the good old Texas Western-style horse drag or the superhuman achievement against the otherworldly creature.[347]

Dragons spew fire.

To face the monster, George was also the patron saint of a town at the foot of Mount Vesuvius in Italy.[348]

The dragon symbolized an active volcano that the superstitious imagined themselves to tame.

---

[346] Philip I of Hesse (1504 – 1567) the Magnanimous was Landgrave of Hesse.

[347] To be sure that this is contextualized properly, authorities typically relied on popular support, even emperors and popes. They tried to avoid such displays of cruelty because they were well aware that they could stoke compassion. They intended to instill fear and pretend due process. But with displays of brutality, they would light the fire of opposition, and literally advertise the cause of the martyr. That is why no historian was eyewitness when a Christian was dragged behind a horse by the order of an 'authority' in actual power.

[348] San Giorgio a Cremano, near Naples.

Organized religion needs to borrow its heroes from novels and Pagan folk tales. It cannot rely on real ones. They never existed. Even St. Augustine complained about the invention of such martyrs by the church.[349]

Yet, the fictional dragon slayer is a popular subject of venerations and prayers – today.

Muslims have their own folk view of the hero saint: for them, Saint George is a symbol for the mental ward.[350]

At Wartburg Castle, Luther produced a German translation of the Greek New Testament in just seventy days.[351] It became the most widely circulated German translation of the Gospels.

His most important reader was Johann of Saxony the Steadfast, younger brother of the Wise. He played courier for the sheets that Luther had created in his hideout.

The sheer volume of works that Luther was able to pump out is amazing.

With the tools available to us today, we can look up a Greek word for its German equivalent in a matter of a few seconds. Back then, there was none of that, no communication other than by letter or in person, no electricity to light a room or run machinery, no access to historical information other than through rare and precious physical books or archives, simply nothing of what we take for granted today. The most rudimentary technological breakthroughs that would lead to our smartphones were still over 400 years out.

A single search would have cost him a lot of time just to make sure that he used a word correctly. He could not just slap the text down hastily, for the typesetter had to be able to read his handwriting before he went to setting the pages with the newly invented movable type – by hand, type by type, letter by letter. The job was possible only if he never once put the pen down for 20 hours every single day, 7 days a week, 70 days in a row. This left no room, none whatsoever, to look up what other people might have thought about any of the passages that he was working on.

All that said, the idea of translating the Bible into a local language was not new either. The French Waldensians[352] – forerunners of the Reformation – had done it more than 300 years before him.

---

[349]  Augustine, De Obedientia, 16.
[350]  Elizabeth Anne Finn, Home in the Holyland (Nisbet, 1866) 46.
[351]  History of the Wartburg, Wartburg-Stiftung.
[352]  Peter Waldo, the founder of the Waldensians, appears to have commissioned a translation of the New Testament into the Arpitan language (Franco-Provençal) at the end of the twelfth century. As they were

For the first two decades of the century, the Grand Inquisitor Cardinal Cisneros had worked on the publication of the Complutensian Polyglot Bible. It was a monumental task of presenting the Bible in Latin, Greek, and Hebrew. The book contains the Greek New Testament, the complete Hebrew Bible (Septuagint), and the Targum Onkelos. The latter was a Babylonian Aramaic translation of the Torah, which constitutes the first five books of the Bible. At that time, Kabalists were popular, even among Christian scholars. Kabalists allege that the Torah contains encrypted, divine meaning beyond its words. For them, the tiniest decorative markings mattered for their interpretations.

With Cisneros' translation, I find myself in a morass of questions about an apparent Jewish influence in Spain. We may remember that I suspect this Cisneros to be one with the renamed Abrabanel. I ask again: did he convert like Senior had become Coronel? Was he the Deceiver? If so, then the top Jewish leadership had infiltrated the Catholic Church itself only to emerge as its most brutal extremist wing.

Meanwhile, the Edict of Worms was issued. It was a warrant to arrest Luther as an outlaw. His books were banned, and anyone was forbidden under severe punishment to assist him in any way.[353] The man behind the imperial draft? Cardinal Aleandro. The Catholic Church. Luther was wanted as a heretic, one who did not believe as others did; one who spoke up. He was made a criminal through the power of organized crime.

The Lutheran response? Speaking up more.

The German Renaissance artist Lucas Cranach, a friend of Luther's, painted the work *'The Antichrist'* the same year that the Edict of Worms was issued. It shows a man on a throne with the Tiara, the triple crown of Pope Leo. The grand symbol for world governance. Leo was depicted in the process of signing stacks of indulgences – the sort of which had helped build Luther's Saint Augustine Monastery at Erfurt. On a table in front of him, greedy functionaries counted the money made from the sale of the indulgences.

Cranach was also a court painter to the Elector of Saxony, Frederick the Wise, who seems to have protected and cultivated a host of dissidents. Cranach created contemporary impressions of Martin Luther and of the young Emperor Charles. The woodcut illustrations for the Luther Bible were also his. Cranach's

---

turned into heretics by the Catholic Church, their principal error was their contempt for the ecclesiastical power of the Catholic Church and other errors (Rosalind B. Brooke, The Coming of the Friars (Barnes and Noble, 1975) 72-73).

[353] Emperor Charles V, Edict of Worms, 1521.

signature is the best of all: a winged serpent, given to him as a symbol by the Wise.

They sure knew how to make a point of their dissent.

We can put all this now in context when Luther mocked Jews in one of his early sermons for their desire for a worldly reign of their messiah.[354] For denying Jesus Christ, *'they are carriers of sacks, lazy beasts of burden and yoked rogues,'*[355] he thought. While these are clearly not words from scripture, the Reformer was rude to anyone who was not convinced by his line of thought.

In that sense, his argument was as vulgar as it was opposed to the papacy or the Ottoman-Turks.

In other sermons during the same time period, he simply stuck to the biblical tension between Christians and Jews and did not mock them as opportunity arose. Because the dispute between the two religions is so prominent in the Gospels, it would have been hard for him or even impossible to escape the topic. Given the anti-Semitic nature of the Gospels, it is quite impressive how Luther sometimes artfully danced around the toxic themes. If he did hate them, it did not show up strongly in either his early writings or in his masses.

Those who claim otherwise should read his early sermons that focused on Jesus' death and resurrection. If anywhere, it would be here, where Christians traditionally put the blame on Jews for the murdering of Jesus Christ.

Not so Luther.

In the progression of this book, we will learn just what full-blown anti-Semitism looks like. We have seen nothing yet. At this point, he simply thought that Jews and Turks were seduced by the Antichrist,[356] personified in Pope Leo X.

A messiah was roaming the continent. Luther may have referred to real events of his time.

But let me not be mistaken for what was just said: even though the Gospels were evidently the work of Jews and were written against their own – a display of self-hatred – the inherent anti-Semitism in them amounts to nothing less than hate speech by its very definition. Its anti-Semitic function and effect can be measured in numbers: hundreds of millions of lives lost and countless more destroyed.

---

[354] Martin Luther, Sermons, First Sunday in Advent, ca. 1521, translated by John Nicholas Lenker, 58, 61.
[355] Ibid.
[356] Martin Luther, Sermons, Sunday After Christmas of Simeon; of Anna, of the Return of the Parents of Jesus to Nazareth, and the Childhood of Christ, translated by John Nicholas Lenker.

The psychological effect on the people inside the circle of self-hatred is evident throughout the historical record. The self-portrayal of a hated people or a hated religion has the simple effect of its members defending themselves against an – any – imaginary enemy who hates them. They huddle together and segregate themselves from the rest of the community. In turn, they are being hated for provoking hatred against themselves in pursuit of their ultimate goal of bringing about the End of the World, which is supposed to hand to them the imperial crown of world leadership.

Simply put: Jewish self-portrayal of being hated begets anti-Semitism.

Neither Christians nor Muslims have grounds, other than the religiously-induced self-hatred, to hate Jews. After all, Judaism, for them, cannot be untrue in its essence.

Christianity and Islam rest their very foundations on the Truth of that religion.

What they also share, as already laid out, is their desire for the End of the World – on opposing battle fronts.

So, Luther was stuck with the biblical framework, and his religion gave him literally no choice but to embed hatred against Jews in almost every reference to the Gospels where they were spoken of. Since they represented unbelief, he could not help but compare the papacy with Jews, or lump them together with Turks, and extend his mal-wishes to all.

He solved the paradox of the Jewish origin of the Bible like a simpleton: Jews did not understand the Bible correctly – he was the only one who did.

While he could have avoided some of these unnecessary low blows, they served well to pepper his sermons and make them more personal and dramatic.

But, from that perspective, so far, the Reformer was moderate.

A moderate radical, perhaps?

Yet, one may wonder how the bombardment of negative biblical analogies against Jews may have injured the minds of ignorant and superstitious worshippers. The sermons were preached in their language now. If they took them seriously, their respect for Jews was destined to freeze in hell. A common enemy who helped binding a community together!

One could even make up the dishonest illusion that Luther applied the Christian approach of love toward them – were it not for the open agenda to do so in the name of converting them away from their beliefs to his. Love was limited to those *inside* his belief circle and to the moths that flew close enough potentially to be brought in to fuel the holy flame.

In addition, new religious sects typically gain numbers quickly by recruiting outcasts. Welcome slaves to go free. Or thieves. Strength is in numbers. At that time, Jews were systematically persecuted by the Catholic Church. Who would serve better to be loved as a marketing target than Jews, homeless, God-disobedient outcasts in perpetual exile as they were?

Besides, business would be good.

On the other hand, Luther's sermons were part of an effective communications strategy.

Luther standardized the intellectual messages for his professional broadcasters to read during masses. Early forms of newspapers did not exist until after Luther's time. Priests were able to spread imaginary and fake news from their pulpits as their bosses pleased. As discussed earlier, Luther utilized a style of clerical thought control similar to the kind the Catholic Church engaged in at the exact same time.

The upcoming wars were based on two successful camps with conformed thoughts, conformed to what each would think of the other: delusion.

But let me be clear here: in the end, many of Luther's sermons, even early ones, amount to anti-Semitic mind infiltration, if only they served for the 'historical' perspective as the devils who dared to oppose and kill Jesus Christ, to reject the Christian message of love, and for restating the omnipresent biblical hate against Jews.

Even if the context were historical, Luther's perpetual mockeries were spiteful and needless.

## Pitchfork Rebels

Two years later, in 1523, Gutenberg's recently-invented press had printed 300,000 copies of Luther's eight-page pamphlet with his 95 Theses. The number of copies suggests that they were circulated throughout Europe to almost everyone who could read. By oppressing an opponent, the Catholic Church had unleashed a radical – and the first strike hit through a novelty in communications technology, a fledgling form of printed mass media.

This was quite a feat.

Primitive Gutenberg presses had started to appear half a century earlier. Now, over 250 towns were busy with improved machines that could churn out more printed paper quicker. Publishing and the construction and improvement of print machinery had become big business. But we would be mistaken to believe that this was a fast process by any standards. There was no automation at this time. For centuries to come, the print plates needed to be assembled manually, character by character. Each individual page still needed to be printed by adding a single sheet to the machine and then pulling a mechanical lever for the actual print. Since the ink had to dry, double sided printing did not come easily either. Books were bound by hand. They were relatively cheap compared to the handwritten copies before Gutenberg. But Luther's pamphlet would still have cost 100 times more than having it produced with advanced machinery from after the Industrial Revolution.

Given the rapid advance of printing presses, we can appreciate that the papacy may have been concerned with 'fake news.' This is why they attempted to submit all print shops to licensing and censoring requirements. They attempted to crush the earliest sprouts of freedom of the 'press.' Obviously, some did not comply. Idle machines make no money. Outside of the jurisdiction of the Catholic Church, they punched out paper at capacity.

This same year, the Reformer co-published another pamphlet with Philip Melanchthon,[357] one of his most important reform collaborators and a co-founder of Lutheranism. It bore the prankful title *Interpretation of the Two Abhorring Figures, Pope-Ass and Monk-Calf.*[358] This is all information needed to assess its overwhelmingly mindful content. We can be sure that the provocation was met at Rome with fatherly cheers.

Luther's fake news turned into a destructive intellectual anti-force.

---

[357] Philip Melanchthon aka Philipp Schwartzerdt, 1497 – 1560. He was the intellectual leader of the Protestant Reformation.

[358] Philip Melanchthon, Martin Luther, Deutung der zwei greulichen Figuren Bapst-Esels zu Rom und Mönch-Kalbs zu Freiberg in Meissen funden (Johann Rhau-Grunenberg, 1523).

A couple of years after the 95 Theses' distribution, Germany, Switzerland, and Austria were at war with their religious overlords. The Reformation spread north to take hold in Denmark and Scandinavia. During the next two decades, Catholic monasteries were attacked and priests thrown out of their churches and arrested.

It happened so fast because royals saw their opportunity to extend their power. Some national kings also became heads of the churches in their territories. To pay for the cost of internal war, they seized the property of the Catholic Church.

Pope Leo received his appropriate reward for having deployed his gang of inquisitors to extort more money for the monumental construction site of Saint Peter's in Rome and to overthrow royalty. Instead, the latter threw out the Catholic Church altogether.

The answer to the pope's orders was a decisive 'no'.

The oppressive behavior of the Vatican provoked alienation, insurgency, and rejection.

Historians are still fighting over other reasons, but the connection between Luther and the uprisings appears obvious, even though social unrest was in the air before, and other reformers roamed Europe at a dime a dozen. He exploited the well-established communications channels of the Austin Friars and the formerly Catholic churches with the new mass media of printed pamphlets.

Given the distribution of Luther's sermons, the idea that he may have been unimportant does not hold. Then as now, communication was key. Press created followers. Loud press created more followers. Luther was the straw that broke the neck of the Taliban-style oppression machinery that was fueled with the last penny from the faithful poor.

Certainly, Martin Luther's timing could not have been better.

Those who are well informed about church history keep wondering what might have taken the people so long to finally rise up.

The answer is simple: physical and emotional abuse – church terrorism.

Asserting the Truth did not come with flexible minds but instead with extortions in order to get the dead out of the imaginary purgatory.

Things were different now.

Revolt was the order of the day. Led and supported by Protestant clergy – largely recruited from the Augustinian Order – as many as 100,000 insufficiently armed and untrained peasants and farmers lost their lives in the first skirmishes of the Protestant awakening.[359] In their rage, peasants of several towns in the Alsace region went after Jews and drove them out.[360]

From a contemporary sermon by Luther, it can be seen that the Reformer was shaken by the fallout.

But at a time when Germany should have been in deep religious suspense, Luther complained about the lack of piety on the government level. He even mentioned that *'the great majority'* were persecuting and blaspheming the Gospels. What he said cannot easily be put in context. Certainly, he cannot have meant the Catholic Church. A similar remark is extant from the French King. He observed a very low devotion of the laity.[361] Were Humanist and Secular movements in northern and central Europe much further advanced than commonly believed?

Certainly, many progressive ideas originated in northern Europe, while the south was deeply immersed in Catholicism. This north-south slide also came to persist in modern economies, where Catholic southern Europe remained in economic and intellectual slumber for centuries. It is not by chance that European countries like Portugal, Spain, and Italy were and still are on the list of bankrupt nations.

Whatever *'great majority'* of impious forces Luther had experienced, he was opposed to them and was determined to quell them. The Reformer stood at the helm of the anti-progressive forces, against Humanism and Secularism.

Luther also lamented the appearance of new sects, which divided his flock. He thought that his disciples did not pray enough.[362]

It echoes the fears that were expressed in the Fifth Lateran Council over newly emerged biblical interpretations. Yet, these new sects still used the Gospels and were religious. Accordingly, the Reformer could not have meant those as his target of *'the great majority.'* Praying to his own choir, one may wonder

---

[359] Martin Luther, Sermons, Tenth Sunday After Trinity, A sermon on the destruction of Jerusalem. In like manner will Germany also be destroyed, if she will not recognize the time of her visitation. What the temple of God is (1525) translated by John Nicholas Lenker, 11.

[360] Rosheim and Sundgau were two of the targets. Rosheim was spared, while all Jews from Sundgau were driven away.

[361] Francis I in Setton, 1984, 178: La dévotion du peuple est si petite, qu'il ne revient quasy rien d'icelle!

[362] Martin Luther, Sermons, transl. Lenker, 1525: 12, 13. .

what the effect of such wailing might have been other than stoking the fire of hatred against different Christian interpretations.

But here too, Luther wanted to go back to the times of single-minded thought control under one church.

Sects constitute organized religions' natural enemies.

With his sectarian fears, he eyed neither Jews nor the Catholic Church. Since we know that several reform leaders were breaking from the main body of the Catholic Church, he must have referred to his leading contemporaries in protest. As a consequence of this division, he feared that all of Germany could go up in flames.[363] In fact, he thought that God would punish Germany for its shameful transgression of his religion and its withdrawal from it.

In the name of his god, Luther was determined to save Germany from deviating from the only Truth – his Truth.

Luther also accused nobility of being too fast with the sword. They were quick to deploy troops to put unrest down. Protesters had obvious causes, but their governments bled them out.

Luther's strategy, it seems, was to bring the Gospel to areas of Germany that had not yet heard it. His argument was that salvation would have to be brought to the Germans before the destruction of their nation by God, otherwise, all these souls would be lost.[364]

By now, Luther had contracted a full-blown infection of the End of the World. While he thought of earlier problems as a prelude to the end, now it was imminent. Given that his friend Lucas Cranach had painted Pope Leo in *The Antichrist,'* he already had his mind set on his enemies.

They were not Jews.

Since Germany should have been fully catholicized at that time, at least since the Carolingian era 700 years earlier, it was a strange thing for Luther to lament the lack of Gospel penetration in Germany. Nevertheless, Jews were not targeted in his sermon. Instead, he thought their ordeal was in the past and that they had learned from it.

Little did he know.

---

[363]  Ibid.: 14.
[364]  Ibid.: 15.

Nobles who broke from the Catholic bond did so under the slogan *'German money for a German church,'*[365] allusions to both the Catholic tax burden and the Lutheran Protestant Church. It was also an expression of nationalism.

Some nobles may have speculated that they would be taxed less by the new church. However, this expectation would have been rather naive. While the over-taxation in the Catholic network played an important role in creating a schism, so did the enabling and empowerment of the feudal hierarchy by the Vatican. Over taxation is difficult to implement without enforcement by sword. But the loss of priestly concubines, the authoritarian submission of sectarian organizations, and the planned substitution of royalty with clergy may have constituted death knells.

On the other hand, we need to bear in mind that the noble class was created and enabled by the Catholic Church. They could not go it alone. Understandably, they willingly put themselves into a new vehicle that promised even more power to them.

Under cover of the Protestant Church, they could simply go on unabated with their crooked business.

And Luther sucked up to nobility to get his way. He would call them *'serene, highborn Prince, gracious Lord.'*[366]

In the conflict with peasants, Luther was criticized for having taken both positions, condemning the rebellion as breaking the peace and the suppression of the insurrection for its brutality.[367] However, that verdict is doing Luther an injustice. He did not know at this point that his church was to separate completely from the Catholic Church. He wanted to go backward, not forward. He was not wavering, but he had not yet found his full role.

Indeed, at this time, he wrote the ill-conceived pamphlet *'Against the Robbing and Murdering Hordes of Peasants'* in which he accused peasantry of betraying his cause by plundering and pillaging monasteries and castles under the leadership of Thomas Müntzer.[368]

This was another religious radical who was called *'archdevil'* and *'murderer'* in Luther's pamphlet.[369] He thought that *'freedom'* was not meant literally to be for

---

[365]  Roland Bainton, Here I Stand: A Life of Martin Luther (Pierce & Smith, 1978) 76.

[366]  Martin Luther, On war against Islamic reign of terror (On war against the Turk), Vom Kriege wider die Türken, 1528 (WA 30 II, 107-148), Lutherdansk.

[367]  Donald K. McKim, The Cambridge Companion to Martin Luther (Cambridge, 2003) 184-186.

[368]  Thomas Müntzer, ca. 1489 – 1525.

[369]  Martin Luther, Against the Robbing and Murdering Hordes of Peasants (1525) in E.G. Rupp and Benjamin Drewery, Martin Luther, Documents of Modern History (London: Edward Arnold, 1970), pp. 121-6.

all but only for the soul. For the Reformer, there was no *'devil left in hell; they have all gone into the peasants.* [370] The lay men had to submit, he insisted, to the noble authorities and to the church.

By his own definition, Luther was a holy enemy of freedom.

In a sermon, he was also spiteful with the more radical wing of reformers:

> *Do you know what the Devil thinks when he sees men use violence to propagate the gospel? He sits with folded arms behind the fire of hell, and says with malignant looks and frightful grin: 'Ah, how wise these madmen are to play my game! Let them go on; I shall reap the benefit. I delight in it.' But when he sees the Word running and contending alone on the battle-field, then he shudders and shakes for fear.* [371]

The context provides ample evidence that Luther was supporting the establishment that protected him at Wartburg Castle. Nobility could not go it alone, nor could he.

His dream was to become part of the establishment in order to ensure that suckers remained suckers.

Luther succeeded.

Peasants died.

Martin Luther wrote that the ruling class had *just* cause and could retain good conscience to take every action against peasants. [372] Because the Catholic Church was friendly with the Kingdom of France – at least under Pope Leo – Luther wanted to coordinate his protests with the subversive tactics of Frederick the Wise.

In any case, Luther colluded and conspired with his feudal overlords.

He went as far as bragging about having ordered peasants killed [373] to quell the rebellion.

That turns Luther into an accomplice to mass-murder of men who were fighting for freedom. For whichever reasons of self-promotion, from the outset of Lutheranism, the reformist leader acted on no less oppressive ideals than the Catholic Church.

The difference was that he sought nobility as allies while the Catholic Church wanted to get rid of them.

---

[370]  Ibid.
[371]  Philip Schaff, History of the Christian Church, Vol VII, Ch IV.
[372]  Rupp, Drewery, Luther, 1970, pp. 121-6.
[373]  Erlangen Edition of Luther's Works, Vol. 59, 284.

Müntzer was not deterred by bloodshed.

While this figure based his ideas on Protestant ideals, he went further to promote a new world order. This hot head had begun to criticize the Catholic Church a few years before Luther's 95 Theses, but well after Luther had represented the Austin Friars in the Vatican with his opposition to a merger.

The two had met at Wittenberg in 1517, where Müntzer absorbed Luther's thoughts. Anyhow, they did not get along. Riots followed to wherever this guy preached. He formed a religious militia and imagined the Peasant Revolt as an apocalyptic act of God. He made himself a revolutionary leader *'as God's Servant against the Godless.'* [374] Like Luther at the time, Müntzer believed that the End of the World was imminent and that true believers were obliged to help God in bringing about a new era. [375]

According to Luther, the radical rebel saw himself as the new leader emerging after the event of the End of the World. He saw Müntzer as the one responsible for the bloody rebellion. [376]

He must have recognized him as a challenge to his leadership.

In his final act, Müntzer showed up on the battlefield at the head of the Peasants' War. He looked eye-to-eye with Frederick the Wise and Philip I of Hesse the Magnanimous, two of the earliest and staunchest Luther supporters and leaders of the revolt's suppression.

The reformer Müntzer was captured, tortured, and a few days later, executed.

By the forces of the Reformation.

After it was all over, Luther appears to have moderated his previous stance on the End of the World and now looked at the events again as a prelude. [377]

This is not as confusing as it may seem.

Rabbi Abrabanel, the King of the Jews (under suspicion to be Cisneros), had predicted that the beginning of the Messianic Age and the fall of Rome would take place in 1531, which translates into the End of the World a little over a decade out.

Müntzer and the late Rabbinic prophet appear to have been in sync.

---

[374] Tom Scott and Robert W. Scribner, eds. The German Peasants' War: a History in Documents (Humanities Press, 1989) 183.

[375] R.W. Scribner: The German Reformation (London, 1986) 47.

[376] Luther, On War, 1528, WA 30 II, 107-148.

[377] Erlangen Edition of Luther's Works, Vol. 59, 284.

While Luther bragged about ordering the violence and Müntzer may have gone rogue, the role of the Catholic and Protestant churches as the active and violent oppressors of their communities had long passed the threshold of certainty. Even before the Protestant Church had formally constituted itself. The Protestant leader spoke with little ambivalence.

The choice of Martin Luther as the topic of this book '*Holy Enemies of Freedom*' is not by chance. While there are many similar religious revolutions in history, namely three that are connected to the foundation of Judaism, Christianity, and Islam, it is a rarity that the circumstances are so clear.

That Luther had no intention of ending up openly hating Jews over and above customary Christian diatribes can be taken from his own works. Synagogues were not on his radar.

Not yet.

As late as 1523, as evidenced by his letters to another leader of the Reformation,[378] Luther was inclusive with Jews, recognizing Jesus as a Jew, and discouraging mistreatment.[379]

A letter from nine years earlier is typically taken as proof that Luther developed anti-Semitism early. That is a willful misreading of his texts. It disregards the larger context and distracts students from the order of events that changed Luther's mind. He conveyed that it was not man's business to convert Jews but God's alone.[380] Blaspheming by Jews against Jesus Christ was part of God's design without which God and the Bible would be proven liars.[381] Jews and their blasphemy were part of the fulfillment of prophecy.

The spiritual problem for him was that Jesus' death was necessary. Without its fulfillment, there would be no salvation. Without all this and without Jews, there could not be a religion that is called Christianity.

From a sermon that was composed just two years later, it can be taken that he, even though the messianic aspirations of Rabbinic leadership could not have escaped him, believed that there was no risk of a new war against Jews.[382]

The future was going to brand him a mastermind, not only of *a* holocaust but of *the* Holocaust.

---

[378] Georg Burkhardt aka George Spalatin, 1484 – 1545, was a leader during the Reformation and tutor of the 'Champion of the Reformation', John Frederick I.

[379] Martin Luther: Letter to George Spalatin, Wittenberg, 1523.

[380] Ibid.

[381] Ibid.

[382] Martin, Luther, Sermons, Twenty-Fifth Sunday After Trinity, The Destruction of the Kingdom of the Jews, the Abomination of Desolation, and the End of the World, 1525, 15-16.

# II: GRANDEUR

## *A Land Grab*

If all this ramble about the End of World and the messianic aspirations sounds unclear, rest assured that you are not alone. Many believers typically rely on a simple layer of superstitions that is derived from a beginner's kernel of scripture.

In order to understand what is going on, we need to get into the heads of the priesthood.

The founding father of all Judaic religions is Abraham. It is alleged that he lived sometime around the second millennium BC.

The word *alleged* alone is enough to brand this exercise as anti-Semitic. The underlying bias of this book is science and evidence, which by nature accepts neither myths nor folk tales as real. This book lays out the biblical foundation of the problems that Martin Luther and his companions were facing.

By not calling the issues by their names, we cannot understand Luther's grievances with his Jewish contemporaries.

The beginning pages of the Old Testament contain the story of how the god of the Israelites created the universe and the first human couple, Adam and Eve. The divinity later realized that having created humanity was a mistake.[383] In fatherly love, this god brought about a flood in order to drown all life except for a few chosen ones who escaped on a do-it-yourself bark.[384]

It is a confounding story in fewer than twenty pages.

The all-powerful god exterminated the entire human race and everything else that walked, swam, or crept.

What is this god of the Israelites?

Martin Luther answered this question in his Catechism: from a god we expect all good and take refuge in distress.

To have a god is to trust and believe.

Faith alone makes both gods and idols.

If the faith is right, then your god is true.

---

[383] Genesis 6:5ff.
[384] Genesis 7:11, Genesis 7:20, Genesis 7:23-24.

If your faith is false, then you have no true god.

God and faith belong together.[385]

You may like to re-read this until you fully grasp its meaning: even in Martin Luther's spiritual world, only faith was able to make gods real.

But then, we need to swap the word *faith* for *fear*. How so? Luther added this: *'Either if you obey Him, rendering love and service, He will reward you abundantly with all good, or if you offend Him, He will send upon you both death and the hangman.'*[386]

Only fear can make gods real.

For Judaic believers, it is self-evident that all other gods and goddesses from Mesopotamia to Egypt and Rome were mythical. Martin Luther's argument was simple: their error was that their faith was false. They did not believe in the only Abrahamic god, but in self-invented nothingness.[387]

Martin Luther included the subtle differences in faith of the Catholic Church in his understanding of *'false worship and extreme idolatry.'*[388]

*'It would be impossible for such a thing to maintain itself if it were not of God,'*[389] Martin Luther argued later in life.

> *No worship of a false god ever endured so long, nor did all the world suffer so much because of it or cling so firmly to it. And I suppose one of the strongest proofs is found in the fact that no other god ever withstood such hard opposition as the Messiah, against whom alone all other gods and peoples have raged and against whom they all acted in concert, no matter how varied they were or how they otherwise disagreed.*[390]

Luther was fully conscious about the destructive force of messianism. Because of the growth of his religion, he marveled at Christians so firmly clinging to it.

All the while, he represented a new religion!

Even after a long career, the Reformer was not thinking through the implications about all older religions, in particular in relation to Judaism. If it were as he said, then the presence of Jews in and by itself would be proof of God's existence and of their superiority.

---

[385] Luther, Large Catechism, 1529, WA 30 I,125-238.
[386] Ibid.
[387] Luther, Large Catechism, 1529, WA 30 I,125-238.
[388] Ibid.
[389] Luther, Jews and Their Lies, 1971, part XII.
[390] Ibid., part XIII.

The Reformer took a shortcut by proclaiming that before becoming Christians, *'we were altogether of the devil, knowing nothing of God and of Christ.*[391]

All of humanity was of the devil before knowing God and Christ. Those not Lutheran Christians were altogether of the devil.

The biblical book of Baruch serves as an exemplary line of argument. To prove the god's existence, belief in the god's deeds is required[392] – yet to be proved. Luther argued that God *'has created heaven and earth; besides this only One I regard nothing else as God; for there is no one else who could create heaven and earth.*[393]

The book of Hebrews sets the belief in the *existence* of God as a specific requirement to be rewarded by God.[394]

Having delivered the circular proof, all other faiths can be declared frauds.[395]

Most readers of the Bible do not seem to be on the alert for motives of power and riches that play out in the sidelines of the stories. Often, they take them as confirmation of beliefs that they already had. Perhaps, they read it like a novel, without grasping that every word comes with purpose and has real-world consequences.

These texts have been refined over centuries to ensure their desired effect while appearing benign to the uninformed outsider.

Casual students of the biblical story seem to overlook that its opening act serves as nothing but the backdrop of a giant land grab. It establishes a specific royal-priestly authority on that land. Its endgame aims at ruling over the entire planet for this same dynasty of royal priests.

Let us not get ahead of ourselves.

According to the Bible, Abraham and his sons were promised the land of Canaan by the god of the Israelites. This was a tribal god among many gods at the time. Abraham's lineage would eventually possess the land, and his successors would become the Chosen People of this god, it prophesied.

In a twisted plot, the first-born Ishmael and his mother were expelled from Abraham's family. His lineage was promised great kingdoms as well. All four, the god of the Israelites, the Promised Land, the Chosen People, and the assurance for Ishmael were the overtures to eternal conflicts.

---

[391]  Luther, Large Catechism, 1529, WA 30 I,125-238.
[392]  Baruch 6:35–40.
[393]  Luther, Large Catechism, 1529, WA 30 I,125-238.
[394]  Hebrews 11:6 (NIV).
[395]  Baruch 6:44–45.

There were two sides to this deal: land on one and unconditional submission on the other.

In order to be assured of Abraham's total obedience, the god of the Israelites commanded the Judaic founding father to sacrifice his second son Isaac.[396] In his faith, Abraham must have lost his good judgment.

He went ahead with the godly order.[397]

There is not a hint of hesitation, no protest, and no negotiation with his god. There was no resistance whatsoever, only full compliance with God's demand.

To what avail?

Just before the murderous act, an angel appeared. Then, the angel called out to Abraham and stopped the killing of the son at the last moment.[398] God's mercy and frightening power presented itself in mysterious ways.

It was nothing but a challenge!

Yet, thanks to the father's blind obedience, the god of the Israelites enforced the earlier promise[399] wherein Abraham's descendants were allowed – commanded – to take possession of the cities of all their enemies.[400]

These promises by God are at the heart of the Jewish desire to return to Jerusalem and Israel.

They view this as the Promised Land.

Angels, like the one that stopped Isaac from being murdered, are another powerful feature of Abrahamic religions. Their nature can only be conquered with faith. No human has ever seen them, but their company is as self-evident as the presence of the god. Benevolent or malicious beings, they master all sorts of improbable and implausible supernatural powers that are limited only by their inventors' creativity.

All it takes to be in awe of them is belief.

There is a fundamental problem with the myth over the promise for the land, still. Somebody else owned the land and lived on it.

They still own it and live in it today.

In other words, the consequences are highly relevant to us moderns.

---

[396] Genesis 22:2 (NIV).
[397] Genesis 22:9-22:10 (NIV):.
[398] Genesis 22:11-22:12 (NIV).
[399] Genesis 12:2-12:3 (NIV), Genesis 12:7 (NIV), Genesis 13:14-13:17 (NIV), Genesis 15:7.
[400] Genesis 22:15-22:18 (NIV).

How relevant?

Let us listen in to a speech, given by Israel's Prime Minister Benjamin Netanyahu before the United Nations' assembly in 2011. In his presentation, he rejected the *'unilateral'* approach of the Palestinians to apply for statehood. Netanyahu said:

> *I often hear them [the Palestinians] accuse Israel of Judaizing Jerusalem. That's like accusing America of Americanizing Washington, or the British of Anglicizing London. You know why we're called Jews? Because we come from Judea.*
>
> *In my office in Jerusalem, there is an ancient seal. It's a signet ring of a Jewish official from the time of the Bible. The seal was found right next to the Western Wall, and it dates back 2,700 years, to the time of King Hezekiah. Now, there's a name of the Jewish official inscribed on the ring in Hebrew. His name was Netanyahu. That's my last name. My first name, Benjamin, dates back a thousand years earlier to Benjamin — Binyamin — the son of Jacob, who was also known as Israel. Jacob and his twelve sons roamed these same hills of Judea and Sumeria 4,000 years ago, and there's been a continuous Jewish presence in the land ever since.*
>
> *And for those Jews who were exiled from our land, they never stopped dreaming of coming back: Jews in Spain, on the eve of their expulsion; Jews in the Ukraine, fleeing the pogroms; Jews fighting the Warsaw Ghetto, as the Nazis were circling around it. They never stopped praying, they never stopped yearning. They whispered: Next year in Jerusalem. Next year in the Promised Land.*[401]

The ramifications are profound.

To stake a land claim, the inventors utilized the cheapest of all possible investments: the making of a scroll. Do you remember the Jewish Oath – the Jewish Oath of Treachery – in the judicial system? The limits are only in the imagination of the beholder. And it costs nothing other than a forger, a piece of paper, and false witnesses.

The politico-economic reality is that the promise to the land marks the beginning and core of this religious tree – not God. It has filled the pockets of the authors of the story as well as those of their children and grandchildren. The same mechanism continues through Christianity and Islam. Enforcement of the land claim is enforcement through organized religion.

It works.

---

[401] Benjamin Netanyahu, Address to the General Assembly of the United Nations, General Debate: 66th session, transcript by the author, September 23, 2011.

Despite the issue that the story is a fabrication,[402] we still need to deal with the fallout of these promises today. But, as Mr. Netanyahu said, *'they never stopped dreaming of coming back.'* Literally, we have a problem of monumental proportions where no party is going to give in easily to the nuisance of facts.

Because God said so.

Abraham's prototype story sets in motion a cycle of violence that is fueled by the biblical 'right' to possess a land that had never been a Jewish property.[403] Since Jews had been dispersed all over the world at the beginning of their fairy tale, they could have applied the same logic of a permanent presence to virtually any city and laid claim to it.

Worse, Abraham was a man with a complex baggage of heirs. Undeniably, his firstborn was Ishmael, who soon vanished from the Bible. But according to Jewish internal logic of faith and law, the firstborn could make a better claim to the land than the lineage through Isaac, the second born.

This is perhaps why one of the first instances of attested early 'Muslim' activities was the transfer of the Promised Land from Isaac back to Ishmael.[404] Likewise, the first religious building that the historical evidence attributes to Islam was on the Temple Mount in Jerusalem, not in Mecca.[405]

Jews take their confidence in the lineage of Isaac because the god of the Israelites had also told Abraham that *'from Isaac will your seed be called.'*[406] Ishmael was not good enough as the firstborn. His mother was *not* from the clean Israelite gene pool.

---

[402] The promise to Abraham contains a paradox that unmasks the story as a fabrication. Just a few pages into the tale, the writers recognize themselves – in a dream – as mistreated slaves, exiled in a foreign nation for 400 years until they are able to come back into their alleged homeland. We are evidently dealing with post-exile wishful thinking from the fourth century BC, at the earliest. It so happened in the myth that Abraham's father was the high-priest of the Chaldeans, presumably Zoroastrians at the city of Ur, which was then at the mouth of the Euphrates River on the Persian Gulf. According to the biblical narrative, it is from there that Abraham set out on his journey. Since Abraham constitutes the beginning of Judaism, there could logically not have been an exile of Jews for hundreds of years before the time of Abraham.
See Genesis 15:12-15:16 (NIV).'

[403] Archaeology has found evidence only of a short but violent period of perhaps less than a hundred years where Jerusalem would have been in 'Jewish' hands, however contested, just before the Roman Empire took over. The simple fact is that we have only faint information about what 'Judaism' may have been at the time or who a 'Jew' was. Experts will claim otherwise. Their opinions are based on nothing but wishful thinking. Nobody is – based on science – able to explain Judaism during the formation of Islam in the seventh century, let alone 600 years earlier. It gets even darker on the other side of our time scale. We simply know too little.

[404] Sebeos' History of the seventh century, 30 (publishing ca. 660 AD), English by Robert Bedrosian (1985).

[405] Pratum spirituale (ca. 639 AD) 100-102.

[406] Genesis 21:12.

The story provides for the intellectual framework to strive for ethnic purity.

Since Abraham constitutes the beginning of the Israelites, Isaac's mother could not possibly have been from the clean gene pool, either. The authors of the Bible found an elegant solution: Sarah was Abraham's half-sister.

But the devil is in the detail. That the seed is called from Isaac does not specify that it refers to the Promised Land. It may just refer to the priesthood, which does not technically own land. Or to something else.

That is not all.

The Ishmaelites are today's Muslims, of whom the Palestinians are a part. Without looking into how the mythical Ishmaelites came to be – well, real *'Ishmaelites'* – the rightful owner of the Promised Land already lives in it.

According to the complexities of the Bible, among the original owners were the Canaanites. Their genes survive today in the Lebanese population.[407]

They owned the land even earlier. Their land was stolen from them by the god-obsessed successors of Abraham.

The Palestinians and the Lebanese are at a disadvantage because most of them are too lazy to study another man's Bible and are content with their Koran, their Sharia law, and their illustrated instruction manuals for rocket-propelled grenades. This shortlist contains all knowledge that Muslims ever need, for example, on how to hate Jews.

But they are missing out on staking the claim to their land on the same great, mythical inheritance that Jews use to their advantage.

The issue is that we cannot go to court with myths. We need evidence – unless the court represents the myths. We have already seen how that works: done deal – with kickback to the judges.

The Palestinians and the Lebanese may also underestimate that they are singled out in the Torah for eternal genocide.[408] The terminal feelings are mutual. In their hearts, the Palestinians will never be able to accept Israel as a nation and vice versa.

---

[407] Marc Haber, Claude Doumet-Serhal, Christiana Scheib, Yali Xue, Petr Danecek, Massimo Mezzavilla, Sonia Youhanna, Rui Martiniano, Javier Prado-Martinez, Michał Szpak, Elizabeth Matisoo-Smith, Holger Schutkowski, Richard Mikulski, Pierre Zalloua, Toomas Kivisild, Chris Tyler-Smith, Continuity and Admixture in the Last Five Millennia of Levantine History from Ancient Canaanite and Present-Day Lebanese Genome Sequences, AJHG, July 27, 2017.
See also Rick Gore, Who were the Phoenicians? (National Geographic, October 2004).

[408] Ezekiel 25:15ff.

It is up to these religious zealots to figure out how to settle on a myth of the Bible without also having to give up the Truth of the Koran.

Throwing bombs is easier than reducing their legitimate case to arguments of 'facts' in mythology. They would have to learn to fend for themselves rather than waiting for some god to provide for them. And learning is hard, in particular when the perceived enemy is highly educated and learns to plot in the crib – from the Bible.

Other than Palestinians, the Israeli government also wants the roughly 200,000 Bedouins in Israel's Negev Desert to give up their land. It intends to 'relocate' them to 'legal' communities, demanding that they surrender their way of life.

Essentially, Israel puts them into ghettoes.

The final solution in their minds is to have all Palestinians deported.

Since I am in danger of appearing to be anti-Semitic again, Professor Ze'ev Herzog of the Tel Aviv University, Department of Archaeology, refutes the historicity to the biblical tales with expertly evidence.

> *It turns out that part of Israeli society is ready to recognize the injustice that was done to the Arab inhabitants of the country and is willing to accept the principle of equal rights for women—but is not up to adopting the archaeological facts that shatter the biblical myth. The blow to the mythical foundations of the Israeli identity is apparently too threatening, and it is more convenient to turn a blind eye.*[409]

I am a humanist, and I have been one all my life. I abhor anti-Semitism, and my real name screams '*Jews*' in Spanish. I look at Switzerland, my birthplace, with disdain for having taken the money of Jews while closing the borders during the Second World War – the boat is full, they said, sending the refugees back into the Nazi gas chambers.

So, do not confuse facing a problem head-on with some sort of an anti-ethnical agenda. After all, this book is about understanding anti-Semitism.

Neither the creation of the Books of Moses, nor the Hebrew Bible, nor the Gospels can be attested to by *any* contemporary evidence. These books are not, and will never be, evidence of facts, until such a time that independent confirmation supports the divine, supernatural, political, or otherwise abnormal claims in these books.

---

[409] Ze'ev Herzog, Deconstructing the walls of Jericho, 1999.

With scripture we are denied the opportunity to verify, so much so that the most precious sections of contemporary documents that could attest to the stories have gone missing. Other ancient evidence of far lesser importance exists in abundance but not the very core; not what the spiritual men and women would have collected and defended with their lives.

Mary's milk jar is a case in point.

Instead, they created a truckload of fraudulent stories and attributed entire books to some holy men who may or may not have existed.

Let me highlight the magnitude of the machinations. One of the later religious frauds included the transfer of the entire Western Roman Empire to the Catholic Church. It is called the Donation of Constantine. This forged document was used by several popes to establish the exclusive authority of the Catholic Church over Western Europe. A fraudulent scroll for an empire? That is how holy these men were when given the opportunity for grand crimes.

What else were they willing to feign?

Everything.

Since there is no evidence of alternate spiritual realities, fabrication is in the nature of religious leaders.

Let me put the spotlight on the spear that supposedly pierced the side of the Messiah Jesus Christ at his crucifixion. Aside from the fact that no soldier would have voluntarily abandoned his weapon, this is an item that would undoubtedly have been safeguarded by earliest followers of Christianity. Indeed, there are several spear relics: the Holy Lance of Rome emerged during the late sixth century; the Holy Lance of Vienna is somehow attached to the seventh century Lombard kings in Italy; the Holy Lance of Antioch had been miraculously dug up at the end of the eleventh century; the Holy Lance of Krakow in Poland appears to be a copy of the Vienna lance; and then there is the Holy Lance in Echmiadzin, Armenia.

The evidence suggests that Jesus has been pierced more than once.

Anyone who has seen any Roman lance of the Christian era does not need to be an expert to recognize that all of these were forgeries, do not resemble Roman lances of any era, and could not have possibly been used in warfare. Their production is so embarrassing that they could not even be regarded as forgeries. They are more like toys or tourist souvenirs.

The Holy Lance in Echmiadzin is the most ridiculous of them all. It is made of a flat parallelogram iron with a *cross* cut into it. Since the cross did not fit on a Roman lance, they simply made up a spearhead to fit the cross. They did not even bother sharpening it. It is the childproof version of the lance that pierced Jesus.

It is irrefutable proof that Jesus was tickled to death.

Regardless of the forgers' financial or spiritual aspirations, the true mystery behind all these relics is why they all appeared so late. Why would they not show up in the historical record right after Jesus' crucifixion?

As a researcher in a subject that involves faith, I do not confuse the absence of evidence with evidence of absence. But the need to postdate documents and artefacts is fairly potent evidence of absence. The impossibility of verification leads to the reduction of the issues to probability and possibility. The results are devastating.

The assertions in these stories are extraordinary, not some abstruse details. No Roman saw anything noteworthy; no Jew took notes; no Persian wrote down how awe-struck he or his Jewish friend was; no Egyptian drew a single hieroglyph; no Greek chiseled a statue.

Even a single independent and verifiable affirmation would be far better than none.

To make myself clear: I personally wish Israel to be here to stay. I have even considered becoming a citizen. Since Israel views critics of its policies as enemies of the state,[410] this is probably too late now.

We will have to find ways for its neighbors and for Israel to peacefully accept and endorse each other's borders. It may need to be enforced by the international community. Insisting on the Truth from myths does not appear to be the most realistic path to peace.

However, just as Iran's theocracy is unacceptable, so is any other nation's. That includes Israel's. They represent the beginning of the endgame of organized religion.

Theocracies, by nature, endanger mankind. The intent to establish a theocracy is a crime against humanity.

As long as they throw salt into the soup, there will be no peace. The soup just does not get any better.

---

[410] Editorial Board, Israel Sees Critics as Enemies, New York Times, April 29, 2017.

Israel is not a theocracy?

That notion is based on naivety.

Have a look at the Hasidic birthrate and their extraordinary rights. They multiply like rabbits and teach their children pretty much no life skills other than what can be found in the Torah, the first five books of the Bible. It is a matter of demographic certainty that they will come to fully take control of Israel[411] within less than a generation – in all likelihood just about now.

This is no different, if I may share this observation, in the Hasidic neighborhood in Brooklyn, New York. While the birthrate of the general population of New Yorkers is roughly 12 per 1,000, the 550,000 Hasidis in New York inseminate an explosive 28. Their concern is not overpopulation but power through shifting demographics. In less than a generation, they will be able to completely corrupt the judiciary system of New York. Better yet, in Israel as in New York, the non-Hasidic populations are suckers.

Zealots often rely on welfare and unmerited other perks on both sides of the Atlantic.

Indeed, in July 2018, Israel's government enacted a racist law that aims at enshrining the right of national self-determination as *'unique to the Jewish people – not all citizens.'*[412] In a nod to America's then president, the air of equality and rights for all residents was eradicated with one clean sweep. Arabic now enjoys special status and is no longer an official language. Israel is on its way to become a theocracy, no longer a democracy.

It confirms some of the worst stereotypes about Jews.

It betrays ordinary Jews.

What are the chances of this idiocracy to stop? Zero.

There is no path to peace – because the Bible says so.

Luther had learned from his studies that there was hardly ever peace in that land.[413] Our religionists will be at each others' throats for another 2,000 years. Probably longer.

But we do not need to wait that long. The next 200 odd years will become disastrous. A deadline of terminal magnitude is approaching for Judaism.

---

[411] Isabel Kershner, Israeli Girl, 8, at Center of Tension Over Religious Extremism, New York Times, December 27, 2011.

[412] David M. Halbfinger, Isabel Kershner, Israeli Law Declares the Country the Nation-State of the Jewish People,' New York Times, July 19, 2018.

[413] Luther, Jews and Their Lies, 1971, part VIII.

Because we are linking the birthrate to the Israeli doomed future, there is another group with extraordinary zeal to increase its numbers: Muslims. As the birthrate in Western post-Christian nations continues to fall, in Muslim nations and poor Catholic countries, it rises.[414] But the big losers in demography are neither Christians nor Muslims. Instead, those who are free from religion will significantly drop, even as their absolute numbers rise.[415] The nones are not interested in the ancient religious command to keep on producing offspring to keep their faith alive – in total ignorance of overpopulation on our planet. And this is not some doom in the distant future. The ultimate clash of religions is in the cards for those already born.

Unfortunately, you have seen nothing yet.

### A New World Order

The idea of the Promised Land started small and progressively expanded over many more promises[416] to finally encompass everything from the Asian side of Turkey and Armenia,[417] down the Euphrates region, the northern Arab Peninsula, the Sinai, and the Levant, including all of Syria, Jordan, and Lebanon.[418]

It also mandates not to enter into any agreements with anyone living inside the greater area of the Promised Land – not ever.[419]

The Bible renders agreements that are contrary to its spirit invalid.

In other words, even if Israel were to be coerced into an agreement, it would be unenforceable before God, as if it were never signed.

The Bible contains an eternal mandate to conquer that land, all of it, never to give back an inch, and to ethnically purify it from every non-Jewish soul.[420]

First in the line of fire: the Palestinians.

> *See, I [God] am sending an angel ahead of you to guard you along the way and to bring you to the place I have prepared [the Promised Land]. Pay attention to him and listen to what he says. Do not rebel against him; he will not forgive your*

---

[414] Pew Research Center, The Changing Global Religious Landscape, April 5, 2017.
[415] Ibid.
By 2055 to 2060, just 9% of all babies will be born to religiously unaffiliated women, while more than seven-in-ten will be born to either Muslims (36%) or Christians (35%).
[416] Genesis 15:17-15:21.
[417] Historically, Hittite and Amorite homelands were on the Asian side of Turkey and in Armenia.
[418] Joshua 13:2.
[419] Exodus 34:15–16.
[420] Josh 13:6.

*rebellion, since my Name is in him. If you listen carefully to what he says and do all that I say, I will be an enemy to your enemies and will oppose those who oppose you. My angel will go ahead of you and bring you into the land of the Amorites, Hittites, Perizzites, Canaanites, Hivites and Jebusites, and I will wipe them out. Do not bow down before their gods or worship them or follow their practices. You must demolish them and break their sacred stones to pieces. Worship the Lord your God, and his blessing will be on your food and water. I will take away sickness from among you, and none will miscarry or be barren in your land. I will give you a full life span.*

*I will send my terror ahead of you and throw into confusion every nation you encounter. I will make all your enemies turn their backs and run. I will send the hornet ahead of you to drive the Hivites, Canaanites and Hittites out of your way. But I will not drive them out in a single year, because the land would become desolate and the wild animals too numerous for you. Little by little [inch by inch] I will drive them out before you, until you have increased enough to take possession of the land.*

*I will establish your borders from the Red Sea to the Sea of the Philistines, and from the desert to the [Euphrates or Tigris] River. I will hand over to you the people who live in the land and you will drive them out before you. Do not make a covenant [agreement] with them or with their gods. Do not let them live in your land, or they will cause you to sin against me, because the worship of their gods will certainly be a snare to you.*[421]

All it takes is unconditional submission to the god of the Israelites, and the Promised Land will be theirs. He will even give them a life of health and plenty.

*I will wipe them out.*

This is an aggressive patron god for a selected few who belong to a small tribe. Even ordinary Jews are not included; only those from the top priestly layers. Everyone who stands in the way of the conquest of the Promised Land is on God's death list.

It is commanded by God.

*Break their sacred stones to pieces.*

The command targets Christian altars also. In return, Christians are obliged to support the desire of Jews for home-going. They are literally praying to another man's god and for another man's land.

---

[421]  Exodus 23:20-23:33 (NIV).

The accusation that Israel intends essentially to absorb most of the Middle East is one of the common fears of Arab countries and of Iran. Yasir Arafat, the former terrorist turned Palestinian leader, famously showed off Israeli 10-agora coins containing a map of Greater Israel under a menorah, the Hebrew lampstand.

Jewish scholars typically deny any such ambitions and declare the commands in the book of Genesis as superseded by other descriptions. Some call concerns about these Jewish desires baseless or fantasies. But the Bible was constructed with this ambivalence in mind. It is part of the intended treachery, thought out by its scribes. This inconsistency, in turn, creates a diluted accusation of Jewish imperialism that often shifts its definitions over which territory these ambitions involve. It allows for exactly this kind of invalid defense, because the Bible says what every generation chooses it to say.

The accusers are confused, Israel claims.

That is the point.

The authors of the Bible commanded over superior intelligence.

The books were created in such a way that they are not easily understandable, and many commandments are presented in multiple versions that bear many possible outcomes. Some call it inconsistent and full of contradictions. Instead, it is genius, intended to mislead. In the Talmud, a large body of Rabbinical wisdom, the biblical story does not even matter. Instead, the Talmudists used the Bible as a key to encode their secret communications. One of their methods to encrypt scrolls was to embed a benign phrase from the biblical text into their cryptic narrative. Only those who were aware of the context of the passage would be able to understand the intended message, which is, by all means, often about the details of an aggressive conquest of the Promised Land and elimination of those who either think differently or live in the land.

Torah commentaries may have served as the communications channels for double agents.

I need to interject that only the level of complexity is unique to the Talmudists, not the principle. Religious writers did tread carefully throughout history.

In a letter, Martin Luther instructed one of his followers on how to preach about specific topics, not to refute the opposite party, and never to call the competitors by their names.[422] This has profound consequences for religious history in general and for Luther's relationship with Jews in particular. If the authors did not name their enemies, they deliberately left escape hatches, providing room for interpretation. In other words, you cannot simply read a text by the Reformer or other religionists without putting it into its proper context. He was keenly aware of his malevolence.

In reality, if Israel is small, as today, then the expressed ambitions sound comparatively benign, a settlement here, another there. But the first wave of religious, ideologically driven Israeli settlers fundamentally believed that they had created *'some sort of stronghold on the land.'*[423]

God's command will come to full force, once greater areas are incorporated and in particular after the Temple Mount is conquered.

It is merely a matter of priorities.

Here is how the settlement process works: as a new settlement is created, the Palestinians in the area are threatened and tormented to make them leave. Acts of vandalism, beatings, threats to life, whichever works. Settlers are armed to their teeth while Palestinians are prohibited from owning guns. Try to strike back if you dare. Try! Israeli Mafia style. Sometimes, they are plainly forced out of their villages with the help of Israeli soldiers, sometimes by the Israeli military, and often by gangs of religious zealots. When Palestinians flee their dwellings for whichever reason and then return, a surprise of Israeli laws awaits them. They cannot reconstruct their demolished houses, not even move a stone without permits. Not as much as putting a tarp over an unroofed structure. But in 2023, permits were only granted to 1% of applicants. It used to be better fifty years ago, 97%. Hence, they are forced to live in ruins – or leave. While settlers can do all this under the protection of Israeli civil and criminal law, Palestinians are subject to military orders and can be indefinitely imprisoned without ever being charged with a crime.[424]

These atrocities are happening under cover of religious freedom.

Under such conditions, try *not* to become a freedom fighter.

---

[422] Martin Luther, Letter to Nicolas Hausmann, February 8, 1534.
[423] David K. Shipler, Arab and Jew: Wounded Spirits in a Promised Land (Times Books, 1986) 144.
[424] This paragraph is a summary of an harrowing article by an witnessing journalist, Megan K. Stack, For Palestinians, the Future Is Being Bulldozed (New York Times, December 9, 2023).

Plotters are rarely stupid enough to reveal their goals in advance. It would otherwise be easy to come to a binding, long-term agreement, quickly and effortlessly.

On the other hand, these mythical commands tempt some religious Jews to look down on everybody else. It forms the perfect cycle of a self-portrayal of being hated, of zealous religious pride, and of a hateful reception by outsiders. Worse, based on these myths, Jews have come to see themselves as a holy people that must not intermix with ordinary folks, almost like a separate species, a race all on its own.[425] They are no longer purebred when crossed with non-Jews. The expulsion of Ishmael was just the first such example. In the biblical book of Ezra, they went as far as separating the purebred from the rest of their 'contaminated' families.

They banished the impure wives and children.[426]

That the holy seed had mixed with the people of the land was viewed as an offence to their god.[427]

Jews promised that they would no longer give their *'daughters to the peoples of the land, nor take their daughters for our sons.'*[428]

Eugenics, for that is what this is, is the selective breeding of a human race, here to Jewish ideals. Civilization has suffered through its consequences last with the Arian race – under Hitler. If you think of it carefully, this man, the incarnation of evil, factually turned the biblical commands, which the god of the Jews was willing to perpetually deploy to the demise of all others, against them.

Hitler simply put Arians first and dehumanized Jews.

The idea of superiority stems from a passage in the Bible that establishes them as the Chosen People of God.[429] The concept fosters nationalistic pride and arrogance.

This superiority complex manifests itself in the disturbingly popular book *'The Kuzari'* by a twelfth-century Spanish Jew.[430] In this book, an imaginary Khazar king converted from Paganism to Judaism.

---

[425] For example: Garcia-Martinez, Dead Sea Scrolls, [4Q396frg1col3 / 4Q397frg5-6], Transcription and translation by J. Strugnell and E. Qimron, late first century BC.

[426] Ezra 10:3.

[427] Ezra 9:1–2.

[428] Nehemiah 10:30.

[429] Exodus 19:3–6.

[430] Judah Halevi, aka Yehuda Halevi, ha-Levi, Judah ben Shmuel Halevi, ca. 1075 – 1141.

The author made a simple statement that Ishmael – today understood as the modern Arabs and Palestinians, among others – was to be condemned from the land because in the biblical story, Ishmael had been banished. He argued that Jews were the preference of mankind, and that neither Christians nor Muslims nor black and white men were a match to them.

No other people could equal Jews, he asserted.[431]

How do Christians feel when they read about the great secondary treatment given to their own by the god of the Israelites? Christians are like the children who always play second fiddle. Stepchildren. They are meant to become the servants of Jews once *all is accomplished*, as their messiah, Jesus Christ, said.

*Do not let them live in your land.*

During the war in 1967, Israel occupied the land of the Palestinians. Mrs. Golda Meir asked the then-Prime Minister Levi Eshkol what to do with the million Arabs then under Israeli rule. He 'jokingly' responded to her that he understood that she liked the dowry, but not the bride. To this, she famously said that everybody would *'love the dowry and for someone else to get the bride.*[432]

This is not some randomly dropped joke.

It sums up the biblical obligation not to allow anyone but Jews to live in the Promised Land. They love the land and want someone else to take the Arabs – because their god said so. Here, Mrs. Meir, who was to become Mr. Eshkol's successor as prime minister, meant specifically the Palestinians. The predecessor of the two, Ben-Gurion, was pretty clear about this: *'The last thing we need is to add them to the Arab [population] of Israel. [...] it will not be easy to get rid of them.*[433]

Such faith-driven statements by people who had lived through the Holocaust are incomprehensible. Inhumane.

The plan was to kick them out of their land, now occupied by Israel.

Prime Minister Benjamin Netanyahu is working hard to make this a reality.

That the Jewish state has since headed toward a theocratic apartheid state is our modern reality. This will not change as long as Israel retains religion at its foundation.

---

[431] Shipler, 1986, 152-153.
[432] Yehouda Shenhav, Beyond the Two-State Solution: A Jewish Political Essay (Wiley, 2013). Ben-Gurion's letter to the editor of Yediot Ahronot, January 6, 1969, Correspondence File, BGA, in Zaky Shalom, Ben-Gurion's Political Struggles, 1963-1967.
[433] Ben-Gurion's speech, May 17, 1966, Speeches and Essays File, BGA, in Zaky Shalom, Ben-Gurion's Political Struggles, 1963-1967.

Golda Meir was succeeded by Yitzhak Rabin who was assassinated in November 1995 at a rally in support of the Oslo Accords that should have initiated an Israeli military withdrawal from Palestinian territories.[434] Why? Under guidance of then U.S. President Bill Clinton, he was about to sign this peace agreement with the Palestinian leader Yasser Arafat (PLO).

One of Rabin's most vicious opponents at the time was none other than the Likud leader and future Prime Minister of Israel, Benjamin Netanyahu. The latter accused Rabin of being out of touch with Jewish values with the proposed peace plan. Netanyahu went as far as leading a pretend funeral procession to protest Rabin. It featured a coffin and hangman's noose.[435]

That the occupation will never be forfeited by Israel is another pillar that is set in stone by the Bible. Not even an inch. Sanctions or boycotts will make no difference. A one-state solution? Jews would be a minority in this one state of Israel. The simple answer is: never. It would create the exact demographic imbalance that the Israeli prime ministers at the time intended to prevent. The Palestinians' case is particularly tragic because the United States of America act as the enablers, thus attracting hatred, violence, and terrorism against itself and the West in general.

If only America was to stand down, we would see a rapid expansion in all directions – according to the eternal plan. The problem is, again, that many people cannot or do not want to distinguish between fact and myth. Could the promise by the god of the Israelites be real?

The consequences are *very* real.

If you wanted to discuss the full extent of God's promise, the first you will face by experts in the field is that – no, no – this is not so clear. Israel is just what it is today and not much more, maybe a few inches here or there – no, no – the original small land of Canaan, which is not clearly defined in the Bible, was the correct meaning. The undivided city of Jerusalem, of course. The Temple Mount.

The Promised Land is whatever the Rabbinic leadership says it is.

For example, the Book of Jubilees was the most popular Rabbinic work until the fourth century AD. It not only included Susa in the inheritance of the land to Noah's grandchildren but also the whole of India.[436]

---

[434] 1995 Oslo Interim Agreement (28 September 1995) II, Article X.2, II, Article XI.2.e.
[435] Ben Caspit, Ilan Kafir, Netanyahu: The Road to Power (Secaucus, 1998) 232.
[436] Book of Jubilees 9:1-9:14.

Susa lies 160 miles east of the Tigris River, deep in Iranian territory. This could one day justify the extension of the Promised Land well past the main borders of the Euphrates River. All a messianic leader needs to do is return to the 'religion of Noah.'

Given the full context of the biblical narrative as well as real history, the Promised Land is fit for an empire, and that is only its middle goal. The ulterior promise gives the rule over the whole world to Jewish leaders.

A new World Order. The King of the Jews is also the king of the world.[437]

The price for the empire? A book that has treachery written all over its mythical stories.

Whatever the ramifications, Jews believe that they have their tribal god on their side and that they have a God-given right to conquer the biblical land. God will make it happen for them, so they think.

Another speech of the former Israeli Prime Minister Benjamin Netanyahu before the United Nations might enable us to understand the nature of the Judaic threat:

*ISIS and Hamas share a fanatical creed, which they both seek to impose well beyond the territory under their control. Listen to ISIS' self-declared caliph, Abu Bakr al-Baghdadi. This is what he said two months ago: A day will soon come when the Muslim will walk everywhere as a master. The Muslims will cause the world to hear and understand the meaning of terrorism and destroy the idol of democracy. Now listen to Khaled Mashal, the leader of Hamas. He proclaims a similar vision of the future: We say this to the West -- by Allah you will be defeated. Tomorrow our nation will sit on the throne of the world.*

*As Hamas' charter makes clear, Hamas' immediate goal is to destroy Israel, but Hamas has a broader objective. They also want a caliphate. Hamas shares the global ambitions of its fellow militant Islamists, and that's why its supporters wildly cheered in the streets of Gaza as thousands of Americans were murdered in 9/11, and that's why its leaders condemn the United States for killing Osama bin Laden whom they praised as a holy warrior.*

*So when it comes to their ultimate goals, Hamas is ISIS and ISIS is Hamas. And what they share in common all militant Islamists share in common. Boko Haram in Nigeria, Al-Shabab in Somalia, Hezbollah in Lebanon, Al-Nusra in Syria, the Mahdi army in Iraq, and the Al-Qaida branches in Yemen, Libya, the Philippines, India and elsewhere.*

---

[437] Daniel 2:44.

*Some are radical Sunnis, some are radical Shiites, some want to restore a pre-medieval caliphate from the seventh century, others want to trigger the apocalyptic return of an imam from the ninth century. They operate in different lands, they target different victims and they even kill each other in their battle for supremacy. But they all share a fanatic ideology. They all seek to create ever-expanding enclaves of militant Islam where there is no freedom and no tolerance, where women are treated as chattel, Christians are decimated and minorities are subjugated, sometimes given the stark choice, convert or die. For them, anyone can be considered an infidel, including fellow Muslims.*

*Ladies and gentlemen, militant Islam's ambition to dominate the world seems mad, but so too did the global ambitions of another fanatic ideology that swept into power eight decades ago. The Nazis believed in a master race. The militant Islamists believe in a master faith. They just disagree who among them will be the master of the master faith. That's what they truly disagree about. And therefore, the question before us is whether militant Islam will have the power to realize its unbridled ambitions.*[438]

While Netanyahu's words appear true, from *his* lips, they are self-serving and devious. Martin Luther would have had something to say about his hypocrisy.

We have already learned that religious Jews see themselves as another *'master race'* that aims at ruling the world. After all, they are the *'Chosen People'* and are singled out for their god's special favors that are in no way distinguishable in madness from the grandeur of militant Islam.

Benjamin Netanyahu was the representative of treacherous hyperbole.

Indeed, the spokesman of ISIS[439] said before he was killed in an American drone strike that the Islamic State could be defeated only if the Koran could be removed from Muslims' hearts.[440] This applies to more Muslims than we wish to acknowledge.

There are many possible leaders of other religious terrorist organizations that can slip into the footsteps of the Islamic State.

For example, Al Qaeda promoted Hamza bin Laden,[441] also known as the Crown Prince of Terror, who was trained from his crib to become a Mujahedeen and a possible successor for his father, Osama bin Laden.

---

[438] Benjamin Netanyahu, Transcript of Benjamin Netanyahu's address to the 2014 UN General Assembly on September 30, 2014 (Haaretz, October 1, 2014).

[439] Abu Muhammed al-Adnani.

[440] Margaret Coker, Eric Schmitt, and Rukmini Callimachi, After the Caliphate, What's Next for ISIS? ISIS 2.0, Experts Say, New York Times, October 18, 2017.

[441] Hamza bin Osama bin Mohammed bin Awad bin Laden, born ca. 1989

In 2015, bin Laden the younger called for jihad on Washington, London, Paris, and Tel Aviv.[442] He was determined to 'accelerate' the destruction of America and the West. Bin Laden was killed during an American counterterrorism operation.

Successors have learned that keeping their names quiet keeps them alive.

As the Islamic State declined, Al Qaeda and the Taliban got stronger.

Encouraged by the Syrian civil war to eventually bring Israel to its knees, bin Laden called in 2017 for lone wolf attacks against Jews, Americans, Westerners, and even Russians.[443]

As sure as 'amen' in the synagogues, churches, and mosques, the terror will continue to rain down on the West.

The ISIS spokesman delivered to us the only path to address the problems in the Middle East successfully: remove the Koran from Muslim minds.

In all fairness, the here-mentioned Hamas, the Palestinian terrorist organization, sees it similarly to the way that Israel does. In their latest amendment to its charter in 2017, it declared that *'no part of the land of Palestine shall be compromised or conceded.'*[444] This, of course, includes the territory of Israel.

At least, they agree on something.

This is pretty much all that is needed to understand fully the complex politics of modern-day Israel, including its offensive settlement strategy, its inhumane treatment of the Palestinians, and its weaponizing of anti-Semitism.

Hamas used to be content with the immediate goal of establishing a Palestinian state, even if it was restricted to the West Bank and Gaza. However, one must not be fooled into believing that they might have changed their thinking. Instead, they just adapted their tactics to the realities on the ground.

Hamas' attack in October 2023 was not only barbaric but also thoughtless, as though Prime Minister Netanyahu (and his predecessors) had not long telegraphed that he would respond with the full and overbearing power of his army – exploiting a window of compassion.

The power imbalance could not be greater.

One commands a superior army with tanks, jets, and nuclear capabilities backed by the superpowers of the United States while the other is on foot and

---

442   Bin Laden: Osama's son Hamza 'issues al-Qaeda message', BBC, August 14, 2015.
443   Dugald McConnell and Brian Todd, Latest al Qaeda propaganda highlights bin Laden's son, CNN, May 16, 2017.
444   Hamas announces a new policy platform, The Economist, May 3, 2017.

153

underground, equipped with 'democratized' weaponry such as pickup trucks, rifles, drones, mobile missiles, and suicide wests.

The Iranian backed Hamas terrorist attacks against Israeli civilians merit a full condemnation and armed pushback.

While the intention here is not to engage in Middle Eastern politics but to focus on the causes and consequences of violent anti-Semitic dogma through the eyes of Martin Luther, it would be disingenuous not to address the crisis under our feet.

Given the catastrophic outlook for the rest of the world, it is very much *our* business how these archenemies will be brought to cooperation and who will own what and under which conditions.

Catastrophic outlook? I said that you might now understand the complex politics of modern-day Israel, but what about tomorrow's? Do we have a looking glass?

I will give you a peek in a moment.

But so far, we can see an unspeakable hatred of mankind.

But that is only part of the story, the beginning. We still have a long path to walk in order to reach the End of the World.

There is still the other side of the coin.

God's deal with Abraham was struck not only with rights but also with obligations. To keep the land, Abraham and his descendants were at first required to accept their god and be circumcised.[445] The fine print was initially unspoken of. As the stakes rose, so did the requirements for God's continued support. To be compliant, the Jews – all Jews collectively – had to fully submit to God and to execute whatever he – it – pleased, even if it was to kill their own sons.

Fail one, fail all.

That is why they are the Chosen People.

Submitting to God is their job.

Their only job.

They failed.

---

[445] Genesis 17:9-17:14.

Jews were known for not ever having fulfilled their part of the bargain, neither individually nor collectively, so much so, that God vacated the Mount and turned his back on them over 2,300 years ago.[446] They are in breach of the imaginary contract. This is why they believe in living in the Diaspora, dispersed all across the world.

There, Jews are generally respected and successful.

The god was never since seen 'again' to this very day, and they lost their land. Forever.

Because of the Jews' failings to fulfill mythical requirements, modern civilization has to suffer under the total absence of the greatest of all, the it-god. In disgust, he refuses to show his face or speak another word.

Ultra-Orthodox Jews think that they can fix their divorce with God. This is why they live in segregated communities. They abuse their children with social quarantine and train them to become Torah-obedient and to multiply like bulls and milk-cows. The more they submit, the stronger they feel that the presence of God and the conquest of the Promised Land are nearing.

The larger their numbers, the more dangerous they become.

First in the line of fire are the lives of their Jewish brothers and sisters who dare to remain in breach of the imaginary agreement.

*All* Jews must be compliant.

Those Jews who refuse to follow the Law to the letter *will* be eliminated. They *must* be eliminated. *All* of them.

For that purpose, Ultra-Orthodox Judaism will need to find and finance someone else to do the dirty job or pretend that someone else did it. This then will be amplified as anti-Semitism. The succeeding compassion will provide for the cover to expand the atrocities.

For better understanding, I will dissect this in a moment.

The behavior of Ultra-Orthodox Judaism is simply criminal – by biblical intent. It is a terrorist organization as well.

Their relationship with their god is irreconcilable, figuratively speaking.

After all, we are still dealing with myth.

---

[446] Jeremiah 12:14–17.
2 Kings 23:27.

## Dynamics of Self-Destruction

Now that we know how it all began and that the ulterior motive was a land grab, we need to learn how the heist is going to be pulled off.

For this ambitious undertaking, a messiah is the central figure and leader. There are others, as we shall see, but he announces the timing and forms global alliances to ensure success in the conquest of the Promised Land.

In the words of Harris Lenowitz, messianism is

> *a doctrine that combines religion and politics in its promise of salvation. Since salvation for the Jews has never been achieved, Jewish messiahs have continued to appear at the darkest moments, as well as at those hours when promise briefly glimmers. When they feel the time is right, when a segment of Jewish society feels a rising existential threat, messiahs take upon themselves their ancient occupation and emerge to lead those who can see only an unacceptable present and an impossible future. [...]*

> *The fact of their death is the proof of their failure. The Jewish messiahs have failed to achieve cosmic redemption; they have failed to guide their followers through the apocalypse to youth, wealth, and eternal life. Nevertheless, the fact that they continue to arise – and we can predict that a Jewish messiah will arise again – suggests that they do achieve what they mean to achieve, they do not fail to be messiahs.[447]*

Lenowitz, in whose honor I have borrowed the title of this chapter and the structure of this book, sees only half the story. But his book, *'the Jewish Messiahs,'* was instrumental for me to recognize the connection between Martin Luther's anti-Semitism and the messianic lineup.

Martin Luther's journey to anti-Semitism will teach us that the dangers lay deeper than we can recognize from the messianic surface. These messiahs were not just whimsical freak occurrences. Instead, they represent an unbroken succession from one messiah to another, right up until today. They are not lunatics gone rogue, but lunatics who are supported by the highest Jewish authorities. Indeed, the Talmud requires 'certification' by sages and the Divine Council[448] in order for a messiah to gain support of the Rabbinic leadership.[449]

Messianism lies at the heart of modern-day Israel.

---

[447] Lenowitz, 1998, 3-4.
[448] The Divine Council is probably the Sanhedrin.
[449] See San 93b, 96b, 98b and Ber 28b, San 98b-99a; see also Ber 34b, Sanh 17b-18a, Baba Bathra 10a, Yoma 86b.

In his book, Lenowitz carved out a cycle of violence that serves as an eye-opening foundation to possible reasons why Jews have been hated and persecuted throughout history.

*Grandeur – Messiah – revolt – war – destruction – compassion – grandeur.*

The *grandeur* is a circular response to the compassionate preferential treatment of Jews as the Chosen People by Christian or Muslim hosts after their (repeated) destruction. The grandeur is nothing less than the claim to world domination.

I repeat: the King of the Jews is also the king of the world.

There are lessons to be learned here for Jews, non-Jews, and for those free from religion alike that might be as important as acquiring wisdom for preventing future religious disasters and holocausts.

Rabbinic leaders recognized that persecution in one place led to extraordinary privileges in another. Granting those privileges was rewarded with economic and political success for the host.

A Jewish contemporary of Luther,[450] who was married to a granddaughter of Abrabanel (who predicted the fall of Rome for 1531), wrote in his chosen home city of Amsterdam – his host:

> *Hence it may be seen that God hath not left us; for if one persecutes us, another receives us civilly and courteously; and if this prince treats us ill, another treats us well; if one banisheth us out of his country, another invites us with a thousand privileges; as divers princes of Italy have done, the most eminent King of Denmark, and the mighty Duke of Savoy in Nissa. And do we not see that those Republiques do flourish and much increase in trade who admit the Israelites?*[451]

After having been expelled from Spain (a phase of *destruction* – a holocaust), we have seen the wave of *compassion* from the Muslim Ottoman-Turks.

Was a phase of grandeur part of Luther's time?

To answer this question, let me first dig into the fundamentals.

---

450  Menasseh ben Israel aka Manoel Dias Soeiro, 1604 – 1657.
451  Manasseh ben Israel, The Hope of Israel (London 1652), printed in Lucien Wolf (ed.), Manasseh ben Israel's Mission to Oliver Cromwell (London 1901) 50-51, in Paul Johnson, A History of the Jews, 1998, 246.

The word *Christ*, means *Messiah*.[452] This is the expected deliverer of the Jewish nation to the Promised Land.[453] Logically, a messiah is only necessary, when Jews do *not* occupy land and Temple Mount. For Christians and Muslims, the Messiah Jesus Christ, has already arrived.

This terminological overlap created confusion when it came to the history of the three Judaic religions.[454]

For Martin Luther, Jesus Christ was the Christian Messiah. The only messiah. Abrabanel, on the other hand, had announced the Jewish Messiah. These two views clashed in Luther's sermons, and they had been subject of the Fifth Lateran Council as well.

In essence, modern Jews are presently waiting for their Christ-Messiah to lead the sack of the temple.

The Bible announced a messiah who would be *like a son of man*, a human messiah who was to establish a Kingdom of the World, the Promised Land, or rather establish a new world order under a Jewish theocrat.[455] Later on arose the prospect of the known world's coming to an end and being re-created by God.[456] It suggests in no uncertain terms that the entire universe should be replaced.

Nothing from before should be remembered.

God had earlier promised that he would *never again send a flood* to exterminate mankind. Unnoticed by the casual reader, the emphasis of the promise was on the flood, not on the extermination.

The End of the World would be the result of a catastrophe similar to the Flood, but just not a flood.

According to the text, God himself would come and send his wrath upon the sinful – you, that is. All of us.

---

[452] *Khristos*, or Christ is the equivalent to the Hebrew word *mashiah* or to the *anointed* (of the Lord). The word seems to have evolved from the term the anointed through the Son of Man, both essentially meaning                        the                        same.
Compare: Ezekiel had received the Word of God (Ezekiel 1:2) and would be addressed by his god as *Son of Man* (Ezekiel 2:1). Daniel would be spoken to as *Son of Man* also (Daniel 7:13 and 8:17). Later, it would come to be a term used for Jesus.

[453] *Online Etymology Dictionary*, www.etymonline.com, keyword "Messiah," accessed October 16, 2009.

[454] Without an explanation of the word Khristos in early primary documents, by itself, it likely refers to the expectation of a redeemer to come for the 'liberation' of Israel for the Jewish people. By the alleged time of the Messiah Jesus, the word Christ had already been in use for perhaps a century. In particular during the first three centuries of our time scale, when historical documents refer to Christ, it is often unclear whether the Jewish Christ to come was meant or the Christian Jesus Christ who had arrived.

[455] Daniel 7:13-7:14 (NIV), Daniel 7:27-7:28.

[456] Isaiah 65:17 (NIV).

This doomsday scenario can only be avoided by submitting to and having faith in the god of the Israelites, while hiding away for just a little.[457] God would then come to establish the kingdom of righteousness,[458] the New Jerusalem[459] in the Promised Land.

In the utopian land, there would no longer be a need for weeping and crying.[460] Children would no longer die. All believers could become centenarians and still enjoy youth in old age. Not reaching 100 years would be considered a curse.[461]

The centenarians would come to die in full bloom of their godly youthfulness!

That sounds worse than the well-earned end of the wrinkly raisins whose minds have slowly faded away. You are warned that the end is near when the teeth remain in the glass.

Hope lies in the crying baby at the death bed.

Never mind the paradox that replacing the universe might not leave much room for humanity's aspirations to the comfort of kings. Since nothing from before could be remembered, this appears rather irrelevant. But it leaves a door open to argue that the End of the World actually had happened – despite the fact that it did not.

We just do not remember.

These dreams are scientifically impossible, except, of course, for changes in territory and world leadership brought about by man.

The missiles are in the air as I speak.

Such prophetic gobbledygook was often derived from dreams. A thousand years before Martin Luther, Pope Gregory, the one with hallucinations about rising souls, took it upon himself to distinguish between dreams by ordinary people and valid ones by holy men, like himself.[462]

Even Pope Leo had been handed down new financial rules in his dreams.

---

457   Isaiah 26:20-26:21 (NIV).
458   Isaiah 32:1 (NIV).
459   Isaiah 65:18 (NIV).
460   Isaiah 65:19 (NIV).
461   Isaiah 65:20 (NIV).
462   Gregory the Great, *Dialogues* (ca. 600 AD) IV:XLVIII.

These utopian promises appear to exert some magic force toward the scientifically impossible. Followers are preparing, nay, dedicating their lives, to achieve this very Kingdom of God and its Promised Land.

Christians and Muslims, as we shall see, go even further. The promise made to them is *eternal* life in the Kingdom of Heaven or in paradise.

In the ambivalent biblical writings, the Messiah needed to be born of a virgin. A sign was promised in which, *'the virgin would be with child and will give birth to a son, and will call him Immanuel.'*[463] This is not a real name but a placeholder for a human *god of all things*. The Messiah can appear with all sorts of encoded name variations.

Clues, such as the virgin birth, are important because any messiah has to follow prophecy in detail – even if he only made them up – for Rabbinic leaders to understand the mission.

There is much more to the virgin birth. It contains a concealed requirement that the virgin comes from the same linage as Moses and Aaron. She is their sister, Miriam. This limits acceptable messianic contenders to a very narrow family tree.[464] In the Babylonian Talmud, she is part of the Sanhedrin.[465] She serves as a representation of the Temple and the Covenant.

Martin Luther explained the necessity of a miraculous virgin birth: the Messiah needs to crush the devil's power over sin and death; from this, it follows that Christ must be born without sin; unfortunately for the requirement of the supernatural event, human nature does not conceive a child without sin.

You did not misread: making love is sin.

No, you did not misread: Luther was clueless about messianic requirements. He did not realize that there were others who were far superior to him at gaming the system.

To avoid a birth corrupted by sin, a special act of God was needed, such that Christ *'is the seed only of a woman and not of a man.'*[466]

A virgin. No, *the* Virgin.

---

[463] Isaiah 7:14 (NIV).
[464] A.J. Deus, The Genius of Miriam (2024) available at academia.edu.
[465] Talmud - Mas. Chullin 92a.
[466] Luther, Jesus Born a Jew, Brandt, 1962: 202.

*She is his true natural mother; yet she is to conceive and bear supernaturally, by God, without a man, in order that her child may be a distinctive man, without sin, yet having ordinary flesh and blood like other men. This could not have been the case had he been begotten by a man like other men because the flesh is consumed and corrupted by evil lust, so that its natural act of procreation cannot occur without sin. Whatever conceives and bears through an act of the flesh produces also a carnal and sinful fruit.*[467]

This is by no means just Martin Luther saying so. The same reasoning is also the foundation of celibacy. Although Rabbinic Judaism denies it because of their hatred for *the* Virgin Mary,[468] it is, indeed, deep seated dogma in all three Judaic religions.

Making love is sin.

The most prominent virgin birth in Judaic history is Jesus Christ's. His supposed years of activity fell into a time when the Temple of Jerusalem was controlled by Jewish leaders.

Therefore, this Christian messiah emerges as a rebel without the necessary messianic cause.

According to the Gospels, Jesus Christ already had a significant impact during his lifetime. However, despite his meeting all prophetic requirements, no independent or internal Jewish evidence confirmed his existence. Yet, there were many messiahs at the time of his assumed life. Even though I fail to understand their causes at a time when Hasmonean Jews were in control, the appearance of Jesus as a messiah at that period was not improbable.

Of the many Jewish messiah claimants at the time of Jesus Christ, hardly any made it into the 'official' list, except for Jesus. Since the more important ones provide great embarrassment for supporters and shocking enlightenment for all others, the consensus only serves to maintain the status quo of refusing to attempt an understanding of what may have been going on.

A messiah or a redeemer – the terms are interchangeable – is one who ultimately *succeeds* in conquering Israel, the Promised Land. Modern Zionism can roughly be understood as messianism. Those who *failed* not only make Judaism look bad, but their chain-appearance also reveals an overly aggressive plot toward the tunnel vision of recapturing Jerusalem for Judaism.

How aggressive? Let us check their daily prayers.

---

[467] Ibid.
[468] Ibid., 208-209.

The most important Jewish prayer is the Shema, constituting the first and last words of any good Jew's day and the daily bedtime prayer for their offspring. Let us pray together with our children for a moment, as Jews do:

> *Hear, O Israel: The Lord our God, the Lord is one. Love the Lord your God with all your heart and with all your soul and with all your strength. These commandments that I give you today are to be upon your hearts. Impress them on your children. Talk about them when you sit at home and when you walk along the road, when you lie down and when you get up. Tie them as symbols on your hands and bind them on your foreheads. Write them on the doorframes of your houses and on your gates.*

> *When the Lord your God brings you into the land he swore to your fathers, to Abraham, Isaac and Jacob, to give you – a land with large, flourishing cities you did not build, houses filled with all kinds of good things you did not provide, wells you did not dig, and vineyards and olive groves you did not plant – then when you eat and are satisfied, be careful that you do not forget the Lord, who brought you out of Egypt, out of the land of slavery.*

> *Fear the Lord your God, serve him only and take your oaths in his name. Do not follow other gods, the gods of the peoples around you; for the Lord your God, who is among you, is a jealous God and his anger will burn against you, and he will destroy you from the face of the land. Do not test the Lord your God as you did at Massah* [the Israelites asked for proof of God over the lack of water]. *Be sure to keep the commands of the Lord your God and the stipulations and decrees he has given you. Do what is right and good in the Lord's sight, so that it may go well with you and you may go in and take over the good land that the Lord promised on oath to your forefathers, thrusting out all your enemies before you, as the Lord said.*[469]

This is how you raise religious extremists.

To be sure, Rabbinic leadership knows how dangerous the business of a messiah is, first and foremost for the entire Diaspora.

When a messiah failed, Jews often became collective victims of holocausts in response to their attempt to bring about the destruction of the world. If he succeeded, though – Jackpot! – the Promised Land. Weighing the risks and tremendous rewards, Rabbinic leaders supported them at first. Since most messiahs have miserably failed and found death instead of redemption, the Rabbinic position is to deny having anything to do with them.

---

[469] Deuteronomy 6:4-6:19 (NIV).

After each disaster – one holocaust after another – they either learned to ignore them altogether, or they declared them as independent and rogue figures whom they were concerned about and opposed to when they first showed up.

Knowing what the consequences of failure were and living at a time where everybody carried arms, they otherwise would not have let any messiah live.

It required a mindset of *grandeur*.

You know where this is going, do you? So you think.

A report from the Jewish historian traitor Josephus[470] confirms that killing all messiah aspirants was indeed their response in the first century. Herod the Great[471] and his successors at the time of Jesus Christ, for example, killed off anyone who dared to stick up his head as a messiah, including John the Baptist, the Gospels' forerunner. If messiahs did not vanish on their own, every single one was killed – with one notable exception: Jesus. This Christ did not merit an entry into Josephus' histories, and the historian knew nothing about him[472] – or anyone else for that matter.

The Messiah found death only in the Gospels, which still made him a failure for not conquering the Promised Land or bringing about eternal life in the Kingdom of God.

For Jews, the Christ-Messiah is the Redeemer of Israel. Christianity and Islam embrace Jesus Christ as the Messiah. Logically, for them, the same End of the World requires a *second* coming.

In early Islam, two types of messiahs were expected.

---

[470] Titus Flavius Josephus, Joseph ben Matityahu, Yosef ben Matityahu (37 – ca. 100 AD), was a Jewish historian and a leader of the Jewish anti-Roman forces during the First Jewsh-Roman War (66 – 73 AD).

[471] Herod, Hordos, Hērōdēs, aka Herod the Great (74/73 – 4 BC), was ruler of Judea 37-4 BC.

[472] Even though academic consensus presents this differently, two paragraphs about Jesus were added into Josephus' text centuries later (Josephus, *Antiquities (93 AD)* XVIII:3 and XX:9:1). The first such paragraph constitutes a break in the flow of Josephus' thoughts. The sentence of the next paragraph starts as following: *"About the same time also another sad calamity put the Jews into disorder [...]"* Only if said Jesus passage is removed does the beginning of this paragraph fit with the calamity of many deaths from the previous one. The smoking gun of the forgery is the phrase *"Jesus, a wise man, if it be lawful to call him a man."* It was not until the Council of Nicea in 325 AD that Jesus was lifted to be God, and it would be the Church Father Eusebius, who attended the council, who would first quote Josephus (or so it is said). Other Christian writers before Eusebius had quoted from Josephus but never mentioned the decisive paragraph. The word *"unlawful"* is the death knell of the fraud. It would not be until Justinian in the sixth century that it would become 'unlawful' to call Jesus a man. The second paragraph is generally viewed as authentic. However, all it needed is the addition of the word *'Christ'* in order to mislead readers. The passage is otherwise embedded in the story about the High Priest Jesus ben Damneus, not about Jesus Christ.

The Messiah of the supreme Sadducee priests from the House of Joseph was anticipated to restore the Temple to its purity and proper worship of God. The Messiah of David came to lead the war with the Iron Rod, which represents the scepter of Davidic royalty. One was the supreme spiritual leader (the Mahdi) and the other led the kingly government and be the warlord (the second Jesus). Paradoxically, *both* these Islamic messiahs come through the maternal family tree of Moses' sister.

Prophet Muhammad himself will be resurrected to become the Mahdi. His task is to fight side by side with the second Jesus against his sectarian opponent – the Antichrist.[473] Scholarship makes no association between Prophet Muhammad and the Mahdi or the Messiah.

It unmasks Islam as fitting the typical Judaic framework of messianism.

In other words, Islam is the result of Jewish messianic success.

Despite contemporary literary evidence of all the necessary components of messianic hopes,[474] the data or such notions are dismissed as Christian hysteria or even as anti-Semitism.[475]

Shi'a Islam has its special type of Mahdi, the Hidden One. His existence is based on the belief that the twelfth Shi'a Imam[476] went into occultation, meaning *hidden away*. He will reappear before Judgement Day. For that reason, rather than being resurrected, he never died.

This belief constitutes the core foundation of Shi'a Islam.[477]

While in occultation, the Mahdi answers the questions of Shi'ites through trusted intercessors, special deputies, as they call them. This is the Supreme Leader of Islam, the equivalent of the Catholic Pope.

Five conditions need to be met for the Mahdi to reveal himself: first, Muslims are practicing Islam in name only; secondly, violence and plague rake away a third of the world's population; thirdly, five corrupt tyrants are ruling, one of them killing children and ripping out bellies of women; fourthly, Syria is destroyed and residents of Baghdad and the Maghreb (North Africa) are afflicted by death and fear; and finally, a fire appears in the sky.

---

[473] Koran 39:32 (Rodwell).
[474] Sebeos' History, ca. 670 AD, English Bedrosian, 1985.
[475] Robert Hoyland, Sebeos, The Jews And The Rise of Islam (1995) 89-90.
[476] Muhammad b. al-Hasan al-Askari, twelfth imam, born 868, went into occultation around 873/4.
[477] Abdulaziz Sachedina, A Treatise on the Occultation of the Twelfth Imāmite Imam (Studia Islamica, 1978) 48, 109–124.

The Mahdi will then come forth in Mecca between the Kaaba and the station of Abraham.

Now, imagine if we could examine a point in history where all three religions and their heretical sectarian offspring brought about their messianic aspirations simultaneously.

Disaster.

That is the period of Martin Luther.

## *The Iron Rod*

Martin Luther was agitated over how the Catholic Church enabled feudal royalty to disown its subjects. In turn, royalty enforced the Catholic Church's oppression of the laity. With the concept of two messiahs from a virgin, we have a slightly modified institutionalized version of the same corruption: the supreme spiritual leader and his temple gang enabled the royal Davidic tax robber dynasties and vice versa. At the expense of a people kept ignorant and in a state of mere vegetation, these two layers filled their bellies with the best food, and their butts sat comfortably on the finest couches.

We have already seen the consequences of accuser and judge being of the same tribe.

This is the kind of imprisonment that encroached on ordinary Jews as well. They voluntarily walked into ghettoes where all their freedoms were stripped away, until they were reduced to exclusively praying and paying to the representatives of their god.

Two fiercely competing branches in Judaism both claim descent through Aaron. This is the brother of the childless biblical superstar, Moses, the leader who brought the Israelites to the borders of the Promised Land in the gruesome but nevertheless mythical Exodus from Egypt. This trek was necessary, because Jews had been enslaved in the land of the pharaohs, as the Bible claims and archaeology rejects.

The Levite Eleazar (through Zadok[478]) is at the foundation of the Egyptian Sadducees from the House of Joseph.[479] The priestly leaders of the Pharisee House of Judah constructed their ancestry through Aaron's son Ithamar, the tribe of Judah, and their King David.

---

[478] Aaron, Eleazar, Phinehas (Chronicles 6:4-8) Abishua, Bukki, Uzzi, Zerahiah, Meraioth, Amariah, Ahitub, **Zadok**.

[479] The House of Korah.

Two messiahs.[480]

It is a theatrical real-life tragedy.

Anyone who wishes to learn about Judaism needs to keep these two and the virgin in mind. It defies consensus that upholds a single messiah. They form the continuance of the older beliefs that have a common origin as far back as ancient Mesopotamian belief systems. Each was willing to scorch the earth for their supremacy over everybody else.

These two lineages are also paramount because their anointment to the priesthood was commanded by the god of the Israelites to last for eternity.[481]

A book – written by themselves – provided them with the privilege that the *'priesthood is theirs by a lasting ordinance.'*[482] Nobody outside of these two can become high-priests.[483]

The hardest issue to wrap our heads around in this messianic interplay is not only that these 'enemies' need to work together but that they are closely related in the same family tree.[484] This royal Hasmonean clan guarded its linages so diligently that it probably does not even show up in the Jewish DNA.

As I said, ordinary Jews are victims all the same.

To understand this better, we need to have a look at parchments that were found in caves near Qumran in Israel, one of which was first discovered by a Bedouin in 1946, or more exactly, by his more curious goat. These Dead Sea Scrolls, as they are called, contain parts of the Old Testament and also other non-biblical texts. They seem to have been brought out of Jerusalem through still-existing tunnels when the city was under siege during the Roman-Jewish wars of the first and early second century.[485]

In other words, we are talking about actual evidence of the period, some of it even carbon dated.[486]

---

[480]   *Cohen ha-Mašíah* literally means Priest Messiah or High Priest of the Sadducees; *Méleh ha-Mašíah* means King Messiah or *'the anointed king'* or King of the Jews from the House of Judah, in the lineage of King David – King of the World.

[481]   Exodus 40:12-40:15 (NIV).

[482]   Exodus 29:8-29:9 (NIV).

[483]   Exodus 29:29 (NIV).

[484]   A.J. Deus, Iran's Poisoned Qibla Arrows (2024) available at academia.edu.

[485]   Norman Golb, On the Jerusalem Origin of the Dead Sea Scrolls, University of Chicago, June 5, 2009.

[486]   The Messianic Apocalypse, has been dated by paleography to 100 – 80 BC and by carbon dating to 93 BC – 80 AD. Ingrid P. Nuse, based on an article by Lasse Biørnstad, Dead Sea Scrolls still conceal many stories, Science Nordic, July 6, 2016.

To make a long story short, at least 500 years before the advent of Islam, some Jewish groups had already been waiting for two messiahs to work together: a priestly Sadducee messiah (Zadok) and a lay messiah from the Pharisee House of Judah.[487]

This may go back even further.

Before the modern era, Judas Maccabeus[488] revolted against Egyptian rule and proclaimed the independence of Israel in the mid-second century BC, initiating the only short era of Israelite independence that is verifiable in the historical record. Judas Maccabeus was considered a messiah, a redeemer of Israel, a christ.[489] With the Maccabee Revolt, Judas initially entered into an alliance with the *Nazarites*.[490] These appear to have been affiliated with the priestly class of the Sadducees.

Forming alliances between Pharisees, Sadducees, and others was standard practice in pursuit of the one greater goal: sitting on the imperial throne of the Promised Land.

One can hardly be successful in these risky endeavors of conquering the world by going it alone. As history tells us in abundance, if they did not end up in the position to oppress the rest of the world, they were roasted.

The duality of the government can also be found in the Torah, the first five books of the Bible. It distinguishes between three main classes of Israelites: Levites, Nazirites, and ordinary Jews of the twelve tribes. The King of the Jews must be an Israelite.[491] But he is placed under the laws of the Levites.[492]

The basic idea of two messiahs may have already existed at the outset of 'Judaism.'

It changes with the biblical book of Judges. There, the Levite Kohanim did not appoint their next warlord. Instead, Judah was claimed to have been appointed by the god of the Israelites itself.[493]

It appears that the Pharisees attempted to get rid of their Sadducee leaders and to usurp the supreme throne for themselves.

---

487  Qumran, Manual of Discipline, 9.11.
488  Judas Maccabeus, leader of the Maccabee Revolt 167 – 160 BC.
489  1 Maccabee 4:11.
490  1 Maccabees 3:49.
491  Deuteronomy 17:15.
492  Deuteronomy 17:18-17:20.
493  Judges 1:1-1:2.

The book of Judges only serves to rationalize the eternal iron rod of the tribe of Judah and its heir, David. All others in this book were not up to the task of ruling an empire, according to its authors.

We cannot be sure how it is all connected without uprooting the whole pile of rubble under which the evidence is buried. However, we can imagine that continuance is likely. In other words, as the roots of the Protestant Reformation had been laid hundreds of years earlier, the roots of Islam can potentially be traced back 500 years before it started or even further, to the very roots of Judaism.

Impossible?

The mills of religion turn very, very slowly. In fact, they grind so slowly that the Koran claims that Abraham was already a Muslim.[494]

Ridiculous? Not any longer.

A dual government was the messianic standard. It was thought that the idea was meant to act like an insurance policy against messianic failure.[495] But the Pharisees (or some Pharisees) wanted to go it alone under the guidance of the House of Judah and King David. When that did not work out, the Sadducees' original concept prevailed.

This is precisely how the founders of Islam had it envisioned.

The on-and-off relationship would perhaps have looked something like modern Muslim Sunnis killing Shi'ites. I would not be surprised to find the ancient divisions of Judaism at the same geographical spots where the Muslims' are today, Shi'ites against Sunnis. Persia (Iran) against all others.

Jesus Christ, the Messiah for Christians and Muslims, stands out for his messianic teachings of goodness, love, and peace.

This notion rests on texts that actually mean the opposite. Experts and believers alike will point in protest to their evidence of Jesus' teachings in the *'Sermon on the Mount.'*[496]

We have an incorruptible expert who said *'that this sermon was principally aimed at and sharply directed against the Jews.'*[497] That should seal the discussion about the loving nature of the sermon.

---

[494] Koran 3:60.

[495] Lenowitz, 1998, 31. [Contrary to the here presented duality to originate from early Judaism, Lenowitz suspects that the doctrine may have been created with the Messiah Simon Bar Kokhba in response to the Christian prophecy of the Second Coming of Jesus.]

[496] Matthew 5 – 7.

[497] Martin Luther, Commentary on the Sermon on the Mount, Translated by Charles A. Hay (1532.

Said who? Martin Luther.

Everyone should be familiar with this short sermon. The text only *appears* to be positive through the eyes of a reader who detaches it from the messianic mission.

This is quite foolish (it is also the point).

After all, Jesus is *the* Messiah.

In the sermon, he promised to *'accomplish all things'* as foretold in the Bible. The promise appears to have been the liberation of the Jews from Roman rule with a strategy of passive aggression to go underground and practice Judaism in secret.

But the accomplishment of all things is nothing other than the conquest of the Promised Land brought about through the minor nuisance of the End of the World with a final world war and the decimation of mankind down to a few survivors.

The Christian text is also an anarchistic masterpiece in subverting an economy by refusing to participate in it. The *'Sermon on the Mount'* is the cornerstone of systemic poverty in Christianity and Islam. Like most of the New Testament, it aims at the Roman *'occupiers,'* even though we can learn from Josephus that Rome had brought peace, progress, and prosperity to an otherwise hopelessly impoverished and zealously violent region – yes, they have been working on their reputation for over 2,000 years.

The Rabbinic leaders preferred poverty for ordinary Jews over being part of a highly advanced Roman civilization.

Jews and Christians alike swore on the Bible that they would never let the name of another god cross their lips.

The gods of all others were myths.

This established a deep rift with the Roman Empire, which required sharing of their Pagan gods and participating in their rituals.

Other than the *'Sermon on the Mount,'* the four short Gospels of the New Testament shine in the absence of Jesus' teachings. Instead, they serve up a cocktail of miracles, demons, and God's punishment for those who do not comply. Such intimidations are concealed; for example, beneath the analogy of Sodom and Gomorrah[498] and Judgment Day.[499]

---

[498] Matthew 10:14-10:15.
[499] Matthew 11:20–24.

That day – who would have thought – signifies the End of the World where all those who are free from religion or are part of a different religion will go to hell or, preferably, perish.

The threat of Sodom and Gomorrah rests on the total obliteration of these two towns and its inhabitants for their people not following the Word of God and for living life outside the norms of biblical expectations.

Abraham's cousin Lot lived there. He was virtually the only resident who would have known about the existence of this god.

After all, Abraham was the first to *hear* words from his divinity.

Here in Sodom, in contrast to his unquestioned submission to his god when he was about to kill his son Isaac, Abraham pleaded vigorously with God not to destroy the city. The final bargain was for Abraham to find ten righteous men for God to spare the cities.[500]

Predictably, he did not.

God's collective deadly punishment came to Sodom and Gomorrah for violating rules and laws neither the residents nor Abraham and Lot had ever even heard of.[501]

These godly regulations were not conceived until the time of Moses.

The cities' residents were wicked or gay. In Sodom and Gomorrah, homosexuality was disciplined with death.

At the same time, the story glorified incest as a means that justified the end of keeping Lot's lineage alive. An intoxicated Lot impregnated not one but *two* of his daughters, supposedly without his knowledge.[502]

The point of this deviation into the double messianic appearance and the threat of Sodom and Gomorrah is that Jesus was the successor of King David. He was supposed to be the warlord with the iron rod, along with a spiritual leader, the Messiah of Zadok (the Sadducees) from the House of Joseph.

---

[500] Genesis 18:23-18:33.
[501] Genesis 19:24-19:26.
[502] Genesis 19:33-19:36.

The idea that he was the warlord came from his own words.

*Everyone therefore who confesses me before men, him I will also confess before my Father who is in heaven. But whoever denies me before men, him I will also deny before my Father who is in heaven.*

*Don't think that I came to send peace on the earth. I didn't come to send peace, but a sword. For I came to set a man at odds against his father, and a daughter against her mother, and a daughter-in-law against her mother-in-law. A man's foes will be those of his own household. He who loves father or mother more than me is not worthy of me; and he who loves son or daughter more than me isn't worthy of me. He who doesn't take his cross and follow after me, isn't worthy of me. He who seeks his life will lose it; and he who loses his life for my sake will find it.*[503]

The love of disciples is meant to be directed toward Jesus Christ, not toward other human beings. Certainly not toward those who would not confess Jesus Christ as their master.

Christians might object that their faith in Jesus induces them to love their enemies.[504] This cannot easily be replicated by somebody outside of the Christian belief system. Instead, the historical record is filled with dead outsiders who stood in its line of fire. People on the receiving end of a peace-loving Christian conquest attest to its militant nature with their broken skulls.

Jesus was the Jewish messianic warlord from the lineage of David, tasked with reconquering the Promised Land from the Romans.

At full disclosure, the respective passage was a call to missionizing on unbelieving targets. The love for your neighbors[505] needs to be understood with this agenda in mind. It was also merely a simplification of the original Ten Commandments from the Bible.

The Messiah himself asked *'if you love those who love you, what reward will you get?'*[506]

A new commandment to love one another was added as part of the secondary text. It explicitly states that the intention was to create an internal doctrinal marker through which everyone should know that the apostles (and Christian followers) were Jesus' disciples.[507]

---

[503] Matthew 10:32-10:39.
[504] Matthew 5:44 (NIV).
[505] Matthew 19:21.
[506] Matthew 5:46-5:48 (NIV).
[507] John 13:34-13:35 (NIV).

Likewise, the New Testament expanded on the rewards where those who blindly obeyed Jesus' commandments would be loved back by God and by Jesus.[508] The meaning of the 'reward' was conversion of non-believers for missionizing through a concept of 'love.'

The authors of the New Testament made it clear that loving one another was part of the communal binding mechanism. It pitted those inside the holy circle against everyone who remained unconvinced, first and foremost Jews.

The word 'love' was abused for ulterior motives: *'If anyone does not love the Lord – a curse be on him.'*[509]

The manipulative slogan resonated. Logically, the writers expanded on the successful motif and provided the audience with what every human loves to hear – love one another and donate everything that you own to the spiritual leaders.[510] From this context, the Christian concepts of kindness, modesty, humility, and truth also emerged.

Upon closer examination, they boil down to passive aggression – bullying.

Martin Luther demonstrates how to increase the pressure.

Sectarianism is a strategic tool that can be summed up in *'Divide and Rule.'* The strategy is deployed today. Look east – then, check your home turf.

While Jesus' Davidic lineage appears to be self-evident to believers, the Gospels sewed confusion. Their authors went to great lengths in listing the family tree of Jesus Christ from Abraham, through David, and finally to his father Joseph. Right after the ancestral lineup, it is explained that Mary was with child through the Holy Spirit *before* the couple came together.[511]

Doctrine commands the Immaculate Conception and Virgin Birth of Jesus Christ to be protected.

The Gospel of Luke contains a second lineage of Jesus Christ . It says that it was *'thought'*[512] that Jesus was the son of Joseph. Not only that. The second lineage varies from the first. It goes all the way to Adam who is designated as *'the Son of God.'*[513]

---

508  John 14:21.
509  1 Corinthians 16:22 (NIV).
510  2 Corinthians 9:5-9:7 (NIV).
511  Matthew 1:18.
512  Luke 3:23.
513  Luke 3:37.

As a human conception, Jesus *could* be from the House of David, although the split 'evidence' is not trustworthy. But with the Immaculate Conception, the Messiah is in the direct lineage of the god of the Israelites, not of King David – unless a Davidic man pretended to be God.

Although modern Western believers want it both ways, it took over a thousand years of bloodshed to settle on duality, which is the doctrine that Jesus is both man and god.

Muslims oppose with their lives the notion that Jesus could have been begotten by God.

We should discard the genealogies and remain in suspense about the ghostly pre-marital lover who could not control himself over Mary's youthful innocence. Unless the spiritual insemination in and by itself is taken as a sign for the lineage of David, Jesus Christ was actually outside of the Davidic branch of messianism even before he was born.

Regardless of all this, academia does not know with any degree of confidence when Jesus actually lived. The absence of evidence during the first century and deep into the second remains troubling. Scientifically, we have nothing that attests to Jesus, the King of the Jews. We do not reliably know who he was or where and when he lived; we do not agree on a sectarian evolution; in most cases, we have no consensus on which evidence rests on mere invention and which is real.

The state of the art is to identify entire books as frauds but to keep on utilizing them anyway. An example is the fourth century fraudster Eusebius,[514] without whom there exists extraordinarily little history about early Christianity and its supposed martyrs, if any.

Let me put this in context.

Martin Luther argued that the Jews had neither king nor kingdom for nearly 1,500 years at the Reformer's time. He thought that this time span was proof of the Messiah's appearance before the destruction of the Temple of Jerusalem.[515]

Did Luther disregard the facts on the ground?

---

[514] Eusebius of Caesarea aka Eusebius Pamphili, ca. 260 – 340 AD.
[515] Luther, Jesus Born a Jew, Brandt, 1962, 214.

After Jesus, Simon bar Kokhba[516] was the next-best-known messiah to appear. Martin Luther commented that bar Kokhba was the Messiah and Akiba the messiah maker.[517] As customary, the boss behind the Messiah was also chief of the sages – the chief of the Sanhedrin.

Here too, the evidence shows a dual government style of the supreme spiritual leader and a Davidic messiah who was not a leader who had gone rogue. Instead, he was under the wings of the highest Jewish authority.

In contrast to many other messiah pretenders, bar Kokhba managed to reinstate the ritual sacrifice on the Temple Mount and to issue his own coins. It indicates a brief period of only a few years where Israelite independence was again achieved.

He was a successful redeemer and messiah of Jews, one who had indeed arrived. Under his leadership, the most important part of the Promised Land had been reconquered, the Temple of Jerusalem.

He was the Christ for whom Jews had been waiting, the King of the Jews.

No Rabbinic leader can claim that Christ had not already arrived. They just reinvented their myths by denying facts.

Someone was offended by the machinations of the messianic pair, Akiba and bar Kokhba. The offended entity was a superpower: the Roman Empire.

Now we can see the dynamics of self-destruction.

In the wake of defeat, bar Kokhba and 400,000 of his followers perished. That is a whole lot of dead followers. Emperor Hadrian, who kicked them off the Mount, is not known for having engaged in ethnic cleansing or for having killed man and mouse, including women and children. Yet, the dead must have encompassed the able men of an entire region, perhaps the whole Levant or even deeper into the Middle East and North Africa.

It is a compassion trap.

The number is grossly exaggerated.

The Talmud suggests a 100-fold embellishment.[518]

---

[516] Simon bar Kokhba (+135 AD), born Simon ben Kosevahon, bar Kosevah, Bar Koseva, or Ben Koseva (Fred Skolnik, Michael Berenbaum, eds., Encyclopaedia Judaica, 3 (Thomson Gale, 2007) 156–157.

[517] Luther, Jews and Their Lies, 1971.

[518] Talmud - Mas. Gittin 57b.

After Jesus Christ's crucifixion, according to the Gospels, there were only a few followers left, *'about a hundred and twenty.'*[519] From a high of about 5,000, almost all seem to have fallen away from the leader and his successors. All that did not matter. Many had already done so while Jesus had been performing his show of miracles.

The gang of a few holdouts were barely noticeable.

However, the number 120 is hardly coincidental with 10 per Jewish tribe, per apostle, forming the Sanhedrin – it intends to say that *all* were on board.

But after bar Kokhba, we could stack up the slaughtered to the height of a mountain.

If only ten percent of the faithful men escaped, there would be ample grounds for a very large Kokhba sect to have survived, over 300 times bigger than Jesus' insignificant band. They would have quickly recovered their numbers by serial-impregnating their polygamist cow-wives who also believed in this Kokhba Christ. They, in turn, would have taught it to their children. Within 25 years, they could have recovered to hundreds of thousands.

It gives us an inkling about the impact that a messiah would have in the real world – one who actually rededicated the Temple Mount, and not Jesus, the one who theorized about it, if one follows the narrative of the New Testament.

In light of this, it is unusual that we cannot identify a Kokhba sect thereafter. Unlike with Jesus, where a sect emerged from a messiah without cause and without a successful conquest, here we have cause and conquest but no sect. The false Kokhba is historically accounted for; the true Messiah, Jesus, is not. The star had real numbers; Jesus did not. The Dead Sea Scrolls know about Kokhba; not a word recounts the Messiah of Christianity.

Kokhba imprinted the rising Star of David on his coins.

Jesus did nothing similar.

After the revolt, the Kokhba sect no longer registered in the historical record, as if it was swallowed by a monster; instead, Jesus Christ's sect emerged in scattered and unclear fragments. But only *after* the Kokhba Revolt. All extra-biblical evidence from before never referred to *'Jesus Christ.'* At best, it referred to *'Christ.'*

It just does not add up.

---

[519] Acts 1:15.

I am not satisfied, simply because Jesus should be there. Obviously, a real messiah would find exposure in the ancient 'news.' The mystery is why the Kokhba sect disappeared without a trace. Or did it? We should not jump to conclusions. Looking at the evidence, it seems that the Rabbinic leadership might have had grounds to reject Jesus. However, they had no reason to deny bar Kokhba as the Messiah.

Luther did not disregard the facts on the ground, but he could not look beyond his bias. He would otherwise have recognized that Christians could not deny that the Second Coming of Christ had already occurred with bar Kokhba, either.

The End of the World had already happened.

Without denying this real-world messiah, Judaism and Christianity would both be dead in the water. Islam would have never been born.

To answer these questions more profoundly, I would need a bigger book than Martin Luther's. But the Reformer has a ready answer, if we lift one of his statements out of its context:

> *After Hadrian had expelled the Jews from their country, however, it was necessary to choose the bishops in Jerusalem from the Gentiles who had become Christians, for the Jews were no longer found or tolerated in the country because of Kokhba and his rebellious followers, who gave the Romans no rest.*[520]

Jews went undercover with Christian bishops, should they have existed. After it went wrong, the Rabbinic leadership denied ever having participated in the folly to provoke the world's mightiest superpower.

The messianic allusion to bar Kokhba later vanished from the Talmud.

As a substitute, his nom de guerre, bar Kokhba (son of a star), literally *'the successor of the Star of David,'* was edited into a derogatory nickname, bar Koziba (son of the lie). They went as far as boasting about killing the failed leader themselves after he had already reigned for two and a half years.[521]

The problem is that the entire historical record has been so manipulated over the centuries that we cannot learn the lessons that would be so important for us moderns to prevent the next religiously motivated massacre. In fact, by the day of Akiva's burial, the next messiah-maker had already been born.[522]

Organized religion will get us in trouble again, sooner or later.

---

[520] Luther, Jews and Their Lies, 1971, part XIII.
[521] Talmud, Mas. Sanhedrin 93b.
[522] Judah, aka Yehudah HaNasi, ca. 135 – ca. 217 AD.

I see. We already are.

Emperor Hadrian razed the Jewish temple only to replace it with a Roman temple of his choosing. He also built a Roman administrative city[523] right over Jerusalem.[524] A humanist and admirer of Greek culture, Hadrian is considered one of the Five Good Emperors, and the building on the Mount must not be viewed in isolation. He also re-built the Pantheon in Rome and erected the Temple of Venus and Roma, a place of worship so large that it took twenty years to complete. He also commissioned a mausoleum for his family – the one now used by the Vatican to imprison its enemies and to be used as a papal fortress in times of trouble. Pope Gregory, the one with flaming souls, had a vision of an angel on top of the mausoleum wiping its blood-dripping sword with its mantle. From this originated the mausoleum's new name, Castel Sant'Angelo.

Since Hadrian must not have known of a sect of Jesus but instead of a sect of Khokba, it appears ironic that the Catholic Church would use this exact castle for securing its popes.

Jews were no longer allowed near the Holy Mount, and Rome instated the death penalty against the practice of circumcision. This is the time in history when 'Christianity' could have had reason to drop the biblical requirement of phallic mutilation.

Those who did not fall during the war took an exit and found themselves in the Persian Empire, in Armenia, in the Arab Peninsula, and preferably somewhere in between the superpowers. Stateless. And without a Khokba sect of the Messiah, son of the lie.

Paradoxically, Hadrian is said to initially having supported the Jewish cause of rebuilding their temple. It is apparent that they did not stop there and that they pushed too far, seceding from Rome, grabbing land that was not theirs, cleansing the land of 'alien' ethnicities, and doing whatever else was commanded in the Bible.

The consequence? Holocaust.

The pattern of history repeats itself as I speak.

---

[523] Aelia Capitolina.
[524] The temple was dedicated to Jupiter Capitolinus.

From then on, with short interruptions, the Temple Mount was off limits for Jews. Such drastic action remained in force for centuries until the 'Muslims' took the land from the Roman Empire. The Romans succumbed to Christianity, so we are told. Yet, Christian rulers came to enforce the three-mile radius as off limits for Jews. Was it anti-Semitism or self-defence?

We have a parallel that might help us understand Hadrian's change of mind: Martin Luther.

Allow me to call it *'Hadrian's Choice.'* It would come to signify Luther's coming out moment.

At first, they may all have been part of a messianic alliance, thus creating a new, ecumenical offshoot. After it went wrong, they pretended never to have participated. They might indeed have put an end to it on their own in order to save their faces in defeat and pretend to be heroes.

After Kokhba, the same ideas continued to foster violent competition.

At the beginning of the seventh century, the Messianic Era in Judaism and the traditions of Prophet Muhammad fell together in the same years.[525]

Of course, early Muslims had a supreme mufti and a government leader, just as in the Jewish messiah duality. The two-messiah concept of Islam represents the customary line in which, in simple terms, the supreme spiritual leaders of the Sadducee House of Joseph were working together with the Pharisee House of David.

The idea of two messiahs was enforced by the second royal dynasty of Islam, the so-called Abbasids.[526] Primary evidence from out of Baghdad from the twelfth century shows how the two messianic branches worked together.[527]

According to the testimony, Prophet Muhammad had ordered the Jewish Throne of David to be raised next to the Caliph.[528]

Indeed, the Koran had commanded it.

> *O David! Verily we have made thee our viceregent upon earth.*[529]

---

[525] The Muslim Prophet also went by 'Kabsha,' a possible tribute to Kokhba. Hence, all this is not mere speculation. Its success might have evolved into Islam by being pushed away (again) through the resistance of more traditional forces of Judaism.
See Sir H.A.R. Gibb, *The Encyclopaedia of Islam*, keyword Khuza'a (Leiden Brill, 1979) 77. [The question for researchers is not *whether* Kokhba and Kabsha are related but *how*.]

[526] We do not yet know what the first dynasty believed in.

[527] The Itinerary of Benjamin of Tudela (ca. 1179 AD), 61.

[528] Ibid., 62.

[529] Koran 38:26 (Rodwell).

That parallel throne was given dictatorial authority over the entire Abbasid administration.[530] Not unlike the Spanish crown rabbi, in Baghdad, the leader was the Jewish 'Head of the Captivity'. He was in charge for all administrative appointments that naturally went to Jewish functionaries, similar to the Spanish 'arrabis.' It included the judiciary and a monopoly of force. Tax farming, of course. Banking. Trade. Everything.[531] They controlled international commerce up- and downriver at the Euphrates and Tigris, at the Nile River in Egypt, and the Red Sea.

This was a religio-political cartel.

Everyone else was left in economic and intellectual serfdom.

The Koran sets this Jewish system as the norm, not the exception.

If that were not enough, the report identifies the caliph himself as a Jewish leader. He was kind with Jews, well versed in the law of Israel, and able to read and write Hebrew.[532] The pilgrimage was to *Baghdad* where the Jewish caliph was venerated like a god, a paraclete, perhaps, and regarded as Muhammad.[533]

In the twelfth century, the Muslim pilgrimage was not only *not* toward Mecca but toward an extraordinary human being in Baghdad (Pumbedita[534]) who pretended to carry the Divine Presence and styled himself as '*Our Lord [Adonenu], light of Islam and glory of* the Torah.[535] In the Hebrew text, '*our Master the Lord of Islam'* is *Adonenu Muhammad*, a Jewish god.[536]

We are talking about a post-apocalyptic King of the Jews.

The primary evidence states plainly that Abbasid Islam in Baghdad equates to Judaism proper.

It has become evident now that all caliphs from the inception of Islam formed an uninterrupted chain of Jewish Muhammads.[537]

It was a New Jerusalem in Baghdad with a new Covenant under Jewish dual leadership, precisely as proscribed by the Bible.

The rest of the population was trampled upon through the oppressive Jewish administrative system. The difference is that caliphal royalty can be identified as

---

[530] The Itinerary of Benjamin of Tudela (ca. 1179 AD), 62.
[531] Ibid., 62.
[532] Ibid., 55.
[533] Ibid., 55-56.
[534] A.J. Deus, The Lost Cities of Baghdad (2023) available at academia.edu.
[535] The Itinerary of Benjamin of Tudela (ca. 1179 AD), 57-58.
[536] For credits and details, see A.J. Deus, Iran's Poisoned Qibla Arrows (2024) available at academia.edu.
[537] Ibid.

Jewish. In Spain, we have suspicions and Marrano links to royal heritage. Now that we have learned where to look, we will find the evidence there as well.

Islam was the Jewish post-apocalyptic dream come true.

This is but a small peak into a world of unspeakable inequality that was so designed by Jewish leaders.

Let us reflect about how they were a magnet of hatred that would endure centuries after Jewish leaders had long abandoned their aspirations to world rule.

Or have they?

Are the fears of the Arab world in any way justified?

We deal with deep-seated cultural trauma that was inflicted by Jewish leaders and their oppressive administrative apparatus.

And it shows in Israel's treatment of the Palestinians.

Even though the report by a Jewish traveler offers no ambivalence, Jewish and Islamic scholars dismiss the fact that Islam was complemented with a Jewish Throne of David as ridiculous or even anti-Semitic. Most have never even heard of a Jewish caliph or never want to hear of one. For fear of repercussions, nobody dares to touch it.

Their history reads like this: wherever economic, political, or religious action took place, the *only* ethnic group that maintained a global network of ultra-loyal connections, was superbly educated, and genius with money and leadership skills *had nothing to do with it.*

Their leaders who brought us Judaism, Christianity, Manicheanism, Reform-Zoroastrianism (yes, I said it), Islam, and more, wash their hands in sanctimoniousness. These leaders and their unsuspecting followers were persecuted indefinitely for no reason at all other than for believing in their god.

Anybody who dares to ask questions is shouted down as anti-Semite.

Since we probably can now safely dismiss God's hand in this swamp, the human leaders constituted themselves through an assembly, a council, also called the Jewish Sanhedrin, during which they mutually appointed and affirmed one another to these lofty positions based on their linage primacy. This Sanhedrin is what we see in the primary evidence from Baghdad.

This is organized crime on a grand scale – a genius religio-political cartel.

This creates a new paradigm where the original Islam was not only just another Judaic break-away, but it was the fallout of one of these messianic periods – a successful one.

The destruction of the entire world bears its signature.

Like in Spain and elsewhere in Europe, the Abbasid Caliphate was a giant Jewish tax farming operation.

Jewish leaders were holy enemies of freedom.

The gravitational forces of this magnet of hatred keep on pulling us down.

On the Throne of David sat the factual Jewish prime minister with tyrannical powers, and the Jewish caliph was the supreme 'mufti', the religious leader, the imam.

There are several messiah episodes throughout history, but we should be able to imagine the basic dynamics of self-destruction as a perpetual phenomenon rather than a one-time occurrence.

Jewish leaders represented an insignificant minority alright; but the minor detail that they were a rather significant *ruling* minority, one that subjugated everybody else, was not handed down through history.

Because of the promised imperial rewards, the biblical mandate is to keep on pushing, regardless of the consequences. The Jewish leadership is determined to climb *back* unto the throne of the world at any cost. No treachery is off the table, even if the path to achieving the goal requires the total destruction of our planet.

That kings, governors, and judges in biblical domains must also be replaced with functionaries from the house of David is so proscribed in the Bible.

> *The oppressor will come to an end, and destruction will cease; the aggressor will vanish from the land. In love a throne will be established; in faithfulness a man will sit on it – one from the house of David – one who in judging seeks justice and speeds the cause of righteousness.*[538]

The Book of Isaiah is blunt about how this would be achieved:

> *By the strength of my hand I have done this [war], and by my wisdom [strategy], because I have understanding [religion]. I removed the boundaries of nations, I plundered their treasures; like a mighty one I subdued their kings.*

> *As one reaches into a nest, so my hand reached for the wealth of the nations; as men gather abandoned eggs, so I gathered all the countries; not one flapped a wing, or opened its mouth to chirp.*[539]

If it were not in the Bible, it would be an anti-Semitic trope.

---

[538] Isaiah 16:5 (NIV).
[539] Isaiah 10:13-10:14 (NIV).

What comes across like boastful words by the god of the Israelites, describes the fundamental understanding of the human authors of the Bible about the power of organized religion. It literally asserts that the power of *their god subverted all nations* that accepted it as the dominant divinity.

They plundered the treasures of nations.

They reached for their wealth.

And their victims neither resisted nor protested.

They were smiling to the vault.

It is quite the achievement that they have not been overthrown more often.

It is just history, is it?

## Perfect Treachery

For the last decades, the Shi'ite Safavid Dynasty had greatly expanded in Azerbaijan and Persia. They wanted nothing to do with Ottoman Sunnis. Safavid Shi'ites not only considered all Sunnis and non-Muslims as unclean but also prohibited Jews from coming into any physical contact with Muslims.[540] Saying it like that hides the fact that Jews are biblically mandated to keep their linage clean and to not intermarry with non-Jews. Whether the Safavids meant to protect the Jewish linage from 'contamination' or keep lowly Muslims away from Jews remains to be answered.

The founder of the Safavid Dynasty[541] portrayed himself as the Hidden Imam to Twelver Shi'ism – the Mahdi – the Messiah of Islam.

God on earth.

He feigned direct descent from Ali, the first imam of Shia' Islam, cousin and son-in-law of Prophet Muhammad.[542] Whether fake or real, because Ali was a Jewish Exilarch,[543] he was therefore Jewish.

The magnitude of betrayal that came with this obvious conspiracy to the subjugated Persian people is beyond imagination.

---

[540] Jewishhistory.org, 1502 – 1736.
[541] Shah Ismail Safavi, ruled as the Persian Shah from 1501 – 1524.
[542] Kathryn Babayan, Mystics, Monarchs and Messiahs: Cultural Landscapes of Early Modern Iran (Harvard University Press, 2002) 143.
[543] A.J. Deus, Iran's Poisoned Qibla Arrows (2024) available at academia.edu.

Their leaders knew how to play with the deadly power of organized religion.

> *But in Persia, the Age of the Mahdi, the Messianic Age, had begun.*
> *The heroic crusaders [ghazi] have come forth with*
> *'crowns of happiness' on their heads.*
> *The Mahdi's period has begun.*
> *The light of eternal life has dawned [upon] the world.*[544]

The Safavids declared Twelver Shia Islam as *compulsory* state religion. Their boss dissolved the Sunni Brotherhoods and ordered the execution of all who refused to comply.[545] In Baghdad, he destroyed Sunni religious sites.

His legendary barbarism rests on a golden drinking cup that had been made from the skull of one of his enemies.[546]

A true religious extremist.

The carefully engineered image of a religious brute cemented the foundation of eternal animosities between Shi'ite Iran, Sunni Muslims, and the rest of the world. This move was designed to bind Persians together against Ottoman ambitions through the weapon of organized religion, exerted upon superstitious subjects.

It worked!

The modern borders of Iran reflect the Safavid Shi'ite mass radicalization of its population.

Before this pivotal change in sectarian adherence, religious positions in the region were not so clear. Persia was not only majority Sunni, but Muslim Ottoman scholars had been educated there. One of the contenders to the Ottoman Sultanate[547] had joined the faith of the *'red-heads'*[548] as follower of the Persian Shah.

Quite obviously, the conversion had imperial motives.

---

[544] Khata'I, Il Canzoniere di Shah Isma'il, ed. Tourkhan Ganjei (Naples: Institudio Orientale) 249:12, in Babayan, Mystics, Monarchs and Messiahs, 2002, 296-297.

[545] William L Cleveland, A History of the Modern Middle East (Westview Press, 2009) 95.

[546] Abraham Eraly, Emperors Of The Peacock Throne: The Saga of the Great Moghuls (Penguin Books, 2000) 10.

[547] Şehzade Ahmet, ca. 1466 – 1513 was Beyazit's firstborn and acted as governor of Amasya.

[548] Qizilbash, Kizilbash, Qezelbash, Qazilbash is an originally perjorative Ottoman-Turkish word for Shia militants who led to the foundation of the Shi'ite Safavid Dynasty in Iran. The 'red head' was symbolized in the headdress of Twelver Shi'ism, a turban with a high pointed crimson peak.

For the Safavid Empire, nothing less than the definition of the correct Islam against Ottoman views, as well as the aspiration to world leadership, was at stake.

The Safavid warrior chiefs constituted an existential threat to the rule of Ottoman-Turks. And they experimented with social engineering.

The Sunni Ottomans came up with a theological answer that turned the Shi'ite Safavids into unbelievers and apostates. Their ruler now had a religious duty to fight them,[549] aiming at the extermination of the dynastic competition.

Indeed, the Ottoman Selim the Grim was able to drive Safavid ambitions back.

Ever since, Turks were watching their Shi'ite back door.[550]

500 years later, still.

The overthrow of Safavid aspirations posed a tremendous problem for a supposed Shi'ite mahdi-messiah: he could not lose. Henceforth, the defeated Safavid leader went into retreat for the rest of his existence as a demi-god. The messianic expectations were then repositioned – re-engineered – and transferred to the next generation of Safavid heirs.[551]

In 1517, the same year that Luther created his 95 Theses, Mecca and Medina fell to the Ottoman-Turks without the need for shooting any arrows. The rapidly growing Portuguese trade empire presented an imminent threat to the two holiest cities of Islam. Fearing collapse, Mecca's Emir, the senior descendant of Prophet Muhammad, sent the keys of the Kaaba, the holiest mosque at Mecca, to the Ottoman Sultan Selim the Grim.[552]

This symbolic handover of the keys made Selim the first 'legitimate' *caliph* of the Ottoman Empire. It marks the formal end of Mamluk and Abbasid rule.

In reality, Ottoman-Turks had just conquered the Egyptian Mamluk Sultanate of which Medina and Mecca were parts. The panicked handover of the keys was preceded by an alliance between the Portuguese and the Ethiopian empires in 1515 that had been forged with the help of Pope Leo X.

Accordingly, the peaceful transfer of the Kaaba is mere legend.

---

[549] Ismail Safa Ustun, PhD diss. Heresy and Legitimacy in the Ottoman Empire in the Sixteenth Century (University of Manchester, 1991) 35-59.

[550] In response to Safavid Shi'a Islam, the Indian kingdom of Bijapur also switched to Sunni Islam. Sultan Ibrahim Adil Shah I (1534–1558) had the names of the twelve Shi'a Imams erased from the Kuthbah and promoted the Sunni religious rite (see Richard M. Eaton, A Social History of the Deccan, 1300-1761: Eight Indian Lives (Cambridge, 2005) 145).

[551] Babayan, Mystics, Monarchs and Messiahs, 2002, 301.

[552] Selim I was Sultan of the Ottoman Empire 1512 – 1520.

The Ottoman Selim the Grim was a religious savage who had before booted his father out of the royal palace. Following his dynasty's harsh tradition, he eliminated his brothers to prevent the throne from being challenged. Avoiding the partition of territories among siblings and leaving only a single dynast in charge constituted one of the key factors of Ottoman success. It protected their domain from being vulnerable through the same Achilles Heel as the fractured feudal system that was upheld by the Catholic Church.

Killing competing siblings was sort of a Judaic royal tradition.

This Ottoman ruler was fabled for a fiery temper. His ministers seem to have been cursed, just for working for him. The reputation of the Grim may have originated with his order to collectively punish 40,000 fellow Muslims – the Safavid Shi'ite[553] competition paid with their lives.[554] As we know from modern experience, ethnic cleansing was a well-honed reciprocation among sects that belong to the religion of peace.

Selim did not have any scruples.

The Sultan assimilated not only Medina and Mecca, but also Jerusalem, which by nature of prophecy, turned him into the Mahdi of Muslims – another Mahdi – at least for the now-dominating Sunni Ottoman-Turks. There are various Sunni sectarian interpretations, but in general, the Mahdi is an ordinary human being who could manifest himself at the side of the Second Jesus. This is in sharp contrast to the Shi'ite version, where he is an un-dead hidden one, essentially a ghost come alive.

Jerusalem gave Selim the Grim a standing above anyone else in the Muslim world, the status of a messiah. He saw himself in the biblical fight between the forces of good and evil. Ever since, Ottoman commanders increasingly focused on messianism and leadership of the world through its caliphate.

The incorporation of Jerusalem into the Ottoman realm also marks the beginning of the forgotten sixteenth century world war.

Earlier, many Jewish refugees from Spain had been welcomed as respected citizens into the Ottoman domain. Through the testimony from the husband of Abrabanel's granddaughter in Amsterdam, we were able to recognize that the extraordinary privileges that could be achieved in the wake of disaster were part of Jewish consciousness.

It acted like a license to keep on pushing further.

---

[553] Qizilbash.
[554] Michael J. McCaffrey, ČĀLDERĀN (Encyclopaedia Iranica, 1990) Vol. IV, Fasc. 6, 656–658.

Under Ottoman-Turkish rule, Jerusalem and Safed turned into major centers of Judaism. Jerusalem Jewry came to play a pivotal role in the Ottomans' further expansion by manufacturing weaponry – weapon dealers – and financing their military campaigns in exchange for more privileges.

We can perhaps imagine what kind of draw Israel had in the messianic context of the predictions of Abrabanel for the beginning of the Messianic Age in 1531.

The only problem: like today, somebody else owned temple and land.

May treachery and encroachment begin.

We might not fully understand it:

our elders looked at Judaism with suspicion and upheld a three-mile circle of prohibition around the temple – for a reason.

You probably do not remember Mahari Minz. He was the Italian super rabbi who had been buried in Padua. Next to him was laid to rest Abrabanel, the King of the Jews. In order to provide an indication of just how connected the top layers of Judaism were, the chief rabbi of Turkey was Moses Capsali. This is the one who helped with rescuing Jews from Spain and moving them to Turkey. Capsali's successor on the Throne of David in Istanbul was Elijah Mizrachi,[555] a rabbi notable for his positive attitude toward Karaite Judaism (Ultra-Orthodox). He was a Greek-born Jew from Constantinople (Istanbul).

He was taught in Padua – by none other than Mahari Minz.

They relied on personal connections and secret communications, embedded in Bible and Talmud commentaries. Nobody suspected anything, even when the couriers were intercepted. It was benign, superstitious chatter, then flying under the guise of religious co-existence.

Captors could torture the messengers and still get nothing out of them.

Jewish leaders coordinated their subversions on a global scale.

Luther wrote about some of the Talmud's encoding principles. Other than for our awareness, the keys to the code of the Talmudic communications are not essential to the Reformer's story, but we have Jewish writers who continued to assert that Rabbinic leaders used layered texts.

---

[555] Elijah Mizrachi, aka Re'em, 1455 – 1526.

*These Talmudists, consider it their duty to propose difficult questions and answer them in a witty and subtle manner, but leave unnoticed the precious pearls that lie upon the bed of the Talmudic ocean, the haggadic passages (similar to Midrash) so rich in beauty and sweetness.*[556]

This passage derives from an overly confident Jewish scholar. It is an affront to moderns who were expected to never understand what he was trying to say. The uninformed would read a witty and subtle text, but underneath, secrets were concealed so nobody would notice.

They had created a Talmudic spider web.

If I had to describe a defining character of Jewish leadership in a single word, then it would have to be *'undercover.'* This is Hasidic doctrine today, Ultra-Orthodox. It stands for *'subversion'* – of your world. Doctrine sometimes calls it *'quietism,'* in the meaning of hushing their goals.

This is why an endless string of secular and religious rulers, starting in the sixth century,[557] over a period of a thousand years, had tried to rid the world of the Talmud.[558] Such stark measures came about because Talmudists were viewed as dangerous extremists. And they were.

And they are.

Trying to argue that these Roman and later Christian leaders had their decisions **not** based on reason and evidence defies logic. Eradicating a *specific* book from the world does not seem to be a trivial decision. It appears more significant than indiscriminately burning entire libraries.

It is the duty of modern science to find answers to these actions in order to help prevent yet another holocaust.

Rabbi Jacob Berab[559] is an example of one who abused the Ottoman-Turkish welcome. He was a son of Spanish refugees. At age eighteen, he became chief rabbi in Tlemcen, the Algerian city that had first received and then persecuted Jews after they were found in royal beds. He must have stood right in the middle of the bloodbath. In 1522, Berab was in Jerusalem. Then he went further to Damascus and Cairo.

---

[556] Isaac Aboab I, Aron ha-'Edut (The Ark of the Testimony) (ca. end of 14th century) preface.

[557] Justinian, Novella 146, addressed to the Praefectus Praetorio Areobindus (553 AD).

[558] Emanuel Deutsch, Literary Remains of the Late Emanuel Deutsch (Murray, 1874) 7.

[559] Jacob Berab, aka Berav or Bei-Rav, 1474 – 1546. He originated from Moqueda near Toledo, Castilian Spain.

In a little over a decade from then, he settled among the largest[560] Jewish community in Ottoman Syria, Safed,[561] with the goal of reintroducing Rabbinic ordination. This signifies the establishment of a central Jewish spiritual leader in the context of wild and extravagant messianic hopes.[562]

He and his pals essentially intended to carve out an independent state of Israel, and therefore to conquer the Promised Land from within their host.

The mortar of their new homes had not even dried yet.

Selim the Grim had left for paradise, and his successor is who we are really interested in: Suleiman the Magnificent.[563] This man, Suleiman, marched his armies up the Balkan toward Vienna, having at this time already sacked most of Serbia and Hungary, approaching Bohemia. Most of North Africa from Egypt to modern day Algeria, at the doorsteps of the Kingdom of Tlemcen, had already been conquered.

Ottomans became a Mediterranean naval power. Only now did the Ottoman-Turkish sovereign grow into an empire, and its monarch was elevated to a king of kings.

Finally, the defeated Mamluk ruler[564] formally transferred the religious leadership over all Muslims to Suleiman.

What a religious feat!

However, there is a concern. Elzearius Horn was custodian of the Holy Sepulchre in Jerusalem between 1725 and 1726 and secretary of the Convent S. Salvatoris between 1737 and 1738. While he is not a contemporary to Selim, in his book he says something extraordinary: the Temple Mount was *'contaminated by the Mohammadean cult during the year 463 AD, and afterwards in the year of Christ 1099 AD.'* He continues that the *'temple was rescued from the Saracens by the Sultan Selim in the year 1517'* but again *'profaned by the impure Turks.'*[565]

Horn knew something that appears to have been lost to history. How Selim and some of his successors are *neither* Saracens or Muhammadeans *nor* impure Turks merely expands the messianic horizon.

No, he was not mistaken.

---

560  Damascus, Jerusalem, Safed, and Tiberias became the four centers of Rabbinic Judaism.
561  Safed was chosen because upper Galilee was part of prophecy in the Zohar wherein the Messiah would appear there.
562  Louis Ginzberg, Jewish Encyclopiedia (1906).
563  Suleiman the Magnificent was caliph of the Ottoman Empire 1520 – 1566.
564  Al-Mutawakkil III was the last Abbasid caliph 1508 – 1516/7.
565  Elzearius Horn, Ichnographiae locorum et monumentorum veterum terrae Sanctae (1744) 33 (Vatican Digital Library) 33-35. https://digi.vatlib.it/view/MSS_Vat.lat.9233.pt.1.

Eudokia (d. 460 AD), wife of Theodosius II, is said to have issued a permit to rebuild the Jewish Temple in 443 AD. The Talmud declares in regard to the beginning of the Messianic era: *"In it is stated that four thousand, two hundred and thirty-one years after the creation the world will be orphaned."*[566] This turns out to be the year 470 AD. The world being orphaned means that they had lost the Temple (again).

That is pretty much all we know.

Horn equates – correctly – the Muhammadeans with Jews but takes preference with Selim's strand of the Ottomans. He is also correct that the Muhammadean cult had already existed during the late fifth century. An inscription in Yemen confirms it. I wish he had made a note of his primary evidence.

Did Selim usurp the Ottoman linage?

The competition between the Catholic Church, the Holy Roman Empire under the Habsburgs, the Kingdom of France, the German Protestant overlords, Safavid Persia, and the Ottomans for leading the entire world in the correct faith was heating up.

Holding the global balance were two rival Muslim leaders who had each made a contract with the Jewish God for the supreme rule of the world. To that end, each had proclaimed a caliphate. Suleiman was portrayed as *'a divinely ordained sultan and caliph who presides over the Ottoman realm with perfect justice and as a ruler who reigns over both spiritual and temporal realms.'*[567] He was *'battling the forces of evil and claiming supremacy over both, Muslims and Christians.'*[568]

The entire world was in agreement: the End of the World had begun.

The Magnificent married a 'concubine' from whom his heir would be born. For this, the ruler passed over another wife who had given him his first son. His concubine wife by the name of Roxelana is of particular interest to the progression of the history of this messianic time.

These guys were famous for their harems that calmed their immense appetites. They did not easily fall for the temptations of lay love. Yet, a contemporary report turns a concubine among so many into the Magnificent's *'most beloved wife.'* She received the title 'Haseki Sultan,' expressing 'exclusivity.'

The others? They meant nothing.

---

[566] Talmud - Mas. Sanhedrin 97b.
[567] Şahin, Süleyman, 2013, 57.
[568] Ibid., 187.

The report claims that she was kidnapped into slavery from her land.[569]

Suleiman's name translates to Solomon, the father of King David; he was literally the pontiff of Muslims; keenly aware of his royal and religious duties, he restored the Temple Mount in Jerusalem.

And we are made to believe that Suleiman was ***not*** careful which mother would carry his heir?

Rest assured that whatever the Catholic feudal system could do with its intermarriages, Muslim Ottomans could do even better.[570]

The story of his two wives comes across as a modified retelling of Abraham's Hagar and Sarah wherein the true firstborn is also passed over in favor of a 'legitimate' Jewish mother.

By default, historians assign her to be Russian Orthodox Christian.[571]

However, with narrowly defined exceptions, Christian priests were not accustomed to children. At least, not without the scandal of having produced a bastard, as they cursed those born out of wedlock.

The girl was unusually well educated. She could read and write. This was at a time when Christians were on the illiterate end of society. Certainly laity and slaves. Jews were generally educated. She became Suleiman's chief advisor and influenced his foreign policy. Roxelana was a Renaissance Secretary of State. Her building projects speak a fairly clear language: she was not Christian.

She originated from the Ukrainian town Rohatyn, and that led to her nickname, 'Roxelana', literally *'the Ruthenian one.'* There, she was captured and brought to a center of the slave trade.

Rohatyn lies approximately forty miles distant from Lviv (Lwow in modern-day Ukraine). The latter city was an important center of Ultra-Orthodox Karaite Judaism. This is the kind that was favored by Elijah Mizrachi, the one sitting on the Ottoman Throne of David. Judaism in Lviv goes back 600 years before Luther. As much as half of its population are believed to have been Karaite Jews. In Rohatyn itself, their presence is verified from the mid-fifteenth century.

---

[569] Mikhalon Lytvyn, De moribus tartarorum, lituanorum et moscorum (on the customs of Tatars, Lithuanians and Moscovians), ca. 1548–1551, in Galina Yermolenko, Roxolana: The Greatest Empresse of the East (DeSales University, 2005).

[570] The idea of slaves ending up under the marital wings of the highest authority should put historians on alert. It occurred repeatedly throughout history, in particular in the court of Prophet Muhammad.

[571] Samual Twardowski (+1661), in Thomas Conley, The Speech of Ibrahim at the Coronation of Maximilian II (Rhetorica: A Journal of the History of Rhetoric, 2001) Vol. 20, No., 266, as quoted in Kemal H. Karpat, Studies on Ottoman Social and Political History: Selected Articles and Essays, (Brill, 2002) 756.

The slave girl's real name was Anastasja Lisowska. That is a Jewish name.[572]

The legends of war tend to be complicated but also liberating. Old baggage could be repacked as new, in particular when the baggage was inconvenient.

Going by the pattern of the emerging design, Roxelana was the daughter of the high priest in the Hasidic Karaite lineage.

Ultra-Orthodox Jewish – Russian Orthodox.

She was not some pretty girl that was picked up on the streets of Rohatyn, which today is in western Ukraine.

She carried the seed of Moses' sister, the symbol of Temple and Covenant.

In the role as Suleiman's wife, Roxelana – the Temple mother – legitimized Ottoman rule beyond man's imagination. She literally was the carrier of the Spirit of God, the Christ, similar to the story of Mary in the Koran.

She gave birth to the next Mahdi – the Messiah – from the Muslim seed of the Redeemer of Jerusalem. For this, one crucial prerequisite is necessary: the lineages of the House of David and Joseph. Nobody in the Sunni Muslim world could dispute the rule of the Magnificent's son by Roxelana.

There was somebody worthy of capturing.

Why not talk about it then? Because in the upper strata, the game is about supremacy, not faith. Suleiman was the Muslim chief, and some secrets to the foundation of their power are better kept to the priestly and royal inner circle.

I can only imagine the betrayal that Muslims would feel if that were public knowledge. How would they square their Jewish leadership with the Koran's command to abuse Jews?

Both the Sunni and Shi'ite Muslim imamate knew exactly what the implications were. Perhaps the French knew as well. They claimed her ancestry to be theirs.[573]

That is how important this slave girl was.

Undercover.

By default, *we* want to know what is happening on the Temple Mount.

Back then, those who left for Italy contributed to a massive brain gain of Greek knowledge for the Renaissance. For Christians who stayed in the city, this defeat signified fulfillment of prophecy. It was an apocalyptic sign of the End

---

[572] Warszawa Archives project.
[573] Joseph de Hammer, Histoire de l'Empire Ottoman (The Athenaeum, 1837) 599.

of the World.[574] Deviating from mainstream thinking, the modern historian Kaya Şahin analyzed period works and found a fusion of Byzantine and Islamic apocalyptic thinking. The conquest of Constantinople was viewed as a sign of the Last Hour.

But to provide for its religious importance, a tradition[575] claims that Prophet Muhammad had pledged to glorify the one commander who would manage to conquer Constantinople.[576] Moreover, the conquest of the Byzantine capital took place thirty-nine years before the 7,000th year of Creation, as calculated by the Byzantine Christian timetable. The 7,000th year of Creation was also to be the last.

The Byzantines were convinced that the reign of the Antichrist – the Ottoman ruler – had arrived. *The scholar and clergyman Gennadios Scholarios, the first Ottoman-anointed Orthodox patriarch, provided the readers of his Chronographia with this crucial information,*[577] he *"consoled himself and his flock with the thought that they did not have long to suffer."*[578]

Muslims had to prepare for the final battles against the *'Blond Peoples.'* These were associated with the Habsburg leadership of the Holy Roman Empire.

Messianic aspirations under Suleiman the Magnificent were not new, but they reached a new level of insanity.

The Ottoman ruler lived under a spell from on high to conquer Rome, then understood as the Holy Roman Empire. All this is not original. It perpetually recurred despite the 'fact' that Muslim tradition upholds that only God knows the timing of the End of the World.

What was novel, though, was a carefully engineered Sunni Ottoman ideology of Islam.

Martin Luther's buddy, Philipp Melanchthon, one of the fathers of Lutheranism, asserted that Ottoman-Turks were Red Jews, one of the Ten Lost Tribes of Judaism. I will get to those later. Indeed, several of the early Turkish tribes that arrived in Anatolia had ridden under the banner of the Star of David.[579] Ottoman leaders used this symbol in mosques and on coins.

---

[574] Kaya Şahin, Constantinople and the End Time: The Ottoman Conquest as a Portent of the Last Hour (Journal of Early Modern History 14, Copyright © 2010, reprinted by permission of Brill) 318.

[575] The authoritative Sunni traditions of al-Bukhari and abu Muslim do not mention Constantinople. The tradition was likely fabricated by Ottoman leaders for themselves.

[576] Şahin, End Time, 2010, 319.

[577] Ibid., 323. For the Greek text and a French translation see Congourdeau, Byzance et la fin du monde, 74-97.

[578] Hanak, Some Historiographical Observations, 43-4, in Şahin, End Time, 2010, 323.

[579] Isfendiyarids, Karamanids, Teke (and therefore also the Hamidids).

Its usage is explained away as popular blue six-edged stars, the Seal of Solomon, because Islam regards this Jewish king as a prophet.

This merits a reality check: the Koran commands Muslims to hate Jews. And they do. Ever since their pious foundation and forever. Yet, they did not recognize that their decoration was the symbol of those most hated? With all the evidence at hand, the interpretation for the seal appears to constitute an excuse for burying the ongoing role of Judaism in Islam.

The obvious defies consensus! No religious leader would mistake the Star of David – the primary symbol of Judaism – for the Muslim 'Seal of Solomon.'

Not even if painted pink. Not then. Not now. Not ever.[580]

Besides, David is even more of a prophet in the Koran than Solomon.[581] Islam attributes the Psalms of David as divine revelation.

Instead, we will later see that a Jewish captain rode under the 'Seal of Solomon.' In addition, Muslims recognize the sign of the false Messiah in this seal.

There exists a piece of evidence that should overthrow all doubt about the Jewish messianism in the Ottoman palace but is generally ignored. With this, it is revealed that Suleiman the Magnificent himself believed in the folly of the Mahdi – or he intentionally created the appearance thereof. What do you think could be the name of his first-born son by the 'Russian Orthodox' slave wife Roxelana?

Şehzade Mehmed – Muhammad, the Mahdi.

That Suleiman named his son Mehmed – the Turkish form of Muhammad – was not by mere accident. According to apocalyptic Ottoman beliefs at the time, a young man by the name of Muhammad would be ruler during end times.[582]

His true objective was to capture Rome and all the lands of the Blond Peoples in a holy war (ghaza).[583]

Although this belief had been used to legitimize an earlier Ottoman ruler,[584] Suleiman renewed the projection of apocalyptic prophecy onto his son.

---

[580] Some churches are also decorated with the Star of David. It is supposed to represent the star of Creation. It can be found more often on Greek Orthodox churches, in particular in the Balkan, less so on Catholic churches.

[581] Koran 6:84-6:87 (Rodwell).

[582] DM/Kaptein,553, in Şahin, End Time, 2010, 347.

[583] Şahin, End Time, 2010, 349.

[584] Mehmed II.

But for this, Suleiman would need to be obsessed with his religion – or with abusing it.

The sultan was also a renowned poet. Here you have it. In his own words:

> *The people think of wealth and power as the greatest fate,*
> *But in this world a spell of health is the best state.*
> *What men call sovereignty is a worldly strife and constant war;*
> *Worship of God is the highest throne, the happiest of all estates.*[585]

Just how much this meant for Suleiman and the caste that enabled his power, was explained by Khaldun, a great and generally respected Islamic scholar of the fourteenth century: the Mahdi will *'rule over the whole earth.'*[586]

Suleiman the Magnificent became the most formidable enemy of Christianity.

The dream was – is – to annihilate the world and enslave it to Islam.

The mysterious maternal lineage is not limited to the Magnificent's wife. It extends through the matrilineal ancestry of several Ottoman-Turkish sultans. It may reach back at least to the conquest of Constantinople in 1453.

The pattern can be found even further back. Out of Baghdad we have the 'slave' girl Sayyida Banafsha.[587] She was brought to the harem of the Abbasid Caliph,[588] himself successor to the before described Jewish Caliph with the parallel Throne of David in the late twelfth century.

The girl rose from 'favorite' consort to be his wife. She failed to give him a boy. What is up with her? She just so happens to be the founder of one of the four major Sunni schools of Islamic jurisprudence, the Hanbali school. A Temple mother.

Her replacement from the harem and mother of the next Jewish Caliph was Zumurrud Khatun.[589] Supposedly, she was a Turkish slave. Devoutly religious, she was involved in the first wife's Hanbali school project. The name of her son? Ahmad[590] – a mahdi. There is more to these harems than pretty girls.

This is not random.

---

[585] Suleiman the Magnificent in Phillip Mansel, Constantinople: City of the World's Desire, 1453–1924 (St. Martin's Griffin, 1998) 84.

[586] Khaldun, *Muqaddimah, 1377*, transl. Rosenthal, 1958, Chapter III.31.

[587] Banafsha bint Abdullah al-Rumiyyah +1201 AD.

[588] Abu Muhammad Hasan ibn Yusuf al-Mustanjid aka al-Mustadi 1142-1180 AD, r. 1170-1180 AD.

[589] Sayyida Zumurrud Khatun aka Umm Nasir +1203 AD.

[590] Abū al-ʿAbbās Aḥmad ibn al-Hasan al-Mustaḍiʾ aka al-Nāṣir li-Dīn Allāh aka al-Nasir 1158-1225 AD, r. 1180-1225 AD.

Suleyman and Roxelana also had a daughter, Mihrimah Sultan. Aaron's and Moses' sister was Miriam. The design included the all-important next generation Temple mother. She would become the wife of the future Grand Vizier Rüstem Pasha – on the Throne of David.

In 1521, Suleiman conquered Belgrade, stoking terror in the superstitious Europeans. Christians literally saw the End of the World approaching. The battlefields were described as the Day of Judgment. Everybody expected that this terminal event would bring about the fall of Rome.

For Suleiman, it was a victory over unbelief and a comfort to the souls of his ancestors. He fulfilled his duty to engage in holy war.[591]

The beast of Doomsday prophecy was knocking on every door.

Indeed, Suleiman was determined to sack Hungary in order to prepare for further conquests into the European continent, which was divided across two major fault lines. The German-speaking areas formed the core of the Holy Roman Empire, which would partially fall to Luther, or rather bleed to the Protestant Church. At its east was the empire's kingdom of Bohemia and the nations in between the world powers, Poland and Hungary. The latter was now unsettled by Ottomans. Italy, Spain, Portugal, and much of the rest of Europe were the large areas subject to continued oppression by the Catholic Church through its terrorist arm, the Inquisition.

To the west of the Holy Roman Empire lay French Catholic France. It stood on its own and was unwilling to submit to the Holy Roman Empire or the Catholic Church in Rome, unless it could control pope and emperor.

Since the French-friendly Medici Pope Leo X would die that year, that prospect was soon to be in jeopardy once more.

Now that Jerusalem was open for business to Jews and with Roxelana's presence, the dedication of the Temple was merely a small step away.

The Temple is the dwelling place of God.

Its seizure is critical for the fulfillment of prophecy.

To let you in on a secret: if enough people believe in a future folly, it can become a self-fulfilling prophecy. A similar process has been repeated many times through two millennia. Were we to learn the lessons, we would be able to do better next time. Unfortunately, organized religion has a vested interest in

---

[591] Tabakat, 63a, 65a–b, in Şahin, Süleyman, 2013, 204.

covering up how their organizations have repeatedly endangered the entire human race in order to follow up on prophecy.

Due to our ignorance, the messianic failure keeps on fulfilling itself.

There is another ingredient.

Because their belief system renders them guests whenever Jews live outside of Israel, they have developed a collective trait that most other religious groups do not have: they do not build on permanence but on mobility. They are preppers, always ready to pack up to head for Jerusalem.

They are well prepared to respond to a calamity to ensure their survival. This factor has had an effect on their wealth.

By necessity to protect their mobile fortunes, they invented practically every financial instrument that was in use at the time. They were able to 'wire' large sums from one corner of the planet to another without ever touching a single coin.

The academic consensus runs along this line: While Jews are in the Diaspora, where they typically do well, something is needed to make them feel unhappy in order for the second condition to emerge: a revolt followed by a persecution; or the loss of too many Jews to humanist thought; or doctrinal infighting; or something similar. Sometimes they do so well that the non-Jewish population becomes suspicious that Jews are being parasites, in particular where they were in charge of administrations. Then hosts bring out fists and stones in order to make living for Jews miserable.

To address the unhappy state of host and 'parasite' under one roof, a forerunner needs to appear to proclaim the Redemption of Israel, the signal to go 'home.' This messenger announces the coming of the Messiah, the Redeemer of Israel.

The consensus is kosher baloney.

If you wish, you can always find something to fret about, individually or collectively. Sometimes you do not know about your acute state of unhappiness until someone, perhaps a Rabbinic leader, tells you about your dire state of gloom.

Let us go and conquer the Promised Land. Instead, the drive to grab the land and Temple Mount is permanent. Logically, the appearance of messiahs is endless until all things are fulfilled.

It is even worse than that. Because it violates the biblical promises and commands when they are not rulers, messianic leaders are perpetually unhappy wherever they are not in charge. This is particularly precarious when the leading family brings forth competing leaders who strive for the same thrones.

The Messiah cannot be just any ordinary Jew. He has to be from the royal Hasmonean bloodline and be approved by the Sanhedrin, which itself needs to be re-established by the god of the Israelites. Its constitution opens the gates to the End Times.[592] The former chief rabbi from Tlemcen, Jacob Berab, was just one of those working on unlocking the doors.

The Messiah needs to carry his and the Sanhedrin's message through the synagogues to the top rabbis of each nation.

Without the support of the Divine Assembly and the synagogues, any aspirant to become a messiah gains no traction.

After all, failure in 'certifying' a messiah has ended in death.[593]

It may be true that messiahs typically had their biggest impact in times of trouble. That is by design.

But when was there not a time of turmoil?

All religious participants, Jews, Catholics, Protestants, and Muslims, based their messianic ideas on the same foundation at exactly the same time. The difference is merely in evolutionary steps, where one would not accept an additional messiah approved by another.

I am not sure whether it is possible to put this in dark enough terms:

They all had the same expectations about the arrival of the Messiah during Martin Luther's lifetime. They were all determined to destroy the others in order to end up as the occupants and leaders of an ethnically-cleansed, righteous utopia – at the expense of everybody else and the total destruction of the world.

Yet, there is another messianic factor, which is perhaps the most important of all. Since it is generally overlooked and willfully misinterpreted, it will come across as fantasy at first.

It lies at the heart of religious fracturing and its violent evolution: the Messiah needs to find partners in leaders of other sects and religions.

One was already in the bag: Suleiman the Magnificent and his Temple wife Roxelana with the Mahdi son.

---

[592] Isiah 1:26.
[593] See Talmud - Mas. Sanhedrin 93b.

Abrabanel's beginning of the Messianic Age in 1531 was less than a decade out. They had to get going in a hurry.

Again, Jewish inventors of messianism were smart and understood that they could not go it alone. After all, Jews are a minority. While the end game is the conquest of the Promised Land and the rule of the world, the strategy includes a 'return' to the 'original' faith of Adam, or Abraham, or whichever biblical point the Messiah and his henchmen in the Sanhedrin may choose.

In its wake, it creates a new, perhaps ecumenical religion, or a new sect under a new law, if we prefer to think so.[594] A new covenant.

In the book of *'the Martyrdom of Bartholomew,'* Jesus was called *'the second Adam.'*[595] The Koran is explicit in calling for the return to the religion of Abraham.[596] It also contains several passages about Muslims having to prostrate to Adam, which all did, except for the devil.[597]

Adam's divinity could be worth another millennium of world wars.

The ritual of bowing down is one of the most visible prostrations when men and women kneel down with their heads to the ground and the hands turned upward, leaving the worshiper in a position of utter defenselessness and unconditional obedience.

In fact, bowing to Adam is the only prostration that the Koran proscribes.

The Muslim prostration is the most objectionable position of submission to modern organized religion.[598] It symbolizes the willingness of believers to forfeit all their freedoms to their religious intercessors.

In this position, they are, indeed, mentally and physically defenseless.

Incapacitated.

It is this new religion, not Judaism, that would seize the Temple Mount at Jerusalem.

It is the moment of reckoning to a perfect treachery, where it turns out that only two can be the leaders: a supreme spiritual Sadducee messiah of the House of Joseph and a sword-wielding messiah of the House of Judah.

---

[594] For example, this is attested to in Jeremiah 31:31-31:33 (NIV).

[595] Book of the Martyrdom of Bartholomew (ca. 500 AD), translated by Alexander Walker. From *Ante-Nicene Fathers*, Vol. 8, edited by Alexander Roberts, James Donaldson, and A. Cleveland Coxe (Christian Literature, 1886). Revised and edited for New Advent by Kevin Knight.

[596] Koran 16:124 (Rodwell).

[597] Koran 38:71-38:74 (Rodwell).

[598] The Catholic Church features an even more extreme version where priests lie flat on the belly with all extremities spread out wide.

It is so prophesied!

This is how Suleiman the Magnificent contextualized Jerusalem in his possession.

Nothing in the world made him surrender the Temple Mount to anyone.

## The Rapture

We still need to investigate how the forces of good and evil will clash at the End of the World and what it means when they do. For this, we will find out what this event spelled for the different parties: Jews who wanted to go 'home' to rule; Christians who were entering into a religious war under Luther's watch; and Muslims who were threatening Europe's borders.

Not only did they all share their longing for the End of the World, but they all did so at this very point in history.

At this watershed episode of history stood two Medici popes, Europe's royals who were in bed with the Vatican, the magnificent Ottoman Caliph Suleiman, the rebel friar Martin Luther with his separatist German overlords, and, we shall not forget, messianic Jews.

Here, the passing of the old and the emerging of the new were defined: the vision of a New Jerusalem that would bring about life in plenty for very few survivors.

Not for you.

In Jewish eschatology (the scholarly term for describing the end time events), the Messiah needs to come no later than the year 6000 AM[599] of the Jewish calendar or 2240 of the Christian time scale.

That gives humanity anywhere from no time to roughly 200-and-some years[600] to prepare for the avoidance of the next holocaust.

We should not belittle the danger that Jews are in. As time progresses, the urge to hasten the arrival of the Messiah will only increase. Since they pretend to have rejected all messiahs who had so far come, Jews are now at the tail end of the period when prophecy *must* be fulfilled in one way or another. If not, the whole Jewish house of cards will fall apart.

In a hurry, people tend to be prone to mistakes.

---

[599]   Talmud – Mas. Rosh Hashana 31a, Talmud – Mas. Sanhedrin 97a.

[600]   The year 2017 is 5777 AM, which started October 2, 2016. It is 223 years to 6000 AM.

In Christianity, there is no such timetable. Christians have been believing since the early days of their religion – so they claim – that the End of the World could happen any day.[601]

Muslims are living through Judgement today.

The authors of the Koran must have thought of the signs as in the past.[602] Indeed, like early Jews and Christians, the first Muslims expected the End of the World to be imminent in their lifetime, a thousand years before Luther. At least, they were hedging their bets, because only their god would know the specifics about its timing.

—— The secret was to be closely guarded and only be revealed to God's Apostle,[603] in our case to Suleiman the Magnificent and his Mahdi son.

The rapture is the day of resurrection of the dead.

The living dead are the warriors for the final war.

But before we go to battle, we would like to know what awaits us on the other side. What are the rewards for dedicating our lives to hastening the End of the World?

Early on in the Bible, the words from the god of the Israelites contain the prototype vision of what will happen after the End of the World in the New Jerusalem: easy food, no sickness, no miscarriages, and a full life span for everybody.[604] This idea was tied to the successful conquest of the Promised Land, provided that all Jews submitted to their god unconditionally. In effect, it was the End of the World for everybody else. Once they arrived in Jerusalem, they could expect a long and healthy life in plenty.

For free. No efforts are required.

But that is not what they got after the few occasions when they actually did grab the land. They bought into a promise that was impossible to fulfill.

Almost every prophecy that addressed the coming End of the World expanded on this prototype. The underlying idea of the Bible is that the Chosen People return to the Promised Land and come to dominate the world. It is a time of salvation for those who accepted the Truth of the god of the Israelites.

The same event is for punishment of those who believe differently or those who are free from belief.

---

[601] Matthew 24:36 (NIV).
[602] Koran 47:20 (Rodwell).
[603] Koran 72:25-72:27 (Rodwell).
[604] Exodus 23:23ff.

For them, a massacre awaits.

The most popular of the Jewish prophecies about what to expect can be found in a short passage in the book of Isaiah:

> *On this mountain [the Temple Mount] the Lord Almighty will prepare a feast of rich food for all peoples, a banquet of aged wine – the best of meats and the finest of wines.*
> *On this mountain he will destroy the shroud that enfolds all peoples, the sheet that covers all nations; he will swallow up death forever.*
> *The Sovereign Lord will wipe away the tears from all faces; he will remove the disgrace of his people from all the earth.*[605]

Imagine this text being read to congregations in synagogues around the world today. It suggests to the audience that they are part of a disgraced people – still at times when there is no sign of such disgrace.

Even though it is now in the utopia of the New Jerusalem, the prophecy's hatred of mankind ramps up.

The Moabites stand for everybody who opposes the Israelite conquest of the Promised Land.

> *This is the Lord, we trusted in him; let us rejoice and be glad in his salvation.*
> *The hand of the Lord will rest on this mountain; but Moab will be trampled under him as straw is trampled down in the manure.*
> *They will spread out their hands in it, as a swimmer spreads out his hands to swim.*
> *God will bring down their pride despite the cleverness of their hands.*
> *He will bring down your high fortified walls and lay them low; he will bring them down to the ground, to the very dust.*

It is not enough to be saved and fed for free at a banquet. Right away, the trampling upon others must begin. Rabbinic leaders call this 'world peace.'

Such is the condition of modern Palestinians.

However, to achieve their goals in Jerusalem, Jews had to meet all conditions of their god. He, God, thought of them as a corrupt and rebellious brood of evildoers.[606] He called them murderers, cheaters, and companions of thieves who love bribes and who neglect their social responsibilities.[607] He regarded them as cowards who run away from their responsibilities in war times.[608]

---

[605] Isaiah 25:6-25:8.
[606] Isaiah 1:4 (NIV).
[607] Isaiah 1:21-1:23.
[608] Isaiah 22:2-22:3 (NIV).

Where could the stereotypes about Jews in Luther's sermons possibly have come from? The Jewish text is prototyping anti-Semitism – unto itself. It opens the door for everyone who repeats these texts to be branded anti-Semitic. And this might be the point of the exercise that describes character traits that, as far we have by now learned, cannot be dismissed offhand in the context of the behavior of the Jewish leadership.

For thousands of years, it has put almost everybody on the defensive.

Then the god of the Israelites reinforced his promises and warned what he would be prepared to do to get relief from Jewish evildoers.

First, the god of the Israelites brought in a big stick and beat everybody down until he was sure of their trembling in fear. All non-compliant Jews were 'impurities' that had to be removed. They can be crossed off the list of those who will live on.

This wrathful termination spree by God concerns everybody, except for a few Ultra-Orthodox Jews, to be precise.

Then he went about promising betterment and establishing the righteous city of faith.[609]

In today's numbers, still, the god of the Israelites was talking in no uncertain terms about more than a billion corpses from those who were free from religion alone and about more than ten million Jews.

It is a curious but important detail that the Sanhedrin (the Jewish supreme court of judges) needs to be 'reinstated' for the Messiah to be successful.

In order to be re-established by the god of the Israelites, the Sanhedrin must 'officially' *not exist* before the End Times. Without this revival, there will be no show. Not surprisingly, this is a theme that re-occurs with messianism.

They thought they could get away with running the Sanhedrin in secret.

Undercover.

Did their god not see that Jewish leaders were trying to betray even their own almighty?

Now that we have this clarified, the book of Isaiah reveals the full extent of Jewish aspirations: world domination.

---

[609] Isaiah 1:25-1:28 (NIV).

*The Lord will have compassion on Jacob; once again he will choose Israel and will settle them in their own land.*

*Aliens will join them and unite with the house of Jacob.*

*Nations will take them and bring them to their own place.*

*And the house of Israel will possess the nations as maidservants in the Lord's land.*

*They will make captives of their captors and ruler over their oppressors.*[610]

The preferred lineage in Isaiah is that of Jacob (the one that had betrayed Esau). The text contains the biblical proscription to form alliances. The alliance itself will carry them to settle their own land, as the Bible calls it.

Then the allies will be betrayed into oppression.

To gather on the Temple Mount serves as a signal that the world rule by Jewish leaders begins. This, in turn, fosters in an age of peace – peace under a single-minded theocratic Truth of Judaism[611] – brought about by killing everybody else.

To be sure that this is understood properly, this world leadership includes every country without exceptions. Any nation that does not allow Jewish leaders to rule with the god of the Israelites oppresses them.

The aspiration of becoming part of the world's ruling family appears to be a strong motivating factor to cling to the religion of Judaism and to raise children to the same extreme purpose.

Envision if it were to succeed.

Imagine if this were the mindset that persists today. If it is, the human race is in trouble.

Indeed, we are.

All others who disagree with the grandeur can, as Moses did, require that the god of the Israelites show itself.[612]

But they must insist, and not be persuaded by miracles that serve only to distract.

Scholars will protest that *not* world domination is meant, but universal acceptance of the god of the Israelites. Of course, villains do not want their plot to be known in advance. Besides, the invalid argument makes no difference. Certainly not for all the dead who were free from religion, were adherents of competing religions, or disobedient Jews.

---

[610] Isaiah 14:1-14:2 (NIV).

[611] Isaiah 2:2-2:5 (NIV).

[612] Koran 2:139-2:140 (Rodwell).

There seems to be good reason to be opposed to this partial kind of Judaism.

It should have dawned on believers after the first unexpected heads rolled on the ground while living in utopia that the promises may not hold water.

They did not worship the god of the Israelites enough.

The Christian version is similar to the one for Judaism with free food and drinks, but in *eternal* life.

The Muslim utopia is distinctly Persian.

> *Surely, among delights shall the righteous dwell!*
> *Seated on bridal couches they will gaze around;*
> *Thou shalt mark in their faces the brightness of delight;*
> *Choice sealed wine shall be given them to quaff,*
> *The seal of musk. For this let those pant who pant for bliss —*
> *Mingled therewith shall be the waters of Tasnim [the river in Paradise] —*
> *Fount whereof they who draw nigh to God shall drink.*[613]

Paradise is a place where their god provides for everything. The bridal couch represents the palaces of princes from where they can *'gaze around'* and reel in girls and global subjects as they wish. The Bible and Koran[614] speak almost the same language about what paradise might look like: *'a land flowing with milk and honey.'*[615]

Similar to Christians who find eternal life in heaven, Muslims believe in literally staying alive forever in paradise. In the end, only the words are different. Meaning and function of the New Jerusalem, Paradise for Muslims, are virtually the same as in Judaism and Christianity with some insignificant deviations in their legends.

It is curious that the glorification of poverty in Islam and Christianity (and the prohibition of alcohol for Muslims) in this life should bring about riches and a fountain of liquor in the next – without cutting a sweat, of course.

However, the Koran expands its interpretation in a significant way. It explains that Muslims, Jews, Christians, and Sabeites have nothing to fear. They will be free of the grief as expressed in the Bible and the Gospels.

There are a few conditions, though: they have to submit to God, do 'right', and believe in the End of the World with its climax on the Last Day.[616]

---

[613] Koran 83:22-83:30.
[614] Koran 47:16 (Rodwell).
[615] Exodus 3:8.
[616] Koran 2:59 (Rodwell).

We should grasp by now that doing 'right' and the Last Day come with a lot of baggage.

The end is terminal, either way.

On Judgment Day, believers – the dead ones, that is – will resurrect.

The theme of resurrection and life after death came to prominence first in the Hebrew Bible,[617] giving Prophet Elijah the power to bringing the dead back to life.[618] This prophet was also the first to be brought to heaven.[619] The prototype legend evolved into a concept wherein humans in general go up to heaven. There, the god of the Israelites watches over the living and the dead.

The idea of Judgment Day is later expanded in the Bible to the day that brings destruction for infidels[620] and a New Jerusalem for believers. Success for this victory is promised through a phenomena of mass resurrections[621] that will raise entire armies.[622]

The most famous resurrection of all times is that of Jesus Christ, three days after his death.

I have already spoken about the lack of independent confirmation of this earth-shattering event. It is not entirely impossible, of course, that only insiders took notice. After all, the Gospel says so. But there is the willfully ignored 'fact' in the Gospel that the resurrection of Jesus Christ was not isolated.

The text lays claim to the resurrection of an entire band of dead guys who walked in the midst of Jerusalem.[623]

The Gospel claims that Roman guards were terrified.

The shock of seeing the resurrected holy men would have frightened the hell out of everyone in and around Jerusalem. The news would have travelled to Rome as fast as the wind could have carried it.

Not so. Nothing.

The 'evidence' of the power of the god of the Israelites over Jesus' and the others' corpses has only one source: the Gospels.

Thousands of witnesses remained silent.

---

[617]  1 Kings 17:17.
[618]  1 Kings 17:22.
[619]  2 Kings 2:1.
[620]  Ezekiel 7:3.
[621]  In more subtle form, the motif of resurrection was introduced earlier (Isaiah 26:19, for example) and would henceforth be exploited.
[622]  Ezekiel 37:9–10.
[623]  Matthew 27:51-27:53 (NIV).

That *the* miracle of all ages – the mass-resurrection – is not supported by an abundance of contemporary testimonies is, well, a miracle. First among the absentees was the Jewish traitor historian Josephus. He was born just a few years after his parents must have personally witnessed an uproar like none before.

The resurrection is the central tenet of Christianity, so much so that if there were no resurrection, then not even Jesus Christ was raised.[624] If the latter were the case, then all Christian preaching and faith is useless.[625] So says Saint Paul,[626] the most important figure of the Apostolic Age,[627] who allegedly authored almost half of the New Testament.

The second most famous resurrection is proscribed in the Koran. Prophet Muhammad is expected to return as the Mahdi.[628] His reappearance is accompanied by whole armies of the un-dead.

After the rapture, Christians and Muslims go to the Kingdom of Heaven or to paradise. Infidels head for hell, where Satan awaits the wicked. This is similar in the Hebrew Bible, where the dead awake to either everlasting life or everlasting shame.[629] For Christians, the only way to evade hell at the End of the World is through believing in Jesus Christ. Only through him are people given eternal life in the Kingdom of Heaven.

These are truly grand promises[630] by all three Judaic religions. Not just life in plenty and without worries but *eternal* life. And it was meant in the sense of never dying or being reawakened to everlasting life.

The Bible says so.[631] The New Testament says so.[632] The Koran says so.[633]

The Bible even established communications between the dead and the living.[634]

---

[624]  1 Corinthians 15:13 (NIV).
[625]  1 Corinthians 15:14 (NIV).
[626]  Saint Paul aka Saul of Tarsus aka Paul the Apostle (ca. 5 – ca. 67) was *not* among the Twelve Apostles of Jesus Christ. After the resurrected Jesus appeared to Paul, Ananias of Damascus appears to have sent him on a mission to preach that Jesus Christ was the Jewish Messiah.
[627]  The Apostolic Age is the period of the Twelve Apostles of Jesus Christ.
[628]  Koran 39:32 (Rodwell).
[629]  Daniel 12.2.
[630]  John 3:14–18.
[631]  Job 33:29-33.30, Daniel 12.2.
[632]  John 8:51.
[633]  The afterlife is one of the six pillars of Muslim beliefs. It is perpetually referred to in the Koran.
[634]  1 Samuel 28:3-28.20.

The books that consistently do *not* say so are those in the Torah, the first five books of the Bible. Accordingly, we find one group that rejects both, the resurrection as well as eternal life: the Sadducees of the House of Joseph, better known as Samaritans.

The Sadducee pretention is particularly interesting in light of their bond with Egyptian mythologies of resurrection and afterlife. Perhaps the most popular myth is the story of Isis and Osiris. The latter was resurrected through the power of his severed phallus. Golden as it was, it helped to conceive their son Horus.

Greeks imagined the resurrection of Attis and others. They were big fans of achieving physical immortality through resurrections.

Whether you may be Jewish, Christian, Muslim, of another religion, or free of religion, we can probably all agree that the Egyptian or Greek ideas about the resurrection and afterlife were purely mythical.

It never happened. Neither in Egypt nor in Greece. Not anywhere else.

However, the success of any religious sect did not actually depend on miracle men. Instead, it was determined by its capability to divide and rule. It needed to seek its roots in the deeply ingrained beliefs and rituals of the religious establishment. Preferably, they sought to oppose religious excess, corruption, and the costliest parts of their rituals.

Luther demonstrated the pattern for us.

In ancient Egypt, the target was the resurrection and afterlife that had at first been a privilege of the pharaohs. For the populace, this was a desirable state of royal existence, but it was also the source of their doom through oppression and over-taxation. This is manifested in grand buildings that were meant to be the gates to the afterlife but were otherwise economically all-consuming without a productive purpose. The pyramids.

Opposing these and proposing lower taxation led to an increase in the power of a newcomer sect.

These were the Sadducees of old.

Their stance is unmasked through the survival of their ancient beliefs in their younger siblings: Judaism, Christianity, and Islam.

The Gospels help us to understand that these were indeed Sadducee Jews who denied the resurrection.[635] But it is not that straightforward, because the Koran accuses them of having pretended to accept the resurrection only to turn

---

[635] Acts 23:8.

around and then deny it again. For this, they deserved to be the inmates of hell.[636] Other than the Sadducees, some Karaite Jewish groups also rejected the resurrection, thereby revealing their kinship.

The only door to the afterlife is through the resurrection.

We have, hopefully, found common ground on the mythology of the Egyptian afterlife.

Why were Adam and Eve banned from the Garden of Eden?

The gods wanted to prevent them from eating from the tree of life. This would have given them *eternal* life, like the gods. The original rejection of eternal life and resurrection in the first five books of the Bible was consistent with the Sadducee's opposition to Egypt's divine royalty.

They simply wanted to climb the pharaohs' throne first to rule Egypt and then the world. Even though it remains a myth, eternal life was wisely denied to humanity by God himself.

The Sadducee priesthood knew to differ.

Here is an example from the Jewish version:

> But your dead will live; their bodies will rise. You who dwell in the dust, wake up
> and shout for joy. Your dew is like the dew of the morning; the earth will give birth
> to her dead.[637]

The resurrection constitutes the very moment of the rapture.

Judaism, Christianity, and Islam share a happy event that has never happened. Their god has a whole lot of divine and strong enemies that kept and keep on working against it, according to the biblical myth.

First and foremost, the god has to deal with Jews who refuse to follow it collectively to the letter.

As long as they do not *all* get in line, the rapture is not going to happen. Which means that it is never going to happen unless they kill *all* dissenters. They will attempt to do just that, meaning that it is still not going to happen if they miss just a single one.

The resurrection also bears no biblical logic that can ever find its resolution.

It does not need resolution. It needs only to serve as the continued source of religious power.

---

636  Koran 64:7 and 64:10.
637  Isiah 26:19.

Like Christians and Jews, Muslims have also reassigned the rapture to different times in the past, in particular to their founding story and to the invasion by the Mongols in the thirteenth century.

For them, it is the Day of Judgment, repetitively spoken about in the Koran to the point of nausea. Prophet Muhammad would be first to be resurrected, and right away, he would have to fight before God against his sectarian opponent.[638]

Suleiman the Magnificent literally believed in just this same folly. He brought the tale to life with his own seed. His son, Şehzade Mehmed, the Mahdi Muhammad, was now an infant.

A short sura in the Koran by the name *'The Resurrection'* sets the bar for Muslims even higher than for Jews and Christians. The moon needs to be eclipsed and the sun and moon brought together, which is when you have nowhere to hide.[639] They have a long list of signs that precede the rapture.

The outstanding feature of this particular sura is that it seems to parallel the book of Revelation, which is the last book of the New Testament. It engages with a heretic who seems not only to have rejected the idea of the resurrection but also to have walked away from the battlefield. It is almost as though the heretic lost patience and wanted to say, *'I am going home; you fooled me; there is no resurrection.'* The opponent thought of the new revelations as fables. The holy text of peace threatened that he would have to carry the burden of all those who he had misled on Judgement Day – in hell.[640]

Given the general intellectual poverty of Muslim fundamentalists, this engagement with an infidel is quite remarkable. The Koran struggled with a Judaic competitor who said that *'God will never raise him who once is dead.'*[641]

So should Muslim believers.

The Koran's authors were quite outspoken about what would happen to those in denial of the resurrection. It is a straight path to hell either by the judgment of God or, if the divinity were to continue its habit of doing nothing, by the imam.[642]

In the latter case, stoning awaits the thinker.

---

[638]   Koran 39:32 (Rodwell).
[639]   Koran 75:7 (Arberry).!
[640]   Koran 16:26-16:31 (Rodwell).
[641]   Koran 16:40-16:41.
[642]   Koran 22:8-22:11 (Rodwell).

In the koranic version of the rapture, much weight is put on the idea of judgement between believers and infidels in regard to their divisions, differences, and variances. While the others essentially exterminate those who refuse to accept the same Truth, the Koran repeatedly disguises it as a sectarian judgment.

Of course, the outcome is the same.

The authors of the Koran often lamented about insufficient belief and sectarian imposters. The Catholic Church and Martin Luther complained likewise about lack of belief and new sectarian sprouts.

As in Christianity, the opposing armies of the Koran are gathered from this unbelieving segment of the populations. As they approach God for judgement, they have no defense for having failed to embrace the divinity's merciful signs, so the Koran says.[643]

The godly signs for believers can be as simple as the very cycle of night and day.[644] Or monsters coming out of the ground when the rapture is at hand.[645]

The rapture will announce itself with a blast of a trumpet, the signal for all to gather for judgment before their god.[646] Then, you will see the mountains collapse in a cloud.[647] That day, the sun will rise in the west.[648]

Whoever did not believe before the miraculous evidence is presented cannot be saved.

The Koran is pretty blunt in its proclamation of the lowest standards of faith. Everything is faith. But that the rapture will indeed come, there can be no doubt. God will, absolutely, resurrect the dead.[649]

The **fear** is meant to be eternal, not the renewal of humanity or the universe through the End of the World.

---

[643]  Koran 27:85-27:88 (Rodwell).
[644]  Koran 27:89 (Rodwell).
[645]  Koran 27:84 (Rodwell).
[646]  Koran 27:89 (Rodwell).
[647]  Koran 27:90 (Rodwell).
[648]  Bukhari, 2007-2009, 8:76:513.
[649]  Koran 22:7 (Rodwell).

### *Monsters at War*

Now, it is time to go to war in order to sort out the Truth.

The Jewish version of the final war starts with a diatribe of curses and prophecies against every conceivable nation. The book of Isaiah is an enlightening lecture about the attitude of Judaism. It shows no tolerance for those outside of this organized religion. They are all arch enemies of Jews, and they do not deserve to live unless they submit to the god of the Israelites. *The earth will be completely laid waste and totally plundered,* [650] so the prophecy goes. God will punish the powers in heaven and the kings on earth. [651]

Their god will also come to *'slay the monster of the sea.'* [652]

The god of the Israelites will march itself against the enemies of the Jews in battle [653] from the *'flowing Euphrates to the Wadi of Egypt* [654] – the Promised Land.

The enemies were the great world powers.

Biblical prophecy can be assigned to anyone as Jewish leaders may please. During Martin Luther's time, these enemy world powers were the Ottoman Empire, the Holy Roman Empire, and the Catholic Church in Rome.

To bring about the successful End of the World, Jewish leaders need to provoke the world powers to go against each other in the Promised Land. And there are external signs to be watched out for. For example, the sun will go down at noon on that day, consequently bringing the entire celestial system into disarray. [655]

In Christianity and Islam, the place of the final battle is Armageddon. In Judaism, it is Jehoshaphat, [656] officially meaning *'Jehovah has judged'* or *'God has judged.'* It also means *'place of the rapture.'*

For all three religions, it is the place of judgement.

Jewish leaders would manipulate the world powers to show up at the place of judgement and then wait for their moment of grand treachery – as the laughing third.

This subversive strategy went wrong many times over.

---

650  Isaiah 24:3 (NIV).
651  Isaiah 24:21 (NIV).
652  Isaiah 27:1 (NIV).
653  Isaiah 27:4 (NIV).
654  Isaiah 27:12 (NIV).
655  Amos 8:9 (NIV).
656  Joel 3:2 (NIV).

It is in play – now!

For Christians, the world will be thrown into total chaos with earthquakes and family members killing each other for differing beliefs.[657]

When the time for punishment by God arrives, the believers will be urged to flee from the cities to avoid being imprisoned or killed by the surrounding enemy armies.[658]

When the Messiah finally arrives in a glorious cloud, the celestial bodies will be shaken and the seas stirred up.[659]

These predictions, Jewish, Christian, or Muslim, on how the End of the World will announce itself are so outlandish that their impossibility is obvious even to high schoolers. The most fundamental followers of any Judaic religion would probably retreat to the claim that these prophecies were not meant literally and that they could never happen as described. Exactly. They are myths, and that includes the Promised Land, the Chosen People, and just about everything else in scripture.

There is no biblical half-myth.

History tells us that there was indeed a great deal of flexibility when the outcome was potential success. Jewish leaders only took word-for-word what they pleased, as long as the end game was never lost to sight: ruling the world from the Temple Mount at Jerusalem.

This myth is in the sole service of the royal Hasmonean family. It is a tool of deceit, treachery, and manipulation to reach for the throne of world power.

Ordinary Jews are victims all the same.

In order to go to the final war, the Messiah will need an opponent worth fighting. In Christianity and Judaism, it is called the Antichrist. In Islam, the Mahdi will clash with the Masih ad-Dajjal, which is the false Messiah, loosely a synonym for the Antichrist.

The idea of an opponent who marches against the one who has been anointed by God originates in the Bible. It warns of false prophets, or one could say as Muslims do, of false messiahs. In essence, anyone who promotes gods other than the tribal divinity of the Israelites or no gods at all is a false prophet. Their spiritual enemies and their false teachings are regarded as satans or demons.

---

657 Luke 21:10-21:19 (NIV).
658 Luke 21:20-21:24 (NIV).
659 Luke 21:25-21:28 (NIV).

For believers, the mythical figures of satans or demons are worse than just dehumanizing opponents. They turn them into monsters. Of all the worst, satans and demons sit at the lowest level. They are the most frightening and dangerous creatures of all: evil cyborgs with super strengths but without emotion or compassion, out to kill and destroy, to tempt and to rape at will. If that does not help, whatever frightens believers most is associated with satans or demons.

Yet, attentive students of the Bible cannot miss that these negative features are also those that otherwise describe the deadly actions and wrathful character of God. Not only enemies of the Chosen People are in the line of fire of the Judaic divinity but also disobedient Jews.

Only the Antichrist is worse.

He is the terror-inducing evil boss who drinks the blood of children to gain more strength.

Historically, blood libel was a recurring accusation. It was raised from religions across the known world against its opponents. It was also a motif in the persecutions of Jews by the Catholic Church.[660]

As an example of such smear campaigns, the Roman Emperor Constantine the Great was reported to have taken a warm bath in the blood of innocent infants to heal his leprosy.[661]

The source for this atrocity is Christian.

Constantine neither suffered from this disease nor did he consider taking baths in children's blood. These are religious lies engineered with the purpose of repulsing a gullible, superstitious audience. The emperor's monstrosity dehumanized religious Pagans and turned them into brute beasts.

Christians simply used the same accusations that had before been brought against them. Their claim is that then-Pope Silvester came to the rescue to heal the emperor with baptism alone.[662]

A miracle.

Here is the real miracle: Constantine was supposedly also baptized by Eusebius – on his death bed![663]

---

[660] Jerome A. Chanes, Antisemitism: A Reference Handbook (ABC-CLIO, 2004) 34–45.

[661] From Zeumer's edition, published in Berlin in 1888, v. Brunner-Zeumer: "Die Constantinische Schenkungsurkunde," translated in Ernest F. Henderson, *Select Historical Documents of the Middle Ages* (London: George Bell, 1910), 319–29.

[662] Ibid.

[663] Isidore of Seville, 560–636 AD, Chronicon. English translation by Kenneth B. Wolf (Tertullian, 2004).

Without any witnesses.

Religious historians could neither agree on how Constantine turned out to be Christian nor by whom he was supposedly baptized. A little detail in the fine print is that Eusebius was an Arian Christian opponent of Western Christianity. They could not agree on the emperor's sectarian creed either. Best of all, Eusebius' single most important work of early Christianity rests largely on forgeries.

Without his works, practically all traces of early Christianity would cease to ever have existed.

The comparative approaches of the claims are tantamount to having the salesman of the holy water for Constantine's baptism accuse his competitors' holy water of being a worthless forgery.

How blood libel serves to enrage the gullible can be witnessed in a modern, non-spiritual context. In 2018, countless were killed in India over rumors about child kidnapping. The dead were the consequence of fake news that spread through social media.[664] The heinous accusations appealed to a core instinct of humanity to protect its children to the point where it overruled reality.

Throughout history, leaders of organized religion were aware of the consequences of such defamations. They weaponized them anyhow.

In the eyes of Christians, the Muslim Prophet Muhammad and his successors later became the focal point of the infant-blood sucking Antichrist.

Of course, Muslim tradition, too, is keenly aware of the Antichrist. It might turn out to be a one-eyed monster. From this then follows that there will be two antichrists shooting lightning rods and plague-diseased corpses at each other.

The acceptance of biological warfare in good old medieval style is all a matter of religious perspective.

According to the Bible, pretender messiahs were sent to test the followers' love of their god. They, the false ones, needed to be killed.[665] The earlier-discussed *'Sermon on the Mount'* lays out that false prophets appear as ferocious wolves in sheep's clothing.[666]

---

[664] Vindu Goel, Suhasini Raj, Priyadarshim Ravichandran, How WhatsApp Leads Mobs to Murder in India, New York Times, July 18, 2018.
[665] Deuteronomy 13:1-13:5.
[666] Matthew 7:15-7:23, see also Matthew 24:21-24:24.

Jesus himself confirmed his love of capital punishment for false prophets or messiah-pretenders in one of his concealed speeches.[667]

The difference between the Bible and the Gospel lies in the broken relationship of Jews with their god. As we already know, their supreme being had long abandoned them. Now, Christian intercessors claimed to be in charge of representing the god of the Israelites for humanity.

The true christ would make an entry with fanfare and glory.[668]

The Antichrist finds his simplistic Christian definition in the Gospels: Everyone who denies that Jesus is the Son of God is the Antichrist.[669]

Most Christians would probably not think twice about shrugging this off. However, the idea of Jesus as God's son is rejected by Judaism. Islam opposes any notion of a son of God. This difference is the very core that sets Jews and Muslims apart from Western Christians and is the ultimate justification of eternal jihad and holy war for more than a thousand years before Luther.

Following the logic of the Gospels – I am – the Antichrist.

With me, all Jews, all Muslims, everybody from other religions, and all those free from religion are the antichrists.

We can find an evolutionary step in the hatred of the Antichrist in a forged letter, allegedly from the second century. The writer condemned everyone who disputed Jesus's *humanity* as the Antichrist.

Everyone who denied the resurrection was the firstborn of Satan.[670]

This hate relationship encompassed more mythical requirements as time progressed.

The hostilities were directed, not only against Jews and Muslims, but also against their own Christian sectarians who begged to differ. Those free from religion and outside of the Judaic mental framework must never be forgotten as belonging on the death list.

The Antichrist is unnamed in Revelation of the Christian New Testament but appears as one or several beasts and a dragon. The latter comes about with seven heads, ten horns, and seven crowns.[671] The authors mixed real but dehumanized

---

[667] Luke 6:23-6:26.
[668] Matthew 24:30-24:31.
[669] 1 John 2:22.
[670] Polycarp, *to the Philippians*, 110–140 AD, XII.
[671] Revelation 12:3.

people[672] with fantasy and monsters. The Antichrist was supposed to snatch the newborn Second Christ from his mother. But the god of the Israelites took the child to itself. A war ensued under the leadership of the warrior Angel Michael, which ended in a bind.

The story serves perfectly to terrify stepchildren.

There is more suffering in this war of monsters.

The first of the beasts came out of the sea[673] and ruled for forty-two months.[674] It took its power from the dragon, *"that ancient serpent called the devil, or Satan, who leads the whole world astray."*[675]

The serpent in the fable is one of the subtle reminders that the first human female, Eve, succeeded in stealing intellect for humanity from the gods. The serpent suggested the crime to her.

Since Martin Luther recognized that dumb beasts cannot be as clever as portrayed in the supposed seduction of Eve, the serpent must have been possessed by the devil, *'a rational, highly intelligent, and mighty spirit.*[676] But Luther insisted that Eve remained the religious carrier of the original sin.

He did not grasp that this *rational,* highly intelligent thing was a human being dressed in snakeskin.

A carnival act. A masquerade.

Luther must have perceived the rise of Ottoman-Turks as a sort of bad omen. That Christians were expedited to heaven by their advances seems to have been a rather tangible disadvantage.

He must have had doubts whether the world might have been a better place if everyone had disobeyed God's commands, in particular those that ruled to trample every non-Jew until their hearts stopped beating. As a man of books, he must have recognized that survivors eventually felt obliged to return the favor and crush Jews.

---

[672] The fact that Revelation is a wartime account that might have been inserted into real history is given away by a remark that Babylon had fallen. It seems to speak about a royal dynasty with ten successors, of which three might have fallen in war. Apparently, the heresy that was targeted in Revelation had been coming out of Babylonian Jewry.
See Revelation 14:8.

[673] Revelation 13:1.

[674] Revelation 13:5.

[675] Revelation 12:9.

[676] Luther, Jesus Born a Jew, Brandt, 1962: 201.

Instead, for Luther, the rational and highly intelligent serpent was *'undoubtedly the devil,'*[677] exclusively *because* it violated God's orders.

Luther demonized women collectively against all reason: *'With their sin they are all under the devil.'*[678]

In the case of Eve, the paradox is that the symbol of the evil serpent actually led to a 'crime' of curiosity to the full benefit of humanity. A benevolent act for humankind was his symbol of evil.

Eve ought to be our mythical superstar.

Judaic disciples are terrified by Satan, who was also a god, as Luther explained.[679] This monster of satanic terror is a polytheist paradox.

It appears that the devil *'will always defeat us; only the power of the word of God can defeat him.'*[680] Our modern Pope Francis said that *'we should not think of the devil as a myth'* and that he is out to *'destroy our lives, our families and our communities.'*[681]

Both, God *and* Satan, seem to enjoy when things go from bad to worse. In the biblical narrative, the two take bets for who will win the seduction contest.

The next beast had *'two horns, like a lamb.'*[682] Its sign, with which followers of this beast were marked on the right hand or on the forehead,[683] was 666.[684] This number in and by itself later caused panic among the superstitious.

The final war against the beast was to be fought in Armageddon and led by a warrior with an iron scepter by the name *King of Kings and Lord of Lords,*[685] the King of the Jews and the King of the World. For this, he would need massive numbers of soldiers. Jews rose the dead, Christians went through the rapture, and Muslims had their Day of Resurrection when all the dead resurrected to join the opposing armies.

The Muslim version of the great war is otherwise along the line of the Christian story. The book of Revelation and the Koran even identify the same enemy armies. These were the eternal rival nations of the Jewish people.[686]

---

[677] Ibid., 202.
[678] Ibid.
[679] Luther, On War, 1528, WA 30 II, 107-148:
The devil, too, is a god and they honor him with this word; of that there is no doubt.
[680] Associated Press, The Latest: Pope Says There Can Be 'No Dialogue With Devil', February 14, 2016.
[681] Pope Francis, Apostolic Exhortation Gaudete Et Exsultate of the Holy Father Francis on the Call to Holiness in Today's World (Vatican, 2018) 161.
[682] Revelation 13:11.
[683] Revelation 13:16.
[684] Revelation 13:18 [from a Jewish and Muslim perspective, 666 means 'One God Only'].
[685] Revelation 19:16.
[686] The enemy armies are Gog and Magog.

But a symbol stands out: the beast of Shi'ite Muslims is depicted with the Staff of Moses and the Seal of Solomon.[687] Shi'ite Safavids used the marker found on some Sunni Ottoman Turkish mosques and attached it to their enemies. The symbolic pair demonized the Sadducee-Davidic alliance in the Ottoman leadership.

The resurrection never happened.

The war at Armageddon never happened.

These events did not even take place in the Bible.

Instead, the beast and the false prophet were captured.[688] Both were thrown into the fiery lake of burning sulfur[689] where the beast was bound in chains for a thousand years.[690] The rest were killed by the iron rod[691] of David, the King of the Jews.

After a thousand years, the beast returned for a short while.[692]

One could expect a wave of superstitions to resurface at the turn of the millennium, when the enemy armies[693] again gather for battle against Jerusalem. Once more, fire was to come from heaven and devour them.

Before it was all going to be over, the coming of the Second Christ was to happen.[694] The Antichrist would find his culmination as the opponent of the Second Christ, who would hold the iron rod,[695] the scepter of David.

The latter was to rule forever,[696] and God was to live among men in Jerusalem.[697]

The revelation that the Second Christ would *'rule all the nations with an iron rod,'* identifies him, here again, as the warlord messiah and redeemer of the Promised Land.

The King of the Jews is the king of the world.

Quite obviously, the origin of the text is Jewish.

---

See Ezekiel 38:1-38:3 (NIV).

[687] Anthony Sean, The Caliph and the Heretic: Ibn Saba' and the Origins of Shi`ism (Brill, 2011) 220.

[688] Revelation 19:20.

[689] Revelation 19:20.

[690] Revelation 20:2.

[691] Revelation 19:21.

[692] Revelation 20:3.

[693] Revelation 20:7-20:9.

[694] Revelation 12:1–5.

[695] Revelation 12:1–5.

[696] Revelation 11:15.

[697] Revelation 21:1–7.

We have already investigated what was to be expected on the other side of victory.[698] The promise of life without work, grief, or suffering never materialized.

However, the most disturbing part is yet to come: the 144,000 survivors are to be Jewish.[699] To be precise, they must be of the Levite priesthood[700] even in the Christian myth of the End of the World.

That Christianity *will* be betrayed is an openly stated goal in the Book of Revelation. Christians are working hard to bring about the End of the World for their salvation in eternal life with the foreseeable outcome that only Jewish priests survive.

The origin of the text is Jewish. Obviously.

It is a classic Ponzi Scheme.

It would be amusing were it not so tragic.

Some modern Christian interpretations of the New Testament wanted to evade such an ending, even though the Book of Revelation leaves no room to argue. The new idea was that nobody would be left behind on earth.[701] However, that is a willful repositioning.

One might think that this folly is exclusive to Christianity.

The same idea, and just as arrogant, can be found in the Talmud. There, only the *invited* will ever arrive at the New Jerusalem.[702]

Should ordinary Jews not think this through and question the odds of winning the lottery to enter the Promised Land?

I hold Jews to a higher intellectual standard, but they are cannon fodder; cannon fodder for their supreme priestly elite.

Human shields.

Their leaders do not care a dot about lowly lives. All they care about is the power that they can leverage either from their taxes or from their deaths. They are not only willing to put all of mankind on the line, but also ordinary Jews – all of them. They are of no importance and of no consequence in the grandiose quest for imperial world power.

---

[698] Revelation 7:14–17.
[699] Revelation 7:3-7:8.
[700] Revelation 14:3-14:5.
[701] 1 Thessalonians 4:17 (NIV).
[702] Babylonian Talmud – Mas. Baba Bathra 75.

Ordinary Jew! You are not invited.

The day they find out will be too late. Jews are puppets of their priestly class as much as ordinary Christians and Muslims are the victims of the same messianic machinations. For the sake of the royal Hasmonean family tree.

The messianic aspirations in Martin Luther's time should now be recognizable for what they were: the love for hatred – loving to hate anyone who dared to disagree with specific myths.

## A Wakeup Call

Predictably, the millennium came and went. The world hung around a little longer. It is surprising, though, that the Christian West was not in uproar around the turn of the millennium. They seem to not have noted the passing of the prophesied end. Their response was to get busy and start building a life. Instead of the End of the World at Armageddon, the period marked the beginning of a long struggle to escape the oppression of the Catholic Church. Like the heretic in the Koran, they started to walk away.

No resurrection? Not with my money.

During this time, Christian pilgrimages to New Jerusalem began.[703]

Since Saint Augustine, Christianity had repeatedly waited for the End of the World. Now believers wanted to visit the New Jerusalem, where the Kingdom of Heaven was supposed to be established. This is where free drinks and food as well as eternal life should have begun, all without worries over insignificant issues, such as health or child survival.[704]

The promises never came through – except for the traders in fake souvenirs. They call them relics.

In contrast, Christianity in the East had fully embraced the idea that this was the End of the World.

All life came to a halt.

They indeed believed that Satan had returned from his confinement. The resulting disaster was inevitable.

Muslims took this seriously.

---

[703] Ralph Glaber, *On the First Millennium* (1044), from C.G. Coulton, ed, *Life in the Middle Ages* (Macmillan 1910) Vol 1, 1-7, text slightly modernized by Paul Halsall August 1996.
[704] Revelation 21:1 – 21:7.

The caliphates in Baghdad and Cairo tried desperately to get the insanity under control. As early as the year 1001, the Muslim Fatimid ruler[705] destroyed thousands of Christian Churches, including some in Jerusalem.

Many believers found solace in drunkenness.

As emergency measures, the ruler interfered with Christian and Jewish rituals, prohibiting the consumption of alcohol. Jews had to wear black turbans[706] and a wooden calf necklace.[707] Christians had to wear an iron cross and special belts.

Christians welcomed death.

In an attempt to safeguard society, Muslim rulers persecuted the Christian population. A superstitious world in which substantial portions of a people thought that life was over and the devil was coming upon them was heading toward disaster. They wailed and whined all day long, dressed in sackcloth, and walked on a tightrope of perpetual collapse.

Many simply fell asleep in the middle of the streets only never to wake up again and to be taken to Satan.

It was Resurrection in reverse.

The administration in Cairo tried to contain disease by collecting the dead from the streets and having them burned. But no hands were available to do any of this dirty work. Dogs and cats were no longer fed and were thrown out into the streets in such numbers that the city had to take emergency measures to have stray animals killed and buried.

Christians had created a living hell for themselves and their Muslim hosts.

Places of entertainment were shut down, and the intolerable mandate for the full-faced veil was made mandatory for all women. Jewesses were obliged to wear one shoe in black and the other in red. Work was shifted to the dark hours. Processions were outlawed.

Churches and convents in Palestine were converted into mosques or destroyed.

Christianity in the caliphate had gone mad.

In 1009, the Church of the Holy Sepulcher in Jerusalem was destroyed. This is believed to be the resting place of Jesus Christ.

---

[705] Abu Ali Mansur Tariqu al-Hakim was the sixth Fatimid Shi'ite caliph 996 – 1021 AD.

[706] A thousand years earlier, the turban had been a distinct feature of the Levite priesthood before the First Jewish-Roman War. See Leviticus 16:4.

[707] The necklace was meant to mock Jewish participation in Moses' story of the golden calf.

Rabbinic leaders on the Throne of David in Baghdad were accused of conspiring to have the church over Jesus' burial ground destroyed.[708] Its ruin served for the later Christian rationale to mobilize for the First Crusade – a holy war to conquer Jerusalem and the Promised Land.

We should now be better able to understand: the immediate reaction of the Catholic Church to the destruction of the Holy Sepulcher was to persecute and expel Jews.[709] There are no reports of retaliation against Muslims, only against Jews.

The enmity appears to have been mutually agreed upon.

While our forefathers convicted Jews of this crime, we do not have the evidence to attest to the reasons for the verdict. But we do have enough evidence that it would be foolish to dismiss the accusations as ridiculous.

Mass delusions bear consequences. They lead to mass graves.

In around 1014, the trauma was all over. The Muslim world returned to tolerating Jews and Christians.

Mainstream historians typically attribute the Muslim atrocities to the eccentric behavior of their leaders. Instead, they attempted to save their domains from total collapse. In the same sweep of madness, the Fatimid caliphate was fully Islamized.

The perception of the dangers that the religious competitors constituted may have been rational – rational in its full-blown irrationality, if that makes any sense.

Perhaps this does: the Shi'ite Caliph in charge was viewed as the Mahdi.[710] They effectively enacted their own Doomsday prophecies on the battlefield of Armageddon.

There is no wiggle room. These are self-fulfilling prophecies that create the dynamics of self-destruction – of mankind, that is.

Still, the End of the World was not near.

Nobody could have escaped the facts of the sun rising and the neighbor happily milking his cows the next morning – at least those cows that had been tended to over the years of collective lunacy.

---

[708] Glaber, 1044, Coulton, *Life in the Middle Ages,* 1910, Vol 1, 1-7, 1996.

[709] Ademar Glaber, *Annales Lemovicenses* (ad an. 1010); *Annales Beneventani* (ad an. 1010) MGH SS III, p.177.

[710] Thomas Patrick Hughes, A Dictionary of Islam, (Allen, 1885) 305.

The paradox needs to be emphasized here that no widespread millennium panic was recorded in the West. What should have destroyed the domains of the Catholic Church did instead terrorize the areas under Islam. The West started economically and intellectually to recover while Islam slid into Taliban style fundamentalism.

Prophecy having been so wrong constituted a wakeup call. For some.

Secularization had begun. Humanitarians were re-emerging. They had been under assault for a thousand years. And they remained so for another thousand.

Around this time, during the twenties of the eleventh century, also emerged the House of Habsburg. This is the dynasty that now ruled the Holy Roman Empire under Charles V.

A feudal count in the Duchy of Swabia erected a castle by the name of Habsburg in a town that now bears the dynasty's name. It lies in modern day Switzerland.

The castle was supposedly named after a hawk, but for the Swiss in me, the sound of its name is something like 'greed castle' from the German word *'haben'*, to have. Have more. History has it that the castle lost its importance in the ever-growing Habsburg power.

They moved to Austria in the late thirteenth century.

The Truth is – my Swiss truth, implanted since birth – that the Habsburgs had their butts kicked by the Swiss. Now this is true: Switzerland is supposed to be the world's oldest living democracy, founded as a confederation in 1291. Its territorial claim lay in the immediate neighborhood of the Habsburg feudal overlords. Such confederations existed before the oath of the Swiss, but this one survived for over 700 years by now and merged into the nation of Switzerland. Its independence was interrupted for seventeen years by Napoleon's invasion. The Swiss democracy is also a special one, a *direct* democracy. The people approve new laws and can propose laws or changes to them for a national vote. It is a system of people's referendums, initiatives, and votes on every issue and on all levels of government. Votes in some cantons are still held by show of hands.

I said *special*, not *better*. All this may not protect Switzerland from the next wave of monsters. Humanity tends to put them in power with popular support. But it survived for quite a while.

Back then, the Swiss rejected Habsburg rule and decided to bleed themselves to freedom. William Tell, a mountaineer and crossbow expert, refused to bow to the Habsburgs who wanted to subjugate the rebellious mountain towns. Tell was arrested and could save himself only by shooting an apple off the head of his son.

He had one shot. And he succeeded.

The rest of the complex myth includes lightning and storms, dark nights, and a boat trashed on the cliffs in order to have Tell freed to kill the Habsburg governor. A sixteenth-century historian-relative of mine spread the invented tale, but that does not diminish my pride in Swiss cheese and chocolate.

The Habsburg Castle was simply too close to the rebellious Swiss for comfort.

It is also true that the Swiss were a fiercely combative nation. There was perhaps little else to do in the Alps. They showed up on practically every battlefield, as winners, of course, and often also as mercenaries. We will meet them again in the paid service of Charles V. Their warlike mercenary function is symbolized, today, on Charles' opposing front as the Swiss Guards in the Vatican.

In its kernel, the Swiss story has been about a fight for self-determination and freedom – at least in its past.

Freedom does not come for free, as the Tell-tale shows. It is a hard-fought-for concept that comes with rights and responsibilities. One of them is to be aware where un-freedom looms and to push against it. We do not need to shoot the crossbow, but it is our generation's responsibility to extend the freedoms for our children and to root out the causes and sprouts of un-freedom.

It is our duty to spread our freedoms to other people who wish to be freed from oppression.

Freedoms never come easy, and we are at risk on multiple fronts of losing them on a large scale, unless we are able to bring freedom to the world on an even larger scale. Moderns are facing forces that aim at depriving us of the freedom to believe or speak as we please within the limitations of respect for others.

I need to briefly return to the millennium scare of the End of the World that never happened. For those who missed the cosmic event, the daily prayer to God stayed, asking him to hasten the End of the World.

Here is the Christian version:

> *Our Father in heaven, hallowed be your name. Your kingdom come, your will be done on earth as it is in heaven. Give us this day our daily bread. And forgive us our debts, as we also have forgiven our debtors. And lead us not into temptation, but deliver us from the evil one.*[711]

Christians pray for the Kingdom of Heaven to come, which is the place where food and liquor come free. They pray with their children that they be rescued from the *'evil one'*, the beast that comes to the battle at the End of the World. Only to hand it to Jewish priests.

Is that how we create the next self-fulfilling disaster?

After the failed event of the End of the World at the millennium, the Catholic Church attempted to reform itself. The topics? Traditional morals, strengthened celibacy, and trying to rid the church of simony. This is the act of purchasing ecclesiastical offices, a definition of systemic corruption. These are, not by chance, the same topics that were discussed during our Fifth Lateran Council in Luther's time.

The corruption has only kept on deepening.

These organizations will counter the accusation of corruption with the half-truth that they rely on alms. It shows best in Islam where alms are mandatory. Or in Europe where governments collect 'alms' for the churches by the billions.

It violates God's Seventh Commandment: thou shalt not steal.

This is not my conclusion. It is Martin Luther's.[712]

History has wonderful ironies in store for us: the pontiff in charge of these failed reforms styled himself Pope Leo IX.[713] The ninth and the tenth attest to the repetitive patterns of history.

This was 500 years before Martin Luther. It should give us an inkling of how little has changed since, once we grasp the full context of the follies during the sixteenth century.

The same powers are still at play today, 500 years after Luther.

To summarize, the End of the World is the conquest of the Promised Land by Jewish leaders, the downfall of all other nations, and Jewish world domination under the theocratic ideals of the god of the Israelites.

---

[711] Matthew 6:9-6:13.
[712] Luther, Large Catechism, 1529, WA 30 I,125-238.
[713] Pope Leo IX was king of the Papal States 1049 – 1054.

Jewish scholars insist that the notion of world domination is ridiculous. They proclaim that all nations should do God's will. Since God is the god of the Israelites, this means the same: a new World Order under the guiding hands of Jewish priesthood and the functionaries on the Throne of David.

Modern jurisdictions across the world will eventually close the loop in the Dynamics of Self-Destruction. They will make religious professionals ineligible for entry into their country and deny them a path to citizenship. Modern France is planning to deny foreign trained Imams to preach their anarchic and extremist views of Islam in the country. Instead, they intend to introduce a national training and certification system.[714] This country has replaced unchecked 'religious freedom' with a focus on secularism.

You think that I might have spoiled the story?

You have no idea what is in store.

Now we are ready to embark on the continuance of our saga that will make us understand why Martin Luther hated Jews so much that he was willing to collectively hurt them.

---

[714] Norimitsu Onishi, Aurelien Breeden, Macron Vows Crackdown on 'Islamist Separatism' in France, New York Times, October 2, 2020).

# III: MESSIAH

## *The Butcher Pope*

At 45, the pleasure-loving Medici Pope Leo was too young to die of natural causes, even though he was seriously obese. Suspicions of poisoning were unfounded – we know. Perhaps he suffocated from deep-pocket syndrome, an inherited disease from his greedy dynasty's mountains of blood-stained gold. It is said that the holy man died of pneumonia. It happened so suddenly that he could not receive the last sacraments.

Christians know that without the last sacraments, his soul was lost forever. Back then, this was a curse upon the deceased. His soul could not ascend to heaven.

That is the bedeviling message that the Vatican intended to embed in Leo's legendary death.

Also unfounded is Martin Luther's hint that Leo might have been a pedophile. After all, the pope demanded chastity from his subjects and celibacy from his priests.

But three days before Leo died, he was 'perfectly able' to sign an alliance against France among the Vatican, the Holy Roman Empire under Charles V, and the King of England. The pope's fever must have put an extraordinarily quick end to his papacy.

From all we know of Leo, he would have rather swallowed poison than sign such a deal against the French.

Some experts claim that Pope Leo's love for France had been wavering. Instead, his reign coincided with a lucky streak by the French King. King Francis' unhappiness about the loss of an empire expressed itself with ongoing military exchanges with the Holy Roman Empire.

The discontent of Charles with the French-friendly Medici Pope marked the end of both, Francis' luck and Leo's papacy.

A fever.

This may have pleased Charles, but now the Medicis were miserable.

Giovanni de' Medici was so depressed about the loss of the Medici Pope that he recruited well-trained, mounted troops from the mercenaries who had been under his command in the service of Pope Leo. The harquebus was then the most modern firearm. It was the first rifle-style weapon with a trigger, more like a handheld cannon that was loaded through the barrel. That thing could explode in the beholder's face at any time. Leo's mercenaries were equipped with the most modern war toys available. Now, guns and other 'hi-tech' weaponry were in the hands of Giovanni's rogue troops. Their attire was black to signal mourning over Leo, hence their name, 'Bande Nere.' Black Bands of Giovanni. Bandits. It speaks for itself that they were deployed for French-friendly popes and in support of French interests against the imperial claims of Charles.

Their tactic was to ambush their victims, rush in on horseback and disappear into the dark of the night.

A terrorist robber band.

A son of 'the Tiger of Forlì', Giovanni de' Medici had inherited Catarina Sforza's anger issues. He was a hooligan, a good-for-nothing street-gang fighter. At the age of twelve, he had already committed his first murder, and a year later, he was banished from Florence for having raped a boy.[715] Today, you can find these kinds of low-lives in the drug-and-prostitution-infested areas of most major cities. Now, he and his 'Bande Nere' troops were free to do as they pleased.

From then on, Giovanni was living the life of a true wild-west outlaw.

Pope Leo's successor was a Dutchman, Adrian VI.[716] Coincidentally, Adrian had previously been the tutor of the young, Spanish-born Charles since the age of seven. Now, as Holy Roman Emperor, Charles V[717] was just twenty-one years old.

Other than the French King, we remember that the emperor's other subversive opponents were Frederick the Wise and his protégé, Martin Luther.

---

[715] Michael Rocke, Forbidden Friendships: Homosexuality and Male Culture in Renaissance Florence (Oxford, 1996) 229.
[716] Pope Adrian VI / Hadrian VI, aka Adriaan Florensz (Boeyens) or Florisze/Florencii, was pope of the Catholic Church 1522 – 1523.
[717] Charles V, ruled the Holy Roman Empire 1519 – 1556.

Before crowning his career as Pope Adrian, the holy man had already made a name of himself as Grand Inquisitor in Spain[718] – another great extremist on a mission to spread the faith by the irresistible love of torture. He had first been co-regent and then successor of the radical Cardinal Cisneros, the Grand Inquisitor (and Abrabanel suspect) under whom 400 monks had fled to the North African Kingdom of Tlemcen. Before becoming pope, Adrian had been the second highest authority in Spain, after Charles.

Certainly, the two knew each other all too well.

Nobility in Spain seems to have acquired a taste for the absence of regents who resided in the Netherlands. They had started to form their own militias and to dream of greater freedoms in the absence of the monarchy. This is also how Cardinal Cisneros had become regent in Spain.

The noble replacement to the throne could only be a loyalist.

Charles, we are reminded, was bribed onto the imperial throne with Fugger money. Lots of it. After the good deed had been accomplished, somebody had to pay up – why not milk the peasants some more? When Charles had to travel to Germany and Austria to be inaugurated as emperor, the Grand Inquisitor Adrian seized power in Spain.

But Castile's parliament refused to comply with the demands to cover the tax blow.

As a result, a series of peasant rebellions broke out, as doctrine calls them. Eventually, all of Spain was in rebellion, including the eastern-most region, Aragon.

But in reality, we are in the fourth decade of the Spanish Inquisition, a weaponized and brutalized version of the Inquisition. This deadly conformation machine was put in motion in the thirteenth century to ensure adherence to the Truth in all territories of the Catholic Church.

The radical Cardinal Cisneros had earlier been Grand Inquisitor of Castile, and Cardinal Adrian – pope in waiting – was Grand Inquisitor of Aragon. Under these two cardinals, the Spanish Inquisition had found the height of its murderous rampage.

After Cisneros' passing, all of Spain had come under Adrian's yoke.

---

[718] Adriaan Florensz had been Grand Inquisitor in Aragon-Catalonia, Navarre, Castile, and León.

A fight for freedom was on, sprinkled with the customary nationalism against a 'foreign' power, meaning the Habsburgs. Charles was a son of theirs. Or half a son. As the grandson in the direct male lineage of the Holy Roman Emperor Maximilian I and born from a native mother, he was half Germanic and half Spanish by birth.

To gain 'legitimacy' for their resistance, the rebels tried to align themselves with Queen Joanna of Castile. She was the mother of Charles and spouse of Philip the Handsome from the Habsburg Dynasty. Adrian, the future pope, threatened her with the loss of Charles' Spanish domains, if she were to support the rebellious factions.

In other words and contrary to the views of some prominent modern historians,[719] the Catholic Church was exerting full control over the rule of the House of Habsburg. While their happiness depended on who was sitting on the papal throne, they were playing along either way. The church was the indispensable ingredient to power.

From the attempt of rebels trying to align themselves with Joanna, it follows that the resistance must have been borne against the Catholic Church rather than against Charles' rule.

Joanna, a highly educated and refined woman, was tutored during her childhood by a Dominican priest, yet another inquisitor. She was fluent in six languages and was instructed in religious studies. Early on, Joanna, not being keen on Christian worship and rituals, became a sceptic.

That should be enough to justify her nickname, Joanna the Mad.

Our earlier blood-friend and Grand Inquisitor, the radical Cisnero, played the decisive role in damaging Joanna the Mad's reputation. To delegitimize her, he called for a regency council. Soon thereafter, the government was 'entrusted' to himself.

Cisnero had her locked up in a convent.

He created the queen who had gone insane.

What else do you expect when accuser and judge are one?

All of Joanna's six children became either queens or emperors. Moreover, Emperor Maximilian I, grandfather of Emperor Charles, placed her on a list of three possible candidates to marry the widowed Polish King.

That is how mad she was.

---

[719] Henry Kamen, The Myth of the Spanish Inquisition (BBC documentary, 1994).

Nevertheless, Adrian, the holy man, kept her locked up in the convent. Any guesses why? The good but skeptical Joanna had developed an affinity for Martin Luther. At thirty-six-years of age, the mature Joanna had been eliminated because of her bizarre beliefs, not because of a mental condition.

And this is also why Spain was in rebellion.

You did not get anywhere when doubting the faith under the Inquisition. They did not tolerate questions. An ordinary woman would have been publicly burned at the stake as a witch. Because of the queen's royal linage and popularity, they could not kill her that easily. Locking her up in a convent and declaring her insane appears compassionate.

Almost divinely so.

Queen Joanna was sent to Saint George's by decree of the Grand Inquisitor of the Catholic Church for being sympathetic to Protestant ideas.

We can perhaps sense the impact that Martin Luther must have had. The Augustinian and Franciscan orders served as his first communication channels.[720] It is astonishing how quickly news was able to travel in those times. It is not credible that Joanna was the only person in Spain infected with the desire to break free from the Catholic Church. Placed in this context, the Spanish rebellions speak for themselves.

The attempt to establish Protestant ideas in Spain might have been eradicated from the history books more thoroughly than elsewhere. In fact, this was consensus until some modern scholars re-examined the evidence to tell otherwise because – surprise – they did not find the evidence. They thought that Lutheranism failed to take root in Spain while there was ferocious repression of heresy in the Netherlands.

Because of this, scholars today are deeply divided over the death toll during the Spanish Inquisition. It is said that 150,000 heretics were 'processed,' and of these, about 3,000 were put to death. What? The Inquisition was not as bad as its reputation? Killing only a few thousand who never did anything wrong except to believe differently was okay?

What, then, would not have been okay? 30,000?

---

[720] In the evidence collected in Spain, we can see that the first appearance of the Lutheran heresy came through these two orders of the Catholic Church in Barcelona, Valencia, Toledo, and elsewhere. See Longhurst, 1964, 25-26.

According to this new research, before the 1560s, there were fewer than fifty cases before the Inquisition that dealt with Protestant beliefs[721] that were soon convoluted with other heresies, such as the Illuminist Movement, for example.[722]

The inquisitors were legal experts, not fanatics, these apologists say, suggesting due process.

Here we are not among those who can be blamed for placing the Inquisition out of the complex context of Spain and the rest of Europe. In fact, the context is crystal clear. It provides for the big picture. Accounting for individual court cases – farces – is the view of an accountant when most transactions are off the books.

History is the study of past events in the context of human development. Without understanding human nature we cannot understand history.

We see little in the court records because the Spanish Inquisition was very effective. Effective in cleaning up the evidence.

It is quite simple: wherever the church was challenged, there was also the Inquisition. For a thousand years before, weeding out heresies was part of the business model.

Without deadly force, it would not have survived.

We will never know the full truth.

Documentation of entire trials has gone missing.[723] Entire towns with their archives and even all their mice have simply vanished. The complete trees of families have been pulled out of the soil, never to root again.

The rule of God is indifferent to the rule of law.

The pretence that the Inquisition was 'somewhat less bloody' than in other places or than its reputation is preposterous. Would it matter if the Holocaust had cost only one million Jewish lives rather than six? Would it be different if it were 'only' 60,000? Let us settle on 6,000.

It would not make Hitler a better man!

---

[721] Henry Kamen, The Spanish Inquisition, A Historical Revision (Yale, 2014) 100.

[722] Longhurst, 1964, 103-115.

[723] Putting this in modern perspective, between 1973 and 1990, the right-wing Junta in Chile, a small country with then roughly 12 million people, managed to render 3,000 humans missing. An estimated 200,000 were driven into exile. In 2015, 43 students vanished in Mexico after they clashed with the police. Despite our modern means and an international team of experts, their whereabouts remained in complete darkness. Obviously, the perpetrators did not care for show trials.

It would neither absolve the German people nor the Protestant Church from their conspiracy with evil.

Here, I am not comparing one persecution with another to determine which one might have been worse. Instead, I simply put the spotlight on the top leadership. It matters not whether they killed 20 or 200 in a year, even 2,000 or more. Just a few were enough to scare the entire population into submission.

In fact, setting examples to frighten the rest was their malicious intent.[724]

Besides, all survivors of such prosecutions must have been traumatized for life. Death would have been the better choice for many.

Having studied countless documents about trials of the Inquisition, I would like to share the feelings of despair that have often arisen in me. As a researcher in systemic poverty and religious violence, I am used to the brutality of reports about terrorism throughout history. But the accounts of these trials are so chilling that my heart sinks to the bottom every time I read another one.

They are not anonymous attacks on crowds.

They are very personal, affecting individuals, often children.

Many elderly, sometimes in their nineties, succumbed to their conditions in jail before their assured verdicts. If you were to read a sample of such court proceedings, I promise you, whether you are religious or not, you will be overwhelmed by the injustice that was served to these men, women, and children. You will not be able to go through these cases without tears. You will side with the accused for a very simple reason. Even the smartest words from them were simply not heard. Their pleas were ignored. Even when they were unwavering Catholics. Their testimony was abused and misconstrued. They were worn down through the most miserable conditions of imprisonment, with lice and rats eating away at them.

They were thrown into torture chambers.

Even though these show trials were given the air of due process, their singular goal was to extinguish the voices of dissent in one way or another. In the end, being publicly burned at the stake provided for the salvation of the poor soul who had gotten between the teeth of the Inquisition.

---

[724] A court case at Geneva from 1553 in which the reformer John Calvin (as persecutor!) betrayed the intellectual writer Michael Servetus into the hands of the Inquistion serves as but one example. Longhurst, 1964, 71.

For students of these real-life horror stories, the only consolation is that the unjust verdicts provide some relief that the suffering of the victim has come to an end.

The scribes must have used their tears as the ink to write down every word of persecutor and persecuted. 'Guilty' of heresy or not, every time the Catholic Church set a victim free, it created new enemies. The Inquisition would have been better off to pray quietly for their corpses to rest in peace.

One example of their determination to reach a verdict at any cost is a case against an unimportant but well-read man by the name of Diego de Uceda. It started at a lower court and went all the way up to the highest court of the Inquisition. He was prosecuted for denying the need of confession, which the accuser appears to have misunderstood. It was a point of discussion in the books of Erasmus Roterodamus,[725] which were at that time officially approved by the Catholic Church.

However, confession was mandatory. Believers disclosed their sins and made amends for them through 'alms.' God absolved sins through the mediation of priests who collected cash from sinners in exchange for forgiveness.

All witnesses attested to de Uceda's good character and unwavering belief in Catholic orthodoxy. This included an archbishop who had discussed with him the matters for which he stood trial. The poor soul had to endure imprisonment for seventeen months without ever knowing what the accusation was that had been brought forth. From his cell, he was dragged out only for questioning by the Inquisition and for appearances before the court.

He did not know what to confess to.

He was then sentenced to torture, during which he confessed to whatever the court wanted him to say. But he recanted. Finally, De Uceda was sentenced to pay a fine. Bare-footed and bareheaded, with wax candle in hand, he had to abjure his heresy in the public square of Toledo and during other public penances.[726]

As I was reading the case, my heart was begging ever more to have the man let go. Please. For God's sake. Have mercy.

Let us reopen the gates to torture, shall we?

---

[725] Desiderius Erasmus Roterodamus (1466 – 1536), aka Erasmus or Erasmus of Rotterdam, was an Austin Friar (he took vows in 1488 at the Augustinian canonry of Stein, in South Holland). He was a social critic, teacher, theologian, and humanist. In order to pursue the position of secretary to the Bishop of Cambrai, he was dispensed of his Augustinian vows.

[726] Longhurst, 1964, 117-134.

Pretending that there is some equivalency, some political correctness, or some fairness in assessing the atrocities of the Inquisition comes at our own peril.

To make it clear: hatred of those of another Truth is part of the communal formation mechanism. As with Hitler, these injustices and their organizations merit nothing but full condemnation for eternity. Luckily, neither the Catholic nor Protestant churches maintain institutionalized networks of terror today.

Imagine if students could have learned about dissent in matters of faith or about how they executed or disowned anyone who attempted to stand in the way. That prospect would only have set the stage for the next wave of dissenters.

Indeed, official history claims that Lutheran groups in Spain were few and far between. Consensus even goes as far as to claim that the term 'Lutheran' was used to describe heretics in general, rather than actual followers of Martin Luther.

Joanna's case speaks volumes.

We can ignore attempts at splitting facts.

I can say this because we have evidence. The Grand Inquisitor Adrian, soon to be pope, wrote a letter to Pope Leo that Luther's translated books had made it into Spain through the Order of Saint Augustine. He issued a command to have them all burned and to criminalize everybody who possessed, sold, or published Lutheran books.[727]

This soon became commonplace.[728]

We know of Lutheran books in Latin and Spanish that were confiscated from ships bound for Spain and burned in the public square.[729] Adrian wrote to Emperor Charles that it was urgently required that the *'obstinate heresies'* of Luther be put down, along with the enemies of Jesus Christ who were following *'that wicked and pestilential man'* – Luther, that is.

---

[727]  A(rchivo) H(istorico) N(acional), AHN, Inquisicion, Libro 317, fols. 182r-v. The letter quoted here is the one sent to the Inquisition of Aragon, in Longhurst, 1964, 13.

[728]  AHN, Inquisicion, Libro 319, fol. 13v in Longhurst, 1964, 16.

[729]  Letter of Martin de Salinas to Archduke Ferdinand, dated Burgos, June 25, 1524, in Antonio Rodriguez Villa, "El emperador Carlos V y su corte (1522 – 1539) segun las cartas de don Martin de Salinas," in Boletin de la real academia espanola, vol. 43 (1903), p. 175 in Longhurst, 1964, 16.

A.J. Deus

A second letter from a committee[730] announced that *'that seducer, not content with having perverted and deceived Germany, is endeavoring with his malignant and diabolical cunning to pervert and contaminate'* all of Spain by smuggling into that country Spanish editions of his heresies and blasphemies.

This was indeed serious: *'From a little spark ... may spring and burst forth a great fire.'* Charles must act immediately in order that *'those damnable and perverse subtleties may cease and be extirpated, so that not only this detestable and corrupt pestilence shall not enter into these your kingdoms and seigniories of Spain, but that by the hand of your Majesty it may be extirpated and destroyed throughout all the world.'*[731]

Despite the most draconic threats and punishments by the Inquisition and despite frequent seizures and destructions, Lutheran books kept on arriving in Spain.[732]

The decision of the Fifth Lateran Council to introduce an approval process for books was implemented with vigor. A veritable underground approach to Lutheran books may have made their lecture even more tempting.[733]

There is no such thing as a 'kind' inquisition. There is only the Inquisition. It criminalized matters of faith. It was organized crime. The organized crime of the Protestant Reformation subverted it.

A gang war.

Now, this book may be perceived as anti-Catholic. For heaven's sake. We are investigating Martin Luther's evolution from protesting the excesses of the Catholic Church to hating Jews. Given that the church oppressed half the world and intended to subjugate the whole planet during Luther's time, it is imperative to highlight its inner workings. We are dealing with facts and with understanding the context as well as we can through lifting the rubble and letting the rats out.

Let us briefly look to Portugal for comparison.

Joanna the Mad had an older sister, Isabella of Aragon,[734] who was married to Portugal's King Manuel the Fortunate.[735] This king was the one responsible for welcoming Jewish refugees into his domain – an estimated 93,000 souls.

---

[730] A committee of grandees of the realm.
[731] Longhurst, 1964, referring to these two letters, which appear in Manuel Danvila, Historia crítica y documentada de las comunidades de Castilla, in Memorial historico espanol, vol. 37 (1898), 580-583.
[732] Longhurst, 1964, 18.
[733] AHN, Inquisicion, Libro 320, fols. 321v-322r and 343r-v, in Longhurst, 1964, 19.
[734] Isabella, Princess of Asturias, 1470 – 1498.
[735] Manuel I aka the Fortunate was King of Portugal and the Algarves 1495 – 1521.

He was also in charge of the Portuguese explorations to India and across the Atlantic.

The Catholic Church, represented by King Manuel's Dominican Confessor[736] – an inquisitor, had arranged Isabella's marriage to the Portuguese King back in 1497 under the condition that Muslims and Jews were to be persecuted in Portugal. Mainstream history describes the laws to completely eradicate all Muslims and Jews from Portugal as Manuel's responsibility.[737]

This is not so.

Other than in the Ottoman-Turkish territories, the status of Muslims and Jews was nowhere greater than in Portugal.

Whoever can dictate conditions is in charge.

Isabella was a grand prize in Iberian noble aspirations. She was also the ulterior chip in the plot of Grand Inquisitor Cardinal Cisnero and in the quest to subjugate all of the Iberian Peninsula.

Isabella had previously been married to the heir-apparent to the throne of Portugal. However, the groom died at age sixteen. It appears obvious that the second arrangement between her and King Manuel served to maintain the royal marriage bonds between Portugal and the rest of Spain. This becomes even more apparent when Manuel was betrothed to Maria of Aragon after her sister Isabella's untimely death.

A match in heaven.

And a religious conquest of the Iberian Peninsula.

The royal temptation was hard to resist. Would he come through with his part of the bargain, he would at least be an accessory to organized crime.

The marriage vows promised the extension of Portuguese royal power into Spain. They allowed its leading dynasty to enter the illustrious club of European nobility, the stratosphere of complicit power. In exchange, the Catholic Church was able to impose conditions.

The 'problem' of the Jews needed to find a 'final solution.' They had to leave *without* their children or convert.[738]

King Manuel the Fortunate liked the brides but did not like the dowry.

---

[736] Friar Jorge Vogado.
[737] António José Saraiva, The Marrano Factory: The Portuguese Inquisition and Its New Christians 1536 – 1765 (Brill, 2001) 10-12.
[738] Steven Lowenstein, The Jewish Cultural Tapestry: International Jewish Folk Traditions (Oxford University Press, 2001) 36.

He did not comply.

He 'arranged' for a grace period of thirty years during which the Jewish faith should not be scrutinized. The two sisters of Joanna the Mad did not insist on the terminal arrangement either.

Maria and Manuel the Fortunate produced ten children. The firstborn son became the next King of Portugal; the first daughter was married to Emperor Charles and consequently became Holy Roman Empress Isabella;[739] two of the younger sons became cardinals of the Catholic Church.

In short, the Catholic Church ordered it – the Fortunate did not enforce the pact.

A riot back in 1506 is enlightening for Manuel's position. It cost the lives of hundreds of Jews during the Lisbon Massacre. Apparently, a Christian in the church of a Dominican convent[740] saw an image of Christ during a Sunday prayer. This was understood by the community as a message from Jesus Christ that was to bring about the end of the drought and plague that had been shaking the city. They were going mad.

A Jewish convert pointed out that it was an optical illusion from a candle.

He paid with his life.

Two Dominican friars – the ones in charge of the Inquisition – took the opportunity to promise absolution of all sins if the worshippers were to go out and take revenge on all converts.

That day alone, 500 former Jews found death in the literal hellfire.

Because he was out of town to escape the plague, King Manuel the Fortunate could have done nothing to stop the bloodbath. As the riots escalated, children and women were dragged from their houses and burnt alive. Their possessions were stolen. 2,000 lives were lost during just three days. It was a massacre of innocent converso Jews.

Finally, the royal guards arrived to rescue the remaining converts. The two Dominicans who instigated the violence were themselves sentenced to be burned at the stake.

Historians emphasize that this event happened under Manuel's watch and before the formal establishment of the Inquisition in Portugal.

---

[739] Isabella of Portugal, 1503 – 1539, was Holy Roman Empress and Queen of Spain, Germany, Italy, Naples and Sicily and Duchess of Burgundy.
[740] The convent of São Domingos of Lisbon.

From the foundation of the Dominican Order, its members were deployed as the terrorist arm of the Catholic Church, the Inquisition. They took advantage of Manuel's being out of town.

It took the monarch only three days to put the fire down. That was incredibly fast, considering that he first had to receive the news and then respond to it effectively.

Had the two Dominicans gone rogue? Probably not. It was their job to weed out 'heresy.' They did whatever it took.

Judge for yourself:

Here was the recommendation of a contemporary Catholic missionary from the furthest corner of the planet to a question about what to do with Christian apostates who reverted to Islam or Judaism: *'For those who do not rightly believe, teaching and preaching would suffice for them, and if that did not profit, burn them as heretics.'*[741] What to do with secret Muslims and Jews? *'And those who did not repent, they might take them and burn them, for such is the use in Frankland and the Church of Rome.'*[742]

There was no hint of compassion.

As if it was no big deal.

The speaker was a subaltern friar sent to spy on Portuguese ambassadors who were on a mission to the emperor of Ethiopia. It was standard procedure across Europe to kill Muslims and Jews – so much so that such heinous crimes against humanity passed the critical examination by inquisitorial censors. They approved the publication of this missionary's horrible passages[743] because they did not see just how repulsive and criminal their actions were. From the highest ranks of the Catholic Church to a lowly friar, they looked at Muslims, Jews, and non-Catholics in general not as humans but as pests to be removed.

It is called *genocide*.

---

[741] Francisco Alvarez, Narrative of the Portuguese embassy to Abyssinia during the years 1520-1527, translated from the Portuguese and edited by Lord Stanley of Alderley (Hakluyt Society, 1881) 243.

[742] Ibid.

[743] All printed books in the realm of the Catholic Church had to be licensed by its functionaries. Francisco Alvarez' reports from between 1523 and his departure in 1526 went missing. The geographer Roberto Almagia (1884 – 1962) found three manuscripts of Francisco Álvares in the Vatican Library that differed from the approved and published version of his work.

There is a modern notion that they did not know any better back then. It is true, there were infinite ways to die. However, the culture of systemic poverty and its related hostile and despotic environment in Europe was then shaped by the Catholic Church alone.

Under the guidance of our modern Pope Francis, the Catholic Church has declared the death penalty as unacceptable in all cases. The pope has opined that capital punishment fosters vengeance rather than rendering justice to the victims. [744] He was particularly concerned about wrongful convictions. While this goodness is laudable, it is also in violation of biblical commands.

As Inquisition trials demonstrate in abundance, sometimes, being denied death is the worse choice.

The same missionary for whom burning heretics was normalized witnessed that one of his Portuguese travel companions and his captain showed '*compassion and virtue*' in freeing an old Jew who had earlier been captured.[745] Because that companion was poor, the captain waived the purchase price for the enslaved Jew.

The difference between the two instances is that one was anonymous and the other up close and personal. The missionary looked right into the eyes of the captive Jew – still a slave after the donated acquisition.

These men knew to differentiate as much as we do today.

A little omission is significant: the missionary did not mention that Portugal was a place of systematic killings. Instead, he singled out the Catholic Church and the Kingdom of France. Since the Inquisition came to provide for another deadly blow on Jews in Portugal, I will return to this nation in due time.

Do you need more facts on the Inquisition?

You had better be sitting.

---

[744] Elisabetta Povoledo, Laurie Goodstein, Pope Francis Declares Death Penalty Unacceptable in All Cases, New York Times, August 2, 2018.

[745] Alvarez, transl. Alderley, 1881, 375-376.

Medina del Campo was a walled town at the side of an artificial, defensive hill in the plains of central Spain. It was distant from any important city. The castle on the hill[746] hosted royal troops for the defense and subjugation of the town below. Across the river[747] lay the ancient market-hall that is still in use today. In Luther's century, the small village had grown to importance through textiles, books, other trades, and banking. Buildings from the time attest to the wealth of the place, exhibited through construction projects with the support of rich merchant bankers.

In the wake of the uprising in Castile, the Grand Inquisitor Adrian oversaw Medina del Campo being set ablaze. He watched it burn to the ground while the people inside were grilled. This vicious act of godly mercy set the hearts of the entire region on fire. The censors of the Catholic Church later claimed that the fire had gotten out of control and that it was only supposed to be a distraction. Were it not for the future Pope Adrian standing at the gates – the Grand Inquisitor at the time – we might take this scenario into consideration. A Franciscan monastery was also engulfed, some of their own, they claim. But we have learned earlier that the monasteries in Spain were rebelling against the reforms in the Catholic Church that aimed at depriving them of their concubines and from their diversity in questions of faith and ritual. This is also why Francisco de Quiñones (educated by the Grand Inquisitor Cardinal Cisneros) was put at the helm of the Franciscan Order. Here, we can confidently separate nonsense and lies.

Adrian chose to smoke his enemies out and made sure that the skulls of those who tried to escape were given a loving blow.

Indeed, the rebels were slaughtered by a professional army under the leadership of the 'Constable of Castile.' The ringleaders were executed on the spot. This anonymous 'Constable' was the second ranking official in Spain, which was none other than our career priest Adrian – the butcher pope.

Of course, we have little evidence to this assertion, other than a painting by a Spanish artist[748] from 200 years later, which cannot serve as proof. From his work, the deep-seated trauma that this savage brought upon the Spanish people can be extracted with ease: there are three prisoners, one with head severed, the next with knife on throat, and the last standing in pride and defiance. A truly heroic Spaniard. The only others that are depicted are two butchers at work on

---

[746] The Castle of La Mota. The castle is prominent for the Italian Cardinal Cesare Borgia. We have heard of him earlier. Cesare was the 'illegitimate' son of Rodrigo de Borja (Borgia), alias Pope Alexander VI. The castle is the location where Cesare was imprisoned after the death of his papal father.

[747] Rio Zapardiel.

[748] Antonio Gisbert Pérez, 1834 – 1901, Los Comuneros de Castilla, 1860.

the prisoners and three Dominican Inquisitors. In the absence of others, one of the latter was the 'Constable of Castile.'

A pure-blood barbarian. The future pope. Adrian.

One of the three rebel leaders[749] was husband to Maria Coronel. This is the revived name from the conversion of Rabbi Abraham Senior to the Coronel nobility – from Senior, the Jewish tax farmer, to Coronel, the Catholic tax farmer. Business was good. The Catholic Church had signed the deal.

Finally, a converso's spouse as a forerunner of freedom.

However, her closeness to Jewish leadership and the succession from the suspect Cisneros to the brute Adrian looms large in Medina del Campo. If this were along my main path of research, I would put my foot down – right here might be the motherlode.

A contemporary proposal[750] indicates that the Spanish population was opposed to an alien leader in the absence of Charles.[751] This is a direct implication of the foreigner Adrian.

In short, the Spanish were against the Grand Inquisitor Cardinal Adrian, who brought about totalitarian oppression.

In 1519, the Kingdom of Valencia in Aragon had been dealing with famine and plague. Its area was also host to large numbers of force-converted Jews and Muslims, all of whom were blinded by messianic hopes to be one day redeemed from their oppressors. To deal with the conversos, Valencia had its own tribunal of Adrian's Inquisition.[752]

As the noble leadership fled the city from the plague, riots led to the overthrow of the royal government. A new, representative government filled the power vacuum, the Council of Thirteen.

After the terror of the Inquisition, they were taking a shot at social reform. The rebels' aim was to put the nobles and the Catholic Church in their place. In their path to freedom stood one man: the highest government caretaker for Valencia who was none other than Adrian of Utrecht – now Pope Adrian.

---

[749] Juan Bravo.

[750] The proposal came from the defiant city of Toledo.

[751] Joseph Pérez, Los Comuneros (Esfera de los Libros, 2001) 53–54.

[752] Sara T. Nalle, Revisiting El Encubierto: Navigating between Visions of Heaven and Hell on Earth, in Kathryn A. Edwards, Werewolves, Witches, and Wandering Spirits: Traditional Belief and Folklore in Early Modern Europe (Truman State University Press, 2002) 79.

By the time Charles and Adrian conquered the Vatican – a considered choice of words – the city of Valencia had been retaken by royal troops and the revolt was soon crushed. The information that has come down to us is unfortunately scant and whitewashed. We can make such an accusation with conviction, though, because the Inquisition was in town.

If we know *anything* about the Inquisition, it is that no noble would have dared to make a move or to come forth with a public proclamation of propaganda without prior approval of inquisitors.

Unless he was tired of his life.

The leader of the Revolt of the Brotherhood, as it was called, was burned out of his home, arrested, and executed.

With exquisite timing, a mysterious leader emerged in the spring of 1522, a messiah – the Hidden One.

I have little to go by. But little sometimes tells a lot.

The Hidden One had a vision from Elijah and Enoch. Jesus Christ made it clear that Elijah had to appear as the forerunner before the End of the World[753] as prophesied.[754] Accordingly, the presence of this prophet was a necessary show of messianic intentions.

As an example of faith for eternal life,[755] Enoch was an unusual character to form part of such an announcement.

For Luther, the important function of this biblical figure was that he had been called to God and had achieved immortality through resurrection. The Reformer's hope was that *'we shall not remain in death.'*[756] Death could, somehow, be beaten. In his work, Enoch is connected to the messianic End of the World only as one who prophesied that the Day of Judgment would come.[757]

Taking the Bible as real evidence, Luther used this prophet among the witnesses for a future life[758] after death,[759] but not as messianic figure. In addition, the Reformer explained how the rabbis viewed Enoch.[760]

---

753  Matthew 11:11-11:14 (NIV).
754  Malachi 4:5-4:6 (NIV).
755  Hebrews 11:5-11:6 (NIV).
756  Luther's Works, Vol. I, 1958332 [lectures about the Book of Genesis].
757  Ibid., 343-344.
758  Ibid., 344.
759  Ibid., 348.
760  Ibid., 349.

The only role that Luther presented was proof of the resurrection of the dead and everlasting life through Enoch.[761]

There are several other Enochs in the Bible, but the one who stands out is Reuben's first-born son Enoch (Hanoch). I will show why my selection fell to Reuben's son, but in short, he and Elijah are directly connected to the End of the World. It appears that Reuben's son is relevant. Rabbinic leaders would pack this Enoch into a messianic message.

The possible identity of Enoch should not blind us to the fact that all – Jews, Muslims, and Christians – were eager to meet their christ-messiah or mahdi. After all, both Muslims and Jews had been thrown out of Spain or were force-converted. Christian Spaniards found themselves under the unexpected yoke of the Inquisition. Consequently, we need to remain open for any of them to come up with some biblical innovations.

On the other hand, the idea of the Hidden One was not new.

Spanish Christians seem to have held a conviction of a Sleeping Emperor of the Last Days for 300 years already.[762] It appears to go back to Emperor Frederick II,[763] the conqueror of Jerusalem in the thirteenth century, and the Spanish King Ferdinand III The Saint.[764] The latter was now revived[765] as the new David. Ferdinand had become a (Syrian-Melchite or Nestorian) Christian folk-saint through the Spanish Reconquista. Remarkably, his tomb features plaques with dates in the Hebrew, Islamic and Gregorian calendars with texts in Hebrew, Arabic, Latin, and Castilian.

Contemporary to Martin Luther, the epithet 'the Hidden One' was used for propaganda by the Inquisitors in the re-conquest of Granada from Muslims. A notable detail is the aspiration of the *current* Ferdinand II of Aragon[766] to '*not only be Emperor but Monarch of the whole world.*'[767] El Católico (the Catholic), as he was called, literally promoted himself as Ferdinand incarnate.

---

[761] Ibid., 351.

[762] Alain Milhou, Colón y su mentalidad mesiánica, 237.

[763] Frederick II from the House of Hohenstaufen was King of Sicily 1198 – 1250, King of Germany 1212 – 1220, King of Jerusalem 1225 – 1228, King of Italy and Holy Roman Emperor 1220 – 1250. Emperor Frederick was not only never emperor over Spain, he was also an outspoken enemy of the Vatican. He is, thus, a strange folk hero for the Spaniards. This mystery seeks resolution.

[764] Ferdinand III was King of Castile from 1217 and King of León from 1230 as well as King of Galicia from 1231 until 1252.

[765] Redivivus.

[766] Ferdinand II of Aragon aka el católico, Ferrando, or Ferran, was King of Sicily 1468 – 1516, King of Castile and León 1475 – 1504, and King of Aragon 1479 – 1516.

[767] Grace Magnier, Pedro de Valencia and the Catholic apologists of the expulsion of the Moriscos: visions of Christianity and kingship (Brill, Copyright © 2010, reprinted by permission of Brill) 72.

El Católico was also grandfather to Charles, now Holy Roman Emperor.

We need no longer wonder where Charles' ambitions to world dominance at all cost were coming from, even if it were achieved through bribery on an imperial scale and with the help of an army.

The phrase *the empire on which the sun never sets* originated in Spain under Ferdinand's grandeur.

The fact that Ferdinand II of Aragon, El Católico, was of marrano heritage, former Jews, translates to the Holy Roman Emperor Charles V to be of Jewish background.

Without intending in any way to debase Jewish achievements, this is confusing. I can only ask the question bluntly: was royalty in Spain at some point Jewish? Not just the crown rabbi and his lethal administration? What was going on in Muslim Spain for almost a thousand years before the Spanish Reconquista is for another book to tell. Did Spain live through a prophetic fulfilment of the End of the World under Jewish leadership?

Not by chance does the Hidden One also have a Muslim Shi'a connotation that relates to the Mahdi. It may have arisen through the strong bond between the (Syrian Melchite and Nestorian) Christian churches in Spain, their Muslim overlords, and Jewish leaders.[768]

In any case, the notion of the hidden savior is essentially the same: a new David, the Messiah with the iron rod.

As it is with superstitions, their origins are not always clear but often feature the kind of love and peace that is brought about by heroes with blood dripping down their swords. Here, in the Grand Inquisitor Adrian's famine-and-plague-stricken Valencia, the Hidden One was a figure who was intent on molesting the tender sensibilities of the faithful of all, Christians, Muslims, and Jews. Whether religion was abused for political goals or politics for religious grand aspirations makes little difference.

In the end, the bloodletting took place with the lowly people.

As the Revolt of the Brotherhood faltered, the Hidden One came to fame through a sermon. Therein, he announced himself to be illiterate. This is a marker that appears with professional prophetic contenders. Prophet Muhammad, for example, is said to having been illiterate.[769]

---

[768] This may also be the path to unlocking Emperor Frederick's mystery as the Hidden One and the one of Jews on royal thrones.

[769] Koran 36:69-36:70.

The aim of the pretention was to suggest that the mission was inspired by God. Force-converted Jews and Muslims picked up on that clue.

The Hidden One unveiled the directions given to him by Elijah and Enoch to save Valencia and to conquer the Promised Land.

Hearsay has it that he was a converso from Andalusia.[770]

Speaking against clerical abuse, the Hidden One is said to have been sent to seek the support of King Charles, now the emperor. In other words, he was attempting to form alliances, even with his enemy overlords. According to the archives of the Inquisition, he intended to seize and sell church properties in order to feed the poor.[771] Similarly, he planned to redistribute wealth from the nobles to the needy. This property confiscation would also finance the holy war to reconquer the Promised Land.

Who can blame the masses that were abused with their deepest desires for freedom? Through the Hidden One, the original rebellion had received fuel from an unexpected source, and the brotherhood's armies quickly found new recruits.

One of the chroniclers who was friendly to the cause of the Hidden One noted that he was creating a new religion and *'was almost adored as God.'*[772] This messiah claimant meant serious business.[773] We have already learned how a messiah needs to proclaim a new religion in partnership with old ones, how a new starting point, for example Adam, is important, and how this *new* religion will conquer the Promised Land.

Yet, it is always interesting to hear how another man's visions about God and his messengers belong into the world of *'not very sane persons.'*[774] A later historian called the Hidden One as *'simple-minded, his sermon is nothing but "heretical nonsense," and his followers are dupes who "swallowed" the whole thing.'*[775]

The Hidden One was not a simpleton. This was no amateur. The story has vital elements of a messianic grand treachery at the cost of ordinary Jews, Christians, and Muslims.

---

[770] Magnier, Pedro de Valencia, 2010, 81 [the converso identity is clearly marked as hearsay by the author].

[771] M. Danvila, El encubierto de Valencia, El Archivo. Revista de Ciencias Históricas, V, 1 (1890) 125, as translated in Magnier, Pedro de Valencia, 2010, 77.

[772] Magnier, Pedro de Valencia, 2010, 89, footnote 26 (Madrid: Editions del Centro, 1975) 228.

[773] Ibid., 84.

[774] Ibid., 90.

[775] Gaspar Escolano, Decadas de la Historia de la Insigne y coronada ciudad y reino de Vanecia (1611, repr., Valencia, 1879) 2:700-9, in Magnier, Pedro de Valencia, 2010, 91.

By the end of the year, the revolt was suppressed, and the Messiah was murdered and *'condemned, posthumously, by the Inquisition of Valencia and dragged through the city. Later, his body was burned and his head placed on the Cuarte gate in Valencia.'*[776] If you would not be scared into submission by this exemplum, you must be one rare and fearless kind of hero.

Several figures claimed that the Inquisition had gotten the wrong guy. Nobody even heard the Hidden One say of himself that he, indeed, was the Hidden One.[777] Only the Inquisition itself used the designation *'the Hidden King'* in its records.[778] But most of these were 'expunged.'

Precisely because of the Hidden One's success, the Catholic Church had to eradicate his traces.[779]

The mystery was never solved but lived on. The crowd believed it anyhow. He must return. One day.

We can contrast the Hidden One with a messianic imposter who appeared in Valencia just seven years later.

The difference is immediately apparent.

One such prophet[780] claimed in the streets of Valencia that he had been divinely inspired and that he could perform miracles. The world would come to an end in 1533, four years after his appearance. His mission was to find a single true follower of Christ. He found none. Jesus would return and an apostolic Christianity would be revamped with the New Jerusalem in Strasbourg.[781]

There was no forerunner. The boastful 'prophet' did not claim that he started out illiterate (although he was trained neither in the Torah nor in theology). He was a false prophet. The Inquisition seized him. He received 100 lashes and was thrown out of Spain.

They did not know that they had let one of the radical leaders of the Anabaptist Reformation go.

---

[776] Magnier, Pedro de Valencia, 2010, 78.
[777] Ibid., 87.
[778] Ibid., 89: El Rey Encubierto.
[779] Ibid., 78.
[780] Melchior of Wurttemberg.
[781] Hugh Chisholm, Melchior Hofmann, Encyclopædia Britannica. 13 (11th ed.) (Cambridge University Press, 1911) 564.
Longhurst, 1964, 28-29.

As promised by the outcast from Valencia, the Anabaptists launched a coup in 1534 in the German city of Münster to establish an Anabaptist theocracy – their New Jerusalem. Except the Bible, they burned all books. Their End of the World had come. A year later, it was all over. The Catholic Church asserted its love over Münster and nailed the leader's genitals to the city gate.

Church historians have since been trying to place the blame for the humanitarian disasters during the Spanish Inquisition on secular forces and Spanish royalty. However, Charles was played by a puppeteer since he could walk – Adrian, the future butcher pope. The Grand Inquisitor. We can appreciate that Charles' mother, a Luther sympathizer, was confined when she should have ruled – by Adrian.

He was the factual king in Spain.

There were only two better positions for him to climb higher: the throne of the empire or the throne in Rome. By pulling the strings for Charles, Adrian had aimed for supreme spiritual leadership.

With the bloodletting, the appetite for liberties in Spain died for centuries to come at the hands of the brutal Inquisition. The area remained a backward-oriented domain deep into the twentieth century. This retro attitude was also dominant in the poverty-stricken areas of the Spanish speaking countries in Central and South America.

This insult to the country and the beautiful people of Spain is, in some ways, doing them injustice. Their contribution to arts, literature, and architecture during the sixteenth century was formidable. The period in art that coincides with the Spanish Inquisition is termed the Spanish Golden Age.

The arts seem to have provided the Spaniards with an outlet for their un-freedoms.

But since we are in the middle of the Renaissance, during which art blossomed throughout Europe, the Spanish paradox is perhaps merely a point of friction on the long path to freedom. The claim of the church to inspiring the Spanish Golden Age is like a father claiming to have rescued the life of his daughter after having beaten her unconscious. Look how beautifully my child can draw! Certainly, the Catholic Church cannot possibly pretend to be responsible for the Renaissance. Not in Spain, nor in Italy, nor elsewhere.

It is liable for having suppressed progress for over a thousand years.

Look at art during the period of the Roman Empire. As the Catholic Church rose, art declined to a kindergarten level. On its way out from the Christian oppression, art started to flourish again.

I have already talked about a few Italian Renaissance Men. There were others. Alfred Dürer,[782] for example, was now in the midst of creating some of his masterworks at Nüremberg. He was influenced by Luther's religious zeal. In other words, the Spanish Golden Age marked an era of awakening that found its counterparts across Europe.

When we look at the arts of the time, depicting rich court life and etiquette, we often feel romance with the Renaissance. Do not get me wrong. The Renaissance is my passion. I love how they made headway against all odds. But this was one heck of a barbaric time, even if one were to turn a blind eye to the victims of internal Christian wars or the spiritual and noble brutes.

One might think that being an outcast was no big deal. Go live elsewhere! That was not so simple. There was no security. The European courts and bishoprics had to travel with entire armies. It took over a month for a letter to get from Paris to Rome, let alone an entourage. To be sure, the letter would not arrive unopened – several times. What information would you have relied on? You were not allowed to read what you wished – should you have been among the few able to read.

Everything was censored and expunged.

Different currencies would bankrupt you along the way. You had no choice but to rely on Jewish money changers. Provisions were in the hands of monopolies controlled by the Catholic Church.

You needed anything? Pay up! You brought along your own merchandise? It was confiscated wherever your wares were desirable. Entire ships of goods were held hostage for trade protection. Why would you think to have been spared? Everywhere one intended to go, letters of safe passage were needed. If you were suspected of carrying state secrets – and you were – you ended up in the torture chambers until the day of your confession, whether you carried secrets or not.

Remember: the organized crime of the Catholic Church was in bed with nobility. It did not follow laws. It made the rules for you, all right. But those rules applied to neither the church nor nobility. Theirs was the honor of bandits. Believe or die.

Anarchy, lived to its fullest potential.

---

[782] Albrecht Dürer, 1471 – 1528.

Flee across the Bosporus? There was no land of freedom either. The world was in the hands of self-aggrandized gangsters who just happened to become bosses of criminal organizations through the power of organized religion and the sword. Sharia Law. Everywhere, people were squeezed beyond the last drop of the lemon.

The beautiful coin of the Renaissance had one heck of an ugly obverse.

Just because criminals love to show off with collections of art does not make them any better human beings.

Organized religion had nurtured the worst of humankind to buoy to the top of the food chain.

Embark to America? There, your welcome would be a shower of arrows. The Inquisition in the south. Protestant passions in the north.

Have a good journey.

If I had said all this about ISIS, everyone would agree. Just because it forms our Western cultural backdrop, we should never be blind to the ugly side of the Renaissance and the eras of its theocratic predecessors. The height of the Renaissance was also the height of the Inquisition.

ISIS were mere amateurs in comparison.

I can now return to the holy man.

Adrian was elected pope by almost unanimous vote, against his will and in his absence.

Come again?

Let me reflect on this for a second.

There is this man, tutor of the boy who became Holy Roman Emperor by means of the greatest bribe in history, this murderous Grand Inquisitor in Spain's slaughterhouse, the second in charge after the emperor himself, and a holy enemy of freedom. And church historians are trying to convince us that he got elected to the throne in the Vatican almost by unanimous agreement. A radical as a compromise candidate? In absence?

Never mind that this supreme spiritual leader was now paired with *his* emperor.

It is no wonder that Martin Luther came to view Adrian as an antichrist. He was, indeed, the embodiment of corruption and Satan personified, were it not for the fact that devils do not exist.

Barely on the papal throne, Adrian forged an alliance between the Catholic Church, England, and Venice against the French. This is perhaps the alliance that Pope Leo never signed, because he was three days from his last sigh in his deathbed.

We are no longer surprised that the French-friendly Medici Pope Leo had succumbed to young age, are we?

This corrupt man stopped for nothing.

In Luther's time, Adrian was, indeed, the Antichrist.

Having been the General Inquisitor of Spain, it also does not come as a revelation that he simply wanted Martin Luther punished for heresy. He had no need to listen.

The punishment for heresy?

Guilty or not: slow roast.

In other words, the pope played shepherd and butcher at the same time.

But Rome did not welcome the foreign pope.

On the Pasquino, an ancient fragment of a group of statues that was only found recently in Rome, protest notes were added. One of them called him *'a traitor'* and the College of Cardinals *'robbers.'*

The writer expressed that the Vatican was in the hands of German rage.[783]

It was just a single note.

Martin Luther's artist friend, Lucas Cranach, produced an illustration of the new pope: a Babylonian whore with the papal Tiara riding a seven-headed beast. Even the cardinals disliked him for his insistence on an alien morality and asceticism (austerity and self-denial), as well as for his attempt to cut down on their privileges.[784] Given his history, I would not have expected anything else.

Neither did the cardinals.

They voted for him unanimously.

Within a few months after Adrian's accession to the papal throne, France went to war against the combined troops of the Catholic Church and the Holy Roman Empire.

---

[783] Ferdinand Gregorovius: Die Geschichte der Stadt Rom im Mittelalter. Band 8 (Cotta, 1872) 381

[784] Albrecht Beutel and Michael Beyer of the Luther-Gesellschaft, Lutherjahrbuch 78. Jahrgang 2011: Organ der internationalen Lutherforschung (Vandenhoeck, 2012) 9.

It did not go well for the French. They retreated and lost their previously French-controlled cities of Milan and Genoa.[785] After England joined the alliance with the Catholic Church, the French were in total defeat.

They were beaten but not dead – yet.

Now the French were looking for allies in Eastern Europe, trying to forge agreements with whomever was willing. Ambassadors of France were deployed to Poland and Hungary, the back doors to the Holy Roman Empire.

One might think that this was a smart strategy.

Emperor Charles had gone even further.

A few years earlier, he had already sent an ambassador[786] to the Persian court of the Shi'ite Safavid Empire. The plan was to squeeze the growing Sunni Ottoman-Turkish threat from east and west. In addition, Charles was also seeking to ally himself with Poland and Hungary against the Ottoman's.

To the detriment of the Americas, Pope Adrian oversaw how Francisco de Quiñones (the disciple of the Grand Inquisitor Cardinal Cisneros) became Minister General of the Franciscan Order. Under his watch, de Quiñones sent twelve Franciscan missionaries to Mexico, among them the first bishop in the future territory of the United States.[787] Another passenger carried the name of a monstrous father: Cisneros.[788]

It foreshadowed bad news.

In their lower deck store compartments, these emigrants brought along African slaves to carry out the hard labors of real life for them. In their eyes, slavery was an expression of the ideal state of New Jerusalem.

The attempt at colonization ended in failure for the colonists. Arrows rained down on them and forced them to retreat to safer ground.

Adrian did not last long as pope.

After less than two years on the throne, he died at the age of sixty-four in the summer of 1523. He succumbed to a fever. Others claim that he may have been poisoned.[789]

---

[785] A contemporary Jewish chronicle suggests that the Jews in Genoa were oppressed. Ha-Cohen, Vol. II, translated by Bialloblotzky, 1836, 30.
[786] The ambassador's name was Knight of Saint John de Balbi.
[787] The Friar Juan Juárez. The first masses in the future continental United States were read at San Miguel de Guadalupe.
[788] García de Cisneros.
[789] Hermann Schreiber, Geschichte der Päpste.

This is supported by the fact that his legacy in the Catholic Church was extinguished. Most of his papers were lost – or were made sure to be lost.

This is how history was engineered.

They even spat Adrian's corpse out of the Vatican.

Adrian was first buried in the Vatican and ten years later moved outside, to the church Santa Maria dell'Anima. This church was originally founded by the Dutch and was now the national church of the Holy Roman Empire, its spiritual center. Luther saw it as a positive contrast to the excess and corruption of the Vatican, almost as one of his own, a German church.[790]

Adrian's burial inscriptions are full of melancholy. The one in the Vatican read: *To the best, supreme God. Adrian VI rests here: he was unhappier about nothing in life but that he had to rule.*[791] And unhappily, the Grand Inquisitor who brought much despair upon so many people longing for freedom, found his end.

The final inscription engraved on his monument in the Santa Maria dell'Anima was: *'Oh pain! How much depends on which time even the best man's virtues fall.*[792] The persecutor's perspective of his life's synopsis could be the summary of Luther's time.

Adrian remained the only Dutch pope, ever, and was also the last pope of the Holy Roman Empire.

Because of tyrants like him, freedom had to keep on pushing elsewhere.

Why did Martin Luther like any of it? Because his intention was to go back to the old, totalitarian state of church control.

His way.

---

[790] Beutel, Beyer, Lutherjahrbuch, 2012, footnote 8, 10-11, translated by A.J. Deus, (WA 4; 425,5-13).
[791] Ibid., 19, translated by A.J. Deus.
[792] Ibid.

## Heap of Ruins

A lucky coincidence with Adrian's final year is Luther's essay *'That Jesus Christ was Born a Jew.'* It provides a timely inventory about Luther's feelings toward the Jewish population. In it, Luther said this:

> *Our fools, the popes, bishops, sophists, and monks - the crude asses' heads - have hitherto so treated the Jews that anyone who wished to be a good Christian would almost have had to become a Jew. If I had been a Jew and had seen such dolts and blockheads govern and teach the Christian faith, I would sooner have become a hog than a Christian. They have dealt with the Jews as if they were dogs rather than human beings; they have done little else than deride them and seize their property. When they baptize them they show them nothing of Christian doctrine or life, but only subject them to popishness and mockery. [...] If the apostles, who also were Jews, had dealt with us Gentiles as we Gentiles deal with the Jews, there would never have been a Christian among the Gentiles. [...] When we are inclined to boast of our position [as Christians] we should remember that we are but Gentiles, while the Jews are of the lineage of Christ. We are aliens and in-laws; they are blood relatives, cousins, and brothers of our Lord. Therefore, if one is to boast of flesh and blood the Jews are actually nearer to Christ than we are. [...] If the Jews should take offense because we confess our Jesus to be a man, and yet true God, we will deal forcefully with that from Scripture in due time. But this is too harsh for a beginning. Let them first be suckled with milk, and begin by recognizing this man Jesus as the true Messiah; after that they may drink wine, and learn also that he is true God. For they have been led astray so long and so far that one must deal gently with them, as people who have been all too strongly indoctrinated to believe that God cannot be man.*
>
> *Therefore, I would request and advise that one deal gently with them and instruct them from Scripture; then some of them may come along. Instead of this we are trying only to drive them by force, slandering them, accusing them of having Christian blood if they don't stink, and I know not what other foolishness. So long as we thus treat them like dogs, how can we expect to work any good among them? Again, when we forbid them to labor and do business and have any human fellowship with us, thereby forcing them into usury, how is that supposed to do them any good? If we really want to help them, we must be guided in our dealings with them not by papal law but by the law of Christian love. We must receive them cordially, and permit them to trade and work with us, that they may have occasion and opportunity to associate with us, hear our Christian teaching, and witness our Christian life. If some of them should prove stiff-necked, what of it? After all, we*

*ourselves are not all good Christians either.*[793]

How, in Jesus' name, did Martin Luther get from this to becoming the world's foremost Jew hater? He recognized that the Catholic Church was wrong in treating them like dogs – sows, actually.

We know that his agenda was their conversion to Christianity. He even says so in this very text,[794] and he may have chosen a gentle approach with this goal in mind. His Christian love for Jews could be suspected as not having been genuine. Yet, nothing out of his earlier writings suggests that this is not how he actually felt.

Was Martin Luther to be overcome by madness? Did Satan perhaps show himself in the guise of a woman? After all, Martin Luther was 39 years old now.

And he was single.

Even though he rejected the concept of celibacy that had been imposed on the clergy of the Catholic Church, he thought himself not ready for a woman in his life, for he did not even sleep in a clean bed: *'I shall never take a wife, as I feel at present. Not that I am insensible to my flesh or sex (for I am neither wood nor stone); but my mind is averse to wedlock because I daily expect the death of a heretic.'*[795]

Throughout the realm of the Catholic Church, millions of girls were forced into monasteries. The rationale for doing so was often to protect family assets from being diluted through marriages. Having to provide daughters with dowries was expensive and a potential existential threat, in particular for nobility.

As nuns, they were involuntarily imprisoned and brainwashed. The inmates' existences were not unlike lives in modern polygamist communities that choose to live in total seclusion – minus the children – minus the men.

Nuns are a unique species. They consider themselves married to Jesus Christ. Their white cuccula symbolizes the wedding dress. Thousands of women were married to Jesus at the same time. They had no issue with the problem that Jesus could not possibly have consented to a vow of marriage. All of it had to take place in a world of pretence.

Getting married to this first century man-god 1,500 years later requires extraordinary mental gymnastics.

---

[793] Luther, Jesus Born a Jew, Brandt, 1962: 200–201, 229.

[794] Ibid.

[795] Philip Schaff, Luther's Marriage 1525, History of the Christian Church, Volume VII, Modern Christianity, The German Reformation. § 77, Christian Classics Ethereal Library, Mullett, 180–81.

The love of Jesus Christ does not impregnate. Not usually. Only in a miracle was the Virgin with child. Was each nun hoping to be selected for the repetition of the tale?

The Cistercian Monastery in Nimbschen, a German town of Saxony, hosted a club of extremists who lived in full isolation with a concept of self-sufficiency and total focus on religiosity. The quiet setting of the cloister, overlooking the Mulde River from a slight elevation in the forest, would almost be idyllic, were it not for its inhumane purpose. The nuns were ruled by a brutal, authoritarian enforcer, an abbess, or in the case of monks, an abbot, denoting *'father'* but really meaning the one *'to hold the place of Christ,'*[796] which is, of course, God, for them.

The monastic origin of the Cistercian Order is French and based on a strict following of the reductionist Rule of Saint Benedict: pax, ora et labora, *'peace, prayer, and work.'* The word *'peace'* here bears the meaning of *'leave me alone'* or perhaps simply of *'sleep.'* The rule manifests the complete rejection of social life: eight hours of prayer, eight hours of subsistence work or sacred reading, and eight hours of a good night's sleep to rest from having exerted oneself in doing absolutely nothing useful.

The miracle man Benedict, the alleged author of the rule for intellectual and systemic poverty, was born with a silver spoon. He was from a noble family and became a teenager well ahead of his age, according to a biography that was invented by the flaming souls' Pope Gregory almost 100 years after the supposed facts. At the age of 14 (!), the immorality of society in Rome so appalled the boy that he dropped out from his studies to become a hermit and to pursue his holiness in the solitude of a cave.

He is known for having rolled in a thornbush in agony over his lust for a girl in order to 'heal' his soul.

Judaic historians typically present Rome as an example of immorality. In doing so, they attempt to contrast the highly advanced Roman society with the piety of their own creed.

However, the last calls for help from the Roman Senate against Christian invaders had gone silent a few years before Benedict's birth.[797] A quarter century before that, the church's Fourth Ecumenical Council of Chalcedon[798] had *'disturbed the entire world.'*[799]

---

[796] Pope Benedict XVI, General Audience, Saint Benedict of Norcia (Vatican, 2008).

[797] From 476 to 493 AD, the Vandal Odoacer was the leader of the *foederati*—Germanic Christian families that lived in Italy.

[798] Fourth Ecumenical Council of Chalcedon, 451 AD.

[799] John, Bishop of Nikiu, Chronicles, ca. 640 – 700 AD, LXXXVIII:16.

Rome was drowning in Christian blood.

What happened is a tragedy.

The stronger Christianity grew, the more Rome crumbled. By the time of the boy Benedict, the city had fallen from 1.7 million inhabitants to less than 50,000.[800] Urban life in Rome had succumbed to faith. Following the advice of Saint Augustine, Luther's idol, scripture was taken like science, and science was rejected,[801] like heresy.

Benedict's Rome was ruled by Pope Symmacchus.[802] His name bears the root to the word simony, and he did, indeed, bribe himself onto the papal throne.[803]

The boy-hermit Benedict may have carried a stick during the years of unrest that followed the usurpation of the papacy by one foreign to his own Truth.

This is why the boy had to leave.

Perhaps to escape jail.

This pope also brought forth a whole library of church fabrications, known as the Symmachean forgeries.[804] His simple strategy was to reject Byzantine spiritual questions by creating Rome's primacy.[805] From Symmacchus forward, Jews were exposed to the methodical wrath of Christians who were made to believe that they had murdered the Messiah Jesus Christ.[806]

The story that had been created to revive the drive for the Promised Land turned against them. Not by coincidence, Pope Symmacchus ruled shortly after a Jewish secession from the Temple Mount was terminated in 470 AD.

The intellectual groundwork for seeking a *'Final Solution'* to the *'Jewish Question'* lies here, 1,000 years before Luther – 1,500 years before Hitler.

---

[800] The reduction of Rome to rubble happened between the early third century and the end of the fifth.

[801] Augustine, *De Genesi ad Litteram* (354 – 430 AD) II, xviii, 37.

[802] Pope Symmachus was pope 498 – 514 AD.

[803] Raymond Davis, The Book of Pontiffs (Liber Pontificalis): The Ancient Biographies of the First Ninety Roman Bishops to AD 715 (Liverpool University Press, 2000) 97. Jeffrey Richards, The Popes and the Papacy in the Early Middle Ages, 476 – 752 (Routledge & Kegan Paul, 1979) 70f.

[804] Catholic Encyclopedia, Pope St. Symmachus.

[805] Consensus insists on Rome having always enjoyed primacy over all else. Their evidence? Forgeries and legends. This historic heist was possible, because the church was in possession of the empire's archives in Milan, Ravenna, and Rome. Like the Jewish leadership after the fall of the empire of Alexander the Great, the Catholic Church could then create a history of its own choosing. Monasteries typically acted as the mass copyists of the frauds. All they needed to do was to edit, inject, and sign off on whatever they pleased.

[806] Johnson, 1998, 164–165.

Henceforth, Italy broke into fiercely competing city-states, modeled after Augustine's Cities of God. This book became the template for the feudal system.

By the time of Martin Luther, the development clock had been turned back by over a thousand years. There was no longer room for reason. Art was blackened. Music went silent. Science was lost. The economy collapsed. Filth and rot became the glorified expression of systemic poverty.

Taliban rule.

Rome an example of immorality?

At Benedict's time, the 'immoral' Rome was Christian.

Our modern Pope Francis' predecessor, Benedict XVI had chosen this papal name for himself to honor his idol.

He thought that the boy *'had a fundamental influence on the development of European civilization and culture.'* He, Saint Benedict, *'gives us a model for human life in the climb towards the summit of perfection.'* And his *'marvelous work'*[807] was instrumental in the formation of Christian Europe, even for the idea of Europe itself. He helped the West to come out of the Dark Ages, the *'black night of history'* as the former pope called it.[808]

Instead, Christian extremists pushed a highly advanced civilization into the Dark Ages, not out of it.

The former pope went even further. He mocked the *'collapse of the great ideologies, now revealed as tragic utopias.'* He wished for an *'ethical and spiritual renewal which draws on the Christian roots of the Continent'* without which *'a new Europe cannot be built.'*

The pope considered Christianity as providing the *'vital sap'* in order to prevent humankind from sliding into yet another utopia. Saint Benedict, said the pope, was the role model from whom we *'can learn to become proficient in true humanism.'*[809]

Monastic life in the image of the hermit Benedict degrades human beings to mere vegetation and to imagination. It robs them of their freedoms and individualities.

These are places of radicalization.

---

[807] Pope Benedict XVI, General Audience, Saint Benedict of Norcia (Vatican, 2008).
[808] Ibid (cf. John Paul II, 18 May 1979).
[809] Ibid.

A little over 50 miles south of Wittenberg, a nun was engineering her escape from the Cistercian Monastery in Nimbschen, Katharina von Bora.[810]

As a child, Katharina was put into a cloister. There, she learned to farm for subsistence and to brew beer.

The confined life of a monastery was not for her.

She heard of Martin Luther's reform movement and contacted the friar for help in plotting a jailbreak for 12 nuns. Katharina did not have to beg for Luther's assistance. He wholeheartedly encouraged them to flee.

His mindset was expressed in a letter in which he reviewed the idea of monastic life. If she had not freely entered, she should call her friends to help in escaping.[811] The former cloister-man made sense. However, under the rules of the Catholic Church, helping refugee nuns who were trying to escape was a crime.

But then Luther made no sense. He added that if she was allowed to leave but had no confidence in her faith, she was still obliged to stay.[812] Escape. But do not escape. As he continued with his letter, he made even less sense:

*The second reason is the flesh: Though womenfolk are ashamed to admit to this, nevertheless Scripture and experience show that among many thousands there is not a one to whom God has given to remain in pure chastity. A woman has no control over herself. God has made her body to be with man, to bear children and to raise them as the words of Genesis 1:1 clearly state, as is evident by the members of the body ordered by God Himself.*[813]

Was he literally suggesting that God had made women to have sex with? Was he looking at females as promiscuous, child-bearing cows? Objects of lust?

He seems to suggest that it was the other way around: men were objects of lust for women.

Since the first female, Eve, gave intellect to humanity, men have looked down on woman as a second class that needed ruling and disciplining.

And have sex with.

---

[810] Katharina von Bora 1499 – 1552.
[811] Martin Luther, To Several Nuns, August 6, 1524, translated from Briefe aus dem Jahre 1524 No. 733 - 756 by Erika Bullmann Flores, Weimarer Ausgabe.
[812] Ibid.
[813] Ibid.

For the Protestant Church, Luther even recommended segregation of men and women.[814]

Taliban style.

At least, Luther recognized that preventing nuns from leaving freely amounted to a criminal act. He saw the freedom to join and the liberty to leave as prerequisites to cloister life.[815]

The dozen nuns hid among herring barrels on a covered horse carriage and fled to Wittenberg. Their reputation galloped ahead of them. In Luther's town, the nuns arrived as vestal virgins, eager for marriage and copulation.[816]

After having been locked up most of her life, at 24 years old, Katharina was ready to embrace love and life. But she faced a troubling decision: she had to get a divorce from Jesus Christ before she could lie in another man's bed.

Two years later, all twelve vestigial virgins were married.

Katharina was last in the Musical Chair.

The runaway girl followed her master's lead and ended up giving birth to six children by Martin Luther.

Two radicals had found their bond in marriage.

The Bonnie and Clyde of the sixteenth century.

Full-breed outlaws.

Luther felt that God had plunged him into marriage unexpectedly.[817] Katharina's upbringing showed itself in the way she supported her husband's vision by raising animals and running a brewery. The union of the couple went well and would come to be viewed as the Protestant model marriage.

As we see so often in history: the outlaws of one are the heroes of another.

A president of the German Reich, Paul von Hindenburg,[818] was a descendant of the Luther family tree.

Irony has it that von Hindenburg was succeeded by Adolf Hitler.

---

[814] Martin Luther, Documents Illustrative of the Continental Reformation, from B.J. Kidd, ed. (Clarendon Press, 1911) 193-202.

[815] Luther, To Nuns, transl. Bullmann.

[816] Ibid.

[817] Philipp Schaff, History of the Christian Church, Vol VII, Ch V, rpt. Christian Classics Ethereal Library, Bainton, Mentor edition, 226.

[818] Paul Ludwig Hans Anton von Beneckendorff und von Hindenburg, aka Paul von Hindenburg, 1847–1934.

In the same year as Katharina's escape from life in a Catholic cloister to life as a Protestant warrior-wife, the Reformer wrote a sermon that was unusual in its language regarding Jews. Previously, he had deployed the customary anti-Semitism of the Gospels, but now, he seems to have been irritated by the stubborn Jewish and Muslim stance against the Christian Trinity. His sermon indicates a path to losing patience.

*They imagine that thus with their wisdom,'* Luther said, that *'they have completely overthrown our faith and exposed it to the derision and scorn of all the world. As if we were all blockheads and egregious fools and could not see their logic as well as they!*[819]

The dispute was not one of reason or science, but whether the idea of the Trinity – the joining of God as father, Jesus as son, and the Holy Spirit as the Word of God – was in conflict with the Jewish and Muslim belief in a single God. The trouble originates in a lack of consistency in the monotheistic stance, which offers multiple layers of divinities, gods, spirits, angels, demons, and devils, that are ransacking the world.

Luther's sermon was more jibe than hatred. You think you are so smart, he seems to have intended to say, but you do not even grasp the most basic concept of the Christian Trinity.

In its essence, the question would be fairly simple, were it not for the complication of having to combine multiple levels of abstractions.

All Jewish, Christian, and Muslim sects have a sort of trinity in common. All know of God, of the human messenger, and of the Word of God. The difference is merely how these three concepts relate to each other. Is the Word of God one with God, or is it one with the human messenger, or perhaps separate from both?

For example, John the Baptist was endowed with the Word of God in the womb of his mother.

Would John be a god?

The Holy Spirit was passed on from John to the adult Jesus upon his baptism.[820]

Would Jesus be human-turned-god?

Would he be all-god or all-human?

Or both?

---

[819]  Martin Luther, Trinity Sunday, The Article of Faith on the Trinity, 1523.

[820]  Matthew 3:16.

The discussion led to the *physical* Jesus finding his definition and his *will* finding a different one.[821]

It did not end there.

Martin Luther bitterly complained that some sects viewed baptism as an external, useless ritual. He insisted that the act of baptizing was *'no human trifle, but instituted by God Himself.'* Baptism is *'truly God's own work.* [822] Without it, he and his followers *'cannot be saved.'* For this, they were willing to *'contend and fight chiefly.'*

The exercise turned into a mortal fight.

For Jews, the Word of God is defined as *'the bond of everything, holding all things together and binding all the parts, and prevents them from being dissolved and separated,* [823] as manifested in the first-born of God. The Jewish Exilarch was endowed with the Word of God or the Christ, if you will. Likewise, the Jewish Sadducee Nasi was instructed by God with the Word of God.[824] They call it the *Shechina.* We have seen earlier that the Sadducee representative of God, the Jewish Muslim caliph in Baghdad, was himself venerated like a god.

Between the two, it was all about who held supreme power over the other, and the conflict was embedded between these intermediaries. Mortal enemies.

This was extended to Mary. It was announced to her by the Angel Gabriel that she was to conceive *'the Word of God.* [825] Mary carried *'in her womb the only-begotten Son and Word of God who is inseparable from them and to become the cause of the Incarnation and his dwelling among human beings.* [826] If Jesus is both human and god, what would his mother be?

In an influential Syrian text, Mary had received the Word of God and was lifted to be a mediator to God.[827] She was also the *'illuminator of all,* [828] which put her at par with the divine son, standing *'to the right of the altar in the Holy of Holies,*[829] *which is truly regarded as being to the right of God.* [830]

---

[821]  The level of complexity about Jesus's will having one or two natures may have found its apex around the middle of the seventh century and may have been ongoing as Islam were to awaken.

[822]  Luther, Large Catechism, 1529, WA 30 I,125-238.

[823]  Philo of Alexandria, De Profugis, in Gerald Friedlander, Hellenism and Christianity (P. Vallentine, 1912) 114–15.

[824]  Deuteronomy 18:18.

[825]  Maximus the Confessor, The Life of the Virgin, transl. by Stephen J. Shoemaker (Yale, 2012) 8, 42.

[826]  Ibid., 13, 45.

[827]  Ibid. 95.

[828]  Ibid., 4, 39.

[829]  This is the inner sanctum of the Temple of Jerusalem.

[830]  Maximus the Confessor, Virgin, Shoemaker, 2012, 7, 41.

As if things were not difficult enough, the inclusion of Mary somehow turned the Trinity into a quartet.

The musical tunes of this fabulous ensemble are written on tombstones.

Being the mother of God created a tremendous paradox, which was resolved by explaining away the obvious:

> *Behold the economy of divine activities and the transformation of natures, for the wondrous son did not make known to the immaculate mother the knowledge of his birth, and in an instant he was inexplicably found outside her womb and settled in her lap, so that just as her conception took place without seed and without awareness, so also the birth took place without corruption and without awareness.*[831]

This notion of Jesus' birth without Mary's awareness enabled a wide range of interpretations from Mother of God to daughter or sister of God. Moreover, as the queen, she held *'authority over all things.'*[832]

What has Mary turned into?

Was she supreme?

An intercessor? God?

Muslims exploited the opening.

Rabbinic Judaism upholds its own form of a Mary substitute, called *Bath Kol,* the *daughter of a voice* in the Talmud. Here we have a Judaized goddess of wisdom.

A daughter of God.

We have already learned about the important linage of Moses' sister as the Temple-mother and stand-in for the Covenant. Except for the linage requirement, Mary's role is similar.

It is no less complex in Islam. There, the divinities of Mary and Jesus are fiercely opposed. Yet, Muslims regard Jesus as the Word of God. In a doctrinal statement, the Koran even accepts Jesus as the *Messiah* in an intercessory role with God,[833] which is nothing but the equivalent to the Christian *Jesus Christ.* But then, Islam rejects intercessors.

While Mary's virginity is accepted, Muslims seem to be ignorant about a birth without awareness.

---

[831]  Ibid., 35, 66.
[832]  Ibid., 10, 43.
[833]  Koran 3:40.

263

John the Baptist – the forerunner of Jesus Christ – is one of the prophets in the Koran. He was the 'verifier' of the Word of God.[834] A human 'prophet' signing off on the Word of God.

It contains a kernel of truth: the Word of God was the word of man in the image of a god. John was its censor.

Judaism and Christianity include the first human, Adam, as the Son of God.[835] Like Jesus, Adam was a recipient of the Word of God through the fruit from the Tree of Knowledge handed to him by Eve. He was a Christ – Adam Christ – in the same way that Jesus was Jesus Christ.

In contrast, Islam rejects the idea of a son of God for any of the prophets or messiahs despite the fact that the Bible says so unambiguously about King David.[836] But then, we have already seen that the Koran famously has Muslims prostrating to Adam, the biblical Son of God. Except for the devil Iblis, all obeyed.

Millions of lives were lost over these questions during the last 2,000 years.

Martin Luther, Jews, and Muslims were still arguing about them.

---

[834] Koran 3:34.
[835] Luke 3:38.
[836] 2 Samuel 7:14 (NIV).

### *Another Forerunner*

After Katharina's flight from the cloister, an extraordinary character stepped into history: David Reubeni.[837]

This man allows us to see the full extent of the dangerous game in play.

Reubeni claimed descent from the biblical tribe of Reuben – made obvious by his choice of name. He said to be from the Davidic King Shlomo of *Habur,* which is believed to be the Jewish oasis of Khaibar.[838]

In the early seventh century, a Jewish army[839] had been led against the followers of Prophet Muhammad. The two leaders who went against this new prophet were Salmon and Hanan the Nasi. In the aftermath of the assault, Khaibar fell to the Muhammadeans.

The presence of a Nasi at Khaibar is problematic because his office had seized to exist 200 years before the appearance of Prophet Muhammad.[840] Either the story of tradition or the resurrected Nasi must therefore be a deception.

Hence, Reubeni's association with *Habur* or *Khaibar* needs exploration.

In the western Arab Peninsula lies the second most important religious center of Islam, Medina. The oldest mosque is situated there. Prophet Muhammad migrated to Medina after having run into troubles with authorities in Mecca, which is today believed to be the birthplace of Islam.

About 100 miles north of Medina lies the oasis of Khaibar, a center of Judaism since antiquity. Amidst a stone desert, the old site of Khaibar is a light forest of date palms that is dotted with ruins of fortresses and run-down huts.

The sun is merciless.

There is a high probability of seeing Fata Morganas, mirages that, not unlike dreams, have often been used for the underpinnings of prophetic visions.

The names of the Jewish leaders in the assault against Muhammadeans, Salmon and Hanan the Nasi, reveal that they must be connected to the ancient Levite leadership. They are better known as the Exilarch Salman al-Farisi (the Pharisee) and his brother and predecessor, Nehemiah ben Hushiel (Hanan). Just a couple of generations before them lies a genetic bottleneck.

---

837 David Reubeni (1490–1535 or 1541).
838 David Reubeni, The Story of David Ha-Re'uveni, as quoted in Lenowitz, 1998, 103-104.
839 The army was staffed with Jews and Mourners of Zion.
840 The Nasi, the highest ranking Sadducee leader, had been expelled from Tiberias by the Byzantine Empire in the early fifth century. This was then supposed to have been the last Nasi, we are asked to believe.

These two were the top Jewish leaders at the time. They carried the Divine Presence and were first in line in the royal Hasmonean lineage. Nobody outside this tree can bring forth prophets and messiahs.

As I have already shown, the most important lineage for Jews is the one through the father of all Judaic religions, Abraham, to his son Isaac and his grandson Jacob. As a reminder, Abraham's firstborn was Ishmael. From his second son, Isaac, were born the redhead Esau and the younger twin brother Jacob.

When Esau was once in dire need, he was betrayed by Jacob, who obtained Esau's birthrights in exchange for a meal.[841] This brotherly let-down rationalizes why Jacob's lineage took primacy over everybody else.

The meaningless treachery over the 'birthright' amounts to something only when we remember that Abraham's inheritance entailed the Promised Land. The birthright was to an empire. The King of the Jews was supposed to be the emperor of the world.

A sandwich for an empire was even cheaper and quicker than an empire for a scroll.

Jacob wrestled with God one night, after which he was disabled[842] and renamed to Israel.[843] As a result, the Twelve Tribes of Israel are embodied in the sons of Jacob, also known as the Israelites or the Children of Israel.

The deceit over the inheritance is a pivotal point in messianic history. Messiahs came to establish a new religion that would go back to Adam, Abraham, or another biblical point. This approach neutralizes the imperial aspirations of the Jacobites. It potentially opens the succession of the Promised Land to anyone – as long as they are coming through the royal Hasmonean lineage.[844]

The Babylonian Talmud insists that the handover to Jacob was voluntary.[845] They rationalized for themselves that the treachery was just.

The linages of Ishmael and Esau might respectfully disagree.

---

[841] Genesis 25:29-25:34.
[842] Genesis 32:25.
[843] Genesis 32:28.
[844] The chosen biblical point can open the inheritance not only to Ishmael for the Muslims, and Esau (for Edom/Rome), but also to all descendants of Adam or Noah, the first and second genetic bottlenecks of the Bible.
[845] Talmud – Mas. Berachoth 7b.

Instead, in a reverse accusation for the arch-betrayal, Rabbinic leaders came to pretend that the redhead Esau – who serves as a nickname for Rome – was responsible for the breach between Judaism and Christianity, which, for them, represents the old way of the serpent.[846] After having suffered injustice from his brother, Esau was branded *'the wicked'* who caused *'a breach in the world.'*[847]

He stood in the way of world governance by the King of the Jews.

Like modern day Palestinians, Esau appears to have refused to roll over.

Five of Jacob's twelve descendants are of particular importance. From Jacob's first wife, they are Reuben (Jacob's firstborn and one of the Ten Lost Tribes in *Habur*); Levi (for the Levite priestly class, the spiritual leaders for all tribes); and Judah (for the successors of King David in Babylon). From his first handmaid was Gad (the 'fortunate' half-Jewish tribe). From his second wife, it was Joseph (in Egypt).

Reuben was the heir apparent to the Promised Land.

He protected Joseph from being killed by his other brothers.[848] The Ishmaelites then carried Joseph off into slavery in Egypt, where he rose to the loftiest ranks in government. Joseph's position suggests that the oppressive Jewish administrative system had already been conceived before the creation of the Bible.

Reuben and Joseph form an important bridge between Jews and Muslims.

The Jewish Levite priestly system is superimposed over all Jewish tribes. Claiming descent from Aaron, they breed among themselves, genetically completely segregated from ordinary Jews. This behavioral pattern is even stronger with the Hasmonean royal linage. It encompasses all Jewish tribes and even extends to other sects, outside of Judaism proper, including Islam.[849]

It cheats ordinary Jews and Muslims out of their lives and livelihoods.

*Habur* is a biblical word that points to the *Khabur River*, which originates in Turkey and flows through the desert of eastern Syria from the north-east into the Euphrates River. According to the Bible, Reuben's tribe was brought to the Khabur River into exile, and this location became its home base.[850]

---

[846] The Sadducees were indeed looked at as the representatives of the serpent – symbol for the Messiah from the lineage of the Sadducees.
See Joseph Jacobs, Albert Wolf, Jewish Encyclopedia, seal: the Hebrew word for 'serpent' has the same numerical value as the word 'Messiah'.

[847] Ha-Cohen, Vol. II, translated by Bialloblotzky, 1836, 181.

[848] Genesis 37:21.

[849] The Itinerary of Benjamin of Tudela (ca. 1179 AD) 32-33.

[850] 1 Chronicles 5:26.

The river also provides for the setting for the book of Ezekiel in the Hebrew Bible as the location of its messianic story. It explains the End of the World, wherein all nations that had troubled the Jews would be devastated[851] – that is *all* nations – and the Temple in Jerusalem would be rebuilt.[852]

For that purpose, the Iraqi-Kurdistan city of Zakho at the river appears to have been chosen by a large Jewish community as *'The Jerusalem of Assyria.'*

Quite a lot about Reubeni's intentions can be deduced from his name alone. An insider would already know: David Reubeni saw himself as another forerunner of the Messiah.

However, Reubeni claimed to be a son of King Shlomo. His elder brother, Yosef, sat *'on the throne in the wilderness of Habur and rules over thirty myriads, over the tribes of Gad and Reuben and the half-tribe of Manasseh [Joseph's first-born].* [853]

A contemporary Jewish chronicler noted that Reubeni was from *'a distant country of India.'* He was introduced as a Hebrew and *brother* of the King of the Jews.[854]

This sounds like a ballgame of a higher league.

Only a royal Hasmonean can be the King of the Jews.

*Indians* used to be a nickname for the disowned tribes of Abraham along the Red Sea,[855] specifically referring to Ishmaelites and Ketuhrans. Khaibar was part of the area of the *'Indians.'* During Luther's time, a book referred to the Emperor of Ethiopia as *'Prester John of the Indies.* [856] The author meant to relate Ethiopia to the lands along the newly discovered sea route to India around the Cape of Good Hope in South Africa – *the Indies.*

Despite consensus, the word *Habur* cannot possibly relate to a river in the Euphrates basin but rather somewhere along the Red Sea.

Reubeni's mission was commanded by the seventy elders of King Shlomo (Solomon), which is nothing less than a revival of the Sanhedrin, the assembly of the highest Judaic authority.[857]

---

[851] Ezekiel 25:1–32:32.
[852] Ezekiel 33:1–48:35.
[853] Aeshcoly as cited in Lenowitz, 1998, 108-111.
[854] Ha-Cohen, Vol. II, translated by Bialloblotzky, 1836, 149.
[855] Sebeos' History, ca. 660 AD, 34. Sebeos had called the inhabitants of the Arab Peninsula *Indians* and the *disowned tribes of Abraham.*
[856] Alvarez, transl. Alderley, 1881, 1 [the author distinguished between *India* proper and the *Indies.*]
[857] The Sanhedrin had formerly been led by a high-priest by the name of Hannanel.

'Re-instating' the Sanhedrin was a pre-condition for a messiah to be accepted and for launching the conquest of the Promised Land. Without the Sanhedrin, there can be no messiah.

It almost seems that David Reubeni had been prepared for his assignment as a substitute for the vanished forerunner Lemmlein and his forerunner Abrabanel.

The mystery of the Hidden One, who was supposedly executed by Pope Adrian's Inquisition in the Spanish city of Valencia, has not been forgotten here. His messianic pair in Spain, Elijah and Enoch, likely referred to Reuben's first-born son Enoch and not to another of the same name.

That is also how the Rabbinic leaders would have understood the connections.

Since I do not have the luxury of being able to present any evidence that ties Lemmlein, the Hidden One, and Reubeni together, this is speculation. But context, timing, and pattern buoy them up as if in a globally interlinked chain.

Luckily, we do not need to rely on suspicions. Reubeni is enough to see through the machinations clearly.

We are being played.

Reubeni's task was to visit the pope and convince him to join in a war against the Ottoman-Turks. They had just conquered more lands from the Christian Republic of Venice. Suleiman's troops continued marching up the Balkan, threatening the borders of Europe.

To impress, Reubeni had 300,000 warriors ready to throw the Ottoman-Turks out of Jerusalem and Palestine.

Ottomans, other than a few other places, were about the only people who provided so many Jews with a safe home. The promise amounts to a rather grand gesture of treachery – against Jews in the Ottoman realm and their friendly host.

If a planned assault by Reubeni and his massive army were to leak to Ottoman-Turkish leaders, the consequences for Jews in their domain would be a self-orchestrated holocaust.

The number of men in Reubeni's alleged army are among the greatest that had been deployed over the ages. Through history, you might see 80,000, perhaps 120,000 men as unusually large imperial deployments. Such a number would later be seen as overwhelming in an assault on Rhodes by Suleiman the Magnificent. Armies of that size on land were unsustainable.

Either he was promising air and did not have any warriors, or he must have represented a large nation. At that time, Khaibar would not have been able to recruit even a tenth of this number of warriors.

Reubeni first travelled to Egypt, disguised as a Muslim Ishmaelite in 1523.[858] There, he seems to have been rejected by the Rabbinic leader for fear of causing harm.[859]

Without success in Egypt, he left for Jerusalem. In a conversation that took place in Gaza, he announced his messianic mission: the End of the World was near; the evil ones would be brought down to earth, and Jews would be uplifted; war would come between the world powers.[860] Reubeni's language was disguised. Those knowledgeable of the Bible could understand what he had meant to convey.

This first stop in Egypt on the trek to Jerusalem tells us that *Habur* is not likely in Khaibar, either. It is more likely on the west shores of the Red Sea, north of Egypt. Perhaps Ethiopia, just as the link to Prester John suggests.

Because the route to Jerusalem had to go through Hebron, he went there first to visit the Cave of the Patriarchs.[861] In Jerusalem, he introduced himself to the guards of the Temple Mount as the son of Prophet Muhammad and the new lord of the Muslims.[862]

This is an extraordinary claim and may just be – a bluff.

Surely, any Muslim guard at the Temple Mount would have immediately killed the imposter. Was the guard even Muslim?

A claim of a Jewish messiah to be of Muhammadean descent is remarkable.

Is it impossible?

Our knowledge of Prophet Muhammad and his actual genealogy was faint until recently. There was no evidence from where he came or where he went.

Now we have it. It is horrifying.

Lofty traditions of the boy Muhammad have been invented. They allege that he was brought up by his uncle with a family tree that is documented to the last leaf. Instead, we know of the Jewish Throne of David under Muslim rule next to the Jewish Throne of Muhammad in Baghdad.

---

858  February 1523.
859  A. Z. Aeshcoly (1940) as cited in Lenowitz, 1998, 108-111.
860  Ibid., 109.
861  Ibid.
862  Ibid., 108-111.

In other words, a claim by a living Jewish leader to Muhammadean ancestry should receive any historian's immediate attention. The claim cannot simply be refuted as false, even though every scholar of note would think of it as ludicrous.

The consequence of Reubeni's claim sends a shockwave through history: Reubeni was from a branch of the House of David – therefore, Prophet Muhammad was in the House of David.

Tradition attributes the prophet to the Hashimite tribe. They did not even attempt to hide their Hasmonean lineage.

After threatening revenge through Reubeni's Ottoman connections at the Throne of David in Constantinople (Istanbul), the guard allowed him to fast and pray for five weeks under the Foundation Stone of the Temple in the Dome of the Rock. He called it the Holy of Holies, which used to refer to the inner sanctuary of the Temple in Jerusalem.

At its center rests the Well of Souls.

This is the dwelling place of God, symbolized with the Foundation Stone in the Holy Temple of Jerusalem.

According to a Midrash commentary, the Foundation Stone is the rock from which *'the world was founded.'*[863] In addition, a black paving stone in the floor marks the gateway to paradise. Christians share in its importance, and some imagine that they recognize Jesus' footprints on the rock as he stood for his sentencing to the crucifixion. After counting down the most holy places from Syria to Jerusalem, a Muslim tradition proclaims that *'the most holy spot on the place of worship is the Dome [of the Rock],*[864] which still stands on top of the Holy of Holies.

Prophet Muhammad ascended from here to heaven.

This is why this piece of property is the most valuable in the world for Jews, Christians, and Muslims alike.

According to the Bible, only the Levite priesthood could enter the Holy of Holies. Everyone else would instantly be stricken to death.[865]

---

[863] Tanhuma Kedoshim 10.

[864] Josef van Ess, 'Abd al-Malik and the Dome of the Rock, in Bayt al-Maqdis, Part 1, eds. Julian Raby and Jeremy Johns (Oxford, Copyright ©1992, reprinted by permission of Oxford University Press, www.oup.com) 89.

[865] Exodus 33:20 (NIV.

The biblical idea of God's dwelling place was that only the Levite High-Priest could consult the divinity. Even for them, entering was a heroic act. In order not to perish, they had to follow strict ritual rules; for example, sounding gold bells to alert the god when entering the Holy of Holies.[866]

The divine regulations to avoid death in this holiest of places reached right down to the underwear.[867]

By praying at the Holy of Holies, Reubeni suggested that he was not only of the Davidic lineage but also of Levite priestly origin. The seventy elders also came to Jerusalem to join in the preparations for the End of the World and for the sack of the Temple.[868]

Every messiah who did not know that the Sanhedrin was essential must have failed to read the Bible. By necessity, and regardless of which messiah it was, if he found support by any rabbi, anywhere in the world, there stood also the Sanhedrin behind the veil.

Moreover, it was a requirement that the seventy would have to stand on top of the Temple Mount.

If Reubeni had made it up, the rabbis would have known of the bluff for lack of confirmation from the seventy elders.

This happy gathering of the forerunner and Sanhedrin on the Temple Mount is such a big deal that there must be more to it.

What was going on up there?

The Holy of Holies is where the Dome of the Rock today stands over the Foundation Stone. It is maintained that it was built toward the end of the seventh century and richly decorated with mosaics and Islamic inscriptions that were signed off by Caliph 'Abd al-Malik. The building dedication was later overwritten by Caliph al-Ma'mun.

It turns out that the Dome of the Rock and the al-Aqsa Mosque could not have stood in their present form until after the Crusades.[869] During the Christian occupation, the builder was inscribed on the outside to be Caliph Umar. Christian inscriptions decorated the inside. Three witnesses, all contemporaries to one another, attest to it. Further witnesses still attest to Umar even while Reubeni showed up.

---

[866] Exodus 18:34-18:35 (NIV).
[867] Exodus 28:42-28:43 (NIV).
[868] A. Z. Aeshcoly (1940) as cited in Lenowitz, 1998, 108-111.
[869] A.J. Deus, The Jewish Serpent King (2023) available at academia.edu.

The interior mosaics with al-Ma'mun's dedication are attached to the interior octagonal arcade. Even from a primitive sketch, the unique design of the mosaics is immediately recognizable. They are made of crowned, demon-like figures that resemble flowering branches.

After a thousand-year search, the first representation of these designs appears on a pilgrimage certificate from 1544-45, merely two decades *after* the Sanhedrin cozied up on the Temple Mount. In addition, windows high up in the dome are decorated with a long inscription that prays for Suleiman and is dated to 1528 AD, cutting the timeframe down to a few years.

Internal and external renovations were ongoing during the Sanhedrin's presence on the Temple Mount. Indeed, with the Sanhedrin still on the Temple Mount, Suleiman would come to restore its water system in a project that would last from 1530-37. It appears as though they were preparing for a reintroduction of ritual sacrifices. Moreover, the crown-designs can be attributed to Suleiman himself and to several contemporary rulers who submitted to him, portrayed in an assembly around the Foundation Stone. One of the subordinate crowns belongs to Emperor Charles V. Hungary was conquered. It is symbolized with another crown.

The presence of Suleiman's and Charles' crowns tells us that the gang on the Temple Mount thought of both empires as having submitted to them.

The work for these mosaics does not seem to show up with Suleiman's costs for the ongoing renovations. It was perhaps expunged in favor of a seventh century creation.

Messianic Jews took possession of the Temple Mount under the watch of Suleiman. The Sanhedrin made itself comfortable in the Dome of the Rock. David Reubeni is under the Foundation Stone. Suleiman's Temple wife Roxelana and his Mahdi son had already been a dark omen.

The mosaics depict world rule by the Jewish God that is represented by Jewish leaders.

The Jewish Serpent King.

They prayed for the annihilation of the world and for the Messianic Age to begin.

### Spinning the Web

The butcher pope's successor held on to the papal throne a little longer, almost eleven years. He was another Medici, Giulio di Giuliano de' Medici, nephew of Lorenzo the Magnificent and cousin of the late Pope Leo X. About ten years earlier, he had been named Archbishop of Florence, the Medici Dynasty's home town.

As corrupt dynasts have it, Giulio was made cardinal by none other than his cousin.

Before that, he was a member of the Knights Hospitaller.[870] This was a radical para-military group of the Catholic Church, which competed with the better known Knights Templar.[871] These were powerful men wielding swords.

Giulio had been a knight. A military man. A crusader.

Another extremist.

Anyone with a romantic notion of knights is a victim of the formation of collective memory. We can compare them with modern footage of ISIS fighters in Iraq and Syria. Their pickup trucks can be substituted with horses that are protected with steel mesh and the warriors carrying lances and crossbows.

There was no romanticism. Only fascism.

These religious lunatics chopped off heads that failed to tick alike. Through Muslim eyes, knights represented the ideal jihadist. Blood was in their eyes.

The knights were best buddies with the Vatican.

After Muslims had captured Jerusalem, the headquarters of the Knights Hospitaller moved from Acre, Israel, to Rhodes in the early fourteenth century. Better put, they annexed the island in a four- year-long campaign that stained the soil in red.

A Byzantine citadel from the seventh century stood there, providing the Knights Hospitaller with a formidable fortress. Its palace was fit for imperial aspirations. In it resided the Hospitaller's Grand Master in sheer pomp.

He was a cardinal of the Catholic Church.

---

[870] Knights Hospitaller is the short version for Order of Knights of the Hospital of Saint John of Jerusalem.

[871] The Hospitaller were a professional papal elite army, organized roughly along the rival lines that we see during Martin Luther's time: Papal States, Holy Roman Empire, now united Spanish Crown of Castile and Crown of Aragon, Kingdom of France, Auvergne, Provence, and Kingdom of England. Each group was headed by an ecclesiastical prior.

The year before Giulio di Giuliano de' Medici became Pope Clement VII,[872] the 600 knights and 5,000 Rhodians who were stationed in the fortifications at Rhodes faced Suleiman the Magnificent. The leader of the Ottoman-Turks was accompanied by 400 ships and a massive contingent of over 100,000 Muslim soldiers.[873] Suleiman threatened to leave not even a single cat alive if the defenders resisted.[874] He meant business.

This was holy war – jihad – against holy warriors of the Catholic Church.

The then-pope, Julius II, ordered all knights to defend Rhodes and to focus all forces on this crusade.[875] During his last days, he was still dreaming of wresting Constantinople and Jerusalem back from Muslims. But the Ottoman assault was at an unprecedented scale. The bombardment by the artillery was more ferocious and greater than against any other town previously.[876] Such was the brave resistance of the knights to fifteen broad attacks during six months that the assailants lost a staggering number of men to combat and disease. It was said that 80,000 died, perhaps even thousands more.[877]

The rate of decimation in large armies was astounding.

Papal reinforcements never arrived. The knights ran out of ammunition and able-bodied men. Rhodes fell. The might of the rising Ottoman Empire became undeniable. Ottoman-Turks had risen to become the controlling naval power in the Eastern Mediterranean.

With the help of Jewish leaders.

After a period without fixed headquarters, the defeated Knights Hospitaller finally moved to Malta,[878] the island between Italy, Tunisia, and Libya.

Fighting seems to have been in the blood of the de' Medici. So was corruption and nepotism. As Giulio di Giuliano rose to be pope, he rehired Giovanni's 'Bande Nere' troops and liberated the bandits' commander from his debts.

Now that the pro-French Medicis were back in power, they could ally themselves with France and plot again for the demise of Emperor Charles.

---

[872] Pope Clement VII, aka Giulio di Giuliano de' Medici, was pope of the Catholic Church 1523 – 1534.
[873] Baron Balfour and Patrick Kinross, The Ottoman Centuries: The Rise and Fall of the Turkish Empire (1979) 176.
[874] Hammer, Histoire Ottoman, 1837, 599.
[875] Raynaldus, ad ann. 1506, nos. 6-7, vol. XX. p. 36, in Setton, 1984, 39.
[876] Jacques de Bourbon, Oppugnation, 1527, fols. 20, 21 in Setton, 1984, 210.
[877] Setton, 1984, 214.
[878] In 1530, Charles V made a grant to the Knights Hospitaller for their headquarters in Malta.

The Jewish ringleaders who were hunkering down on the Temple Mount in Jerusalem were the priestly class with divinely inspired scriptures in hand. They positioned themselves as the Chosen People in the Promised Land, as the spiritual and secular leaders of the world. After a last great war at Armageddon, they would end up being the only survivors. All others, including all ordinary Jews, were the disposable collateral damage of a mythical idea that we can only view today as a call to self-destruction.

After a sign from God, Reubeni took off for Rome to continue his mission.[879] Sent as an ambassador on official business by a Jewish Kingdom – and secretly by the Sanhedrin – David Reubeni attempted to forge an alliance with Christian kingdoms against the Muslim Turks: the Papal States in Italy, the Holy Roman Empire, the kingdoms of France, the Republic of Venice, the Kingdom of Portugal, the 'Empire' of Ethiopia, and/or Reubeni's brother's unknown Jewish Princedom, where the lost tribes of Reuben and Gad lived.

However, we are in midst of a culture of treachery. Reubeni was a double agent, dancing at two weddings or more.

In a letter about Reubeni, an anonymous Rabbinic author spoke in cryptic language that only sages, learned Jewish leaders, could understand. He did not seem to trust the knowledge of the sages, so he marked the important passages with *'enough said.'* The author claimed to have met Reubeni. The latter was sent by the 250-year-old Hannanel, the then-leader of the Sanhedrin. The anonymous author presented his argument with the important symbol of the River Sambation, which identified – as already discussed – the location of the Ten Lost Tribes of Israel.[880]

An Ashkenazi tradition mentions the 'little Red Jews' (Die Roite Yiddelech). They lived beyond the Sambation River *whose foaming waters raise high up into the sky a wall of fire and smoke that is impossible to pass through.* [881] The legendary Red Jews were supposed to invade Europe when the End of the World was near.

---

[879]   Ibid., 108-111.
[880]   Adolph Neubauer, The Jewish Quarterly Review (Nutt, 1889) 200.
[881]   Moses Rosen, The Face of Survival, Epilogue 'The Recipe' (1987).

The Lutheran founding father, Philipp Melanchthon, had thought of Ottoman-Turks as Red Jews. Others thought that they were originally the Khazars.[882] The latter's ruling elite appears to have 'converted' to Judaism in the eighth century.[883]

On the western side of the Euphrates River, there were supposedly no Jewish tribes.[884]

Since the river stopped flowing every Sabbath, we can be certain that it was a mystical symbol for a secret location. The letter hinted at the shortest way to get from Reubeni's supreme leader to Damascus in Syria. It was through Egypt, not from the east. Reubeni's first stop was there.

Legend or real, Christians had ample reason to be concerned.

The former Sanhedrin's leader, Hannanel, was also known as Armilus, which is a symbolic play on a terrible figure for the End of the World. Born of Satan and a virgin, the legendary,[885] leprous, and crippled king would come to kill the Messiah of Joseph – from the Egyptian lineage that had been saved by the Ishmaelites, the later Muslims.

Armilus, in turn, would be slain by the Messiah of David.

The synagogues had not only retained the knowledge about the occurrence of a messiah who had attempted an alliance with Rome 250 years earlier, but the Rabbis revived the memory and tied it to their new hero.

What happened, back then?

In around 1280, a Jew by the name of Abulafia[886] had set out to find the River Sambation. He attempted to convince Pope Nicholas[887] in Rome of the need to liberate Israel – the meaning of which was to take the land from under the feet of those who lived there – in order to give it to the Chosen People.[888]

---

[882] Another contemporary historian mentioned the 'Red Jews' as a Jewish sectarian group that distinguished itself through its red garment. They were allegedly a militant Jewish group that was present in Europe. See Aegidius Tschudi, Chronicum Helveticum, ed. Johann Rudolf Iselin, 1734, Vol. 1, 377-378.

[883] Peter B. Golden, The Conversion of the Khazars to Judaism, in Peter B. Golden, Haggai Ben-Shammai, András Róna-Tas, The World of the Khazars: New Perspectives, Handbook of Oriental Studies (Brill, 2007) 149.

[884] Neubauer, Jewish Quarterly, Nutt, 1889, 200.

[885] Armilus might reach as far back as to the evil principle in Zoroastrianism, Ahriman, or beyond.

[886] Abraham ben Samuel Abulafia, 1240 – ca. 1291.

[887] Nicholas III, aka Giovanni Gaetano Orsini, was pope 1277 – 1280.

[888] His appearance was not rogue. In Sanhedrin 97b, the Babylonian Talmud responds to a question about when the world would come to an end with four dates, 8500, 4231, 7000, and 'after' 5000. Abulafia was born in 5001 AM, i.e. 1240 AD. 4231 AM refers to 470 AD, which marks the Nasi's expulsion from the Byzantine Empire ('4231 years after the creation the world will be orphaned') and the 'offical' end of

Abulafia followed a specific messianic model,[889] wherein the focus was on studying. The demand for the pope to assist in Israel's liberation was then understood as a prerequisite for the Messiah to be accepted.[890]

As it often works with self-fulfilling prophecy, a vision had earlier overcome Abulafia in the middle of a public appearance.[891]

God commanded him to go and convert the pope to Judaism.[892]

Good luck. Off he went.

The pope ordered him burned.[893]

But that did not work out as planned. Three days later, according to the after-the-fact tale, Pope Nicholas died of plague. The pope was carried to his own funeral and Abulafia was recognized for divine intervention.

The conquest of the Promised Land was as near as 1290.[894]

The Messiah passed away the year after the supposed Redemption of Israel never came to be.

Reubeni now conveyed that this messiah had never died.

And this was probably a fact: Abulafia's death was immediately followed by the '*Prophet of Avila,*'[895] carrying forward the light of Christ. The conquest of the Promised Land was postponed by a mere five years.

But the ram's horn was not blasted then either.

As we have already seen, we can find a similar concept of undead redeemers in the Mahdi of Muslims and in the Hidden One from Valencia. The difference is that the Mahdi was the redeemer of Islam whose reappearance coincided with the Second Coming of Jesus. In the event of the End of the World, the two went to war against the Antichrist.

---

Talmudic redactions. Abulafia's presence is an indication that the Talmud was still in revision in the thirteenth century.

[889] Rabbi Moses ben Maimon aka Maimonides, Rambam (Rabbeinu Mōšeh bēn Maimon), ca. 1135 – 1204, was a Sephardic philosopher and Torah scholar, astronomer, doctor and physician. Born in Córdoba, he lived in Morocco and Egypt and was buried in Tiberias.

[890] A.H. Silver, A History of Messianic Speculation in Israel (Beacon, 1927).

[891] Abulafia's vision is claimed to having occurred in Capua, Italy.

[892] Jerry Rabow, 50 Jewish Messiahs: The Untold Life Stories of 50 Jewish Messiahs Since Jesus and how they Changed the Jewish, Christian, and Muslim Worlds (Gefen, 2003), 47.

[893] Sefer ha-edut [Book of Witness], Monatsschrift für Geschichte und Wissenschaft des Judenthums 36 (1887) 558, in Lenowitz, 1998, 96.

[894] Rabow, Jewish Messiahs, 2003, 48: one Jubilee (fifty years) after the fifth millennium from Creation. [Abulafia is said to having been born in the Jubilee year 5000 since Creation.]

[895] Nissim ben Abraham, the 'Prophet of Avila' was active from 1295.

Armilus appeared even earlier for the foundation of proto-Islam with his phonetic twin Hermolaos. There, he represented the Deceiver from the House of Joseph who announced the arrival of the Second Coming of Jesus Christ. It again unmasks Islam as a success of Jewish messianism.[896] The slight repositioning of Armilus appears to rest on Ottoman preferences.

The legend of Armilus has a real name, Salman al-Farisi (the Pharisee). He was the first 'convert' to Islam. He was also Exilarch Hanamel and brother of the Jewish Exilarch Nehemiah ben Hushiel (Hanan) who seceded from the Persian Empire while dedicating the Temple Mount. The latter is the man who morphed into the Muhammad of Muslim tradition.[897]

These two are Jewish descendants of the Hasmonean-Hashimite Mar Zutra who forms the *only* lineage that can provide for Jewish messiahs, nasis, exilarchs, and Muhammads.

Obviously, another messiah was announced by Reubeni in preparation for a renewed attempt to re-conquer the Promised Land.

Egypt finally joined Reubeni's cause after the Sanhedrin had corresponded with its Rabbinic leader in Egypt.[898] The messianic mission had received confirmation from the Sanhedrin.

At the same time, the Jewish community in Turkey was awed by the appearance of a twelve-year-old whose name it was forbidden to write.

The twelve-year-old is possibly the beginning of a royal era.[899] It could signify a symbol for the Christ, the Messiah.[900] The fact that his name was forbidden could be a sign that he carried the Word of God.

This is not by chance.

Reubeni had to follow prophecy.

The book of Isaiah had announced a son of a virgin by the name of Immanuel. His name translates loosely to *god of all things*. Isaiah also said that *'before the boy knows enough to reject the wrong and choose the right,'*[901] the nations that stood in the way to their Promised Land would be devastated.

---

[896]  A.J. Deus, Doctrina Jacobi: The Deceiver's Deception (2021) available at academia.edu.

[897]  A.J. Deus, Iran's Poisoned Qibla Arrows (2024) available at academia.edu.

[898]  Neubauer, Jewish Quarterly, Nutt, 1889, 200.

[899]  It might be an allusion for the biblical King Solomon, the son of King David, who may have ascended to the throne at a young age. Likewise, King Manasseh of Judah ascended to the throne at twelve-years-old.

[900]  Neubauer, Ten Tribes, transl. Lenowitz, 1998, 111.

[901]  Isaiah 7:16.

The 'twelve-year-old' was either destined to become the King of the Jews on David's Throne[902] or the new Muhammad.

A similar language is used in the Jerusalem Talmud[903] for the appearance of the Messiah.[904] It signifies the transfer of authority. The Christ is representative of the Word of God, which is, in one form or another, attached to the Messiah or a prophet.

The importance of the transfer of authority is that whoever bears the Christ is the boss of the sect, and whoever bears the Christ *and* conquers the Promised Land is the Messiah who rules the world.[905]

For this transfer, we need to imagine a beam of light coming from heaven upon the Messiah with all the knowledge that God wanted to transmit to the religious leader.

This is why they are typically portrayed as illiterate – waiting for the Word of God.

One might think that Suleiman possessed the Promised Land and that he had a son on his lap by the name of Şehzade Mehmed, Muhammad. But that would make the plot too transparent.

For the followers of Reubeni – global Jewry – it was a signal to put aside the Bible and dust off the daggers.

That Jewish leaders in the Ottoman Empire were involved to the extent that they brought forth one of the two necessary messiahs plus the Temple mother is disturbing. After all, they have been welcomed with open arms as citizens when they have been in dire need.

As the new Ottoman Caliph's efforts to denounce Christian blood libel against Jews (the preposterous accusation of murdering Christian or Muslim children to use their blood in Jewish rituals) would later show,[906] the life of *ordinary* Jews in a sea of religious hatred was not easy.

---

902  Isaiah 9:6-9:7.

903  The use of the same cryptic models of the Talmud conveys that the anonymous author as well as Reubeni himself were masters in the Talmudic texts.

904  Schwab, JT Berakhoth, 1886, 44-45.

905  The anonymous letter used verses from Genesis with a technique where the quote itself was not of the essence, but rather what preceded it: God's covenant with Abraham for the Promised Land. In order to figure out what was being said, Rabbinic leaders simply memorized the entire Bible. When faced with a quotation, they could insert the blanks on-demand. We have already learned how the covenant and the Promised Land need to be understood as an eternal command for conquest and ethnic cleansing.

906  Mansel, 1998, 124.

Was the same generation of Jews who had previously been rescued now collectively turning against its host in the name of biblical prophecy?

On the other hand, for Ottomans, the Mahdi alone was not enough. He needed to ally himself with the Messiah in order to go to war against the Blonde People – Rome.

Reubeni had him handy.

The game was rigged: let the two big guys fight it out and have 'David' move in between as the laughing third. This foul-play works as long as nobody spots the cards in the sleeve – and that is our modern problem with some organized religions in general and with Israel's religious right-wing leaders in particular.

This must not be misunderstood as singling out Israel for some sort of cheap polemic – as the center of the biblical story, Israel singled itself out thousands of years ago. Nice clothes will only serve to better hide what is supposed to remain concealed.

Since Jewish leaders had weaponized religion, the Bible and the Talmud came back repeatedly to haunt ordinary Jews.

The anonymous author established Reubeni as a prophet and forerunner who was able to foretell the re-conquest of the Promised Land – the End of the World. For this to come true, the Messiah's coming was necessary on the Christian side, as well as the Mahdi and the Second Jesus in the Muslim area.

If Reubeni could pull this off, the clash of civilizations would be perfect.

The same author also referred to *'the evil decree,'* which was a reference to the prohibition of Jews to visit the Temple Mount. He predicted that the Jews would soon be redeemed and that repentance and charity would annul the zone that was off-limits.[907]

The Roman Emperor Hadrian had bulldozed Jerusalem in the early second century, only to erect his own temple on the Temple Mount. Jews had been forbidden to approach the place since.[908]

As it is often with predictions, they are truer when uttered after the fact.

The 'zone' had already been cancelled with Suleiman's conquest.

The letter ended with a tragic note by the copyist:

*Righteousness, righteousness you shall pursue so that you may live and inherit the land.*[909]

---

[907] Neubauer, Ten Tribes, transl. Lenowitz, 1998, 111-112.
[908] There are a number of temporary exceptions.
[909] Neubauer, Ten Tribes, transl. Lenowitz, 1998, 111-112.

We can only imagine the turmoil that the global Jewish community was in. The news of Reubeni as a forerunner as well as a 'twelve-year-old' messiah reached them across the world within weeks.[910]

Also, Abrabanel's prediction for the beginning of the Messianic Age in 1531 and the passing of Halley's Comet were less than nine years out. Likewise, after the capture of Constantinople, religious authorities of Ottoman-Turks had calculated the beginning of the tribulations that lead to the Last Hour would start around 1494-95 AD.[911]

Nothing had happened since.

Capsali's nephew Elijahu published his Hebrew chronicle at this time. He documented how Jewish leaders plotted the messianic events at Suleiman's doorsteps right under his nose: *'He [Suleiman] is the tenth king [sultan] of the Turks, and the tenth one shall be holy to the Lord (Leviticus 27:32); in his days Judah shall be delivered … and a redeemer shall come to Zion (Isaiah 59:20).*[912] Suleiman believed of himself to be *'the world emperor and messiah of the last age.*[913] He was supposed to be the second Solomon, not a Jewish redeemer.

The apocalyptic fever now reached a full-blown hysteria.

It would be hard to reject Reubeni as not being the real deal.

Before traveling to Rome, Reubeni stopped at Venice and was received by the head of the Jewish community in the Ghetto of Venice. He was sent on his way with assurances of support and manpower.[914]

This head was Abrabanel's successor. The 'Rabbi of Venice.' He was the highest Jewish authority in Europe.

The beast was sucking up explosive fuel. As it moved its strategy forward, it was ever more energized.

The story in a contemporary Jewish chronicle is different from Reubeni's account. There, he started in Portugal and went through Spain to Avignon and then to Italy, through Bologna, Ferrara, and Mantua.[915] He drew large crowds of hopefuls everywhere he appeared.

---

[910] They communicated with each other frequently through Talmudic commentaries.

[911] Şahin, End Time, 2010, 342.

[912] Elijahu Capsali, Hebrew Chronicle (1523) in Gülru Necipoglu, The Dome of the Rock as Palimpsest (Harvard, 2008) 68.

[913] Sena'i, Chronicle (1540) in Gülru Necipoglu, The Dome of the Rock as Palimpsest (Harvard, 2008) 68.

[914] A. Z. Aeshcoly (1940) as cited in Lenowitz, 1998, 112.

[915] Ha-Cohen, Vol. II, translated by Bialloblotzky, 1836, 149.

While his route is not all that important, the deviations of the stories should prompt researchers to be on alert. This is the territory of history that has been engineered.

Not only Jews but also Christians wanted to get in touch with Reubeni. The superstitious news about this holy messiah forerunner travelled far ahead of him and infected much of the continent's religious underground, Jews, former Jews, and perhaps even Christians.

According to Reubeni, he finally arrived at the gates of Rome in 1525 where he was received by the Catholic Cardinal Egidio di Viterbo.

This happened to be Luther's archenemy. He had been the one willing to sell out his Austin Friar friends and who had opened the Fifth Lateran Council in Rome.

It turns out that Cardinal Viterbo had been taught by at least three Jewish teachers, Rabbi Yosef Ashkenazi,[916] Baruch di Benevento, and Elia Levita.[917] The latter suggests Levitical priestly class. While he was also an Ashkenazi, a German Jew, the Levites own the right to spiritual and secular leadership over the Jews through the lineages of the two sons of Aaron. As a young man, he had been among the expelled Jews that had arrived in Italy from the area of Nuremberg.[918]

David Cameron, the former British Prime Minister[919] of our time is one of Elia Levita's descendants.

The Augustinian Cardinal Viterbo was a Christian Kabalist who hosted Levita in Rome for ten years. Di Benevento, on the other hand, had taught in the Naples residence of Samuel Abrabanel, who was one of the three sons of the prophetic Isaac Abrabanel. Another of these sons, the Hebrew Lion, Judah Abrabanel Leone Ebreo was also well-acquainted with Egidio Viterbo.

It was a small world.

Reubeni managed to convince di Viterbo and an assembly of other cardinals and officers of the church to arrange for an audience with the new Medici Pope Clement VII.[920] Reubeni followed the protocol of Abulafia to demand help in the liberation of Israel from the pope.

---

[916] A. Z. Aeshcoly (1940) as cited in Lenowitz, 1998, 112-113.

[917] Eljahu Ha-Levi aka Elia Levita Ashkenazi, Eliyahu haBahur (the Bachelor), Elye Bokher, 1468-1549. For a biography of Elia Levita see The Massoreth ha-massoreth of Elias Levita: being an exposition of the Massoretic notes on the Hebrew Bible: or the ancient critical apparatus of the Old Testament in Hebrew (Longmans, 1867) 1-84.

[918] Elia Levita was born in Neustadt, near Nuremberg.

[919] David Cameron was prime minister of the United Kingdom 2010 – 2016.

[920] Clement VII, born Giovanni de' Medici, was pope from 1523 – 1534.

It fulfilled a prerequisite for the messianic mission.

The papal audience was granted.[921] Twelve Jewish elders – symbolizing the Twelve Tribes of Israel – were already present at Cardinal di Viterbo's home. From there they went over to the pope's living quarters.

The involvement of Jewish leaders at the Vatican even before a meeting between Reubeni and the pope is astonishing.

This subversion is so genius that it escapes our wildest imagination.

Reubeni's plan on the Italian side of the plot was to appease quarrels about the Duchy of Milan between the French King and the Holy Roman Emperor in order to form an alliance against Ottoman-Turks – the friendly host of so many Jewish survivors of the expulsions from Spain, Tlemcen, and elsewhere.

How would he do that?

The timing of Reubeni was brilliant. Clement VII had three main problems, the Lutheran revolution, the division between King Francis of France and Emperor Charles, and the Ottoman-Turkish threat.

In a melancholic letter, the pope expressed his concerns about the ferocity and long duration of inter-Christian wars. Almost all European nations were devastated. The might and military machinery of the Turks was about to bring the destruction of the Catholic Church. He thought that the fortunes of Christendom were being dashed to the ground and destroyed.[922]

He believed that the End of the World was at hand.

Reubeni offered hope in two of these issues. Although it is not clear in which form he would have helped to appease the European royals, we might be able to sense the power of the global Rabbinic network with its financial muscle.

The pope thought that a pan-European undertaking might not be possible – because he had his own agenda of Catholic conquest of the Holy Roman Empire. He suggested rallying the Portuguese instead.[923]

Since being a pope requires the highest degree of fundamentalist beliefs in the fulfillment of prophecy, one should not be surprised that he embraced Reubeni's mission. As we had heard before, not only Jews, but also Luther and Müntzer believed in the coming End of the World.

---

[921] A. Z. Aeshcoly (1940) as cited in Lenowitz, 1998, 112-113.

[922] Pope Clement VII, Arch. Segr. Vaticano, Arm. XLIV, tom. 9, fol. 59', December 22, 1524, in Setton, 1984, 226.

[923] A. Z. Aeshcoly (1940) as cited in Lenowitz, 1998, 113.

By nature of its position, the Vatican had also been infected by the silly expectation.

We can be certain that the papacy had no clue about Reubeni's hidden agenda. As a forerunner or a messiah, he would have ended up torn to pieces. It appears that Martin Luther also remained ignorant of the secret.

The global Jewish network operated undercover.

Like Rabbinic leaders themselves, the conspirators in the Vatican – including the pope – had ulterior motives.

Never mind that Reubeni and the pope would each have intended to play their own fiddle on the Temple Mount. The pattern was always the same: leverage divisions, promise allegiance in return for unprecedented privileges, and play the game with the intention of coming up on top.

The strategy went wrong so many times throughout history that it is astonishing that modern societies uphold religious freedom for such organized crimes. Instead of protecting the freedoms of humanity, they serve as civilization's Achilles heel. They are holy enemies of freedom.

Of course, one could think that Reubeni's story was only a bluster.

The church records contain an entry on February 4, 1525 describing indeed a visit of a Hebrew-Arabian embassy and confirming the pope's preference for the involvement of Portugal and Ethiopia.[924]

The Ethiopian Queen Eleni had already sent an embassy in 1512/13.[925] With the help of the Medici Pope Leo X, an alliance between the two nations had consequently been established. At that time, Ethiopia was threatened by the Muslim Adal Sultanate, which was located at the Horn of Africa, modern-day Somalia.

Since the Portuguese were engaged in trading with India through the Gulf of Persia, they would indeed come to the defense, as they had under Queen Eleni.

Then the bluff reveals itself.

---

[924] Raynaldus, Annales Ecclesiastici, translated by A.J. Deus. Lenowitz misplaced the papal memorandum to 1526. Instead, the Latin original is dated to February 4, 1525 (Annales ecclesiastici Caesaris Baronii, CLEMENTIS VII ANNUS 2. — CHRISTI 1525, Febr. 4, 93: Hebraeorum Arabum legatio ad Ponttficem. — Obita est hoc anno Haebreorum Arabiam incolentium apud Sedem Apostolicam legatio [...]).

[925] Under Matthew the Armenian. His embassy to Portugal brought along a piece of the True Cross. Matthew died upon his return to Ethiopia.

A significant detail has been omitted from Reubeni's story. The introduction in the church records is followed by a speech in the name of *'David Alnazarani Abbassiae'*,[926] the King of Ethiopia, Dawit II[927] of the Solomonic Dynasty.

Now, the puzzle comes together.

In the just-before discussed meeting with the pope, Reubeni referred to the legendary figure (Petri) Prester John.[928] In order to establish the alliance between Portugal and Ethiopia, Queen Eleni had sent a *'letter of Prester John'* to Pope Leo.[929] A contemporary missionary related *'Prester John of the Indies'* to the Ethiopian court of Queen Eleni[930] as well as to *'this King David Prester John.'*[931] Chosen for the throne at age eleven,[932] and enthroned at twelve (!),[933] Dawit was a nephew of the previous emperor[934] and son of Queen Eleni.[935] He was called *'son of Israel.'*[936]

Was the twelve-year-old who had earlier been hailed in Turkey and whose name it was forbidden to write a reference to the Ethiopian King Dawit II? Was Suleiman aware of him?

---

[926] Annales ecclesiastici Caesaris Baronii, CLEMENTIS VII ANNUS 2. — CHRISTI 1525, Febr. 4, 93: Charissimo in Christo filio nostro **David Alnazarani Abbassiae, et AEthiopiae** regi illustri.

[927] Dawit II ruled the Ethiopian Empire 1501 – 1540.

[928] That the legendary kingdom of Prester John could have been in Ethiopia appears in the European consciousness from about the thirteenth century. See Joe Thornton, A Cultural History of the Atlantic World, 1250 – 1820 (Cambridge University Press, 2012) 16–17.
In the next century, he was recorded as the Patriarch of the Ethiopian Church. Rober Silverberg, The Realm of Prester John (Ohio University Press, 1996) 164–165. [This fiction writer claimed that the name was given to the leaders of the Solomonic Dynasty at the Council of Florence (p. 189).]

[929] Again under Matthew the Armenian.

[930] Alvarez, transl. Alderley, 1881, 20.

[931] Ibid., 143, (Francisco Alvarez, Delle Navigationi et Viaggi, Obedienza del Prete Ianni, 1524, translated by Giovanni Baptista Ramusio, Volume 1, 3rd Edition (Giunti, 1563) 260: Signor David , Re della grande, & alta Ethiopia volgarmente detto il Prete Ianni [...])

[932] Ibid., 143.

[933] Ibid., 307.

[934] Ibid.

[935] Ibid., 223.

[936] Ibid., 147.

A short biography of David of Abbysinia[937] says that Dawit sent another embassy from his capital Barrara (probably a phonetic corruption of Dabra Tabor[938]) to Pope Clement VII in 1533.

In fact, the Ethiopian Solomonic Dynasty has long claimed direct descent from King Solomon and his son, King David. Even in the twentieth century, the Rastafari movement saw the crowning of Emperor Haile Selassie I[939] as the Second Coming of Jesus. They viewed him as God incarnate.

Therefore, Reubeni's *'seventy elders of King Shlomo'* refers to this dynasty. The Ethiopians were connected to the Jacobites from Egypt, presumably through Joseph. It is these two linages that form a bridge to Islam.

The prester was also supposed to be head of the Nasara, Christians of Saint Thomas, or the Syrian Orthodox Church.

The Koran offers them as partners in the formation of Islam. Reubeni's middle name confirms just that: *'David Alnazarani Abbassiae,'* David, the Nasara from Ethiopia.

Behind the emperor stood a Christian priest, the confessor to Prester John.[940] Similar to the Catholic puppeteer rulers in Europe, this confessor was second after the emperor.[941] He also seems to have been second in command.[942]

It is Ethiopian doctrine (as is Coptic) that priests can be married[943] provided that they do so before being ordained. This would have made them sympathetic to a major stance of the Protestants. We know of a few Jewish converts who had influenced the Reformer. The omnipresence of Rabbinic leaders makes it seem unlikely that they were not actively part of Luther's Reformation also, even of his inner circle.

---

[937] Jean-Jacques Boissard, Leben und Kontraseiten der Türkischen und Persischen Sultanen, von Osmane an, bis auf den jetzt regierenden Sultan Mahumet II. (Diterich von Bry Leodien, 1596) 258. [It contains a portrait of Dawit II from the 1590s' that is marked with 'David Beldugian.' This same biography clarifies that the Ethiopian Emperor was called by the names Acegua, Neguz, or Beldugian. The Germans called him Prettergiam, which is a linguistic corruption of Prester John, (page 259) as is Beldugian. John and Gian are translations of the same name. On a map of East Africa that was prepared by the Portuguese just two decades later, 'Preste' was the Emperor of Ethiopia at a time when these two nations worked together. In other words, it was by this name that the Europeans knew the Emperor of Ethiopia. (Alvarez, transl. Alderley, 1881, 188-189)]

[938] History is not made easier by the habit of early authors in printed books to spell names phonetically.

[939] Haile Selassie I aka Tafari Makonnen Woldemikael, was Ethiopia's king 1916 – 1930 and emperor 1930 – 1974.

[940] It is unclear whether he was also the Patriarch of the Ethiopian Church (the Abima).

[941] Alvarez, transl. Alderley, 1881, 168.

[942] Ibid., 403.

[943] Ibid., 57.

Nevertheless, it was not David Reubeni who showed up before the pope but an ambassador[944] who presented Dawit II to be a Hebrew man from the desert and the *'mountain of Thabour'*.[945] Therefore, the Vatican's *Thabour* can be identified as *Debre Tabor* in Ethiopia which is also Reubeni's *Habur*. It is not the fortress town of Khaibar in the Arab Peninsula.

Debre Tabor is a city up in the mountains of Ethiopia that has long been used as an imperial retreat in the event of crisis.[946]

The meaning is now clear: Dawit II, the Ethiopian Emperor from *Debre Tabor*, was David Reubeni from *Habur*. And he was Prester John, ruler over the Nasara. He represented the ruling linage of the former Nasara of the Koran and was related to Muhammad, indeed.

While this is not the place to explore this detour, the consequences of these details cascade through the fragmented past of Ethiopia and illuminates it in unprecedented ways.[947] It is like a time rupture, reaching back to the foundation of Islam and the location of the Sanhedrin, the Exilarch, and the Nasi.[948]

All of a sudden, the idea of a Jewish king with Muslim and Christian roots does not sound as bizarre as it initially did.

It appears that the Ethiopians had been both Jews and Christians all along – the Nasara. Perhaps even Muslims. While this may sound strange, it is not unique. The Islamic tribe Banu Hashim, from which Prophet Muhammad is said to have originated, likewise claimed Jacobite and Ishmaelite descent through their maternal and paternal bloodlines. Again, in the middle sat the linages of Jacob and Joseph on the path to Islam.

The Muslim Banu Hashim, of course, are the Hasmonean royals who rule over *all* Abrahamic tribes. That is why they can be Jacobites and Ishmaelites all at once.

---

[944] Perhaps the Portuguese missionary, Francisco Alvarez.

[945] Annales ecclesiastici Caesaris Baronii, CLEMENTIS VII ANNUS 2. — CHRISTI 1525, Febr. 4, 93.

[946] Against consensus, the claim here is that this city acted in this function a few hundred years earlier than it is commonly assumed. It appears that the court moved around the country in tents and used monasteries and churches as their hospices, leaving no royal structural traces behind. See Alvarez, transl. Alderley, 1881, 219.

[947] Unfortunately, the history of this Solomonic empire between the appearance of Prophet Muhammad in the seventh century and the Zagwe Dynasty from the late tenth century is in the dark.

[948] According to the account of Dawit II, Ethopia was cut off from Rome in the seventh century. Indeed, when the Muslim Abbasid Dynasty took control of the young caliphate, the last of the Umayyad leaders (Marwan II aka Marwan ibn Muhammad ibn Marwan or (Marwān bin Muḥammad bin Marwān bin al-Ḥakam) was Umayyad Caliph 744 – 750) is said to having fled to Ethiopia. Compare Francisco Alvarez, Delle Navigationi et Viaggi, Obedienza del Prete Ianni, 1524, translated by Giovanni Baptista Ramusio, Volume 1, 3rd Edition (Giunti, 1563) 259.

David Reubeni represented the continuance of the koranic Nasara in Ethiopia.[949]

Undercover.

The Ethiopian king was also connected to Muslim prophecies of the End of the World. A tradition proclaims the appearance of Al-Harj, which means 'killing' in the Ethiopian language. This Al-Harj would be responsible for the loss of religious knowledge,[950] which ties him to the House of Joseph – the House of Deceivers.

It signifies the establishment of a new religion and the extinction of the old.

In other words, Muslims were already waiting for David Reubeni – Al-Harj.

The treason against ordinary Jews, Christians, and Muslims that comes with their voluntary reception of messiahs is beyond comprehension.

Another Muslim tradition says that one with two lean legs would come from Ethiopia and destroy the Kaaba in Mecca.[951] Being thin or short legged appears to be a signal of a significant opponent, perhaps even the Antichrist. In contrast, one with long legs or one whose legs would miraculously lengthen in front of witnesses would be a messenger of God.[952] We will see how this prophecy neatly fits in with David Reubeni.

He was playing all his cards well. Very well.

But now we are enabled to look into his sleeves. Luck has it that a missionary diligently took notes.

An Ethiopian mirror of the Muslim Al-Harj tradition was recorded just a couple of years before the appearance of David Reubeni. The contemporary patriarch related that it was prophesied that Ethiopia would submit to the Catholic Church in Rome during his lifetime. The Kingdom of France was expected to join with Ethiopia and Portugal to destroy Mecca and conquer Cairo.

---

[949] I have written a paper 'The Nasara in the Koran' (A.J. Deus, The Nasara in the Koran, academia.edu, 2016) in which I insisted that the existence of the Nasara since long before the advent of Jesus Christ was not in question. Only their whereabouts from the fifth century onwards was a mystery. The Nasi had found shelter under the Exilarch of the Babylonian Jews in the fifth century. This may have led to a short-lived alliance between the two, eying the Temple Mount in Jerusalem. The result of this pact may constitute the earliest root of what would later become Islam – a new religion that attempted to unite five core sects. First the Nasi and then the Exilarch's family fled later into the Arab Peninsula. Tradition claims that the first group of 'Muslims' headed for Ethiopia, where they found protection.

[950] Bukhari, 2007-2009, 9:88:187.

[951] Bukhari, 2007-2009, 2:26:661.

[952] Ha-Cohen, Vol. II, translated by Bialloblotzky, 1836, 162.

Given a French-friendly Vatican, the participation of Portugal in this dream pact is remarkable. It lays bare the macro-religious environment that pits the pro-French faction against Habsburg imperialists.

The Patriarch of the Ethiopian Church (the Abima) appears to have conspired to subvert his host nation. His intention was to pull Ethiopia away from the Coptic Christian Church in Cairo – now under Ottoman rule – to the French-friendly Catholic Church in Rome.[953] The Portuguese embassy suggested that the patriarch should encourage Dawit II to help wrest Jerusalem from the Ottoman-Turks.[954]

During the three years before first appearing in Jerusalem and Rome, Dawit II expressed concerns over the advances of Ottoman-Turks into the Arab Peninsula. He was hoping for Portuguese troops to build fortresses. In return, he promised men and provisions.[955] In 1521, Dawit II sent the Portuguese embassy back to Europe to formally ask for military assistance from the Portuguese King.

However, the following year, the emperor was unimpressed by a map that had been drawn. He was concerned that Portugal was too small to possibly defend the Red Sea against Ottoman-Turks and other Arab forces.[956]

The emperor seems to have sensed the magnitude of the opportunity at hand and started to devise a plan to extend his alliance.[957]

Finally, he thought of dispatching an embassy to the Vatican[958] and of offering assistance and men to the Portuguese governor of the Indies for a war against the heretical Muslims.[959] His plan was that European armies would sail with their war ships, while the soldiers of Ethiopia would march by land.[960]

Even a concealed pilgrimage to Jerusalem through Cairo was part of the account.[961]

This is the European side of the story.

---

[953] Alvarez, transl. Alderley, 1881, 254-255.
[954] Ibid., 264.
[955] Ibid., 204.
[956] Ibid., 311.
[957] Ibid.
[958] Ibid.
[959] Ibid., 374.
[960] Ibid.
[961] Ibid., 345.

The only element missing was that Dawit II personally left for Jerusalem. The text was expunged by the censors of the Catholic Church at exactly the point where this would have occurred.[962] Indeed, excerpts archived in the Vatican Library confirmed the existence of differing versions.[963]

A couple of years later, an embassy from Dawit II delivered a letter to the Portuguese King that appealed to the monarch's pride. Should he conquer Jerusalem, nobody would be greater than him. There would be no other name but his alone.[964]

They played the grandeur of the Portuguese and Ottoman rulers all at once – and the Vatican; and the French. None could have known of the heavenly glory that was promised to the others.

What a dangerous house of cards! Fall one, fall all.

Holocaust is written all over it.

Dawit II offered men *'like the sands of the sea,'* financing, and provisions.[965] In return, the Portuguese would provide modern weaponry and training. The missionary with the message, Francisco Alvarez, was also to meet with the pope at Rome.

An Italian translation contains some of the missing elements from Alvarez' expunged notes. Among them is a copy of the letter from Dawit II to Pope Clement VII for the meeting in early 1525 and the pope's reply.

According to the letter, Ethiopia was cut off from Rome in the seventh century. The emperor had conserved the related books from Pope Eugene[966] in his archive.[967] Like his incarcerated papal predecessor,[968] Eugene is said to have refused to submit to the orders by the Patriarch of Constantinople[969] about questions of Jesus' will.[970]

---

962 Alvarez's story is interrupted in the spring of 1523 and continues without connection with his departure in 1526.
963 The geographer Roberto Almagia (1884 – 1962) found three manuscripts of Francisco Álvares in the Vatican Library that differed from the approved and published version of his work.
964 Alvarez, transl. Alderley, 1881, 393.
965 Ibid., 399.
966 Pope Eugene I aka Eugenius I was Pope 654 – 657 AD.
967 Alvarez, Viaggi, 1524, transl. Ramusio, 1563, 259.
968 Pope Martin I was Pope of the Catholic Church 649 – 655. He was arrested in 653 under suspicion to having been in communications with the Umayyad Saracens.
969 Patriarch Peter of Constantinople, 656–666 AD.
970 It may not be obvious that these are – should the Vatican ever release these books – documents that could enlighten modernity about events during the rise of Islam. The documents could enlighten moderns what the Catholic Church of the seventh century looked like.

Dawit II acted as though he had submitted to the Vatican.[971] Of course! He wanted the pope's cooperation for a suicidal mission. While he complained about never having received answers to earlier letters, he vowed that it would not be difficult to defeat the enemies of faith and gain access to Jerusalem.

For this, he suggested that the pope order peace among the divided European royals and go to war to root out Islam.[972] This could easily be achieved with Christian unity. The Holy Sepulcher in Jerusalem would be his. Instead of offering numerous foot soldiers, Dawit II complained that the Christian disunity led to his requests for assistance to be ignored.[973]

Contrary to the entry in the Vatican Library, the pope agreed to the plan to unify Christian rulers and to provide any assistance necessary.[974]

Why would the Catholic Church censor a work about a Jewish Messiah? Other than outright embarrassment for having supported the scheme, the Papal States suffered from a self-inflicted shortage in Christian scribes. A Jewish censor would have performed his job to perfection.

But all this is irritating. Despite all claims to the Solomonic lineage, Dawit II was not supposed to be a Jew. Ethiopia is believed to having been close to Jacobite or perhaps Syrian Christianity.

Indeed, a contemporary embassy to Ethiopia recognized a novel kind of Christianity in one town. Jews were absent.[975] The travelers thought that its inhabitants would be a worthy target for Catholicism.[976]

In some Ethiopian places, a layer of Islamic customs seems to also have been buried in their rituals. According to the missionary, they entered a church only barefoot, as Muslims enter their mosques.[977] Like them, the Ethiopians fasted during the day and ate at night.[978] They even used velvets from Mecca to cover their cloisters and circuits.[979]

The author of Dawit II's biography reported that the Ethiopians used temples with rituals and baptisms not unlike those of the Catholic Church. They used the Old and New Testament, including the Paulinic epistles, which was noteworthy for the author.

---

[971] Alvarez, Viaggi, 1524, transl. Ramusio, 1563, 259.
[972] Ibid., 260.
[973] Ibid.
[974] Ibid., 261.
[975] Alvarez, transl. Alderley, 1881, 406.
[976] Ibid., 9.
[977] Ibid., 29.
[978] Ibid., 30.
[979] Ibid.

The function of 'market churches' was similar to mosques that served as places for trade. Curiously, Christians only traded in low values and food. Merchants were generally Muslims.

However, they hated each other so much that Christians, like Jews, did not touch edibles from Muslims.[980]

Except for clergy, it was custom for men of wealth to have multiple wives, and they could separate at will. However, it appears that the Ethiopian Church at the time attempted to forbid the practice only recently against a more traditional view of the emperor.[981]

They circumcised both men and girls.[982]

Sabbath *and* Sunday were sacred.[983] Muslim enemies exploited the fact that Ethiopian Christians, like Jews on Sabbath, would not fight on either of these days.[984] The former was clearly tied to the Jewish Bible and maintained by the 'Christian' leaders of Ethiopia.[985]

These were recognized as Judaizers.[986]

The link to the papacy[987] could possibly have been established during recent generations.[988] Ethiopia had previously viewed both the Roman and the Egyptian papacy as heretics.[989] Yet, toward the end of the fourteenth century, Ethiopia was subject of the Egyptian Jacobite Church.[990] At this time, church customs appear to still have been in flux.[991]

But Jewish history recognizes David Reubeni, aka Dawit II as one of theirs.

How could this be?

Is it possible that covert Jews were leading entire nations, even occupying the seats of patriarchs and emperors, even popes? I demonstrated the alienating bond between the Temple-mother Roxelana and Suleiman the Magnificent, who now portrayed himself as *'the conqueror born under an auspicious astrological conjunction*

---

[980]   Ibid., 336.
[981]   Ibid., 45.
[982]   Ibid.
[983]   Ibid., 11.
[984]   Ibid., 110.
[985]   Ibid., 34.
[986]   Ibid.
[987]   Ibid., 252.
[988]   Ibid., 243.
[989]   Ibid., 253.
[990]   Khaldun, *Muqaddimah, 1377*, transl. Rosenthal, 1958, Chapter III.31.
[991]   Alvarez, transl. Alderley, 1881, 245.

*and thus destined to rule over the whole world.* [992] I also highlighted the ancestry of some of Portugal's and Spain's royals, including Emperor Charles' lineage.

Is this no more than malicious suspicion?

Let me rephrase the question: is it possible that the last 2,000 years brought forth *not a single* patriarch, pope, bishop, king, or even emperor from the only ethnic group that operated an ultra-loyal global network, was superbly educated, and skilled in leadership, trade, and finances?

Now that we have a better context, the answer is simple: absolutely not.

For at least a thousand years before Martin Luther, Jews were collectively the best educated people on the planet. The rest were largely illiterate. There is no probability that Jews did not climb to any of these positions, either covertly or overtly. Instead, Jewish leaders had created multiple versions of the New Jerusalem for themselves, in the Ottoman Empire, in the Iberian Peninsula, across the rest of Europe, in Ethiopia, and in other places. True to prophecy, everybody else was either reduced to serfdom or rooted out. Jewish leaders controlled the judicial, fiscal, and executive branches of administrations and filled its ranks with their own. Historians may not have looked closely enough, and we currently do not understand what happened and why this information would have been erased from the historical record.

The organized religions of Christianity and Islam forced their subjects to live in abject poverty and illiterate ignorance. In doing so, they created dependencies on the literate population of the competing mother-religion, Judaism. The influence of a literate minority in the top layers of feudal social hierarchies was of outsize magnitude. They could potentially monopolize trade, banking, armed forces, learning, government administration, religion, and the making of kings. This includes weapons and slave-warrior trades no less than financing of wars on all sides, tax farming, the creation of religious divisions – and even the shaping of history.

I do have a notion, though: it went wrong. It ended in disaster. It destroyed entire civilizations – every single time.

It remains under-appreciated that the fulfillment of a New Jerusalem also constitutes the end of prophecy. Without its perpetual and violent renewal, Christians, Muslims, and ordinary Jews would eventually wake up to a reality of having been cheated out of their beliefs, savings, livelihoods, and children.

All that remains of old is the Levite priesthood and the Hasmonean royals.

---

[992] Şahin, Süleyman, 2013, 189.

It almost appears as though Luther's time constitutes this kind of an awakening from a Judaic nightmare, literally, the Renaissance.

Certainly, in his letter to the Portuguese governor of the Indies, Emperor Dawit II had himself presented as a Jew and successor of King David.[993] The previously quoted biography of Reubeni lays it out for us:

> *Although Christ is not unknown among the Abissinians along the coast, the people are Jewish, in fact even circumcised.*[994]

They were Jews who had endorsed Jesus Christ[995] – Jewish Christians or Christian Jews. Crypo Jews.

More precisely, like Luther, they rejected changes to Christology and church doctrine that had been introduced at the Fourth Council of Chalcedon from back in Augustine's fifth century.[996] That council had affirmed that Jesus' mother Mary was the Mother of God. The creed was flat-out rejected by the Persian version of Christianity and ultimately by Islam. It had also been rejected by Egypt and Ethiopia at that time, likely even by Rome under Pope Eugene and his predecessor.

This was the council that plunged the entire world into chaos.

Given this context, I continue with Reubeni's version of the story.

He was represented in the Vatican for a second meeting by the leader of Italian Jewry, Daniel da Pisa, a banker. It appears to have taken almost a year to forge the alliance for the messianic cause of Reubeni.

But Italian Jewry was by now fit for war with hearts of lions.[997]

With the backing of a banker of Italian Jewry, subversive support from at least the Egyptian, Syrian, Turkish, Portuguese, Spanish, French, and Italian Jewry, and a pact with Portugal and the Catholic Pope, Reubeni and his Sanhedrin bosses had all the ingredients necessary to unleash a re-conquest of the Promised Land – the Redemption of Israel and the beginning of the End of the World.

Credit has to be given to them for being cautious and secretive in their impatience.

---

[993] Alvarez, transl. Alderley, 1881, 368.

[994] Boissard, Persische Sultane, transl. Robert M. Kerr, 1596.

[995] The Christian writer would have naturally thought of Jesus Christ rather than the Jewish Christ.

[996] Alvarez, transl. Alderley, 1881, 207.

[997] A. Z. Aeshcoly (1940) as cited in Lenowitz, 1998, 113-114.

Meanwhile, France was able to sign an alliance with Poland. One might think that France was lucky, until we learn that the driving force behind the deal was Queen Mother Bona Sforza, a highly educated woman who was married to the widowed Polish King.

Do you remember 'The Tiger of Forlì?' Yes, that was Caterina Sforza, wife of the French-friendly Giovanni de Medici 'delle Bande Nere.' The Tiger's father was Bona Sforza's grandfather, and they seem to have been bred for character. We should not be surprised that Bona was a fierce opponent of the Holy Roman Empire. Like the elder, she was hot tempered and energetic. She was disobedient and wanted to achieve things her way.

Since the Sforza family had lost Milan and Naples, the dynasts were working on regaining control and trying to extend their influence through establishing family bonds.

Back then, marriage into the sphere of royals was a complicated business of tactical deals and trades with girls intended to bring advantages to both families involved. But as in Spain previously, the Polish nobles did not appreciate the ascent of a Sforza son to the throne.

He was not purebred, but half a foreigner.

It was a native father whose heir was from a foreign girl. Yet, Bona knew what mattered was power. Her goal was to amass as much as possible to ensure her children's future.

Bona Sforza was also in contact with Roxelana, wife of Suleiman the Magnificent and mother of their Mahdi heir. These women appear to have been ahead of their time.

Were they shaping the inconceivable?

### Free Will

As leader of the Protestant Reformation, Luther was busy with his family and with fighting with people who had slightly differing religious ideas. With one of his enemies, the Dutch Desiderius Erasmus Roterodamus, he argued *ad nauseam* that free will does not exist.[998] Luther thought that free will brought about sins and those, in turn, made it impossible for humans ever to stand before God.[999]

Erasmus was an Austin Friar who favored integration of his order with the Catholic Church. His Augustinian vow was later dispensed with. We heard of him earlier in a case about an innocent and ignorant victim that had been scarred for life by the Inquisition.

Erasmus and Luther respected each other in their enmity. The latter thought highly of Erasmus for his level of learning. Erasmus understood that many of Luther's reforms were necessary.[1000]

However, the argument of the two about free will was self-defeating. The problem of predetermination, the foreseeing guidance of humanity by God, vs. free will, is one of clever design. Whatever humans might try to receive favors from their god, the outcome is always the same: humans never get to stand before their gods. Sooner or later, one of God's many commandments will be broken, even if only in thought. The more fundamentalist believers become, the less likely it is that they can ever march up to the throne of their god to be accepted into the Kingdom of Heaven – or thrown to hell.

The Catholic Church did not appreciate Luther's ideas. It had turned free will into a money machine to sell indulgences. Free will was official church dogma. You sinned through free will – you paid up for redemption.

Luther's rejection of free will was a continuance of opposing curiosity.

His version was no less irrational than Erasmus' defense of the Catholic's. With Luther's predetermination, everyone's life is set in stone already before birth. This concept requires no effort. Not even those who are free from religion can be excluded from the benefits of predetermination. Life is pre-programmed whether lived or not. There is nothing one can do to alter the course toward purgatory, heaven, or hell.

Not even Jews.

---

[998] Martin Luther, The Bondage of the Will (1525), translated by Henry Cole (London, 1823) Discussion, Sect. LXXXII.

[999] Ibid.

[1000] Mark Galli and Ted Olsen, 131 Christians Everyone Should Know (Holman Reference, 2000) 344.

This discussion is not new. It goes back to ancient civilization. Persian Zoroastrianism[1001] seems to have been based on the concept of free will. The ancient Greeks banked on fate. Then as now, the chasm of faith lay at the Bosporus.

The spiritual rift had been dug by religious professionals. It fuels hatred toward one another.

In all this, Luther did not need to think much. He strictly followed Saint Augustine. The Catholic Church trailed the saint where that served its treasury.

Augustine offered up a mind-boggling argument for the difference between self-determination and the will of God. He abused Cicero's[1002] ancient writings, which also centered on fate against free will, leveraging the tension between realism and spiritualism.

Augustine argued that there are two wills, one good (fate) and the other wicked (free will), but only the good is from God.[1003] Believers can escape God's will by turning into wicked beings of their own will. Every suffering that is not due to man's free will is God's will.[1004]

His conclusion was that man needs to submit to God's will, without any compromises.[1005] Better yet, displaying no will at all is the way to avoid sin, according to Augustine.

As Luther said, free will makes it impossible for humans ever to stand before God. This explains why fundamentally religious nations tend to host a high percentage of idle hands. This, in turn, begets systemic poverty, involuntary for the people in most part, but deliberately induced by the religious leadership. Many believers from such countries are useless in their jobs, almost as if in a modus of minimum intellectual effort and no physical strain.

Did priests commit crimes against innocent children by their own free will or through predetermination? Which path did they choose for the successive cover-ups and obstructions? Was it God's plan or theirs?

---

[1001] Zoroastrianism was an ancient monotheistic religion that predated the Jewish Torah. Their single God Ahura Mazda was an all good creator without evil and they believed in the free will of humanity.

[1002] Cicero, 106–43 BC.

[1003] Augustine, *The City of God* (354–430 AD), V:9.

[1004] Ibid., V:10.

[1005] Ibid., XI:10.

Augustine was declared a heretic by Greek Orthodoxy, which was then the dominating universal church. Greeks did not require a subscription to the official faith in order to earn God's gift of salvation. The mercy of God was for all, and free will was of the individual, over which God had no power.

But in the Rome of Augustine's era, very few voices of dissent would make it into the archives of modernity. There, before the advent of Islam, strict adherence to predetermination was the rule.

Luther's way.

The Koran has its own logic about the guiding hand of God.[1006] God's will is all-encompassing and includes God's responsibility for violence and war. Given the role of imams and caliphs as direct representatives of God, this is a dangerous mix. However, contradictions are readily at hand. *'God changes not what is in a people, until they change what is in themselves.'*[1007] There is predetermination, but then there is also free will. This is not unlike the Jewish Pharisee position.

Similarly, the Syrian Christian Church (Melchite) advocated free will of the individual, opposing Saint Augustine's ideas.

We have a timely testament from a man associated with the first 'Muslim' caliphate.[1008] He differentiated between nature, necessity, spontaneity, fate, chance, and intent.[1009] According to this author, you cannot have it both ways: free will and predetermination.[1010] Predetermination was restricted to matters that are not subject to the human free will. He attributed the good outcomes to cooperation with God and the bad to abandonment by God.[1011]

The concept of free will could have made its way from the Syrian churches to Spain and finally into Italy. This is perhaps why the Catholic Church may at some point have adopted the doctrine of free will.

This might be a preposterous thing to say. However, if one follows the evolution of these spiritual ideas, then a great sectarian conflict emerges that explains the existence of the papacy's location in Avignon (now in France) in much clearer terms than the whitewashed version of history.

---

[1006] Koran 11:120.

[1007] Koran 13:11.

[1008] John of Damascus, *The Fount of Knowledge* (ca. 740 AD), On Heresis, in Frederic Chase, *Fathers of the Church* (1958) Book Two.

[1009] Ibid.

[1010] Ibid., Book Two, 264.

[1011] Ibid. Book Two, 262.

We have testimony from a famous Muslim scholar who recognized only three relevant Christian groups: Melchites in Rome, Jacobites in Egypt, and Nestorians in the Persian territories.[1012] Barely a century before Luther, this scholar did not see 'Catholics' because the popes of the Catholic Church were hiding in Avignon at the time of his writing.

Luckily, we do not need to be concerned here about this confusing era.

In effect, Luther ended up with the pure Augustinian interpretation that should have been the position of the Catholic Church. In contrast, the Catholic Church ended up in compromise, adopting the Syrian Christian (Melchite) version of free will.

Moreover, Martin Luther advocated that disciples should elect their own clergy. This was not new either. It was the approach of Pope Leo I in the fifth century, and therefore policy of the original Universal Church.[1013] Luther's and Leo's idea was that it raised parishioners' enthusiasm by letting them believe that they had a say in their fate.

Luther eventually came to realize that this did not work and he reversed course.[1014]

In other words, the historic paradox emerges again: Luther's church was closer to the pure Catholic Church, while Rome seems to have assimilated Syrian Christian (Melchite) traditions. Likewise, the Spanish Reconquista must have had to do not only with hunting Jews and Muslims but also with weeding out the Melchite Christian, Nestorian, and other 'heresies,' as the Catholic Church would see them.

They cleaned up, thinking that no trace was left behind.

These points of friction about questions regarding spirituality had existed for hundreds of years before, and they remained a cause for hundreds of years of conflict.

If one were to look closer, the question of free will found a resolution in the earliest pages of the Old Testament, where Eve disobeyed the command of God. The Koran is also clear about the command: *'but draw not nigh this tree, lest you be evildoers.'*[1015] God expressed himself in no uncertain terms. Eve's disobedience that led to the original sin – of inducing humanity with intellect – was undoubtedly based on free will, although on a pre-intellectual level.

---

[1012] Khaldun, *Muqaddimah, 1377*, transl. Rosenthal, 1958, Chapter III.31.

[1013] Pope Leo I, Letter XIV (446 AD).

[1014] Diarmaid MacCulloch, Reformation: Europe's House Divided, 1490–1700 (Allen Lane, 2003) 164.

[1015] Koran 2:33.

But in the end, we need to realize that the argument remains a circular question of faith and dogma.

Predetermination serves as an excuse for one's weakness. Under predetermination God punishes humans for sins that are outside of individuals' control. Not even the original sin could have occurred.

Reubeni was welcomed by King John III of Portugal the Pious[1016] in 1525, carrying letters of recommendation from the pope. Portugal had just risen to become a world power – with the help of Jews who had fled from Spain. It showed the seeds of a secular awakening.

King John the Pious was the firstborn to the Portuguese King Manuel the Fortunate. Father and son had so far resisted persecuting Jews in Portugal. So far, all signs point at Portugal being the last stronghold that opposed the Spanish Reconquista of the Catholic Church.

The same year when Reubeni showed up in the court of Portugal, King John the Pious was married to Emperor Charles' sister Catherine (herself a daughter of Joanna the Mad). The following year, Emperor Charles married John the Pious' sister Isabella. By all means, the dynastic bonds again came at the price of submitting to the demands of the Catholic Church.

The Portuguese John the Pious was made king on the checkered board of the Catholic Church as designed by the butcher pope, the former Pope Adrian.

A Christian monk in Portugal dared to deny that Reubeni was the Messiah and of the lineage of David. In front of everyone, Reubeni threw the doubter out the window and killed him. This crime pleased the 'great judge,' the head of Portuguese Jewry.

One might wonder how he got away with murder

The Jewish subversion at the court in Portugal must have been profound.[1017]

Instead, following his own story, David Reubeni's fame kept on growing. The Portuguese Marranos venerated him like a king[1018] – the King of the Jews. The prevalence of pretend converts must have been great, and Reubeni made it clear that they indeed had previously converted to Christianity to blend in. He was so steadfast on his mission that he even rejected an offer to become a Portuguese prince in exchange for converting to Catholicism.

---

[1016] John III aka the Pious was King of Portugal and the Algarves 1521 – 1557.
[1017] A. Z. Aeshcoly (1940), The Story of David Ha-Re'uveni (Jerusalem, 1994) 62-130, as cited in Lenowitz, 1998, 114-115.
[1018] Ibid.

Instead, we have already seen that, as Dawit II, he pretended to be a member of the Catholic Church.

To Jews, he explained that they would need to be patient with coming to Jerusalem because great wars had to be fought – by others.

If they only were patient, the Promised Land would be brought to them.[1019] Reubeni's saga has a Muslim prince pronounce to him that the *'end of the reigns of the Christians and the Ishmaelites has come, and within three years all the kingdom of Edom [Rome] will be in the hands of the king of the Jews in Jerusalem, and all the nations will come back to the one faith.'*[1020]

This reflects, first, the previously mentioned meaning of the Muslim tradition that proclaimed the appearance of Al-Harj, the destroyer of religious knowledge. Secondly, it insists on the return to 'one' original faith, a crucial messianic ingredient.

The grandeur is astonishing.

The goal was nothing less than taking over the world and establishing Jerusalem as the imperial center of world governance. The tactic was to let empires clash to create the opening.

Divide and rule. As prescribed in prophecy.

Self-fulfilling prophecy.

Dismissing all this as a mere tale of a lunatic gone rogue comes at the peril of entire nations – and moderns continue to be unaware of the dangers of our time.

Reubeni had gained the pledge of Portuguese Jewry to supply finances and manpower. The mission was clear: they wanted to conquer the Promised Land and to bring down Rome (Edom) and the Ottomans – Reubeni was the man to do it.

The strategy: burn down Rome first, then the empires.

---

[1019] Ibid.
[1020] Ibid.

## A Deal with the Devil

The soul of Luther's mentor Frederick the Wise ascended to heaven in 1525, and his earthly remains were buried at Wittenberg. Mary's milk jar had bought him 100 years of protection from the infernal purgatory. He had done all things according to the prescriptions of the Catholic Church, including paying a fortune for the rarest of relics.

His collection had grown to be worth almost two million years of purgatory evasion. However, if there was the ever so smallest error in the plan on how the soul should meet up with God, he never reached his goal. But since he had supported the excommunicated Martin Luther, it is not likely that his relics helped him make it to neverland.

While Martin Luther was busy with family and organizing his new Protestant Church, history was shaping itself with or without him. He created a new supervisory church body, the Consistory. This was sort of a more decentralized anti-organization to the Vatican, which allowed the regional churches some leeway.

This was not new, of course. It was similar to the preexisting organizational structure of the Augustinian monasteries.

The successor of Frederick the Wise was his younger brother, elector Johann of Saxony the Steadfast. At Wartburg Castle he had been Luther's courier for his translation of the New Testament.

Working together with him, Luther initiated a *'development towards a church government under the temporal sovereign.'*[1021] His solution was that church and state were to be one – the opposite of the plans in the Catholic Church. Like that, they could tax the communities for the Word of God and for the sword of the nobility at the same time.

There was not an inkling of separating church from state. It would have ruined the prospects of the Protestant Church.

The goal was a counter-theocracy to subvert the Holy Roman Empire.

Upon his rise to the elector, the Steadfast abolished the ceremonies of the Catholic Church and confessed Lutheranism. Since the Protestant Church was now beginning to cut its ties with the Catholic Church, it had neither assets nor income – other than what Lutherans seized from the Catholics and imposed anew.

---

[1021] Brecht, Luther, transl. Schaaf, 1985–93, 2:267.

Luther later complained that the populace refused to pay up and was not able to *'support one respectable preacher, where formerly they filled ten fat paunches.*'[1022] It appears that the sheep was happy to run away from the popists. It was also ready for a run past a new religion, straight to freedom.

Not on Luther's watch!

Those who paid the bills wanted nothing to do with any of this. It shows how state coercion is necessary for extortion by organized religion to find its full, destructive potential.

In order to build strength, Johann of Saxony the Steadfast entered a Protestant treaty with Philip I of Hesse the Magnanimous, the one primary beneficiary who was a teenager when he first started to support Luther. Under the Steadfast's leadership, other provinces soon followed. The sovereign – himself – held exclusivity over appointing or firing clergy. Luther was colluding in planning a coup. They aimed at nothing other than deposing both the monopoly of the Catholic Church over the spiritual world *and* the worldly forces of the Holy Roman Empire.

A super-monopoly in the form of a state-church was emerging.

Pope Clement VII had previously made a secret pact with the French for the papal forces to stand down should Emperor Charles request support. As part of the deal, French troops assisted in the re-conquest of Naples by the Catholic Church. So did Giovanni de' Medici's 'Bande Nere' troops. But the undertaking went sour. The French commanders had divided their forces for the march on Naples. Thousands of Swiss mercenaries had to return home in order to defend their homes. Giovanni was wounded and had to retreat with his troops. He soon died of his injuries.

The final battle at Naples lasted only a few hours. It was a slaughter-fest. The French troops were obliterated, and King Francis was incarcerated.

The war was over.

The political landscape had undergone an earthquake.

Imprisoned with the King of France was a double agent: Cardinal Hieronymus Aleandro. He was the radical and leading prosecutor against Martin Luther at the imperial Diet of Worms before Charles. After being liberated for ransom, Aleandro was put in charge of opposing Luther's reforms in Germany.

The French King was defeated, all right. But he was not dead, yet.

---

[1022] Luther, Large Catechism, 1529, WA 30 I,125-238.

The King of England, Henry VIII, was now eager to invade the headless French territories. However, going back to war was expensive and required the approval of parliament. The proposal failed to gain the required authorization for extra taxes. The treasury had already been depleted by ongoing warfare. So the king devised a new idea: to levy one-third of the goods from the clergy of the Catholic Church and a tenth from the laity.

The plan also failed.

Henry's dream of an invasion was dead.

The Kingdom of France lived to see another day.

Widowed at 19, Louise of Savoy was Francis' mother. We recall that her great-grandfather was Antipope Felix V,[1023] then head of the House of Savoy. Her father and brother had later stepped into the dynastic leadership. Like our other examples of outstanding Renaissance women of the feudal houses, she was well educated and well read.

She was also clever and power-hungry.

Louise's husband[1024] was a promiscuous scumbag who appears to have had illegitimate children wherever he could spread his genes. He had maintained his own sort of harem and raised children from multiple women at his court. Louise must have thought that this was normal royal behavior.

Now that her son was imprisoned in Madrid, she was hell-bent to make sure that King Francis remained the legitimate heir of the Kingdom of France.

For this, she needed friends.

For over a century, France had been in alliance with the Kingdom of Scotland. In essence, the pact had been to invade English territory if one of the partners were attacked by England.

Louise had one card to play. And she played an excellent hand.

It took patience and determination. Six months after the Naples disaster, she had her first agreement sealed. Other than some irrelevant territorial settlements, the key to the *Treaty of the More*, as it is called, was assistance by England in securing the return of the French King and the prevention by the French of the Scottish leadership's returning home.

Louise allowed England to close the threat at its backdoor.

---

[1023] Amadeus VIII, Duke of Savoy, was antipope as Felix V from 1439 to 1449.
[1024] Louise of Savoy had married Charles of Orléans, Count of Angoulême, on 16 February 1488 in Paris.

The chief negotiator for the deal that betrayed Scotland, and the person who would come to be responsible for the recovery of the Kingdom of France, was Cardinal Thomas Wolsey,[1025] an alter rex, almost monarch, but not quite king. He was factually in control of state and church in England, because young Henry VIII showed little interest in government affairs.[1026] The king was out hunting – mistresses.

Cardinal Wolsey was the Catholic leader behind the King of England – until he died on his way to be prosecuted for treason.

On Henry's path to emancipation, England, too, had its puppeteer that controlled its royal leaders. The Catholic Church was in a position to manipulate royal houses across Europe.

The problem of the church was its factionalism of pro-French and pro-Habsburg (German and Spanish) popes who ascended the Vatican's throne through corruption. Not that we should forget the third problem: the German Lutherans and their insurrectionist royal overlords.

Or the ongoing subversion by Jewish leaders.

Historians emphasize Wolsey's support and role in the earlier war against France by joint forces of the Holy Roman Empire and the Kingdom of England. However, on the shoulders of every man of power sits an opportunist devil with a fiddle that plays its own tune.

Having been elevated to cardinal by the Medici Pope Leo X, it was not by accident that Wolsey had become the chief proponent of the deal with Louise for France. Wolsey was also the negotiator for the earlier Anglo-French treaty of 1514 that brought peace between France and England.

As part of this pact, the earlier French King had married King Henry's sister.

Since the French King had died without a male heir, Louise and Francis from a different family branch of the same dynasty seized the opportunity to step in and climb onto the throne.[1027]

---

[1025] Thomas Wolsey aka Woolsey or Wulcy (ca. 1473 – 1530) was Cardinal of the Catholic Church 1514 – 1530 and Lord Chancellor, the English King's chief advisor, 1515 – 1529.

[1026] Oxford Dictionary of National Biography, Henry VIII (2004).

[1027] The Capetian Dynasty and the House of Habsburg (Austria) were the two most powerful European royal families from the late tenth century up to the French Revolution. The modern King Felipe VI of Spain and Grand Duke Henri of Luxembourg are members of the Capetian Dynasty. The House of Habsburg is now extinct.

The primary achievement of Wolsey, although short lived, was the *Treaty of London*, which had been ratified by Pope Leo X the year before Charles bribed his way to become ruler of the Holy Roman Empire. The intent was to appease and unify Europe in order to concentrate the forces against the rising Ottoman-Turkish threat.

The pontiff of the Catholic Church was engineering peace while aiming for going to holy war.

Wolsey was the peacemaker.

It was not meant to be that way, though. Christians kept picking Christians. Even more so after the 'election' of Charles to become emperor.

The task that finally broke the straw in the relationship between Wolsey and King Henry was a tax plan, which was called *'a benevolence.'* Wolsey was assigned to push it through. The plan failed, as did all initiatives under the leadership of Wolsey that were going against France. Instead, peace with France was achieved.

This is what Wolsey had on his mind all along.

In consequence, we have Louise's *Treaty of the More* between the kingdoms of England and France, securing the north-west flank. But her son was still imprisoned and was forced to agree to the Treaty of Madrid. With it, he lost territory to the Holy Roman Empire and had to swear off his Italian ambitions – with crossed fingers.

Francis had no intention of being part of anything with Charles. Before signing the treaty, he had it notarized that his signature would be written under duress.[1028] Francis and Charles 'agreed' to join forces to repulse and ruin the heresy of the Lutheran Sect.[1029]

Simultaneously, the Catholic Church was trying to extinguish the fires of passion from Spain to the Netherlands and from Germany to Bohemia through its terrorist arm, the Inquisition.

Martin Luther had made it to the top of the European agenda. He now embodied the cause of division and war among European royalty. He stood in the way of assembling Europe's Christian forces for the Crusade against the Ottoman Empire.

Since France was situated in between parts of the Holy Roman Empire, Louise had to figure out how to neutralize her main enemy.

---

[1028] Setton, 1984, 239.
[1029] Ibid., 238.

She was willing to make a deal with the devil.

After the treaty with England was sealed, Louise looked through the Holy Roman Empire's backdoor: Suleiman the Magnificent.

The Antichrist.

The idea of a military alliance with France suited Suleiman the Magnificent on his march up the Balkan just fine. His answer to Louise was baffling, not in the way he agreed, but how he presented himself. He saw himself as *'the dispenser of crowns to the monarchs on the face of the earth, the shadow of the God on Earth,'* listing all the domains that had been annexed by force with the pride of a child.[1030]

Certainly, such an alliance would ensure that Emperor Charles stayed embattled with the French while Suleiman was knocking at the eastern borders of Christianity. Crowning her efforts, Louise sealed the Franco-Ottoman alliance against the Holy Roman Empire.

It lasted for centuries.

This alliance turned out to be particularly fruitful for France. In essence, it created a trade monopoly. Christianity in Turkish territories came under French control. These privileges endured until the twentieth century.

To add injury to the scandal, Louise was not the first to envision an alliance with a Muslim 'enemy.' Before Charles became emperor, someone who pulled the strings for the boy had already sent a Maronite Christian emissary[1031] to the Persian Safavid ruler. The Maronite – his sect is another offshoot of Syrian Christianity – represented Charles and the King of Hungary in order to combine forces against the approaching Ottoman-Turks.

The strategic idea was the same: squeeze the enemy from two sides and fall into its back with the aim to divide the forces of the target. The hidden agenda of Charles' tutor was to seize the throne of the Holy Roman Empire in the event that their bribes might not have worked. Since they did work, the alliance with Persia amounted to nothing.

Instead, Charles' tutor became the butcher pope Adrian.

The hostilities between Shi'ite Persia (Iran) and the Sunni Ottoman-Turks do not need explaining. They are subject of our modern daily news about their bombastic lifestyles.

---

[1030] Suleiman the Magnificent, answer to Francis I of France, February 1526, in Roger Bigelow Merriman, Suleiman the Magnificent 1520 – 1566 (Read Books, 2007) 131.

[1031] Petrus of Monte Libano.

Their Muslim sectarian conflict reaches back to the foundation of Islam, perhaps even earlier. But as already mentioned, the Safavid ruler[1032] now marked the *'end of time'* – the beginning of the End of the World – and positioned himself as the *'shadow of God on earth.'*[1033] He was the representative of his divinity on earth and the future leader of the universe.

Now there were two shadows of God.

One after the other of Luther's contemporary royal and religious leaders across the old world seems to have suffered from religious grandeur.

Civilizations were marching toward Armageddon to sort this out.

A year later, the Kingdom of Hungary was attacked by Suleiman the Magnificent. An already weakened nation ended up torn apart. Before this campaign, the Venetians were informed that the prophecies of an ancient book foretold that Suleiman *'would conquer many lands, eventually capture Rome and establish the dominance of a single religion.'*[1034]

All aimed at the same destructive goal.

After the fall of Constantinople to Ottomans in 1453, the conquest of the *'Red Apple'* – Rome or the Christian capital, Vienna[1035] – was expected to happen soon.

In order to further cement legitimacy of Ottoman rule, messianic aspirations and the fulfillment of prophecy became ever more urgent. One of Suleiman's chief secretaries described his boss as *'the messiah of the End Time,'* himself a mahdi, and *'the master of the auspicious conjunction.'* The latter were individuals who were born under a conjunction of Saturn and Jupiter.[1036]

Peasants who were supposed to fight in the Crusade against Ottoman-Turks ended up revolting against nobility. They had failed to provide for leadership and provisions. By the time the Papal Bull for the Crusade had been revoked and the peasants were ordered home, the kingdom was in full rebellion.

The papal strategy had gone awry.

Those who had to pay the price for the folly were peasants.

---

[1032] Shah Tahmasp I ruled Sfavid Iran 1524 – 1576.

[1033] Babayan, Mystics, Monarchs and Messiahs, 2002, 302.

[1034] Cornell Fleischer, Shadows of Shadows: Prophecy and Politics in 1530s Istanbul (IJTS 13, 2007) no. 1–2, p. 55, as paraphrased in Şahin, Süleyman, 2013, 58-59.

[1035] John Victor Tolan, Gilles Veinstein, and Henry Laurens, Europe and the Islamic world: a history, translated by Jane Marie Todd (Princeton, 2013) 181-184.

[1036] Tabakat, 134b, 135a, in Şahin, Süleyman, 2013, 61.

Suleiman's plan for the decisive battle appears to have come from a private soldier[1037] – and from on up high. Ottomans had gained the upper hand through Prophet Muhammad's intercession. The Prophet, his companions, and the hidden saints of Islam had risen from the dead in order to dress their swords in the blood of the infidel enemy. Muslims could be stopped neither by fortifications nor weapons.[1038]

The heavens were rigged against Christians.

Luther kept himself busy with the internals of the emerging Protestant Church. His strategy was clever. All complexities around the faith should be drastically reduced in order to influence the young and allure to simpletons.[1039] He broke the rule of reading mass in Latin. Mass in the German language was supposed to be a *'public stimulation for people to believe and become Christians.*[1040]

It spoke to simple minds.

Explaining the abstractions of faith in any language made little difference. What mattered was the differentiation from the Catholic Church.

Luther's orders should not amount to a form of church law. Nobody should be forced to believe. Instead, joining his version of the Truth was a matter of liberty and of the better argument.[1041]

However, his mass was not about the liberty of mankind but about the *limits* of its liberties. We will learn shortly how his definitions of liberties were meant to be oppressive and against any freedom of the individual: believe or leave.

Luther was acutely aware that the Protestant Church could end up with the same corrupt institutionalization as the Catholic Church. In contrast to his competition in Rome, he specifically labelled his orders as sort of non-binding, but still binding until changed.[1042]

Yet, the evidence of centuries of religious violence is overwhelming. The Protestant Church was unable to live up to Luther's standards.

Besides, we should not forget who Luther was: he was right.

Always.

---

[1037] Hammer, Histoire Ottoman, 1837, 599.
[1038] Tabakat 150a, 419a, in Şahin, Süleyman, 2013, 204.
[1039] Kidd, Reformation, 1911, 193-202: So much for daily Divine Service and for teaching the Word of God, specially with a view to influencing the young and alluring the simple.
[1040] Brecht, Luther, transl. Schaaf, 1985–93, 2:255.
[1041] Kidd, Reformation, 1911, 193-202.
[1042] Ibid.

He set out to structure masses while leaving only minor deviations to the clergy. Luther could not trust that they would see the big picture as only he could.

Intending to safeguard the preachers from fanaticism and sectarianism,[1043] he thought that they were good for nothing and that the common people were completely ignorant about Christian doctrine.[1044]

This was a striking insight by the Reformer with a new, fanatic sect.

If the peasants knew nothing and the clergy was too dumb to teach, how then could it have mattered what they believed in? How could they lose their lives over religious dogma when they had no clue, as Luther observed? The answer, unfortunately, is obvious: the people were expected to follow religious authority without question. Before, the authority was the Catholic Church. Now, it was Luther's Protestant movement.

It was conceived in German nationalism.

Easter and the suffering of Jesus Christ before the crucifixion (the Passion) should still be celebrated, according to Luther. It should be simpler, though, like a normal week with sermons. The dark sadness of the Catholic Church was to be replaced in the Protestant churches with an outright celebration of Jesus Christ. Rituals would be stripped down to the essence, and the paintings in the places of worship should be covered up.[1045]

Across the northern half of Europe, early Protestant mobs went out to attack Catholic churches and to destroy their treasures of art and relics. The medieval 'iconoclasm' manifests itself in modern Protestant churches that are bare of art. The center of all things was the cross.

There emerged his Augustinian City of God.

The Catholic Church had increasingly used paintings to teach the Gospel to its illiterate disciples. With a new kind of iconoclast, again, Luther went back to the old ways, while Rome was abusing the arts of the Renaissance for its own purpose.

Luther's tone toward Jews still did not change. In fact, they were not mentioned at all, other than perhaps being included in Luther's overarching theme of luring those of other beliefs in with gentle temptation.

---

[1043] Ibid.
[1044] Michael A. Mullett, Luther, Quoted from Luther's preface to the Small Catechism, 1529 (MacCulloch, 1986) 165.
[1045] Kidd, Reformation, 1911, 193-202.

To reach out to prospective converts, he encouraged all Protestant disciples to learn the Bible so they could teach its wisdom. The Christian laity was illiterate at the time. If only they were to read the Bible, they would become believers. Part of his plan was to establish Protestant schools to teach children not only the Bible but also languages. In the spirit of the time to explore and subjugate the New World, he aimed at enabling disciples to convert prospects in foreign lands.[1046]

Luther's intention was to raise an entire generation of sectarian extremists and teach them from an early age only what was necessary for missionizing upon those who believed otherwise or were free from religion.

His oversight was that learning to read fosters critical thinking. Not in many. Perhaps in very few. One in a million who could think outside of the box would eventually come to make a huge difference in the further evolution of mankind.

Higher education absent of indoctrination subverts organized religion[1047] and is against its self-interest.

Luther viewed older non-Christians as lost souls. Nothing could persuade them to change their spiritual minds. He had long written them off. The future lay in infiltrating the minds of children.[1048] He put his investments where they were most promising to be effective.

It worked.

The next generations of 'educated' believers came to battle it out.

Here, Luther followed the example of Jews who had brought forth Europe's intelligentsia through relentless learning. The Catholic Church had previously decided at the Fifth Lateran Council to approach education through children. The Reformer thought that the attraction of his version of faith was so strong that the simple laymen would voluntarily flock to it. But for that, we must be alert, it took state coercion to get children behind the Lutheran school desks.

Once the youngsters were infiltrated, they would have already lost their freedom of choice.

Had Luther by now reduced his hopes ever to be able to convert Jews?

It would be strange if he did see non-Christians as not worth the effort if it did not include Jews. If any, his complaint had long been that they were a stubborn people, unwilling to accept his Truth.

---

[1046] Ibid.
[1047] Pew Research Center, The Age Gap in Religion Around the World, June 13, 2018.
[1048] Ibid.

### *War is Love*

Martin Luther's new movement faced stiff headwinds. A conference of imperial nobles was held at the Diet of Speyer. Its majority was Catholic. In front of this hostile audience, Johann of Saxony the Steadfast and Philip I of Hesse the Magnanimous had to defend the Lutheran heresy and its reform efforts. In light of the looming Ottoman Turkish threat in the east and the opponents' French allies in the west, the two noble Protestant leaders showed defiance.

It had already become impractical for Emperor Charles to prosecute Luther. The meeting came to the conclusion that a council of the Catholic Church should be convened where questions of church reform would be addressed through majority decisions – a show council.

In the meantime, a non-action treaty was agreed upon to maintain the status quo. It was a sort of ceasefire. But its formulation left much room for regional maneuvers: *'every State shall so live, rule, and believe as it may hope and trust to answer before God and his imperial Majesty.'*[1049]

The idea was not religious freedom, but a period during which no significant changes would be implemented, while imperial allegiance was upheld.

For a short period, it removed the peril to Martin Luther's life.

The ambivalent decisions of the council acted like a rocket booster for reform movements. Barely a couple of months later, Philip I of Hesse the Magnanimous called for the Synod of Homberg to settle Protestant and territorial questions.

This synod ran into sharp opposition by the Catholic Church, denying the council jurisdiction over ecclesiastical questions.

Although the synod was not a success, Protestantism started to show signs of adolescence. Yet, Luther and his friends had a price to pay. We shall see the real-world consequences.

Bloodletting.

Nevertheless, the foundation had been laid for what would come to be known under the term *'Cuius regio, eius religio,'* meaning *'whose realm, his religion.'* The idea was, again, not religious freedom. For Luther's subjects, it was Lutheranism or the boot to exile. For the Catholic Church, it was Catholicism or ending up on the skewer of the Inquisition.

For the cohesion of the Holy Roman Empire, it was terminal.

---

[1049] Diet of Speyer, August 27, 1526.

Freedom was reduced to two choices, of which Lutheranism was the more precarious. The 'choice' was not in the hand of individuals but of nobility for their subjects. Any other attempt to freedom meant sure death by the wrath of both competing holy institutions or by imperial thumbs down.

The idea was in alignment with the concept that Luther had devised with Johann of Saxony the Steadfast, *'a church government under the temporal sovereign.'*[1050]

As a consequence, the non-decisions of the Diet of Speyer triggered a wave of nobles to seize the opportunity and to make themselves head of state and church.

They could do so with Luther's church.

Not so with the Catholic Church.

The crossroads to reformation was not in the cross. It was on the roads to more power for nobility. The reward was a double treasury of the spiritual and secular world.

Two hands of gold.

In the eye of Christianity, the threat of the Ottoman Empire was ever more advancing toward Armageddon and the End of the World.

In the same year that Luther formulated his abstract vision of joining religion voluntarily, he wrote the treatise *'Whether Soldiers can be in a State of Grace.'* In it, he argued for just war in the name of God.

Not surprisingly, the style was, again, Augustinian. In order to be successful in war, fighters needed to be equipped *'with a good and well-instructed conscience.'* Belief provides for courage and an easier victory, which would be granted by God.

Within months, Luther's approach of loving conversion or a push into exile made way for holy war.

While joining the religion of love was voluntary, opposing it was met with the love of arms. The concept to expel or terminate all non-compliant subjects was already born before Luther's anti-Semitic outbursts.

---

[1050] Brecht, Luther, transl. Schaaf, 1985–93, 2:267.

Luther's double standard is here unmasked in a single paragraph:

> *For he who fights with a good and well-instructed conscience can indeed fight well;*
> *since it cannot fail that where there is a good conscience there is also good courage*
> *and a bold heart, and where the heart is bold and the courage assured there is the*
> *fist the stronger and both man and mount the more spirited, and all things turn out*
> *better, and all chances and affairs lead the more easily to the victory, which*
> *accordingly God grants.*[1051]

Luther's conscience and fame seem to have gone to his head. He now saw himself as one to whom God had given the light.[1052] The extremist saw himself as being born a prophet.

A new Vicar of Christ. A second pope.

Technically, Protestantism had evolved between the messianic fronts.

A new religion had been conceived.

To put it mildly, it is disturbing how Luther bragged about how *'the civil sword and authority have never been so clearly described and so finely eulogized'* as they were by him.

He thought it was a badge of honor to be singled out *'as seditious and hostile to authority.*[1053] It was Luther and his companions who were indeed hostile to authority – the rebel did not seem to remember[1054] – but in the same breath, he declared that the government that he conspired with would be God-given and, thus, be absolute.

To solve the Gordian Knot, Luther resorted to contrasting the spiritual Kingdom of God, where Christians do not fight, with the earthly governments of the real world, where Christians need to pick up the sword.[1055]

Those in authority had the right to call their cause just.

God, according to Luther, was the boss of both worlds, spiritual and civil.[1056]

It is nothing but a farce to seduce an illiterate population that was addicted to both superstition and authority.

---

[1051] Martin Luther, Can Soldiers Be Christians, 1526, translated by Prof. W. H. Carruth (University of Kansas, 1899) 525.

[1052] Ibid., 526.

[1053] Ibid., 527.

[1054] Ibid., 530.

[1055] Ibid., 529.

[1056] Ibid., 529.

The question to be addressed in Luther's writing was whether a Christian could *'slay and stab, rob and burn'* in war. As it was ever so often through history, he was opportunistic and could adapt to changing circumstances, like a flag in the wind.

The Protestant Church now opposed the concept of early Christians to *'never slay or harm anyone.'*[1057]

This latter approach was never in the spirit of love, either, even back then. Instead, the refusal to serve in the armies of the Roman Empire was part of the Christian strategy of social and economic rejection with the goal of subverting its government. Its approach was based on passive aggression.

Luther had it the other way around, as first worked out with Johann of Saxony, the Steadfast. Government represented the authority, and it had the right to recruit Christian soldiers for just war. The fighters' duty was to submit and to contribute with their faith and life to the success of the bloody undertaking.

The sheep had to march along and jump from cliffs as their noble masters commanded from their comfortable palaces. In this context, Luther rationalized his stance against peasants in the earlier Peasant Revolt. Even when the authorities did wrong, they still had the right to oppress rebellion.[1058]

In a puzzling side note, Martin Luther defined the God-given division between peasants and nobles: Tillage is to provide, warfare is to protect.[1059]

The feudal world was normal for Luther. Outside of the monastery, he had never experienced anything else.

The feudal system had encroached upon society over centuries. Part of its structure had been inherited from the Roman Empire and substituted with the emerging city states in the image of Augustine's City of God. The idea was that regional authorities would be appointed by the Catholic Church and armed to ensure adherence to its changing creeds. Preferably, the men in charge originated from ecclesiastical families. Since the armed forces were to be paid for by the people, their leaders were also given authority to levy taxes. Over time, the peasants were disarmed, and the warrior class increasingly held a monopoly on force, wealth, and leaders' networks.

---

[1057] Ibid., 526.
[1058] Ibid., 537.
[1059] Ibid., 540.

Then they became 'nobles' who would uphold the rules of inheritance that were controlled by the Catholic Church.

Who was obliged to protect the nobles' exorbitant lifestyles with limb and life?

The peasants.

This unhealthy symbiosis between nobility and the Catholic Church was to the detriment of the people. Challenging either of the two triggered armed protection of one another.[1060] Faith determined the relationship between peasants, rulers, and the Catholic Church. It disowned the lay population.

Luther was determined to keep it that way.

It laid the foundations for class warfare in the French Revolution and in the rise of Marxism and Communism. They aimed at bringing the nobles back to the ground.

But the Reformer was not a dimwit.

To make sure that everything depended on the judgement of the Protestant Church, he introduced a concept of war that was *not* just. In that case, good Christians had to refuse military service,[1061] even if they risked being executed for their refusal. It would make them martyrs.[1062]

Only one person could at that time make the call on whether a war was just: Martin Luther.

The control mechanism through the faith of the Protestant Church was designed from the beginning to be totalitarian. In other words, without the approval of the Protestant Church, no ruler could count on recruiting Protestant troops. Without the approval of the ruler, no doctrinal changes to Luther's original creeds could be made in the churches. This same ruler selected or dismissed the clergy.

The open door of Luther's just war came to not only rationalize religious wars against the Ottoman Empire but also against the Catholic Church.

---

[1060] Jean du Tillet, Sommaire de l'Histoire de la Guerre faite contre les Heretiques Albigeois, extraicte du Tresor des Chartres du Roy par feu Jehan du Tillet (1590), sigs a7, D5.

[1061] Luther, Soldiers, 1526, transl. Carruth, 1899, 541.

[1062] Ibid., 541.

> *For since the sword is appointed by God to punish the wicked, protect the good, and maintain peace, it is sufficiently proven that warfare and slaying is appointed by God, and all that warfare and justice bring with them. What else is war but punishing wrong and evil? Why do we fight but to have peace and submission?*[1063]

This is the definition of charity, love, and peace.

He, Luther, had elevated just war between an army of crusaders and an army of jihadists to normalcy. We can perhaps see the subtle struggles in the minds of opposing warriors in combat: would the gods bring about success? Could good training and battle axe in hand be more promising?

As long as you hold the axe, there has never been a more convincing argument than a split skull.

End of dispute.

Under the title *'War as a Work of Love,'* Luther compared the slaying and robbing as a work of love with the task of a physician who cuts off a limb to save a man's life.[1064]

> *For if the sword did not keep the peace, [...] everything in the world [would decay in riot]. Therefore such a war is nothing else than a small and brief breach of the peace to prevent a long and limitless breach of the peace, a small misfortune to prevent a great one. [...]*
> *Thence doth God honor the sword so highly that he calls it His own ordinance, and will not have it said or thought that men invented or ordained it. For the hand that wields this sword and slays with it is no longer the hand of man, but the hand of God, and it is not man, but God, who hangs, breaks, beheads, slays, and makes war.*[1065]

The Reformer argued that war should be only defensive in nature.[1066] However, Luther's reasoning was deep in Muslim jihadist territory.

They were on such a slippery slope that it destroyed the image of Christianity as a religion of love.

It was an unintended stroke of genius: war is love.

---

[1063] Ibid.
[1064] Ibid., 527.
[1065] Ibid., 527, correction of the translation by A.J. Deus; the German original reads: Denn wenn nicht das Schwert entgegentritt und den Frieden bewahrt, müsste alles, was es in der Welt gibt, im Unfrieden verderben.
[1066] Ibid., 353.

Let me contrast this with the Koran:

> *Then, when the sacred months are drawn away, slay the idolaters wherever you find them, and take them, and confine them, and lie in wait for them at every place of ambush. But if they repent, and perform the prayer, and pay the alms, then let them go their way.*[1067]

> *The believers fight in the way of God, and the unbelievers fight in the idols' way. Fight you therefore against the friends of Satan; surely the guile of Satan is ever feeble.*[1068]

> *You did not slay them, but God slew them; and when thou threwest, it was not thyself that threw, but God threw, and that He might confer on the believers a fair benefit.*[1069]

> *Leave is given to those who fight because they were wronged — surely God is able to help them — who were expelled from their habitations without right, except that they say "Our Lord is God." Had God not driven back the people, some by the means of others, there had been destroyed cloisters and churches, oratories and mosques, wherein God's Name is much mentioned.*[1070]

Martin Luther mimicked some of the wording of the Koran, including the advance pardon for killing in warfare, even though he might not have been familiar with the Muslim scripture at that point in his life. Like the Koran, Luther positioned war as a means of defending the peace, meaning the religious monopoly.

The trouble is that peace between organized religions is not the norm.

War is.

Finally, the barbarity of the Koran found its match in the Reformer.

Indeed, Suleiman the Magnificent recognized the similarities between Luther's Protestantism and Islam. Lutherans did not worship idols, believed in one God and fought against pope and emperor.[1071]

---

[1067] Koran 9:5.

[1068] Koran 4:78.

[1069] Koran 8:15-8:17.

[1070] Koran 22:40. The consensus attributes this verse to Muhammad sanctioning assaults on trade caravans and unto Mecca. This view ignores the larger picture of the historic setting with the Persian King Xosrov and the Eastern Church. The belief in the one God was going to provide for superpowers in the fight against the unbelievers.
Koran 8:65.

[1071] Kemal H. Karpat, The Ottoman state and its place in world history (Brill, 1974) 53.

But as in Christian tradition, Luther saw in Suleiman a tyrant,[1072] the Antichrist.

When we try to understand Protestant fundamentalism, we do not need to look far for a radical element that reinterpreted scripture. It sits right in front of our noses. Its name? Martin Luther.

Some 500 years after Martin Luther, 1,400 years after Prophet Muhammad, 2,000 years after Jesus Christ, and 2,200 years after the Pharisees threw the Sadducees over the Temple walls, it should dawn on moderns that the eternal danger might be difficult to confront.

It is not just history.

Their just wars are unjust on either side.

Whatever Martin Luther was preaching to fire up the courage of the Christian crusaders, Suleiman the Magnificent was not scared. He personally moved his armies north along the Danube River. The estimates of the Ottoman troop size range from anywhere between 50,000 to 100,000 Muslim soldiers.

Most of Suleiman's advance faced little resistance.

Utterly unprepared and prone to tactical error, Hungary and Croatia collapsed after a short key battle. The antiquated army of the Hungarians faced a disciplined enemy that was equipped and trained for modern Renaissance warfare. Despite the Hungarians' winning an initial battle, the war was all over in a day. The Catholic Archbishop[1073] in charge of the front had failed to fall back to await reinforcements. Faith had trumped reason. The fleeing Hungarian King drowned in a river crossing. His old-fashioned, heavy equipment cost his life. Approximately 1,000 nobles and 14,000 Hungarians never left the battlefield on their feet.

This major victory over an important Christian nation by the Magnificent could have been achieved only through the intervention of God. This strengthened Suleiman's claim to divinely anointed leadership over the entire world.[1074]

Well, it may have taken a little more than the help of a god. Jews had stayed in Budapest. After God heard their cries, the Rabbinic leaders of the synagogue went out to meet Suleiman. Falling down before his feet, they *gave the city into his hand.*[1075]

---

[1072] Luther, Soldiers, 1526, transl. Carruth, 1899, 538-539.
[1073] Archbishop Paul Tomory of Kalocsa aka Tomorri of Kolozinsi [ben Meir] was a Franciscan Friar.
[1074] Şahin, Süleyman, 2013, 66.
[1075] Ha-Cohen, Vol. II, translated by Bialloblotzky, 1836, 58.

They could pretend not to have had anything to do with the conflict and to having supported the winner all along. Falling down before Suleiman was even cheaper than a scroll or a sandwich to maintain the oppressive administrative order.

Orchestrated from the Temple Mount in Jerusalem, the messianic game was played well.

Ottoman-Turks were now the masters in the Balkan. While Budapest fell only temporarily at this time, Suleiman was knocking on the doors of the Holy Roman Empire. Luther blamed the clergy of the Catholic Church for the losses. The Hungarians even killed their cardinal for it, Luther said.[1076] He did not seem to have suspected Jewish involvement, even though Jews were expelled from the city as soon as Suleiman had been pushed back.[1077]

We have a better grasp now for these actions. The border region between Christianity and Islam provided for blood swamps for centuries to come.

The glory of Hungary was forever lost.

It shows in the mosaics inside the Dome of the Rock, which were then not yet completed. The crown of Hungary is part of the artistic design as one of the subjugated nations.[1078]

Meanwhile, Pope Clement was trying to cut loose from the uninvited and uncomfortable interdependency between the Vatican and the Holy Roman Empire under Charles.

After Hungary fell into disrepair, two competing kings watched over the land. One was from the Holy Roman Empire.[1079] The other was a vassal of the Ottoman-Turks.[1080] Suleiman allowed the kingdom to remain Christian. Thrilled, the pope, together with Venice, Bavaria, and Louise of France, recognized the new Christian vassal king.

This became the Franco-Hungarian alliance – between the lame and the blind.

But, on rare occasions, two weak partners can make up for their respective shortcomings. This may particularly have been true in this case where the pope suddenly found himself on the side of the Ottoman Empire.

---

[1076] Luther, On War, 1528, WA 30 II, 107-148.

[1077] Jewishhistory.org.il, 1526 November 9, Hungary and Croatia.

[1078] A.J. Deus, The Jewish Serpent King (2023) available at academia.edu.

[1079] Ferdinand I was king of Bohemia and Hungary from 1526, king of Croatia from 1527, and, as successor of Emperor Charles V, Holy Roman Emperor from 1558 – 1564.

[1080] John I, John Zápolya aka John Szapolyai was King of Hungary 1526 – 1540.

In his relentless campaign against Charles, Pope Clement was willing to sacrifice an entire Christian nation to Muslims. Prompted by this alliance, the two vassal kings quickly went to war against each other.

Proxy war. Moderns know all about it.

In a fight over Milan, the pope also took the side of the Kingdom of France. This is no surprise. After the devastating defeat at Naples, he had formed the League of Cognac, involving the Papal States, the Kingdom of France, the Republic of Venice, the Duchy of Milan (with the Sforza clan), and the Republic of Florence (his Medici Dynasty).

Louise finally managed to get Francis freed.

Two of the king's sons were given as collateral hostages to Charles' court. In the wake of the treaty, Francis seized the assets of his main competitor to the French throne. For this reason, the leader of the noble House of Bourbon[1081] defected to the imperialists.

Immediately, they went back to work together against Charles.

According to consensus, in 1527, Charles won a Pyrrhic Victory in northern Italy.

His luck had run low ever since his puppeteer, the former Pope Adrian and architect of the massive bribes, died. The Fugger bills hit home. Charles was unable to pay for his army. In desperation, his troops were promised loot, similar to Muslim law.[1082] Soldiers received a share of the booty from conquered cities. Disgruntled by a looming peace treaty, which would have deprived them of their payday, they broke ranks, joined up with angry peasants, and marched to Rome. They left everything along their route burnt and devastated. Girls were abducted and raped by soldiers, and peasants were used as pack-mules. The Italian Peninsula was in uproar, and revolts broke out everywhere.

Finally, the wild troops sacked Rome in a single day. And the pillaging and promised looting began.

A Jewish and a German chronicle tell otherwise.

---

[1081] Charles III, Duke of Bourbon, 1490 – 1527.
[1082] Setton, 1984, 262.

The leader of the approaching troops was the head of the noble House of Bourbon, the one who had earlier defected from the Kingdom of France to the imperialists.[1083] He approached the city but was shot.[1084] The city was then conquered and pillaged. That tells us half of what we need to know.

The other half is that behind the fall of Rome stood an insider, Cardinal Pompeo Colonna, an imperial loyalist and one of the most influential members of the nobility in Rome and Naples. His family traced its roots back to the Julio-Claudian Dynasty, the first dictators of the Roman Empire. Blue blood; tyrannical blood. Never mind that the last of this dynasty, Nero, was a Jewish 'proselyte'[1085] and father of one of the most important Jewish sages, Rabbi Meir. He showed up next to Rabbi Akiva and Simon bar Kokhba during the Jewish Bar Kokhba Revolt in the second century.

Almost two decades earlier, Colonna had to flee Rome, because he was the ringleader of a conspiracy against then-della Rovere Pope Julius II. Offered a papal pardon, he refused. When Pope Julius finally died, Colonna amassed armed forces and marched into Rome, leading to the 'election' of the French-friendly Medici Pope Leo X and the successive appointment of Colonna as cardinal. At Leo's death, Colonna conspired against the next Medici aspirant and for his own ascent to the papal throne. Instead, the Medici rose, and Colonna was rewarded with the post of Vice Chancellor. This was the most lucrative of all seats in the Vatican, except for the throne itself.

Sometimes, the ecclesiastical machinations in the Vatican were truly miraculous.

Corrupt.

The guy held his position at the Vatican until he could stab Pope Clement in the back. Just after the League of Cognac was formed, when he was needed in the direst of times, Colonna seems to have been absent or ill, or anything, just not to be in Rome. He was plotting a coup upon Rome to bring the pope back into submission to the emperor.[1086] Clement got wind of it and came to a truce with Colonna in which a gullible pope retired his forces to their local bases.[1087] In bad faith, Colonna entered Rome at the head of 3,000 infantry and 800

---

[1083] Ha-Cohen, Vol. II, translated by Bialloblotzky, 1836, 69.
    See also Sebastian Franck, Chronica Zeitbuch und Geschichtsbibel, (Beck, 1531, p. 232-236) with the same version.

[1084] Ibid., 70.

[1085] Talmud - Mas. Gittin 56a.

[1086] Ferdinand Gregorovius, History of the City of Rome in the Middle Ages Volume VIII part 2 (London, 1906) 498-503.

[1087] Ha-Cohen, Vol. II, translated by Bialloblotzky, 1836, 65.

cavalry. After that, Clement in some way regained the upper hand and sent his troops to set the towns of the Colonnas on fire.[1088]

Cardinal Pompeo Colonna was thereafter stripped of all his privileges.[1089]

Finally, Colonna reappeared for the sack of Rome. He had planned it as an insurrection, which included the renewed betrayal of a treaty with the papacy.[1090] He showed up with Bourbon at the gates of Rome with a disciplined force of thousands of men[1091] and assumed control. The German chronicle states that Colonna arrived eight days after the conquest – just in case it went wrong – and took over.[1092]

The broken promises and betrayals of this holy man could fill a book; his family tree's a very large book.

The Jewish chronicle says about the events that the troops were German Lutherans. How were these indeed Lutherans and not just the imaginary product of religious polemics? They not only raped the women in the city but also ravished the nuns, *'and squeezed the breasts of their virginity, and plundered their whole property.'* They destroyed and looted the places of Catholic saints and threw their bones *'into the mire of the streets.'*[1093]

During the riots, the remains of Pope Julius II, Leo X's predecessor, were desecrated. Saint Cajetan, protagonist at the Fifth Lateran Council and persecutor of Martin Luther found himself tortured.[1094]

Cardinal Egidio Viterbo, the Augustinian aspirant to the papal throne, was also hit. His library was part of the rubble. The career of Luther's archenemy was over. Viterbo went into exile in the Italian city of Padua, only to die a few years later. Fittingly, he was buried in the Basilica of Sant'Agostino – St. Augustine – in Rome.

---

[1088] Ibid., 66.

[1089] Guilelmus van Gulik and Conradus Eubel, Hierarchia catholica III (Monasterii 1923) 279.

[1090] Federico Stefani and Guglielmo Berchet, I diarii di Marino Sanuto: (MCCCCXCVI-MDXXXIII) dall' autografo Marciano ital. cl. VII codd. CDXIX-CDLXXVII (Visentini, 1892) XLV, 39.

[1091] Ibid., 165, estimated by Fra Angelo Maria da Orvieto, friar of S. Pietro in Vincoli. Ibid., 134: Another report says that 'Cardinal Colonna has entered with easily a thousand peasants.' Ibid., 167: another monk estimates 12,000 men.

[1092] Sebastian Franck, Chronica Zeitbuch und Geschichtsbibel, (Beck, 1531) 235.

[1093] Ha-Cohen, Vol. II, translated by Bialloblotzky, 1836, 72.

[1094] Michael Mullet, The Catholic Reformation (Routledge, 2002).

The Jew Elia Levita, the man with the name with the key to spiritual leadership, who had enjoyed Viterbo's palace for a decade, was now exiled to Venice – into the ghetto. Jews were expelled from Florence – among the expelled Jews: the Medicis – yet again.[1095]

The German Chronicle adds that papal guards wanted to transfer the papacy to Martin Luther – with the help of then present cardinals and bishops. This action seems to have been the mockery of the day.[1096]

All this turns the sack of Rome into less of a random pillage than commonly portrayed. They were Lutherans, indeed: identified by their targets. The assault had been carefully planned and orchestrated.

This is the price that Luther and his protectors had to pay for the non-action treaty that had been signed the previous year: armed troops. His writings that defined war as a work of love came to full fruition at Rome. Peace had merely been abused to prepare for war.

It amounted to a blood bath.

The nightmare in Rome was burnt out by two friends of wars: a plague and a bribe. The plague raked away countless victims, sometimes hundreds in a single day. Nobody could be found to bury them. The dead were thrown down the Tiber River.[1097] Even the occupants of the Castello Sant' Angelo, where Pope Clement had sought refuge, were not spared.

The ranks of defenders and assailants alike were thinning out by the infection of the tiniest of creatures, bacteria by the name of Yersinia Pestis.

We all understand the consequences, I suppose.

The prophecy of the fall of Rome had come through.

The first 'Red Apple' had fallen without direct Ottoman-Turkish involvement. They were busy conquering Bosnia, Croatia, and Slavonia – heading for Vienna, the second 'Red Apple.'

Luther himself had plucked the fruit.

The King of the Jews, Rabbi Abrabanel, had predicted the beginning of the Messianic Age and the fall of Rome to occur a little later, in 1531, the year of the passing of Halley's Comet. But that would be splitting hairs. Following Abrabanel, Reubeni, too, had predicted the fall of Rome. Burning the Eternal City to the ground came easier to Reubeni than he might have thought. He was

---

[1095] Jewishhistory.org.il, retrieved September 22, 2017.

[1096] Sebastian Franck, Chronica Zeitbuch und Geschichtsbibel, (Beck, 1531) 234.

[1097] Sanudo, Diarii, XLV, 432, in Setton, 1984, 282.

not even there. We can only imagine the energy that was now directed toward Reubeni. The prophecy was true: the End of the World was at hand.

The whole world believed it.

Pope Clement's life was ransomed, and when all was over, the political landscape in Italy had again completely shifted. Rome – for the good Christians that the assailants were – was cut down by 80% with some 10,000 left murdered.

Somehow, Cardinal Colonna and Pope Clement resigned themselves to distrustful cooperation. Nevertheless, Colonna never returned to Rome.[1098]

If it was not already powerless after the Naples' debacle, now the papacy was more dependent on Emperor Charles than ever before.

Triggered by the pope's inability to act against Charles' interests, the English Reformation started soon thereafter, which put English Christians at war with themselves for the rest of the millennium.

It is simmering in Ireland today. Five centuries later.

With Europe's balance of power shattered, France quickly signed a deal with England to resist further advances of the Holy Roman Empire under Charles.

Once more, it did not go well.

Sooner rather than later, the Kingdom of France had to bury its hopes to regain a foothold in Italy.

The new goal of the French was peace with Charles. Louise engineered a new pact with her sister-in-law for the latter's nephew, Charles. Similar to the previous agreement, with the Peace of the Ladies, France had to desist. But it lived. It was removed from the pope's League of Cognac.

The Papal States, Venice and Florence now stood alone against the Holy Roman Empire, albeit all of them bankrupt.

Rumor had it among the invaders at Rome that a Spanish relief army was on its way to free Pope Clement. Their leader was Francisco de Quiñones, general of the Franciscans and former disciple of the Grand Inquisitor Cardinal Cisneros.

Quiñones had been among Luther's persecutors at the Diet of Worms. He was an imperial loyalist, bent on arresting the pope rather than freeing him.

---

[1098] Paolo Giovio, Pompeii Columnae Cardinalis vita () 203.

Whatever the truth about de Quiñones' relief army, it appears that he was indeed in Rome as the lead ambassador in the negotiations between Pope Clement and Emperor Charles.

The pope had to agree to crown Charles as the official Holy Roman Emperor. The ceremony took place a few years later. De Quiñones became a cardinal of the Catholic Church. Henceforth, he was known as 'Cardinal of the Holy Cross,'[1099] an apparent allusion to a holy war that was supposed to be launched against the Ottoman Empire.

The fall of Rome was the signal to prepare for a meetup at Armageddon to wage the final war.

Viterbo's demise brought more power to Martin Luther and strengthened his leadership over the global network of Augustinian monasteries. Sure enough, Luther's supporting nobles took advantage of Charles' gratitude.

This same year, Johann of Saxony the Steadfast – brother and successor of the Wise – established the Lutheran Church as his state church and had himself made chief bishop.

State and church were one.

A theocracy.

It was born corrupt.

At this junction, a scholar by the name of Molla Kabiz appeared in Constantinople, an obvious nickname of contempt. Do you remember Simon bar Kokhba's derogatory renaming to bar Koziba (son of the lie)? Add to this that Prophet Muhammad had been called by a name of similar phonetics, Kabsha, in his early days.[1100] The scholar merely fits a rabbinic pattern, where Kabiz stands for the lineage of King David and Molla for a messianic figure. In a near contemporary history, he was called Mulcarabum (Mulca the Arab).

This man was highly esteemed in Constantinople as 'the Prophet of Damascus,' and he was promoted by Grand Vizier Ibrahim Pasha,[1101] Suleiman's right hand[1102] on the Jewish Throne of David. Since the recent converts from Orthodox Christianity to Sunni Islam were open to new ideas, he proposed a new religion where Jesus Christ enjoyed supremacy over Prophet Muhammad and all other prophets.

---

[1099] The name derives from Santa Croce in Gerusalemme.

[1100] Gibb, 1979, 77.

[1101] Pargalı Ibrahim Pasha, aka Frenk Ibrahim Pasha, the Westerner, aka Makbul Ibrahim Pasha, the Favorite (1493–1536), grand vizier to Suleiman the Magnificent (1523–1536), and governor of Egypt (1525)

[1102] Boissard, Sultane, 1596, 243.

This is not as outlandish as one might think.

In the Koran, Muhammad is merely regarded as 'the Prophet', while it singles out Jesus as the Messiah.[1103] Jesus is the Christ-Messiah of Christianity and also of Islam. For Muslims, the Word of God is one with Jesus Christ (it was placed in the Virgin Mary's womb).[1104] The spirit came upon the 'Muslim' apostle *after a flight.*[1105]

Molla Kabiz's proposal was the apparent result of a fusion of Byzantine and Islamic apocalyptic thinking.[1106] If not the new religion under Luther, it is the element that was missing so far: a new religion that would emerge after the End of the World.

To cut the legends short, a tribunal failed to refute Molla Kabiz's arguments and released him.[1107] Allegedly, he had challenged Suleiman's position as *'the Shadow of God on Earth.*[1108]

Setting him free was perceived as a mistake.

The story turned into his pursuit and imprisonment. To a Muslim, Prophet Muhammad must be greater than any other messenger of God. The judge said to him: *'You have heard the faith of the congregation of the orthodox followers of the Holy Prophet. You know that no man who has been illuminated by this glorious faith and afterwards denies the truth of God can be permitted to live. Do you agree to leave all error, and to walk in the truth?'*[1109]

Based on Sharia Law, Mollo Kabiz was found a heretic by the chief judge and ordered executed: *'The sentence of the Law is that he die!'*[1110]

This religious argument was irrefutable. Mollo Kabiz was there and then terminated. Some noble spectators spat on the martyr.

They silenced him with the power of beheading.

His positions have never been refuted by Muslim scholars.

Except that they have.

---

[1103] Koran 9:30-9:31.
[1104] Koran 21:90-21:91 (Rodwell).
[1105] Koran 9:25-9:26.
[1106] The analysis of the modern historian Kaya Şahin had offered just that.
[1107] Şahin, Süleyman, 2013, 73.
[1108] W. L. Kingsley, An Unnoted Martyr (New Englander and Yale Review, Volume 53, 1890) 216.
[1109] Ibid., 219.
[1110] Ibid.

While not consensus, an element is sticking out from the inscriptions inside the Dome of the Rock on the Temple Mount: the simultaneous diminishing and lifting of Jesus, not to a higher level but to the same level as Prophet Muhammad. It appears to be a compromise between Mollo's proposal and the Ottoman naysayers.

The clarification – the refutation – hangs on the inner octagonal arcade of the Dome of the Rock.[1111]

Instead of the official tale, a sixteenth century historian tells a much different, more enlightening story of Mulcarabum. He had been trying to motivate Suleiman for war against the Persians by turning the latter into heretics.

The Magnificent obliged.[1112]

Together with the proposal for a new religion, this puts Mollo Kabiz solidly into messianic territory.

His death was probably an invention on the path to messianic immortality.

My distrust rests in what happens next.

As the forerunner, Reubeni was obliged to present a messiah. Still in Portugal, he found a partner by the name of Solomon Molcho.[1113] A Marrano-Christian, Solomon is said to having been the court historian of the King of Portugal.[1114]

Contrary to what we are encouraged to believe, this was no ordinary man. The description of a contemporary Jewish chronicle turns him into a successor of the priestly lineage of the House of David that fled Jerusalem after its destruction in the first and second centuries.[1115] The two were one – Mulca and Molcho are phonetically too closely related for comfort. Indeed, before joining with Reubeni, Molcho had been in Edirne, an early Ottoman capital.[1116] In other words, Molcho carried the soul of Mulcarabum.

The subversion of the world through the network of the messianic leadership was perfect.

Incredible, but perfect.

Anyhow, the meeting of the two sounds more like an arranged marriage than a chance encounter.

---

[1111] A.J. Deus, The Jewish Serpent King (2023) available at academia.edu.

[1112] Boissard, Sultane, 1596, 243.

[1113] Solomon Molcho aka Sholomo Molcho (1500–1532), originally named Diego Pires.

[1114] A.Z. Aeshcoly, The Story of David Ha-Re'uveni (Jerusalem, 1994) 93-94, as cited in Lenowitz, 1998, 116.

[1115] Ha-Cohen, Vol. II, translated by Bialloblotzky, 1836, 151.

[1116] Louis Ginzberg, Jewish Encyclopedia Joseph B. Ephraim Caro.

Instead, it is said that Molcho had converted back to Judaism. After spiritual dreams, he got circumcised and pronounced himself the Messiah, prophesying that the messianic kingdom would arrive in 1540.[1117] The righteousness would come to Israel, and God's judgement would ravage all other nations. All non-Jewish families would be brought down.[1118] The dead of the world would awaken from the dust by a perfect resurrection.[1119]

Reubeni thought of Molcho's approach as imprudent, endangering himself as well as Jewish and Marrano communities.

From a passage in a poem by Molcho, we can learn that he was excited about the fall of Rome.

> *The nations will fight*
> *but men of might will put the stranger to flight.*
> *And then will be the time*
> *of cities the prime,*
> *to flush Rome – Edom's pest –*
> *from out of the Nest.*[1120]

They were willing to scorch the earth in their passion for the Temple Mount at Jerusalem.

Without question, the status of Reubeni and his messiah must have been immense, not only among Jews but also for others who were susceptible to supernatural forces – *all* others.

Reubeni was unstoppable, and the team was on a mission to make itself known to the European leaders.

The first stop was a symbolic gesture to confirm Molcho's messianic standing.

For this, he had to be found among beggars in the ransacked Eternal City. So, he put on sackcloth and made sure to do just that.[1121] This is how prophecy fulfilled itself. Yet, Molcho also predicted the flooding of Rome (which indeed occurred in 1530), a pair of comets (which did appear in 1531, as already calculated by Abrabanel), and an earthquake in Portugal (which appeared in 1536).

---

[1117] Isidore Singer, Phillipp Bloch, Molko, Solomon (Jewish Encyclopedia, 1901-1906).

[1118] Ha-Cohen, Vol. II, translated by Bialloblotzky, 1836, 165-166.

[1119] Ibid., 170.

[1120] Molkho, The Beast of the Reed, ed. Aeshcoly (Jerusalem, 1994) 14, in Lenowitz, 1998, 120.

[1121] Ha-Cohen, Vol. II, translated by Bialloblotzky, 1836, 160.

Jews were great astronomers and in particular observers of comets. There is no secret to the star prophecy other than that it was the rocket science of the time. The prediction of unusual heavenly objects was how 'prophets' could cement their fame in front of an ignorant people. It is then of little importance that other prophecies were post-event predictions. Modern science with all its computing power and satellites is still unable to foretell either floods or earthquakes.

Molcho's inspiration can only have come from the god of the Israelites.

Some truths were mixed with lots of lies, which appeared truer when delivered as a package. The more outlandish a lie, the more fanatical were its defenders.

Indeed, the author of a contemporary Jewish chronicle was unable to hold back his excitement. He presented Molcho as illiterate in *'the law of the Lord.'* Upon his circumcision, God provided him with the necessary wisdom, and he became *'wiser than all men in a very short time.'* [1122] The text fits the pattern of messianic acknowledgement. *'For the spirit of the Lord spake in him.'* Later, the chronicle would admirably comment on *'his spotless soul.'* [1123]

While one is tempted to be amused by the folly, in the aftermath, hell will freeze over.

By some miraculous intervention, despite the obvious fallacy, Molcho must have gained the pope's trust and protection from the Catholic Inquisition.[1124] Finally a worthy messianic pair that could straighten out the troubles with Martin Luther, Emperor Charles, and the Ottoman Empire, all at once.

It was supposed to remain a secret between them.[1125]

It was probably also a secret between Suleiman and Mollo, the Mulcarabum. According to Molcho, the pope was impressed with the prediction of the appearance of the two comets.[1126]

From a contemporary German chronicle, we learn that there were multiple competing prophecies in play that the author dismisses as superstitious nonsense. One foresaw that the Turks would throw the pope off his throne and put an end to the Holy Roman Empire.

---

[1122] Ibid., 151.

[1123] Ibid., 191.

[1124] Matt Goldish in Frederick E. Greenspahn, Jewish Mysticism and Kabbalah: New Insights and Scholarship (New York University, 2011) 122.

[1125] Ha-Cohen, Vol. II, translated by Bialloblotzky, 1836, 177.

[1126] Ibid., 179.

Another prediction was coming forth through papal channels in Rome. It was supposedly dated to 1440 AD. It foretold that Charles would be able to subdue all his enemies, including the Balkan, the Turks, and Asia. He would put his crown down on the Mount of Olives in Jerusalem.[1127]

Superstition is *not* nonsense when coming from superstitious leaders.

Clement was not alone in his love with Molcho's mission. Italy's nobility appears also to have been infatuated with the messianic pair,[1128] even though Molcho himself expressed that they were dragons who would be destroyed.[1129]

Rome was a city, he boasted, that was *'destined to become desolate, and whose land will be burning pitch.'*[1130] It would become a possession of the New Jerusalem, he exclaimed.[1131]

There must have been various layers of messages. One was for the Rabbinic leaders and a different one for pope and nobility. It is unimaginable that the audience would have let such threats pass unpunished.

Nobody other than the rabbis must have known that Reubeni and Molcho were working as a messianic pair.

The following year[1132] – but without implicating anyone – Luther came down with diarrhea after consuming Kosher food at a banquet. It is copied *ad infinitum* that Luther had written a letter to his biographer and fellow reformer Melancthon, suggesting that the Jewish community had attempted to poison him. This was often taken as a turning point in Luther's treatment of Jews. However, with the best of my efforts, I was unable to verify this letter. Thirteen years later, Luther indeed warned Melancthon to be on guard for poisoners at banquets. But he meant it in general and did not direct suspicion at Jews.[1133]

We can make of this event whatever we wish. Neither Luther nor we today have any evidence of the diarrheic causes, and the master appears to have been able to distinguish between suspicion and criminal fact.

Many wish that Martin Luther had died that night. It would have prevented his anti-Semitic writings from ever being published.

---

[1127] Sebastian Franck, Chronica_Zeitbuch_und_Geschichtsbibel (Beck, 1531) 252.
[1128] Ibid., 151.
[1129] Ibid., 153
[1130] Ibid., 153-154
[1131] Ibid., 159.
[1132] 1528.
[1133] Martin Luther to Philip Melanchthon, April 21, 1541.

However, if Jews had indeed tried to get rid of him to please the pope (and the emperor) and schmooze themselves into an alliance (or two) – the context does not render this scenario impossible – then his death would have concealed involvement of Rabbinic leaders in one of the greatest turning points in history. If Jewish bosses did *not* try to assassinate him, then we still would want to know what may have made him change his mind.

After all, Luther was the intellectual father of Hitler's anti-Semitism.

However, it should be clear by now that anti-Semitism was not new. This book started out with a holocaust from before Luther's mission had started. Distant from his whereabouts. Hatred of Jews was not Luther's invention. Instead, it was created by Jewish leaders for their ordinary followers as part of their dreamt-up collective memory. The biblical mechanism to bind a people through the – mythical – image of being hated before they even existed as a nation had a fatal flaw. The imaginary hatred turned into real hatred the moment a breakaway sect no longer saw itself as Jewish. John the Baptist was a Jew. Jesus Christ was a Jew, born of Mary, a Jewess. Simon bar Kokhba was a Jew. David Reubeni was an Ethiopian Jew with a claim to descend from Prophet Muhammad (a Jewish exilarch). Solomon Molcho was a Jew from a lineage that may go beyond John the Baptist. The Gospels – written by Jews – took the self-portrayal of being hated to distinguish the newly-born Christianity from Judaism, Pharisee Judaism, to be precise.

The imaginary had turned against them in a very real and deadly way. Mountains of Christian masses of either Egyptian, Greek, Russian, and Syrian churches in the East, or the Catholic Church, and now also the Protestant Church reminded their disciples of the fake fact that Jews had killed the Jew Jesus Christ. If not for that, Jews were worthy of being hated for being wicked. Or just for being Jews.

They were hated for denying the Truth of a history that they themselves had invented.

However, that is merely scratching on the surface of deep-seated historical trauma that is buried under the reasons for this self-portrayal as a hated people. We have already learned about Jewish dictatorial administrative networks that acted as magnets for hatred. They have a deeper history than we can imagine.

The self-described hatred appears to have served as a very clever justification for atrocities committed against the rest of the population because – well – they were hated.

In essence: had Luther not written his anti-Semitic works, someone else would have come to fill the void. History would not have deviated an inch from its course. Even if Luther had never been born, the Protestant Reformation would still have occurred. Not a single war would not have been fought. The trajectory had already been set before Luther was conceived.

This is not to be mistaken for predetermination. Luther's protector, Frederick the Wise, would have simply picked another man for his machinations.

Luther's diarrheic mess was irrelevant for the historic trajectory. He made it out of the toilet alive. Before dying, he had much larger problems to deal with.

Creating a church was not as simple as one might think. Take a couple of churches and declare them independent of the Catholic Church but true to its noble overlords. Luther had to define what the Protestant Church stood for.

That should be easy enough.

But for a religious sect to be emancipated, it needs to sharply distinguish its marketing policies from the mother house from which it broke off. It needs to engage in division. Without a unique selling proposition, there would simply be no Protestant Church. What? You are the better Catholic Church? In this endeavor, the Reformer faced headwinds from many directions.

Such relevant questions about how repentance would be positioned for the forgiveness of sins would divide him from other reformers. How was faith related to work in Luther's world wherein faith alone justified everything?

How was myth linked to the real world?

# IV: REVOLT

## *The Antichrist*

In the meantime, the French had made advances back into northern Italy all the way down to Naples. It is like a broken record: it did not go well. Shortages of supplies caused starvation among both the imperialist defenders inside the city and the French assailants outside its walls. The soldiers were increasingly bogged down by filth and debris. The French had cut off the city's water supply and rerouted the aqueducts into their camp. The *almost-victorious* French army found itself in the midst of a self-created swamp.

Back then, they did not know much about the agents of disease.

The source of life turned on them. The stagnant water became the polluted home of mosquitoes. Typhus, malaria, dysentery, and plague decimated them. The city itself was dry and almost untouched by the onslaught of disease.

During those times, plagues were not always brought about by the whims of nature. Infection has a long history as a biological weapon. Diseased corpses were catapulted over city walls. Typically, Jews were blamed for poisoning the water supply. Whether this bears any truth, the cruelty of organized religion had no bounds even at terminal risk to their own foot folks. Of course, it was easier to suspect Jews from Germany than to listen to the advice to light fires around the camp and to drain the swamp.

In the end, the dead remained unburied.[1134] The stench must have been unbearable. The French victory disintegrated at Naples in the face of their inability to put together even small bands of soldiers. The imperial forces took back the countryside unopposed. On their flight back to the ruined and depopulated city of Rome, dead Frenchmen littered the roads. The few who escaped from Naples were robbed and stripped nude by peasants along the way.

No love-preaching Christian dared to lend a helping hand.[1135]

Charles' strategy to hold the Vatican hostage paid off immensely. He ended up the unexpected victor. Florence and Venice trembled in fear.

However, the renewed French advance on Naples was not an isolated event.

---

[1134] Setton, 1984, 306.
[1135] Sanudo, Diarii, XLIX, 15-16, letter dated at Naples on September 17, 1528, in Setton, 1984, 310.

While the Naples' disaster went down, Suleiman planned his next assault on Hungary. Europe was panicking. But it remained divided in its noble enmities. In a language blossoming with papal affection, Pope Clement described Ottoman-Turks as a fatal virus, a pest, and plague that could spread more widely.[1136] The papal words reflect the true feelings of believers of one sect against the leaders and members of their competing sectarians and religions.

But the pope had no real force to offer in defence of Christianity against the oncoming Turkish tide.

What would Luther see in all this chaos? Could he grasp clearly who was playing whom? Was he among the played?

In 1529, Suleiman the Magnificent besieged Vienna in Austria – nothing less than the capital of the Holy Roman Empire – the second 'Red Apple.' From the larger context, we can see that Suleiman's ambitions did not lead to this event by chance. The intent to invade Europe and to overthrow Christianity is written in the charter of Islam. With Rome's fall, Hungary's earlier defeat, and the sack of Constantinople from 1453, the signals to bring down Edom (the Roman Empire) had been sounded.

The path to ruling the entire world led through Vienna.

Since the Holy Roman Empire had exhausted its strength in its conflicts with the Catholic Church, Suleiman's timing could not have been better.

Naturally, Emperor Charles was concerned about Ottoman advances toward his capital. In response, he sent an ambassador[1137] to the Persian Safavid ruler, asking for assistance.

In preparation for the earlier Ottoman advances, Luther had written *'On War Against the Turk'* during the last couple of years. Due to a mishap, the work was published only now.[1138] It was a damning call to real war for the Holy Roman Empire that should be kept separate from the spiritual war that Luther was fighting.

His responsibility was prayer and repentance. Charles' was blood.

His prayers called for the bleeding.

---

[1136] Acta Tomicana, X, no. 350, pp. 334-336, in Setton, 1984, 320.
[1137] The name of this delegate was again knight of Saint John de Balbi, the emissary who had been sent a few years earlier.
[1138] Martin Luther, Letter to Nicolas Hausmann, February 15, 1529

Some reform preachers maintained that Ottoman-Turks had been sent by God for the punishment of the sins of Christianity. Battling them back would be to resist the will of God. They thought that Christians should not fight Ottoman-Turks and should neither be rulers nor bear arms.[1139] Luther was offended not only that his radical teaching would bring forth such ideas, but also that the blame for bloodshed was laid upon him.[1140]

The notion that Christians should not be rulers is an alarming proposition. Following Revelation, this suggests a state of existence on the other side of the End of the World, in New Jerusalem.

It advocates a voluntary submission to the sole survivors of the final war: the top Jewish leaders.

Luther had indeed been excommunicated by Pope Leo X for having said, among other transgressions, that *'to fight against the Turk is the same thing as resisting God, who visits our sin upon us with this rod.'*[1141] He did not deny having said that, but he now proclaimed that the situation had changed.[1142] Back then, pope and clergy were like God on earth, according to Luther, while nobility had been *'oppressed'* by the Catholic Church.[1143]

The Catholic Church created nobility and controlled it. The pope was in power. But with the Reformation, this was no longer the case, Luther asserted. Worldly governments had to organize themselves as independent of the representatives of God on earth. In Martin Luther's vision, the Protestant Reformation empowered nobility to do just that.

We have learned how the core teachings of the New Testament indeed advocate passive aggression and follow the principles of predetermination. This latter leads to the End of the World with the final war at Armageddon and to New Jerusalem. Luther must have understood his own teaching in the same way as preachers and disciples did. If he meant anything different, then he was unable to explain his spiritual abstractions for lay people.

The peasants of the time, even if they learned to read the Bible in their mother tongue, did not understand the bigger picture of hatred and corruption. For them, it all needed to be simple. We heard from Luther that they had no clue anyway.

---

[1139] Luther, On War, 1528, WA 30 II, 107-148.
[1140] Ibid.
[1141] Ibid.
[1142] Ibid.
[1143] Ibid.

Preachers could tell them whatever they wanted the Bible to say. The laymen would believe what was coming upon them from the pulpits.

Back then, it was no different than it is today. People were just trying to fit in. For the peasantry, it did not really matter which faith they followed, as long as they were left in peace. By all means, they could as well have lived the same lives and prayed to the same god under Muslim Ottoman rule. Were it not for the cross and the moon, most could probably not tell a Protestant church from a Muslim mosque. Christianity, or now the Protestant Church, really only mattered to the people in its relationship to nobility.

Logically, Luther addressed his booklet *'On War Against the Turk'* to nobles, not to peasants.

He was damning his opponents to hell and denied them repentance or forgiveness.[1144]

Islam's Koran is filled with such diatribes.

Since punishment, such as the calamities of the End of the World, can matter only to believers, one may wonder how effective Luther's tirades were. He did not care so much about being excommunicated from the Catholic Church. Why would his opponents be scared by his threats? But it shows how leaders spread boundless hatred.

The concept of turning the other cheek,[1145] of course, works only for those who are a minority, hopeless to win over those who rule. It is designed as a tool of pride and passive aggression,[1146] not for pacifism. Its sinister meaning is at its best in the passage wherein you go two miles if someone *forces* you to go one.

However, Luther was now in a position of power.

For him, a new paradigm emerged, one of not giving back an inch of spiritually conquered territory and disciples.

Luther resolved the paradox in 'reasoning' that there was an earthly government that was obliged to protect its people and go to war when necessity called. A heavenly government did not have any obligations that mattered. In that, he proposed nothing less than a form of dual government, as is prevalent in Judaism and Islam.

The final say was to be with the supreme spiritual leader – Martin Luther.

---

[1144] Ibid.
[1145] Ibid.
[1146] Matthew 5:38-5:42 (NIV).

It is a subtle departure from his earlier stance on unifying both the spiritual and temporal world under one sovereign leader, then Johann of Saxony the Steadfast, chief bishop of the Lutheran Church and head of Saxony.

The Reformer accused the Catholic Church of having deserted their spiritual calling by meddling with secular governments and participating in war. He was of the opinion that Christianity forbade them to do so.[1147]

> *Because the papists reject it, arbitrarily and without Scripture, the Turk must take its part and prove it with the fist and with deeds. If we will not learn out of the Scriptures, we must learn out of the Turk's scabbard, until we find in our hurt that Christians are not to make war or resist evil. Fools must be chased with clubs.*[1148]

He thought that participation in war by clergy of the Catholic Church was the reason for the losses to Ottoman-Turks. Instead, the papacy was to stick to praying while leaving the fighting to earthly rulers.[1149] Luther maintained that the losses found their cause in the papal disobedience to God and the Canon Law.

They should be taught a painful lesson.[1150]

The Reformer had a peculiar kind of logic. He recognized that warfare was a different job than praying to a god. War was rather real and required another kind of training than his. Yet, he put his advice into a book addressed to those responsible for warfare.

For Luther, to urge the earthly authorities to go to war against Ottoman-Turks was a spineless position. *We* must go to war. *You* go! Going to war and calling to war is the brother of committing violence and inciting violence. The difference is one of scale.

The club-swingers are not the ringleaders.

The preachers are.

His concealing of the call to war with the responsibility of a spiritual veil is hypocritical. Christians do not kill. They must run from the battlefield. But feudal nobles are not real Christians. They must protect Christians with Protestant soldiers. They must kill but not in the name of Jesus Christ. Crosses are forbidden on flags of war.

---

[1147] Luther, On War, 1528, WA 30 II, 107-148.
[1148] Ibid.
[1149] Ibid.
[1150] Ibid.

Luther was merely trying to teach Charles his final lesson about how David, the mythical[1151] King of the Jews, dealt with a competitor for the tillage of a girl's garden – a married woman.

King David, the exterminator in the Promised Land,[1152] the Son of God,[1153] had been in lust with her. In order to conquer her lawn, he sent her husband to the battlefront, where he was expected to fall. He obliged. Now, David could console the widow's grief. The result of the obvious betrayal and adultery was an heir.

But the god of the Israelites did not punish King David for either of the two crimes. The reason that the king eventually fell out of God's favor – despite the promise that God's love would never be taken away from David[1154] – was that the king had ordered a consensus.[1155] The latter would have allowed us to see how many Jews there were. Or how few.

Priestly minds experience extraordinary difficulties in dealing with immediate crisis. They are *not* King David with the slingshot who killed Goliath.

But the analogy shows that Luther was a brownnose.

His intentions with Emperor Charles were diabolic. Only the emperor and the Christian nobility had a mandate from God to oppose Ottoman-Turks, according to the Reformer.[1156]

God's directive was, of course, to be approved by Luther.

It was a double game.

Together with Johann of Saxony the Steadfast and Philip I of Hesse the Magnanimous, Martin Luther had worked for a long time on subverting Charles' throne. Utterly ill equipped, opposing the advancing Suleiman the Magnificent on the battlefield was a suicide mission. No Christian of note believed that such a war could be won. Certainly not Luther. The text about Charles' taking on his sovereign responsibility was but another evil plot to have the emperor dangling on a spear.

---

[1151] There was no mighty King David, no Israelites, and nobody else of their family tree. The whole story was an invention. *A* David may have existed but not *the* David.
See Israel Finkelstein and Neil Asher Silberman, The Bible Unearthed: Archaeology's New Vision of Ancient Israel and the Origin of its Sacred Texts, (Simon and Schuster, Copyright © 2002, reprinted by permission of Simon and Schuster) 132.

[1152] 1 Samuel 27:9.

[1153] 2 Samuel 7:14.

[1154] 2 Samuel 7:15 (NIV).

[1155] 1 Chronicles 21:7.

[1156] Luther, On War, 1528, WA 30 II, 107-148.

Luther had indeed learned a thing or two from King David's example: send the despised competitor to the battlefront, and the 'bride' is yours. In this case, the bride was the Holy Roman Empire.

Since the Vatican held all the power before Luther helped break its spine, it continuously engaged in bloody warfare against fellow Christians. It was intent on maintaining its absolute control through the support of loyal dynasties.

Bishops and cardinals marched onto the battlefields to face Christians. They were holding on to Vatican flags and swinging deadly weapons.

Martin Luther viewed Suleiman as *'a pirate or highwayman'* who had no right to attack lands that were not his. As though conquest had anything to do with 'rights.' The Protestant chief had no doubt that the Ottoman leader was punishing the world in the function of *'God's rod and the devil's servant.'*[1157]

It speaks for itself that all Christian ideals were buried in an instant when another faith threatened to overcome Luther's creed. As Pope Leo had suggested, he *wished to be wiser than he should be* by establishing his just war doctrine. In the process, Luther deployed the well-tested mechanism to create his hatred against mankind by dehumanizing his opponent.

As always, Christian laymen had to pay the price.

Protestants had to place their lives into Luther's hand and go die in his name. He required from his followers that they had to be first in line to move onto the battlefield in order to smite the devil. This was sort of a spiritual shock-and-awe strategy. The idea was that Christian soldiers would be able to startle Suleiman so much that the Protestants could *'take the rod out of God's hand.'* Ottomans would then have to fight with their own strength,[1158] without God's help.

The devil of the Judaic religions *'is a spirit who cannot be beaten with armor.'* For the earthly devil Suleiman, *'Christian weapons and power must do it.'*[1159]

To be more persuasive with the superstitious population, Luther instructed his preachers to highlight the people's sins and ingratitude. God's punishments that would be brought upon them by advancing Ottoman-Turks were justified.

In pursuit of terrifying the poor peasants, it was explained in the churches how frequently God's wrath had come upon the earthlings for their sins. This was enforced with examples, such as the Flood, the story of Sodom and

---

[1157]  Ibid.
[1158]  Ibid.
[1159]  Ibid.

Gomorrah, the entire population of which had been totally obliterated, and the misfortune of Jews.[1160]

Luther and his priests were drumming up the End of the World.

This is part of the core mechanism of how the Reformer abused his influence and power for hatred of mankind and violence against anyone who did not agree with him.

> *Read the histories of the time and you find that the principal business of popes and bishops has been to set emperors, kings, princes, lands, and people against one another, even themselves to fight and help in the work of murder and bloodshed. Why so? Because the spirit of lies never acts any other way.*[1161]

Who says so? Martin Luther.

Before the Protestant Church even reached maturity, he was on the same slippery slope that the Catholic Church had occupied for centuries. Here, it is particularly tragic, because the poor people understood the Word of God – Luther's words – in their native tongue for the first time.

Because they could not tell the difference, they swallowed the frog whole.

The spirit of lies never acts any other way?

The work of murder and bloodshed?

It is organized crime.

Luther was in such a position of power that war without the support of the Protestant Church was futile. The leadership of the Holy Roman Empire was in disarray and was discouraged by previous internal and external losses.

Luther had become the recruiter for holy war. Extremism showed its ugly face in its very definition.

Let us pray.

> *O help us, dear God the Father; have mercy on us, dear Lord Jesus Christ!*[1162]

Now we know what the fearful prayer means: A battle cry.

Just a little later, Luther accused the Catholic Church of ordering Christians to bear arms and to make war. The clergy's duty should have been to preach and pray.[1163] He, Luther, maintained about himself that he preached peace and

---

[1160] Ibid.
[1161] Ibid.
[1162] Ibid.
[1163] Ibid.

obedience and that the earthly rulers had *'to do their duty and maintain peace and justice'*[1164] – meaning: go to war.

Besides making war, murdering, or robbing foe and friend, Luther accused the Catholic Church of burning, condemning, and persecuting the innocent, the pious, and the orthodox. The pope was the Antichrist and Suleiman the devil.[1165] *'Both shall go down to hell, even though it may take the Last Day to send them there.'*[1166] To that end, he was willing to scorch the entire planet and bring it to the End of the World.

We can recognize Luther's definition of peace:

> *Where the spirit of lies is, there is also the spirit of murder, though he may not get to work or may be hindered. If he is hindered, he still laughs and is jubilant when murder is done, and at least consents to it, for he holds it right.*[1167]

Following Luther's logic, all religious sects carry the spirit of murder. They all are tantamount to organized crime.

There is only one exception: his.

Catholic researchers will protest that his is the view of a polemic enemy. Instead, Luther was a first-hand witness of how the Inquisition brought persecution across Europe in their Taliban ways.

He was a target.

Then Luther destroyed the notion that the subjects in the Ottoman domain had enjoyed some sort of religious freedom. He denied this by saying that Christians in the Ottoman Empire were not allowed to *'openly confess Christ or preach or teach against Mohammed.'*[1168] If you put the truth that bluntly in a printed book: of course not! We can see it today in majority Muslim nations the world over. Why, for Allah's sake, would they allow to have their impoverished minds subverted by another religion? He asked, *'what kind of freedom of belief'* this was supposed to be.[1169]

Further dehumanizing them, he called Ottoman-Turks a *'barbarous and wild people'* who were under *'severe rule,'*[1170] which prevented Christians from preaching by force.[1171]

---

1164 Ibid.
1165 Ibid.
1166 Ibid.
1167 Ibid.
1168 Ibid.
1169 Ibid.
1170 Ibid.
1171 Ibid.

He genuinely thought that there should be some kind of freedom in Muslim countries that would allow him to incite hatred.

The will to teach *against* religious dogma in foreign lands provides us with one of the keys to understanding atrocities by organized religions throughout history. The problem is not that the target defended itself, but that it punished entire communities of the religious competition. Had they singled out the priestly class and locked them up, it would have become less of a problem. They might even have done so – initially. The response of the community is predictable: sectarian unrest and bloodshed. The soldiers of the provocateur became the target. In an unavoidable cycle of self-destruction, the communities ended up persecuted. They acted as human shields.

Luther's argument was merely expedient. The Catholic Church had silenced Muslim calls to prayer across Europe. Some 200 years before the Reformation, the Council of Vienna[1172] criticized Muslim rituals, outlawed the calls to prayer, and ordered the destruction of their mosques and minarets.[1173] There was no such freedom to preach against the Son of God for Muslims in Luther-land. The process of converting mosques to churches was still ongoing in his time.

Peace, at last. Established through destruction.

Luther had no intention of reintroducing such liberties. He did say, though, that *'the authorities should not interfere in peoples' faith.'*[1174] This included Muslims, Jews, and those free from religion alike.

Was this a moment of weakness in Luther's mind?

In just a few years, Luther himself came to call for the expulsion of both, Turks and Jews.

We need to look elsewhere for what Luther may have had in mind. In the foreword to his *'Small Catechism'*, the intent of this newfound *'freedom of religion'* dawns upon the student. Nobody should be forced to believe, but if you do not fully endorse all of Luther's teachings, then you are not a Christian.[1175] Further, if you are not a true Christian, you are free to leave your Protestant hometown.[1176] The reformer made sure that this was preached viciously from the pulpits of Protestant churches. *Liberty* was in the eye of the religious beholder. It meant something completely different from how we wish it to be understood today. Freedom of religion was reduced to becoming an exile. For those who should

---

[1172] The Council of Vienna took place in 1311 – 1312.

[1173] Council of Vienne (1311-1312) Canon 25.

[1174] Luther, On War, 1528, WA 30 II, 107-148.

[1175] Martin Luther, Small Catechism, 1530.

[1176] Luther, Small Catechism, 1530.

not exercise their freedom to leave, the Protestant community would demonstrate what passive aggression feels like.

The bully was preaching from the altar in the Protestant Church; the herd of sheep was pushing its dissidents over the cliff.

The process might have been subtle, at first. But the tragedy of communal boundaries in organized religion was that their function led to genocide. Just because they did not believe alike, they did not deserve to live a decent life, go to school with the others, or have a shot at a good job.

Just as the Catholic Church recognized that imams in the mosques were preaching against Christianity, so did Muslim leaders grasp that Christian preachers were subverting their governments. Jews do not need singling out in their subversive efforts.

Luther went on to say that the Protestant Church *'must pray against the Turks'* as if they prayed *'against the Devil himself.'*[1177] The vicious cycle of hatred against Muslims had been started over a thousand years earlier. Luther had no problems in maintaining the status quo of abhorrence.

In order to strengthen his message, Luther studied the Koran.[1178] *Reading* the Koran would be a better description. That made him the Protestants' foremost expert on Islam. But as far as we know, he never as much as met a Muslim. And he did not seem to have spent a lot of time trying to make sense of the Muslims' holy book.

Of course not. There were no longer any Muslims in Europe to meet. The Inquisition had 'processed' them all.

One example needs to be put on the table:

> *[…] it has been commanded to him [Prophet Muhammad] to bring the world to his faith and if the world is not willing, to compel it or punish it with the sword; and there is much glorification of the sword in it. Therefore, the Turks think their Mohammed much higher and greater than Christ, for the office of Christ has ended and Mohammed's office is still in force.*[1179]

We have already seen that the conquest of the entire world was first mandated by Jewish leaders for themselves, then for Christians by Jewish leaders, and now to Muslims by Jewish leaders. Conquering the entire planet by hastening the End of the World is in the standard repertoire of all Judaic religions. The motives lie

[1177] Luther, On War, 1528, WA 30 II, 107-148.
[1178] Ibid.
[1179] Ibid.

in the profits. But, in the eye of the Christian Luther, Islam *'is the chief doctrine of the Turkish faith in which all abominations, all errors, all devils are piled up in one heap.'*[1180]

For the sake of peace, let us agree that Muslims may indeed view Muhammad as being higher than Jesus Christ. However, in the Christian view, Jesus is higher than all the prophets combined in Judaism, a position that irresponsibly offends Jews and Muslims.

Christianity flat out declines even to entertain Muhammad as a prophet.

Solomon Molcho's proposal for new religion where Prophet Muhammad is accepted but Jesus Christ is of higher standing than the Muslim messenger seems rather conciliatory.

But Luther called for extremist measures, including that a Christian would *'rather be dead than alive under such a government, where he must say nothing about his Christ, and hear and see such blasphemy and abomination against Him.'*[1181]

We are in the territory of jihadists. Martyrdom. Out in the open.

The Truth is self-evident.

When Luther declared that no kingdom has ever come up to become so mighty by murder and robbery as that of Ottoman-Turks,[1182] he was in error about historic facts.

At least one has: the Catholic Church.

Another had already started under Luther's watch: the Protestant Church.

The Jewish faith as well as Christianity were designed to overturn existing governments.

Islam is no different, except for different governments.

It is enlightening when a man of faith discusses another man's religion.

The point that drove it home for the disciples listening to the masses in the Protestant Church was that Islam despises women and marriage. They can take ten or twenty wives and sell them cheap, like cattle.[1183] This surely enraged Christian hearts against the approaching Muslims. If they could not care less about the wrath of whoever's god was coming at them, the calamity of losing wives and daughters to Muslim savages needed to be prevented at all costs.

---

[1180] Ibid.
[1181] Ibid.
[1182] Ibid.
[1183] Ibid.

They were imagining serial rapists. Churchgoing women made sure that their husbands understood their duty to go to war, even though some of these men have been in Rome for the ravaging of its city nuns.

But then wives, daughters, and sons became prey of clergy men.

They preyed from behind.

Furthermore, and in direct consequence to the fall of Rome, Martin Luther built his argument on the 'fact' that they were now living through the End of the World. This self-defeating vision was shared by Muslim Ottoman-Turks, by the Catholic Church, and Jews alike.

The Second Coming of Jesus Christ was at the door.[1184]

The entire world was working toward the final war at Armageddon. Fear had taken over. The monsters were about to come out from under the bed. The faithful flock was in panic. If all else fails, threaten the superstitious disciples with the beast of the final war. It prevents lay people from making a decent living. Terror grips the minds of believers. Working for tomorrow is futile. No! it is mandated by Jesus' own words![1185]

This is why Europe had lain in ruins for hundreds of years before Luther.

Ottoman-Turks were mighty and well equipped. They had a standing army that could bring 300,000 or 400,000 men to battlefields, Luther thought. He saw the previous inter-Christian warfare as child's play in comparison.[1186] It was necessary, according to Luther, for all nobility and kings to rally behind Emperor Charles and for the emperor to take his responsibility as captain over all of them.

Luther's power over the government showed its muscle in the churches. He called for unity of the seculars.

At the same time, he never buried his rebellion from the Catholic Church in the name of the needed unity for a focused defense. The only hope was for all nobles to stand together and for divided Christian leaders to pray for them,[1187] if from different spiritual centers.

The historical evidence is without ambivalence: wars were won or lost with or without conflicting prayers. They failed to stop praying against each other.

---

[1184] Ibid.
[1185] Matthew 6:33–34.
[1186] Luther, On War, 1528, WA 30 II, 107-148.
[1187] Ibid.

In all this, Luther was a religious opportunist. He used the threat of Ottoman-Turks to divert the nobility's attention from harassing the sprouting Protestant Church to going to the final war at Armageddon.

Luther's greatest hazard was not an impending attack by Ottoman-Turks but the Catholic Church. His enemies sat in the city of Speyer in a conference to figure out how to get rid of him[1188] and of the religious menace of his Swiss reform competitor, Ulrich Zwingli.[1189] Emperor Charles' idea for the second Diet of Speyer was to reverse the policies of religious tolerance as expressed earlier.

The devilish scheme was to reinstitute Catholicism as the only religion in all provinces of the Holy Roman Empire.[1190]

As the leader of the Protestant league, John the Steadfast confessed Lutheranism at the meeting and defended the interpretations of the earlier conference that had promised church reformation. However, the power of the majority was stronger. Further reform was prohibited until a council organized by the Catholic Church was convened. Several reform sects were prohibited, and violations were subject to capital punishment.

This prohibition through the power of the majority did not come easy to Charles. The affected sectarians launched mass protests – hence the name *Protestants* – a love fest. An appeal was sent by the leaders of fourteen imperial cities. It was signed by six influential princes. Wittenberg, Martin Luther's base, was not on the list of appellants.

Followers of the reform movement from Switzerland were put under threat of death.

Not so for Luther's.

His efforts against the Turks and the Catholic Church in support of Charles may have provided Lutherans with a competitive advantage for their sectarian movement. It was a win-win proposition. If all went well, the Ottoman-Turks and the pope would be obliterated in the Last Judgement.[1191] If not, Charles would either fall in battle or have an accident. Food poisoning, perhaps.

Luther's hands were clean,[1192] either way.

---

[1188] Ibid.

[1189] Huldrych Zwingli, Ulrich Zwingli, 1484 – 1531, was the leading reformer in Switzerland.

[1190] Karl Brandi, The emperor Charles V; the growth and destiny of a man and of a world empire (Cape, 1939) 300.

[1191] Luther, On War, 1528, WA 30 II, 107-148.

[1192] Ibid.

The Reformer's imperial support was nothing but mean-spirited, sharply-calculated expedience. By now, Luther had grown to outdo the extremism of Savonarola in Florence.

Luckily for Luther, the conference amounted to nothing for his movement.[1193]

Suleiman, as magnificent as he may have been, remained the Antichrist and was preached against from the pulpits of Protestant and Catholic churches alike as the devil incarnate.

The beast was on the move.

Superstition constitutes a powerful wall against aliens. It has been deployed for this purpose for at least 7,000 years. There was no shortage of willing volunteers to enlist in suicide missions to achieve salvation through martyrdom.

The war unfolded in unexpected ways.

The farther north Suleiman advanced along the Danube River, the deeper he found himself in religiously rebellious country. The populations were already in uproar over the new kind of Christian religion that Luther and other reformers had brought about.

Just a decade earlier, Vienna was in rebellion over Protestantism. Several reform leaders were executed then. This ensured Catholic supremacy over the capital.

Many were already proficient in wielding clubs.

Although Suleiman the Magnificent had managed to besiege Vienna, the capital of the Holy Roman Empire, he was unable to finish the job.

The assault on Vienna turned out to become a case study in the limitations of Renaissance warfare.

It was not easy to move large troop contingents to distant lands and keep them supplied and maintained. Because of torrential rains, the campaign had been hampered and delayed from the beginning. Camels, which were not suited to the climate, died along the way. Cannons became stuck in the wet ground. The march was treacherous. Soldiers got sick. They arrived at their target destination neither in full numbers nor in the best of spirits.

According to Luther, Ottoman-Turks destroyed the city and then ran away before the Germans.[1194]

This was the folk story for the superstitious.

---

[1193] Martin Luther, Letter to Martin Link, 1529.
[1194] Martin Luther, Letter to John Lange, 1529.

In reality, the Ottoman-Turkish troops were surprised by early incoming winter weather that worsened their already precarious situation. Muslims were not accustomed to such miserable conditions. After a final all-or-nothing assault, which did not bring the hoped-for success, they decided to retreat for the time being. Heading south turned out to be an even bigger disaster than the march toward Vienna.

Luther was cheering.

He regarded it a miracle of his god.[1195] It would only strengthen his resolve.

Nevertheless, Suleiman sold his campaign to Vienna as a success. Back home, elaborate celebrations included the circumcisions of three of his sons.

Among the three was Mehmed, the Mahdi.

After the repositioned embarrassment, Suleiman entered into an alliance with Somalia's radical imam, The Conqueror,[1196] against Ethiopia. A collapse of Dawit's Empire (David Reubeni's) could be averted only through the standing alliance with the Portuguese.

Did the Ottoman ruler smell foul play?

Was Suleiman disappointed that the gates of Vienna had not been opened from the inside? The city's Jews had been annihilated and their synagogue destroyed a century earlier. Back then, they were accused of having collaborated with and helped arm the Hussite Bohemian Reformation, Luther's forerunners.

We are told that only few Jews lived in the capital during Charles' reign.

---

[1195] Martin Luther, Letter to Nicolas Hausmann, 1529.
[1196] Imam Ahmad ibn Ibrahim al-Ghazi, The Conqueror, was the ruler of Somalia 1527 – 1543.

### *Radicalizing Children*

Luther showed a remarkable focus on building his church. He brought forth the large and small Catechisms, which were teaching materials for preachers and memory cards for the disciples, all written in various languages. They were especially designed for the young and gullible.[1197] The idea of a catechism in the local language was not new. Like the translation of the Bible, the French had created their local catechism earlier. The Swiss Ulrich Zwingli had done so four years before Luther, but his works were now prohibited. A legitimate replacement was opportune.

Luther's plagiarized 'idea' was to create a familiar environment with standard texts that the people could memorize.[1198]

For his plan, Luther devised the simpler *'Small Catechism'* and the extended *'Large Catechism.'* The small one was *'Protestantism for Dummies.'* The large served to provide for *'a richer and fuller knowledge'*[1199] of Luther's teachings. To help in the learning process, many of Luther's books were decorated with woodcut illustrations that related biblical stories.

We have seen the precursor for teaching through Renaissance art that had been commissioned by the Catholic Church.

For whatever sense that made to Luther, putting pictures in religious books was all right. Hanging them in churches was not.

He thought of his pastors as nothing, a horde of incompetent idiots, living *'like dumb brutes and irrational hogs.'*[1200] Martin Luther was a reactionary, showing all the symptoms of a true religious tyrant.

He may have been arrogant, but he was no simpleton.

He put the blame for the *'deplorable, miserable condition'* of Christianity on the Catholic Church and its bishopric.[1201]

But the accuser was sitting in the same boat. At the risk of their own demise, its passengers were willing to set their vessel afire mid-sea in order to throw all dissenters overboard.

---

[1197] Luther, Small Catechism, 1530.
[1198] Ibid.
[1199] Ibid.
[1200] Ibid.
[1201] Ibid.

Here was Luther's plan:

> *But those who are unwilling to learn it should be told that they deny Christ and are no Christians, neither should they be admitted to the Sacrament, accepted as sponsors at baptism, nor exercise any part of Christian liberty, but should simply be turned back to the Pope and his officials, yea, to the devil himself. Moreover, their parents and employers should refuse them food and drink, and notify them that the prince will drive such rude people from the country, etc.*[1202]

Luther did not mean 'learning' in general but learning his catechism. The implication is that those who were unwilling to learn – his catechism – were to be shown out of town and country.

He advocated total sectarian segregation.

Closed communal boundaries help to keep the flock away from those who could disrupt the community with new ideas. Not to engage with the latter is one of the core principles of organized religion. It can push communities into a self-defeating tunnel vision.

His argument was that this would not restrict the freedom to believe as you chose, because you could simply move somewhere else. However, any town's Protestant laws superseded the individual freedom of choice.[1203]

His fanaticism challenged the extremism by the Inquisition.

Those who were 'talented,' meaning the most obedient to the Word of God, could go on and study for whatever need there may be.[1204] But it is apparent that breaking from the Christian model was against Luther's goals. It is also no different from what the Catholic Church had in mind with 'education.'

With the help of the printing presses, an age of propagandist mass indoctrination had begun.

The novelty was that Luther targeted the entire population, not just the privileged. He intended to raise a new generation that was able to memorize religious texts to become worthy missionaries and church clerks.

Parents who did not send their children to Bible school acted *'as the worst enemies both of God and of men,'* said Luther. *'God will punish them terribly for it.'*[1205]

---

[1202] Ibid.
[1203] Ibid..
[1204] Luther, Large Catechism, 1529, WA 30 I,125-238.
[1205] Luther, Small Catechism, 1530.

To enforce obedience, Luther's Catechism was to be taught with examples of God's wrath against the non-compliant and of blessings for unconditional love for God.[1206] Whoever was not convinced by his teaching and not inclined to godliness, he would *'hand over to the hangman and to the skeleton-man.*[1207] This is a cartoonish expression for the impersonation of the Angel of Death. True to the basic concept of one body in church and state, this threat also extended to nobility.

Luther linked misfortune of all sorts with disobedience to his god or to civil authorities.[1208] Indeed, the only way society could find its way back to religious fundamentalism was through enforcement by the wrath of both, church and state.

Luther required total submission of the populace in a time where the free spread of information was accelerating through printed books.

Luther's impressive focus on creating a catechism that was almost free from the immediate worries of the day is admirable. With Turks in retreat, there would have been plenty of distractions that could have made the Reformer incorporate references to contemporary events.

One unfortunate exception was his wish to *'vanquish the Turks.*[1209] It constitutes the foundation of the distrust that Protestant Europeans came to harbour against the Turkish people, even today.

A few decades later, the Vatican published their competing catechism to program Catholic children.

Collateral damage to more common literacy was that humanism and secularism were also fueled.

The *'Large Catechism'* was completed before the small one, but the latter tells us most of what we need to know.

In the *'Large Catechism,'* Luther put down two passages that appear angrier than he normally wrote.

In one instance, Luther accused Jews of commonly and ordinarily bearing false witness.[1210]

---

[1206] Ibid.
[1207] Luther, Large Catechism, 1529, WA 30 I,125-238.
[1208] Ibid.
[1209] Ibid.
[1210] Ibid.

The other was addressed to both, heathens and Jews. He unleashed a short diatribe on how his god would overthrow *'all false worship, so that all who remain therein must finally perish.'* His rants were spiteful, targeting Jews for boasting *'defiantly of their Mammon,'* their wealth. They would *'be wrecked, with all in which they trusted; as all others have perished who have thought themselves more secure or powerful.* [1211]

Before, he had been swearing at Jews. But now, it was a death-wish, uttered by the Protestant leader. It was different from the earlier call to banishment. Now, non-compliance by Jews and heathens was terminal.

It was religious hatred and a call to violence exemplified.

Luther called for his god to *'deal a smashing blow and punish them.'* Those who hated his god *'fairly merit wrath,* [1212] as apparently brought upon these non-believers by the empowered Protestant bishops of nobility and its noble cronies.

Blood was flowing down the curbs. Luther was encouraging more of it.

The death wish emerges while David Reubeni and Solomon Molcho were high with their messianic mission. I will show that Luther was aware of the messianic presence amongst the ashes of Rome.

Luther continued to look at former Catholic clergy with disdain. Many priests were now Protestants under his domain. But some pastors and preachers were negligent in their duties, according to Luther, and ignored his (!) teaching *'from sheer laziness and care for their paunches.'* [1213]

Of course, they did not accept the Lutheran teachings without grumbling. Those, he called *'shameful gluttons and servants of their own bellies who ought to be more properly swineherds and dog-tenders than care-takers of souls and pastors.* [1214] They were neither inclined to buy Luther's books nor to read them. He called the rites of the Catholic Church *'unprofitable and burdensome babbling.'* Because the preachers were not familiar with his interpretation of the Gospel, Luther thought that they should feel shame. *'Like pigs and dogs they retain no more of the Gospel than such a lazy, pernicious, shameful, carnal liberty!'* [1215]

Luther repeatedly called those who did not study his Catechism daily, *'lazy paunches or presumptuous saints* [1216] for pretending to learn too quickly. The arguments of one of his competitors were *'silly prattle.* [1217]

---

[1211] Ibid.
[1212] Ibid.
[1213] Ibid.
[1214] Ibid.
[1215] Ibid.
[1216] Ibid.
[1217] Ibid.

Even among nobility, *'some louts and scrimps'*[1218] could be found, according to Luther, who thought that preachers and pastors were no longer needed. In the modern world of the sixteenth century, everything could be learned from books, they thought.

In consequence, by lack of support, some parishes fell into disuse, and preachers went hungry.

Luther saw this as a disgrace.

We can see in Martin Luther's evolution that *learning* had nothing to do with what moderns understand it to be. In Luther's world, learning was mass conformation. He had discovered a tool for indoctrinating the entire population through its children. With this, he could build critical mass in religious intolerance and bring forth his vision of The City of God. This would manifest itself in a series of little provincial theocracies under the rule of nobility and his umbrella – back to the good old times of the oppressive feudal system.

Learning was restricted to inseminating thought with the Word of God as explained in Luther's Catechism.

The sixteenth century was decisive in establishing the path to the freedoms of modernity. Even though the true revolution was in the explosion of the new mass media – the printed book. For few, it brought an attitude of exchanging and welcoming ideas that they did not necessarily agree with.

It almost seems as though modern mass media and social media are now hampering the exchange of ideas for the masses. This, in turn, provides a fruitful soil for a renewal of religious extremism, alternative realities, and conspiracy theories even in the West.

There is yet another parallel, more painful and more immediate: the rise of modern mass media, radio and movies. It does not seem by mere coincidence that Adolf Hitler and the other despots at the time, Stalin, Mussolini, or Franco, were masters of propaganda. Commercial radio broadcasting began in their lifetime. So did movies, which then started to play synchronized sound.

What might be in store for us moderns with the advent of social media has already been lived through during Martin Luther's time. Despots are on the rise all over the planet. Fascist ideas are supported in the voting booths. Our freedoms are under full-on assault – many of us have already handed them over voluntarily.

---

[1218] Ibid.

In order to foster Protestant fundamentalism, the teachings of Luther's Catechism were to be hammered into children's minds. Old dogs and rascals could be made neither obedient nor pious, according to Luther. In contrast, young saplings could be bent and trained.[1219]

To start with, they would learn the daily prayer, which calls for hastening the End of the World: *'They kingdom come.'* The methods back then distinguished themselves markedly from those to teach children in the modern West.

> [The prayer of 'Our Father' and the Ten Commandments] are the most necessary parts which one should first learn to repeat word for word, and which our children should be accustomed to recite daily when they arise in the morning, when they sit down to their meals, and when they retire at night; and until they repeat them, they should be given neither food nor drink. Likewise every head of a household is obliged to do the same with respect to his domestics, man-servants and maid-servants, and not to keep them in his house if they do not know these things and are unwilling to learn them. For a person who is so rude and unruly as to be unwilling to learn these things is not to be tolerated [...][1220]

That is how you condition a dog.

If youngsters *'transgressed'*, they should be punished with the rod.[1221] This was indeed my experience as a Catholic child. Luther's was a time when organized religion no longer enjoyed the high social status that its leaders wanted it to have. They were determined to force it back onto their subjects.

Modern Protestants learn his Catechism today. In 2015, the modern televangelist Pat Robertson advised this in response to the grievances of a Christian mother over unbelieving family members: *'Somebody take that kid to the woodshed and let him understand the blessings of discipline.'*[1222]

Physical punishment was the lesser crime.

Indoctrinating children is the graver sin.

How did Luther reconcile his punishing indoctrination campaign with the Christian concept of offering the other cheek? He swore at his enemies and wished them killed. Almost in the same breath, he talked about how the origin of murder was forbidden as much as murder itself was. He called for his subjects to *'have a patient, gentle heart, especially toward those who give us cause to be angry.'*[1223]

---

[1219] Luther, Keeping Children in School, 1967, 213-57.
[1220] Luther, Large Catechism, 1529, WA 30 I,125-238.
[1221] Ibid.
[1222] Pat Robertson in an interview on the Christian Broadcasting Network, 2015.
[1223] Luther, Large Catechism, 1529, WA 30 I,125-238.

His Christian kindness was meant to be confined to compliant members of the Lutheran community. After all, he had also called for total segregation and expulsion of all non-Lutherans. There was kindness only for those who agreed, and violence against all others.

The rule was also a matter of obedience by the common folks upon whom it should be *'impressed.'*[1224] The concept of total submission even extended to prohibiting the refusal of aid when a religious member needed it.

Yes, he created a rule to help a fellow Protestant Christian.

It does not come so naturally with a Catholic.

Or a Muslim. Or a Jew.

The hypocrisy of Luther's treachery against an all-inclusive and tolerant civilization lies exactly in submissive goodness within sectarian communal boundaries and the outright refusal even to engage in discourse with the 'other.' There, the love of the 'enemy' starts with passive aggression and progresses into refusal of aid and militant sectarian violence.

An implied death wish.

Martin Luther said that our whole life should be built on the foundation that it *'may be pleasing to God.'* From this *'good work'* should arise. He added *'that outside of the Ten Commandments no work or thing can be good or pleasing to God.'*[1225]

The Ten Commandments are sort of a mixed bag:[1226] 1) I am your God; 2) you shall not have other gods; 3) no idolatry; 4) do not tempt God's name; 5) honor your parents; 6) do not kill; 7) no adultery; 8) do not steal; 9) no false witness; 10) do not desire another man's wife. None of them appear to contribute to a more positive attitude toward a greater spirit of humanity.

Even the religious can draw no special benefit from them.

On the contrary.

The first four commandments are divisive in nature and intolerant of other beliefs. They only work for the interests of a community with *specific* beliefs. The other rules are common sense for any decent human being.

---

[1224] Ibid.
[1225] Ibid.
[1226] Exodus 20.

According to Luther, Christians are divided and separated *'from all other people upon earth. For all outside of Christianity, whether heathen, Turks, Jews, or false Christians and hypocrites, although they believe in, and worship, only one true God, yet know not what His mind towards them is, and cannot expect any love or blessing from Him; therefore they abide in eternal wrath and damnation.'*[1227]

Luther wrote yet another propaganda piece. In this, he discussed his doctrines of public ministry on how the Protestant preachers *'should exhort people to keep their children in school.'*[1228] It is a shameful attempt to force his doctrines upon young, impressionable minds.

Masquerading as a sermon and addressed to his pastors and preachers, Luther's text sets out to complain that Satan had deceived the common people so much that they were no longer willing to keep their children exposed to religious instruction at school. Instead, the focus had shifted to making a living and getting rich.[1229] This was satanic for Luther.

When he complained that the youth *'learn nothing and know nothing,'* he was referring to biblical proficiency. Those free from religion appear to have started to learn arithmetic and reading, but when it came to indoctrination, they seem to have taken their children out of school.

I have touched on it before, but the impression returns repeatedly through Luther's texts that northern Europe may have been more secularized during the Renaissance than we are led to believe. Of course, this could merely be a matter of perspective, where a few strove for making a living.

They were setting *'a bad example for all the other good citizens.'*[1230] For Luther, this was *'a real masterpiece of the devil's art.'*[1231]

In saying so, he shamed parents into submission by putting the burden of responsibility for a worsening world – for sin, death, hell, heresy, error, contention, war, and strife – onto them. Even the empire itself and the Kingdom of God would go down to destruction, along with the Christian faith, he threatened.[1232]

---

[1227] Luther, Large Catechism, 1529, WA 30 I,125-238.
[1228] Luther, Keeping Children in School, 1967, 213-57.
[1229] Ibid.
[1230] Ibid.
[1231] Ibid.
[1232] Ibid.

The refusal to helping his god's cause amounted to souls' eternal damnation in the abyss of hell.[1233] The security for wives, children, houses, homes, and property was at stake. It was the responsibility of those who refused to cooperate if this security were lost.[1234] The Reformer applied similar principles to education as he did to war.

His playbook was very limited, indeed.

Limited to faith.

In all this, Luther maintained a disgraceful submission to the feudal class. They were busy with being heirs, he thought. Poor people do not need heirs. He reasoned that the children of the poor should not be educated in making a living but rather in becoming doctors of holy scripture and in becoming ordinary pastors.[1235]

Let the poor keep poverty to themselves.

The Reformer complained about some universities and boys' schools that had been backed by the Catholic Church being so deserted that it distressed him.[1236] He recognized the necessity of making recruitment into the priestly class a priority. As a convincing incentive, the conformed poor were promised occupation in the churches. How could he otherwise fill the open ranks of pastors and preachers, just a few years down the road?[1237] As a bonus, church servants did not need to worry about anything.

The table was already set for them in the short-staffed parishes.[1238]

More jobs were made available for the mass-conformed, first and foremost in government organizations, where good Protestants could replace Jews. We must not forget that the head of the state was now also the head of the church. In this way, the government could choose its staff based on orthodoxy.

This was an effective strategy for a nationalist church organization.

The most pressing problem that Luther saw was that after death, people would appear before God unprepared. This would render them as wild as Turks. With this denigration, the Reformer attempted to emphasize the uselessness of Islam.[1239]

---

[1233] Ibid.
[1234] Ibid.
[1235] Ibid.
[1236] Ibid.
[1237] Ibid.
[1238] Ibid.
[1239] Ibid.

In response to this barbaric fear, his model for schooling children was to raise them for God's service. Nothing else. In his mind, the End of the World could be brought about only with such a stringent approach.

Those who did not comply would be *'completely rooted out – you, your children, and everything else.'*[1240] Luther's threat was eternal damnation in hell.[1241]

Peace, said Luther in the same train of thought, *'is really a fruit of true preaching.'*[1242] War and sectarian unrest are the result of false preaching, according to him.[1243]

As was said earlier, Martin Luther was all about submission to God and against the rise of humanity to orient itself toward making a living. There was no distinction between making an honest living and worshipping money.

For Luther, it was all the same.

It signified the loss of the world in which religiously *'ignorant louts'* were raised to become *'utter asses.'*[1244] He compared those who focused on making a living with *'hogs wallowing forever with their noses in the dunghill.'* They were either crazy or without love for their children.[1245] Should preaching and church law fail, Luther was convinced, business would also go down.[1246]

Luther offered no intellectual insight into why the loss of preaching should have an adverse effect on business.

It was so because he said so.

Since he first portrayed himself a prophet,[1247] he had become a know-it-all. Prophet Luther.

His religious evolution comes across like the creation of a 'correct' religion in the mold of Persian Safavids and Ottoman-Turks. The sole object was world power – through social engineering in order to subvert the Holy Roman Empire. He was correct, though. Only a prophet could bring about such changes. From then on, he promoted himself increasingly as being enlightened from on high.

---

[1240] Ibid.
[1241] Ibid.
[1242] Ibid.
[1243] Ibid.
[1244] Ibid.
[1245] Ibid.
[1246] Ibid.
[1247] Ibid.

For humanity, making a living constituted the beginning of a long struggle out of the oppression of organized religion. Opposing this drive, Luther wanted a more stringent control of society by his church. Many wanted none it – Luther frequently suggested *'almost all.'*

It is not by chance that Luther was called out by secular humanists for not teaching good works. In retaliation, the rebel prophet responded with his customary diatribes: *'They are like the cawing of jackdaws and ravens, though not as good. For the daws at least like to caw; they do so gladly. But the sophists take no pleasure in their croaking; they caw reluctantly, like the hoopoes and owls.'* [1248]

Those who refused to send their children to religious school, he called *'pious hypocrite and unproductive weed.'* [1249]

Secular humanists promoted the teaching of critical thinking and innovation. They started to oppose preservation of unhealthy religious tribal warfare or political absolutism.

Once they got the facts straight, multiple valid solutions emerged on how to address even seemingly insurmountable problems.

Most of the time.

---

[1248] Ibid.
[1249] Ibid.

### The Messiah in Luther-land

With the imperial victory over France, Pope Clement and King Francis had no choice but to submit to Emperor Charles. But it speaks for itself that the French-friendly Vatican and Francis continued to subvert this relationship.

Francis was now married to Charles' sister Eleonora, the widow of the King of Portugal. For this, Pope Clement had to remove the matrimonial barriers of the third and fourth degrees of consanguinity.[1250]

Declared *'legally elected'* by Clement, Charles became the last emperor to be crowned by a pope.[1251] The public spectacle took place on Charles' thirtieth birthday.

The two met at Bologna where Charles kneeled before the Holy Father to kiss his foot. He was then crowned King of Lombardy (Milan is its capital) and Roman Emperor. The jeweled crown symbolized world rule. The people who lined the streets to watch the procession were shouting with joy.

They were motivated by gold and silver that was being thrown into the streets.

The coins had previously been extorted from them.

Among the illustrious invited guests was Rabbi Joel of Rosheim,[1252] a sort of king of Ashkenazy Jews, and Cardinal Hieronymus Aleandro, one of Luther's archenemies.

Thereafter, Charles forced Clement to excommunicate the Christian Ottoman Vassal King in Hungary, whom the pope had earlier recognized. Given the harsh consequences for an excommunicated leader, it turned out to be a mistake of monumental proportions. The kingdom had been guaranteed to maintain its Christian culture, if only through paying the Muslim head tax.

But now all cards were on the table.

Before this decision, Lutherans were under threat of life and limb.[1253] Now, their persecution stopped.

Lutheranism became the nobles' fad of the time.

---

[1250] Setton, 1984, 328: the papal dispensation is dated February 18, 1530.
[1251] Michael Erbe, Die Habsburger 1493 – 1918, Eine Dynastie im Reich und in Europa (Kohlhammer, 2000).
[1252] Josel or Joseph of Rosheim, also Joselmann, Yoselmann, or Joselin, aka Joseph Ben Gershon Loanz or Joseph ben Gershon mi-Rosheim, 1480 – 1554.
[1253] Edict of Diet of Hungary, 1523, in Andrew Pettegree, The early Reformation in Europe (Cambridge University Press) Article 48 (54):1523.

The reaction in Istanbul to the peace of Bologna tells us everything we need to know. The words came from the Grand Vizier to Suleiman the Magnificent:

*The faith of Christians was writ in snow, that of the Sultan [Suleiman] in marble, and [that] there must needs be but one monarch in the world, either the emperor or his own lord.*[1254]

This grand vizier, Ibrahim Pasha (Abraham, it may be noted), thought very highly of himself. Yes, that is the grand vizier who had sponsored Molla Kabiz, Mulcarabum (Mulca the Arab), the Messiah who was to morph into Solomon Molcho.

The grand vizier was so full of himself, indeed, that he claimed to be the ruler of the Ottoman Empire. It was he who exercised the power. He controlled all the offices and all the kingdoms of the Sultan. War and peace were in his hands, even if Suleiman the Magnificent decided otherwise.[1255]

One might think that such grandeur would mark Ibrahim's death-sentence.

However, the grand vizier was sitting on a parallel throne. A dual government with Suleiman holding the supreme spiritual lead with Ibrahim wielding the Davidic sword. The iron rod. His claim to superiority over government affairs is not unusual. It is as it should be in Islam. The Throne of David is commanded in the Koran.

We know nothing about Ibrahim's heritage, other than that he is claimed to having been an Orthodox. It is another historic lapse in placing 'Orthodox' into the camp of Christianity. He was supposedly from a town called Parga in northwestern Greece. This town had acted as one of few refuges for persecuted Jews from Spain.

We do know that Suleiman had him executed a few years later. While we do not know the details, we will soon find out why.

This Grand Vizier Ibrahim Pasha claimed something extraordinary. In a meeting with imperial ambassadors that took place in Istanbul, he boasted that he himself was responsible for the inability of the Catholic Church to hold a general council. How could he make such a claim? Did he use the Jewish Rabbinic network to subvert the church organization? Was he manipulating the Lutherans? Was he part of the messianic plot?

Undercover?

---

[1254] Sanudo, Diarii, L111, 8, in Setton, 1984, 338.
[1255] Setton, 1984, 375.

At the same meeting, the grand vizier opined that neither the pope nor Francis were on the side of Charles. They would never come to love the emperor, he prophesied.[1256] He was not mistaken about that.

However, Charles had a plan to change these parameters. The city state of Florence was now the only place of overt resistance against the imperial forces. Venice was feigning neutrality. The emperor could potentially take care of these two by influencing the pope's will. In order to stop the subversions of Clement, Charles spent five months with the pope under the same roof at Bologna.[1257]

Charles had Pope Clement on a rope.

But an even bigger conflict kept Charles preoccupied with internal strife: the Lutherans. Except for sheer luck, the emperor could hardly engage in external warfare. Trying to 'unite' the Germans under the Catholic Church may not have been the smartest of his moves. Just to deal with his enemies who had turned 'friends,' he would have had his hands full. Former enemies make for unreliable allies. They might as well watch him walk into a trap. Even encourage him to do so. In particular, when war had them all ruined.

How much the Catholic Church felt the pinch of the Lutheran rebellion could be measured in money. According to rumor, the Vatican's income had fallen by over half,[1258] and that is probably still optimistic. The endless inter-Christian wars must have taken a heavy toll on population and income.

Nevertheless, we can learn from a diplomatic brief from Regensburg to Venice that Charles wanted to challenge Suleiman on the eastern borders of his empire…

> *… and not to leave until one of them becomes the victor, for in overcoming the enemy he will acquire the further merit of fighting for the faith, the state, and glory for himself and his posterity, and dying he will achieve at least the salvation of his soul and the glory of the kingdom of heaven.*[1259]

The minds of grandeur agreed to a God-commanded world rule. To this end, they were willing to give it another try and clash at Armageddon.

But church business had to be taken care of first.

---

[1256] Setton, 1984, 380.

[1257] Eduard Vehse, Memoirs of the Court and Aristocracy of Austria, Volume 1 (Nichols, 1894) 61.

[1258] Cf. Sanudo, LIII, 15-16, in Setton, 1984, 339.

[1259] Sanudo, Diarii, LVI, 17, in Setton, 1984, 358.

In the spring of 1530, Emperor Charles called for the long-promised church conference to address questions of sectarian divisions, war against the Ottoman Empire, and other political matters. At this time, Martin Luther was again an imperial outlaw. In his place, Johann of Saxony the Steadfast and Philip I of Hesse the Magnanimous attended the Diet of Augsburg to defend Protestant beliefs.

They came prepared.

For this meeting, Luther and a few of his closest theologians worked out a document that became known as the *'Augsburg Confession.'* It is the most important document of the Reformation and consists of twenty-eight articles that amount to a statement of faith. Besides the removal of outwardly rituals, they insisted on the sacrament wherein Jesus Christ's body and blood is factually present in the bread and wine. As had long been custom in Ethiopia,[1260] priests would be allowed to marry.

They were still envisioning *one undivided* Christian church. It would be located wherever the Gospel was preached correctly. In addition, only those who were *'rightly called'* would be allowed to preach publicly.

This *one* church was *not* the Catholic Church.

It was supposed to be another show trial anyway, with a predetermined outcome. But the script had been badly prepared by the Catholic Church. The *'Pontifical Confutation of the Augsburg Confession'* was never properly published. The meeting ended again in a non-decision. This was perhaps the best outcome for the Protestant movement, and the lengthy process gave Luther a break to further expand his propaganda machinery.

The Republic of Florence got decisively beaten that same year. However, Emperor Charles did not seem to have had his senses together. He installed Allessandro de' Medici the Moor as the leader of the city. This man is believed to having been an illegitimate son of the Medici Pope Clement VII.[1261] The office for Florence's lead was purchased by the Vatican, so the legend goes.

Unknowingly, Charles could have been in for a surprise were it not for the medieval practice of forging family loyalties through arranged marriages. It was part of the complex pact between Charles and the exhausted Clement.

---

[1260] Alvarez, transl. Alderley, 1881, 191-192 .

[1261] Catherine Fletcher, The Black Prince of Florence: The Spectacular Life and Treacherous World of Alessandro de' Medici (Bodley Head, 2016) 16, 280-81.

Allessandro the Moor married an illegitimate daughter[262] of the emperor. The deal included the restoration of the Papal States to a now subordinate Vatican – a manifestation of Protestant ideals.

Soon thereafter a distant cousin assassinated Allessandro in the name of the Republic of Florence.

The intention of the pope remained to forge peace in Europe in order to bring war to Ottoman-Turks. However, he might have had the same Davidic treachery in mind as Luther before him: send the emperor to the front lines. Regardless, since everyone's strengths had been spent, the prospect of an uneasy peace might indeed have been at hand.

The Protestants did not play along.

Charles could not achieve religious and political unity in his empire. On the contrary, it was marching toward breaking to pieces with reformers turning up the heat. Protestant leaders refused to comply with imperial directives and prepared for violent defense. Their basis was that the emperor had overstepped his rights in trying to prohibit the new faith, thus providing for the rationale for just war, yet again. Obedience but disobedience. Their only principle was that whoever challenged their combined religious and noble power merited armed love.

Martin Luther and his pals had gone militant against Charles.

This was the defining moment for the final separation of the Protestant Church from the Catholic main body. They would soon stand apart.

Johann of Saxony the Steadfast and Philip I of Hesse the Magnanimous formed the Schmalkaldic League, a rebellious alliance against the imperialists. The King of France supported the league with money and cannons.[263] Under the condition that the Lutheran *'Augsburg Confession'* was embraced, everyone could join. This ensured rapid Protestant growth in Germany at the cost of the Catholic Church.

Breaking with Charles, the League reached higher: replacing the Holy Roman Empire.[264] This was the moment of coming out.

The only one who seems to have been unaware of these goals all along was the emperor himself.

---

[262] Margaret of Austria (1522-1586) was a daughter of a beautiful servant, Johanna Maria van der Gheynst, with whom Charles V had a love affair.
[263] Setton, 1984, 386-387e.
[264] John Merriman, A History of Modern Europe, Volume One: From the Renaissance to the Age of Napoleon (Norton, 2009) 110.

Surrendering to the new reality of imperial supremacy, the pope issued the Papal Bull Intra Arcana, which essentially handed power over the New World to Emperor Charles. Defenseless 'Barbarians' in the newly acquired territories were to be missionized upon with all zeal, if need be *'by force and arms.'*[1265] The Catholic Church was determined to bring its 'culture' to the Americas. This strategy had begun as Franciscan missions during the previous three decades. It found a highlight in former Pope Julius II's establishment of the first dioceses of *Spanish rule* – as history came to portray the deadly mission – including one in Puerto Rico (Catholics would come to be among the persecuted in the British North American colonies).

The Americas were on a path to death by faith that was expanded to unspeakable proportions.

All 'Barbaric' civilizations in the Americas collapsed.

Apologists go as far as proclaiming that conversions were prohibited by Canon Law. They assert that the meaning could not possibly have been militaristic conversions.

Christians should know better: in ever so many occasions, the dead speak for themselves. The Papal Bull also included Charles' right to appoint priests to his liking and a promise to recant papal excommunications or suspensions that might contradict Charles' selections.

We already knew from the context that the papal signature did not come voluntarily.

But that does not absolve the Catholic Church from its collusion and leadership in the terror that overcame the Americas. As the example of Portugal showed, they could have refused to follow through. First, they did not. Second, with their behavioral patterns, they would have unleashed the same terror upon the New World anyway.

Interestingly, many conversos sailed along to the newly discovered continents. An example from Mexico demonstrates that some purchased so-called certificates of 'Purity of Blood', attesting to their families' continued Catholicism for at least four generations.[1266] These certificates were obtained through briberies. Organized crime. In the new territories, the pure-blooded were raised to high ranks and even became governors.[1267]

Bribes paid off handsomely.

---

[1265] Pope Clement VII, Papal Bull Intra Arcana, May 8, 1529.
[1266] Jewishhistory.org.il, 1523 Mexico.
[1267] For example, Jewishhistory.org.il, 1522 Gil Gonzalez de Avila (Central America).

The French King was back to plotting harder against the empire. He wished that Ottoman-Turks were all-powerful and willing to go to war against the Holy Roman Empire.[1268] Suleiman the Magnificent was indeed on the move again. His goal was once more to sack Vienna with a massive army. It was relayed through the diplomatic channels that there would be only one true monarch in the world, either Charles or Suleiman.[1269]

Biblical prophecy was about to fulfil itself.

Learning from the last retreat, the Ottoman timing for the challenge was better. The campaign was designed to be *'a show of force and a long procession through Southeastern and Central Europe, rather than a campaign with specific military objectives.*[1270] This romantic portrayal of Suleiman's intentions does not hold water. Entering Belgrade, Suleiman showed off a crown made in Venice that was supposed to symbolize that his rule surpassed the triple crown of the papal Tiara, as well as Charles' imperial crown.

It was a quadruple crown.

To end the dispute, Suleiman invited Charles to the Final Battle – Armageddon – to settle their aspirations once and for all. In a letter, Suleiman expressed that it was Charles that he was after and that he was otherwise seeking peace with everyone.[1271]

Just how peaceful Ottoman-Turks were is written in their history of jihad.

The speed of their advance toward Vienna was astonishing.

The Holy Roman Empire was under assault from three sides. But to fend off the Ottoman-Turks, Emperor Charles conceded to the Religious Peace of Nuremberg. In light of the common enemy, the internal threat to the Lutherans was substantially reduced.

For then.

In October of 1530, an already-shattered Rome was battered by torrential rains. The Tiber River overflowed and ruined the Eternal City, yet again. Palaces collapsed, and provisions were washed away. Houses and shops crumbled.

[1268] Roger Crowley, Empire of the sea (Faber & Faber, 2008) 66, Francis I to the Venetian ambassador.
[1269] Şahin, Süleyman, 2013, 82.
[1270] Ibid., originally quoted from Ágoston, Information, Ideology, and Limits of Imperial Policy, 100–101. For the symbolic nature of the campaign also see Murphey, Süleyman I and the Conquest of Hungary, 214–16; Özlem Kumrular, Campaña de Alemania: Rito, arte y demostración, in L'Empire Ottoman dans l'Europe de la Renaissance…, eds. Alain Servantie et. al. (Leuven: Leuven University Press, 2005), 191–214.
[1271] As quoted from Von Gévay, 1-5, no. XXV, pp. 87-88, in Setton, 1984, 364–365.

The messianic pair, Reubeni and Molcho, buoyed ever higher.

The prophecy had come true.

It was a widespread Christian belief that this was a punishment from God.

Jews, instead, thought of the Lord as just. Not a single Jew had drowned.

Only one old Jewish woman died that day. *'It was the finger of God.'*

The miracle of the wonderful fall of Rome must be told to the children of all coming generations of Jews.[1272]

They prided themselves for not having warned the gentiles.

After Rome had been devastated twice, Luther held lectures on the Book of the Galatians. In its preface, the Reformer pointed out a direct contrast between Jews and Catholics. He thought that the madness of the synagogue was mere child's play in comparison.[1273] Jews at least took Jesus Christ for a thief who deserved to be crucified, whereas the Catholic Church regarded Jesus as a fable.[1274] From the context, it is not surprising that Luther was still focused on competing with the Catholic Church and its Antichrist, the pope, as well as with the Anabaptists. However, in a passing remark, he asked whether his *'bitter conflicts and so many sharp battles against the Jews'* were not known to his audience.[1275]

Such 'battles' against Jews manifested itself in these lectures. Therein, he cited Saint Paul for the children of Abraham being those who believe, not those in the biblical prophet's literal linage. Because Jews did not believe, being of the seed of Abraham was of no consequence. Logically, the inheritance of the Promised Land belonged to Christians who believed.[1276]

All Luther needed to do was to allow for *Abraham's seed* to be a *parable* for the *faithful* as the heirs of the world.[1277]

He simply applied the parable style of Jesus Christ to Abraham.

His anger was a response to the real-world messianic events.

The biblical inheritance of world leadership marks the cornerstone to all conflicts in Judaic religions, including all current ones in the Middle East. The End of the World with the total destruction and the final war at Armageddon has but one purpose: to claim the inheritance of the Promised Land. The idea

---

[1272] Ha-Cohen, Vol. II, translated by Bialloblotzky, 1836, 134-135.
[1273] Martin Luther, The Letter to the Galatians, lecture 1531 (1535).
[1274] Ibid.
[1275] Ibid.
[1276] Ibid.
[1277] Ibid.

wreaked havoc on the entire known earth for almost 2,000 years before Luther and continued to do so for 500 years after him. It will scorch the earth for generations to come.

This very question hit home literally under Luther's feet.

The whole manipulation circus, the treachery, and the betrayals were motivated by the one goal: conquest of the Promised Land. Perhaps Luther was not completely out of his mind after all when he sharpened his focus like a laser on denying the Jewish inheritance.

The timing of his denial is remarkable.

He directly addressed Reubeni's and Molcho's claims. Knowing of their presence, he would come to directly refer to them.

Luther faced *'Hadrian's Choice'*.

He purposefully packaged his message within the biblical narrative, taking the Bible for laws, which he could present like a court case. As the 'lawyer' – and judge – of the Protestant Church, he would need to refrain from striding too far from the 'evidence.'

But his inclusion of the Christian Gospels in his arguments against the Jewish claim to the Promised Land was a stretch, to say the least. Arguing with a 'local' law of faith that does not apply to aliens of another faith who want to live in a faraway land makes little sense. Having earlier claimed that faith should be voluntary, Luther had no jurisdiction over his adversaries by his own ideology – other than sending them to exile in the Promised Land. In the one outcome of the case, the Rabbinic leaders could claim their inheritance of the world; in the other, where faith alone was the guiding hand,[1278] the true and only church of God, Luther's Protestant Church, could do the same.

Why was this important?

In a letter that was styled as a battle cry, he literally took the position that Christ had begun to reign.[1279] The Second Jesus had arrived.

The world would go up in flames either way.

Martin Luther was already working on arriving at his darkest moment.

Most of Luther's teachings against Jews so far were merely self-inflicted through scripture, which had been written by Jewish leaders. But now it was different. His anti-Semitism was turning personal.

---

[1278] Ibids.
[1279] Martin Luther, Letter to the Leipsic People who were Banished for the Gospel, October 4, 1532.

In contrast, Jews claimed that the Holy Books were written by the hand of God. It was God-inflicted anti-Semitism – written down by Jewish scribes, the left and right hands of God.

Luther was cognizant of the Jewish desire for a messiah to bring about the End of the World and the conquest of the Promised Land. He noted that, according to Jews, their messiah had not yet come, and he thought of his coming as a detestable dream.[1280]

The contradiction in Luther's thinking was that the Second Jesus can only have arrived if the Jewish Messiah was present. He knew that they were in Rome, but he did not seem to have taken them seriously. Were Reubeni and Molcho playing Jews, Catholics, Protestants, and Muslims, all at the same time?

The Reformer went further in enforcing the abolishment of Moses' Law. Jesus Christ and Moses could not agree, he said.[1281]

This provides for a key to fully understand Martin Luther: faith alone is the defining element, not laws, not outwardly appearance, not belonging to an ethnic or racial group, but nothing other than faith[1282] – in the Lutheran interpretation of Augustinian Christianity, that is. We can see this theme throughout his works. It is the pivot from which all understanding springs, including his anti-Semitism.

However, we must not fail to note that this anti-Semitic outburst came together with the League having risen to challenge the Holy Roman Empire. Martin Luther's Reformation was now in a position of real power. It made a dramatic difference to what this leader of the Protestant Church could say.

There is more to it.

Rabbi Josel of Rosheim wrote in his memoirs that there was an outcry against Jews in 1529/30, because they were accused of being in treasonous communications with Ottoman-Turks. In consequence, Emperor Charles prohibited the presence of Jews in Württemberg and other German territories.

Indeed, in a decision by Charles to grant safe-conduct for a number of ships, the monarch refused, *'saying that the galleys carry Moors [Muslims] and Jews, who are his enemies and [come and go] as spies.'*[1283]

---

[1280] Luther, Galatians, 1535.
[1281] Ibid.
[1282] Ibid.
[1283] Sanudo, Diarii, LIV, 428 in Setton, 1984, 347.

After Rosheim wrote an apology to the court of Innsbruck, their privileges were reinstated there.[1284] Rosheim probably appealed against collective punishment, which is always a powerful argument, and insisted on papal and imperial privileges that had formerly been granted to the Rabbinic leadership.

Nobody at the imperial court appears to have sensed that Jewish leaders had been working together all along through an ultra-loyal network across the Diaspora. Those who knew did not tell.

The outcry was not based on rumors. It was real. The treachery was orchestrated by none other than David Reubeni and Solomon Molcho. Luther's hateful language was not accidental. The accusation of treachery was common wisdom, and this news reached Luther. After all, leadership depends on the flow of information.

Rabbi Josel von Rosheim was an important man of his time, a money lender. He rose to become a defender of Jews at the imperial court. In this function, Rosheim had attended the coronation of Emperor Charles in Bologna. He helped to stop the anti-Semitic plans of the former Jew Pfefferkorn, whose pamphlet we had looked into earlier. His defense was so effective that Pfefferkorn was burnt and torn to pieces with red-hot pliers.[1285]

Rosheim soon became the leader of the Jewish communities in Lower Alsace, situated along the Rhine River in modern France, and then of all Jews in the Holy Roman Empire as well as in Poland. This rabbi was the 'Regierer',[1286] the ruler, sort of a king of the Jews, the one in command of the German and Polish Jews, the Ashkenazys.

We will hear from him again.

For a while already, Luther had seen himself as a prophet.

Now, he paralleled himself boastfully with Saint Paul, who had attracted the hatred of Gentiles and Jews alike.[1287] I am Martin Luther, he said, repulsed by the world.[1288] I am like Saint Paul.[1289] *'Am I therefore become your enemy because I tell you the Truth?'*[1290]

---

[1284] Joseph of Rosheim, The Historical Writings of Joseph of Rosheim: Leader of Jewry in Early Modern Germany, transl. A.J. Deus.

[1285] Sebastian Franck, Chronica Zeitbuch und Geschichtsbibel, (Beck, 1531) 224.

[1286] Because this designation was perceived as an insult to the imperial court, the crown fined Josel von Rosheim (see Ludwig Feilchenfeld, Rabbi Josel von Rosheim (Heitz, 1898) 12-15.

[1287] Luther, Galatians, 1535.

[1288] Ibid.

[1289] Ibid.

[1290] Ibid.

He meant to say, *'Do not mess with me and my religious community.'*

His successes had gone to Luther's head.

Grandeur became his principle.

He topped his lecture off by portraying not only himself as hated, but his entire community as well. I have shown before how this is part of the religious binding mechanism. Hate and being hated. It provides for common enemies.

Being hated and persecuted was to be rejoiced, *'for they are a seal and most sure testimony of true doctrine and faith.'*[1291] Obviously, the portrayal of self-hatred was not by accident, neither for Protestants nor for Jews. It is one of the most dangerous tools in the arsenal of organized religion because it appeals to the most basic of human instincts. It triggers unmerited compassion.

It works.

And in the same breath, Luther legitimized the Promised Land for the Chosen People.

Persecuted Jews were testimony for their Truth.

The Reformer brought forth over twenty preface commentaries during that year and the following two.

In a preface to the biblical book Prophet Ezekiel, Luther repeated his denial of the wish for a messiah to them. Jews injure themselves with their messianic dream.[1292] His arrival had already been biblically fulfilled under the Persian Emperor Cyrus almost 2,000 years earlier.[1293] Because of that, he argued 'logically,' Jews could not insist on the old covenant because they did not want to accept the new one under Jesus Christ.[1294]

There was another covenant, which Luther rejected as casually as Jews did away with Jesus Christ: the covenant with Prophet Muhammad. However, Luther appears to have been unable to think through his own logic.

We can be sure that the Rabbinic leadership fully embraced Luther's grandstanding with peaceful quietism.

---

[1291] Ibid.
[1292] Ibid.
[1293] Martin Luther, Preface to the Prophet Ezekiel, 1532.
[1294] Ibid.

Another man then published an anti-Semitic book, *The Whole Jewish Belief.*[1295] It was written by a Jewish convert to Lutheranism, Anton Margaritha, born to the top Rabbi in Regensburg.[1296]

He was the author of the before-presented account about the events leading to the expulsion of Jews from his city. His work is credited with having shaped Luther's anti-Semitic position. The Reformer indeed referred to him.[1297]

However, Luther had come to his conclusions independently. Luther's evolution and what led to his position are directly tied to the active messianic pair.

Jewish commentators brand Margaritha's work as libel.[1298]

It found its inspiration in hatred.

But this is illogical.

After all, the whistleblower was not only Jewish, but also from a prominent family of the Talmudic authority at the time.[1299]

The denouncers went as far as belittling his knowledge of Hebrew, even though he was a teacher of that language at the universities of Leipzig, Augsburg, Tübingen, and Vienna. His errors and misunderstandings of theology were portrayed as total ignorance. But his arguments lack convincing refutation by his decriers. Supposedly, he had parroted another anti-Semitist who had written a pamphlet against the Jews for a Catholic bishop a few decades earlier.[1300]

Because Margaritha was criticized for lack of knowledge, for abusive translations, or for orthographic errors (!), we *must* examine his booklet.

Assessing his work is not made easy because Margaritha spelled out words phonetically and mixed some Yiddish into the text. Even to put his work into proper modern German would be a challenge.[1301] His style left open a ready flank of attack against his intelligence.

---

[1295] Margaritha, Jewish Belief, 1544.

[1296] Ibid., 110.

[1297] Luther, Jews and Their Lies, 1971, part X.

[1298] Joseph Mieses, Die älteste gedruckte deutsche Übersetzung des jüdischen Gebetsbuches a.d. Jahre 1530 und ihr Author Anthonius Margaritha (Löwit, 1916)

[1299] Ibid.

[1300] Ibid., 26, and footnote 3.

[1301] The critics seem to have missed that the author thought of his own German so poorly that he promised never to write again in that language. Margaritha, Jewish Belief, 1544, 258.

From his work, it is apparent that he had learned some sort of household wisdom from his prominent parents – or he played with his readers. The privilege of having grown up in a Talmudic home did not make him an expert, of course. As an example, he had been taught – as perhaps a mother would teach her son – that Jews had black hair because they hid it under their hats and because they did not eat pork.[1302] Also, his text unmasks a mind that had been raised in segregation, not unlike some modern Ultra-Orthodox Jews.

However, he knew enough to be able to lay down the Thirteen Rules of Ishmael on how the secrets of the Talmud would be elucidated.[1303]

Margaritha's *The Whole Jewish Belief* is an entirely different genre than Luther's works. Luther criticized Jews for their failure to convert and their insistence on the inheritance of the Promised Land. Margaritha's work is a Jewish critique from an internal perspective. He rarely made references to the news of the time.

Luther's was the broad horizon of an army general, Margaritha's the narrow outlook of a foot soldier.

The book starts out more descriptive than Luther's vendettas. At times, it is even hilarious, in particular when the author compared Jewish with Christian superstitions – were it not so tragic. For example, he described how Jews slaughtered a cock and fed its entrails to ravens. The ritual ensured that Jews' sins were sent to hell in their stead.

He portrayed this as ridiculous. For Christians, Jesus died for the sins of his followers. Jews laughed at the notion that a man could have suffered for another or have carried his sins. If a man was hungry, they said, another could not eat for him. Hear, blind Jew, Margaritha retorted, with your Talmud, which has darkened the Truth with your cocks: a cock could not carry your sin. A person sinned.[1304]

Since the discourse refuted both Jewish and Christian beliefs, his faith must have made him blind to logical thinking.

When he described how Jews viewed Christians as unclean and did not wish them well,[1305] Margaritha merely spelled out a part of the mechanism to form communal boundaries. Perhaps he did not understand all the fine points of the Talmud, and maybe he mistranslated some of it – all of which is in doubt

[1302] Ibid., 20.
[1303] Ibid., 129-135.
[1304] Ibid., 50-56, argument against the Jews.
[1305] Ibid., 26.

because of his heritage. When a son criticizes his father for his crimes, a kernel may turn out to be true.

Noteworthy is Margaritha's style and cadence of dramaturgy. Unlike Luther's, his work is difficult to 'appreciate' without the full picture. His text is a description of the banalities of rituals, customs, and prayers. It is beefed up with accounts about the hatred of Jews for their Christian hosts. It also attempts to explain – with counter-hatred – why Jews were deplorable because of it.

This is how Jews hate us, he elaborated, and they deserve to be hated back.

This hatred against all outsiders and a drive to become the rulers over everybody else comes to a climax in Margaritha's account over the aspiration of Jews to return to the Promised Land.

Jews wished to sprinkle Christian blood on the walls, meaning to kill them.[1306] That Jewish leaders aimed at the destruction of the *'seed of Esau'* can indeed be taken from the Talmud.[1307] It is academic consensus that the successors of Esau, the Edomites, have always been equated with Rome by the Talmudists.[1308] They were later symbolically connected with Christianity as Rome's successors. But frankly, nobody appears to have been interested in better understanding this strange connection between Esau and Rome. This is not the place to explore it, but: what is behind it?

Although I hold the Jewish leadership to be of unsurpassed intelligence, this transfer of hatred from Rome to Christianity was perhaps an unfortunate error in judgment. If it was not real. It put Esau back in charge over Abraham's inheritance to the Promised Land, for which he had been betrayed by Jacob.

The effect is – following Talmudic logic – that Rome (and later Christianity) were the rightful owners of the Promised Land.

Like Luther, Margaritha trailed the prescriptions of the Gospels, which viewed Jews as dumb, blind, and stiff-necked for their refusal to accept Jesus Christ as the Messiah who had arrived.[1309] Their superstition was foolish and their interpretation of scripture erroneous.[1310]

Jews were bragging about being the masters of Christians, who they viewed as their servants.[1311]

---

[1306] Ibid., 69-70.
[1307] Talmud – Mas. Pesachim 5a.
[1308] Talmud – Mas. Gittin 57b.
[1309] Margaritha, Jewish Belief, 1544, 13.
[1310] Ibid.
[1311] Ibid., 30.

The whole week, Jews would think of nothing but usury and of buying and selling goods for profit.[1312] While modern Westerners no longer have issues with profits, the problem with usury is a particularly vulnerable flank for Judaism. In his argument, Margaritha quoted from the Bible that usury was prohibited among Jews but was encouraged with strangers.[1313]

Christians were not their brothers in flesh or in faith and were free game.

Jews would lend to many nations, but they would not borrow from them.[1314]

Jews prayed for the riches of the entire world to be handed to them and wished for the destruction of Christians, whom they called Edomites, he said.[1315]

They asked for a great war between Christians or with Ottoman-Turks,[1316] hoping that they would fall to the enemy and perish.[1317]

Margaritha promised to come forth with another document about how the usury of Jews was damaging Christianity. His intention was to give Christian rulers the strength to prohibit and weed out the menace.[1318]

Taking away the lending for interest from them and making them work, he argued, would be the key to their willingness to convert to Christianity.[1319] Allowing their usury strengthened their belief that they were the Chosen People and that their god had not left them.[1320]

The fact that Christianity accepted them as the Chosen People only strengthened their resolve.[1321]

The idea of a chosen people is the mother of supremacy, division, racism, and genocide – and anti-Semitism.

The trouble with the hopes of Jews was, as Margaritha observed, that they were dependent on the fulfillment of the commands of the god of the Israelites by the entire Jewish community. Fail one – fail all. Since Jews had been unsuccessful in keeping the divine commandments for 1,500 years, these privileges were null and void, and their god threatened to have them live in

---

[1312] Ibid., 31.

[1313] Deuteronomy 23:19 – 23:20 (NIV).

[1314] Margaritha, Jewish Belief, 1544, 94.
  Deuteronomy 15:6 (NIV), see also Deuteronomy 28:12,

[1315] Ibid., 32.

[1316] Ibid., 33.

[1317] Ibid., 66.

[1318] Ibid., 98.

[1319] Ibid., 159.

[1320] Ibid.

[1321] Ibid., 159.

servitude.[1322] Logically, this line of business with money for interest should be prohibited for Jews, and they should perform ordinary work instead, Margaritha advocated.[1323]

So says the Bible also.[1324]

The Jewish apostate also commented on the persecution that others suffered who tried to expose Jewish machinations. Instead of accepting testimonies of whistleblowers, cheap excuses by learned Jews were believed, he said.[1325]

Margaritha's hatred of his father's co-religionists is sickening.

However, claiming that this work was decisive in Luther's coming determination against Jews makes little sense. He may have picked up a couple of pointers, and in his book *'Schem Hamphoras,'* Luther even recommended Margaritha's work. However, the blueprint to Luther's anti-Semitism was in the Jewish messianic machinations and the Bible itself.

The Bible is designed to put everyone on the defensive.

In an environment of widespread anti-Semitism, the former Jew's booklet merely confirmed common conceptions. And it contains a kernel of truth with which we have already become familiar.

Obviously, Margaritha's work was *intended* to be critical of Jews, but other than many hateful slurs, his work was broadly descriptive, and it addressed real concerns of Christianity at the time. Moreover, he did not want Jews to be expelled or killed.[1326]

His intention was to have them converted to Christianity.

The vehicle for opposition against Jews was rather the new mass media of printed books and a new interest in learning. It is much easier to fool an illiterate population than one that starts to take an interest in its affairs.

Having said that, in evaluating the causes for anti-Semitism, we need to look at the intentions and differentiate hatred from real concerns, from biblically induced self-hatred, and from mere ritual or cultural comparisons.

If organized religions agree on one theme, it has got to be to hate each other – and Jews.

---

[1322] Ibid., 95.
[1323] Ibid., 97.
[1324] Deuteronomy 28:43 (NIV) and Deuteronomy 28:68 (NIV).
[1325] Margaritha, Jewish Belief, 1544, 71-72.
[1326] Ibid., 160.

The ruler of the German Jews, Joel of Rosheim, appeared before the emperor at Augsburg to dispute Margaritha's work, claiming that Margaritha himself had contributed to the expulsion of the Jews from Regensburg, even before converting to Christianity.[1327] I lack insights, but it ended in the latter's arrest and ejection from the city.[1328] It seems as if the author had put his own fate into his book: the cheap excuses of one smarter than him must have led to his exile.

During the same show, Rosheim refuted that Jews had caused the religious divisions that led to Lutheranism.[1329] This is an eye-popping accusation. Can we easily dismiss this?

What was the role of Jews in Luther's inner circle?

I now return to the news from David Reubeni, the Jew and forerunner, and from Solomon Molcho, the Messiah.

The papacy maintained secret agents across its domain at the time. Solomon Molcho had travelled to Regensburg under papal protection (!). He was promoted as the leader and the Messenger of God who promised to march ahead of all the armies against Ottoman-Turks.

The Rabbinic leader, Josel of Rosheim, packed up and fled the country in fear of the consequences of the messianic visit. But then he *'was forced to come back'* to the imperial court to attend the meeting between Charles and Molcho. At least, that is what he said after the fact.

He was lying.

Other than from the context of his rise, Rosheim stated that Molcho sanctified the religion of Israel by turning back many from sin,[1330] meaning that he was able to bring former converts and Christians back to Judaism. This had indeed happened all along the path of the pair and was a major frustration for Martin Luther.[1331] He also used a corruption of the Messiah's last name *Molqo*, which is a code word for *heretic*. But then he combined it with his best wishes for Molcho, that he may rest in the Garden of Eden, in paradise.

We have seen this sort of trickery already with Simon bar Kokhba (son of a star) who morphed into bar Koziba (son of the lie). The coded word *Molcho* on its own is a corrupted abbreviation of *Moshiach*, the Messiah. We can be sure that Rosheim was aware of its meaning. Here we have Molcho (Son of God) turning

---

[1327] Ludwig Feilchenfeld, Rabbi Josel von Rosheim (Heitz, 1898) 117, transl. A.J. Deus.

[1328] Ibid., 118.

[1329] Ibid., 119.

[1330] R. Josel of Rosheim, memoires, from Aeshcoly in Movements, p. 426, as quoted in Lenowitz, 1998, 121.

[1331] In his Chronica, Franck takes note that many Lutherans fell violently off in favor of Ludwig Zwingli, Sebastian Franck, Chronica Zeitbuch und Geschichtsbibel, (Beck, 1531) 442.

into Molqo (heretic). I have touched on the rabbinic pattern in Molla Kabiz's name before. The latter represents merely an after-the-fact Muslimified combination of the two. Molcho and Molla (Mulcarabum) were the same person. It literally means the same for all three, bar Kokhba, Molla Kabiz, and Molcho: the Messiah was outcast *after* his failure.

We should not trust a word of his memoirs.

The influential twelfth century Jewish scholar Maimonides made it clear that their leaders needed to stop their false messiah claimants and put them in chains. There appears to have been but one contemporary Rabbinic physician[1332] who tried to hinder the pair in their mission. This account cannot be trusted either. This man was a 'gaon,' the top Jewish spiritual leader in Italy and later physician to Pope Paul III.[1333]

Otherwise, all we see is after-the-fact denunciations.

Perhaps a pretend flight. Well-advised cowardice.

Rosheim did not tell us one word about the causes of the expulsion of Jews from Regensburg other than that *'the Regensburg community was expelled and uprooted from all the splendor and from our most precious properties — our most valuable.*[1334] Since he omitted that Jews had been at each other's throats, this was willfully misleading. He did not miss the causes. He was the top Jew of Germany, the regent.

His text was intended to trigger unmerited compassion.

The messianic pair were received by Emperor Charles at Regensburg in Germany in 1532, where they offered a military alliance to the Holy Roman Empire in its fight against the advancing Ottoman-Turks.

We remember that the Throne of David was sitting next to Suleiman and that Ottoman Jewish leaders were implicated. Also, Jews enjoyed unprecedented freedoms in Jerusalem as well as Ottoman citizenship. With his apparent support of the Sanhedrin on the Temple Mount, Suleiman had ordered large scale renovations that included the Dome of the Rock and the al-Aqsa Mosque.

David Reubeni and Solomon Molcho, the Jewish messianic leaders, were offering to betray the friendliest Muslim host of so many Jews.

The Sanhedrin prepared for the End of the Word. They were all in on it.

---

[1332] Jacob Mantin from Venice, Jacob ben Samuel Mantino, +1549.
[1333] Gotthard Deutsch, Isaac Broydé, Jewish Encyclopedia, Jacob ben Samuel Mantino.
[1334] Rosheim, transl. A.J. Deus.

Their cronies over at Istanbul had offered the same assistance to Suleiman the Magnificent, who started to be portrayed as *'the ruler of the inhabited world.'*[1335] While we are not in possession of evidence that Reubeni ever visited the Ottoman leaders, a contemporary Jewish chronicle shows that Solomon Molcho had indeed travelled to Turkey.[1336] He stood at the show-trial as Mollo Kabiz (Mulcarabum). It was instigated by the Grand Vizier Ibrahim Pasha on the Ottoman Throne of David.

It was a grand treachery in the making. Rabbinic leaders attempted to betray Charles, Suleiman, and Clement all at once – and ordinary Jews. Perhaps even Luther.

They were working together on a global scale.

We have seen how Reubeni offered assistance to the pope in his fight against Charles. We learned how they were active at the Throne of David next to Suleiman. And we now have Reubeni's offer to Charles against Suleiman.

If all worked, the End of the World was at hand. The planet would burn up to ashes. As prophesied, the only survivors would be Jewish leaders, some of whom were already waiting on the Temple Mount for the fulfillment of the dream. The laughing third would take over the Promised Land – Reubeni.

What would happen if this plot were to fly in their faces?

The reputation of Jewish treachery had arrived at the imperial court before the orchestrators stepped into Charles' space.

Rabbi Joel Rosheim's report indicates that the pair was received in Germany with suspicion.

The man standing there as the secret representative of Pope Clement was none other than Cardinal Hieronymus Aleandro, declared enemy of Martin Luther. Back in 1521, he had discovered that Spanish editions of Luther's works were printed in Antwerp. He celebrated his find with a great public bonfire – fueled by Luther's books.[1337]

But this was Martin Luther's turf now.

---

[1335] Şahin, Süleyman, 2013, 189.

[1336] Ha-Cohen, Vol. II, translated by Bialloblotzky, 1836, 151
From Molcho's own letter, ibid., 155.

[1337] Bataillon, vol. 1, p. 132. Cf. Henry C. Lea, A History of the Inquisition of Spain, New York, 1922, vol. 3, p. 413 in Longhurst, 1964, 16.

Cardinal Aleandro reported to the pope that he did not want a Jew to accomplish the defeat of the Ottoman Empire or sack of the Temple Mount.[1338]

God forbid; a Jew!

The cardinal believed that a Jew would bring dishonor over Christianity, because Christians had to put their entire faith into Jesus and not into a Jew. In his lectures about the Galatians, Luther thought alike.

What did Christian leaders think a messiah would be, other than a Jew?

The imperial functionaries were working hard in the background to derail the messianic plans. But their motivations were unbelievably cruel, as can be taken from a letter to Pope Clement from the envious Aleandro. He made it clear that it was better to be defeated by Ottoman-Turks than to hand a victory to Jews.[1339] As an imperialist, the cardinal knew nothing about the pope's hidden mission. And he was clueless about the grand subversion in play.

On the other hand, Luther knew for a long time about the position of the French-friendly papacy and was aware that the French as well as the Catholic Church would refuse assistance in a war against Ottoman-Turks with Charles in the lead.[1340] It should be appreciated that Luther's focus remained on the Catholic Church as his main enemy, rather than on Jews.

He did not see this messianic plot coming.

Because every messianic adventure needs to follow the biblical pattern, were it not for his blind faith and hatred, it should have been easy to detect.

Who would deliberately send their own to death rather than see the competition saving them? These religious fanatics were distrusting of each other and were jealous to the point of self-destruction.

It must be acknowledged, though: these Jewish leaders showed extraordinary courage despite all odds being rigged against them.

And rigged they were.

Over generations, Jewish leaders had rigged the game for their purposes.

---

[1338] Hieronymus Aleander, special representative of Pope Clement VII in Germany, from the translation of the Italian in H. Fraenkel-Goldschmidt, R. Josel of Rosheim (Jerusalem, 1996) 183-184 as translated by Lenowitz, 1998, 121.

[1339] Ibid., 122-123.

[1340] Martin Luther, Letter Nicolas Amsdorf, 1532.

Being a messiah is a risky business. In the event of the successful conquest of the Promised Land and the rededication of the Temple Mount in Jerusalem, the rewards are imperial, literally. The successful messiah is the ruler of the world, the King of the Jews – and ruler over all emperors and caliphs.

It was not meant to be. Not this time.

Solomon Molcho did not make it to the beginning of the Messianic Age. Someone was willing to sell the mission out. Some Jews wanted to poison him.[1341] Allegedly. Being persecuted with the help of a Jewish (!) physician from Venice,[1342] the Holy Roman Emperor, Charles, had him burned at the stake in the northern Italian city of Mantua in November 1532 after learning that the Ottoman army had retreated.[1343]

It takes *one* good man to stand in the way of evil.

By the way, Molcho got terminated? We need to pay attention. While the sources do not reveal the reasons for the imperial verdict, something must have spooked Charles. It was certainly not the act of offering the help of Rabbinic leaders in the empire's struggle against Ottoman-Turks. And Charles did not take killings lightly. After all, the double agents in his own ranks were alive and well. He even refrained from eliminating King Francis of France when he had the opportunity to rid himself of his staunchest opponent once and for all. Charles was obviously aware of the treacherous game that was being played by Jewish leaders. Molcho was probably recognized as the mastermind and sentenced to death for treason. He may have been sacrificed for the survival of David Reubeni.

As Dawit II, he may even have been perceived as one of the victims.

The plotter for the Promised Land had fallen into his own ditch.

The fact that Emperor Charles did not exile the entire Jewish community shows that he was a man of restraint. His decisions were measured and well thought through.

One might expect that the grandiose games stopped here.

However, for believers, Molcho had not died. The flames could not have done him harm. The man was dead, but the spirit lived on.[1344] For others, he was a martyr gone to paradise. He would soon reappear. Another hidden one.

---

[1341] Ha-Cohen, Vol. II, translated by Bialloblotzky, 1836, 175.
[1342] Ibid., 173-174.
[1343] Joseph Ha-Cohen, A pue offering, in Lenowitz, 1998, 120.
[1344] Joseph Ha-Cohen, 'Emek ha-Bachah', in Lenowitz, 1998, 120.

The belief that he lived on was fueled by the pope himself. He appears to have found a worthy substitute who ended up charred on Molcho's stake. Of course, there were also immediate successors[1345] who proclaimed themselves messiahs in order to continue the mission.

Only God knows.

We have it from the ghost of Molcho's own hand that some sources had conveniently compounded multiple stories in order to have the mission live on. Pope Clement had pretended to give the Messiah up to the angry mob.

Another was grilled in Molcho's stead.[1346]

How many lives does this cat have?

The superstitions never ended, even with the after-the-fact rejections. The admiration of Rabbi Rosheim spinelessly turned to never having supported the cause. That is how it was lost.

Molcho resurrected in a miracle – with ample precedence: the Mahdi, Jesus, Daniel.

Had Reubeni and Molcho succeeded in their mission, once more, the entire world would have been uprooted.

By the time Solomon Molcho found his stand-in at the stake, Suleiman's assault on Vienna had already been called off – for then. A direct confrontation with Charles' forces awaiting Ottoman-Turks at Vienna was averted. Persian Shi'ite Safavid Muslims had attacked the east of the Ottoman Empire, opening a second front to which Suleiman needed to pay attention.

Armageddon could wait another day.

The recently reignited Sunni-Shi'ite rift between Ottoman-Turks and the Safavid Persians called for the blood of the newly faithful brothers. The distraction led to a hit-and-run retreat of the Safavid fighters.

Nevertheless, Hungary was now in firm control under the Ottoman vassal king. With Suleiman's retreat, the services of the Messiah were no longer in demand. At least not with Charles. The emperor's grip over the rest of Europe had only strengthened as collateral damage of the Ottoman campaign.

We can be sure that Martin Luther knew what was going on in Regensburg and Mantua.

---

[1345] The immediate successors were Isaac Lurya and his disciple Hyyim Vital Calabrese.
[1346] Ha-Cohen, Vol. II, translated by Bialloblotzky, 1836, 177-178.

## Rise of Hatred

During the year of Molcho's official demise and the previous year, Martin Luther created the *'Commentary on the Sermon on the Mount.'* This sermon was supposed to be the foundation of Christian love. Instead, his language became ever more spiteful and vulgar. He called his opponents' ideas *'their ass's cunning and devil's dung,'*[1347] Luther had turned into someone who genuinely hated Jews.

He had a real anger issue.

We have heard earlier that the Reformer portrayed the *'Sermon on the Mount'* as specifically directed against Jews. This was a sharp departure from his contextual application of the anti-Semitic biblical diatribes.

Here, Luther was the intellectual father of his own smears.

Luther thought that the opening of the sermon was kind and sweet to Christians, but vexatious and intolerable for Jews. The sermon rejected and condemned their doctrine and their way of living.[1348] He singled them out for being in error for their focus on mammon (money), on making a living and amassing wealth.[1349] The sermon was out to overturn their *false notion and tearing it out of their hearts.* [1350]

Their errors would make them become avaricious and care only for themselves.

Christians were supposed to be poor, otherwise they could not make it into the Kingdom of Heaven. Following Augustine's concept of predetermination, wealth was God's arrangement.[1351]

Luther had become a grand inquisitor against Jews.

The Reformer advocated that he who forsakes all possessions, including wife and children, shall be recompensed a hundred-fold and achieve eternal life.[1352]

In contrast, nobility could not be poor in Luther's vision. They needed possessions to fulfill their 'duties.'

---

[1347] Luther, Sermon on the Mount, transl. Hay, 1532.
[1348] Ibid.
[1349] Ibid.
[1350] Ibid.
[1351] Ibid.
[1352] Ibid.

After the Catholic Church and its nobles had stolen the land from under the feet of the peasants, to put this in a sermon is astonishing.[1353] In his extremist quest, Luther had no shame in leveraging the network of the establishment that sucked blood from its people.

But at least, he clarified that to have riches, to be cheerful, or to eat and drink well, were not sins. It may explain the difference in prosperity between Protestant and Catholic denominations. It was an unintentional loophole for the individual to get somewhere other than scooping dung.

Even though it took ages, Luther's mistake constituted the death knell for Christianity.

To be a Christian means that you are persecuted by those who do not believe as you do, Luther argued. The devil does not allow it otherwise. As a worldling, you are a friend of the world, free of trouble.[1354]

In fact, in the face of their persecution by the Catholic Church during the previous 300 years, the Waldensians had pursued their faith in secret across Europe.[1355] That year, they decided to come out of their holes and join the Protestant movement. Luther had them validated.

In his commentary, Luther portrayed Jews as having hearts of ice and stone. Falling into the deepest Jewish stereotypes, they were caring only for themselves, ignoring the injury of others, and despising everyone else. All the world must serve Jews, said Luther, but they were not obliged to give anything or serve anybody.[1356] They perverted and corrupted the law, and Luther had come to set things right again, just as he did with the Catholic Church.[1357]

We have not yet seen what a man with a heart of ice sounds like.

The messianic pair had been travelling under the protection of the Catholic Church – Martin Luther's archenemies. Undoubtedly, the couple had been announced with great fanfare well ahead of their arrival at Charles' imperial court. Luther must have known for some time that they were coming.

He would come to settle on an even darker opinion of Jews.

Evidently, Reubeni and Molcho provided for the main spark – not the only one – for Luther's change of mind.

---

[1353] Ibid.
[1354] Ibid.
[1355] Pope Innocent III had the Waldensians declared heretics at the Fourth Lateran Council in 1215. Pope Innocent VIII had ordered their termination in 1487.
[1356] Luther, Sermon on the Mount, transl. Hay, 1532.
[1357] Ibid.

Yet, it is our misfortune that his doctrine continued never to call competitors by their names.[1358]

The plan of the Rabbinic leadership was to have other nations go to war for them with the intention of sacking the Promised Land and secede from the Ottomans from on top of the Temple Mount.

It was treason against mankind.

It would not come as a surprise if their leaders' machinations were to backfire.

The Messiah was now presented as dead.

However, David Reubenis's fate was not a done deal. Under guard, he was exiled to Spain. Vanishing from the history books, his whereabouts are open to ongoing speculations. Supposedly, he was rotting behind Portuguese bars until he was poisoned a few years later. Others claim that he was burned.[1359]

Not so fast.

Now that the tables had turned, in 1533 the troubled pope received another delegation from Portugal carrying a message from the Ethiopian Emperor Dawit II, by Jews known as David Reubeni. While the papacy was obsessed with keeping a hold on its theocracy, with Reubeni and Molcho, it had been subverted and compromised.

With the hope to regain some sort of relevance, Pope Clement supported an alliance between Ethiopia and Portugal in the name of converting the Moors of North Africa, the area of the Gulf of Persia, and India to build up the numbers of future warriors in the name of Christ.

Ethiopia's chips on the poker table: conversion of Dawit's empire to the Catholic Church.[1360]

For the goal of seceding from the Temple Mount, he was willing to pretend to believe in Catholic Christianity and to promise Christian rule over Jerusalem. Since Dawit would now be a Christian, he meant *his* Christian rule.

The plan remained to go to war against the 'superstition' – the Vatican's illuminating word choice for its Judaic competitor – of the Muhammadean Ottoman-Turks in order to eradicate Islam.[1361] For this, Dawit offered provisions and hundreds of thousands of soldiers.

---

[1358] Martin Luther, Letter to Nicolas Hausmann, February 8, 1534.
[1359] Jewishhistory.org.il, 1524 David Reuveni (Italy-Portugal).
[1360] Caesaris Baronii, Annales ecclesiastici, CLEMENTIS VII ANNUS 10 — CHRISTI 1533, 21, 22.
[1361] Ibid, 23.

Completing the circle of evidence that Dawit and Reubeni were one, in the understanding of the Vatican, it was Dawit who had brought forth a 'celestial miracle' – a comet.[1362]

Ensuring success in overturning the Muslim enemies, the churches in Egypt and Syria had also expressed their 'friendship.' The two Christian denominations in North Africa and the Levant attempted to subvert the Ottoman Empire from the inside.

As Reubeni's story continued with Dawit II, it appeared that he might not have been imprisoned in Portugal, but rather protected from Emperor Charles' sword by the Catholic Church and by Portugal.

Besides, the official end of Reubeni's mission was forged into the historical record by amateurs. They forgot to edit the messianic messenger out of the story of some of his enemies. According to one of these, Reubeni increased his influence after Molcho's death – and the Italian rabbis took him seriously.[1363]

The pope never knew anyone by the name of Reubeni, only Dawit and Prester John, even though Reubeni's external story is the Vatican's internal version of Dawit. In the guilt of the consequences, reality was broken into seemingly unrelated fragments that should no longer be understood without reassembling them in their proper context.

Right after this visit of the Vatican by Dawit's delegation, the Holy Roman Empire pleaded for armed assistance from the papacy for a renewed fight against Ottoman-Turks on the Hungarian border. While forging a master plan with the Portuguese and the Ethiopians, Pope Clement claimed depleted resources and sent his prayers to Hungary for good luck.[1364]

In his quest to regain status and pay back Emperor Charles, the pope was willing to sacrifice an entire empire. He was content to let Hungary, Austria, and Germany go up in flames. His hope was double-edged: on one hand it would solve the imperial overstepping by Charles and on the other, it would get rid of Luther and his growing Protestant Church.

The pope probably did not know that war fosters religiosity.

---

[1362] Ibid.
[1363] Richard Gottheil, Jewish Encyclopedia, Azriel Ben Solomon Diena (Dayyena), Rabbi at Sabbionetta.
[1364] Caesaris Baronii, Annales ecclesiastici, CLEMENTIS VII ANNUS 10 — CHRISTI 1533, 31.

In a letter from the governor of Mantua – this is the place where Molcho found his imaginary end – Charles had been warned that Germany was part of a coup-attempt by global conspirators. The letter alleged that Bavaria, Würtemberg, and Hesse would create disturbances in Germany, while France, England, and several princedoms would form an alliance against Charles.

France would even pay for Ottoman armies to invade Christendom.[1365]

What had happened shows that the fronts had only hardened.

The French, the pope, and Venice were in a forced alliance with Charles, all right. But that did not hinder them from harboring their own aspirations.

Perhaps illustrating the love between Clement and Francis best was their *voluntary* dynastic inter-marriage.[1366] The groom had to be shuffled a little, because the bride was not the prettiest. Both were fourteen at the time. It mattered little. She gave birth to three French kings, and laid the foundation for all French kings, from the seventeenth century up until the French Revolution, bearing Medici blood.

The following year, France was on the move again. This time with the support of an Ottoman-Turkish fleet. Suleiman and Francis had formed a kind of brotherhood.[1367] The idea of the Franco-Ottoman Alliance between the French and the Ottoman-Turks was to expand the co-operation with England and with the Lutheran defector states.

The secret alliance was supposed to have the Holy Roman Empire in its grasp and to obliterate it completely. Also, the Peace Treaty of Constantinople was forged between Hungary and the Ottoman-Turks to temporarily shut down the hostilities with the Holy Roman Empire at that front.

The plan was for an attack on northern Italy by the French and on southern Italy with a fleet from Ottoman Istanbul and Algiers.

The assault was to be executed in two years by Suleiman's leading grand admiral, Barbarossa.[1368] The latter was freshly promoted to this position as a strongman at sea. Suleiman made him Grand Admiral and Chief Governor of North Africa.

[1365] Governor of Marano wrote to Charles V, Holy Roman Emperor, Calendar of State Papers, Spain, Volume 4 Part 2: 1531-1533 (1882), pp. 858-868.

[1366] The marriage between Henri II d'Orléans and Catherine de' Medici was performed by the Medici Pope Clement VII on October 28, 1533.

[1367] Merriman, Suleiman, 2007, 140: [Suleiman said that] 'he could not possibly abandon the King of France, who was his brother.'

[1368] Hayreddin Barbarossa, ca. 1466 – 1546.

His background is obscure.

His mother was the widow of an Orthodox priest. His father's first name was Yakup, of Albanian descent. Like his father, all his brothers bore names from the Torah: Ishak, Oruç, and Ilyas. In English: Jacob, Isaac, Aaron, and Elijah. Such collections of biblical names would not typically be found in Christian or Muslim families.

This man was essentially a Renaissance pirate, raiding Christian territories along the coasts of Italy, Spain, and southern France. He recruited local converts, former Jews. Once in Ottoman government service, the looting became state-sponsored and legit. He was the embodiment of a daredevil. In his raids, he had captured Algiers from the weakened Spaniards and made himself sultan – the pirate Sultan Barbarossa. He even sacked Tlemcen, the city from which Jews had been expelled earlier. In Ottoman service, Barbarossa participated with his ships in the capture of Rhodes.

We think that our modern planet is small and interconnected. But it was no larger back then. Rhodes, as we have learned, was the island from which the Knights Hospitallers had been driven. Part of the knights then was Barbarossa's contemporary Medici Pope Clement VII.

That was a really small world.

There was another pirate in the service of Suleiman. He was known as 'il Zudio' – his name translates to 'the Jew.'[1369] He was a Jewish corsair who was second in command to Barbarossa.[1370] His flag was the six-pointed Star of David, which Zudio called 'the Seal of Solomon.'[1371]

The venture was ambitious. The men were mighty: the lame, the blind, the Jewish pirates, and the Antichrist.

A first attack on Italy failed on a stalled French invasion from the north.[1372] But these were not men to give up easily.

These were men of faith.

---

[1369] His name was Ciphut Sinan of Smyrna aka Sinan Reis.
[1370] Jewishhistory.org.il 1538 Sinan Reis (Ciphut Sinan).
[1371] Ibid.
[1372] In 1533, Suleiman sent his cavalry to Otranto in southern Italy. Soon after, he withdrew.

At the same time and as a contextual consequence of sympathy for the Franco-Ottoman Alliance, England was breaking off from the Catholic Church. We remember that Emperor Charles was now master over priestly appointments. This would have provided him with a tool to spiritually subvert England and other nations. Henry VIII had long recognized the threat of high treason and made consecration of bishops independent of papal approval. Putting at the leadership of the English Church a bishop who agreed to annul Henry's marriage led to the excommunication of both, king and bishop by Pope Clement. To this, Henry responded with the Act of First Fruits and Tenth, redirecting the revenue streams of the Catholic Church to the English Crown. Not a single penny ended up in the pockets of the pope. One year later, the Act of Supremacy established the Church of England as entirely independent from the Catholic Church.

The Anglicans were born – to kill Anglo-Saxons.

Over in Spain, the Inquisition began to show its fruits. Most of the followers of Erasmus Roterodamus (despite prior church approval of his books) and of the Illuminist Movement had either fled, were in jail, or were erased from the birth records. They were processed with the brute instincts of the Inquisition. The traces of these movements were almost completely eradicated from Spain.

Almost.

Eliminating Luther's competition may not have been the best of ideas. It helped fuse his reform movement and made it ever stronger.

Blood energized it.

Meanwhile, an unusual man showed up at Luther's doorsteps.

The deacon Michael the Ethiopian[1373] spent an entire month at Wittenberg and met with Luther several times. At the end of this visit, the Reformer wrote a letter of recommendation in which he attested to the compatibility of his movement with the Ethiopian Church.[1374]

This is hardly a coincidence.

Was the Ethiopian father on a mission to bring Luther into Dawit Reubeni's orchestra?

Were they offering to become Catholics? Were they offering to become Protestants?

---

[1373] Michael the Ethiopian, aka Abba Mika'el, aka Michael the Deacon, *ca. 1500 AD.
[1374] Martin Luther, Recommendation, Wittenberg, July 7, 1534.

At the same time?

## Turning Up the Heat

Two of Luther's great enemies died in 1534. First to go was Saint Cardinal Cajetan, Dominican Master-General of the Inquisition. Like many works since Gutenberg's printing press, those of Cardinal Cajetan were 'expunged' thereafter. Unless we will find a stash of unedited originals at some point in the future, we will never learn the Inquisitor's true positions. It prevents modern researchers from putting the pieces of history back together.

Cajetan died in August.

The Medici Pope Clement VII fell ill in the same month. Right after appointing four French cardinals, he left for sainthood in September at the age of 56. The rumor went that the pope consumed poisonous mushrooms.

Did Cajetan perhaps eat at the pope's table?

Clement's successor was Pope Paul III,[1375] already of retirement age. He had been appointed cardinal by the Borgia Pope Alexander VI. The then-freshman Cardinal Farnese was a brother of Borgia's mistress, Giulia the Bride of Christ. This nickname bears deep meaning. The pope claimed to carry the Christ. He was an intercessor with God. Modern popes still see themselves likewise – minus the bride. Farnese, the Borgia 'brother-in-law,' had been educated at the University of Pisa and later at the court of Lorenzo de' Medici the Magnificent. Having fathered five children with his concubine, the new pope brought along some experience that seems to have been rooted in real life.

We know little about Pope Paul, but measured by the palaces that he ordered built while cardinal, he and his seed were uniquely greedy. His grandson was awarded not just one benefice but sixty-four. A benefice was an endowment of territory for the purpose of doctrinal submission of its population and transfer of revenue streams to the Catholic Church. Essentially, Pope Paul turned his grandson into a member of the feudal nobility.

And a tax farmer.

We have already seen how the noble club had been fashioned and managed by the Catholic Church. The converted tax farmer Coronel, the Grand Inquisitor Cardinal Cisneros, and the rise of the Farnese grandson are just cases in point.

---

[1375] Alessandro Farnese, 1468 – 1549, was Pope Paul III 1534 – 1549.

A quick look at the Palazzo Farnese in Rome, which today hosts the French embassy, teaches us moderns everything that we need to know about where the indulgences for lowly sins ended up. This palace and the Villa Farnese just north of Rome, originally envisioned as a fortified castle, attest to a lifestyle worthy of royalty. These buildings project nothing but power and feudal pomp.

To portray the elevated status of the enriched Farnese Cardinal to have become pope, he commissioned Michelangelo to carry out architectural refinement of his palace in Rome. The Renaissance artist received other jobs from him, even his last frescoes. Among the most important Farnese appointments given to the master was the architecture of St. Peter's Basilica, the heart of the modern Vatican itself.

The bills were paid for by the alms of the poor. At knifepoint.

By the same token, Pope Paul invested family members to dukedoms – by means of armed forces of the Papal States. Nobility multiplied by papal nepotism. On the other hand, he appears to have been just about the only one who would have been somewhat acceptable to both, the imperialists and the French. But since he was already sixty-six years old, he may have been elected to bank time. Nobody could have expected him either to be effective or to last for another fifteen years.

Yet, his name is forever tied to church 'reform,' as they call it.

It should be called for what it was: suppression of heresy and freedom.

Pope Paul III was a seasoned diplomat and master of propaganda.

He had been at the helm of the efforts to distribute printed books that were censored – expunged – by the Inquisition. His intention was to control the human spirit through an effective censoring apparatus. Like his predecessors, he wanted to unite Christian nobles for his quest to go to war against Ottoman-Turks.

As a diplomat, he feigned strict neutrality – toward Emperor Charles.

Luther had published his German translation of the New Testament in 1522, and he and his collaborators completed the translation of the Old Testament in 1534, when the entire Bible was published.

Some modern scholars claim that Luther started to confuse Jews, papists, sectarians, and Turks in his later life, accusing them of favoring the Antichrist, which Luther personified as the pope. We can now see that this is not so. In his arguments, he named the pope, Turks, Jews, and sometimes Anabaptists or heretics in general in one breath. These four were his main enemies all along, and this collective disagreed with the teachings of the Protestant Church in one way or another. Luther did describe the Catholic Church as *'our Jews'*. But it is made clear that his discourse was held with precision.[1376] There was no difference between papists, Jews, Turks, or heretics, in his view, because they did not rest on faith but on specific works, ceremonies, and rituals that enforced outside appearance.[1377]

We also know from a delegate of the Catholic Church who met Martin Luther at Wittenberg that the reformist was not confused. He described Luther as having demoniacal eyes, speaking very bad Latin, and being intolerably arrogant.[1378]

The rebel leader was sharp as a knife.

Luther was not alone in this 'confusion.' The French King had called the Catholic priests the real Turks to be feared in Europe, referring to the period under the former imperial Pope Adrian VI. King Francis had then also denied certain canonical 'rights' to the papacy and had threatened to withdraw French obedience from the Catholic Church.[1379]

Instead, Pope Paul III had a novel trick up his sleeves.

A Basque nobleman by the name of Saint Ignatius of Loyola[1380] had found a new way to follow the teachings of Jesus Christ. As a consequence, a new competitor sprang to life that year: the Jesuits. Ignatius had previously been wounded[1381] in the struggle *against* the re-conquest of the Catholic Church in the northern Spanish Kingdom of Navarre, then an ally of France.

He and his founding brothers were force-converted disciples of the Catholic Church.

His Jesuit spiritual enlightenment fell together with anti-Protestant persecutions in his area. In response, a new Luther was born: Ignatius. His new 'discoveries' meant absolute self-denial, glorification of poverty, chastity, and obedience to the pope of the Catholic Church. His extremist sect was approved by the Farnese Pope Paul III.

Its religious foundation was based on Saint Augustine.

---

[1376] Luther, Galatians, 1535.

[1377] Ibid.

[1378] Nuntiaturberichte, I-1, no. 218, pp. 539-47, letter of Vergerio to Ricalcati, dated at Dresden from the residence of Duke George of Saxony, 13 Novermber, 1535 in Setton, 1984, 405.

[1379] Setton, 1984, 218-219.

[1380] Saint Ignatius of Loyola, 1491 – 1556. He was the first Superior General of the Jesuits. The foundation included the Spaniards Francis Xavier, Alfonso Salmeron, Diego Laynez, and Nicholas Bobadilla, the Savoyard Peter Faber, and the Portuguese Simão Rodrigues.

[1381] In the Battle of Pamplona in 1521, then part of the collapsing Kingdom of Navarre.

The Jesuits became the popes' missionaries, and its noble leader was canonized as a saint – the patron saint of soldiers.

According to one of his biographers, Ignatius was *'a fancy dresser, an expert dancer, a womanizer, sensitive to insult, and a rough punkish swordsman who used his privileged status to escape prosecution for violent crimes committed with his priest brother at carnival time.'*[1382] Back then, these must have been valued as excellent prerequisites for spiritual leadership.

Ignatius was almost a copy of Saint Augustine, Martin Luther's role model.

The Basque's miraculous conversion to spiritual leader came about during his recovery from injuries from which he emerged limping. One leg had become shorter than the other. Sleeping around was off the table. A new purpose in life was necessary.

Thus, his devotion to God was shaped in the image of Francis of Assisi, the idol of our modern Pope Francis – a Jesuit.

The Jesuits introduced a new ritual: as if Jesus Christ's body and blood were not enough, they imagined themselves as actually partaking in Jesus' story as they read the Gospels.

The Virgin Mary with her child Jesus had appeared to Ignatius in one of a series of visions during a stay at a Benedictine abbey[1383] in Spain.

Henceforth, the Jesuit leader was hell-bent on converting infidels in the Holy Land.[1384] Now, the noble man made a living with (voluntary) begging, practicing (voluntary) asceticism, praying, and organizing his new Jesuit Order in the footsteps of totalitarian dictators.

With multiple visions, this man was on his path to madness.[1385] Likewise, his listeners did show signs of insanity, particularly devout women: *'One fell senseless, another sometimes rolled about on the ground, another had been seen in the grip of convulsions or shuddering and sweating in anguish.'*[1386]

It did not take long until the Basque attracted the attention of the Inquisition. But he was later released.

---

[1382] Joseph N. Tylenda (transl.), A Pilgrim's Journey: The Autobiography of Ignatius of Loyola (Liturgical Press, 1991).

[1383] This was the Spanish Benedictine Santa Maria de Montserrat Abbey, about thirty miles west of Barcelona.

[1384] James Brodrick, Saint Francis Xavier (1506–1552) (Burns, Oates & Washbourne, 1952) 47.

[1385] Jean Lacouture, Jesuits, A Multibiography (Counterpoint, Copyright © 1995, reprinted by permission of Counterpoint Press) 18.

[1386] Ibid., 27-29.

Yet, there were underpinnings of grander church politics in the background. One of the early followers was Saint Francis Borgia,[1387] a great-grandson of the Borgia Pope Alexander VI (who had promoted the Farnese to become cardinal). He was now the most important functionary of Emperor Charles. He, Borgia, became the third Superior General of the Jesuits. His brother[1388] became 'Consultor' to the Spanish Inquisition.

The simple question that needs to remain unresolved in the context of Martin Luther is whether the integration into the Catholic Church had been the intention of the Jesuit founders from the beginning. After all, the alliance with Portugal and France, as well as their background as Basque rebels, speaks a different language than voluntary submission. The Borgia leader may have provided for the possible pivotal moment to a change of heart. Moreover, the Farnese Pope Paul's neutrality is here unmasked as a farce.

It was the moment of laundry.

One of the co-founders[1389] of the Jesuits was appointed by Pope Paul to head the missions to the New World on Portuguese ships. Francis Xavier was viewed as a new Saint Paul – yet another one – and became the patron saint of all foreign missions.[1390] When he was still a boy, his brothers had been under siege by none other than the Grand Inquisitor Cardinal Cisneros in their Basque resistance against the Catholic Church. In defeat, the future Jesuit leader's land and castle were confiscated.

We can appreciate the loving relationship between these leaders.

It makes no sense: while they were force-converted, they remained religious extremists on the other side. Professional extremism was their job.

Xavier's Jesuit awakening finds its roots in the University of Paris where he obtained a Master of Arts degree. There, he was a roommate of Ignatius.[1391] As a good Jesuit man with a Christian heart, he approved of the persecution of the Eastern Orthodox Church. And he initiated[1392] the horrors of the Goa Inquisition, during which apostates[1393] in the far-away lands of Portuguese India were persecuted.

---

[1387] Saint Francis Borgia, 1510 – 1572. He was canonized in 1670 by Pope Clement X.

[1388] Tomás de Borja y Castro, 1551 – 1610. He became Consultor de la Inquisición Romana in 1571.

[1389] Saint Francis Xavier, 1506 – 1552. He was canonized by Pope Gregory XV in 1622.

[1390] Pope Pius XI, Apostolicorum in Missionibus, December 14, 1927 (Papal Encyclicals Online, retrieved 2014).

[1391] James Brodrick, Saint Francis Xavier (1506–1552) (Burns, Oates & Washbourne, 1952) 40.

[1392] Ronald Daus, Die Erfindung des Kolonialismus (Hammer, 1983) 61-66.

[1393] H.P. Salomon, I. S. D. Sassoon, Antonio Jose in Saraiva, The Marrano Factory. The Portuguese Inquisition and Its New Christians, 1536–1765 (Brill, 2001) 345–347.

His intention was to hound those who fell off their earlier conversions.

This tells us everything we need to know: another monster.

First the Portuguese – supposedly Catholics – forced them to convert, and then Jesuits of the Catholic Church persecuted them for having fraudulently converted?

Ordinary people could never win.

People.

Hindus, Christians, or those free from religion. And Jews. For all we know, they were charred for a dime a dozen.

Hundreds of Hindu temples were destroyed.

About 20,000 innocents were tried by the Inquisition, so the official record goes. Listening to Jesuit masses was compulsory. Reading Hindu scripture and rituals were punishable by an affectionate hug from the Angel of Death.

Even their native language and names were outlawed.

The East Syrian Christians (Nasranis) had before the arrival of the Jesuits maintained a stronghold community in Goa with hundreds of thousands of disciples. They were now also persecuted for Nestorian heresy.[1394]

Eventually, this would lead to their breaking off again, never to return to the Vatican.[1395]

This same year of the Jesuits' founding saw again intensifying exchanges between the Holy Roman Empire and the Ottoman-Turks. Suleiman the Magnificent had a large fleet built over the winter.

In alliance with the Kingdom of France and under the command of the pirate Sultan Barbarossa and his companion 'il Zudio,' the Jewish corsair, the Italian coast was raided under the flag of the Star of David or perhaps the Seal of Solomon.

They even landed at the Tiber River.

Rome was terrified by the approaching hordes of the Antichrist.

The Italian island of Malta was the new home of the Knights Hospitaller. Its members were exempt from ordinary military service, because their historic mission was to wage terrorist attacks on the infidels on both land and sea.[1396]

---

[1394] Lauren Benton, Law and Colonial Cultures: Legal Regimes in World History, 1400–1900 (Cambridge, 2002) 122.

[1395] See the Coonan Cross Oath of 1653.

[1396] Setton, 1984, 352.

Barbarossa was able to establish a strategic naval base at Tunis, just south of Malta. This provided Ottoman-Turks with control over the east-west passage in the Mediterranean Sea. Luckily for pope and empire, the eastern Ottoman front with Persia held the world powers somewhat in balance.

The following year, Emperor Charles organized an expensive counter-offensive against Barbarossa in cooperation with the Farnese pope and the Knights Hospitaller. The pope preached for a crusade and provided finances and a few galleys; the emperor was to lead the Crusade against Tunis.[1397]

However, the cost of war was a heavy burden on the empire.

The French, as could be expected, denied assistance and entered the previously secret alliance with the Ottoman-Turks formally. The French strategy was to occupy the Mediterranean islands of Sicily and Sardinia and continue to raid the Italian coasts around Genoa. They intended to force the city-state into submission to the Kingdom of France.[1398]

Despite the French itch on his back, Charles recaptured Tunis.

This prompted Charles to brag about having defeated Ottoman-Turks and to elevate himself as the protector of Christianity.

The successive celebrations at Rome required the demolishment of more than 200 ancient houses and a number of churches to create an unobstructed route for the emperor to the Vatican.[1399]

Within a couple of months, an otherwise ruined city turned into the symbolic New Rome.

Barbarossa resurfaced raiding the Spanish coast. Un-dead.

It was only a matter of time until Suleiman the Magnificent would attempt to add the Protestant defectors of the Holy Roman Empire to his alliance with France and England. As a proxy, the Kingdom of France finally entered an alliance with the Schmalkaldic League.

Satan himself now had new, albeit unofficial friends – the Luther League. Was this arranged by Michael the Ethiopian who had just paid Luther a visit?

Suleiman, Francis, the Farnese Pope Paul and Luther had the same goal: bring down Charles.

---

[1397] Ibid., 396.
[1398] Military instructions to Jean de La Forêt, by Chancellor Antoine Duprat (copy), 11 February 1535.
[1399] Setton, 1984, 396.

In a string of rapid successes, the Protestant alliance expanded significantly through southern Germany. Several cities subscribed to the *'Augsburg Confession.'* They broke from the Catholic Church. Its 'property' was simply expropriated. Some of the resulting funds were used for relief of the systemic mass poverty that had been induced by the violent conflict between the Catholic Church and the Protestants.

The luck on the eastern front of Suleiman the Magnificent with the Mahdi son by his side did not run low, either. He captured Baghdad, the world's largest center of Islam. In order to directly address the Shi'ite need for divinely inspired evidence, both the conquest of Baghdad and the size of the Ottoman army were portrayed as miracles.

Legitimacy was engineered at will.

Ottoman-Turks now controlled the areas of the Euphrates and Tigris rivers and lower Mesopotamia. In this way, the Magnificent had unrestricted access to the Gulf of Persia.

But his goal of destroying the elusive Shi'ite Safavid enemy could not be achieved. Suleiman's forces needed to retreat to Baghdad for the winter.

Predictably, another miracle occurred in Baghdad. The tomb of Abu Hanifa, the intellectual father of the Hanifa legal school of Islam, was 'discovered.' Having captured several important Shi'a shrines empowered Ottoman Sunnis to claim that the Twelve Imams had denied their support to the Shi'ites.[1400] In an apparent attempt to further legitimize Ottoman power through organized religion, Shi'ite mosques were converted.

The Ottoman ruler's standing as a saint and prophet was indisputable.

The entire Promised Land was his. His son, the Mahdi, had worked his miracles. However, to fulfill the prophecy of the End of the World, Suleiman still had to bring down the Holy Roman Empire.

The time was ripe. In alliance with King Francis of France, Suleiman the Magnificent, could finally challenge Emperor Charles, yet again.

Little did he know that Jewish leaders were engineering secession from the Temple Mount in Jerusalem.

---

[1400] Şahin, Süleyman, 2013, 100.

Luther held lectures on Genesis in 1535 and the year thereafter. It resulted in the first Lutheran commentary on Genesis,[1401] written from notes by his audience, not by Luther himself. It was also heavily edited.[1402]

The Reformer now dehumanized Jews in the context of having adopted alien rituals and ceremonies. He said that after despising the Temple, they expanded their outwardly signs by bringing *'their sacrifices under trees and in groves, until in the end inhuman parents sacrificed their own children.*'[1403]

Luther overstepped the boundaries to open anti-Semitism.

Such disgraceful accusations have been used throughout history to vilify religious opponents. It was abused by Pagans, Jews, Christian sectarians, Muslims, and by many other denominations.

Instead, the natural inclination of life is to protect its offspring, come what will. Luther, a learned man, was aware of the allegation's historical use as well as we are today. That they were sacrificing their *own* children was his innovative novelty.

The anti-Semitic attack came during a lecture about hating other people's myths and superstitions in favor of his own. The community not only believed it but was also shocked by and alienated from Jews. The Reformer claimed that this would have never happened if Jews had faith in the Word of God.

His accusations were not directed against Jews alone but continued against the Catholic Church as well. Had Catholics appreciated the power of baptism, then there would have been no monks, no purgatory, or other abominations.[1404]

Luther was not done with the Jews. His style still mostly derived from the biblical narrative. But he would stride further and further into the territory of endangering the lives of the entire world Jewry.

In a passage that deals with a conflict between Adam and Eve's children, Cain and Abel, the rebellious teacher selected a verse from the Psalms. These are poems or songs from and about King David. The Psalm that Luther was dealing with, is about David's complaint to God that wicked and deceitful men had defamed him without cause. David then asked God to punish the deceivers and to help him. There is no word about who the deceivers were in this Psalm. In

---

[1401] Luther's Works, Volume I, Lectures on Genesis, Chapters 1-5, Edited by Jaroslav Pelikan, translated by Georg V. Schick (Concordia, 1958).
[1402] Ibid (cf. Luther's Works, 13, Introduction, pp.xi-xii).
[1403] Ibid., 249.
[1404] Ibid., 250.

the passage in question, David asked God to make the accuser's children wandering beggars and to have them driven from their homes.[1405]

What Luther made out of this is horrifying.

He turned it into letting Jews never find a secure place and forcing them to keep on wandering from one host country to another. They would never know where to turn for refuge.[1406] The only way out of their misery was to convert to Luther's style of Christianity.[1407]

A Lutheran holocaust was shaping up.

With the appearance of Reubeni and Molcho, Luther rapidly evolved from his approach with Christian love to deeply ingrained anti-Semitism. He hated Jews for their leaders' sharing beds with Ottoman-Turks and the Catholic Church. They were willing to cuddle up with his enemies if only to harm one of their common spiritual opponents.

In his later sermons, Luther also introduced such a deep-seated hatred toward the Turks that a cultural barrier remains between Turkey and Germany today. The distrust led to the European Union's refusal to accept Turkey as one of theirs. The failure to integrate the first Muslim nation into Europe was a mistake of historic proportions. It was pretty much immediately clear that the West had to pay an enormous price and will continue to do so for generations to come. Integration would have created exactly the kind of bridge that the world so desperately needed.

It will be a long time for another such opportunity to offer itself.

Luther said of the Turks that they were devoted to exterminating Christians and were in their hearts enemies of Christ.[1408] This observation is correct. With *Turks* he meant *Muslims*, but since he said Turks, the damage was eternally inflicted upon that nation.

They belong to the devil, Luther swore.[1409]

The hatred against Turks was fueled not only by sermons of Luther but also by many of his other later readings. He is one of the fathers not only of anti-Semitism but also of modern Islamophobia.

Ordinary moderns still pay for the consequences today.

---

[1405] Psalm 109:10 (NIV).
[1406] Luther's Works, Vol. I, 1958314.
[1407] Ibid.
[1408] Martin Luther, *Luther's Epistle Sermons*, Vol. III, Twenty Third Sunday After Trinity, Righteousness of the Law Opposes the Cross, 1535, translated by John Nicholas Lenker (The Luther Press, 1909).
[1409] Ibid..

In traditional religious fashion, his intellectual framework of hatred targeted all who did not believe as he did — including the Catholic Church. Luther said about its functionaries in one of his masses that they were *'simply abandoned knaves, living shameless lives of open scandal, avarice, arrogance, unchastity, vanity, robbery and wickedness of every kind.'*[1410]

We have seen that Luther's view was realistic. But his methodology was appalling. Instead of reason, he deployed hatred and created the same binding mechanism that Jewish leaders used of a hated people who would love to hate everybody else – because they were hated.

Luther's plan was to purify the church and return to the genuine faith, as he saw it. His ideals were based on the principles of poverty[1411] even more than the sixteenth-century Catholic Church, which was losing its grip on an outdated business model.

He was tirelessly threatening with the coming End of the World.[1412]

Poverty was king.

The emptiness of art in modern Protestant churches is intended to create the appearance of poverty, exactly in contrast to the wealth of art in places of worship of the Catholic Church. Luther had no part in the humanist advancements of the time. On the contrary. He hated it. He hated all its proponents. His intention was to push the faith a few hundred years back into its good times of 'faith alone' as the driving force to salvation.

In one such mass, Luther demonstrated the power of conformation that faith exerted on him. When he was an Austin Friar, his thoughts were so thoroughly focused on rituals and prayers that he would have readily picked up the first stone to be thrown at himself for his execution or gathered the wood for having himself burned at the stake.[1413]

All he did was exchange one faith for another.

Through the progression of Luther's works, we can recognize that the order of the day was reformation of the Catholic Church with the goal of regaining uncontested power. There was also an undercurrent of attempts to subjugate diverging sectarian Christian approaches, in particular of the Spanish flavor, into one 'reformed' Christianity. All of that was not his doing. The question of how

---

[1410] Ibid.
[1411] Ibid.
[1412] Ibid.
[1413] Ibid.

to reform the church divided the clergy, and many disagreed with breaking tradition, abandoning old habits, and introducing new ones.

These are just the basics of the risks that come from attempting to reform organized religion.

Through the rejection of his ideas as an insider of the Catholic Church, Martin Luther was pushed ever further into the fringes. Until the bond finally broke. His only options were to fight or to die. He questioned the authority of the Catholic Church, which was based on the handover to Saint Peter.

There was no real alternative except to emerge as a separate church. Questioning church authority came with the trivial problem that he, Martin Luther, had no authority either. Even less so. But he had no choice but to reject papal supremacy in Rome to justify the establishment of a nationalistic German church for Germany.

In this sense, his impact in the historical progression was perhaps irrelevant, indeed. We can see that the influence that the order of events had on the rebel preacher was far greater.

Luther did not define the time. The time defined Luther.

His timing was epic.

As he matured, the radical Augustinian monk became an even more extremist reformer, protected by the subversive powers of the day. He was a man of evil spirit and sheer arrogance. It was his imagination that brought about spite and hatred against anyone who disagreed with him.

But, unfortunately, when it comes to Jews, imagination created the most powerful cocktail of hatred when reality hit home: the grand treachery of Reubeni and Molcho.

At that exact junction, it even pleased a Jewish chronicler that the Reformer removed the statues from the churches and stopped the veneration of saints.[1414]

The Jewish writer did not know that Luther was coming after them.

---

[1414] Ha-Cohen, Vol. II, translated by Bialloblotzky, 1836, 320.

# V: WAR

## *Jews and Their Lies*

Now, the master Luther went to work to establish his greatest legacy: '*On the Jews and Their Lies.*' He created an anti-Semitic book beyond anything imaginable.

Luther's opening statement was not written by someone who was confused. Therein, he complained that those miserable and accursed Jews would not cease to lure Christians to themselves. He intended to warn his disciples away from their poisonous activities and was in disbelief that Christians could be duped by Jews into accepting Judaism.[1415] His book against Jews seems to be a direct response to a treatise in which a Jew engaged in dialog with a Christian. Unfortunately, we are blind to who its writers were or what its content may have been. The Jew thought that they had the stronger argument and could destroy Christianity.[1416] Luther was under the impression that '*this impenitent, accursed people who give God the lie and haughtily despise all the world*' conspired to Judaize all of mankind.[1417]

He saw it correctly that they were conspiring to Judaize the entire planet. But he did not understand the 'rules' of the 'game'.

'*On the Jews and Their Lies*' was addressed directly to the German people.

Luther did not intend to talk *with* Jews but *about* Jews.[1418]

In other words, it was intended to be anti-Semitic.

Jews were no longer God's people, Luther argued, in addition to the wrath that was brought upon them.[1419] He packaged his frustration with Jews around their unwillingness to accept Jesus as the Christ, together with the Father and the Holy Spirit, the Trinity. One key sentence perhaps says it all: '*Moses was unable to reform the Pharaoh by means of plagues, miracles, pleas, or threats; he had to let him drown in the sea.*'[1420]

---

[1415] Luther, Jews and Their Lies, 1971, part I.
[1416] Ibid.
[1417] Ibid.
[1418] Luther, Jews and Their Lies, 1971, part I.
[1419] Ibid.
[1420] Ibid.

This is a malicious distortion of the story with the pharaoh, but we can see the deadly consequences that lie in the message: Jews deserved to die for not accepting Lutheranism.

This misrepresentation of the pharaoh's role provides us with a glimpse at how religious scripture can be taken at will and turned into whichever is opportune. A pharaoh was the equivalent to the pope of the Catholic Church, sort of an Egyptian pontiff. Long before Jews, Christians, or Muslims, Egyptians had believed in resurrection and afterlife. Indeed, descriptions of their customs from the sixth century BC are almost indistinguishable from descriptions of Judaism.[1421]

The tribal god of the Israelites is claimed to be omnipotent. He issued commands to anyone, including Pagans or non-Israelites, just to name a few. In a biblical passage,[1422] this god personally handed out a command to the pharaoh.[1423]

This has implications: God is all-powerful.

The general idea of Moses' play was that Jews were held as slaves in Egypt. According to the Bible, the Egyptian ruler thought that Jews had allied themselves with their enemies. Moses, the great Jewish Prophet, premeditated the assassination of a guard and fled thereafter. He returned as a redeemer of the Jews.[1424] Moses, the assassin, had been commanded by the god of the Israelites to lead them into a land flowing with milk and honey.[1425] This, of course, was supposed to result in the conquest of the Promised Land, a country they knew nothing about.

It is an apparent precursor to the messianic model. That Jews had been involved in the royal palace since Moses was in his crib indicates that they had been 'slaving' to maintain an oppressive administrative system. The latter can be traced past Moses' assumed lifetime and YHWH's first archaeological evidence all the way back to the third millennium BC. It operated during the Ptolemaic and Roman eras in Egypt and in the Persian Achaemenid Empire. And elsewhere.

Instead of simply commanding the pharaoh, as it could have, the god of the Israelites equipped Moses with supernatural powers to perform tricks to impress with the power of his god. This included witchcraft such as turning a staff into

---

[1421] Herodotus, Histories, II.
[1422] 2 Chronicles 35:20–24.
[1423] Necho II was king of the Twenty-Sixth Dynasty of Egypt from 610 BC–595 BC.
[1424] Exodus 2:11–12.
[1425] Exodus 3:7.

a snake,[1426] turning the river Nile into a stinky glut of blood full of dead fish,[1427] and sending a plague of frogs.[1428]

After Moses's god sent a plague of gnats,[1429] the *magicians* – a derogatory nickname of Egyptian priesthood – surrendered to the supreme power of his god.[1430] But they did not quit their resistance. Not yet. They came up with their own magic that challenged the kind offered by Moses.[1431] So, the unsuspecting population had to endure many more tricks that were sent by an unwarranted wrath of God: swarms of flies that ruined the land;[1432] a killing of all livestock, except for those of the Israelites;[1433] an outbreak of boils on all men and animals;[1434] the worst hailstorm ever seen;[1435] a locust plague;[1436] and total darkness for three days.[1437]

Finally, the pharaoh gave in to the tremendous power of Moses' god and let the Israelites go.[1438]

But it was not enough.

One more humanitarian disaster had to be unleashed only to make a point of God's supremacy: it manifests itself in the most important Jewish festival, Passover, as discussed earlier. Celebrated today by Jews as some kind of an achievement of freedom, God went on to kill all firstborns – children – in the land of Egypt, man and animal.[1439]

Jews were protected from the heavenly wrath by writing a secret Hebrew mark in blood to their door posts.[1440] It is the same symbol that today marks practically every Jewish household around the world.

Ordinary Egyptians received neither a warning nor a life-saving opportunity to submit to the god of the Israelites.

---

[1426] Exodus 7:10–12.
[1427] Exodus 7:20–22.
[1428] Exodus 8:6–7.
[1429] Exodus 8:17–18.
[1430] Exodus 8:19.
[1431] Exodus 7:22.
[1432] Exodus 8:24.
[1433] Exodus 9:3.
[1434] Exodus 9:10.
[1435] Exodus 9:18.
[1436] Exodus 10:4.
[1437] Exodus 9:22.
[1438] Exodus 9:27.
[1439] Exodus 12:12.
[1440] Exodus 12:7.

To celebrate this day as though it brought anything good to humanity or to themselves is a shameful manifestation of hatred of mankind, all mankind other than Jews.

Every time the mark is placed on a doorpost, they consent to none deserving to exist other than Jews. Modern Jewish thinking reads it something like this: *'[…] without the experience of that returning group from Egypt, we might not have had the ethic of caring for the stranger.*[1441]

'Caring' for Palestinians seems to bear a different meaning.

But all these killings of innocent life and all these humanitarian and natural disasters were not necessary. Why not? First, no real animals were harmed in the tale's progression. Secondly, and this is the moral of the story, God – it is hard to 'believe' – personally commanded the pharaoh to refuse the departure of the Israelites.[1442]

This whole rampage was for nothing but for showing off the immense power of the god of the Israelites.

As the highest authority of the Protestant Church, *the* religious expert of his time, Luther did not miss this portrayal of Jewish invincibility. But the story was not over yet. When the pharaoh finally did let them go, he changed his mind again and pursued the Israelites with the Egyptian army. Moses and his followers were rescued through a miracle, the Parting of the Red Sea. The water magically opened a dry path for the Israelites to pass through safely. God drowned the pursuing army, to the last man – and horse.[1443]

This god's power is awesome.[1444]

There were, according to the Bible, thousands of witnesses on both shores.

The text claims over 600,000 grown Israelite males on the trek, plus the uncounted Levites.[1445] That amounts to two or three million Israelites in total. Not to mention the millions of directly affected dwellers at the Nile River. Or the Egyptian widows and orphans – other than the firstborns.

Here is the miracle: nobody thought any of the disasters as noteworthy. Not an Israelite. Not an Egyptian. Nobody. There is no memorial. Not a scribble of a child. Not even a single word.

---

[1441] Richard Elliott Friedman, The Exodus (HarperCollins, 2017) 9.
    Copyright (c) 2017 by Richard Elliott Friedman. Courtesy of HarperCollins Publishers.
[1442] Exodus 11:9–10.
[1443] Exodus 14:28.
[1444] Exodus 14:18.
[1445] Numbers 2:32 (NIV).

That does not mean that the Sadducee Levites did not come from Egypt or had not lived there and ran their administrative deep state at some point. After all, the original Levitic names are of Egyptian origin.

Their origin would barely be a kernel of truth in the story.

What did Luther say again? *Moses was unable to reform the Pharaoh by means of plagues, miracles, pleas, or threats; he had to let him drown in the sea.*[1446] The entire seed, all of the branches and the roots of those who cannot be reformed, here Jews collectively, need to be eliminated to the last man.

That is anti-Semitic Luther logic.

The core problems that Luther had with Jews was that they could not accept Jesus Christ as the Messiah and stole his disciples. Instead, he thought, they were boasting of being the only noble people on earth. Their claim was to be of such noble birth that God was obliged to establish them to rule over the entire world and over the spiritual world as well.[1447] They looked down on non-Jews as not human, poor worms.[1448] In their religious world, those who were not circumcised were a stench in their nostrils.[1449] Their raving follies were mad and stupid.

Jews thanked their god for being humans and not animals; for being Israelites and not non-Jews; and for being men and not women.[1450] In that order. Luther perceived this as inexpressible presumption.[1451]

Luther accused Jews of being so lowly that they did not even invent this folly but borrowed the barbarian fool's boast from the Greeks. The Catholics fancied themselves likewise as the only human humans while all others were non-humans.[1452] If Jews were to drop this boasting about their nobility, their entire religious system would topple, Luther asserted.[1453]

In this respect, the rebellious Reformer saw clearly: that declaring a person to be nobler than another by reason of birth was a fountain of inequality.[1454] No human is born differently, he proclaimed.[1455] Had he applied this to nobility in general, then his insight would have been revolutionary for his time.

---

[1446] Luther, Jews and Their Lies, 1971, part I.
[1447] Ibid.
[1448] Ibid.
[1449] Ibid.
[1450] Ibid.
[1451] Ibid.
[1452] Ibid.
[1453] Ibid.
[1454] Ibid.
[1455] Ibid.

However, he only envisioned this in context with the *'devilish arrogance'*[1456] of the Jewish claim to their birthright, and, in consequence, to world leadership. For this, *'they would have to be hurled into the abyss of hell.'*[1457]

Regardless of whether the Rabbinic leadership had been working on subverting the entire world, the collective call to hating and hurting Jews was a crime against mankind.

This Jewish claim to world leadership was complicated by the biblical grand treachery of Esau's birthright that had passed to Jacob for a meal[1458] or of Abraham's firstborn, Ishmael[1459] who had simply been passed over. He likewise argued that God commanded the circumcision to entire household of Abraham, including servants and Ishmael, spanning the Abrahamic tree, not just the branches through Isaac.[1460]

Well argued with biblical 'evidence,' for Luther, it was a matter of faith, not of birthright and circumcision.[1461]

He knew his Bible well and was a master at exploiting its weaknesses.

Since the price of becoming emperors over the whole world was as cheap as feeding a foreskin sandwich to a brother in dire need or a scroll together with a couple of false witnesses, the 'birthright' of the Jews should indeed be laughed at.

Perhaps, we should not laugh. Luther has fallen for the cunning play.

The pretention is that Esau was thrown under the bus by Jacob. Instead, an uninterrupted messianic chain emerges. In it, Esau plays the invisible role of the Deceiver. He manipulates his targets, becomes spiritual leader, and calls in the King of the Jews with his administrative system that tramples everybody else down

The hatred against Jews is part of this genius tragedy.

Ordinary Jews are oblivious to the machinations of their leaders. Whenever they thought that there were too many Jews, they divided and sacrificed them. This ensured their continued rule. They did not care whether they reigned over Jews, Christians, Muslims, or some other Adamic religions.

As long as they rule, they sit on comfortable couches.

---

[1456] Ibid.
[1457] Ibid.
[1458] Ibid.
[1459] Ibid.
[1460] Ibid., part II.
[1461] Ibid.

It is a warning to modernity to never – ever – allow the Sanhedrin to take possession of the Temple Mount. Once they do, it will already be too late, and the next disaster will unfold.

We are going to witness it.

Anyone making such claims to world leadership should be politely shown the door.

> *And these dreary dregs, this stinking scum, this dried-up froth, this moldy leaven and boggy morass of Jewry should merit, on the strength of their repentance and righteousness, the empires of the whole world – that is, the Messiah and the fulfillment of the prophecies – though they possess none of the aforementioned items [the Promised Land, penitence, and merit for the Messiah] and are nothing but rotten, stinking, rejected dregs of their fathers' lineage!*[1462]

But by debasing Jews, Luther lifted himself and his followers into the same lofty position of supremacy as Jewish, Catholic, and Muslim leaders before him. In a dangerous vicious cycle, they ended up owning the Truth – each one of them different – and they all strove for world supremacy.

Over the centuries, each has honed a subtler defense to pretend that this is not so.

The problem is not with the worshippers, but with the ringleaders.

The game is so dangerous that it threatens all of mankind. Listening to Martin Luther makes it clear that there is no exception: owning the Truth comes at the expense of eliminating the untruth. That costs lives. The preferred tactic is always to eliminate the weakest first.

In the Reformer's view, Jews with their ideas of world domination based on their birth *'would merit that thunder and lightning strike down from heaven and that sulphur and hellfire strike from below.'*[1463] The same boast from other religious or secular groups befits similar retribution. But Luther had no patience for mythical meaning.

The punishment of Jews was supposed to be real.

As so many times in history, the grandeur of setting themselves above all others as the Chosen People has brought them to this watershed moment. The tragedy is that Luther's foul arguments were striking in their validity from a biblical perspective.

---

[1462] Ibid., part VIII.
[1463] Ibid., part I.

Rabbinic leaders themselves had provided the causes for Luther to turn against all Jews. This was not so much due to their 'failure' to convert to Christianity but to being *'arrogant rascals.'* They were a *'malicious, stiff-necked people that would not be converted from evil to good works by the preaching, reproof, and teaching of the prophets.'*[1464]

According to Luther's interpretation of the biblical account, Jews killed most of the prophets, including Jesus Christ.

> *The entire course of the history of Israel and Judah is pervaded by blasphemy of God's word, by persecution, derision, and murder of the prophets. Judging them by history, these people must be called wanton murderers of the prophets and enemies of God's word. Whoever reads the Bible cannot draw any other conclusion.*[1465]

Luther portrayed Jews as *'real liars and bloodhounds'* who vengefully yearned to slay all non-Jews. They expected of their messiah to *'murder and kill the entire world.'* Often enough they have made the messianic attempt, Luther argued, *'for which they have got their snouts boxed lustily.'*[1466]

The inconceivable reality is that his assessment was broadly correct.

However, he applied it collectively to *all* Jews.

Criticizing a religion for what it is and inciting hatred for an ethnicity to be sent into a holocaust are two entirely different ball games. But we can also see how dangerous the portrayal of self-hatred by Jews in scripture is. Luther had used it before. We can now see how easy it was for the spiritual leader of the Protestant Reformation to flip from a policy of marketing the goodness and principle of love to Jews to showing them what this really meant.

Luther was also a learned man, and through learning so much about the biblical world, he developed an ever more fanatic tunnel vision. Finally, his patience with Jews ran out, and he turned against them.

It would lead to a veritable business boom – in the industries for coffins and mass graves.

If only his work had focused on the differences between Christianity and the Jewish faith and how Christians felt about it, the discourse could have turned out to be profitable. But despite his anti-Semitic diatribes, Luther's work was everything but confused.

---

[1464] Ibid., part II.
[1465] Ibid.
[1466] Ibid.

He was quite sharp about comparing Jewish and Catholic rituals and declaring them void and empty of faith. The outward separation of rituals from faith was a perversion of his god's Truth. Christians merited all devils – Prophet Muhammad and the Catholic Pope – to come upon them.[1467] Jews likewise severed outwardly symbolism from faith. The Muslim Turks were fooled by the devil, anyhow, addressing events contemporary to Martin Luther.

If evil exists, we are right in the bloodsucking heart of it.

These extremists called each other out for radicalism but failed to see that they were not the exception to the rule.

Only they represent the one true faith – each one of them individually.[1468]

The Protestant preacher concluded that Jews had been expelled from Jerusalem for over 1,500 years for a reason and that they had lost their claim to the land of Israel. The Jewish call for the Promised Land was getting on Luther's nerves. He thought that enough was enough.

Now that we know that the appearance of David Reubeni and Solomon Molcho before Emperor Charles immediately preceded Luther's hatred of Jews, it is clear that his pain was real and contemporary. While earlier parallelisms might have felt coincidental, now we know that Luther had not picked his topics by chance. During his entire life, he responded to real challenges.

Luther had merely begun his hatefest.

They were like an incorrigible whore and an evil slut, he thought. When the god of the Israelites punished them *'through the prophets, they contradicted him, killed his prophets, or, like a mad dog, bit the stick with which they were struck.*[1469] The Reformer was at his most effective where he described what Jews thought of his Christian followers: *For they are full of malice, greed, envy, hatred toward one another, pride, usury, conceit, and curses against us Gentiles,*[1470] meaning all non-Jews.

The problem of the Jewish usury monopoly provided for an open door to hatred by people who were indebted to Jews. Even though the usury laws had seen times of harsher enforcement and were at the tail end of their Christian life span, Luther used the trick repeatedly.

---

[1467] Ibid.
[1468] Ibid., part III.
[1469] Ibid.
[1470] Ibid.

The breath of Jews *'stinks with lust for the Gentiles' gold and silver; for no nation under the sun is greedier than they were, still are, and always will be, as is evident from their accursed usury.'* They would be happy with the coming of the Messiah, because he would divide *'the gold and silver of the whole world'* among them. Luther presented them as a people with insatiable greed.

The German princes and rulers sat there and snored *'with mouths hanging open'* and permitted *'the Jews to take, steal, and rob from their open money bags and treasures whatever they want'* until they were *'beggars with their own money.'* [1471] Thieves would be hanged, but *'when a Jew steals and robs ten tons of gold through his usury, he is more highly esteemed than God himself,'* [1472] Luther charged.

> *Moreover, they are nothing but thieves and robbers who daily eat no morsel and wear no thread of clothing which they have not stolen and pilfered from us by means of their accursed usury. Thus they live from day to day, together with wife and child, by theft and robbery, as arch-thieves and robbers, in the most impenitent security. For a usurer is an arch-thief and a robber who should rightly be hanged on the gallows seven times higher than other thieves.* [1473]

Such language is criminal, not only in its intent to incite hatred, but because Luther was asking for the killing of all Jews.

How would his disciples receive this?

We know that nobility and citizenry at that time ate out of Luther's hands. They were so infatuated with him that he could have sent them into a flaming pit.

Those who refused were kicked out of Protestant communities.

Luther went as far as to suggest that Jews understood prophecy in nothing but to satisfy their bottomless greed. [1474] Because they are so noble and circumcised, they are entitled to take all the gold and silver from non-Jews. They are *'stiff-necked, disobedient, prophet-murderers, arrogant, usurers, and filled with every vice, as the whole of Scripture and their present conduct bear out,'* [1475] Luther denigrated them.

The business with money had indeed been theirs for a long time.

Better yet, even though the Jewish financial monopoly over Christianity and Islam was an original invention of Jewish leaders – usury was to be outlawed, except for Jewish business with non-Jews – Christianity and Islam accepted the

---

[1471] Ibid., part VII.
[1472] Ibid.
[1473] Ibid., part VIII.
[1474] Ibid., part III.
[1475] Ibid.

madness. Of all things, did they not know that the one in control of finances is the master? Why would they ever have allowed Jews to impose such usury laws upon them if they applied only to non-Jews?

Using figurative speech and Jewish symbolism, Luther compared them with *'a sow that wallows in the mire'*[1476] and speaking to them about their useless outwardly piety was *'much the same as preaching the gospel to a sow.'*[1477] He had long overstepped the boundaries by inciting such hatred against the collective community of Jews, portraying them as *'arrogant saints and damned blasphemers and liars.'*[1478]

His work stands out as the most anti-Semitic ever written.[1479] The criminal intent was not clouded by other writers before him.

The responsibility was his.

His alone.

Luther turned to his main message about Jews asking for their messiah.[1480]

To begin, he made it clear that the god of the Israelites had promised the coming of the Messiah after the tribe of Judah lost the Kingdom of Israel. This, he laid out, had already happened under King Herod in the first century. God made this promise of the coming of the Messiah unconditionally, he argued.[1481]

However, even though all Judaic religions share the vision of the return or coming of the *Jewish* Messiah, Jews insisted on their monopoly on him. They alone should be masters of the world. The accursed non-Jews should be servants and hand over all their wealth to Jews, while they should *'let themselves be slaughtered like wretched cattle.'*[1482]

And then Martin Luther referred to David Reubeni and Solomon Molcho.

Some contemporary Jews said that the Messiah was *'in the world secretly, sitting in Rome among the beggars and doing penance for the Jews until the time for his public appearance is at hand.'* For this, Luther mocked Jews as below Jewish, as men *'of the arrogant, jeering devil.'*[1483]

We remember that Luther refused to call competitors by their names.

There was *one* messiah among the beggars in Rome: Solomon Molcho.

---

[1476] Ibid.

[1477] Ibid.

[1478] Ibid.

[1479] Nuremberg Trial Proceedings, Vol. 12, p. 318, Avalon Project, Yale Law School, April 19, 1946.

[1480] Luther, Jews and Their Lies, 1971, part IV.

[1481] Ibid., IV.

[1482] Ibid., VI.

[1483] Ibid., V.

The Virtual Protestant Museum states that Luther wrote the work in 1534 and adds that this was at the time that Johann of Saxony the Steadfast expelled Jews from his territory,[1484] which occurred in 1536/7, according to Joel Rosheim.[1485] We cannot be sure about the exact dates, but the passage about a hidden messiah in Rome in Luther's anti-Semitic tirade was in reaction to Solomon Molcho going up in flames. He may have kept on 'refining' it over a longer period.[1486]

The mere thought of this collision is so uncomfortable, so horrifying, that it is simply inconceivable.

What must not be true cannot be true.

This is no attempt here to vindicate the Lutheran attacks. Quite the contrary. The only purpose here is to understand why Luther came to his conclusions.

The answer that we receive is so terrible that it is painful to write it down.

Luther's hatred originated in the biblical presentation of Jews as a hated people and the respective enforcement in the New Testament. The activities of David Reubeni and Solomon Molcho were the main triggers for a fatal change of heart inside Luther's world of myths and miracles that had become real.

The messianic illusions that came along with the two stirred Jewish and converso communities to become imprudent. They converted back to Judaism. Luther's paying disciples were stolen away.

Their machinations did not fail to reach the Protestant leader.

Previously, Luther was ignorant about the full extent of the messianic activities and treacheries that were going on undercover.[1487] Now, Luther came to realize that Jews were subverting the entire Protestant society.

---

[1484] The Virtual Protestant Museum, retrieved May 18, 2017.

[1485] Rosheim, transl. A.J. Deus: In the year 5297 (1536/37) Duke Johann of Saxony declared us unprotected, and refused permission for the Jewish people to set even one foot's breadth in his land.

[1486] On Jews and Their Lies was published in 1543. In March 1538, Luther sent out a letter with copies of 'two pamphlets against the Jews.' Since these can be none other than 'On the Jews and Their Lies' as well as Shem Hamporas, Luther must have been working on these for some time before. His original German edition shows the year 1542, but this appears to have been a sloppy last-minute edit. In the same passage and in similar thoughts around the middle of his book, he also calculated the years since the destruction of Jerusalem in 70 AD to have been 1,468. Thus, he had his work first ready for publication in 1538 as written in the previously mentioned letter, which makes it apparent that the dates of writing would otherwise be misplaced.
For the two pamphlets, see Martin Luther, Letter to Nicolas Hausman, March 27, 1538.
For the calculation of the publication see Luther, Jews and Their Lies, 1971, part I, and part VI.

[1487] Luther, Jews and Their Lies, 1971, part XI.

The trouble is that he was correct – by one third – in his conclusion but unbearably incorrect in his collective verdict against the entire Jewish Diaspora.

Ordinary Jews, Christians, or Muslims are utterly unaware of their leaders' diabolic plans.

The other two thirds are that Christianity and Islam subverted societies of others in like manner.

The failing of David Reubeni and Solomon Molcho did indeed have an effect on Jews. A couple of years later, Luther served up an anecdote wherein a rabbi confided to the Reformer that he had waited for the coming of the Messiah until that time. But now that they had failed, the rabbi came to the conclusion that Jesus Christ must be the Messiah.[1488]

But even if Jews did not accept Jesus Christ as the Messiah, even if there was no secret messiah in Luther's time, their messiah had already come in the figure of Simon bar Kokhba. He was supposed to be the lord of the world. But it did not happen. Emperor Hadrian put an end to ambitions to world rule and the Temple of Jerusalem.[1489] The story of the defeat of messiah and Jerusalem was *'sufficient witness that all of Jewry understood that this had to be the time of the Messiah.'*[1490]

Luther's assessment and line of argument was, as far as the religious progression is concerned, correct. Without complete denial of their own history, no Jew can claim that the Messiah had not already come. I have before touched on the paradox of a vanished Kokhba sect where Christianity miraculously emerged.

In context of the messianic dreams of Jews, Luther cited a rabbi who declared that nothing would change with the advent of the Jewish Messiah, *'only the Jews will be the masters and will possess all the world's gold, goods, joys, and delights, while we Christians will be their servants.'* We have already seen that the Reformer saw this correctly. But he was spinning his ideas further, claiming that Jewish aspirations for world leadership coincide with the teachings of Prophet Muhammad of Islam. *'If he were a Jew and not an Ishmaelite, the Jews would have accepted him as the Messiah long ago, or they would have made him the Kokhba.'*[1491]

What if he were a Jew?

---

[1488] John Aurifaber, Table-Talk of Martin Luther (Eisleben, 1566) translated by William Hazlitt (The Lutheran Publication Society) DCCCXXI.

[1489] Luther, Jews and Their Lies, 1971, part VIII.

[1490] Ibid.

[1491] Ibid., part XII.

David Reubeni had claimed to be of Muhammadean descent. It was noted earlier that the birth of Islam fits the pattern of Jewish messianism. Moreover, tradition suggests that Prophet Muhammad had an alias, ibn Abu Kabsha,[1492] a derogatory nickname, we are told. We have heard that before. Blowing all linguistic prudence to the wind, then *Kokhba* and *Kabsha* sound like prophetic twins. In good old Talmudic custom of tongue in code, the insulting *Kabisa* fits the deprecating *Kabsha* even better. Luther did not know, but with his speculation, he got more than he asked for.

We have seen from the evidence out of Baghdad that Prophet Muhammad was indeed a Jewish messiah. In fact, only Jews can be messiahs. And only royal Hasmonean Jews. With the evidence that Islam was able to maintain its Jewish messianic success for over a thousand years, no Jew can ever claim again that the Jewish Christ has not already arrived.

The messianic linage goes through at least two genetic bottlenecks. The first is with Herod the Great and the second is with the Hasmonean Mar Zutran family that constitutes all Jewish exilarchs and nasis since. The Hasmonean Mar Zutran Nehemiah ben Hushiel (Hanan) turned into Prophet Muhammad of tradition from the Banu Hashim (Hasmonean).[1493]

The encoded Jerusalem Talmud Berakhoth says that different religions came together and formed an alliance, with Pharisee and Sadducee Jewry as the ringleaders.[1494] The Jewish Academy of Caesarea ended up leading the 'Muslims.' The winners in the master game of world conquest were Jewish leaders of a spinoff with a new religion: Islam.

The tragic consequence is that the leadership of Shi'a and Sunni Islam is Jewish – today – and so is the former leader of the Islamic State who had killed himself during an U.S. raid, Abu Bakr al-Baghdadi al-Husseini al-Hashimi al-Qurashi. This modern world's enemy claimed to be a Quraysh, thus a Sadducee, a Jew.

The Jewish primary witness Benjamin of Tudela says so in the twelfth century without ambivalence.

Islam equates to successful Jewish messianism.

Adam was the first Jewish Messiah, Jesus Christ was the Jewish Messiah, Simon bar Kokhba was the Jewish Messiah, Muhammad was the Jewish Messiah, Abrabanel wished to have been the Jewish Messiah. There were many

---

[1492] *Bukhari*, ca. 864 – 870, 2007-2009, *6:60:75*.

[1493] A.J. Deus, Iran's Poisoned Qibla Arrows (2024) available at academia.edu.

[1494] A.J. Deus, MHMT/MHMD And A Seed Of The Koran. A Historical Context in the Jerusalem Talmud? December 18, 2015, available at academia.edu.

other Jewish messiahs in a long, uninterrupted lineup, some of whom we have met as Luther's contemporaries. All of them were Jewish by biblical design. After the fact, they were repudiated by Rabbinic leaders as false messiahs. The global Rabbinic community carried the pair David Reubeni and Solomon Molcho. The latter was immediately renounced as soon as the mission had turned sour.

They must do so. Judaism would otherwise collapse.

The after-the-fact rejection of the real messiahs resets the clock: let the game over the conquest of the Promised Land begin, yet again.

In a debate with three Jews, Luther found himself faced with the argument that they believed *'their rabbis as we do the pope and the doctors.'* He thought them harmless. But he later heard that they called Jesus Christ a hanged highwayman. After this experience, he said, he did *'not wish to have anything more to do with any Jew.'*[1495]

Until this experience, the master was willing to work on their 'salvation'.

But now, he quit.

He proclaimed that Jews had neither messiah nor scripture.[1496]

Unlearned Christians would understand one thing:

Have nothing to do with any Jew.

We have discovered earlier that two messiahs need to arrive in the Christian engagement with Islam: one of the Sadducee House of Joseph and one of the House of David. Most Christian denominations focus only on the latter. So did Luther.

In his logic, he brought forth something truly illuminating: if what Jews say about the Messiah were true, then there must be a House of David reigning contemporary to his time. There must be an heir somewhere, such that the House of David *'never stood empty no matter where this heir may be.'*[1497] Luther was unable to fathom that the Sanhedrin and the House of David could have survived in Ethiopia, perhaps since the time of Prophet Muhammad. He did apparently not know that David Reubeni brought exactly that to the table.

*'Now let the Jews produce such an heir of David,'*[1498] Luther dared their leaders.

---

[1495] Luther, Jews and Their Lies, 1971, part V.
[1496] Ibid.
[1497] Ibid.
[1498] Ibid.

In the Catholic Church, the messianic hope is symbolized in the eternal light, a candle that should never be extinguished.

The fundamental error that Luther committed was that he interpreted Jewish texts for them as the only Truth, rather than listening to them about how they understood the Word of God. He also did not seem very well versed in the histories (or rather traditions) of Judaism and Islam in context of Christianity. Otherwise, he might have been able to see through the plot that had been brewing in his lifetime.

His approach turned him blind to the thinking of others.

Luther's charge that Jews were *'ignorant teachers and indolent pupils of Scripture*[1499] was based on his not knowing enough about the secret machinations of Rabbinic leaders.

What if the House of David never died out?

Indeed, the Talmud claims that it endures through all generations.[1500] What if rabbis did not want him to know that the House of David had survived all along?

What is the big deal with this?

It is difficult to express, but had Luther stayed calm and refrained from the anti-Semitic jargon, we could understand better that his complaints were grounded on the reality of competition with his movement.

The throne of David shall be forever, as long as the sun may shine.

Without end, the House of David will claim their right to world leadership. And for eternity, they will subvert entire civilizations in order to achieve their goal.[1501]

Humanity has a problem of monumental proportions, one that it does not need on top of all the other problems of real-world significance.

Luther had just gotten warmed up.

> *Shame on you, here, there, or wherever you may be, you damned Jews, that you dare to apply this earnest, glorious, comforting word of God so despicably to your mortal, greedy belly, which is doomed to decay, and that you are not ashamed to display your greed so openly. You are not worthy of looking at the outside of the Bible,*

---

[1499] Ibid., part VI.

[1500] Sanhedrin 97b in the Babylonian Talmud states that *'Abaye said: The world must contain not less than thirty-six righteous men [tzadikim] in each generation who are vouchsafed [the sight of] the Shechinah's countenance.'* One of them is the Tzaddik of the Generation (Tzadik Ha-Dor), meaning that there is a living messiah at all times.

[1501] Luther, Jews and Their Lies, 1971, part V.

*much less of reading it. You should read only the bible that is found under the sow's tail, and eat and drink the letters that drop from there. That would be a bible for such prophets, who root about like sows and tear apart like pigs the words of the divine Majesty, which should be heard with all honor, awe, and joy.*[1502]

Luther had lost all restraint, calling Jews ignorant, stupid asses who were like talking to sticks and blocks.[1503] For him, they were the devils incarnate.[1504]

They had learned to hate non-Jews as children.

Now, it was part of their nature and life. Luther could easily anger any Jew by claiming that he was a co-heir in the Kingdom of God. He was met with a nasty rebuff and received the glance of death from them.[1505]

But Luther advised his disciples to be careful. Next to the devil, he said, they *'have no more bitter, venomous, and vehement foe than a real Jew who earnestly seeks to be a Jew.'* In the history books, they were often accused of contaminating wells or of kidnapping and piercing children. It was irrelevant, according to Luther, whether these accusations were true. They did *'not lack the complete, full, and ready will to do such things either secretly or openly where possible.'*[1506]

They performed good deeds merely for expediency, Luther assured his audience.[1507]

Indeed, 'good deeds' are part of the price to pay for the hoped-for success in religious, criminal, or political careers. These are stone-cold investments in the pursuit of power.

Luther pointed out – correctly – that it is *'no sin for a Jew to kill a Gentile,'* but it is *'only a sin for him to kill a brother Israelite.'* Likewise, it is no sin to break a promise with a non-Jew, whom they look down at as cattle, Luther said. Stealing from or robbing a non-Jew amounted to rendering a service to God.[1508] *'They are steeped in greed, in usury, they steal and murder where they can and ever teach their children to do likewise,'*[1509] the Reformer continued.

---

[1502] Ibid.
[1503] Ibid.
[1504] Ibid.
[1505] Ibid.
[1506] Ibid., part VII.
[1507] Ibid.
[1508] Ibid.
[1509] Ibid.

Turning to the priestly class of the Sadducees, Luther thought that they were the greatest abominations – horrible and monstrous sows. The reason for his anger was that they *'did not believe in the existence of any angel, devil, heaven, hell, or life after this life.'*[1510]

This is a remarkable thing to say. First, Luther was not incorrect in his assessment of their beliefs. Secondly, they sound rather down-to-earth.

However, they are the ones playing the role of professional deceivers – the devils incarnate.

The Sadducees were those who had led the composition of the first five books of the Bible, called Torah or Pentateuch. They only believed in those five books. This group rejected oral traditions, mainly the rest of the Bible and the Talmud. It had originally created the god of the Israelites as one of many gods in the Divine Council – an ancient human interest-group stoked by real religious leaders in flesh and blood, who played the role of representatives of gods of their time.

It was meant to be a global cartel of spiritual masters.

The leader of the Sadducees was the Nasi, who was comparable to the leader of the Pharisees, the Exilarch. Both competitors were endowed with the Word of God, or so they claimed. When there have been large conflicts in the history of the last 2,000 years, the two were not usually far away. During Luther's time, the pulling power of the Sanhedrin with the Nasi and Exilarch at its helm is obvious.

Never mind that they also composed the Koran.

War and death were the consequences.

Luther thought that Sadducees were less honorable than Pagan philosophers. *'They teach that man by nature is obliged to serve his fellow man, to keep faith also with his enemies, and to be loyal and helpful especially in time of need.'* He believed that some of the Pagan works contained *'more wisdom and more instruction about good works than can be found in the books of all the Talmudists and rabbis and more than may ever occur to the hearts of all the Jews.'*[1511]

Since Christianity had been created to subvert the Roman Empire and its Pagan values, the disciples of the Catholic Church and now also Martin Luther's would naturally be inclined to reject Roman culture based on nothing other than

---

[1510] Ibid.
[1511] Ibid.

faith. Putting Sadducees below Roman Pagans is akin to judging them the lowest spirits possible. Christians at the time did not fail to note the implication.

But here again, this was not a confused man speaking. He was quite awake in his assessment of the wisdom that could be found in Paganism also. After all, as I noted earlier, the Judaic religions are participants in Pagan cultures. They included repackaged polytheist elements.

But Luther kept on pushing his hatred upon Jews, now against the entire community, not just Sadducee leaders. They curse all non-Jews and wish them every misfortune, he said. *'They rob us of our money and goods through their usury, and they play on us every wicked trick they can.'* In the end, Jews still claimed to have done God a service. *'And they teach the doing of such things.'* No Pagan ever acted in this way, Luther proclaimed, except Satan himself.[1512]

Luther was not confused.

> *'But our bastards and pseudo-Jews think they must curse us, hate us, and inflict every possible harm upon us, although they have no cause for it.'*[1513]

He genuinely hated every single Jew for them cursing all non-Jews. The circle of hatred worked for the religious communities as intended. As the fronts hardened, the communities became more resilient about owning the only Truth. *'No house was ever disgraced more than this holy house of God was by such vile sows as the Sadducees and Pharisees.'*[1514]

There you have it: Luther hated all Jews. He had learned it from the Bible. Now, he put his feelings into his own words.

No work of Luther was free of bias. But here, he went further. He made up that early Christians had been dragged out before the judges by Jews, and they had them killed.[1515] From this, Luther resolved that Jews were behind the killings of Christians, rather than Romans (as per Christian tradition).

From the context of their mutual hatred, such behavior is in the realm of the possible. However, I am not aware of any such reports that would not come from Christian scribes regarding Christians having been killed for their faith, let alone having been betrayed by Jews. Quite the contrary. The evidence points at a symbiosis between 'Judaism' and 'Christianity' – whatever these two were – where Christians shared synagogues with Jews.

---

[1512] Ibid.
[1513] Ibid.
[1514] Ibid.
[1515] Ibid., VIII.

Christians started out as subjects of Jewish leaders, precisely as Jewish messianism was biblically designed.

The emancipation of Christianity from Judaism took hundreds of years and was still ongoing at the turn of the fifth century, if not later.[1516] To be sure, as in Islam today where Shi'ite Muslims prefer to kill Sunni Muslims, the historical record is peppered with Christian sectarians killing other Christian sectarians.

In Judaism, we see Pharisees preferring to kill Sadducees through mutual religious terrorism. The slaughtering of members of other religions tends to have been executed on battlefields, in Holy War, Crusade, or Jihad.

But let us reflect on what Luther just said: Christians had been dragged out before the judges by Jews in order to have them killed. Let me rephrase this to make the consequences clear: Jews had been dragged out before the judges by Christians in order to have them killed.

This single swap is good for six million Jewish souls lost in less than a decade.

Furthermore, Luther called Jews out for speaking in secret code meant to bedevil Christians and all other non-Jews. For example, they replaced the common *welcome* with a linguistic corruption that was meant to welcome a devil. Christians were made to feel welcome by Jews, while in reality, they were *'calling down hellfire and every misfortune on our heads.'*[1517]

They called Jesus Christ *'a whore's son,'* the Reformer said, *'who conceived him in adultery with a blacksmith.'* Mary was renamed by a *'malicious rabbi'* to *haria*, a corruption from the German *Maria*, meaning a *heap of dung*.[1518]

The source of this information was Sebastian Münster, himself a convert to Lutheranism from having been a disciple of the Jew Elia Levita. Yes, that is the ancestor of David Cameron. Levita was the Jew who found himself in the Ghetto of Venice after enjoying Egidio Viterbo's palace for a good decade. The latter had earlier introduced David Reubeni to the pope.

Luther's source was more reliable than we wish for.

But again: how deeply did Rabbinic leadership penetrate and subvert Luther's inner circle?

---

[1516] See Saint Chrysostom, Homilies Against the Jews, Adversus Judaeos "Autumn 386", translated by Paul W. Harkins, The Fathers of the Church (Catholic University of America Press, 1979).

[1517] Luther, Jews and Their Lies, 1971, part X.

[1518] Ibid.

Luther recognized that such speech had its origin in *'sheer hatred and spite, solely for the purpose of bitterly poisoning the minds of their poor youth and the simple Jews.'* [1519] This should have been an eye-opener.

However, the Reformer could not see that he was applying the same principles. He could not recognize that he was inciting his disciples and German youths with the same hatred.

He called for violence against all Jews.

Instead of receiving instructions from God, Luther asserted, Jews hoped to instruct God to exterminate all non-Jews *'so that they can lay their hands on the land, the goods, and the government of the whole world.'* In Luther's time, rabbis preached in their synagogues *'every Saturday and daily in their homes'* that *'sword and war, distress and every misfortune may overtake'* all accursed non-Jews, apparently referring to the conflict between the Holy Roman Empire and the Ottoman-Turks. *'They teach, urge, and train their children from infancy to remain the bitter, virulent, and wrathful enemies of the'* non-Jews. [1520]

This was not some abstract monologue. Luther intended to speak about his countrymen, the contemporary Jews of his time. [1521]

The Reformer did not seem to realize that he fueled the same mechanism of infiltrating the minds of children with hate doctrines.

Those responsible were sitting at the very top of the chain of command.

When it comes to hatred, no man is excused for remaining seated when he should stand up. Inciting hatred and violence is inexcusable for speaker and listener alike.

As the master taught, doing and consenting deserve equal punishment. [1522]

Then Martin Luther showed them the door. But how!

They could leave to their land, the sooner the better. Jews were *'a heavy burden, a plague, a pestilence, a sheer misfortune for our country.'* As proof of their deserving to be thrown out of Protestant Germany, he cited how other places had already done so during his lifetime: France, Spain, Bohemia, Regensburg, Magdeburg, and other places. [1523]

---

[1519] Ibid.
[1520] Ibid.
[1521] Ibid.
[1522] Ibid., part XII.
[1523] Ibid., part X.

The kingdom where persecutions against Jews brings enlightenment to us was Portugal. I will get to it shortly.

He thought it ridiculous that Jews acted as though they were held captives in Germany. Even though Luther understood that their tongue was in code, he missed that the internal Jewish meaning of 'captives' or 'slaves' was that the Diaspora was *working* for and profiteering from the messianic administrations that pushed everyone else into serfdom.

For him, they were free – free to leave.

> *Since it has now been established that we do not hold them captive, how does it happen that we deserve the enmity of such noble and great saints? We do not call their women whores as they do Mary, Jesus' mother. We do not call them children of whores as they do our Lord Jesus. We do not say that they were conceived at the time of cleansing and were thus born as idiots, as they say of our Lord. We do not say that their women are 'haria,' as they do with regard to our dear Mary. We do not curse them but wish them well, physically and spiritually. We lodge them, we let them eat and drink with us. We do not kidnap their children and pierce them through; we do not poison their wells; we do not thirst for their blood. How, then, do we incur such terrible anger, envy, and hatred on the part of such great and holy children of God?*[1524]

How? Read the Bible!

No interpretation is necessary.

Jews hate Christians and Muslims from the bottoms of their hearts because they learn to do so through the Bible. Hatred has been indoctrinated into them from the cradle. Luther was telling us in his own words why Christians were supposed to hate Jews, from the deepest crevasses of their skulls.

Do we need to talk much longer about why Muslims take delight in blowing up teenagers who are leaving a concert? Read the Koran!

> *Now tell me whether they do not have every reason to be the enemies of us accursed Goyim [non-Jews], to curse us and to strive for our final, complete, and eternal ruin!*[1525]

What shall we do with Jews?

---

[1524] Ibid.
[1525] Ibid.

You might not like Luther's fatherly advice of spreading his love:[1526] Burn their synagogues and schools to the ground;[1527] destroy their houses and lodge them in barns,[1528] today known as concentration camps; confiscate all their prayer books and Talmudic writings,[1529] book burnings in our modern lingo; put their rabbis' teachings under capital punishment;[1530] deny Jews safe passage; those who pass through are collaborators, anyway;[1531] forbid them the practice of usury and seize all their wealth (use it for bribing potential converts);[1532] force Jews to work, or eject them from the country;[1533] cancel all their privileges;[1534] torture them until they confess, or keep them incarcerated forever.[1535]

Can you feel the love of Adolf Hitler for Jews?

Holocaust.

One might think that this one word sums it all up, if only we were to understand cause and effect of a catch twenty-two where hatred is the principal mechanism that organized religion works with.

Not to forget the magnet of hatred through oppressive tax farming and administration.

In the twentieth-century aftermath of the Second World War, Protestant Britons brought Jews back to modern day Israel. It did nothing but renew the 2,000-year-old cycle of violence.

In all this, Protestants as well as all others should be able to recognize that Martin Luther and his Reformation did not contribute to peace and prosperity. Quite the contrary. Luther's path was back to a past with a totalitarian religious society. Other than possible collateral damage from some of the decisions that had been made – such as openly disobeying the Catholic Church – we must look for the progressive forces elsewhere. For example, one such place to look would be contributions to economic and cultural awakenings that Jewish and Muslim converts to Catholicism and Protestantism might have brought. Many may have turned into covert humanists.

---

[1526] Ibid., part XI.
[1527] Ibid.
[1528] Ibid.
[1529] Ibid.
[1530] Ibid.
[1531] Ibid.
[1532] Ibid.
[1533] Ibid.
[1534] Ibid.
[1535] Ibid., part XII.

I would not be surprised to have this found to be the number one driving factor in the formation of the modern world as we know it.

But before anyone celebrates, 500 years of religious wars and holocausts separate the modern West from Martin Luther.

Religious freedom, of course, is a one-way street for believers. You are free to believe. But please! Not here. Do not teach otherwise under our noses. Do not sing your own praises. Do not revile the true faith, and do not attempt to lure others to your false beliefs – *'that is a far, far different story.'*[1536]

Hatred and violence await you there.

Allow me to draw your attention to the beautiful quote from Martin Luther at the beginning of this book: *'My friend, it is not a question of what you know or what you wish to know, but of what you ought to know, what you are obliged to know.'*[1537] I had you miss the context. Now you have it. Being part of the book *'On the Jews and Their Lies'* makes its beauty crumble into its chilling meaning.

> *As it happens, not only the Jew but all the world is obliged to know that the New Testament is God the Father's book about his Son Jesus Christ. Whoever does not accept and honor that book does not accept and honor God the Father himself.*[1538]

The quote contained the essence of Luther's message of hatred and violence against Jews, Muslims, and any other religion or sect that did not understand the New Testament as the master did. The targets included the Catholic Church and all who were free from religion.

Jews, according to the Reformer, are not worthy of uttering the name of God within hearing distance of Lutherans. Those who hear the name of God from a Jew must inform the authorities or throw sow dung at the Jew and chase him away without showing mercy.[1539] Since Jews would then go underground, Luther's recipe was to shortcut the process and simply get rid of them altogether: *'they must be driven from our country.'*[1540]

So much for replacing the dark rituals of the Catholic Church with celebrating the message of love by Jesus Christ.

> *Dear Lord God, keep your Messiah, or give him to whoever will have him. Instead, make me a sow.*[1541]

---

[1536] Ibid., part XI.
[1537] Ibid., part XII.
[1538] Ibid.
[1539] Ibid.
[1540] Ibid.
[1541] Ibid.

The icing on the cake is when the extremist proclaimed that Christianity had achieved its dominance solely through application of the word. No violence was necessary.[1542]

We can see clearly now.

Preaching to smoke them out is not the same as smoking them out. Sending papal armies is not the same as wielding the sword.

The word of love alone would have done it all.

But Luther was not done with demonizing Jews.

He wrote yet another diatribe against them. His book *'Schem Hamphoras'* is an additional rant about Jews' inability to accept Jesus Christ as the Messiah.

Luther was convinced that Jews needed to believe whatever their rabbis said.[1543] But he was not thinking things through. If that were said the case, then nobody can assume that the Truth in the Torah was God-given. It says whatever the rabbis say.

In this work, Luther explained the meaning of the Gematria in the Talmud, which is one of the methods of encoding and decoding the underlying text. Indeed, the Talmud provides for a visible layer to read and a secret layer for Rabbinic experts to decipher. It even mocks non-experts arrogantly by saying that they can read it, but they cannot interpret it. Its authors thought of them as fools walking in the dark.[1544]

The Talmudist leaders were builders of a trap who needed to be indicted. Instead, those who tried to prevent others from falling into this pit were persecuted.

In the second part of *'Schem Hamphoras,'* Luther investigated the two different lineages of Jesus Christ in the Gospels. He was out to prove that Jesus Christ descended from the House of David and that he fulfilled all the prophecies that identified the Messiah. Jews – whom he called *'evil boys'*[1545] – deny this. His arrows went to the heart of the ongoing messianic competition.

The book is a trove of hate.

---

[1542] Ibid.

[1543] Luther, Schem Hamphoras, transl. A.J. Deus, 1543, 26.

[1544] A.J. Deus, MHMT/MHMD and a Seed of the Koran, A Historical Context in the Jerusalem Talmud? (2015).

[1545] Luther, Schem Hamphoras, transl. Deus, 1543, 97.

> *That is why we need to step on the heads of the poisonous and thorny serpents and respond accordingly despite the Devil's stomping and fuming.*[1546]

However, toward the end of *'Shem Hamphoras,'* Luther made an odd remark that Jews were too powerful.[1547] He had mentioned early in his career that he had to be careful with how he spoke about Jews. We learned about a penetration of administrations by Jews in Germany and elsewhere. The Reformer might have referred to the power that these positions may have provided them, which included the judicial system. Luther complained that he had to recant some of his translations, in particular a section from his German Bible that referred to David.[1548] It appears that Rabbinic leaders had been tracking Luther closely and dragged him before Jewish judges when opportune.

He finished the book with a statement that he did not want anything further to do with Jews. He would no longer write about or against them.[1549]

The damage was already done.

In all this, we must not forget that Martin Luther had also replied to a Jewish pamphlet whose writer and content are unknown to us. Its mission was to convert Christians to Judaism by showing that the latter had the better Truth. At the same time, Luther faced large Christian followings of David Reubeni and Solomon Molcho. In droves, they had openly converted to Judaism. Their success in 'stealing' his disciples angered Luther.

The mutual hatred of religious competition gave him such a headache that he created the foundation of modern anti-Semitism.

The underlying accusations were real. Not new. But real.

Even though we should not foolhardily rush to judgment, now we can perhaps envision that the Alhambra Decree from 1492, which ordered the expulsion of practicing Jews from Spain, might indeed partly have been a reaction of a Jewish messianic attempt to convert Marranos back to Judaism and to subvert the Catholic Church.[1550] Ottoman and Mamluk aggressions against Europe may have played their part. Jews may have been suspected of betraying their hosts and to abuse their administrative positions.

---

[1546] Ibid., 86.
[1547] Ibid., 187.
[1548] Ibid.
[1549] Ibid., 189.
[1550] Isabella I of Castile and Ferdinand II of Aragon, Alhambra Decree, March 31, 1492.

The top leadership of this administrative deep state might have ended up being the same with the Spanish Inquisition – a transfer of terror through crypto conversion. This rabbit hole deserves deep exploration. Should the Catholic Church have been infiltrated, the 'whole truth' might offer an escape hatch from its responsibility.

Luther did not invent the problem of financial enslavement of his disciples by Jews. It has been a recurring theme throughout history. It was a self-made biblical monopoly that hit all non-Jews who submitted to Judaic religions. Their former and current position as tax farmers meant, factually, nothing other than financially enslaving the population.

For Luther and his followers, it was real.

And it backfired. Again, and again, and again.

Ordinary Jews kept on paying with their lives. The bosses got away.

The accusation of Jewish treachery was real also. We could see it unfolding under Luther's feet. We can see it today in the unhealthy back and forth between Israel and Palestine.

Or in daring America to take out Iran.

The evidence from Luther speaks clearly : Luther himself was hell-bent to subvert and destroy Emperor Charles by weakening the Catholic Church; the latter wanted to defeat the Antichrist who had appeared with Ottoman-Turks; Islam was determined to obliterate the Holy Roman Empire with its seat in Vienna; Rabbinic leaders intended to play the world powers against each other in order to move into the Promised Land as the laughing third.

These are not just neighborly skirmishes but global insanities on a grand scale.

How the extremist Reformer responded to all this finds no excuses for those who belong to his dominion, none whatsoever. There are no justifications for the Holocaust or any holocaust. By being part of a Lutheran sect, all disciples conspire with Luther's anti-Semitic attacks, if only through their unacceptable silence.

Their only defense, thus far, may be that they might have not understood it in this way. My friends, it is not a question of what you know or what you wish to know, but of what you ought to know, what you are obliged to know.

Now you know.

Knowledge is humanity's only hope to confront the madness that has decimated mankind over thousands of years.

The story could end here.

But you might like to know what else Luther had in store for the coming decade.

What happened to the Mahdi?

Or to the Jews?

What about the End of the World?

### Bind Him Up in Hell

Martin Luther had become an anti-Semitic activist. Within a few months of Solomon Molcho's death, Jews were persecuted in the area of Johann of Saxony the Steadfast – Luther-land. The Protestant leader thundered against Jews in south-eastern Germany, Brandenburg, Saxony, as well as Silesia.[1551]

Luther had found his life's mission in having Jews persecuted.

Two years later, Jews were prohibited from setting foot in Saxony.

Rabbi Josel of Rosheim attempted to intervene with Martin Luther to no avail. The Reformer refused to lend a hand,[1552] and Rosheim could not even get an audience with the Steadfast. That is how much Martin Luther had become the gatekeeper for access to nobility. In his memoirs, Rosheim commented that Luther – *'may his body and soul be bound up in hell!'* – was responsible for the Jewish calamities in Saxony.[1553] He called Luther by the name *Lo Tohar*. This is another Talmudic phonetic corruption of his last name. It means approximately the same as *The Fool*. Rosheim petitioned the city council of Strasbourg to prohibit Luther's anti-Semitic works. This was granted only after a Lutheran priest called for murdering Jews.[1554]

We need to reflect on Luther's policies from years back. Because the focus was on Jews, it is easy to forget that their general expulsion was not the product of Luther's anti-Semitism but of his longstanding views that those who did not agree with Lutheranism should simply leave. That would impact anyone, including Catholics and Anabaptists, for example. Combine this with the oppressive Jewish administrative hate magnet and a financial monopoly. With his anti-Jewish propaganda, which surfaced with the treachery of David Reubeni and Solomon Molcho, this turned into a deadly cocktail. It reflects his

---

[1551] Robert Michael, *Holy Hatred: Christianity, Antisemitism, and the Holocaust* (Palgrave Macmillan, 2006) 117.

[1552] Luther's letter to Rabbi Josel as cited by Gordon Rupp, *Martin Luther and the Jews* (London: The Council of Christians and Jews, 1972) 14, this text cannot be found in the English edition of Luther's works.

[1553] Rosheim, transl. A.J. Deus.

[1554] Michael, *Holy Hatred*, 2006, 117.

progression from a persecuted minority to a position of power and the persecutor. Regardless of sectarian affiliation, this process is attested for in history perpetually. As an identifiable community, Jews were a welcoming target for the extremist Luther. They willingly contributed to their own tragedies through their self-portrayal as a hated people and their stubborn pursuit of the arrogant myth of the Promised Land for the Chosen People.

They saw their suffering as God's will.

Not to forget: they had supposedly killed Jesus and insisted on his not being the Messiah.

There is another factor when assessing Luther's rise to anti-Semitic stardom that is routinely swept under the rug. I have discussed it at length to help us to understand where Luther came from.

The Inquisition.

Asking where the Catholic Church stood in all this, the answer is straightforward: Luther's time is also the era of the Inquisition's peak of religious atrocities. Luther was emboldened by anti-Muslim and anti-Jewish policies of the Catholic Church, which blanketed all of Europe. He spoke the way he did because it was normal in his day. I doubt that Luther would have come so far without the deep-seated anti-Semitism of the Catholic Church that had engulfed the entire Western civilization with the exception of a few places of refuge.

We have a testimony from a Portuguese captain of the time. He called Jews traitors and liars. They had no balls and no honor.[1555]

The policy was on its way to America.

None of them had an excuse for their crimes against humanity. The difference between Luther and the Catholic Church is that the latter did a better job in wiping away the evidence.

Of course, after losing the Messiah, Rabbinic leaders went right back to their plot. This time, Rabbi Josel of Rosheim was directly implicated. Supposedly in an inter-Jewish dispute that arose in Bohemia, Rosheim happened to be elected to assist the great rabbi, the Gaon, the Jewish spiritual leader behind the veil, in drawing up new ordinances for Jewish communities.[1556] The great rabbi was Rabbi Abraham ben Avigdor.[1557]

---

[1555] Captain António da Silveira, Letter to Hadim Suleiman Pasha at the Siege of Diu, 1538, in Gaspar Correia (1558–1563) Lendas da Índia (Academia Real das Sciencias de Lisboa, 1864) book IV, 35.

[1556] Rosheim, transl. A.J. Deus.

[1557] Rabbi Abraham ben Avigdor, d. 1542.

The word *gaon* stands for the Jewish leader sitting on the Throne of David, and *Avigdor* is another name for *Moses*. He was none other than the new messiah of the Ashkenazy and Polish Jews. It appears that the troubled communities intended to forge a new inter-sectarian alliance.

Eight years later, Jews were thrown out of Bohemia, and Rosheim blamed the Sadducees for this, accurately symbolized in his memoirs as *'the snakes, the fiery serpents.'*[1558] The alliance and the new ordinances did not work out. They departed from the path that had been agreed upon.[1559]

Of course, Rosheim denied any participation.

It is not just Christian or Muslim sectarians that do not get along with each other. Jewish sects are not role models of peaceful cooperation either.

With the intervention of Emperor Charles, Pope Paul was pressured to call a general council in response to the rise of the Protestant Church. The emperor intended to reunite all sectarians, including the Protestants under one, reformed Catholic Church. Charles obviously did not understand the basic mechanisms of organized religion. He hoped to leverage the united religious hierarchies to provide even more power to the imperial throne.

Therefore, the pope appointed a commission to review the abuses of the Catholic Church.[1560]

Then and now, a commission is the most primitive excuse for doing nothing.

The report was supposed to be confidential but was leaked. It essentially confirmed Luther's concerns and recommended abolition of the abuses[1561] – as though the Catholic Church has not pretended to abolish its abuses time and again. The Reformer translated the report into German, took his stabs at it, and published it as his personal vindication.

The Catholic Church was using foxtails instead of brooms, he said.

Just as Luther's original spark was a leak, so was the one that led to the Counter-Reformation by the Catholic Church.

But the Catholic Church was actually using brooms. And they were performing a clean sweep.

In Portugal.

---

[1558] Rosheim, transl. A.J. Deus.
[1559] Ibid.
[1560] Consilium de Emendanda Ecclesia, Romæ, 1538.
[1561] J. le Plat, Monumenta ad historiam Concilii Tridentini (Leuven, 1782) ii. 596–597.

We remember that Jews had fled there for cover from the Spanish Inquisition. King Manuel of Portugal the Fortunate had failed to enforce his obligation to persecute them.

Their grace period was over. For good. Two years earlier, Pope Paul – mainstream history tells us that it was Manuel's fault – promoted a man by the name of Diogo da Silva[1562] to be the Grand Inquisitor of Portugal to bring the Inquisition to that nation and into the New World.

How do we know that this was Pope Paul's game and not the king's?

First, the arrival of the cult of the Brotherhoods of the Divine Holy Spirit[1563] in the Portuguese dominions of the New World ahead of the Inquisition provides us with an important clue that the 'Christian' population and nobility in Portugal may previously not have voluntarily submitted to the Catholic Church. Likewise, for the previous 200 years, Portugal had not participated in the persecution of the Knights Templar Order for heresy. There, the order lived on undisturbed.

Some Knights Templars were accused in the torture trials of the Inquisition for venerating an idol known as Baphomet.[1564] This is a French Talmudic corruption, meaning *the Beast* – Muhammad.

A god.

Christians praying to Muhammad? This is not as fantastic as one might think. Religious communities, which came in between the sectarian battle fronts, sometimes sought compromises, in particular in messianic contexts.[1565] However, Knights venerating Muhammad in a concealed manner might simply originate from former Muslims who had been force-converted and then became part of the order. As confusing as this is, in the interest of focus, I need to leave it at that.

Nevertheless, Christian Knights Templar who venerated Muhammad as an idol are quite something.

---

[1562] D. Miguel da Silva (Diogo Miguel da Silva), 1480 – 1556, was a son of one Diogo da Silva, the First Count of Portalegre, Portugal.

[1563] Irmandades do Divino Espírito Santo.

[1564] Peter Partner, The Murdered Magicians: The Templars and Their Myth (Barns & Noble, 1993) 138–144.

[1565] Together with what had been earlier said about the influence of the Syrian Melchite Church in Europe, this evidence from the trials could serve to unravel the history of the Iberian Peninsula. However, the chain of cross-insemination needs to be firmly established first.

Now, the Knights Templars sailed under a new name in Portugal.[1566] They rose to great wealth during the Age of Discoveries. How this change of identity came about provides us with more clues.

Of course, it has to do with the End of the World.

Back in the late twelfth century, a man by the name of Joachim of Fiore[1567] took the Book of Revelation and predicted that the End of the World would occur in 1260. After that, a new age would usher in the rise of a new religion that would unify all believers and infidels alike. The Catholic Church would be replaced by the Order of the Just. It would constitute the New Kingdom of the Holy Spirit. Universal love and freedom based on the Gospels would rule.

Love and freedom for those who voluntarily submitted, that is.

Its leader ruled the world. Fiore was considered a prophet and a saint.

He was denied beatification.

The mechanisms are familiar.

The Knights Templars had just established the Kingdom of Cyprus. They could govern this territory on their own. From this, they expanded so-called Crusader States along the Levant.

But they could not hold on to them.

A century after Fiore, the Florentine philosopher Dante Alighieri[1568] placed Fiore as a prophet into paradise.[1569] Dante was one of the Catholic Pope's mightiest enemies at the time. He was armed – with a pen. The holy man – the Vicar of Christ – was placed into hell. In his book *De Monarchia,* Dante argued against papal power. The church was a system of organized crime that extorted money from the poor. That was *his* choice of words. It did not help those in need, he maintained.[1570]

Dante envisioned a unified empire in the ideal of ancient Rome.[1571] The exclusive way to resolve disputes was through a high secular power, not through the Catholic Church.[1572] He, too, was dreaming of world governance, but by a secular monarch and a government in the service of the people. The ancient

---

[1566] The Order of Christ with the Cult of the Holy Spirit.

[1567] Joachim of Fiore, aka Beatus, Joachim of Flora, Gioacchino da Fiore, 1135 –1202.

[1568] Dante Alighieri, also known as Dante 1265 – 1321. He was an Italian poet.

[1569] Dante Alighieri, Divine Comedy (ca. 1308) XII, Translated by Charles Eliot Norton (1999).

[1570] Dante Alighieri, *De Monarchia* (ca. 1308) II:XII.

[1571] Ibid., I:VIII.

[1572] Ibid., I:X.

Roman Empire was God-given.[1573] The Catholic Church had to stay out of it, except for matters of spirituality.[1574]

Dante was an Italian supremacist.[1575]

His popular work, *The Divine Comedy*,[1576] was possibly inspired by Arab writers.[1577]

Several popes came under attack by his pen. Two were destined for hell because of simony, the selling of influential church positions, and other offenses.[1578] Another was placed near the gates of hell, and the last was in purgatory for too much liquor.

The four holy men could have stolen the jar of milk from the breast of Jesus' mother Mary back from the deceased. It would not have helped them. They never made it to the Kingdom of Heaven.

The four had a communality that may have attracted Dante's rejection of their pontifices: all took actions against the Spanish Crown of Aragon and in favor of the French House of Anjou. The Crown of Aragon then occupied eastern Spain, parts of southern France, Sicily, Corsica, Sardinia, Malta, and southern Italy. Soon thereafter, the Vatican was occupied by anti-popes. The Catholic popes were forced to move to Avignon (now in France). This period is called the 'Babylonian Exile of the Church.' It is also the time during which a report has reached modernity that the Syrian Melchite flavor of Christianity was not only dominant but also had its seat in the Vatican in Rome.

Fiore's 'prediction' for 1260 indeed fell together with the End of the World.

Only it never happened.

In the autumn of that year, the Mongols, who had already devastated the Holy Land, were destroyed by Muslim Mamluks. In the wake of this war, one stronghold of the Knights Templar after another fell to the Muslim conquerors. The knightly strongmen with the rest of the Christian Crusaders were kicked out of the Middle East.

---

[1573] Ibid., II:IV.

[1574] Ibid., III:XII.

[1575] Ibid., II:III.

[1576] Dante Alighieri, Divine Comedy: published from about 1308 (Inferno), 1314 (Purgatorio), through to 1321 (Paradiso).

[1577] Miguel Asín Palacios, Islamic Eschatology in the Divine Comedy (1919). Palacios thought that Muslim works from Ibn Arabi were used and also that the "Night Journey of Muhammad to Heaven" (Kitab al Miraj) had served as an inspiration.

[1578] Dante Alighieri, Divine Comedy (ca. 1308) XIX, Translated by Charles Eliot Norton (1999)s.

Their tell-all symbol: Crown, scepter and orb. At the time of Dante, the knights were aspiring to a new monastic world governance[1579] in the image of Fiore.

The Knights Templar had become a danger to the power of the Catholic Church. This was the reason for their persecution.

Dante's descendants had miraculously survived the End of the World.

However, Joachim of Fiore's influence was significant not only for the Franciscan Order (the order from which monks had fled to Muslim North Africa) but also for the Knights Templar.[1580]

After Manuel the Fortunate, the knightly order came under visible persecution by the Inquisition of the Catholic Church in Portugal.

In other words, Portugal was a target in the re-conquest by the Catholic Church and also the main target by the Inquisition. The Knights Templars[1581] had been driven east through France and Spain to Portugal, their last holdout. Portugal's original faith had been brought through Germany, France, Italy, and Spain with the migrating Germanic tribes. They had adhered to beliefs that were likely shaped through the writings in the New Testament by Saint Paul.[1582]

After the arrival of the Arabs in the Iberian Peninsula, we are left in the dark about what might have happened to these Christian communities. How and when did the Melchite Syrian Church penetrate south-western Europe?[1583] In addition, evidence about Portugal's conversion from their original style of Christianity to Catholicism is pretty much absent.

Even though it might be difficult to fathom, what we believe to know are mainly fantasies that were created after the re-conquest. The whole 800-year story of the Reconquista is a myth.[1584] The first whitewashed histories of Iberia appeared right then, during the lifetime of the Portuguese Grand Inquisitor

---

[1579] Sean Martin, The Knights Templar: The History & Myths of the Legendary Military Order (Oldcastle, 2014) Fall and Trial.

[1580] This included the Cult of the Holy Spirit, with their order of Christ, and the Order of Montesa.

[1581] The Order of Christ.

[1582] Departing from academic consensus, their beliefs appear to originate with the Ulfillas Bible from around the middle of the fourth century. Ulfilas (ca. 311–383, aka Ulphilas, Orphila, Wulfila ['Little Wolf']) was a disciple of Eusebius, one of the most fundamental Arians of the time. Ulfilas' teaching was based on Eusebius's translations, fabrications, and collections of the Bible, emphasizing a new form of Arianism. It embraced the Paulinic letters.

[1583] Modern historians call the sectarian flavor of Christianity under the Muslims 'Mozarab,' a confusing term, which is understood as akin to Eastern Syrian Orthodoxy or perhaps the Paulinic type of Christianity of the Germanic tribes. In any case, it was not Catholicism.

[1584] Martín M. Ríos Saloma, La Reconquista. Génesis de un mito historiográfico (Historia y Grafía, 30, 2008) 191–216.

Diogo da Silva. It is little wonder that nothing can be found about a Syrian Christian influence in Spain. Bishops and church councils – whether real or invented – provide no information about the level of penetration by the respective 'Catholic' sectarians in the Iberian Peninsula.

It is taught in history lessons for amateurs not to abandon questioning simply because something is not there. What could be the motives why it is not there? The easy way out is to keep on parroting histories that make no contextual sense.

Assuming that pathological liars and criminals were at work is more difficult, but it may lead to the lessons necessary to avoid the repetition of humanitarian disasters that are based on differences in faiths that were created by Jewish leaders with the agenda to divide and rule.

Secondly, we have no knowledge about who this Grand Inquisitor da Silva was. He is rooted in mystery. Somewhat. He is another one of those tricks with two different personalities that were really one, the Portuguese Ambassador to the Vatican in Rome and also the Portuguese Archbishop.

Manuel the Fortunate had sent him to Rome as ambassador to the Vatican. He worked in this role from 1514 with the Medici Pope Leo X, the Butcher Pope Adrian VI, and the Medici Pope Clement VII. Manuel had opposed da Silva's promotion by the Vatican to the position of cardinal. After the Portuguese King's unfortunate death in 1521, the current Pope Paul III finally elevated the 'ambassador' to become bishop of Ceuta, archbishop of Braga (the Catholic head church for all of Portugal), and to be Cardinal Diogo da Silva. The Portuguese crown under King John III of Portugal the Pious, who had received Reubeni, took this promotion as treason.

One da Silva was stripped of his Portuguese nationality and the other became cardinal.

Two stories. One man.

The treasonous move with da Silva had been designed by Pope Paul III to subvert Portugal.

Mainstream historians suggest that the Grand Inquisitor Cardinal da Silva was not the first in charge of the Holy Office, but rather Henry,[1585] the fifth son of King Manuel. At this time, Henry was supposed to be Grand Inquisitor (whatever that meant for him), only to become cardinal of the Catholic Church later. Over thirty years out, he was going to be Cardinal King of Portugal – the Chaste.

---

[1585] Cardinal Henry the Chaste, 1512 – 1580, was King of Portugal and the Algarves 1578 – 1580.

But here is the problem: Henry the Chaste rose exactly when Manuel's fifth son presumably disappeared on the battlefield. The son was barely twenty-one years old. The crown was open for grabs – or was forced open.

With the charge of blaming Henry, we need to recall that the Catholic Church claimed the 'right' to appoint Europe's kings and the world's emperors.[1586]

Once in power, the pope could put anybody on the Portuguese throne that he wished.

You need evidence?

For its power, the Vatican insisted on an age-old Papal Bull. The pope alone *'may be permitted to depose emperors.'* All princes shall kiss his feet. The pope is the judge to be judged by no one.[1587] He is the stalwart of the Truth.

Henry's predecessor's untimely death smells awful: he was trying to drive back on the power of the Inquisition and banned its customary confiscations of properties.

The pattern of a disobedient king who came to a sudden end has been repeated over and over again.

The death of the young man? Foul play by the Catholic Church?

Ignoring these ambitions came at a price: book burnings, Inquisitorial trials, persecution of witchcraft and sexual crimes. The consequences were brought to their homes by the Inquisition.

Now, it was Portugal's turn.

Whichever the case is with Henry's ancestry, this man was under the power of the Catholic Church. Until the ascent of Henry the Chaste, Portugal had been building a global empire in which the sun never set. With his ascent, Portugal's slide into deep Catholicism was ushered in – until the sun set. For countless.

With the spotty information that has come down to us, the body count is well over 30,000 inside the small Portuguese mainland alone.

Portuguese royalty had tried to keep the Catholic Church at a distance. The papacy subverted the last European stronghold that provided protection for Jews and usurped it.

---

[1586] We have testimony from a respected Muslim source that the pope indeed empowered emperors. Khaldun, *Muqaddimah, 1377*, transl. Rosenthal, 1958, Chapter III.31.

[1587] Pope Gregory VII, *Dictatus Papae*, 1075, from Brian Tierney, *The Middle Ages, Volume I, Sources of Medieval History* (McGraw-Hill, 1999) 121-122.

Portugal remained Europe's most culturally, intellectually, and economically backward oriented country for hundreds of years. The Inquisition kept on trying cases up until the nineteenth century.

The poor kept on footing the bills.

With coins and blood.

Not that the perpetrators were unaware of the injustice. A letter that begged for war funds, which was sent from the Senate of Venice to the pope, grumbled that *'the poor will always be exploited and burdened beyond what is right.'*[1588]

Their behavior came about with intent and awareness.

At least the taxes to the Catholic Church – alms, they called it – were at the time of the letter adjusted to be based on 'known' income. Those were mandatory 'alms,' similar to the practices in Islam and Judaism.

The lemon had already been squeezed dry.

The Catholic Church was looking for ways to extract more of the precious juice.

A friend and co-Reformer of Luther, Johannes Agricola[1589] evolved reform ideas further and became now a focus of Luther's scorn. Agricola proposed that Christians who acted on faith alone were no longer bound by the Law of Moses. Christians needed only the Gospel, he maintained. However, Agricola's proposal is not as bizarre as it seems. Early Christianity was without the Law of Moses (the Pentateuch/Torah/the first five books of the Old Testament) until perhaps the early fourth century. This is a tangent that I am not exploring other than noting that it kept Luther busy with disputations, an open letter,[1590] and another book.[1591]

Fitting into Emperor Charles' plans, Agricola and other reformers were part of a proposal to bring the Protestants back under the authority and doctrine of the Catholic Church. The Protestant belief about justification (by faith alone) was tolerated – for then.

The attempt to reconcile the churches under the guiding hand of Pope Paul III turned Agricola and his unifiers into enemies of the Protestant Church.

---

[1588] Sen. Secreta, Reg 58, fol. 64', dated September 3, 1537 in Setton, 1984, 411.
[1589] Johannes Agricola, aka Schneider, aka Schnitter, aka Magister Islebius1494-1566.
[1590] Martin Luther, Letter to C. Güttel Against the Antinomians, 1539, Luther's Works (Fortress, 1971) 47:107–119.
[1591] Martin Luther, On the Councils and the Church, 1539, Luther's Works (Fortress, 1971) 41, 113–114, 143–144, 146–147.

Luther was probably angrier about the challenge to have the rug pulled from under his leadership than about the status of the Law of Moses. With his Catechism, Luther had already established independence from the Old Testament.

Charles' plans were crossed by Luther's Schmalkaldic League, which now protected itself with armed forces. The Reformer wanted to push through stricter, more fundamentalist Protestant rules. Thanks to advancing ailments, his plans for the revised Schmalkald Articles were stalled until almost the end of the century. Henceforth, the Lutherans systematically overthrew bishops and nobles loyal to the Catholic Church.

Like Jews, Catholics were among the persecuted in Luther's domain.

Convert, leave, or die.

Lutheranism thus spread through much of Germany – by armed forces. In Luther-land, Catholics no longer dared to stand by their faith.

The plan to reconcile the religious divisions between the Catholic and Protestant churches also failed because they could not agree on a combination of 'faith alone' with good works. The Catholic Church rejected the compromise altogether, and Luther insisted on the admission of 'guilt' by Rome for having misunderstood the Gospels hitherto.

He may not have been confused.

But he was not bound to realism.

The idea of the council was quite simple: bring love to Europe's royals under the guidance of the pope with the goal of bringing Christian holy war to the Muslim Ottoman-Turks.[1592] Peace through war. As collateral damage, Pope Paul hoped for the fall of Charles in battle and the suppression of the Lutherans as a recently arisen, pestiferous heresy.

The Germans were smarter than that. They smelled a double-deal and wanted nothing to do with the council.

In the meantime, the English King Henry VIII had proclaimed himself master over the Church of England.

He wanted nothing to do with a council either.

The meeting was postponed and planned to be relocated to a 'neutral' city in the Kingdom of Venice. And postponed again.

---

[1592] Ehses, Conc. Trident., IV. 54, lines 3-9, Vienna, December 14, 1536, in Setton, 1984, 415.

All the while, the Catholic Church was falling to pieces.

Sure enough, Suleiman the Magnificent was ready for battle once more. In alliance with the Kingdom of France, the Ottoman leader mobilized 300,000 men and invaded parts of southern Italy under the admiralty of Barbarossa.

The plan was for a Muslim force to descend on Italy from the south and sack Naples. The Kingdom of France would move an army of 50,000 men into Italy from the north.[1593] Rome was again in End-of-the-World mood and fortified its cities in a hurry. However, hindered by imperial forces, the Kingdom of France again failed to deliver on its obligations. With 10,000 slaves in tow, Suleiman thus abandoned the Italian assault and directed Barbarossa and his fleet with 25,000 sailors to the Greek Island of Corfu, which was then in Venetian hands.

Due to an epidemic that decimated Suleiman's ranks, he had to abandon this new plan as well.

The world failed to end.

When the French troops finally made it into Italy, Suleiman was long gone.

In the wake of the exchanges, Emperor Charles expelled *all* Jews from Naples.[1594] Since the Kingdom of Naples was part of the French-Ottoman strategy, the pattern emerges again. While evidence about Charles' reasoning is absent, the context is sufficient for the suspicion that treachery must again have been at the heart of their misfortune. The phenomena had global dimensions. The tragedy is that Charles lost his patience with them as well.

He had faced *Hadrian's Choice*.

It hit Jewish communities collectively, rather than just their ringleaders. Naples had been the center of Italian Jewry until that time. For a couple of hundred years afterwards, Jews were no longer allowed to return there.

By harassing Corfu, Suleiman had unwittingly broken the Ottoman-Turkish peace treaty with Venice. It had kept its promises for almost forty years.

In order to fend off the menace, the Farnese Pope Paul III and the Republic of Venice formed another Holy League of war with the Knights Hospitaller in Malta, to which Spain joined. Following Reubeni's original recipe, the pope also made peace between France and Emperor Charles. The Truce of Nice ended their violent exchanges.

---

[1593] Against fairly clear evidence, some historians think that the troop movements were unrelated. See Letter from the governor of Marano to Charles V, November 9, 1533 in Calendar of State Papers, Spain, Volume 4 Part 2: 1531-1533 (1882), pp. 858-868.

[1594] Rosheim, transl. A.J. Deus.

Together as one happy family, they could focus on what mattered most to them: bringing war to their common enemies, Ottoman-Turks, Lutherans, Anabaptists, Zwinglians, Calvinists, and those free of religion.

Their intention was to show mercy in their enemies' quick deaths.

They assembled a huge fleet under the command of a Genovese admiral[1595] in the service of Emperor Charles. Luther commented in a letter that French and Venetian fleets were indeed successfully combined against the Ottomans.[1596] However, King Francis was never committed. He soon returned to the alliance with Suleiman.

The forces met near Corfu the next fall.

Playing with gunpowder was a dangerous business. It did not go well. The forces of the Catholic Church could not put their Christian cannon fodder on land. They died by the droves and were constantly repulsed back into the sea through the stronger Ottoman prayers.

Assistance came to Muslim jihadists from effective artillery.

Nevertheless, Christians were eager to be expedited to the Kingdom of Heaven. Under the proud banner of the cross, the holy warriors showed courage. They prayed for martyrdom and prepared for an all-out attack. With a fleet less than half the size of their assailants,' the Muslim forces surprised the Christian fleet before its soldiers got off their knees.

49 : 0.

The Christians lost 49 ships. Barbarossa not one. 400 Ottoman warriors died, and 3,000 Christians were taken prisoners – future Muslims.

In the face of humiliation, the fleet under the ripped flags of the Catholic Church sailed home. The defeat soon led to a new peace treaty with the Republic of Venice under which the islands in the Aegean, Ionian and eastern Adriatic Seas were forfeited to the Ottoman Empire. Hat in hand, substantial reparations were paid.

Suleiman was master over all of the eastern Mediterranean.

It did not matter how hard they tried, the world refused to end – except for the martyrs: over 20,000 Ottoman-Turks and over 3,000 Christians who were strewn across the blood-soaked battlefield in the Siege of Castelnuovo alone.

These neither made it to paradise nor to the Kingdom of Heaven.

---

[1595] Andrea Doria, 1466 – 1560.
[1596] Martin Luther, Letter to Jacob Probst, 1538.

Their prayers had gone silent. Without a resurrection, the world lived on.

Nothing was left untried by Charles. An assault on Algeria failed because of bad weather. He even made an offer to Barbarossa for the position of Admiral-in-Chief and rule over the Spanish holdings in North Africa. In the end, Suleiman the Magnificent prevailed. Charles was forced to return the land to France that had previously been theirs.

Charles' low amounted to Luther's high.

Emperor Charles was increasingly occupied with the raging Protestant conflicts in Germany. The reform movement had infested most of Germany. Denmark and Brandenburg also joined Luther's Schmalkaldic League.

The imperial subversion as originally designed by Frederick the Wise with Luther as his protégé and puppet was profound.

After months of negotiations for Protestant assistance against the Ottoman Empire, the Lutherans achieved a breakthrough. With the Agreement of Frankfurt,[1597] no further attempts to forcibly convert those who had subscribed to Luther's *'Augsburg Confession'* were undertaken. Lutherans promised to cease further spreading their creed. Differences in faith were to be resolved in councils.[1598]

The agreement came with crossed fingers – on both sides.

The pipedream of a unified Catholic Church was broken. The opposing sides went their separate ways. Lutherans were determined to turn back the clock of the evolution by a thousand years. Back to Augustine. For the Protestants, everything that was introduced thereafter was unnecessary ballast.

The Catholics had no intention to reform. They wanted to reunite the heretics under the banner of the Vatican's Tiara. Neither they nor the Lutherans thought that matters of Christian faith were negotiable.

Never.

The pope regretted ever having sought to forge peace among European royalty in pursuit of holy war against Ottoman-Turks. The consequence of it was slowly losing the papal position as supreme monarch who could 'bind and loose' kings and emperors at will.

The infallibility of popes eventually made way for the separation of church and state. To arrive there was still a long and rocky path.

---

[1597] The Agreement of Frankfurt dates April 19, 1539.
[1598] Setton, 1984, 452.

As every so often throughout history, the Truth of some Christians collided with the Truth of other Christians. All the while, Muslims were tearing down their borders – and Rabbinic leaders kept on playing them all.

Centuries of wars failed to sort it out.

Could the dead have been avoided?

Yes.

If they would have known what must be known.

That, of course, is easier said than done.

### Table Talk

A Lutheran reformer diligently took notes from one of Luther's Table Talks. The diatribes that Martin Luther unleashed on Jews had become repetitive. But the master's audience was so captivated that nobody dared to speak until spoken to. The continued Jewish boasting about being Abraham's children[1599] made him think of them as a miserable people. They were not permitted to trade or to keep cattle, he said. They were only usurers and brokers.

In rare detail, Luther explained just what this meant.

Rabbinic leaders lent out 100 and ended up with returns of 2,000. Little wonder that he called Jews *'a pernicious race, oppressing all men by their usury and rapine.'*[1600] Luther may not have fully understood the business of high finance, and we do not know any details about the deals in question, but even our modern sense of shrewd business practices is taken aback by this. We complain about a 20 percent interest rate as being abusive profiteering. How about 2,000 percent? However, Luther appears to have viewed the Jewish faith and usury as inseparable.[1601]

Indeed, Jews faced an imperial edict that would have deprived them of their economic foundation. All money transactions were planned to be prohibited for them. As chief of the Jews in the German lands, Rabbi Josel of Rosheim was able to avert the danger that loomed over the collective Jewish community.

At this time, Rosheim appears to have grown into Luther's Jewish main adversary.

---

[1599] John Aurifaber, Table-Talk of Martin Luther (Eisleben, 1566) translated by William Hazlitt (The Lutheran Publication Society) DCCCVII.

[1600] Ibid., DCCCXX.

[1601] In his contemporary Chronica, Sebastian Franck (1531, p. 249-50) makes a similar observation wherein farmers would have to pay back 200 or 300% of the original loan. However, in the same breath, he also reports of price increases in wine of 5 to 600%.

Jews in Frankfurt – the place of the Lutheran breakthrough – now wore yellow rings on their coats. They could not own houses, not even the ones they lived in. Mortgage business had become hazardous to them.[1602]

Yet, ordinary Jews were made to believe that better times would come through the End of the World. After all, their suffering was part of prophecy. The worse it got, the more they believed in their version of God.

Jews and Christians agreed as little as cat and mouse, Luther demonstrated with the example of a converted rabbi. They hated *'Christians as they do death; it galls them to see us.'* Morphing faith and finance, Luther wanted to prohibit their practice of usury.[1603] They were full of superstitions, eating nothing that a Christian killed or touched. They drank no wine.[1604]

Luther was still hopeful that Jews might recognize the superior understanding of the Old Testament by the Lutherans over the abominations and profanities of the Catholic Church, as he saw it.

As evidence, he cited an anecdote of a Jew who was willing to convert. That Jew first went to Rome only to come back to enthusiastically be baptized by the Protestant Church.[1605] Hearing his preaching might persuade them to come over to his faith. Perhaps a few rabbis, at first, would eventually trigger a mass conversion.[1606]

What was Luther thinking?

How could he expect that turning them into the boogieman would be some kind of constructive strategy for converting Jews? Producing crypto-Jews perhaps. We can only imagine what Rome must have been preaching to make Protantism look attractive for Jews.

Luther insisted that the succession of the Covenant between God and Abraham for the Promised Land was a folly akin to the claim to Christian leadership by the Catholic Church. The old Covenant had long been replaced by a new one, he argued.[1607]

---

[1602] John Aurifaber, Table-Talk of Martin Luther (Eisleben, 1566) translated by William Hazlitt (The Lutheran Publication Society), DCCCIX.
[1603] Ibid., DCCCXXIII.
[1604] Ibid., DCCCVIII.
[1605] Ibid., DCCCXXV.
[1606] Ibid., DCCCVIII.
[1607] Ibid., DCCCX.

It is not surprising that Luther hardly ever left the line of reasoning of the Bible. He took it literally. He correctly asserted – following the Bible – that Jews had been rejected by God because of their faithlessness to their divinity.[1608]

The glory of the Temple of Jerusalem had been destroyed, and in this event, its authority to world leadership had been transferred to Jesus Christ, and with this to Christianity[1609] – and now to him. Jesus Christ was the new King of the Jews, constituting the only righteous branch of the lineage of King David. If there was another, he dared them, he should show his face.[1610] Instead, when they learned that the Messiah Jesus Christ changed their laws contrary to their expectations, they crucified him.[1611]

Never mind that Luther reversed the order of events. Jesus Christ was crucified *before* Jews lost the Temple of Jerusalem.

The authority of the House of David was transferred to a dead man.

After they lost the Temple in Jerusalem, Jews had been despised for 1,500 years. For that long, they had been rejected by God.[1612] Luther thought that this should be their extermination.

He accused Jews, as people of books, of using Christian scriptures as weapons against Christianity,[1613] as though Luther, the Catholic Church, or Islam did not act in the same way.

In an encounter with two Jewish rabbis, Luther was personally offended for being asked to remove a passage that referred to the crucifixion of Jesus Christ in a letter of safe passage for the two.[1614]

Luther was in a position of power.

Granted. The rabbis' behavior was shrewd. It was along the lines of one of the worst of Jewish stereotypes. It was like asking our modern Pope Francis to take his cross off while at the same time applying for free access to the Vatican library. It is so deeply offensive that, if I had been in Luther's shoes, I would have abused *my* power. Luther probably put the pen down, ripped the draft to pieces, and sent the two on their way with his wishes.

They asked for it.

---

[1608] Ibid., DCCCXI.
[1609] Ibid., DCCCXII.
[1610] Ibid., DCCCXVI.
[1611] Ibid., DCCCXXIV.
[1612] Ibid., DCCCXVII.
[1613] Ibid., DCCCXIV.
[1614] Ibid., DCCCXV.

The two ended up being Christian converts the very next day.[1615]

Conversion by sheer stupidity.

I pointed it out before: the Renaissance was not a time of peace and security. If anything, this example shows how it was impossible to travel without approval of a journey from the highest offices.

The dangers lurked just about anywhere.

Luther said that complaints about Jewish superstitions had been part of the social fabric of Germany and Italy since ancient times.[1616] For this, he cited a contemporary example of how Jews delighted in tormenting Christians and treating them as dogs.

A Jew had offered a talisman to a noble of Saxony that would protect the wearer against injury from swords or daggers. The nobleman tested the talisman out on the salesman.

With his sword.[1617]

Death by sheer stupidity.

On rare occasions, Luther showed a macabre sense of humor.

He compared Jews to one of their heroes who was able to throw huge rocks at his enemies. Unfortunately, one of the rocks fell on the hero's neck. Since then, he could never rid himself of the itch[1618] – the itch of Jews, as Luther saw it. He also showed some admiration for Jewish history and the great religious men that Judaism had brought forth.

In comparison, for the Reformer, Western Christianity had but one thinker of note: Augustine[1619] – other than himself.

In all this, we can recognize that Luther did not learn much – other than hating Jews – since he left the Saint Augustine monastery at Erfurt. By now, the audience knew what to expect of their leader, and nobody put a stop to his tirades.

He was not alone.

---

[1615] Ibid., DCCCXVII.
[1616] Ibid., DCCCXIII.
[1617] Ibid., DCCCXVIII.
[1618] Ibid., DCCCXIX.
[1619] Ibid., DCCCXXII.

Luther's right hand, Philip Melanchthon, wrote a pamphlet that reminded nobility of their obligation to extinguish all heresy and to establish the pure teachings and the correct rituals of the Protestants.[1620] Ethnical cleansing took the subtle argument of daggers. He rejected the notion that the reign of Moses would be re-established by Jews. The Ten Commandments applied to all of mankind. Their violation of the First Commandments and others by Jews needed to be disciplined.[1621]

Melanchthon put nobility to the task of punishing those who did not believe or who cursed God and thought of the Christian Religion as fools' work and monkey play.[1622] He demonstrated how a lineup of emperors prohibited non-Christian worship and how they made sure that sacrificial practices came under the severest punishment.

Such bans were still imperial law in Luther's time.[1623]

One emperor[1624] even had churches of heretics demolished to make sure that nothing of their worship could survive.[1625] These emperors served as good role models and as a reminder to nobility that their duty was to enforce the laws – unjust and oppressive rules that are an embarrassment to humanity.

In return, these leaders had been richly rewarded in wars, he argued.

The Jewish Empire had been torn apart by God since Solomon, Melanchthon interjected. Directly referring to Jews, he threatened that those nobles who did not comply would meet the wrath of God.[1626] Augustine, as well as Melanchthon, had taught that the annoyance of those who refuse to follow the Truth would be eradicated by force.[1627] It was the law – not only against Jews – that blasphemers were to be punished and killed.[1628]

The religious leadership was in charge. If nobility wanted to stay relevant, it had to follow their rules.

---

[1620] Philip Melanchthon, Dass die Fürsten aus Gottes Befeh und Gebot schuldig sind/ bei ihren Untertanen Abgötterei/ unrechten Gottesdienst und falsche Lehre abzutun/ und dagegen rechten Gottesdienst und rechte Christliche Lehre auf zu richten (Wittemberg, 1540) 24.

[1621] Ibid.

[1622] Ibid.

[1623] Ibid.

[1624] Theodosius the Great aka Flavius Theodosius Augustus was emperor of the Eastern Roman Empire 379 – 392 and over the whole empire until 395.

[1625] Philip Melanchthon, Dass die Fürsten aus Gottes Befeh und Gebot schuldig sind/ bei ihren Untertanen Abgötterei/ unrechten Gottesdienst und falsche Lehre abzutun/ und dagegen rechten Gottesdienst und rechte Christliche Lehre auf zu richten (Wittemberg, 1540) 24.

[1626] Ibid.

[1627] Ibid.

[1628] Ibid.

Melanchthon distinguished himself through a more polished style. His words to bring persecution upon those who believed differently sound almost comforting in their deadly righteousness – compared to Luther's lowly diatribes.

His text attests that Luther was not senile. His younger crony had the same destructive ideas, and he dared to put them in print.

Torture and death to those who thought differently.

He also spoke out against a church council. There could be no middle path. Nobility had to take a side, he urged, either with the persecutors of the true teaching or with the pure and truthful Protestant Church.[1629] Melanchthon accused Cardinal Hieronymus Aleandro of being a tyrant who had many Lutherans strangulated.[1630] He said that the Catholic Church had promised betterment. Instead, it accelerated persecution of its opponents.[1631]

The Catholic Church agreed with the Protestant Church on two issues: both owned the Truth; and everyone who refused to line up behind them merited death.

It is astonishing that Melanchthon's polished slander did not address any rational arguments. He could have argued that Lutherans were a minority in a sea of the Catholic Church. Like Jews, minority Protestants deserved protection and special privileges. He did none of that. Melanchthon was unable to argue outside of the realm of hatred.

For Jews, another messiah appeared in Portugal in 1540, 'the Messiah of Setubal,' Ludovico (Louis) Diaz. Apparently, he first announced that he was a prophet, and later he claimed to be the Messiah. A formerly converted Portuguese Jew, a Marrano, he was described as a poor, uneducated shoemaker. Diaz's magic was in miracles alone – or his stories thereof.

We would, of course, believe all this, were it not for the pattern of illiteracy and his choice of name. Ludovico is a Germanic name, indicating a famous warrior. Diaz is a common surname in Portugal. It has its origin in the central Spanish region of Castile from the Visigoth period. However, it also means *son of Jacob*. This choice does not allow us to draw any conclusions other than putting us on alert.

---

[1629] Ibid.
[1630] Ibid.
[1631] Ibid.

But Marranos and some Christians in Lisbon and Setubal did: he was hailed as the King of the Jews, the Messiah. During his appearances, crowds were determined to kiss his hands.[1632]

Other than that being 'uneducated' is a recurring motif among messianic aspirants, one might think that such a dumb fool could not win followers among the learned. The physician to the bishop Don Alfonso, brother of the archbishop of Portugal, was among those who obeyed the Messiah's command to circumcise themselves. Apparently, there was a greater conspiracy at play, which is not going to be addressed here in detail. In short and as can be expected, it did not turn out to become the hoped-for conquest of the Promised Land. Diaz was arrested by the Inquisition.

After his release, the Messiah went right back on his mission. He and his disciples ended up at the stake, burned alive in 1542.[1633] This Ludovico Diaz was in another account 'confused' with David Reubeni.[1634]

Did Reubeni stand behind it all?

Martin Luther continued his anti-Semitic storm. Asked how Jews should be baptized, he added to his explanations that he would take a pretend Jewish convert, *'tie a stone around his neck, and hurl him into the river; for these wretches are wont to make a jest of our religion.'* This would validly baptize the pretender.[1635]

A prominent German atheist wrote to me that *'the wish of destruction is not the destruction itself.'*[1636] This man had been awarded doctor of theology and then left the Protestant Church over the results of his critical studies in Christianity. This anecdote demonstrates just how strong of an imprint religious indoctrination leaves on the minds of individuals and, in consequence, on the collective memory of humanity.

For moderns, the evidence is in: when a political or religious leader incites hatred in order to divide and rule its citizens, the outcome can be counted in pipe bombs – at first.

---

[1632] Rabow, Jewish Messiahs, 2003, 53.

[1633] A.Z. Aeshcoly, Messianic Movements in Israel (Jerusalem, 1956) 435, as cited in Lenowitz, 1998, 98.

[1634] Ibid.

[1635] John Aurifaber, Table-Talk of Martin Luther (Eisleben, 1566) translated by William Hazlitt (The Lutheran Publication Society) CCCLV.

[1636] Joachim Kahl, email to A.J. Deus, December 21, 2017.

### The Mahdi's Last Words

Sometime before 1543, Martin Luther wrote *'Last Words of David.'* The work of the Reformer was no less sharp than ever. This book discusses the specific question of the Messiah and denies the Jewish idea that this should be a mortal or corporal and earthly king.[1637] It confirms Luther's knowledge that Jews were playing the game on both sides. Luther referred to them as *'that scum of the Jewish race who are now mingled with the Turks at Buda[pest] in Hungary.*[1638]

The armistice between Emperor Charles and Caliph Suleiman did not last.

Charles had gone on the offensive against Hungary upon the death of its imperial king. For this, he needed the support of the Protestants. Once more, Lutherans found themselves jubilant. In exchange for money, weapons, and Christian expendables, Charles removed the territorial and legal restrictions from Lutheranism.[1639]

Henceforth, Protestants could also be employed at the Imperial Supreme Court.

While the pressure against Luther's heresy – by definition – was easing, Emperor Charles then also halted persecution of Lutherans in the Netherlands. Nevertheless, religious opponents still engaged in Bible burnings.[1640]

The entire civilization was on a slippery slope toward deeper religious fundamentalism.

Suleiman personally led the defense of Budapest. The result of yet another catastrophic defeat were 16,000 Christian souls who never made it back home. It led to the final annexation of Hungary by the Ottoman Empire. Suleiman was still determined to bring the Holy Roman Empire down.

Luther was upset that Jews were embedded with Ottoman-Turkish troops. As a way of showing mockery and insult, it has been said that some Jews publicly carried a crucified cat around Budapest. This is just a detail that may or may not have happened. But the double play was perceived as despicable. No, the double play was treasonous.

Like any other leader of powerful nations, Suleiman needed to watch his back.

---

[1637] Martin Luther, Last Words of David (1543), in Select Works of Martin Luther, translated by Henry Cole (Bensley, 1824) 218.

[1638] Ibid., 274.

[1639] Setton, 1984, 460.

[1640] Martin Luther, Letter to Anton Lauterbach, 1542.

At one point, the Reformer questioned whether they were really Jews or just pretended to be. Because they insisted that God's promise was to Jews alone, *'these very dregs of the Jewish nation in our day'* cursed and insulted Christianity. Yet, said Luther, by their cursing the nations, all nations were cursed by the seed of the Devil, the Jews.[1641]

Luther lashed out at them for their arrogance in not understanding his Truth. They *'deserve to be laughed at by all, no less than that frog, which, as the German proverb goes, having by chance espied a farthing, sat upon it, and being as proud of it as if it had gotten all the riches of Persia.'* He mocked Jews with sarcasm for portraying Christians as *'poor miserable, blockish, leaden-headed'* and for bringing forth arguments that Christians *'never could have thought of before.'*[1642]

Even now that Jews were in a miserable exile, they ceased not *'to burn with rage wherever they assemble together in their conventicle.*[1643] The Reformer thought that Jews were out to harass Christians *'to vent the foam and poison of their enmity.*[1644] Luther was out to destroy them. The mutual hatred was mutually agreed upon.

He was right. Jews were wrong.

*'Let us now away with them!'*[1645]

In all of this, Martin Luther may never have been aware that a messiah had been travelling to Germany.[1646] The mission was undercover. Only Rabbinic leaders knew, and they kept their secrets well.

For Luther, the central question of enmity appears to have remained faith. He accused Jews and Muslims alike of zealously advocating their beliefs with their puffed up and conceited opinions and wondered why they did not feel *'thunderstruck and terrified'* and why they did not see their *'whole fabric of the world'*[1647] tremble in light of the Lutheran logic. For him, Jews constituted the *'pest of the human race.'*[1648]

It is the stubbornness of the Truth that continues the human tragedy brought about by organized religion. It will go on until God judges the Jewish nation and destroys it with the fire of his wrath.[1649]

---

[1641] Kenneth M. Setton, The Papacy and the Levant, Volume III (The American Philosophical Society, 1984), 278.
[1642] Ibid., 310.
[1643] Ibid., 334.
[1644] Ibid., 226.
[1645] Ibid., 230.
[1646] Ibid., 233.
[1647] Ibid., 252.
[1648] Ibid., 332.
[1649] Ibid., 333.

Luther had nothing good to say about Prophet Muhammad either. From the *'chambers of the Muhammadean brothel,'* that *'filthy fellow, who dared to call himself a prophet of God,'* exerted such a masculine strength that it would not suffice for one night.[1650] The Koran tastes and stinks of Muhammad's filth, Luther judged, and it had no other source than the stinking and abominable orgies of drunkards.[1651]

In all this, Luther never forgot to remind his community that they were different. They were the good ones. They were wearing white robes. They owned the Truth. They were made to feel good about calling for the deaths of Jews and Muslims.

The evil ones, manifested in Suleiman the Magnificent, had renewed their pact with France. Europe was at religious war. One way or another, the Holy Roman Empire had to be dismantled for prophecy to fulfil itself. Assisting each other, French troops harassed Spain, the Netherlands, and England, while Ottoman-Turks built a landing harbor at Marano in the Italian Adriatic Sea under the admiralty of Barbarossa, the pirate Jew. Francis helped Suleiman in the Levant with galleys and in his further push west in Hungary with artillery units. But because Ottoman Egyptians opposed it, the operation was delayed. At the same time, France was in trouble again with Emperor Charles' forces.

In all this, Martin Luther showed unshakable principles. When this man hated, he did so passionately and relentlessly. He expressed himself in a letter that he would gladly go onto the battlefield as a mighty warrior and injure Ottoman-Turks himself. The Muslim enemy, he thought, had *'all the devils in hell on his side.'*[1652] If he could have, he would have gone out to kill. The only excuse that stood between his word and a sword was his age – perhaps – he was only sixty years old by now.

If the role model of the Protestant Church proclaimed such aggression as laudable, it does not take rocket science to figure out that he found hordes of enthusiastic martyrs.

The Catholic Church was not sitting around idle, either. Pope Paul III ordered a crusade against the Kingdom of Tlemcen. A crusade, to be sure, is not a kind of pilgrimage where the faithful hold up their crosses in love for their neighbors and pray for the good fortune of the distant kingdom's citizens. The swords were sharpened for piercing skulls that had no clue about their differences in faith.

---

[1650] Ibid., 316.
[1651] Ibid., 316-317.
[1652] Martin Luther, Letter to the Elector John Frederick, 1542.

They simply split the argument.

However, Pope Paul's plans were crossed. On his way to Marseilles and to bombarding the city of Nice, the pirate Barbarossa stopped at the mouth of the Tiber River, the gates of Rome.

The End-of-the-World tremors in the Vatican were tremendous.

Suleiman was successful in Hungary. With heavy casualties on both sides, he took the city of Esztergom further up the Danube River. He was thus able to secure central Hungary through Budapest.

The ruler was impressed by the Hungarian engineering skills. Inside the city's fortifications stood the country's tallest church and its largest building. Esztergom was at the time an important religious center and the seat of the Catholic Church in Hungary. The basilica had been built of red marble by Italian masters just over three decades earlier. Today in its former glory, its sheer size and form, in the style of a mixture between a Roman temple and an imagination of the Temple of Jerusalem, is impressive, indeed. It is so big that the massive fortifications upon which it was built look like miniatures. Thanks to its universal Judaic appeal, it was converted into an Ottoman mosque.

During the siege – in long standing Muslim tradition – the cultural heritage, as depicted in numerous statues of saints, was shattered to pieces. They looked at them as forbidden icons.

In our time, we have witnessed the disappearance of cultural heritage with the modern Taliban and the Islamic State. Not to mention a chain of wars.

The assailants did not seem to have treated their victims with tender, peaceful care either. Martin Luther noted in a letter that Ottoman-Turks had massacred 3,000 citizens of a town, including the elderly and pastors. Their corpses were heaped over the town walls.[1653] We already know that we do not need to believe everything that this man said.

The memory of the city is quite different. Those who intended to betray the defenders into the hands of Ottoman-Turks were put out of their dishonor. But Muslims did, according to their own account, desecrate the tombs of a lineup of Hungarian kings as bearing signs of a faith doomed to hell.[1654]

---

[1653] Martin Luther, Letter to Justus Jonas, 1543.
[1654] Şahin, Süleyman, 2013, 113.

The trouble with their success is that the god of the Muslims did not seem to have appreciated Suleiman's friendship with the French Christians. Suleiman's son died there a young man after accompanying his father to the Hungarian frontier at Esztergom.

The Mahdi was dead – peace at last. In paradise.

At least on this front.

The death of the Mahdi at the age of twenty-two marks the end of Suleiman's advances toward the capital of the Holy Roman Empire, Vienna.

For Ottoman-Turks, the End of the World was called off.

The messianic claims were relinquished. Suleiman now retreated and engaged in elevating himself through propaganda. The Ottoman ruler, *'by virtue of his exploits, had superseded the glory of all the legendary Persian kings. Thanks to divine support, he equaled the military successes of Muhammad and attained the stature of Solomon. Even the Caesar of the Christians [Charles V] had become one of his slaves.*'[1655]

At that time, nobody was checking facts.

Suleiman had become the 'Second Solomon.' From then on, the apocalyptic nature of his rule was dismissed, and the focus shifted to his military successes of the past and his role as *'the abode of kings, the refuge of sultans, the distinguished ruler whose retinue is formed of kings.'*[1656] He was the only representative of true Islam.

In his newly found submission to the will of God, his greatest duty was to *'treat his subjects with munificence and justice and to ensure peace and security in the realm. This duty can only be fulfilled through respect for the Sharia and the abrogation of injustice and heresy from the face of the earth.'*[1657]

The repetition of the atrocities in the name of the Truth was perpetual.

The protection of non-Muslims was no more.

By Francis' hospitality, Barbarossa was wintering in Toulon. He continued to terrorize the coasts of Spain and Italy.

Francis was keenly aware that letting the French Christians intermingle with the 30,000 Muslim forces might be a bad idea. To prevent difficulties, he ordered the customary religious segregation. He did not wish his Christian subjects to be set on fire by Muslim thought.[1658]

---

[1655] Ibid., 116.

[1656] Tabakat 364b, in Şahin, Süleyman, 2013, 191.

[1657] Tabakat 437b–438a, in Kaya Şahin, 192-193.

[1658] Instruction of Francis I to his Lord Lieutenant of Provence, in Harold Lamb, Suleiman the Magnificent - Sultan of the East (Read Books, 2008) 229.

Soon thereafter, King Francis of France helped to forge a truce between Caliph Suleiman the Magnificent and Emperor Charles V. In the successive negotiations, Hungary was recognized as belonging to the Ottoman Empire. Tribute was to be paid to Suleiman. France and the Holy Roman Empire also entered a treaty, the Peace of Crépy.

Francis and Charles called the End of the World off.

Rabbi Jacob Berab was the one who had earlier moved to Jerusalem and created the foundation to formally re-establish the Sanhedrin in Israel (again). Now, the institution moved from the Temple Mount to Safed. Official history places this move a few months earlier.

However, it did not come voluntary. The messianic mission had failed. They were thrown off the Temple Mount.

In the Dome of the Rock, they left behind the famous mosaics that would later falsely be attributed to the Umayyad leader 'Abd al-Malik.[1659] The artwork signifies that the rulers of the world had submitted to the King of the Jews, including Emperor Charles and Suleiman. They had been rooting for the End of the World to happen, and they envisioned themselves in the New Jerusalem.

None of the twenty-five rabbis who were present had opposed Jacob Berab. The names of some members of the Sanhedrin have come down to us. Of these, we know the chief Rabbi of Jerusalem Levi ibn Habib, Rabbi Joseph Caro[1660] who had received the Holy Spirit and was a follower of Solomon Molcho, Hayyim Alshich, Levi Najara and his son Moses Najara I of the influential Najara Dynasty, Rabbi Moses of Trani who was the Safed rabbi for fifty-five years, and Rabbi Yosef Sagis.

Their actions betrayed the Ottoman host. And Emperor Charles. And the pope. And ordinary Jews. And ordinary Christians. And ordinary Muslims. And everyone who failed to believe.

The Rabbinical Court in Safed represented not only Jews in the Levant but of the entire global Diaspora. A Jewish traveler reports during the 1560s of a community in Safed that flocked around the *Divine Presence* (!) that was 14'000 strong and divided into eighteen schools.[1661]

---

[1659] A.J. Deus, The Jewish Serpent King in the Dome of the Rock, Primary Evidence: 'Big Daddy' of Inscriptions a Colossal Fraud (2022) available at academia.edu.

[1660] Joseph ben Ephraim Karo aka Yosef Caro or Qaro, HaMechaber (the author), Maran (our master), 1488 – 1575, was the successor of Rabbi Jacob Berab to lead the Rabbinical Court. He was author of the Shulhan Arukh, the most important code of Jewish law, for which he had been receiving visits from the spirit of the Mishna (Lenowitz, 1998, 127).

[1661] Zachariā Al-Ḍāhrī, Sefer Hammusar, ed. Yehuda Ratzaby (Ben-Zvi Institute, 1965) 116–117.

A new messiah was then in Safed. The Jewish leadership revived its push for the End of the World.

World peace meant renewed trouble for Martin Luther.

Having gotten rid of the main sources of conflict, Emperor Charles signed the Treaty of Speyer with Denmark, a member of the Schmalkaldic League. In the deal, the Danish King was recognized by the Holy Roman Empire over his rival. In exchange, Denmark pledged to stand down in the conflict between the League and the Catholic Church.

Charles was able to amass his forces against Luther without major hindrances or distractions. Woe to Christians who now focused on their own. Martin Luther saw in this the coming of the End of the World.[1662]

One may wonder how the Kingdom of France was able for so long to exert such an important influence over the rest of Europe, which was at least five times its size. Other than with loans from the Ottoman-Turkish treasury, how did they pay for all this? Who was the invisible hand of high finance?

One hint is sometimes sufficient to unravel an entire history: Joseph Nasi.[1663]

His last name goes down like milk and honey.

This man later came to be appointed Lord of Tiberias,[1664] representing the highest authority of the Torah. He was the Jewish Nasi. But he was also a Marrano, a convert from Judaism to Catholicism – and back. After Charles had decided to confiscate the fortune of his family, Joseph Nasi escaped to Portugal[1665] – Portugal of all nations!

Now we know that Charles had good reason for his actions against this dynasty.

They were financing his French archenemy, who accompanied us through Luther's entire public life.

We can now also appreciate that a Marrano who came out as the Nasi constituted a clear and present danger to the Catholic Church.

If you convince your bride with a dagger, you should not be surprised that you end up sleeping with the enemy.

---

[1662] Kenneth M. Setton, Lutheranism and the Turkish Peril (Balkan Studies, 1962) 164.

[1663] Dom Joseph Nasi or Nassi, aka João Miques or Micas, Dom João Migas Mendes, Giuseppe Nasi, Yasef Nassi, 1524 – 1579.

[1664] Naomi E. Pasachoff, Robert J. Littman, A Concise History of the Jewish People (Lanham, Rowman & Littlefield, 2005) 163.

[1665] Ibid., 162.

To understand it better, I need to make a detour. The Jewish Benveniste/Mendes clan was the most important to arrive in the Netherlands after the Alhambra Decree led to their expulsion from Spain. Their influence extended across Europe and to the Ottoman Empire.[1666] Through marriage, Aunt Gracia (Mendes Nasi)[1667] had entered a lucrative business in spice and gem trading. And banking. But they were not poor self-starters. This dynasty goes back to French Narbonne of the eleventh century, where they were tax farmers. As they moved to Aragon and Castile in Spain, they again became tax farmers of the Knights Templar.

Strangely enough, this means that they were already tax farmers in Spain *before* the Spanish Reconquista. For whom were they farming taxes, then?

But it goes even further back.

The Nasi in Narbonne was already prevalent in the Frankish Kingdom during the eighth century. The city of Narbonne was the most important Jewish stronghold in Europe at the time, originating in a Jewish migration to this region after the First Jewish-Roman War. Then in Spanish Arab hands for four decades, they first shot the there-stationed garrison in the back – friendly fire – only to surrender the city into the hands of the Frankish Kingdom in 759 AD.[1668] Since the local Gothic and Gallo-Roman population and nobility were opposed to the approaching Franks,[1669] we need to call this by what it was: treachery.[1670]

This act of treason led to Jewish privileges under the French domain and to religious and judicial (!) autonomy. It was akin to an independent Jewish state in Narbonne with a regional Jewish King.

The result attests to the motives.

---

[1666] Ibid., 161.

[1667] Gracia Mendes Nasi aka Hannah aka Beatrice de Luna 1510 – 1569.

[1668] The Nasi Makhir ben Yehudah Zakkai of Narbonne (aka Makhir ben Habibai of Narbonne or Natronai ben Habibi aka Theoderic IV of Narbonne [725 ~ 765 AD or 793 AD) collaborated with Pepin the Short who was King of the Franks 751 – 768.

[1669] Ian Meadows, The Arabs in Occitania (Saudi Aramco World, March-April 1993) 44: 24–29.

[1670] As treasonous as the actions of the Nasi leadership were, the larger contextual changes need to be highlighted briefly. This is not the place for details, but for researchers, it is important to note that the surrender of Narbonne coincides with a dramatic change in Arab Spain. No contemporary writer took note of the religious adherence of the first-generation Arabs who occupied Spain during the previous half century. Now, an identifiable Muslim force swept across North Africa and Spain. They squeezed whomever had been holding Narbonne from their backs in the south while the Franks were pushing from the north. Since we do not know whose soldiers were standing at the walls in Narbonne against the Franks, we can also not be entirely sure who had been betrayed by Nasi leaders other than that they belonged to the first 'Muslim' generation, the Umayyads.

Prominent Jews from Baghdad came to resettle in this French city and establish a major Jewish learning center there. The Nasi successors and the Frankish kings still remained friends in the tenth century. From the eleventh century, the title of the Nasi is also confirmed in Aragon, and Barcelona.

We can learn what these 'privileges' meant when the Nasi had to flee from Narbonne to Girona in Spain.

For their arrival in the eighth century, they struck a deal to finance the Franks in return for a monopoly in tax farming. This included ever expanding territories, in particular the lands that came under Frankish control from which the Saracens had been pushed back: southern France, Girona, Barcelona, Zaragoza, and more.

Again, their function as tax farmers constituted a magnet of hatred.

So, what was going on in Narbonne? A primary witness tells us how important Narbonne was, in the twelfth century, still. Barely 300 Jews were enough to manage the entire European Diaspora from here. The Divine Presence for European Jewry, the Word of God, the Shadow of God, an intercessor not unlike the Catholic Pope, sat here. Jewish leaders were then in control of the port in Marseille and the Rhone River traffic, essentially the Mediterranean trade from the Islamic world to the economy of France. The treasury of the Vatican was in the hands of Jewish leaders.[1671]

There is massive financial and political power buried under the fact that Jewish leaders simultaneously controlled the treasuries in Rome *and* Baghdad, in Spain, France, and elsewhere.

After over four hundred years in Narbonne, the office of the Nasi moved across the southern border to Girona in Spain in 1194 AD, shortly after our witness had passed through.

An anti-Semitic incident fourteen years earlier helps us to understand this move.

Things had fundamentally changed north of the Pyrenees.

King Philip Augustus of France[1672] imprisoned all Jews, had them dispossessed, force-converted to Christianity, or deported.[1673] Given the centuries' old Jewish presence in France, this is a whole lot of Jews in jail. We

---

[1671] The Itinerary of Benjamin of Tudela (ca. 1179 AD) 1-8.
[1672] Philip II, 21 August 1165 – 14 July 1223 AD aka Philip Augustus was King of France from 1180 to 1223 AD.
[1673] Jim Bradbury, Philip Augustus: King of France 1180–1223, The Medieval World (Routledge, 1997) 53.

can put one and one together and see a cruel Philip who tortured Jews just for being Jews.

Christians were enriched at the expense of Jews, so the tale goes.[1674]

Instead, a humanitarian emerges.

Philip helped *free* (!) his French towns from 'seigneurial authority.' He robbed the Jewish leaders from their lucrative and corrupt tax-farming business, fired the Jewish administrators, and supported an emergent Christian Bourgeoisie.

Why might he have done that? Because the leaders of this genius Jewish system had no moral limits to their abuse of the oppressed French population. The Bible commands it thus.

His portrayed 'anti-Semitism' was national self-defense against a group with double loyalties – with their primary loyalty not in their host's interest.

Philip probably did not incarcerate *all* Jews – maybe all Jewish *leaders* and perhaps for a reason – and perhaps not *only* Jewish leaders, unless they still controlled one hundred percent of the administration.

In one town, the French King had 99 Jews burned alive – a credible number for those who cannot count to 100.[1675] As customary in history telling, the reasons remain untold. Jews were perhaps killed for being Jews? Knowing how historical numbers are inflated, perhaps 9 leading Jewish criminals were prosecuted and given a death penalty? Because the facts are left out, we cannot tell the difference whether we are played for compassion.

That does not mean that some of the nouveau Bourgeoisie had not used some trickery to shake their Jewish ancestry. There was just too much money involved. After all, the same people tend to sit at rulers' tables before and after revolutions – the learned ones. But they were moving away from being crypto-Jews who had before been intent on applying the Biblical recipe to subvert the entire Kingdom of France.

The king's actions were necessary to remove a criminal mafioso-system and replace it with something that smells like the beginnings of *freedom* from oppression and extortion.

There is nothing wrong with being a Jew or any other ethnic group. Anyone, Jew or not, who thinks to be better than everybody else because of their blood should be brought back to earth.

---

[1674] Ibid., 52.
[1675] Ibid., 266.

Those who pray for the return of this system are complicit in the next *real* anti-Semitic event.

After the Nasi *fled* to Girona, Philip allowed (some) Jews to return. A French administration with illiterate Christians was hard to operate.

It should no longer be a surprise that Spanish Aragon was a hotbed of messianic agitators to conquer the Promised Land from under the feet of its non-Jewish citizens. The headquarter was there. The Jewish top leadership has been rocking the entire planet in the service of their overtly pious mission for hundreds of years – forever, actually.

From Girona they maintained and expanded their extortion business:

Vidal Benveniste de Porta[1676] became treasurer of Barcelona, Girona and Lerida, Spain. He was the chief tax collector of Spanish Catalonia (Aragon and Castile) side by side with the Knights Templar who helped squeezing coins at sword point.

How Vidal Benveniste could be treasurer in Barcelona when Muslims preach to hate Jews should by now be transparent. They were farming taxes for themselves – under cover of an Islam with a Jewish dual government.

Then we have Isaac Benveniste Nasi[1677] the physician from Narbonne of the king of Aragon. He was the father of Sheshet Benveniste Nasi,[1678] also a physician and political advisor to the kings of Aragon. He lived first in Barcelona and later in Zaragoza (whence comes Abulafia).

In the second half of the fourteenth century to the beginning of the fifteenth, we have Vidal Benveniste 'de la Cavalleria'. The *Cavalleria* was an 'honorable' title for having been tax farmers.[1679]

The Benveniste/Mendes clan.

Their terror regime caused deep seated historical trauma in every Christian and Muslim community in the Iberian Peninsula. We have already learned that these communities were managed by a Jewish functionary of the crown, called *'arrabi'*[1680] or also *al-Arabi*. They were in charge of the judicial system, including enforcement. And tax collection. And banking. The military, of course. Slave

---

[1676] Vidal Benveniste de Porta +1268 AD.
[1677] Isaac ben Joseph Benveniste Nasi died 1224 AD.
[1678] Sheshet Benveniste Nasi ca.1131-1209 AD.
[1679] Encyclopaedia Judaica.
[1680] Jonathan Ray, Jewish Communal Organization and Authority, The Sephardic Frontier: The Reconquista and the Jewish Community in Medieval Iberia (Cornell University Press, 2006) 124–128.

trade. The apex of this genius corruption is that the crown rabbi oversaw the kingdom's audits of the arrabi administration[1681]

We have seen it as the modus operandi for centuries in Aragon, Castile, Granada, Navarre, Toledo, and elsewhere. In Portugal. In France and Germany. In Istanbul and in Baghdad. And we are merely at the beginning of discovery.

We find them with Muslim names, as Sulayman ibn Yaqzan al-Kalbi al-Arabi (no, al-A'rabi does not mean 'the Bedouin') who was governor of Barcelona and Girona in 777 AD, or his contemporary governor of Zaragoza, Husayn of Zaragoza. History forgot to hand down their Jewish names.

Enough! How is this even possible?

A Persian Metropolitan from the late eighth century explains the basics: Jews have one law wherever they could be found. Christianity's laws were in chaos, different everywhere, even from city to city. They depended on one's social status.[1682]

The difference is that one group is cohesive, highly educated, and loyal to a single Jewish leader who rules over large domains. The other group is entangled in division.

But here it gets fascinating: the legal uncertainty in the Christian world was broadly managed by Jewish feudal overlords in the judicial system. Without any basis in fact, the cohesive group that had cohesive laws must have given incohesive laws to the incohesive group.

They must not have been able to stop laughing.

The archaic system of achievement for one ethnic group over all others was genius – genius, and a mortal threat to all other ethnic groups.

Their system of privilege was so stable in their own interest that it endured over hundreds of years.

Let us take the Spanish city of Segovia.

From here, the voyage of Christopher Columbus was financed.

There, the crown rabbi of castile lived in a 'house' large enough to later accommodate a full-blown monastery. That was the dwelling of Rabbi Senior who had morphed into the Catholic Coronel. Just a stone's throw away, the Crown of Castile lived in the Alcazar of Segovia, a huge castle towering over the

---

[1681] Cardozo de Bethencourt, J Leite de Vasconcellos (ed.), Inscriptions Hébraïques du Portugal [Hebrew Inscriptions of Portugal] (Museu Ethnográphico Português, 1903) 8 (2): 37.

[1682] Isho'bokht, Persian Metropolitan of Fars (ca. 730-780), Composition on the Laws (Corpus iuris, 1.1.8-10) 206-207.

town below. Which of the two might be bigger, king's or rabbi's, is difficult to tell.

Were they equals?

The Old Jewish Quarter housed a large Jewish community. The state of populist education has it that Jewish quarters were like Jewish ghettos that were imposed by Christian authorities to segregate them. Given that this was Muslim territory and that the Puerta de San Andrés is a city gate that was controlled by the Jewish quarter, it was the other way around.

During these centuries, the 'ghettos' did not serve to keep Jews locked in – it served to keep non-Jews – who were herded like cattle – out.

The wolf[1683] is sold for sheep.

To live in the impoverished medieval towns as non-Jews was the opposite of what their modern charm might suggest.

Two words come to mind, feudal and serfdom, defining Europe from the ninth century. It is no coincidence. From the fifteenth century onward, the system was overthrown with rivers of blood inflicted by those intent on hanging on to their oppressive privileges.

Remember this next time you marvel at medieval castles in Europe.

I wonder how long it will take for European citizens to come to a reckoning that their taxes are feeding royal overlords whose riches and privileges find their roots in this genius system.

In 1492 AD, it was Spain's turn to change.

The Alhambra Decree led to the expulsion of Jews and is portrayed as one of history's greatest anti-Semitic catastrophes.

In the business of ruling others, one must be surprised for *not* having been overthrown more often. The most despicable part is that the Jewish leaders pulled all Jews along through the manger.

That is the backstory of Joseph Nasi's and the Benveniste/Mendes clan's tremendous wealth and influence that came to the Netherlands after the Alhambra Decree.

We are dealing with the top of the cream.

Joseph Nasi's importance was the fruit of his aunt, Gracia Mendes Nasi. Her success rested on the laurels of this very old, leading Jewish dynasty. In the wake

---

[1683] 'Wolf' is a concealed Talmudic name for Benjamites.

of the Portuguese Inquisition, she fled to Antwerp. Joseph had to take care of her financial affairs in Portugal from where they financed ships in the nation's discovery missions.

Gracia was well versed in business by bribe.

This is how they were able to form state-supported monopolies that created immense – illegitimate – riches for them. When Joseph finally needed to flee Portugal in 1546, he ended up in the court of King Francis of France.

Ten years out, Joseph married Gracia's daughter.

This Nasi also had a hand in the Sanhedrin.

In order to attract settlers to Tiberias, he financed the manufacture of textiles and books there. With the help of his immense fortunes, the Jewish leadership was hoping to renew the conquest of the Promised Land from within.

It is difficult to grasp what the Mendes' wealth may have meant at the time. A Persian historian from the eleventh century described a vast Jewish trade network that spanned the known world through a trading company:[1684] They were born traders.[1685] Among everything else, they were weapons dealers and engaged in human trafficking. They were slave traders.

The banking system of Jewish leaders was so highly developed that a check could be made out in Persia and cashed in Spain – 900 years ago.

Now that the Mahdi of the Ottoman-Turks was gone, the race was on for a worthy replacement. The two final rivals were Selim and Bayezid, both sons of the Temple mother Roxelana. Joseph Nasi put his cards on Selim – the Sot (the drunkard) – or perhaps on both.

But first, there was a problem of a musical chair to be solved.

It is all popular hearsay, not historical evidence. The rightful heir after the Mahdi should have been Mustafa by Suleiman's first harem wife.[1686] Roxelana had supposedly forged a court alliance against Mustafa with her son-in-law, the Croatian Rüstem Pasha,[1687] in favor of her own sons. The pasha was grand vizier of the Ottoman Empire at this time. And he was married to the world's most important girl: the Temple mother Mihrimah Sultan. In order to understand just how close the pasha was to the sultan, we need to take note that he was later

---

[1684] The Radhanite trading company.
[1685] Abu'l Qasim Ubaid'Allah ibn Khordadbeh (ca. 820–912 AD).
[1686] Mahidevran, aka Gülbahar ca 1500 – 1581.
[1687] Rüstem Pasha Opuković, ca. 1500 – 1561, grand vizier of sultan Suleiman the Magnificent, married to Mihrimah Sultan, ca. 1522 – 1578, daughter of Roxelana. Mihrimah was the most powerful princess in Ottoman history during the Sultanate of Women.

buried to the left of the Mahdi – the side of the heart of Suleiman's favorite son. The pasha warned Suleiman that Mustafa intended to kill the sultan.

Mustafa was eliminated from the dance.

His execution led to widespread riots – and this tells us one more time that there might be much to be learned about Suleiman's chief wives and his grand viziers. Why would ordinary Muslims or nobility care so much which of the Magnificent's sons would ascend to the throne? These fights were instigated by noble ringleaders from these families that wanted to climb to the top.

A possible explanation could be found in a diplomatic remark from a couple of years later wherein Suleiman's wife Roxelana was thought to be ruling the sultan. With the death of the Mahdi, the Magnificent had lost his edge. It was believed that he had been bewitched *'by means of a Jewess,'* a favorite of Roxelana.[1688] She and her son-in-law, the Grand Vizier Rustem Pasha, appear to have come in control of the Ottoman state.

That Suleiman had been building on Bayezid is believed to be because of the latter's appointment to rule the Ottoman-Turkish European holdings from Edirne. Roxellana did not live to see which one of her sons succeeded to the presumed leadership of the world. But Suleiman had already changed the governorships of his sons.[1689]

From there, the story of how Selim grabbed the throne becomes legendary. To make it short, I skip to the low point of the drama. Somehow, Bayezid ended up in Persian captivity. His father, the Magnificent, seems to have been willing to pay for his son's return and reconfirm a treaty between Ottoman-Turks and Persian Safavids.[1690]

The war was over. The world could live on.

When Bayezid was finally freed, he was garroted,[1691] an elaborate form of medieval strangulation.

Having won the favor of the harem in Constantinople,[1692] Joseph Nasi's gamble paid off handsomely. He gained the trust of Suleiman, became a primary adviser, particularly in foreign affairs, and joined the high ranks of ministers.

---

[1688] Letter from Cervini to Alessandro Farnese, January 15, 1546, in Setton, 1984, 493.

[1689] Şahin, Süleyman, 2013, 146.

[1690] Collin P. Mitchell, The Practice of Politics in Safavid Iran: Power, Religion and Rhetoric (Tauris, 2009) 126.

[1691] Ibid.

[1692] Naomi E. Pasachoff, Robert J. Littman, A Concise History of the Jewish People (Lanham, Rowman & Littlefield, 2005) 162.

Almost the entire Cyclades Archipelago (the islands in the Greek Aegean Sea) was given to him to enrich himself through tax farming.[1693]

This man, Joseph the Nasi, could rely on a vast pan-European Jewish network, which reached from the Ottoman Empire to Italy, Portugal, Spain, France, the Netherlands, and beyond, even into the New World. He is bragged about for being so well connected that he was also 'friends' with a next Holy Roman Emperor.[1694] Later in life, he 'encouraged' the Netherlands to revolt against Spain. For this, he promised the support of Ottoman-Turks. And money, it needs to be presumed. It would start the Eighty Years War.[1695]

By the end of Luther's century, Jews were able to open a synagogue in Amsterdam and publicly confess to their Jewishness.

War. Privileges. Treachery is written all over this man's biography.

Joseph the Nasi also tried to betray the Cypriots who were under Venetian rule. His negotiations with the Jewish community of Cyprus to submit to Ottoman-Turks were uncovered.

In its wake, the Jewish population was expelled.[1696] One of his relatives was arrested for attempting to set fire to Venetian armories and shipyards.[1697]

It was just a rumor.

But it is not a mystery how this man persistently showed up with the winning team: he financed both sides. I originally thought that a Jewish group could have financed one party and a different one its opponents. They could have done so without knowing each other. This is not so. For example, in a conflict over the leadership in Moldavia, this single Jewish leader backed both sides.[1698] This anecdote lays bare the extent of the treacherous mechanism.

In short, Joseph the Nasi was a monster playing games with beasts.

---

[1693] William Miller, The Latins in the Levant, a History of Frankish Greece, 1204–1566 (Dutton, 1908) 637–643.

[1694] Jewishhistory.org.il, 1520 – 1579 (7 Av 5339) Don Joseph Nasi (Joao Migues, Duke of Naxos).

[1695] Naomi E. Pasachoff, Robert J. Littman, A Concise History of the Jewish People (Lanham, Rowman & Littlefield, 2005) 162.

[1696] Dan Urman, Paul Virgil McCracken Flesher, Ancient Synagogues: Historical Analysis and Archaeological Data (Brill, 1995) 62.

[1697] Ibid., 63.

[1698] Constantin Rezachevici, Evreii din ţările române în evul mediu [Jews in Romanian Lands in the Middle Ages] (Magazin Istoric, September 1995) 59-62: [This episode concerns the two Moldavian princes Alexandru Lăpuşneanu and Jacob Heraclides].

These guys enabled the feudal system with their finances. Ordinary Jews, Christians, and Muslims deserve our compassion. They had no idea that they were the pinballs in a game of insane aspirations that were packaged in soothing words.

The feudal system was rigged against them.

Whatever happened, they had to foot the bills. Even in the best case, they faced excessive prices through monopolized trade in favor of Jewish financial wizardry.

Either way, they paid. Often with the blood of their children.

Other than through bribes and the pressures from indebtedness that could be exerted on an overextended nobility, how did Jewish leaders achieve such extraordinary privileges? Compassion after a holocaust was certainly playing an important factor. For example, at around the time of the treaty with Denmark against Luther's Schmalkaldic League, Emperor Charles also entered a new deal with the German Jews. We could, if we wished, embed this in the context of the ongoing pan-European persecutions of Jews.

On a closer look, there is a pattern.

On one side of the equation was a hefty bribe, packaged as a contribution to the war against the Kingdom of France. On the other was permission for Jews to charge higher interest rates than Christians.

The argument by Josel of Rosheim went that the former were, collectively, paying much more (not higher) taxes than the latter. But, of course, they were paying more taxes than Christians. Rabbinic leaders were the tax farmers of Christians!

Higher interest rates pushed the vicious circle further. It meant more trouble for the borrowers – and more hatred against everyday Jews.

Was this some kind of extraordinary stupidity on behalf of Christian nobility and population?

Indeed, in Luther's sixteenth century, as we have seen in abundance, Jews were learned, and Christians were generally illiterate. But this was changing fast. And money could not have been that stupid, could it?

Yes, it could. We are reliving it today.

Perhaps the most important factor of this success is the ultra-loyal Jewish Diaspora – loyal to the cause of the Promised Land; disloyal to their hosts. When excesses in one place led to their expulsion, the Diaspora went to work to receive them with privileges.

Let me guide you through the mechanism when it comes to money in Judaism, Christianity, and Islam.

It starts out early on in the Bible where rules for foods were established.[1699] As noted earlier, some of these were in the name of getting ahead at all costs and the expense of others. For example, eating cadavers is prohibited, for understandable reasons. Yet, it is specifically sanctioned that Jews can sell spoiled meat to foreigners.[1700]

Treachery as a God-commanded cultural prerogative.

This laid the foundation of the worst of Jewish stereotypes. And it is taught to children in Jewish schools – today. Since Christians and Muslims were exempt from these rules by their respective scriptures, these religious laws remained exclusive to Jews. Notably, the texts of these new religions bore the signature of Jewish leaders.

Likewise, usury was strictly prohibited for Christians and Muslims. However, it did and does not apply to Jews. The Bible forbids the lending of money for interest to the poor.[1701] But then comes the hammer: this applies among Jews but not to foreigners.[1702]

If I were to reduce the core motivation of the entire pile of biblical trickery to the two most important issues, then it would be this and the land grab from which to build a global empire. It literally creates a banking and administrative monopoly for Jewish leaders.

Wherever a Judaic religion governed, the organized crime of Jewish minority leaders prospered, even if the majority had applied the same biblical standards to itself, since brothers were prohibited to lend for interest. It only worked for Jewish minority leaders, never for the good of the society as a whole.

---

[1699] Deuteronomy 14:1–20.
[1700] Deuteronomy 14:21.
[1701] Exodus 22:25.
[1702] Deuteronomy 23:20.

To make sure that this is understood properly, it did not work for ordinary Jews either. They were just as much victims as lay Christians and Muslims were. It worked only for the Jewish nobility, the priestly class, rabbis, Levites, Nasi, or Exilarch. The leadership swam in gold and diamonds. Ordinary Jews paid the price in the later ghettos – playing the role of human shields for their bosses. These clueless Jewish disciples wasted their money and prayers on their priestly parasites.

Case in point: Gracia Mendes Nasi lived in a palace outside of the Venice Ghetto's walls.

Even today, Muslims suffer from the usury law through restricted access to credit. Over millennia, Jewish leaders successfully exploited the opening and lent for interest to Christians, Muslims, and others, who were 'foreigners' to them, even if they had been citizens of the same nations for generations.

They were biblically encouraged to build financial empires that aimed at sucking the blood out of entire civilizations – that were biblically enslaved.

These money-lending operations created immensely influential financial entanglements that could impose their will directly upon governments. As they lent money, as collateral they were rewarded with trade monopolies and tax farming.

The planet's most lucrative business.

World domination came through five aggressive components: God, messiahs, the Diaspora, monopolies, and money. God and the conquest of the Promised Land led by the Messiah served to sow division in order to keep the money flowing into the pockets of the Jewish leadership.

Ordinary work was for ordinary people.

It was not stupidity. It was organized religion. Christians and Muslims glorify poverty. Jews do not.

Jewish leaders were raking it in.

People who make money from nothing are considered smart. They were even smarter. They took the money from those who made it from nothing and sent them right back to starting over with nothing.

It is genius.

Now we can understand what Martin Luther meant in a letter to warn the elector of Brandenburg of Jews. The Margraviate of Brandenburg was neighbor to Saxony, the land of Luther's protector Johann of Saxony the Steadfast. In this letter, the Reformer said that the Jewish practice of alchemy was a deception, *'for all know money cannot be made by such sophistry.*[1703]

In the context, it means nothing other than an accusation of medieval style money laundering.

The rationale was that Jewish money came from alchemy, produced out of a chemical soup. In reality, it concealed the sources of the Jewish money that was used to bribe left, right, and center.

Luther was genuinely concerned that Jews would bankrupt the Margraviate of Brandenburg.

The problem is horribly obvious: In his assessment of the financial consequences, Luther was correct.

## Dying in Hatred

Time was slow in the sixteenth century.

Martin Luther was still concerned about the passivity of Europe's nobility in regards to the conflict with Ottoman-Turks. Word did not seem to have reached him that the Mahdi had died and that Emperor Charles' diplomacy had trumped bombardments. But the news of persecutions against Protestants in the Netherlands and new areas that joined his cause travelled fast.[1704]

In the same token, Luther was convinced that the papal promises for a council would never amount to anything.[1705] We have already heard from Melanchthon that the Protestant leaders opposed a council altogether. When the holy men did come together, he thought that the subaltern composition of the council was laughable. The members of the council did not know what to do.[1706] His futile arguments paint over the fact that such a council would be rigged against the Protestants.

Against all odds, Pope Paul got the Council of Trent started.

---

[1703] Martin Luther, Letter to the Elector Joachim II.
[1704] Martin Luther, Letter to Herzog Albrecht of Prussia, May 2, 1545.
[1705] Ibid.
[1706] Martin Luther, Letter to Nicolas Amsdorf, July 17, 1545.

With few participants, it stood in the name of restoring the Christian world. This meant nothing other than a mission to destroy the Lutheran heresy. Sure enough, one of the first orders of business was to declare sects with doctrines diverging from those of the Catholic Church as anathema.

This council stands at the beginning of the Counter-Reformation by the Catholic Church. Brought about by external pressure and inter-sectarian wars, it culminated in the Thirty Years' War a century later.

Let me explain the papal hatred of Lutherans with money.

Pope Paul pledged 800,000 ducats for the destruction of heresy in Germany.[1707]

To put this meaningless sum into perspective, just a few years earlier, the same pope had granted Venice 90,000 ducats in one year. The next year, when it became necessary to fend off a massive world-war style assault by Ottoman-Turks, he was reluctant to increase the payment to 200,000 ducats per year and negotiated for a loan instead of a subsidy in the midst of an emergency.[1708]

Money talks – if ever, then especially here.

These guys failed even in the single task that they were responsible for: preparing for Armageddon.

They were proficient at destroying their own.

Pope Paul's love for humanity was also emphasized in his slavery decrees. He not only affirmed the buying and selling of slaves but also abolished the policy that slaves could claim their freedom by converting to Christianity.

Paul's decree was not a novelty, though.

After the fall of Granada, the then-Pope Innocent[1709] had been donated 100 Moorish slaves. He did not set them free but distributed them among his cardinals. Innocent is also the pope who had ordered the destruction of the Waldensian sect.

Half a century earlier, another pope legitimized the enslavement of anyone who was deemed an enemy of the Catholic Church.[1710] That earlier papal decree constitutes the beginning of the black slave trade. These edicts amounted to

---

[1707] Setton, 1984, 484.
[1708] Ibid., 438.
[1709] Pope Innocent VIII, aka Giovanni Battista Cybo or Cibo, 1432 – 1492.
[1710] Pope Nicholas V, *Papal Bull Diversas* (1452), from Diana Hayes, *Reflections on Slavery*, in Charles E. Curran, *Change in Official Catholic Moral Teaching* (1998).

systematic ethnic cleansing operations against Jews, Muslims, Pagans, Christian sectarians, and the Protestant Church.

And any skin color other than white.

Black and red looked down the blue steel of loaded barrels.

When Luther learned about the mission to the Ottoman ruler by the pope, Charles, and Francis to forge a treaty, he was appalled that the devil's demons would dare to make a pact with the Antichrist. For this offense to Christianity, he was hoping for the End of the World to come upon his enemies.[1711]

Luther, the bringer of a new Christian religion, was opposed to peace. A global peace treaty deprived the Reformer of his best poker card to obtain privileges for the Protestant Church through division and war.

In early February 1546, Luther complained to his wife Katherine that he had passed through a village where many Jews lived. He thought that a cold wind in this town had threatened to turn his brain into ice. He was on his way to help expose Jews in a neighbouring district.[1712]

A week later, he wrote to his wife that he had made good on his promise to smoke his opponents out. But he was surprised that no one harmed Jews. He was hoping somehow to set boundaries for Jewish pride. They posed as god. On account of their pride, they could not remain in heaven, he said.[1713]

On February 18, 1546, Martin Luther preached four sermons, one of them containing his final warning against Jews.[1714] He thundered that they should not be permitted to live among Christians if they did not willingly accept Jesus Christ as the Messiah.[1715] If they refused, Luther would turn them into scapegoats:

> *They are our public enemies. They do not stop blaspheming our Lord Christ, calling the Virgin Mary a whore, Christ a bastard, and us changelings or abortions [Mahlkälber: mast calves]. If they could kill us all, they would gladly do it. They do it often, especially those who pose as physicians—though sometimes they help— for the devil helps to finish it in the end. They can also practice medicine as in French Switzerland. They administer poison to someone from which he could die in an hour, a month, a year, ten or twenty years. They are able to practice this art.[1716]*

---

[1711] Martin Luther, Letter to Nicolas Amsdorf, July 17, 1545.

[1712] Martin Luther, Letter to his wife Katherine, February 1, 1546.

[1713] Martin Luther, Letter to his wife Katherine, February 7, 1546.

[1714] Martin Brecht, Martin Luther, 3 vols. (Fortress Press, 1993) 3:350.

[1715] Weimar Ausgabe 51:194–196; J.G. Walch, Dr. Martin Luthers Sämtliche Schriften, 23 vols. (Concordia, 1883), 12:1264–1267.

[1716] Ibid.

Any Jew who did not convert, he said, was malicious. They would not stop blaspheming Jesus Christ, sucking you dry, and killing you, if they could. This is – literally – how he showed Jews how refined Christians applied the art of love.[1717]

Shortly after the echoes of his words fell silent, Martin Luther died in sheer hatred.

He was sixty-two years old and had wasted his limited intellect on religious division and hatred against Jews, Catholics, Turks, and anyone who disagreed with him.

The Council of Trent proceeded.

Doctrines were reworked, dogmas adapted to the new realities. Discipline and the corruption of the administration were addressed by enforcing a rigid hierarchy.

Of course, the council was rigged.

The papal legates constituted the majority blocks[1718] and managed the whole show. As a result, the liberal reformists lost out in both, voices and votes.

No one, the council decided, was allowed to interpret scripture in any other way than it was taught by the Catholic Church.[1719] By the same token, the printing of sacred books was subject to approval and censoring by Vatican functionaries.[1720] Punitive blasphemy rules were introduced.[1721]

Preachers and preaching were now subject to licensing through each Catholic Bishopric.[1722] Eventually, the church learned that priests that were not properly indoctrinated were prone to defection. Henceforth, it made precise conformist instruction of the priesthood a priority.

It was called 'focussing on spiritual life.'

Luther had shown the way: in seminaries, young priests learned how to deceive unsuspecting targets out of their freedoms.

The Counter-Reformation was not an intellectual awakening to the realities of this world, but rather the simple determination to weed out heresy with the power of armed force in a pact between the Farnese Pope Paul and Charles. The

---

[1717] Ibid.
[1718] Setton, 1984, 495.
[1719] Council of Trent, Fourth Session, April 8, 1546, edited and translated by J. Waterworth (Dolman, 1848) 19-20.
[1720] Ibid., 20.
[1721] Ibid., 20-21.
[1722] Ibid., Fifth Session, 27-29.

armed forces were provided by Jesuits, the new order that was unleashed by Pope Paul himself.

Nevertheless, doctrines were now voted upon, rather than decreed by the pope. This was a sea-change. But as usual in organized religion, the church-leaders were determined to make Catholicism what Lutheranism was not.[1723]

Addressing the Lutheran concept of Justification by Faith alone, the council prohibited its teaching, preaching, and belief.[1724] Pope Paul was unwavering in implementing thought control. He wanted to hammer its doctrines into the subjects' minds. The best way to enforce them was through the Inquisition.

You better knew your thoughts before you heard your words.

But the reason why the Protestant Justification by Faith alone was unacceptable for the Catholic Church was simple: money. Faith alone is nothing without charity[1725] – filling the pockets of church functionaries. Packaged in a lengthy and confusing discourse, they called this church tax *'charity'* or *'good works.'* Hence, Justification by Faith *and* Works.

I am not going to examine the further details of the Council of Trent.[1726] However, you may remember what I had earlier said about the original sin, where Eve had Adam eat some fruit from the tree of knowledge. That this act of bravery by Eve would have positively affected all of mankind – by instilling intellect – was then declared anathema.[1727] Catholics were obliged to confess that Adam had lost his holiness at that infraction – because of Eve – thus deserving the wrath and the introduction of death by God.

Moreover, the original sin was not a matter of the individuals, Eve and Adam. Instead, it was a matter of all humanity for eternity.[1728]

It was a collective verdict for a crime that never happened.

As stated early in this book: the misogynist doctrine is the mother of treating mothers as calf-bearers in Judaism, Islam, and Christianity. Women were supposed to remain second-class maidservants to their husbands.

Things went from bad to worse for the Protestant Church.

---

[1723] Setton, 1984, 496.

[1724] Council of Trent, Sixth Session, January 13, 1547, edited and translated by J. Waterworth (Dolman, 1848) 27-29.

[1725] Ibid., 35.

[1726] If anywhere in history, the Syrian Melchite influence over the Catholic Church could have been buried around here. In consequence, the Inquisition would be particularly harsh in Spain.

[1727] Council of Trent, Fifth Session, June 17, 1546, edited and transl. J. Waterworth (Dolman, 1848) 22, 1.

[1728] Ibid, 2.

That summer, the inter-Christian Schmalkaldic War broke out. Luther's protectors Johann of Saxony the Steadfast and Philip I of Hesse the Magnanimous decided to challenge Emperor Charles before he could amass troops against their league.

Charles was prepared.

The pact between Pope Paul and the emperor to destroy the Reformation had become bloody reality.

> *In the name of God and with the help and assistance of his Papal Holiness, his Imperial Majesty should prepare himself for war, and equip himself with soldiers and everything pertaining to warfare against those who objected to the Council [of Trent], against the Smalcald League, and against all who were addicted to the false belief and error in Germany, and that he do so with all his power and might, in order to bring them back to the old faith and to the obedience of the Holy See.*[1729]

Every German, noble or layman, who did not recant ended up with his house in ashes. Buried under the rubble was his entire family, including the house-rats.

Germany was at war – with itself.

The commander-in-chief was the pope.

The League went sour, and both leaders ended up imprisoned. All but two German cities submitted to the Catholic Church. Martin Luther's Wittenberg fell without a fight. Years later, after being freed, Philip I of Hesse the Magnanimous spent the rest of his life trying to forge an agreement between the Protestants and the Catholic Church.

It was too late. The sprout of religious diversity was pulled out of the ground.

But more seeds had been planted.

Since Charles was now becoming too strong, just a couple of days before his final success, the ongoing Council of Trent was moved to Bologna. Pope Paul must have allied himself with Satan. He withdrew his troops from the German imperialists in mid-battle. The pope's plan was to betray the emperor and deliver him to the Kingdom of Heaven.

Charles survived one more time.

He had seven lives.

This single mistake to abandon Emperor Charles in mid-battle constitutes the pivotal moment for the birth of the secular West.

---

[1729] F. Bente, Historical Introductions to the Symbolical Books of the Evangelical Lutheran Church, in the Concordia Triglotta (Concordia, Copyright © 2005, reprinted by permission of Concordia) 113.

Bologna, being in the Papal States, was unsafe for imperial delegates. In other words, whatever the minutes of the council say about the reasons for the move to Bologna was a cover-up. Being victorious, Charles could have simply 'democratically' overwhelmed the council. The papal treachery was designed to prevent this. It broke the pact between the Vatican and the Holy Roman Empire once and for all.

In an effort to make good on the offence, another lie was packed onto the first decision to move. Apparently, typhus had hit Trent, which prompted the delegates to flee so fast that they first sat down and wrote a decree to hasten the previous decision to move.[1730]

Those who supposedly agreed to the decree had already fled. They were smart enough at that time to know that the way to contain disease was through quarantine,[1731] not through spreading it by flight.

In consequence, the Schmalkaldic successors were able to regroup only to keep on fighting for centuries.

Many of the leaders of the Schmalkaldic League had fled to England where the English Reformation began. It did not foster in some sort of an age of freedom, either. For example, one of the reformers who went to the island excommunicated a disciple and burned him at the stake.[1732]

The accusation?

Arianism – teaching that Jesus Christ was a mortal.

This was not the Inquisition of the Catholic Church. This was Protestantism in England, which was on its way to Anglicanism – and America.

At the same time, the Inquisition was in full swing in the rest of Europe.

The Council of Trent was moved back to Trent, but after Charles was beaten by the Schmalkaldic successors,[1733] the council fell apart.

The pope never wanted it in the first place.

---

[1730] Council of Trent, Eight Session, March 11, 1547, edited and translated by J. Waterworth (Dolman, 1848) 67-68.

[1731] Alvarez, transl. Alderley, 1881, 384.

[1732] Jan Laski, aka John Lasko, 1499 – 1560, was a former pastor of the Protestant Church and now a member of the congregation Strangers' Church of London in London. He had George van Parris excommunicated, who was a member of the preacher's congregation. He had him burned at the stake for Arianism.

[1733] Maurice, Elector of Saxony who was cousin of both Johann of Saxony the Steadfast and Philip I of Hesse the Magnanimous

In the end, the Catholic Church sought to maintain its power through force that was ordered and directed by the pope himself.

The holy man's plan failed.

The term *Counter-Reformation* is misleading. *Restoration* would be more fitting.

After ten years of more war, the Lutheran faith came again to be recognized by the Holy Roman Empire. The back and forth continued to cost lives up to the twentieth century. Think of Ireland.

The Thirty Years' War came to be one of the most destructive religious insanities between the Catholic Church and the Protestants in the history of Europe.

Eight million perished.

Josel Rosheim continued to play his own game. By supporting Emperor Charles with German Jewry, he could reinstate some of the previously granted privileges. He also acted as a spy, sending a message to the emperor that Saxony was preparing to invade Austria. Charles escaped[1734] and showed his thankfulness with a special protection by imperial order.

Francis of France died in 1547.

A formal treaty was signed between Emperor Charles and Suleiman the Magnificent shortly thereafter. The Ottoman-Turkish conquests in the Balkan were now Suleiman's to keep, and he could turn his focus against Safavid Persia.

The Farnese Pope Paul III died the next year.

This extraordinary pope had lived to see the start of the 'reformation' of the Catholic Church for which he had worked all his life, beginning with the Borgia Pope Alexander VI. Rarely before then had a pope died at over eighty years of age. Few would make it there after him.

He went straight to Hell.[1735]

His successor, another Paul,[1736] had been friends with Saint Cardinal Cajetan, Dominican Master-General of the Inquisition. The Roman Inquisition was kick-started by this pope. Mainstream historians portray his inquisitorial initiative with the false equivalency of some sort of bureaucratic tribunal. The inquisitors were advised by experienced scholars and international consultants, they maintain. The implementation was less harsh than in Spain.

---

[1734] Deutsch, Feilchenfeld, in Singer, Encyclopedia, 1901-1906.
[1735] Pope Paul's bronze tomb rests in the St. Peter's Basilica.
[1736] Pope Paul IV, born Gian Pietro Carafa, was pope of the Catholic Church 1555 – 1559.

The riots, uprisings, and wars in the Catholic realm that raged for the next 400 years speak for themselves.

They were holy enemies of freedom.

Do you want just one example from this pope?

All right.

He ordered that the Jewish quarter was to be walled as a ghetto in the eternal city. His rationale sounded eerily similar to Martin Luther's.[1737]

The restrictions on Jews were draconic – and exposed one more time the worst Jewish stereotypes. Forged agreements were outlawed, and contracts required to be in the local language.[1738] The sale of collateral for defaulted loans was now regulated. No longer could Jews enrich themselves through the failure of their debtors. Interest had to be computed pro rata.

Finally, some sensible financial regulations were introduced, even though they pulled the rug from under Jewish financial networks.

Little did the pope know that every regulation comes with loopholes.

By the same token, Jews were collectively forced to wear funny yellow hats, and were only allowed to trade in non-essential foods and secondhand clothes.[1739]

Henceforth, Jews in the Papal States were confined to the ghettos of Rome, Ancona, and Avignon. These were the only three places in the Papal States where Jews were allowed to stay. They were in total segregation from the Christian population.

Their physicians were prohibited from tending to sick Christians.[1740] One synagogue per ghetto. The rest were destroyed. One entry gate. One exit. Closed at night.[1741] Violations were prosecuted as crimes.[1742]

The Jewish Ghetto in Rome remained operational until the dissolution of the Papal State over 300 years later. It was formally abolished by Italy in 1882.

Only seven years after the abolishment, a strong-willed boy was born in the Upper Austrian town of Braunau am Inn.

He came to turn the clock back – Germany first.

---

[1737] Pope Paul IV, Cum Nimis Absurdum [Since it is absurd], July 17, 1555.
[1738] Ibid., 6-8 and 12.
[1739] Ibid., 9.
[1740] Ibid., 10.
[1741] Ibid., 1-5, 11.
[1742] Ibid., 14..

Does it ring a bell? Redemption through suffering. Adolf Hitler.

One might think that Jews – of all people – would have learned to abhor the display of religious symbols. Not so. Funny hats continue to be worn with pride.

In 1558, Emperor Charles was buried in the chapel of the Monastery of Yuste. His final resting place became the monastery El Escorial in Spain. That location used to be a center of oppression by the Catholic Church.

The Magnificent, Suleiman, died in his battle-tent in Hungary.[1743] The holy leader succumbed to natural causes. His death was kept secret in order to prevent the Muslim troops from running away.

Only two years later, 'religious freedom' was legislated for the first time anywhere in Christian Europe. The 'freedom' was for the leaders to choose, not for ordinary people to be free. It came from an unexpected place: eastern Hungary, Transylvania. Neighbors of Dracula. Local Ottoman leaders had long understood the power of division and supported Lutheran reform movements in Hungary – fools call the evil game Muslim religious tolerance.

It is not by chance that this location also brought forth new Protestant sectarian offshoots who denied the Holy Trinity – a mainstay of Muslim complaints against Western Christianity. They call it Unitarianism. It is closer to Islam than any other Christian denomination outside of Christian Arianism. Shortly after an ordered expulsion of Calvinist and Orthodox preachers failed through lack of enforcement, every ruler was allowed to choose his own religion from a limited list: Catholicism, Calvinism, or Lutheranism. The Hungarian innovation was finally extended to all Christian religions, as long as it was not Christian Orthodoxy, Islam, or Judaism. Abuse of competing preachers was now outlawed. Threatening other rulers because of their dissenting beliefs was no longer tolerated.

The edict proclaimed that *'faith is the gift of God.'*[1744]

But the Act of Religious Tolerance and Freedom of Conscience did not absolve congregations from their responsibility for preachers who incited hatred or violence: *'they shall be permitted to keep a preacher whose teaching they approve.'*

Today, the awareness of implied consent appears to have vanished from the minds of the faithful.

---

[1743] During the Siege of Szigetvár on September 6, 1566.

[1744] The Edict of Torda, Act of Religious Tolerance and Freedom of Conscience, 1568, as cited in Charles A. Howe, *For Faith and Freedom: A Short History of Unitarianism in Europe* (Skinner House Books, 1997) 99.

When talking about Luther, we cannot fail but to be in awe of the pivotal time that this was.

A contemporary of Luther was the Polish doctor in the laws of the Catholic Church, mathematician, and astronomer, Nicolaus Copernicus.[1745] His book On the Revolutions of the Celestial Spheres was delayed for fear of repercussions by the Inquisition.

It was published just before his death and marks a major event in the history of science. This man's life was dedicated to extraordinary learning against all odds. His studies of antiquity may have opened his mind to the possibility of other worldviews.

Even though earlier thinkers were fairly advanced in their models, the prevailing belief in Luther's time was that earth constituted the center of the universe. The Lutheran founding father, Philipp Melanchthon, thought of Copernicus' ideas to move the earth and stop the sun as absurd.[1746]

Copernicus' heliocentric hypothesis, where earth revolves around the sun, came to revolutionize astronomy to what we understand today. To get there, it would still require later innovators, such as Galileo Galilei or Isaac Newton to properly explain the Copernican system.

The Catholic Church claims that Copernicus's ideas were received at the Vatican with enthusiasm. It was only with Galileo that it would become apparent how the Catholic Church posed a danger to Copernicus. Over half a century after him, the Roman Inquisition investigated heliocentrism and found it to be *foolish and absurd in philosophy, and formally heretical since it explicitly contradicts in many places the sense of Holy Scripture.*[1747] Galileo was to be found *'vehemently suspect of heresy.'*[1748] The then-pope[1749] ordered him to abjure, curse and detest his teachings that the sun stands still and that earth is not at the center of the universe. The astronomer had no choice but to recant. The publication of his books was prohibited.

E pur si muove – and yet it moves.

---

[1745] Nicolaus Copernicus, 1473 – 1543.
[1746] Philip Melanchthon as quoted in Czesław Miłosz, The History of Polish Literature (University of California, 1983) 38.
[1747] Maurice Finocchiaro, Defending Copernicus and Galileo: Critical Reasoning in the Two Affairs (Springer, 2010) 74.
[1748] Ibid., 47.
[1749] Pope Paul V, born Camillo Borghese, was pope 1605 – 1621.

# VI: DESTRUCTION

## *Hadrian's Choice*

The endless atrocities during Martin Luther's time were guided by popes, patriarchs, rabbis, caliphs, other religious leaders, and the Protestant Reformer himself. Luther was one of the ringleaders of religious hatred. His diatribes against Jews, the Catholic Church, and the Muslim Ottoman-Turks have survived in detail.

This is not unique to Luther's time.

When Judaism first entered the historical record, it did so with militancy, terrorism, and war. Ever since the beginning of Christianity, one overarching theme runs through its past: violence, holy wars, and crusades. Islam was born of Jewish leaders in jihad. The battles of peace were not fought with folded hands but with folded steel. Not only would Jews, Christians, and Muslims collectively hate Jews, Christians, and Muslims, each would excel in hating their own sectarian kind even more. Indeed, as can be witnessed in the modern-day bloodshed between Shi'ites and Sunnis, the preference is to kill each other's sectarian brothers for ever-so-slight deviations from the Truth.

For that end, competitors are called 'heretics.' In its original Greek meaning, heretics were from a *'school of a man's choice.'* The freedom to choose, so to speak. However, in Judaic religions, it identifies enemies of faith. Those who choose a different school.

Our historical records went through phases of religious monopolies. Also, over long stretches, the Jewish Diaspora recruited the only people who could write for religious monopolies. The result is a whitewashed version of the past. It attempted to paint over the shame of self-inflicted humanitarian disasters and to portray wishful thinking about righteousness and love for peace and charity.

The leading role of Jews was deleted but not successfully erased.

The righteous were those who followed strict doctrines of a given Jewish sect. All others, including other Jewish sects, were to be hated and not tolerated in the Promised Land. Modern Ultra-Orthodox Jews go as far as to deny even Jewishness to their sectarian competitors, in particular American style Reform Judaism that diminishes messianism – as it should.

The concept of self-hatred in the Jewish belief system triggered a particularly dangerous vicious cycle. It begot hatred. The Jewish religion literally invited anti-Semitism.

No. It ignited it.

It ignites it.

The treacherous 'undercover' approach of Jewish leaders divides all hosts for the purpose of making 'Judaism' the leader of the entire planet. It does not help to foster trust.

The successful Messiah brings about 'world peace,' they insist.

Love was for those Christians who belonged to the same community of faith. The others were to be expelled, particularly those of other Christian sects. The branding of Jews[1750] in the Gospels as a target for derision and hate provided for the foundation of eternal anti-Semitism by Christianity. It was strongest where oppressive Jewish administrative systems were maintained that pushed everybody else into serfdom. Eventually, they were overthrown with hatred that Jewish leaders themselves had invited through their actions.

At the heart of many holocausts were hosts who defended their nations against abuses of this feudal system.

Those who reject the Jewish insistence on being the rulers are anti-Semites.

The claim to peace in Islam was and is restricted to those in the same Muslim sect. All others were wished dead, including and specifically Jews.

The open concept of jihad in the Koran is particularly disturbing as is the total destruction of mankind in the Christian Revelation or the eternal mandate to reconquer the Promised Land for the Chosen People.

In Islam, the hatred was fueled by a religio-political cartel that was maintained by Jewish leaders from this religion's inception. The Caliph represented the Nasi in a chain of Jewish Muhammads. The Exilarch sat on the parallel Throne of David. It was the Jewish post-apocalyptic dream come true under a new covenant, precisely as proscribed in the Bible.

That Jews are targeted as a hated people in the Koran is a cunning deception to redirect from the fact that the Koran and Islam were purely Jewish post-apocalyptic operations. And to keep dissenting Jews, in particular secular Jews, in line.

---

[1750] In particular Pharisees.

All of this has an unavoidable outcome: religious wars and ethnic cleansing. It has repeated itself many times.

Letting Jewish, Catholic, Protestant, and Muslim history evolve in tandem, unveils a disturbing unifying goal: all strive to bring about the End of the World to establish a sole Truth. The highlight of their shared and eternal death-wish is a final war between the armies of Christians and Muslims. Jewish leaders pretend to participate in this war – undercover – on both sides. Betraying left, right, and center. They are the ones to come out on top, not only as the sole, righteous survivors but also as the rulers of the world in the name of the god of the Israelites. This privilege is not meant to benefit ordinary Jews. The sole survivors of the End of the World are to be the Levite top layer of the Judaic hierarchy. The one percenters.

Only they can provide for the leader of the world – the King of the Jews.

Not the lowly Jew. He serves as nothing but a human shield.

Cannon fodder.

The King of the Jews must come from the royal stock of the Hasmoneans, the Banu Hashim in Islam. None other can be messiahs.

Because of the Mar Zutran genetic bottleneck in the royal Hasmonean linage, all future Jewish messiahs must come from its tree.

Jewish, Christian, and Muslim scriptures were written by Jewish spiritual leaders. We have witnessed through Luther's life how they manipulated all sides to bring about the End of the World. They actively contributed to their own holocausts with an incredible high-stakes game.

Their financial wizardry helped lift Jewish leaders into the most influential and lucrative positions in government, including and most importantly, tax farming. With a careful examination, we can see how Jewish leaders financed opposing sides. With huge margins, they could afford to have one side lose everything. They still came up profiteering big, not to mention the privileges that resulted from these deals. Tax farming was collateral.

The biblical constructs create a financial monopoly that benefits only the Jewish leadership. The financial and hierarchical enslavement of sub-Judaic religions – such as Christianity and Islam – was designed as the centerpiece around which the successor religions were built.

It appears as though Judaic religions were shaped with the motive of forming and protecting Jewish financial monopolies and the related power structure of its leaders. The concept of treachery flies in the face of human justice. Entitlement and profiteering stuck as the worst Jewish stereotypes.

Financial enslavement of Christians and Muslims by Jewish leaders is not a myth. We have seen through the evidence that it led to expelling and persecuting all Jews collectively for said reasons.

The usury laws of Christianity and Islam, combined with their glorification of poverty, set these two on a path of economic and intellectual poverty. The legal mess provided a fertile ground for evasion and exploitation. Judaism does not have such problems. For a long period in Western Christian history, they were almost the only people who could read, write, and compute. They had a uniform legal system across the globe. Moreover, Jews were working together in a hyper-loyal, global network, the Diaspora, in pursuit of shared goals. In other words, Christianity created dependency on the Jewish intelligentsia. Muslims need to figure out how to live with the fact that Jewish leaders had created the Koran to mislead them.

Islam is the post-apocalyptic New Jerusalem coming to life.

Many of Islam's single-Truth nations can brag about low literacy and high poverty.

A ninth-century writer from the 'Muslim' Spanish territory reported that only one in 100 Christians was able to write.[1751] With twenty-nine percent, even modern-day Afghanistan is better off.

The Bible, the Gospels, and the Koran are designed by Jewish authors with that goal in mind. Uneducated disciples make good extremists and are easy targets for tax farming. No wonder that Jewish leaders were able to rise to the loftiest positions and manage to subvert governments and even entire civilizations. By design, the biblical constructs lined their pockets for thousands of years. The obvious income inequality, in turn, attracted attention and, of course, hatred.

Abuses by Jewish leaders over centuries created a hatred for Jews that lies in deep-seated cultural trauma.

The coin of anti-Semitism has two sides.

It is a miracle that this system has not been overthrown more often.

When the Catholic Church was in power, the inequality was part of doctrine. The last penny was to flow into the treasure chests of the church and its feudal overlords; nothing to the people. Everything from the people.

---

[1751] Indiculus luminosus 854 AD.

The common conception that the art of financing was pressed unto Jews by Christianity and Islam rests on false assumptions.

Scripture was *designed* to have it 'pressed' on them.

When it comes to hating, humans appear to be more at ease to direct their scorn at ethnic groups rather than at a specific individual, in particular when that person is influential and rich. Wishing an anonymous group dead is easier than looking a victim in the eyes. As the inter-religious conflicts show, targets of hate do not need to be in a minority. But in Luther's time, we talked a lot about tax farmers. Many of them were Rabbinic or Sadducee leaders. We could also see how, under pressure, they converted to the local religion but often concealed a continuance of their former beliefs. Force-converted, they retained their privileges and lucrative positions. They remained in power to subvert local religions and governments. Some morphed into nobility.

Gene technology will change our perception and lift the veil about just how deeply Jewish leadership penetrated European intelligentsia. As a matter of fact, it matters not. But in order to learn valuable lessons from history, these facts are hugely important.

It is quite startling to find former Jews as some of the most atrocious elements when it came to 'unifying' a territory under their newly acquired religion. One might think that forced conversion would bring forth freedom fighters, not inquisitors. When multiple stories were lumped together in one narrative, as they have been in the historical record, the picture got blurry very quickly. However, it almost seems as though violence was part of their job description. They just changed employers.

The unification of a people under one organized religion was more important than the fine points of religious doctrine themselves. After all, ordinary people do not fight with the logic of the word, but with the sword.

The word came from on high.

Whatever they said must have been worth dying for.

A contextual approach lifted another man out of Martin Luther than the one we commonly wished to have known. Gone is the underdog. He turned out to be a monster who merits only full and unconditional global condemnation. This man knew how to leverage hatred and hasten war. To his 'defense', it is also obvious that the historical trajectory would not have needed Luther. His presence was irrelevant. Another in his place would have been compelled to take the same steps. The powers of Jews, Christians, and Muslims to bring about the End of the World were greater than him.

At the core of the End of the World that all Judaic religions strive for sits the Messiah or rather two messiahs. For all, they must come from the branches of the Sadducees and of King David – Jewish leaders – for whatever sense that might make for Christians or Muslims.

Laity belonged into serfdom. The Bible says so. All Judaic believers, including ordinary Jews.

We have seen how Jewish bosses were masters of deception and concealment. It was not in the open, but it penetrated and subverted royal palaces around the known world. It even occupied some thrones. Ethiopia was just one. Portugal and Spain may have been others. Charles' linage. The heritage of Ottoman sultans. Abbasid Islam.

Undercover.

This is the reason why this worked for so long. Secrecy. Concealment. Deceit. The Diaspora. Undercover.

It is the very definition of 'Deep State'.

Had the successes of Jewish messianism and its real-world consequences been common knowledge, messianism would have failed to work its magic any longer.

The concept of the Jewish Messiah – there is none other but a Jewish messiah – contains the mechanism of self-destruction, not only for the collective Jewish communities, but for the world as a whole. A string of messianic pearls came down to Luther's time. One after another. This string reached uninterrupted into the past and continues.

Up until today.

The appearance of the messiahs brings forth a matter-of-fact explanation of the cycle of violence:

*grandeur – Messiah – revolt – war – destruction – compassion – grandeur.*

Together with offensive financial practices and rigged administrative systems, it serves for an eye-opening foundation for reasons why Jews were hated and persecuted throughout history. The 'grandeur' is a circular response to the compassionate preferential treatment of Jews by Christian or Muslim hosts after their (repeated) destruction. It leads to nothing less than a perpetual resurfacing of the claim to world domination: the King of the Jews is also the king of the world.

It continues into our present time with modern Zionism, which started around the late eighteenth century. Some authors attempt to position Zionism as a secular movement and Israel as a democracy. Perhaps undercover. Moreover, some proclaim that Zionists came to the land of the Palestinians with peace and brotherhood with the Arabs in mind.

Given that Zionism cannot be detached from the Promised Land, a concept of *secular Zionists* is rather outlandish.

The standing biblical mandate to eradicate all non-Jews from the Promised Land, and the treatment of modern Palestinians tells us how peaceful and secular the intentions of Zionism are.

The origin of Zionism falls into a phase of European liberalism where Jews participated in civilization as any other human being. But Jewish leadership refused to have their folks integrated into the general society. They were in fear of losing their paying members that provided them with a human shield.

Instead, they arrived with a religious agenda of cleansing the land from non-Jewish elements.

Jews came to Palestine, stole the property of Palestinians, and called it Israel. Some land was purchased, some was cheated and bullied away. But in compassion and guilt after the Holocaust, the international community looked the other way. Jews see this as a command from God. They see the Holocaust as part of God's design. As Hitler saw himself fighting in God's name against them, so they place themselves into the fulfillment of God's plan for the re-conquest of the Promised Land.

The diagnosis is simple: insanity.

The idea that Palestinians have to submit to Israel violates the basic concepts of a home for Jews as set out by the Balfour Declaration[1752] during the First World War. It was then understood that the civil and religious rights of existing communities in Palestine would not be compromised.

The idea of a 'national home' for Jews came up in Britain to court American Jews for war support.[1753]

Money, money, money.

We have seen the pattern before.

---

[1752] Arthur James Balfour, Secretary of State for Foreign Affairs, Letter to Lord Rothschild, November 2, 1917.

[1753] David M. Halbfinger, Balfour Declaration of Support for Jewish Homeland Still Divisive at 100, New York Times, November 3, 2017.

Through the assistance of a precursor of the United Nations — pressured by three terrorist organizations, the Zionist Irgun paramilitary, the radical Lehi Fighters for the Freedom of Israel, and the Haganah paramilitary — the world had facilitated a sanctuary for Jews to *share* with Palestinians. This decision was taken without the consent of either Palestinians or the surrounding nations.[1754]

It is also against the will of hard-core Ultra-Orthodox rabbis.

They refuse to recognize the legitimacy of a Jewish state before the arrival of the Messiah. Correctly so. But ever since the Second World War, Orthodox Jews have been quarrelling and rebelling against the world's will, and their neighbors have been intent on wiping them off the face of the earth.

The modern scholar Harris Lenowitz has investigated the most important messiahs in history. His conclusions are quite bluntly titled 'The Dynamics of Self-Destruction':

> *Despite the variety of details in the messiahs' lives and circumstances, one concludes, after reading all the accounts of them in succession, that they possess at least one feature in common: the messiah's failure to achieve his stated promises; from the beginning of every account, disaster is present and only awaiting its turn to appear. Hasidism [Ultra-Orthodox] spreads the risk around, multiplying messiahs and lowering the degree of disaster, less intent apparently on its own end. But a reckoning remains to be made with the part it played in the Holocaust. One tzaddik – the Satmar rebbe – ordered his following to remain steadfastly in Hungary, where they would be killed, and he then fled Europe. No messiah succeeds in leading his followers and the world to a harmonious existence – not on the political level, where independence and autonomy inside or outside Israel is not regained by the Jews; and certainly not on the cosmic plain, where disease, violence, and death endure as principal features of the human universe. No messiah is able to soften these perdurable actualities. The messiahs, during their lives, and the followers, after their leader's death, must push the successful fulfillment of their programs forward into the future in order to maintain themselves as microsocieties in the present, but their efforts merely inflect the unavoidable death of the messiah and the eventual collapse of his movement, leaving rationalizations on the ruins of the unattainable hopes they have raised.*[1755]

Lenowitz puts the blame on Hasidic Judaism, the Ultra-Orthodox sectarians.

However, the Messiah is not the cause of the failure.[1756]

---

[1754] After the fall of the Ottoman Empire, Syria and Mesopotamia, i.e. Iraq, were also created.
[1755] Lenowitz, 1998, 263-265.
[1756] Ibid..

The Messiah is a mere symptom of the Truth.

The Zionist movement was already successful before the two world wars. It was their long-time goal to establish a Jewish state. As we have seen, again and again in an unending river of blood. In 1897, the first Zionist Congress in Basel, Switzerland, which was a meeting of various Zionist groups throughout the world, put forth its program on how to establish a Jewish home in Palestine. It included the modern settlement policies, a global Jewish federation, and the strengthening of religious Jewish feelings.[1757]

The idea then was to buy up land in Palestine, little by little,[1758] and grow a Jewish state from within by betraying their Palestinian host country and seceding from it. For this purpose, they established financing arms, the Jewish Colonial Trust and the Jewish National Fund. Palestine was the target of carefully engineered treason. Ever since, Jews across the world have donated feverishly to achieve their goal.

Even schools were part of the plot. A Jewish children's song referred to a memorial box for donations to bring about the Redemption of Israel.[1759] The blue box showed a map of Palestine marked with all the land that had already been purchased or expropriated.

They were busy buying up Palestine, inch by inch – a re-conquest of the Promised Land through the Jewish financial machinery. These were *not* rogue microcosms. One look at the Wailing Wall in Jerusalem tells a different story.

Jewish leaders worked together through the ultra-loyal global network of the Diaspora to eliminate Palestine.

Following the Balfour Declaration, the British Mandate in 1920 established a home for the Jewish people in Palestine under international administration. The Ottoman Empire had been partitioned at the end of World War I. Syria and Lebanon were managed by France. Jews and Palestinians were supposed to live alongside each other.

The international commitment had already been subverted before it had been assigned to Britain.

---

[1757] Basel Programm, 1897.

[1758] Exodus 23:30.

[1759] *The Memorial Book for the Jewish Community of Yurburg, Lithuania* (Assistance to Lithuanian Jews, 2003), 356. Translation and update by Joel Alpert, Zevulun Poran, Josef Rosin, and Fania Hilelson Jivotovsky.

The few Jewish arrivals had no intention to share the holy land with Palestinians who were then a vast majority. Rising anti-Semitism in Europe brought more Jewish immigrants to Palestine. Tensions rose, leading to the Arab Revolt in Palestine. The trickle of arrivals gave way to a torrent during the Holocaust.

While millions of Jews were killed, Jewish paramilitary groups staged an insurgency against British rule. Over the heads of the Palestinians, the United Nations then created a plan that envisioned a two-state partition in economic union. The United Nations was the trustee of Jerusalem.

From a position of weakness, the Jewish leadership accepted the plan – with crossed fingers. The Palestinians rejected it. They did not want to receive more Jews at the expense of having to give up their homes. They feared that Jews wanted to take the Temple Mount, one of Islam's holiest sites. Although not publicly spoken of at this time, for Jews, that the Temple Mount is theirs, is non-negotiable. David Ben-Gurion, Israel's first prime minister, had earlier expressed himself that *'we shall fight in the war against Hitler as if there were no white paper, but we shall fight the white paper as if there were no war.'* In talmudic tongue, he meant to reject agreements that limited Israel's expansion.

Israel declared independence and went to war shortly thereafter. For Israelis, this is the War of Independence. For Palestinians it is Nakba, the disaster. The first 700,000 Palestinians were displaced, meaning pushed out of their land.

The international community put the humanity of Jews over the humanity of Palestinians to the point where the humanity of Palestinians was no more.

This is the world we have lived in ever since.

It is horrible: the messianic highlight – Doomsday – is manifested in the Holocaust itself. The disaster is in the end of millions of Jewish lives, its success is in the establishment of Israel – the very goal of messianism that creates an expectation for a new beginning out of the ashes of disaster.

Jewish messiahs were not some lone lunatics but, chosen ones who were supported by the highest authorities of Judaism, the Sanhedrin. They were the Nasi, and the Exilarch. The mission was carried by the global Jewish leadership in the Diaspora. The messiahs reflected the self-destructive hope and outlook of *all* Jews.

They turned against the messiahs only after they had failed.

Ordinary Jews ignore that the Pheonix rises from the ashes with a new covenant, a new religion. Jews are to be betrayed all the same.

The modern Lubavitcher Rebbe is one such messiah who carries forth this suicidal spirit.

It is simple: The Torah provides Jews with an eternal mandate to reconquer the Promised Land. Before we knew that Islam was one such successful Jewish conquest, we all believed that it took Jewry almost 2,000 years to get to the point of establishing the seed state of Israel.[1760] It started even before the Jewish reign in the Ottoman realm came to ruin. Regardless, the mandate stands to conquer all of the Promised Land, inch-by-inch. That entails just about everything west of the Euphrates River, or perhaps even further east, past the Tigris River.

It was not enough that the Abbasid Caliphate and the Ottoman-Turkish realm lived in the Jewish post-apocalyptic dream. The Jewish leadership aimed at the entire world. Since the Second World War, Judaism has been hard at work to achieving its reason of existence, yet again: God's covenant with Abraham for the re-conquest of the Promised Land in return for absolute obedience to the Jewish priesthood as the representative of their divinity. Once the Temple is seized, Redemption will be near. It will mark the dawn for the conquest of the rest of the Promised Land. And a death sentence for all Palestinians on this land. And secular Jews.

Lebanon and parts of Syria are next.

It will not end there.

It cannot end there – until all kingdoms and nations are subject to Jewish leadership.

The Bible commands thus.

Martin Luther was a spiritual father of Adolf Hitler, and he ultimately provided for the religious justifications for the Holocaust. Now, we can understand better why this might have been so.

It appears miraculous that the coincidence of Luther's change of heart with Reubeni's presence has not made headlines for the last 500 years. It explains with cutthroat directness why Luther hated Jews. Willful ignorance has prevented humanity from understanding the plots that led to repeated holocausts against the Jewish people. It also led to the loss of hundreds of millions of Christian and Muslim lives that could possibly have been saved through an understanding of the mechanisms.

---

[1760] With a main intermezzo in the seventh century and several other short-lived attempts.

On the flip side of the religious atrocities, three factors created cracks of liberty for new humanistic and secular worldviews to sprout: Luther's success, combined with the new 'social media' that sprang from the printing presses, and the notorious internal disunity of the Catholic Church. Almost reaching its oppressive goal of a reunified European theocracy, the betrayal of the emperor on the battlefield against Protestants by the pope put an instant end to the unification of Europe under the Catholic Church.

This one 'mistake' is perhaps the pivot that helped create the free West, which we enjoy living in today.

As we have learned from Luther, organized religion is freedom's enemy. It is intolerant by design. There is only one Truth. The Truth needs to be defended with the blood of its disciples. Sure, there are moderate religious voices that we would hope to amplify. However, they are utterly irrelevant. The ones on the extremes know exactly what they want. Through their relentless stubbornness across generations, they win over peaceful majorities. Given the opportunity for a united Catholic front, organized religion could have easily crushed the sprouts of freedom. And it could have continued its policies in the New World.

To put it in the words of George Orwell, *'to see what is in front of one's nose needs a constant struggle:'*

> *'[…] We are all capable of believing things which we know to be untrue, and then, when we are finally proved wrong, impudently twisting the facts so as to show that we were right. Intellectually, it is possible to carry on this process for an indefinite time: the only check on it is that sooner or later a false belief bumps up against solid reality, usually on a battlefield.* [1761]

When evil shows its true face, it may already be too late.

It is only a matter of time until we face *'Hadrian's Choice'* again. After having first fed the monster, the only way to tame it will be through apocalypse.

This time around, we are armed to the teeth with the nuclear potential to leave merely 144,000 survivors behind, if any.

---

[1761] George Orwell, In Front of Your Nose (Tribune, 1946).

## The Holocaust

Jews, Catholics, Protestants, and Shi'a or Sunni Muslims, including their sectarian flavors, each based their religions on hating and excluding everyone outside of their communal boundaries.

Protestants came to hoist Adolf Hitler into power, acting as enablers for the Holocaust. We can now understand why Protestants were enthusiastic about the Nazi regime and supported anti-Semitic policies.

One of the most prominent German Luther scholars declared in 1933: *'We Christians greet the rise of Adolf Hitler as a gift and miracle from God.'* From a distributed mass that was read in the centralized Protestant churches of Bavaria, Germany, we learn that *'A state which begins once again to govern according to God's command may expect not just the applause but the joyous cooperation of the church.'* [1762]

The initial spark of the mechanism that led to the rise of Hitler is now visible: a single man who was willing to openly fuel hatred and nationalism for evangelicals to idolize the Führer. Like an out-of-control pandemic, the infection was contagious across the globe.

The Protestant Reformer had it all figured out for them.

The disease spreads until it burns out.

Then the vicious cycle re-starts.

Compassionate human nature allows it, even, supports it.

Heinrich Himmler, the man who directed the construction of the German concentration camps – industrial extermination facilities – admired Martin Luther,[1763] even though Himmler was a devout Catholic. His biblical foundation, combined with an interest in anti-Semitic literature, created this beast and nurtured this sick mind. Himmler had been dreaming of a military career. But it did not materialize. He was stranded.

Were it not for the support of the Protestant Church, he would not have become commander of Hitler's SS.

Moderns prefer to forget that Adolf Hitler was elected democratically.

---

[1762] Robert P. Ericksen (Kurt Mayer Professor of Holocaust Studies at Pacific Lutheran University) in Peter Hayes, John K. Roth, *The Oxford handbook of Holocaust studies* (Oxford University Press, Copyright © 2010, reprinted by permission of Oxford University Press, www.oup.com) 253-254.

[1763] Marc H. Ellis, Hitler and the Holocaust, Christian Anti-Semitism (NP: Baylor University Center for American and Jewish Studies, 2004), Slide 14.

The rise of the Nazi regime is a case study in the failure of democracy and the decisive role of organized religion in its downfall. Protestants did not vote for the Nazis *despite* anti-Semitism but **because** of it; not in complacency but in full consciousness of an oncoming wave of terror against Jews. When opposition was still possible, the search for official Protestant criticism or opposition to the Nazi regime is almost in vain. Public dissent against the mistreatment of Jews and other groups was practically non-existent.[1764]

The Nazi Party harvested a disproportionate number of voter support from Protestants. The difference was a full quarter![1765] Twenty-five percent. Had Protestants voted like Catholics, the National Socialists would have lost more than half of their votes, and they would have never made it into power.

The outcome was dependent on local clergy. Wherever Catholic priests opposed official warnings of the Catholic Church against National Socialism, their parishioners voted like Protestants. The same could be observed after the opposition by the Catholic bishopric had been given up.[1766] They all voted for Hitler, and all Catholic resistance collapsed after the Enabling Act in 1933. According to the German bishopric, warnings against National Socialism were no longer necessary.[1767] They had accepted that a monster had risen to power. And now, they supported it. Right after the abandonment of opposition by the Catholic Church, Catholics and Protestants joined the National Socialists in equal numbers.[1768]

The influence of leaders of organized religion tends to be underestimated. The religious elite held and holds significant sway over its parishioners.[1769] In this case, it helped to create a global nightmare.

But before Catholics cheer, there are some issues that need to be pointed out. Nine out of ten Germans approved of the Nazi policies. Catholics had their establishment party. Protestants did not. This alone may explain the difference.

If it serves the power of organized religion, an unimaginable concentration of character defects in one single man who violates every one of their ideals becomes irrelevant.

---

[1764] Ibid., 254.
[1765] Jörg L. Spenkuch, Philipp Tillmann, Elite Influence? Religion and the Electoral Success of the Nazis (March 2017) 10.
[1766] Ibid..
[1767] Ibid. (Scholder 1977, p. 320).
[1768] Ibid., 13.
[1769] Ibid., 15.

After the Enabling Act, neither Catholics nor Protestants had a party of their own. In consequence, the same electoral behavior emerged: all supported evil alike.

Pope Pius XII allegedly excommunicated Hitler and other Nazi bosses in 1931.[1770] According to documents in the Vatican archives, an Italian historian found evidence that Mussolini 'secretly' requested the excommunication of Hitler in 1938.[1771] These papers were part of a regular process through which documents are unsealed after a period of seventy years. Mussolini did not need to ask for another fascist's excommunication after the pope had already done so. The same evidence suggests that the Vatican thought of Hitler at first as a passing phenomenon.

At a time when humanity needed most for someone to stand up against evil, being at odds with the friendship between Mussolini and Hitler, the pope chose to do nothing.[1772]

There was no excommunication.

Diplomatic relations between Vatican and Hitler were not broken off.

How the Catholic Church fought against Hitler's plans, while the Protestant Church supported them, remains murky and questionable. They chose silence even while knowing that priests were imprisoned and up to 6,000 Jews and Poles were killed in furnaces at the Belzec concentration camp in Poland – daily. Rather than being religious rebels and freedom fighters against Hitler, they sat on the comfortable chairs of party establishment.

That is a whole different story with its own shameful mechanism.

After all, the Catholic Church was as much anti-Semitic as Luther was. In fact, we have seen how the Catholic Church had created a culture of anti-Semitism from which Luther merely arose as a symptom.

We were incapacitated to see that this visible anti-Semitism was then grounded in the necessity to overthrow the Jewish administrative systems that had penetrated and subverted most, if not all of Europe. I suspect that the Catholic Church was embarrassed about having tolerated or introduced this deep state in the first place.

---

[1770] Klaus Scholder, The Churches and the Third Reich. 2 vols. (Fortress Press, 1988) 150-162.
[1771] Emma Fattorini, Hitler, Mussolini and the Vatican: Pope Pius XI and the Speech That was Never Made (Polity, Copyright © 2011, reprinted by permission of Polity) 147
Original publication in Italian, copyright © 2007 by Emma Fattorini, from Pio XI, Hitler e Mussolini, La solitudine di un papa, by permission of Einaudi.
[1772] Ibid., 149.

We marvel at heroic individuals who rescued some Jews and fostered an underground resistance movement. As inspiring as these stories are to us moderns, such courage was rare[1773] and remains so.

Taking action on the ground was dangerous.

Scholars are largely divided over Adolf Hitler's religious background. Christian academics typically prefer him to have nothing to do with their religion. But Hitler was not what we wish him to have been. He was the fire-spewing dragon that he was, and he flew high by the support of the Protestant Church and through lack of sustained opposition by the Catholic Church.

By knowing that his mother was a staunch Catholic and his father anti-clerical, we can get a grasp of Hitler's mindset. This mixed household might as well have been Protestant with a strong belief in a church subservient to the state. Naturally, that would cause friction with all religious organizations, but the emerging Protestant Church had already shown the way under Luther.

It may be hard to imagine, but the boy Adolf was singing in the church choir and looked up to his priests as representing the highest human ideal worth striving for.[1774] According to his own account, he excelled in his favorite subject, history, from which he drew lessons for his time.[1775]

When Joseph Goebbels noted in his diaries that *'the Fuhrer [was] a fierce opponent of all that humbug,*[1776] referring to a discussion about the Vatican and Christianity, Hitler criticized the power that the Catholic Church exerted in politics. This appears only natural, since the Catholic party initially supported their own candidate.

Hitler was the mirror of the anti-clerical stance that he learned from his father.

The monstrous consequences are obvious in his collaboration with the Protestant Church.

In his book, *'Mein Kampf,'* Hitler referred several times to his Christian beliefs. We can, of course, choose to doubt his words and intentions. It matters not that the Fuhrer's motives may have been expedient.

Of course, he was religiously as opportunistic as most modern politicians.

---

[1773] Ibid., 258.
[1774] Hitler, transl. Murphy, 1939, Chapter I.
[1775] Ibid.
[1776] Joseph Goebbels, The Goebbels Diaries 1939–41, translated by Fred Taylor (Hamish Hamilton, 1982) April 29, 1941.

We can take from the Goebbels diaries that Hitler was deeply religious. But after having learned about the End of the World insanities in all three Judaic religions, we also know what Hitler had in mind when he came across as anti-Christian, viewing Christianity as a symptom of decay and a product of the Jewish race.

That Christianity and Judaism would in the end be destroyed gives us an indicator that Hitler had the End of the World in mind, true to the biblical manuscript.[1777]

> *The Jewish doctrine of Marxism repudiates the aristocratic principle of Nature and substitutes for it the eternal privilege of force and energy, numerical mass and its dead weight. Thus it denies the individual worth of the human personality, impugns the teaching that nationhood and race have a primary significance, and by doing this it takes away the very foundations of human existence and human civilization. If the Marxist teaching were to be accepted as the foundation of the life of the universe, it would lead to the disappearance of all order that is conceivable to the human mind. And thus the adoption of such a law would provoke chaos in the structure of the greatest organism that we know, with the result that the inhabitants of this earthly planet would finally disappear.*

> *Should the Jew, with the aid of his Marxist creed, triumph over the people of this world, his Crown will be the funeral wreath of mankind, and this planet will once again follow its orbit through ether, without any human life on its surface, as it did millions of years ago.*

> *And so I believe to-day that my conduct is in accordance with the will of the Almighty Creator. In standing guard against the Jew I am defending the handiwork of the Lord.*[1778]

We can recognize a deeply religious man. It spoke loud and clear, years before Hitler came to power. Moreover, for someone like Hitler, it was easy to complement religious radicalism with fanatical nationalism. The results were tragic.

We have seen it under Martin Luther.

Does money talk?

Hitler introduced the compulsory church tax in Austria.

End of debate.

---

[1777] Ibid., December 29, 1939.
[1778] Hitler, transl. Murphy, 1939, Chapter II.

There are a couple of disturbing thoughts that this provokes. Was Hitler correct, after all, in his assessment of the menace of Judaism, but incorrect in his conclusions and actions? Did Hitler's National Socialism in effect save Europe from Marxist Communism? Have China, the Soviets, and others fallen prey to a Jewish 'conspiracy' under cover of Marxism?

It sounds awful.

Marx was indeed from a paternal linage that had supplied a century of rabbis in Trier. On the maternal linage, we find a Dutch rabbi. Marx's father had converted to Lutheranism to escape anti-Semitism. At the age of six, Marx was baptized Lutheran together with his mother and five of his siblings.

The Jewish background of Marx was part of a German Nazi propaganda piece from 1940, a movie Der Ewige Jude, the eternal Jew. In it, Jews were accused of working together in a global network to exploit the weaknesses and divisions in Germany and in every other nation. They were out for themselves and not interested in the common good. Equated with rats that bring along disease, Marx and other Jews were accused of bringing divisions to the German people and to subverting them for their gain.

Let us listen in for a moment how problems of fact were used by the Nazi regime to stir hatred against all Jews:

*Although they were a small minority, they knew how to terrorize a great tolerant Nation. For every 1,000 Germans there were 10 Jews, or better said, for every thousand disunified Germans who fought among themselves were 10 Jews who, despite business competition, all had a common goal: exploiting the Germans.*

*The Jewish merchants crowded into the cities. Three-fourth of all Jews lived in the big cities but not to work in the factories. They left that to the Germans.*

*For every 1,000 workers in Berlin there were 2 Jews. At the beginning of 1933, of 100 state prosecutors in Berlin, 15 were Jews. Of 100 judges, 23 were Jews. Of every 100 lawyers, 49 were Jews. Of every 100 doctors, 52 were Jews. Of every 100 businessmen, 60 were Jews.*

*The average income for a German was 810 Marks. The average income for every single Jew was 10,000 Marks. While millions of Germans fell into unemployment and poverty, immigrant Jews acquired fantastic riches in a few years, not through honest work but through usury, swindling, and fraud. We are only reminding of names like [inaudible, Goshtoritz] who lightened the Berlin treasury by 12.5 million Marks. The Jew [inaudible, Kutitzka] defrauded Prussia of 14 million. The Jew Baumann cheated the same state out of 35 million, not to mention the inflation profiteer Mendelsohn, the Jewish racketeer [inaudible Katenel En Bogan], and all the rest of them.*

> *Jews are most dangerous when permitted to meddle in a people's culture, religion, and art, and to pronounce their insolent judgment on them. The concept of beauty of Nordic men is incomprehensible to the Jew by nature and will always remain so. For the purity and neatness of the German concept of art, the Jew, without roots of his own, has no feeling. What he calls art must gratify his deteriorating nerves. The stench of disease must pervade it. It must be unnatural, grotesque, perverse, or pathological. These feverish fantasies of hopelessly sick minds were once extolled by Jewish art critics of German public life as high artistic expressions. Today it seems incredible that such pictures were once bought by nearly all our galleries. But Jewish art dealers and critics praise them as the only real modern art. German cultural life was niggerized and bastardized. Painting, architecture, literature, and music suffered as well. For more than a decade, Jews wielded their profane power as art dealers, music publishers, editors, and critics. They decided what would be called art and culture in Germany.*[1779]

While the resulting horrors are unfathomable, we must not be blind that these accusations were stereotypes, alright, but some of them were not just anti-Semitic. The *intention* of the piece and its structure is anti-Semitic. Some accusations are not, in particular the extraordinary penetration of learned professions by Jews. As modernity shows, learned people do not strive for factory jobs, Jews or not. There would be nothing wrong with striving for the intelligentsia were it not for the context of a hangover from the Jewish feudal administrative system in Germany.

We have not only heard similar stories from Martin Luther, but the evidence shows such accusations across Europe and Islamic nations. Germans had a lot of catching up to do. First, they had to wake up from the Christian ideal of being illiterate subjects of the priesthood. Then, they had to get to a Jewish level of learning. This provided Jews with competitive advantage over centuries – just as designed by the Judaic scriptural constructs.

Moderns understand the power of culture war. We are living it – again.

The Nazis used a kernel of truth to create the most poisonous mix of hatred. They exploited a deep-seated cultural trauma that had been inflicted on the German people through the centuries' long oppression by the Jewish administrative system.

Holocaust.

---

[1779] Der Ewige Jude, The Eternal Jew (Nazi Movie, 1940), ca. 33:00.

But let me move away from a humanist perspective and look at the problem through the eyes of the religious. Is it possible that such horrors could be repeated? The answer is straight forward: absolutely.

They are working on it.

Hitler's Holocaust changed the trajectory of the world – only for a while.

We need to ask similar questions for the presence of Martin Luther. His success created an unbearable paradox for modern Westerners. Had the anti-Semite failed, would Europe have continued to live under the yoke of a united Catholic Church? The latter may have reformed a little, but it would likely have retained its power to oppress the populations of Europe and the New World.

Jews would have been persecuted many times over, even without Luther. Were it not for Luther's attacks, the anti-Semitic work of another could have served the same destructive purposes.

This man, Hitler, needed to learn nothing new from what he had acquired in his parents' household. True to the biblical script, he was keenly aware that he would eventually create a conflict with the church.[1780] With this in hand, it would merely be a toddler's hop to Hitler's viewing himself as a prophet.

On one occasion, Goebbels noted that Hitler hated Christianity for crippling everything that is noble in humanity.[1781] Hitler was incorrect insofar as he did not include Islam. He may not have done so, because he thought that the Mohammedan religion would be more compatible with the German people than Catholicism – or because he was too intellectually lazy to learn about it. Like Luther before him, Hitler may have been referring to the Catholic Church, not to Christianity as a whole.[1782]

When Hitler was about to annex Austria in 1938, he berated the Austrian chancellor because the Habsburgs and the Catholic Church had sabotaged every national idea in Germany's history.[1783] This was not Luther speaking here, but Hitler. Nothing like a papal betrayal stood in the Fuhrer's way, and we are now enabled to put one and one together. Instead, as late as in December 1941, seven Protestant regional confederations consented to the Nazi policy of requiring Jews to wear a yellow badge. Luther provided their justification for preventive measures against Jews and for having them thrown out of Germany.

---

[1780] Goebbels, transl. Taylor, 1982.
[1781] Ibid., April 8, 1941.
[1782] Ibid., April 1941.
[1783] Adolf Hitler in William L. Shirer, The Rise and Fall of the Third Reich (Secker & Warburg, 1960) 325–329.

Hitler's point of criticism was more focused on the way the Catholic Church addressed anti-Semitism. He thought that their approach was well meant but ineffective.

> *Through this shilly-shally way of dealing with the problem the anti-Semitism of the Christian-Socialists [the Catholic party] turned out to be quite ineffective.*

> *It was anti-Semitic only in outward appearance. And this was worse than if it had made no pretences at all to anti-Semitism; for the pretence gave rise to a false sense of security among people who believed that the enemy had been taken by the ears; but, as a matter of fact, the people themselves were being led by the nose.*

> *The Jew readily adjusted himself to this form of anti-Semitism and found its continuance more profitable to him than its abolition would be.*[1784]

It does not take rocket science to recognize that Hitler's anti-Semitism was merely an extension of an already existing religious base that hoped for wiping out the 'menace' of Judaism. The German population was still being traumatised by Jewish elements that continued to exploit them.

> *[The Jewish person's] life is of this world only and his mentality is as foreign to the true spirit of Christianity as his character was foreign to the great Founder of this new creed two thousand years ago. And the Founder of Christianity made no secret indeed of His estimation of the Jewish people. When He found it necessary He drove those enemies of the human race out of the Temple of God; because then, as always, they used religion as a means of advancing their commercial interests. But at that time Christ was nailed to the Cross for his attitude towards the Jews; whereas our modern Christians enter into party politics and when elections are being held they debase themselves to beg for Jewish votes. They even enter into political intrigues with the atheistic Jewish parties against the interests of their own Christian nation.*[1785]

There is one source and one source only for this scourge: the Bible.

Hitler was merely another executioner.

There was nothing perverted or caricatured in Hitler's religious thoughts.

If societies fail to take these leaders by the ears, they will continue to lead entire nations by the nose.

---

[1784] Hitler, transl. Murphy, 1938, Chapter III.
[1785] Ibid., 307.

Some say that there is a world of a difference between Luther's belief in salvation and Hitler's racial ideology.[1786] But we have come to learn that this is not so. The very foundation of Judaism is racism – against all other races. We have also seen that Luther's later diatribes against Jews had nothing to do with salvation. Luther's anti-Semitism was expressing racism in its purest form. He wished them gone. He hoped for their synagogues to be burned to the ground. He wanted them to find a home nowhere.

Luther's *intent* was no less evil than Hitler's.

His death wish did not extend further than his territorial area in Germany, because one man stood in his way: Emperor Charles.

> *I would like here to appeal to a greater than I, Count Lerchenfeld. He said in the last session of the Landtag that his feeling 'as a man and a Christian' prevented him from being an anti-Semite. I say: My feeling as a Christian points me to my Lord and Savior as a fighter. It points me to the man who once in loneliness, surrounded only by a few followers, recognized these Jews for what they were and summoned men to fight against them and who, God's truth! was greatest not as a sufferer but as a fighter. In boundless love as a Christian and as a man I read through the passage which tells us how the Lord at last rose in His might and seized the scourge to drive out of the Temple the brood of vipers and adders. How terrific was his fight against the Jewish poison. Today, after two thousand years, with deepest emotion I recognize more profoundly than ever before the fact that it was for this that He had to shed his blood upon the Cross. As a Christian, I have no duty to allow myself to be cheated, but I have the duty to be a fighter for truth and justice.*[1787]

We can count the meaning of Hitler's words in bones.

If the notion that Hitler's known masterplan included the destruction of Christianity – he meant the power of the Catholic Church[1788] and the differences in the treatment of Jews – is based on reality, then the actions of the Protestant Church are even more understandable through Luther's eyes.

In 'secret' table talks, Hitler was indeed critical of Christianity.[1789] But the source of *secret* conversations appears questionable in the first place. It may tell us that Hitler – like Luther – may have evolved over time.

---

[1786] Martin Brecht 3:351.

[1787] Adolf Hitler in Norman H. Baynes, The Speeches of Adolf Hitler: April 1922-August 1939, Vol. 1, Munich, April 12, 1922 (Oxford University Press, 1942) 19.

[1788] Ian Kershaw; Hitler a Biography (Norton, 2008) 290.

[1789] Norman Cameron, R.H. Stevens, Gerhard L. Weinberg, H.R. Trevor-Roper (2007). Hitler's Table Talk 1941-1944: Secret Conversations (Enigma, 2007) 48, October 14, 1931.

His early words demonstrated sincere belief in Christianity. Nazi dogmas were born from Christian ideals. It had been laid into the monster's crib. The anti-Semitic stance was built into the Gospels and the Old Testament alike. Fueled by cultural trauma, Hitler and his Nazi apparatus were products of Christianity.

Love for your own – death to all others.

And they were a product of true Judaism – death to everybody else.

I personally know Christian ministers, priests, and other functionaries that are critical of their own religious organization. As much as the faithful wish this to amount to a posthumous extradition of Hitler from their community, such disapproval neither disqualifies this man's religious upbringing nor his own religiosity. It does not paint over the enthusiastic embrace of this monster by the Protestant Church. Even Pope Francis reproached his own religious organization at times. It cannot serve to cleanse the Catholic Church of its collusion with Europe's fascist regimes, not just with Hitler's.

Could the Holocaust have been prevented? Absolutely not. For this to have happened, a thorough understanding of messianism and its tragic self-fulfilling prophecies that continue to come down upon Jewish people would have been a prerequisite.

Can future holocausts be prevented? Unquestionably: learn.

The horrifying abuse and killing of Jews during the Third Reich had the effect of raising compassion for them and increasing external and internal opposition to the inhumane practices. The horrors provided one of the keys of the intellectual framework for the formation of allied forces against the evil Third Reich. It culminated in the foundation of today's Jewish state of Israel in the land of the Palestinians. This represented an immense leap forward for the formerly persecuted.

It was the biblical motive relived.

The Christian historian Paul Johnson brings it into context for us:

> *The Holocaust and the new Zion were organically connected. The murder of six million Jews was a prime causative factor in the creation of the state of Israel. This was in accordance with an ancient and powerful dynamic of Jewish history: redemption through suffering. Thousands of pious Jews sang their profession of faith as they were hustled towards the gas chambers because they believed that the punishment being inflicted on the Jews, in which Hitler and the SS were mere agents, was the work of God and itself proof that He had chosen them. According to the Prophet Amos, God had said: "You only have I known of all the families of*

*the earth, therefore I will punish you for all your iniquities." The sufferings of Auschwitz were not mere happenings. They were moral enactments. They were part of a plan. They confirmed the glory to come. Moreover, God was not merely angry with the Jews. He was sorrowful. He wept with them. He went with them into the gas chambers as he had gone with them into Exile. That is to state cause and effect in religious, metaphysical terms. But it can also be stated in historical terms. The creation of Israel was the consequence of Jewish sufferings.*[1790]

The Holocaust led to the creation of Israel.

The killing frenzy still rings through eight decades later in the West's compassion toward Jews. Like cattle, Jews were poisoned and burned with the organizational efficiency of German slaughterhouses. An estimated two-thirds of all Jews living in Europe were systematically exterminated. The apologist behavior is reflected in today's courts, which still award retributions to Jews from those who exploited the Holocaust.

Jews continue to be protected by the West.

At the same time, the Middle East is outraged about the presence of an Israeli state in their lands.

On the other hand, we now know that the Jewish leadership does not care about the cost of their pursuit. As long as it leads to climbing to the top of the Temple Mount, every means is on the table, even if the whole world needs to be laid in ashes. Indeed, total destruction is the biblical plan.

Proponents of messianic grandeur are simply criminals and of the same class as despots with weapons of mass destruction.

I may have to state it expressively: this is not to rationalize or trivialize the evil actions of Nazi Germany or the Zeitgeist behavior of other nations that reduced their Jewish populations. Irrespective of religion or ideology that may have provided for the cause, whatever they did was inhumane, horrible, and objectionable on every level of thought and action. I am thankful to the allied forces of Britain and the United States for their intervention to bring them down.

However, Luther's story is a warning for the future: when religious organizations flex their political muscles, they represent the number one hazard to bring about humanity's self-destruction. The Nazi actors ended up in jail after it was too late. However, the enablers walked free – all of them.

---

[1790] Johnson, 1998, 519.

From their Protestant pulpits, the mantle of religious freedom provided cover for their engagement in passive aggression. After the deadly facts had hit home, they pretended that there was nothing they could have done. They were praying hard to oppose the atrocities, they said.

Right away, they created an Orwellian history in favor of their religion, misrepresenting everything that could shed a negative light on them.[1791] Or a true light, for that matter. They were *'impudently twisting the facts so as to show that [they] were right.'*

The Protestant Nazi enthusiasm was pushed out of sight in the process of self-cleansing.[1792]

The Catholic Church failed to stand up to evil. If the beast had supported *their* party, they would have closed eyes, ears, and mouths and catapulted Hitler into office just as well. Nations around the world should have introduced comprehensive regulations to ensure that monsters can never again be supported.

The failure to do so represents a mistake of historic proportions.

Instead, it took the Catholic Church a full two decades after the Holocaust to come up with some sort of justification and repositioning. On October 28, 1965, Pope Paul VI declared in his Nostra Aetate that it was true that Jewish authorities had pressed for the death of Jesus Christ. However, not all Jews can be charged with what happened, in particular not Jews of today. In effect, he broke with the Council of Trent in which collective responsibility for Eve's original sin was confirmed upon all generations of humanity. Jews should not be rejected or accursed *'as if this followed from the Holy Scriptures.'* We have seen the evidence from the Catholic Church as Martin Luther saw it. Jews *'do not teach anything that does not conform to the truth of the Gospel,'* he said.[1793]

> *Furthermore, in her rejection of every persecution against any man, the Church, mindful of the patrimony she shares with the Jews and moved not by political reasons but by the Gospel's spiritual love, decries hatred, persecutions, displays of anti-Semitism, directed against Jews at any time and by anyone.*[1794]

It is a rather fanciful repositioning for a new beginning.

---

[1791] See The Protestant Church in the Third Reich: Handbook of the Kirchenkampf (1956).

[1792] Ericksen, *Holocaust studies*, 2010, 261.

[1793] Pope Paul VI, Declaration on the relation of the Church to non-Christian religions, NOSTRA AETATE, October 28, 1965.

[1794] Pope Paul VI, Declaration on the relation of the Church to non-Christian religions, NOSTRA AETATE, October 28, 1965.

## *It Is Just History*

Enough of all that stuff of the past. It is just history. Or is it?

Today, we can applaud the religions of charity, love, and peace for settling their disputes once and for all. We are all one happy, global family.

I am being sarcastic.

After the attacks on the World Trade Center and the Pentagon in September 2001, President George W. Bush is said to have discovered his life's mission that day. *'He became convinced that God was calling him to engage the forces of evil in battle.* [1795] We now know what these words meant for this deeply religious president. Misled by fabricated claims of weapons of mass destruction, Bush engaged in a campaign against the 'Axis of Evil.' In his ignorance, he willingly took the risk of a clash of civilizations — the End of the World.

It would be unfair to Bush to be silent over the modern history that preceded the attacks in 2001. As was demonstrated, the Middle East has been prone to religious madness throughout its past.

There were three events that shaped the violence of the modern Middle East: the founding of Israel, the Revolution in Iran in 1979, and the invasion of Afghanistan by the Soviet Union in the same year. These events fueled the Mujahideen. In the nineteenth century, this prominent jihadist guerilla group had battled the British, which then held the colony of British India, bordering to Afghanistan. Like ISIS, the Mujahideen welcomed religious 'freedom fighters' from all over the world.

After the Soviet Union withdrew from Afghanistan and disintegrated in 1989, the Mujahideen felt emboldened. They thought of themselves as having beaten the then all-powerful Russians out of their country. And they credited themselves for having caused the collapse of a superpower. Anyone who tangled with them became a target in an increasingly globalized jihadist religious struggle.

Foreign powers were looked at as colonialists that plundered their (oil) resources and supported local dictators. One of their fundamental beliefs was that Jewish and Christian countries conspired to destroy the religion of Islam.

Today, they are still motivated by the same fears. Of course, nobody admits just how correct they are in their assumptions.

They think of themselves as being treated as the 'Meddle' East.

---

[1795] Tom Carver, BBC, *Bush puts God on his side*, April 6, 2003.

As a consequence of the fight against the Soviet Union, the Sunni militant Islamist organization al Qaeda was formed by Osama bin Laden, the mastermind behind the attacks upon New York in 2001. During the Soviet-Afghan War, Bin Laden had been supported by the United States, then led by another profoundly religious man: President Ronald Reagan.[1796]

Those who did not know that already need to let that sink in.

This constitutes the seminal moment for a precursor of the Islamic State (ISIS), the *Sunni Organization of Monotheism and Jihad.* There are others, but bin Laden's group stood out in competing for the trophy of the most outrageous violations of human nature, directed first against their Shi'ite co-religionists, against more moderate forms of Sunni Islam, and then against everybody outside of the territories that are under the spell of the Koran.

President Bush's invasion of Iraq in 2003 was supposed to be a bold response to the disaster in New York. It opened a full-on jihad against America's presence in the Middle East and against the Shi'ite majority in Iraq, fueled in large parts by trained former Sunni members of the Iraqi army. Under Osama bin Laden, the *Sunni Organization of Monotheism and Jihad* merged with al-Qaeda and became al-Qaeda in Iraq (AQI).

As the U.S. withdrew under President Obama, AQI morphed into the Islamic State (ISIS) under Abu Bakr al-Baghdadi (Caliph Ibrahim) and slipped into the void left behind by the departing American led 'coalition.' As Syria fell into civil war (triggered in part by Obama's promises made in Cairo to support people's drive for freedom), ISIS expanded vastly with its signature violence.

Unlike other jihadist terrorist groups, ISIS aimed at expanding its territory. For this, it would recruit just about anybody willing to carry a gun. Since Syria has turned into a land of a proxy war (which the Middle East has been for over a century), ISIS's expansion was virtually guaranteed.

The idea of ISIS was to build a new caliphate, a unified national identity, which spans all majority Muslim countries.

Should Muslims ever succeed in unifying Shi'ites and Sunnis, this would represent the worst nightmare for a world entirely unaware of its danger. A unified Islam would immediately turn its attention toward Jerusalem and attempt to blast the Jewish State of Israel off the map.

It turned out that Iraq and Iraqis had nothing to do with any of this. Nevertheless, they ended up being bombed back into the Dark Ages.

---

[1796] Ronald Wilson Reagan was president of the United States 1981-1989.

Here is the problem: When the leader of the free world does not base his decisions on facts and the lessons from history, the entire world is put at risk.

The paradox is unfathomable: America should not have gone in – but they could not leave either.

U.S. President Trump, a brilliant master in the art of manipulating religious men, forced an unnecessary hand to completely withdraw American troops from Afghanistan.

The Taliban were emboldened.

Trump's announcement of a deadline removed critical contractor logistics, maintenance support, and surveillance from troops that were routinely engaged in fights with the Taliban. Practically overnight, strong American air support had changed into no-engagement. The Taliban had nothing to fear from the air. Technical issues grounded vehicles and aircraft dependent on maintenance that had been contracted out. Before, the Afghan Army was on the offensive; now it had entered a vicious cycle of endless losses. Their president, the commander in chief, fled the country. They fought until their ammunition ran out, even after the Taliban had entered Kabul.[1797]

Within weeks, the disabled Afghan Army was overrun by the Taliban.

Instead, the televised images in our heads are branded by a collapsed Afghan Army that failed to take a stand, imprinted with footage from a C17 transport carrier with refugees hanging on for dear life, some of which fell to death or were crushed inside the fuselage.

The next deeply religious U.S. President, Joe Biden, was left with few choices. Reversing course would have meant restoring a collapsing Afghan Army and sending in American troops. Biden's only viable option was to try to extend Trump's May deadline to August 2021 and seek to withdraw American and allied troops with as little carnage as possible.

On his visit to Egypt in the spring of 2017, our modern Pope Francis warned against violence and terror in the name of religion. He said that religious leaders had an obligation to denounce violations of human dignity and human rights and to expose attempts to justify hatred in the name of religion.

He thought of these as idolatrous caricatures of God.[1798]

---

[1797] Sami Sadat, I Commanded Afghan Troops This Year. We Were Betrayed (New York Times, August 25, 2021).

[1798] Jason Horowitz, Pope Francis, in Egypt, Delivers a Blunt Message on Violence and Religion, New York Times, April 28, 2017.

These words came within the context of a government crackdown on religious terrorism against Egyptian Christians. He hoped to exploit the weakness of the Coptic Church in Egypt for a merger with the Catholic Church with the aim to expand the power of the papacy. He holds similar ambitions with more conservative elements in the Anglican churches in England.

During this same visit, the Grand Imam, Ahmad al-Tayeb, advocated that the West should not hold the collective of Islam responsible for crimes of small groups of followers.

If the imam does not want to be held accountable for the atrocities of those who read the Koran, he should rip out the offensive pages from his disturbing scripture. It would be reduced to a handful of pages. The rest constitutes an utterly hostile assault against those who fail to believe in their Truth.

Turning to President Abdel Fattah el-Sisi, Pope Francis said that history would not forgive preachers of justice who practice injustice or those who talk about equality but discard those who are different.[1799]

Freedom, as we know it, has grown from between the fronts of organized religions.

On the following, we can probably agree with Pope Francis:

> *'Demagogic forms of populism are on the rise. These certainly do not help to consolidate peace and stability,' he said. 'No incitement to violence will guarantee peace, and every unilateral action that does not promote constructive and shared processes is in reality a gift to the proponents of radicalism.* [1800]

The result of political support by organized religion is coming home in a political shift to the right that is reminiscent to many of Hitler's rise. Their leaders are aware that all concentrations of power deprive individuals of their freedom to do as they choose. Yet, the religious upper class insists on voting for its party leaders despite their obvious rot and filth.

I appreciate the difficult task of this pope. However, one pope will not change the trajectory of the Catholic Church. One rabbi will make no difference. One imam is like a drop in the river of history's blood.

Theocracies are enemies of freedom. Women, homosexuals, non-religious, and even the religious of foreign creeds are directly hurt by them.

---

[1799] Ibid.
[1800] Ibid.

In that sense, one more messianic couple is offered to better understand modern atrocities: the American Schneersohn Rebbes. As an activist Russian Orthodox rabbi, Yosef Yitzchak Schneersohn (Joseph Isaac) lived through the horrors of the world wars. Arriving in New York in 1940, he set out to build Orthodox Jewry in the United States. On the site of a deserted Arab town near Tel Aviv, he also established a Hasidic village, Kfar Chabad.

Hasidic Judaism is a subgroup of Haredi Jews, known as the Ultra-Orthodox. Officially, it goes back to a parallel messiah in Ukraine and Russia, Israel Ben Eliezer, the Baal Shem Tov of the eighteenth century, and his successors. The Schneersons were at the spiritual helm of Hasidic Judaism when Jews were restricted to the Pale of Settlement.[1801] From the late eighteenth century, Jews were not allowed to live anywhere inside Imperial Russia except this designated region. We have learned that Hasidic leaders were around long before.[1802] Similar to Luther's time, the Jewish upper strata, the noble leaders, were excluded from these restrictions.

Ultra-Orthodox Jews claim to have no identity without a state of Israel. In contrary, Jewish identity and success lie exactly in their status in the Diaspora without a state. They maintained their identity through the privileges that had been showered upon the Diaspora. Throughout history, Ultra-Orthodox Jews have shown that they are flexible to declare new spiritual hubs anywhere.[1803] We have seen it in Amsterdam, Baghdad, Tlemcen, and in Zakho. Location is not a limiting factor to establishing world domination.

Instead, the existence of a Jewish state exposes its theocratic nature. It might as well constitute Judaism's death-knell – the end of prophecy.

Schneersohn's son-in-law, the Russian-American Menachem Mendel Schneerson, the Rebbe, became one of the most important Rabbinic leaders of the twentieth century after fleeing Europe in 1940 as well. The Rebbe was interested in making the world a better place and eliminating suffering.[1804]

Sounds good, does it?

This is limited to nobility of Ultra-Orthodox Jews.

---

[1801] The Pale of Settlement existed 1791-1917. It encompassed a large region in the west of Imperial Russia. This included Belarus, Lithuania and Moldova, parts of Ukraine, eastern Latvia, eastern Poland, and western Russia.

[1802] Josel Rosheim, king of the German Jews, visited the new Hasidic messiah (Rabbi Abraham ben Avigdor ) right after the stand-in for Shlomo Molcho had been roasted on the stake.

[1803] Baghdad, Basra, Edessa, Haran, Samarra, Sana'a, and Sippar, only to name a few of the hotspots.

[1804] Rabbi Menachem Mendel Schneerson, *Sefer Hama'amorim Melukot Al Seder Chodshei Hashana* Volume 2 (Kehot Publications, 2002) 271.

Suffering ends with a death blow. He imagined *'a redemption of such magnitude and grandeur through which the purpose of the suffering, the harsh decrees and annihilation of exile will be understood [...]'.*[1805]

The Rebbe was another messianic contender in the name of conquering the Promised Land.

I look up to former U.S. President Jimmy Carter as a role model for humanism and peace. He is also a deeply religious man who stood at the beginnings of the modern evangelical voting bloc that exposes the vulnerability of democracies to homogenous religious groups. Precisely because of his beliefs, Carter could not see through the Rebbe's machinations.

Instead, Carter honored the Rebbe's birthday as Education and Sharing Day for the thousands of religious schools that he established.

Honoring a fanatic for raising the next generation of religious extremists was not Jimmy Carter's smartest decision.

We can now better appreciate this in the context of the wave of compassion that followed the Second World War and the Holocaust. It is not Jimmy Carter's fault. Everybody in the West thought alike and ignored warnings from the East.

Like collective punishment, collective compassion or guilt that continues generations after the facts may not be appropriate. At some point, we must return to seeing each other eye to eye in mutual normalcy and friendship.

According to the Rebbe, the Messiah was human. He appears in every generation. He thought his generation was the most likely to achieve the goal of the Redemption of Jerusalem. However, since Zionism had fundamentally changed the landscape and Israel was firmly established, he chose to change the dialogue: *'we must stop insisting that Judaism is in danger, an assertion that does little but place Jewry on the defensive. We need to go on the offensive.*[1806]

We now know where this is leading: the next holocaust.

Palestinians suffer from this change in policy to this very day. They are held captive in slums on their own land. We remember Israel's Prime Minister Golda Meir, who liked the dowry but not the bride. Instead of imprisoning these figures for hatred of mankind, they were honored for their outward appearance. Behind the veil, they prepare for conquering the Temple.

It will come at the cost of millions of lives.

---

[1805] Ibid., 404.
[1806] Gershon Kranzler, Jewish Life, Sept.–Oct. 1951.

Palestinians hate Jews, and they cannot accept an Israeli state that keeps on pushing them further off their land. Jan Fermon, the secretary general of the International Organization of Democratic Lawyers in Brussels brought the paradox to the point:

> *The U.S. for the past 70 years has supported aggression, blockades, settlements and occupation. [...] Even under international law, Palestinians, being occupied, have the right to fight back. You can't simply say, 'Oh, if they do they are terrorists.*[1807]

It should be obvious who the aggressor is. However, we have learned that the root is much deeper. Even if Palestinians would have been treated in the kindest possible way, the Koran and Sharia Law still obliges them to hate Jews from the bottom of their hearts. They do not even know why. They just do. The Koran, written by Jewish leaders, indoctrinated this hatred against themselves into Muslim minds.

Hatred and compassion were designed as cold-blooded tools for manipulation.

It works: the land is lost either way.

Iranians and Lebanese are with them against Israel. We no longer need to wonder why.

At Iran's annual conference in support of Palestine in February 2017, Iran's supreme leader, Ayatollah Ali Khamenei, sounded the horn of battle against Israel, calling the Jewish land dangerous and a cancerous tumor. He thought that *any* compromise with Israel would be a grave mistake.[1808]

Khamenei has nothing to worry about. Israel is not going to violate its God-given mandate never to enter into any agreements with anyone who has a foot on the Promised Land. In order to make compromises a matter of impossibility, the Israeli government introduced a referendum in 2010 for mandating that *'any peace deal involving the ceding of territory annexed by Israel — namely East Jerusalem and the Golan Heights — must be put to a national referendum.'*[1809]

What are Israel's peaceful intentions?

---

[1807] Thomas Erdbrink, At Tehran Gala, Cakes, Fruit and Anti-Israeli Slogans, New York Times, February 21, 2017.

[1808] Ibid.

[1809] Isabel Kershner, Israel Enacts Bill to Force Referendum on a Treaty, New York Times, November 22, 2010.

Perhaps, they follow the meaning of the Talmud: '*Scripture says Love thy neighbor as thyself: choose an easy death for him.*'[1810]

They agree on at least something.

Khamenei recognized that a united stance of Islam against Israel would be overwhelming: '*The issue of Palestine can, and should be, the pivot of unity for all Islamic countries.*'[1811] The supreme leader assessed correctly that the turmoil and crises in the Middle East have undermined Muslim unity in support of Palestine.

Westerners fail to appreciate just how dangerous this is. Muslim disunity is in the interest of both Israel and the West.

A united Muslim front would indeed be an intolerable threat. Not because of Arab or Persian people.

Because of their religious leaders.

Ayatollah Ali Khamenei is one of the most dangerous men on earth. We need to take into consideration what he said about Palestine.

At the same conference, Ramezan Abdullah, the secretary general of the Islamic jihad warned that the '*Palestinian people should prepare themselves for the downfall of Israel,*' pointing out that his group did not share the interest of the United States in a two-state solution. '*Palestine belongs to the Palestinians, not the Jews,*'[1812] Abdullah exclaimed.

If we look at the historical and biblical context, then Abdullah has no point. Islam was Jewish. But the desire for a Jewish homeland would not be easy to accommodate anywhere.

Israel is here to stay and to be protected – but there is a veto against its theocratic and ethnic nature.

Ultra-Orthodox Judaism and similar extremist sects in Israel (and globally) are terrorist organizations when terrorism is defined as any act that is intended to cause harm to innocent people. Messianic organizations are terrorist organizations. They intend to destroy the world.

The hatred, divisions, wars, atrocities, and holocausts will never end.

Religious freedom and free speech *of the individual* are sacrosanct. By principle. Individuals are free to believe whatever they wish. However, organized religions and theocracies are different. They need regulations.

---

[1810] Talmud - Mas. Sanhedrin 45a.
[1811] Ibid.
[1812] Ibid.

For years, Israel's Prime Minister Netanyahu has been encouraging the United States to threaten Iran over its nuclear program. His strategy of division and distraction from continued encroachment on Palestinian land has always been obvious.[1813] Pushing the United States into a war with Shi'ite Iran, which is embedded in a sea of Sunni neighbors – all aspiring to nuclear power — does not seem to be a sensible approach for peace in the Middle East. Netanyahu wanted to put Americans on the front lines — cannon fodder – in order to expand the Promised Land.

Meanwhile, Israel grew the largest nuclear arsenal in the East. How can we trust that this weaponry will be used with the utmost restraint and only when all other options are exhausted?

Here is a teaser for the true mindset of the current elite: at the end of 2014, Israel's minister of the economy and the leader of the Jewish Home Party, Naftali Bennett, promoted a full annexation of the Palestinian territories in light of the evolution in the Middle East with ISIS and Hamas.[1814] In his plans, the Palestinians would have political 'independence' under Israeli law and military 'protection' with Israeli soldiers. After his election to replace Netanyahu as prime minister for a brief time, he said that Israel is *'the precise anchor of stability, of willingness to do the job to keep this area safer.'*[1815] Instead, he perpetuates a shadow war with Iran and refuses to even negotiate a peace deal with Palestinians. Bennett opposes their sovereignty. He wants their land. He promotes a full annexation of the Palestinian territories and subjugation of the inhabitants.[1816]

The aim is military sovereignty while pretending to provide citizenship to some, but not to others, to secure Jewish 'democratic' majorities. The writing on the wall is the Jewish post-apocalyptic dream come true once more.

While still Israel's education minister, Bennett expressed his feelings in biblical lingo:

> *From the ruins of Amona we will move to build a new settlement. From this mountain we will move towards applying Israeli sovereignty over Judea and Samaria.*[1817]

In other words: the re-conquest of the Promised Land was restarted.

---

[1813] Reuters, Netanyahu to Press U.S. For Military Threat on Iran, New York Times, November 7, 2010.

[1814] Naftali Bennet, For Israel, Two-State Is No Solution, New York Times, November 5, 2014.

[1815] Patrick Kingsley, Isabel Kershner, New Israeli Leader Backs Hard Line on Iran but Softer Tone With U.S. (New York Times, August 24, 2021).

[1816] Naftali Bennet, For Israel, Two-State Is No Solution, *New York Times,* November 5, 2014.

[1817] Oren Liebermann, Euan McKirdy, Israel to build entirely new settlement in West Bank, CNN, February 1, 2017.

Bezalel Smotrich is Israel's finance minister. He openly laments that Israel's founders did not *'finish the job'*, meaning to remove the Palestinians with the intent to transfer the land to Israelis. He thinks that there is *'no such thing as a Palestinian people.'*[1818] Smotrich is co-founder of an NGO called Regavim which applies this train of thought. His goal is the displacement of the Palestinian people from every speck of land that he considers to be the ancient homeland of Israel.

If given the opportunity, the entire Middle East will be subjected to slow genocide.

After the horrendous terrorist attack by Hamas in October 2023 that took over 1200 Israeli lives, Israel struck back with disproportional force and in blatant violation of the laws of war, killing more than twenty times as many civilians – ten times as many Palestinian children alone. In November 2023, Prime Minister Benjamin Netanyahu made it clear again that Gaza needed to be de-radicalized and demilitarized. Israel will maintain control in Gaza for as long as necessary, he said, referring to Judea and Samaria, a concealed term for the Promised Land.

He would never forfeit security control over Gaza to any other authority.[1819]

Netanyahu laments that Palestinian children are taught to hate Israel.

The Bible teaches Jewish children to hate non-Jews.

Meanwhile the American thinking goes along the line that a one-state solution that deprives so many Palestinians of their rights would be inconceivable. Israel will not agree to anything else but that. And that is the worst case.

The best case is to rid the land of them all.

Relocate them to other countries – a war crime.

From the perspective of world stability and peace, it is not only Palestine that needs to be de-radicalized and demilitarized — it is also Israel.

Remember: never again!

---

[1818] Megan K. Stack, For Palestinians, the Future Is Being Bulldozed (New York Times, December 9, 2023).
[1819] NBC, Meet the Press (November 28, 2023)

Benjamin Netanyahu spoke for the third time to the U.S. Congress in March 2015. The main topic was Iranian nuclear ambition. The speech was revealing. There, he thundered how Iran and ISIS were competing to impose a militant Islamic empire on the entire world. They just disagreed on who should become the emperor, Netanyahu proclaimed. There is no place for Christians or Jews and no rights for women or freedom for anyone.[1820]

The Israeli Prime Minister was correct.

But he forgot to mention that Judaism aspires to the same kind of world domination, representing a third party that cannot agree on who will be the ruler of the global empire. Netanyahu and Bennett constitute the spear of militant Judaism. They want to create a combative Jewish empire, first in the region and then the entire world. Israel and Iran just disagree among themselves who should be the ruler of that empire.

Later in his speech, Netanyahu added a casual biblical warning that Israel will stand even if it has to stand alone. Moses, he said, brought his people from slavery in Egypt to the borders of the Promised Land. The Israelites should be strong and resolute in their conquest and neither fear nor dread their enemies.[1821]

To be clear, Moses' message was to conquer the Promised Land from the Sinai to the Euphrates and terminate every non-Jewish inhabitant in it.

Add to this that Israel's leader likened himself to the Maccabees. He claims direct ancestry to the Polish–Lithuanian Vilna Gaon. I suppose that concealed claim would render him of the royal Hasmonean linage.

Netanyahu's speech was bold in crying out against an aggressive Islamic regime while at the same time promoting his own Jewish imperial agenda. It is just the same idea in different clothing. Their common denominator is that the Islamic Republic, the Islamic State, or the Jewish State represent a threat to each other. By design of their religions, they can no longer coexist.

They constitute a threat to the planet.

The then-present representatives of the U.S. Congress did not have their guards up, because many of the spectators were also women and men of faith. That a new messiah should come from Jews, from the House of David, is only natural for them. They do not seem to have been able to translate the biblical mysteries into the language of assault that it really was.

Instead of being shouted down, Netanyahu received standing ovations.

---

[1820] Benjamin Netanyahu, Address to Joint Meeting of Congress, March 3, 2015.
[1821] Ibid.

The Democrats' House leader, Ms. Nancy Pelosi thought that the Israeli had insulted the intelligence of the United States in regard to the threat posed by Iran.[1822] The then-president of the United States, Barack Obama, recognized the Israeli leader's appearance as theater.[1823]

But it was a mortal threat.

Here is what is at stake: Netanyahu and Bennett are masters in dividing parties and diverting attention from greater dilemmas, Palestine, for example.[1824] Their ulterior interest is the further conquest of the Promised Land and the Temple Mount. The best ways to achieve these goals are to encourage large parties to go to war against one another or to subvert the American government to the same end.

By a just-in-time unveiling of a stash of documents, Netanyahu and American Orthodox Jewry were able to embolden the American government in its quest to get out of the Iran Nuclear Deal.[1825] The latter, imperfect as it was, had been intended to halt Iran's ambitions for nuclear armament and, more importantly, to draw the Shi'ite country into a global dialogue to weaken its extremist theocratic regime. In turn, exiting the agreement without an alternative in place emboldened Netanyahu and Bennett.

The very day after the American president pulled out of the Iran Nuclear Deal, Israeli fighter jets attacked Iranian positions in Syria. Following the Israeli Maxim, *'if there is rain on our side, there will be a flood on their side,'*[1826] Israel responded with a flood of fighter jets to twenty missiles that had been directed from Iranian positions inside of Syria toward the recently annexed Golan Heights. The Iranian-made missiles failed. Iran is unable to engineer anything that could be called high-tech, such as cars (!), missiles, or nukes. Their scientists have long been exported – to America. The clash appears to have started with an Israeli bait attack on Syrian territory in the Golan Heights. These were known to the Israeli government as *'Chess.'*[1827]

They looked at deadly force as chess?

---

[1822] Peter Baker, In Congress, Netanyahu Faults 'Bad Deal' on Iran Nuclear Program, New York Times, March 4, 2015.

[1823] Peter Baker, In Congress, Netanyahu Faults 'Bad Deal' on Iran Nuclear Program, New York Times, March 4, 2015.

[1824] Roger Cohen, Bibi's Tired Iranian Lines, New York Times, October 3, 2013.

[1825] Roger Cohen, Trump to Iran: America's Word is Worthless, New York Times, May 9, 2018.

[1826] Isabel Kershner, Israeli Warplanes Hit Dozens of Iranian Targets in Syria, New York Times, May 10, 2018.

[1827] Isabel Kershner, Israel and Iran, Newly Emboldened, Exchange Blows in Syria Face-Off, New York Times, May 11, 2018.

This is not to favor Iran. It is an evil theocracy. In this face-off, it has openly threatened the existence of Israel. However, we are discussing anti-Semitism here, which naturally puts Israel into the spotlight.

But I am not sure whether the world understands the full implications of Israel's founding charter *'as envisaged by the prophets'*[1828] of Judaism. It mandates the conquest of the Promised Land and cleansing of all non-Jews from it.[1829]

The ethnic cleansing does not involve only Palestinians. They represent merely a symptom. Any non-Jews are not welcome.

Many decades have passed since the Israeli occupation of the Golan Heights, a Syrian territory that had been seized by Israel in 1967. The heist was never recognized internationally. Five years into the civil war in Syria, Prime Minister Benjamin Netanyahu declared in 2016 that the land would never be returned. According to him, it was integral to Israel since ancient times.[1830]

It is as simple as that.

This language of occupation, annexation, and cleansing is justified by the biblical Promised Land.

Little do moderns know that all of Syria is part of that promise.

And much more. Until there is nothing left to take.

The most contentious issue is east Jerusalem with the Temple Mount. Israel will never agree to a division of the Holy City. The Palestinians insist on the eastern half for the capital of their state.

'Unofficial' comments by Israeli government members make it clear that the dream is hushed, but it is an undeniable goal to sack the sanctuary as soon as opportunity strikes.

David Cameron, the prime minister of Great Britain, said in 2016 in response to a question in the House of Commons that he was shocked by what he recognized as encirclement of East Jerusalem by Israel.[1831] Cameron has not forgotten that he is in the lineage of the Jew Elia Levita, the one who had enjoyed Egidio Viterbo's palace in Rome before ending up in the Ghetto of Venice.

---

[1828] The Declaration of the Establishment of the State of Israel, May 14, 1948.

[1829] Joshua 13:2-13:6.

[1830] Isabel Kershner, Israel Will Never Give Golan Heights to Syria, Netanyahu Vows, New York Times, April 18, 2016.

[1831] Isabel Kershner, Benjamin Netanyahu Rebukes David Cameron for Criticizing Israel, New York Times, February 25, 2016.

Mr. Netanyahu lashed out at Cameron that he seems to have forgotten some basic facts about Jerusalem. Israel was the only protector of the holy sites from being ignited by Hamas or the Islamic State, he said[1832] This is so patently fabricated that it should be transparent for all the world.

Sooner or later, the Temple Mount will be Israel's – and then the world will be ignited.

As a reminder, Jewish leaders succeeded in occupying the Temple Mount before. The consequence was the creation of Islam, an aggressive religion of jihad that put the world on fire, indeed. They must do so under a new covenant.

It is biblically mandated.

The encroachment occurs also in subtler forms. After the founding of Israel, churches had leased vast swaths of land to Israeli settlers via the Jewish National Fund. Typically, such deals were signed for ninety-nine years, at the end of which the land with all buildings would fall back to the churches.

Big mistake!

Granted, that land was stolen before – from the people. Now, it is stolen back by Ultra-Orthodox Jews. To finance their operations, some churches sold leased land to private investors, netting in the hundreds of millions. Israel intends to confiscate such properties, even if deals were made years back.

At the time of publishing this book, the respective bill was hushed. But with a similar approach, about 800 km² of land in the West Bank have been seized to create 'parks' which would then be abused for illegal Jewish settlements.

With the exception of actual places of public worship, all church property would be confiscated. Meanwhile, Ultra-Orthodox settler organizations continue to strategically buy up real estate in East Jerusalem only to harass its non-Jewish neighborhood residents into leaving town.

The Greek Orthodox Patriarch Theophilus III said that the Christian community in Israel faced systemic discrimination. *'This reminds us all of laws of a similar nature which were enacted against the Jews during dark periods in Europe,'* he said.[1833]

With our current approaches, the oncoming train cannot be stopped.

---

[1832] Ibid.

[1833] Sue Surkes, Tamar Pileggi, After Holy Sepulchre Shuttered, Bill Allowing Seizure of Church Lands Shelved, The Times of Israel, February 25, 2018.

Perhaps it can. Listen to what Netanyahu had to say:

> *You know, I have learned something from history, and I think you have too, you know, when you have an aggressive tyrannical regime with a murderous ideology, you know, stop it in the beginning. Don't let that tyranny grow and expand. Don't let that aggression conquer more and more territory. So yes, you have to take a stand. We take a stand. I think that's the way to prevent war. If history has taught us anything, it's that opposing such tyrannies and their aggression early on actually prevents catastrophe, and if you don't, you invite the catastrophe.*[1834]

This message should be prescribed for all scripturally inspired nations, including Iran, Israel, and other ideologically driven aspirants to regional or world leadership.

I repeat: the facts speak of a different ownership of the contested land. In 1999 Ze'ev Herzog of the Department of Archaeology in the Tel Aviv University in Israel was surprised that no public outcry followed his myth-shattering findings. *'Any attempt to question the reliability of the biblical descriptions is perceived as an attempt to undermine "our historic right to the land,"'* he said. He was met with hostility or silence. And not only by Orthodox or secular Jews, but also by Christians![1835]

The trouble with this is that it undermines the religion of Jews and the state of Israel. Without the claims of the Old Testament, the foundations of their houses go missing.

The concept of time for Jewish leadership is biblical.

However, the pressing deadline for the Messianic Age to begin within just over 200 years may change their willingness toward taking ever greater risks. They have been relentless and think long-term — very long-term, so much so that they encourage large families for Ultra-Orthodox Jews to fill the future ranks of the elite with their own.

> *When the state was founded in 1948, David Ben-Gurion, the first prime minister, granted full-time yeshiva students state financing and exemption from army service to refill the ranks of Torah scholarship destroyed in the Holocaust.*[1836]

---

[1834] Interwiev of Benjamin Netanyahu by Chris Cuomo, CNN, May 10, 2018.
[1835] Herzog, 1999.
[1836] Isabel Kershner, Some Israelis Question Benefits for Ultra-Religious, New York Times, December 28, 2010.

The goal in the mind of Ultra-Orthodox Jews is the establishment of a Jewish theocracy that will rule the world.[1837] The Messiah must arrive before the year 6000 AM,[1838] which ends in the year 2240 AD.

The majority of Jews in Israel are secular. Unfortunately, the peacefulness of them will lose in the face of growing zealotry and the rabbit-like birthrates of Ultra-Orthodox families. Most of us will see it in our lifetime. To subvert a democracy, a majority is not needed. A strictly *obedient* alliance of minorities can threaten majorities simply by deploying divisive strategies and forming a voting bloc.

Where this leads to is made clear by a modern Jewish Ultra-Orthodox sect, called Sicarii. Their name is borrowed from a first-century Jewish terrorist organization with the goal of wresting Judea from the Roman Empire.

At the end of 2011, Ultra-Orthodox Jews were in a standoff with more moderate Jews about implementing more stringent religious rules. They threw rocks and eggs at the police while shouting at them 'Nazis'. Female reporters were called *'whores'* with the derogatory Yiddish *'shikse'*. They do not even want to hear the voices of females.

Meanwhile, the ultra-Orthodox community is exploding through their extraordinary birthrates.[1839]

No, I am not talking about Islam.

Ultra-Orthodox groups.

Ultra-Orthodox Jews are about a tenth of modern Israel and do not consider more liberal Jews or Reform Judaism as Jewish. They define politics and the flow of Israeli thought in respect to the most fundamental issues that fuel the crisis in the Middle East. The suspension of a plan to create a space for men and women to pray together at the Wailing Wall speaks loud and clear. If Ultra-Orthodox Jews have their way, Israel will live biblically, including the debasing of the female gender as eternal punishment for their original sin.

The future of Israel has full gender segregation in its cards.

---

[1837] The seeming paradox with Ultra-Orthodox Jews in Israel is that 60% live below the poverty line, half don't work and most don't serve in the military. In the effort to repopulate Ultra-Orthodox ranks, the Israeli regulations essentially force them not to work and dedicate themselves to religious studies if they don't want to lose their exemptions and the financial support from the mainstream population through government stipends. Outside of Israel, Ultra-Orthodox Jews tend to be as successful in making a living as the Torah prescribes.

[1838] Talmud – Mas. Rosh Hashana 31a.

[1839] Isabel Kershner, Israeli Girl, 8, at Center of Tension Over Religious Extremism, New York Times, December 27, 2011.

These are not fringe views. In a desperate appeal, the president of the World Jewish Congress expressed his concerns over the threat by Ultra-Orthodox groups to the Jewish nation. He saw Israel's capitulation to religious extremists as a source of alienation through the pressures exerted by Ultra-Orthodox minorities. Referring to a possible path to peace with Israel's neighbors, he said that Israel might face the stark choice between granting Palestinians full rights, in consequence ceasing to being a Jewish state, or ceasing to being a democracy.[1840] The trouble is that ordinary Jews – even the non-Orthodox president of the World Jewish Congress – do not realize that Israel was born a theocracy.

How the 550,000 Hasidic Jews in Brooklyn, New York, live gives us an eye-opening taste. How do they make a living with so many not willing to engage in 'ordinary' work? Look no further than the enablement by New York itself. They know just as well as the polygamist Mormon communities how to exploit the system to their advantage.

Jews around the world have reason to fear for their lives – stabbed in the back by their own Ultra-Orthodox extremists who hold power in Israel. Or in New York. And elsewhere. They will be first in line to be betrayed into another holocaust by their brethren.

Why the West does not have its defenses up against Ultra-Orthodox Jewry is made clear by the former Knesset speaker, former head of the Jewish Agency, and author of the book *'Defeating Hitler,'* Avraham Burg. He is a respected Israeli dissident with a French passport.

> *But the worst kind of Jewish fundamentalism is insidious. It looks nothing like Al-Qaeda — it's not a crusade against the West or a campaign for theocracy, so often we don't see it and fail to protect against it because it maintains an oddly democratic facade.*

> *This invisible Jewish neo-fundamentalism is rooted in fear. And it is this fear that rights all the wrongs of Israeli policies and justifies the occupation [of Palestine]. What is this fear? It is old and it is Jewish: it is the fear that every enemy is a new Hitler, that behind every threat lies the potential for a new Holocaust. Now more than ever these fundamentalists want us to believe that we have to "look out for us and our own." Otherwise, who knows? The next Kristallnacht might come straight out of Ramallah.*

> *And so democracy remains a value until there is enough of a threat — real or imaginary — to warrant its suspension. Similarly, equality is considered the*

---

[1840] Ronald S. Lauder, Israel's Self-Inflicted Wounds, New York Times, March 18, 2018.

*highest value, up to a certain demographic percentage. When these fears are strong enough, discrimination against non-Jews becomes warranted — even necessary — and any progressive principle can be placed under caveat. Democracy, for the invisible fundamentalist, turns out to be something more akin to a preference than an obligation.*

*This democracy-eliding fear is insatiable, and its greatest victory is it has been superimposed on our hope. The words "to be a free people in our land" in the Israeli national anthem have become hollow and meaningless. The original meaning is more than just political emancipation. It entails freedom from debilitating fear, the freedom to determine our destiny with vision, not to succumb to circumstances helplessly. It means freedom from Orthodox dictates and freedom from oppressing others. Alas, we are not free. There is no freedom of religion when the Orthodox impose their version. There is no independence for the state when it occupies another land. Judaism is a kidnapped civilisation.*

*Seventy years ago Israel's founders wanted to create an alternative to the eastern European shtetl — one place that would be free of fear for Jews. But their Zionist hope has turned into our Zionist fear.*

*And, unhappily, this dread lives on both sides of the Atlantic. Increasingly, many Jewish establishment organisations — the political and religious, most of the official voices of worldwide Jewry — embody the same embarrassing duality. In as far as they deal with domestic issues, they incline towards moderate, inclusive and tolerant. But when it comes to Israel, most of them transmogrify into bloodthirsty hawks: extreme, religious right-wingers. They claim to stand for liberal values while pledging allegiance to a deep, archaic tribalism. And in the battle of values, tribalism wins. No wonder they no longer represent the majority of Jewish individuals abroad who divorced themselves from this fundamental hypocrisy.*[1841]

Avraham Burg's assessment is striking in its naiveté, and I am hopeful that many Jews think just like that. They believe in a benign foundation of the state of Israel for a free people as we in the West might wish to understand it.

Israel was designed with a different kind of freedom in mind. The freedom to conquer the throne of the world.

Fear is just one of the ingredients of the religious game of 'undercover' death to anyone who thinks differently.

It never meant for Burg to be master of his own destiny.

---

[1841] Avraham Burg, Jewish Fundamentalism, The Economist, online debate, August 7, 2012.

The behavior of Jewish leadership, as described by Burg, confirms nothing but the worst stereotypes of Judaism. It comes at the peril of all, including liberal thinkers like Burg and the majority of ordinary Jews.

In the opening statement by Rabbi Daniel Gordis, opposing Burg's ideas, a frightening verification of the just quoted mechanism was given:

> *Contemporary Jewish life is replete with examples of political extremism and religious fundamentalism. Before we despair, however, we would do well to recall that Judaism's instinctive moderation has long been one of its most salient characteristics. In Jewish history's fierce ideological battles, moderating middles have typically emerged victorious.*
>
> *In 2010, an Israeli rabbi ruled that Jews ought not to sell or rent property to Arabs and two other rabbis published a book, "Torah Ha-Melekh" (The King's Law), arguing that Israeli soldiers could intentionally kill Palestinian children. But upon learning of the ruling on not renting property to Arabs, rabbis around the world responded with disgust. When the book was published, the authors were almost prosecuted for incitement.*[1842]

The façade is moderate and friendly. The heart is of stone. Corrupt. Treacherous.

And deadly for Palestinian children.

While acknowledging Jewish political extremism and religious fundamentalism, Gordi argued that it all is not as bad as it may seem. However, despite the worldwide 'outcry' of rabbis, Jews refuse to rent property to Arabs. Despite the call to violence against Palestinian children, the authors of *The King's Law* were only *almost* prosecuted — but they were not. It is with exactly this double-edged hypocrisy that Ultra-Orthodox groups can subvert the rest of Judaism and drum up anti-Semitism and create another holocaust.

Instead of understanding their own history, Israelis feel threatened and think that they need to push their agenda even harder.

This evolution leads to a self-fulfilling prophecy with a clear trajectory: Armageddon.

The bullish voices of the fundamentalists are a core ingredient to the mechanism of self-destruction. Fundamentalism is the norm, not the exception, and moderation has always been in the face of death. The religiously peaceful majority follow extremists for the latter's courage to assert themselves and for the majorities' love for peace.

---

[1842] Daniel Gordis, Jewish Fundamentalism, The Economist, online debate, August 7, 2012.

We can see clearly now: religious militancy is stronger than secular reason. In fact, peaceful majorities are irrelevant in shaping the trajectory of history. They are pushed around like herds of sheep.

One of their über-Rabbis was Ovadia Yosef, who died in October 2013. The outpour of grief at his funeral procession brought Jerusalem to a near standstill. 700,000 (!) lined the streets of the Holy City. That is almost 10% of the population of Israel. Rabbi Yosef was the spiritual leader of Ultra-Orthodox Shephardies, and with his black turban, he would have been indistinguishable from Muslim imams from the Middle Ages.

Benjamin Netanyahu thought of Yosef having been one of the wisest men of his generation. He advocated *true* peace, which means peace under the terms of Israel. His dark sides are reported as if they amounted to nothing. His sermons were uploaded to YouTube and served to target supposed enemies of Israel, political rivals, and, of course, homosexuals. When then Prime Minister Ariel Sharon planned to withdraw from Gaza in 2005, the wisest man threatened with God's wrath. Sharon would receive God's blow, die, and not awake. He also hoped that Iran's president would get sick and stuck the word 'evil' unto President Mahmoud Abbas of the Palestinian Authority. Yosef prayed for God to strike Ishmaelites and Palestinians with a plague. He wanted the 'evil haters' of Israel dead.[1843]

These are the charitable words from a religious leader of Israel.

One of the wisest men of our generation was not only filled with unspeakable hatred against mankind, but he also preached about it under the mantle of religious freedom.

Why do modern societies tolerate such obvious hate speech?

Why, for God's sake, would such qualities be celebrated in commemorating the spewer as if nothing better of his personality would have stood out? In the rosiest of possible interpretations, this is complicity.

Such people need to be kept in check through international laws that criminalize *public* hate speech and their radical organizations.

Instead of being hailed, the wise man Yosef should have been jailed – cut off from any communication with the outside world. He and his ilk should have never been able to board an aircraft or cross any borders. And never be.

---

[1843] Isabel Kershner, Rabbi Ovadia Yosef, Spiritual Leader of Israel's Sephardic Jews, Dies at 93, New York Times, October 7, 2013.

The current Chief Rabbi of Israel is Yosef's son Yitzhak Yosef, another saint who is proud to not have graduated from high school. He was exclusively 'educated' in yeshivas. Math, science, English and other subjects as required in Israel's Education Ministry's curriculum are nonsense. The Torah is the only education necessary. According to his wisdom, religious Jews must keep themselves segregated from traditional or secular Jews to avoid being influenced. It is unbearable for him to having to live among secular Jews,[1844] and he wants to challenge Jewishness of immigrants by requiring DNA tests. He thinks that some of them coming from the former Soviet Union are religion-hating Communists. Black people are monkeys. Women who do not submit to the Jewish dress code are animals.[1845]

Non-Jews should be expelled to Saudi Arabia.

He promised to do just that when the Messiah arrives.

Disregarding Israeli rules of engagement, he proclaimed that anyone who comes to attack a soldier must be killed. Later he specified that they must be put in prison for life if they no longer have a knife. They can kill them when the Messiah comes.[1846]

So the father, so the son. A fine extremist.

And you allow him to visit your country? Under what pretense? Religious Freedom? Free Speech?

700,000 showed up for his father's funeral. How many more will be at his?

If we fail to put guardrails on him and his delusional subordinate leaders, *all* Jews will end up paying with their lives.

The Israeli Prime Minister Arial Sharon, while defense minister and then not yet on Yosef's hitlist, pursued the conquest of Lebanon in order to expel the Palestinians to Jordan. The plan was sold as the removal of P.L.O. artillery that posed a threat to Israel. Sharon's vision included the annexation of the West Bank.

He imagined that the Palestinians would overthrow Jordan and would as a result no longer demand a Palestinian state in the West Bank.[1847]

---

[1844] Kobi Nachshoni, Chief rabbi: Better to live abroad than among secular Israeli (Ynetnews, 5 July 2021).

[1845] Sam Sokol, Israel's chief rabbi shrugs off math, science studies as 'nonsense' (Haaretz, 2021).

[1846] Toi Staff, Chief rabbi: Non-Jews shouldn't be allowed to live in Israel (The Times of Israel, March 28, 2016).

[1847] Ronen Berman, How Arafat Eluded Israel's Assassination Machine, New York Times, January 23, 2018.

On the eve of the Israeli election in 2015, Prime Minister Benjamin Netanyahu clarified that there would be no Palestinian state and that no Palestinian land would be evacuated.[1848] To stimulate last-minute turnout, he even warned that Arab voters could influence the outcome of the elections after the latter had formed a surprise alliance.[1849]

Netanyahu confirmed Avraham Burg's fears and unmasked the lip-service democracy that included Arabs for show. As long as Arabs remained disorganized and dispersed minorities, all was fine. But the hawks came out once the 'others' dared to stick their heads out and organized themselves.

The unfortunate fallout from Netanyahu's long leadership is that he is at the epicenter of rising anti-Semitism around the world.

His posturing, maneuvering, and finally showing his true intentions provided those who oppose Israel, Judaism, or Jews with the justification for their hatred. He is the polarizing figure that has been re-elected in a democratic process in Israel, equating him with '*the Jews.*' This is self-endangering and self-destructive for all children of Israel.

There was no better way to isolate Israel globally than to re-elect Netanyahu. This is how an everyone-is-against-us paranoia can turn into a self-inflicted self-fulfilling prophecy.

Netanyahu is a religious fanatic whose age-old strategy is to have others blow up the world in order to get his feet on the Temple Mount. He has no issue with millions of Palestinians living in conditions that are reminiscent of concentration camps under Hitler's Nazi regime.

The Bible absolves him.

The 'New Anti-Semitism' needs to be partially understood in this context. A large portion of its rise can directly be linked to outbursts of violence between Israel and Palestine.[1850] Another part is related to wearing the Star of David or skullcap in Muslim areas. Or to reactions to Islamophobia among Jews. The deep-seated historical trauma resurfaces with every incident. In the face of the humanitarian disaster in Palestine, we cannot possibly expect Muslims to roll over.

The remedy is simple: do not wear offensive religious symbolism.

---

[1848] Jodi Rudoren, Netanyahu Says No Palestinian State if He Is Re-Elected, New York Times, March 16, 2015.

[1849] Yousef Munayyer, Netanyahu's Win Is Good for Palestine, New York Times, March 18, 2015.

[1850] Adam Nossiter, 'They Spit When I Walked in the Street': The 'New Anti-Semitism' in France, New York Times, July 27, 2018.

The most important advisor to the former leader of the free world was an Orthodox Jew. The latter is known to be so close to Benjamin Netanyahu that his parents had him clear the bedroom for the Israeli leader to stay overnight. This advisor was in charge of peace negotiations between Israel and the Palestinians. It is probably not exaggerated to assume that nothing good could have come from these buddies.

Was the former president of the United States of America a subverted puppet of Israel's expansionist agenda? Who else has been meddling in the American election? Who has an interest in destabilizing the world?

We fail to appreciate just how dangerous this relationship is.

Not surprising, in defiance of a United Nations' Security Council resolution, Israel signed off on 2,500 new Jewish units in the West bank settlement on the fifth day of the Trump presidency. Two days earlier, on the third day, 566 units had been approved in East Jerusalem.

This decision had been held off for a long time because of objections by every American president since the 1960s.

Amid worldwide condemnation, Israel escalated its determination under the trade winds of the American administration. It essentially legalized almost 4,000 settlement units retroactively that had previously been illegal. The settlers can simply claim 'in good faith' that the former owners of the land had been unknown. Even if the Palestinian owners were known, the government could have given the original holders alternative plots of land or otherwise compensated them.

A fleck of desert for an oasis. Ofir Akuni, a minister from the Likud party, said that the law was a demonstration of *'the connection between the Jewish people and its land. […] This whole land is ours. All of it.*[1851]

We can see clearly now. It is just history. And its patterns repeat themselves.

How? When?

During his campaign for the presidency of the United States, Donald Trump pledged to give Israel the freedom to negotiate with the Palestinians as they pleased, and he promised to move the American embassy from Tel Aviv to Jerusalem. Under his administration, the United States would *'recognize Jerusalem as the undivided capital of the State of Israel.*[1852]

---

[1851] BBC News, Israel passes controversial law on West Bank settlements, BBC, February 7, 2017.
[1852] Alana Wise, Trump tells Netanyahu he would recognize Jerusalem as Israel's capital, Reuters, September 25, 2016.

He did so on December 6, 2017:

*In 1995, Congress adopted in Jerusalem Embassy Act urging the federal government to relocate the American Embassy to Jerusalem and to recognize that that city, and so importantly, is Israel's capital. This act passed congress by an overwhelming bipartisan majority. And was reaffirmed by unanimous vote of the Senate only six months ago. [...]*

*Therefore, I have determined that it is time to officially recognize Jerusalem as the capital of Israel.*

*Ever since then [the recognition of Israel by the United States of America] Israel has made its capital in the city of Jerusalem, the capital of the Jewish people established in ancient times. [...]*

*However, through all of these years, presidents representing the United States have declined to officially recognize Jerusalem as Israel's capital. [...]*

*We want an agreement that is a great deal for the Israelis and a great deal for the Palestinians. We are not taking a position of any final status issues including the specific boundaries of the Israeli sovereignty in Jerusalem or the resolution of contested borders. Those questions are up to the parties involved.*[1853]

All checks and balances were removed.

Senate and House had indeed voted for the Jerusalem Embassy Act in 1995.[1854] It was a mandate that *'(1) Jerusalem should remain an undivided city in which the rights of every ethnic and religious group are protected; (2) Jerusalem should be recognized as the capital of the State of Israel; and (3) the United States Embassy in Israel should be established in Jerusalem no later than May 31, 1999.*[1855]

All presidents since the Act have argued that it infringes on foreign policy, which is the responsibility of the White House. They thus signed a Presidential Waiver as foreseen in the act when it was *'necessary to protect the national security interests of the United States.*[1856]

At the opening ceremony of the embassy, two notorious evangelicals delivered sermons, John C. Hagee, a megachurch televangelist, and the leader of one of the largest Southern Baptist churches, Robert Jeffress.

---

[1853] Donald J. Trump in Full Video and Transcript, December 6, 2017.
[1854] The approval was overwhelming: Senate 93-5 and House 374-37
[1855] Jerusalem Embassy Act of 1995, Section 3.
[1856] Ibid., section 7.

During a mass in 2008, Jeffress had preached that Islam and Mormonism were heresies *'from the pit of hell.'* Only those who follow Jesus Christ will be saved. *Judaism — you can't be saved being a Jew. You know who said that, by the way? The three greatest Jews in the New Testament: Peter, Paul and Jesus Christ. They all said Judaism won't do it. It's faith in Jesus Christ.'*[1857]

Hagee had said in the late 1990s that the Holocaust was part of God's plan. *'How did it happen? Because God allowed it to happen [...]. Why did it happen? Because God said my top priority for the Jewish people is to get them to come back to the land of Israel.'*[1858]

We now know where we are heading, do we? Holocaust.

Since the Palestinians claim east Jerusalem as their capital, the decision to move the embassy provided fuel for further violence.

Within days, Netanyahu urged the annexation of Jewish settlements in the West Bank,[1859] and Israel's right pushed for legislation to make a two-state solution impossible. Ratification of a peace agreement now requires a two-third supermajority in parliament.

> *'We are telling the world that it doesn't matter what the nations of the world say,' Public Security Minister Gilad Erdan told more than 1,000 members of Likud's central committee on Sunday. 'The time has come to express our biblical right to the land.' [...]*
>
> *Daniel Seidemann, director of Terrestrial Jerusalem, which focuses on the Holy City's fate in a potential two-state solution, said that 'what was winked and nodded about before is now being acknowledged publicly: 'We have no intent of sharing this land with anybody else except as a barely tolerated minority.' [...] 'The map of external pressures has changed dramatically,' said Menachem Klein, a political scientist at Bar-Ilan University. 'Instead of Obama, we have Trump. The European Union is divided, Brexit occupies the British agenda, Germany has coalition problems. There's no consensus in Europe, no single policy putting pressure on Israel. So this is a very easy arena in which we can go ahead.*[1860]

Even though the former president said that no final decision has been taken in terms of the specific boundaries in Jerusalem, in November 2019, the White House no longer viewed Israel's occupation of the West Bank as illegal.

---

[1857] Matthew Haag, Robert Jeffress, Pastor Who Said Jews Are Going to Hell, Led Prayer at Jerusalem Embassy, New York Times, May 14, 2018.

[1858] Ibid.

[1859] David M. Halbfinger, Emboldened Israeli Right Presses Moves to Doom 2-State Solution, New York Times, January 1, 2018.

[1860] Ibid.

The trajectory is obvious: The Temple Mount is encircled.

Now we have context for the Iranian backed Hamas terrorist attacks in October 2023 against Israeli civilians. Firstly, they merit full condemnation and armed pushback.

But we must not be blind: the only way to peaceful co-existence is a two-state solution that needs to be imposed and enforced by the international community. Both sides have no interest in ending the quarrel until the other is extinguished. The Temple Mount must be protected as neutral ground. Failing to do so will awaken large parts of the worldwide Jewish Diaspora into a messianic nightmare with New York ahead of all falling into chaos. Israel will keep on expanding into neighboring countries. It will trigger a messianic disaster of global proportions with the unavoidable consequence of another holocaust, one like none before.

Read the Bible!

The final months of 2023 have also been instructive how anti-Semitism was abused as a tool to shape public opinion. Anyone who dared to speak up in defense of the Palestinian people who have lived for decades under Israeli repression was branded anti-Semite. Even university leaders who were seeking context were pushed out of office. If that is not their job, then I do not know what is.

The smallest confrontation with any Jew is drummed up as anti-Semitism.

We have also seen that some of the largest anti-Semitic events in Martin Luther's environment had more to do with self-defense than with anti-Semitism. Anything that did not privilege Jews above all others appears to have been declared as anti-Semitism. Inviting Jews to lay down their supremacy and to join humanity as one of the many in a meritocracy is viewed as anti-Semitism. Criticism of Israel's behavior is anti-Semitism.

It is as though we should not be surprised that we have so *few* clashes between Palestinians and Israelis in North America and Europe.

It took the American President Biden two months to start seeing the consequences and to question his unconditional support for Israel, a support that has its origin in his religiosity. His former boss in the Whitehouse was more reserved about Israel's operations.

Biden should have known better.

The conflicts and excesses have accompanied him throughout his long political career.

What gets lost in all this is that genocide of the other is scripturally mandated by God for both. But one commands a superior army with tanks, jets, and nuclear capabilities while the other is on foot and underground, equipped with 'democratized' weaponry such as pickup trucks, rifles, drones, mobile missiles, and suicide wests. And with junk from Iran.

Hamas' attack was not only barbaric but also outright stupid, as though Prime Minister Netanyahu (and his predecessors) had not long telegraphed that he would respond with the full and overbearing power of his army – exploiting a window of compassion.

Put yourself into Palestinian shoes.

Would you be sitting at home praying in silence for God's help when your neighbor encroaches on your land? When you are being systematically pushed out of your home and being deprived of basic human freedoms, even basic necessities with a legal system rigged against you?

The legal system was designed precisely in that way as we have learned.

That the land of the Palestinians belongs to Jews alone rests on mythical fancy. Any city in the world with a long-established Jewish diaspora could be claimed as ancestral land of the Jews. Were Palestinians to put some effort into studying the Bible, they might discover that their ancestral claim is *older* than the one of the Jewish people, either through Ishmael or the Philistines.

When biblical myths should be grounds for land claims, what about the lands of the natives in the Americas? They have a factual ancestral claim to their homeland. Are they going to get it back?

## Charity, Love, and Peace

Abuse of religious power through supposedly secular political organizations is ongoing in Protestant-led England. It oppresses the religious feelings of Catholics in Northern Ireland. We have seen the beginning of their end 500 years earlier during Martin Luther's lifetime.

The IRA is the Irish terrorist organization that has unleashed its deadly force of love for decades. It is dedicated to Irish — Catholic — independence. The violence often comes from both sides. The Protestant-controlled police are reputed for their excessive brutality against Catholic protesters. Even today, Catholics refuse to submit.

The Irish Republican Army (IRA) is fighting it.

The IRA under Sinn Fein officially renounces terrorism today. However, it leaves violent actions to more radical terrorist groups and is suspected of pulling the strings for attacks from behind the scenes.

Even in the twenty-first century, Irish Christian minds are still divided over such sectarian differences that only few can explain.

The power of organized religion is only waiting for its moment to grab the moral supreme lead when opportunity strikes. It will do so in moments of despair – even if it has to bring those moments about by its own doing and at the cost of millions of lives and livelihoods.

The survival of the organization justifies the disposal of individuals, non-members and members alike.

In South Korea too, host of some of the largest Protestant megachurches, we can see sectarian animosities flaring up among Christians in the midst of Buddhists and Confucians.

Today.

When the Catholic Pope Francis visited Korea in 2014, the Presbyterian Rev. Song Choon-gil fired up his Protestant disciples who were rallied a few blocks from the papal mass. He called the pope an enemy king.

Protestants sounded the trumpets of spiritual war against the idol worship and satanic forces of Catholicism.[1861]

---

[1861] Choe Sang-Hun, Papal Visit That Thrills Catholics Is Unsettling to Protestants in South Korea, New York Times, August 16, 2014.

South Korea is a modern, industrialized and urban society, which has caught up to the twenty-first century. Its population is highly educated and technologically advanced. It boasts the world's eighth highest median income.[1862] Among the least ignorant people on earth, South Koreans rank third (the United States holds the position of thirty-fifth out of forty).[1863] Almost sixty percent do not register with religious organizations. According to various research organizations, their capital, Seoul, comes in seventh among the most sustainable cities in the world. It is number six in the world's leading cities, and it ranks fifth among the planet's largest economies.[1864]

Obviously, the animosities between Catholics and Protestants can flare up at a moment's notice, even in seemingly advanced societies.

At the heart of the issue lies the simple principle in this business of competing for other sects' paying members. It is quite surprising that some of the recruiting efforts are made by intimidating non-believers with the threat of hell blared through megaphones in streets and subways.[1865] Yes, I am still talking about South Korea.

They pose a clear and present danger to all of us.

Even in the conflict of Ivory Coast, a former French colony in western Africa, religious power held the key. Laurent Gbagbo, the past President of the country, was obsessed with his Christian beliefs. His Protestant pastors said that only God alone could remove his power. Laurent Gbagbo was hailed as God's representative on earth. The winner of the election in 2010, his successor Alassane Ouattara, was portrayed as the devil.[1866]

The months-long stalemate between God's representative and the devil led to countless deaths and brought the country to the brink of civil war. Who exactly was that devil? A Muslim. The conflict was a continuance of a decade-long struggle for religious supremacy in the country. Sarcastically speaking, Western societies are so much more advanced that this could never happen here.

It already happened.

---

[1862] Gallup, Worldwide Median Household Income, 2016.
[1863] IPSOS, MORI Perils of Perception Survey, 2016.
[1864] Sustainable city index 2016, Arcadis.
Institute of Urban Strategies, The Mori Memorials Foundation, 2015.
Global Metro Monitor, Brookings, 2015.
[1865] Choe Sang-Hun, Papal Visit That Thrills Catholics Is Unsettling to Protestants in South Korea, New York Times, August 16, 2014.
[1866] Venance Konan, "In Ivory Coast, Democrat to Dictator," New York Times, April 7, 2011.

Laurent Gbagbo was in the custody of the International Criminal Court for crimes against humanity. Even though he denied all charges, he was exactly where he belonged. He was later acquitted and returned to Ivory Coast in 2021 where he launched the African People's Party.

As for the Middle East, we cannot fail to note a significant difference between Martin Luther's time and our present. The Muslim holdings were largely controlled by two dictators who were representatives of the god of Shi'ite Safavid or Sunni Ottoman Islam – as they had engineered it. The shadows of God. Today, Islam is a collection of failed states and despotic regimes. We can recognize that the Christian powers of the time had no interest in a stable Islam and vice versa. Today, the short-sightedness of Western politics and the far-sighted tactics by the Ultra-Orthodox leadership might likewise not bring about long-lasting resolutions that could foster peace among and with Muslim nations.

After all, a strong Islam can only be a vicious enemy of the West. A weak and conflict-laden Islam will serve well.

In particular Israel.

However, we have seen that social engineering was practiced on all fronts. People tended to submit to whatever their bosses mandated for them. They had no choice. Their alternatives were to leave or die.

The excuse is valid only for the past.

The Muslim Middle East has awakened from its pipe dream of the Arab Spring. The education of young minds in the area is in the firm grip of religious establishments. Many countries censor literature and ideas. We have seen its beginnings with the disbursement of printing presses five centuries earlier.

For example, Saudi Arabia's Ministry of Information and its religious police ban the Bible (which is actually a paradox, because the Koran includes the Bible and the Gospels in its foundation). In Malaysia, the Department of Islamic Development has protected the purity of faith by outlawing over a thousand books, including Charles Darwin's *'On the Origin of Species.'* This is little different from the Inquisition, and it creates fertile grounds for intellectually impoverished Muslim extremists.

Islam does not nurture advanced thinking. It factually outlaws curiosity.

The only thing worse than an illiterate terrorist is a terrorist who has been conformed in the school system of single-minded extremists.

What the competitors in Luther's time were able to achieve 500 years ago, modern societies should be able to change more effectively with the means at our disposal today. Islam is in need of a fundamental intellectual overhaul in order to kick-start some hope of liberating these countries from their religious oppressors' tunnel vision. The root of their underperformance lies in religiously monopolized education.

Children that are indoctrinated are robbed of their freedom to choose a religion of their liking or no religion at all. There is no freedom of religion – or any other freedom – where young minds are abused for the purpose of expanding the number of members in organized religions.

The West needs to launch a systematic education offensive wherever Western aid or boots are on the ground. Children must be kept away from indoctrination by any religion or other fanaticisms – including our own.

Children have a beautiful capacity to look beyond the color of skin.

A secular education storm is needed, a transparently executed propaganda initiative in the service of freedom, if you will. If children in poor countries are provided food and essential social services in their schools, their parents will voluntarily enroll them. This is what drives the children into the madrasas, the houses of Islamic brainwashing. Such a project lasts at least a generation.

This is too expensive?

It is cheaper to help children dream of what they could become than bombing entire nations back into the Dark Age. Besides, the strategy of bombs has long failed to bring forth change for the better.

In Kosovo, we can witness the eternal hatred between majority Muslims and their Serbian rulers (or former rulers). While the Constitution of Kosovo guarantees freedom of religion and its leaders claim to be part of a secular society, the tiny country is 96% Muslim. On the other hand, its Serbian overlords are 91% Christian. It is little wonder that the region is a hotbed of ethnic tensions.

Their supposed tolerance is intolerable.

Since the 'liberation' of Kosovo in 1999 by a NATO alliance led by the United States, the country has become increasingly radicalized, not the least through the Wahhabism *'Wahnsinn'* ideology that was sponsored by Saudi Arabia (*Wahnsinn* is a German word for insanity).

Kosovo happens to have been the country with the highest per capita sympathizers for the Islamic State, ISIS. Yet, as discovered in 2015 through WikiLeaks documents, Saudi Arabia dispatched a network of *Islamic centers and Saudi-trained clerics that spans Asia, Africa, Europe, and likely also in North America. In New Delhi alone, 140 Muslim preachers are listed as on the Saudi Consulate's payroll.*[1867]

In other words, the Arab Islamist regime was bringing peace to our planet through financing the radicalization of Wahhabism wherever they found an opening in religious freedom.

In Kosovo, for example, Wahhabis first subverted traditional congregations. Then they started infiltrating them with radical ideas. This created divisions and hatred and forced disciples to choose.[1868]

The mechanism stayed the same throughout history. Their eyes were set on a long-term goal. They worked toward it by subverting a related sect through humanitarian work and social programs for women, orphans, and the poor.

Along came hidden agendas.

Here the Sunni Wahhabis undermined the less radical Sunni Hanafis with the goal of taking over an operational basis. At first, there were only a few. Because radicalism is aggressive, loud, and bullish, it is also attractive for the young and hotheaded.

Once it established a bridgehead, its attractiveness was suddenly magnified, and recruitment became self-perpetuating, like an epidemic.

By the rule of the stronger bully, the strategy is programmed to win.

With the war in Syria, young Muslims were pushed to take up arms to join the fight. Every Muslim must take part in jihad. Not to do so is a great sin.

*The blood of infidels is the best drink for us Muslims.*[1869]

Once the moderates woke up from their happy lull, it was too late to avert the disaster. Their response can be summed up in three words: radicalism begets radicalism.

Evidently, wars were not won through peaceful prayers, but through shock and awe.

---

[1867] Carlotta Gall, How Kosovo was Turned into Fertile Ground for ISIS, New York Times, May 25, 2016.
[1868] Ibid.
[1869] Ibid.

But if they can radicalize women and men through Saudi-trained clerics, the West can extinguish the fire by sending an entire army of secularly trained teachers. Teaching children that they can shape their own lives can change their perspective.

No child should be left to hawks.

In defense of Saudi Arabia, it appears that change might be on the horizon.

Mohammed bin Salman (M.B.S.), who became Crown Prince in 2017, introduced changes toward a more open approach. He allowed women to drive and to attend dances, concerts, and even soccer games. As if any of this would not be part of basic human rights. More importantly, he had clerics arrested who refused to fall in line with a more tolerant version of Islam. And he has taken away the arrest powers of the religious police.

There is a glimmer of hope.

As we have seen in Luther's age, it appears that most of the clergy can be made to conform with reasonable government restrictions.

Bin Salman engages in social engineering, and the West can learn from his mistakes in order to do a better job in cooperation with all religious organizations.

Having said this, bin Salman is a dictator.

The power of the Saudi royal family, Al Saud, rests on religious leaders from the Al ash-Sheikh family, descendants of Wahhabism's founder.[1870]

Criticizing medieval style royalty still merits dismembering. In August 2017, his administration arrested several non-violent civil society activists.

The prosecution demands capital punishment by the sword.[1871]

Of course, moderns are not blind to the assassination of a dissident journalist in the Saudi embassy in Istanbul or the kidnapping of Lebanon's prime minister.

The war in Yemen is not only a tragic humanitarian disaster but also an embarrassment to modern Western nations that have little choice but to act as bystanders to Saudi Arabia's massacres – with little will to confront them.

There is not a single word in the Koran that promotes peace among those who believe differently or do not believe at all.

---

[1870] Muhammad ibn Abd al-Wahhab, 1703 – 1792.
[1871] F. Brinley Bruton, Saudi Arabia seeks 'unprecedented' beheading for woman activist, NBC News, August 22, 2018

Muslim apologists frequently quote a fragment from a dialogue that suggests that if you kill one person, it is as though you kill all of humanity. The quote is taken out of context. It is embedded in the story of the first sons of Adam and Eve. Cain murdered his brother Abel. From this followed that killing one of the two would be akin to killing all, or half of humanity.[1872]

The Koran specifically addresses the *'children of Israel'* rather than Muslims. This detail changes the meaning of the text fundamentally. Immediately after this verse come the exceptions:

> *Of old our Apostles came to them with the proofs of their mission; then verily after this most of them committed excesses in the land.*

> *Only, the recompense of those who war against God and his Apostle, and go about to commit disorders on the earth, shall be that they shall be slain or crucified, or have their alternate hands and feet cut off, or be banished the land: This their disgrace in this world, and in the next a great torment shall be theirs –*

> *Except those who, ere you have them in your power, shall repent; [...]*[1873]

In short, there is no message of peace. Only those who repent get away with their lives, i.e. the converts to Islam. All others are committing offences by having distorted the message of the Bible and the Gospels, meaning Jews and Christians.

There is a vast body of Sharia traditions that often conflict with the Koran.

Can we find a message of peace there?

Of course not.

In jihad, Sharia Law and the Koran speak one language: believing Muslims follow the Imam's call to jihad.

Only who this leading Imam should be is not clear.

The choice of the boss remains the core reason for division and bloodshed between Shi'ites and Sunnis.

---

[1872] Koran 5:32 (Rodwell).
[1873] Koran 5:33-5:35 (Rodwell).

The Sunni scholar Bukhari authored thousands of Hadiths (Sharia traditions). He highlighted how Jesus's Second Coming was a common belief among Muslims and Christians.

> *By Him in Whose Hands my soul is, son of Mary [Jesus] will shortly descend amongst you people as a just ruler and will break the Cross [the Christians] and kill the pig [the Jews] and abolish the Jizya [the tax that was imposed on non-believers]. Then there will be abundance of money and no-body will accept charitable gifts.*[1874]

In plain words, Muslims are waiting to overthrow those who venerate Jesus as a god on the cross and to cleanse their world of Jews, pigs as they call them – the sows on the German churches.

It represents quite literally the goals of ISIS.

They are in possession of divine mandates to kill each other. It continues today among Palestinians and Israelis and among Shi'ites and Sunnis.

The answer to the paradox of a 'religion of peace' appears to lie in how humans think about claims in context of beliefs rather than in the more complex scenarios of reality. The vast majority of the world's population longs for peace. Since every religion preaches peace – among themselves – it is reasonable to assume that worshipers desire to portray this image outwardly, even though sectarian animosities perpetually demonstrate the opposite. In other words, belief is 'poisoned' by claims that are untrue but are accepted inside of religious communities.

Even worse, organized religion exploits the human 'truth bias.' That is the tendency to believe others even if we are told explicitly that half of what is said was untrue.[1875] After all, the source of the 'poison' is the trusted sectarian priestly hierarchy. 'Come, join the community, and you will find peace,' they appear to say while thinking that staying outside of their group is at your own peril. In consequence, the sectarian followers filter out bad news and look at the sunshine of their religion as something you need to be part of in order to find peace.

Luther demonstrated for us that a temporary period of war was justified for finding peace in the unity of faith. The result was permanent war.

Simply put: we all want peace.

Many leaders of organized religion torpedo it.

---

[1874] Bukhari, ca. 864 – 870, 2007-2009, 3:34:425.

[1875] Bella DePaulo, I study liars. I've never seen one like Donald Trump. Washington Post, December 8, 2017.

The Islamic State is habitually portrayed as a reaction to liberalism, to democracy, or to interventions by the United States. These are overstatements.

Since the First World War, the superpowers have tried to stem the natural order of the Middle East by imposing artificial border lines and supporting dictatorial minority regimes. They did not want another Ottoman Empire, let alone a strong one.

The Islamic State was the consequence of Islam's inner tensions.

Neither Shi'ite nor Sunni religious leaders can be content with being marginalized by either sectarian, secular, or oppressive politics. For that reason, new blood rises with ambitions to overthrow an unjust, or worse, an unholy government. After mass arrests in 2013, Sunnis started to support the advance of the Islamic State, which quickly overran more than a third of Iraq and parts of Syria roughly along the Euphrates and Tigris River.

Most of the terrorist attacks since 2011 have occurred among Muslims who remain divided along sectarian lines, in particular Sunnis (Saudi Arabia, ISIS, Hamas, Brotherhood, Al-Qaeda) against Shi'ites (Iran, Bashar al-Assad, Hezbollah) and to a lesser degree against the Jewish state of Israel.

The terrorist attack by Hamas in October 2023 broke that 'norm'.

The leaders of the Islamic State would not have blinked if given the opportunity to reduce the world's population by 200 million Shi'ites.

The vision of the Islamic State was simple: the End of the World, brought about under the world leadership of Abu Bakr al-Baghdadi – al-Baghdadi was a self-declared Quraysh (and thus of Jewish origin), a Korahite, and he was viewed as the eighth caliph. The twelfth will be the Mahdi, who will clash with the anti-Mahdi in Armageddon. The latter will originate from the region of Khorasan. In between, the armies of 'Rome' will camp at the Syrian city of Dabiq (which is also the name of ISIS's propaganda magazine), and they will be defeated by the caliphate.

In contrast to the common people, these leaders know exactly what they want, how they want it, and when they are ready to move, or when they need to engage in mass manipulation. In fact, many religious organizations, Islamic or not, maintain parallel legal and governmental structures across the globe that can replace secular structures at a moment's notice. They are not subject to democratic processes. These leaders tread prudently when representing a minority, but viciously when in charge.

Fundamental Islam intends to return to the precinct of the Koran and Sharia Law through jihad. As it stands now, it has no issue with killing. Murdering and enslaving the conquered is part of Sharia. True to the Koran, its fighters do not fear death – they even long for it because it brings them to paradise. The radicals believe that what they do is commanded by the Koran and Sharia, both of which created by Jewish leaders.

Their worldview is limited to nothing more.

It needs to be understood and discussed in the open that 'peace' is a grandiose word in their context that includes only those who are of the same sect and therefore of the same world view. Others are to be excluded, preached against, missionized upon, converted, or, in the worst of interpretations, terminated because of their differing beliefs.

We can continue to pretend that Judaism and Islam have nothing to do with the turmoil in the region.

These new, most radical and ruthless elements seem to spring from in between the divisions. Those are the ones with a good chance to end up ruling, since their brutality and focus as well as anti-Vatican and anti-American posturing helps them scoop up the disenfranchised across the planet.

Further up north, in the triangle between Iraq, Turkey, and Syria, sit Kurds with their own ambitions for a nation. It is another artery that has been bleeding for a century. Kurds too came to realize their chance with the weakening of ISIS.

Tayyip Erdogan, the president of Turkey, seized on any opportunity to oppress the desire of Kurds. Having reluctantly joined the American fight against the Islamic State (ISIS), he knew nothing better than to attack the Kurdish holdouts at ISIS' northern limits and resume the internal war against the P.K.K., the Kurdistan Workers' Party, in his eastern territory. This war lasted three decades and cost about 40,000 lives.

To distract from his own atrocities, Erdogan expressed his displeasure about the behavior of Israel's leadership:

> *"Those who associate Islam with terrorism close their eyes in the face of mass killing of Muslims, turn their heads from the massacre of children in Gaza," Erdogan told a conference of the Eurasian Islamic Council in Istanbul.*

> *"For this reason, I say that Israel is a terrorist state, and its acts are terrorist acts," he said.*[1876]

---

[1876] Reuters, Turkey's Erdogan calls Israel a 'terrorist state,' November 19, 2012.

Israel's hunger for more of the Promised Land – everything from the Euphrates River down to the Sinai – cannot have escaped anyone.

There is no need to further highlight the posturing of the leaders of most modern Islamic states. We can take it from our daily news show of horrors.

That they all envision themselves on the throne of a world empire manifests itself not just through blunt proclamation but also through their extraordinary birthrates. I have already touched on the problem in connection with Ultra-Orthodox Jewish principles. Typically, a high birthrate is linked to systemic poverty. Systemic poverty is also strongly correlated to high religiosity. Religiosity begets poverty, because it glorifies it. It declares poverty as the ideal state of being in the service of their gods. Religiosity begets high birthrates. They are obliged to strengthen their sectarian ranks with children. Both, poverty and high birthrates serve to subvert civilizations systematically and intentionally with religious militancy.

For Arabs, Egyptians, Yemenites, Iranians, Afghanis, Iraqis, Syrians, or many other nations in the Middle East and Africa, the consequence of the high rates of religiosity is that they will vote themselves right back into theocracies.

Currently, the Muslim world is sorting out a larger conflict among the desire of a minority to democratize, the drive to establish ethnic nations, the force of ultraconservative Muslims, and the oppressed, voiceless masses.

Israel has already taken steps to become a full-fledged theocracy.

The further evolution will surely be painful.

Kurds have an obvious right to self-determination. They are among very few people in the Middle East with some chance to establish a democracy. Why? Their religious diversity is unlike any other in the troubled region.

If the West should put its foot down in the Middle East, it ought to be for the Kurdish and Palestinian people.

## *Exit*

Before we even reach its climax, the story should make clear that messianic aspirations represent crimes against humanity. On the other hand, the episode also highlights how religious divisions endanger mankind by providing for the opening to prey on the poor and disadvantaged. Without the expulsion of Jews in Spain, in the absence of a messiah, history might have taken a different turn. But the betrayal of the Ottoman host tells of an unaltered trajectory into the twenty-first century.

Modern civilizations must find a way to work together to improve the conditions of all nations and the planet as a whole.

Less than two weeks after Donald Trump's inauguration, the new President of the United States addressed the National Prayer Breakfast:

> *I will get rid of and totally destroy the Johnson Amendment and allow our representatives of faith speak freely and without fear of retribution. [...]*
>
> *Freedom of religion is a sacred right, but it is under serious threat.*[1877]

Senator Lyndon B. Johnson[1878] had introduced a bill to change the tax code to prohibit non-profit organizations from endorsing or opposing candidates for political office or to otherwise intervene in elections to public office. It broadly includes charitable foundations, universities, and churches.[1879] It was adopted without opposition or even debate in 1954.

Obviously, the mingling in politics of the Protestant Church in Germany and the sixty million consequences, including six million Jews, had left impressions in some statesmen.

The decision was entirely uncontroversial at the time.

Johnson was from a family that belonged to a minority sect, Christadelphians. This is a small group that separates the humanity of Jesus from his divinity. For them, Jesus is immortal, and he will return for the End of the World. A hidden one. They reject the immortality of the soul.

Hopefully, I have made my case convincingly and based on sufficient evidence that letting the amendment be repealed is dangerous. Indeed, even some pastors are concerned that this could fuel partisan super PACs.

---

[1877] Mark Landler, Trump Vows to 'Destroy' Law Banning Political Activity by Churches, New York Times, February 2, 2017.

[1878] Lyndon B. Johnson later became the 36th president of the United States 1963-1969.

[1879] U.S. Code (U.S.C.) 26 U.S.C. § 501(c)(3) Title 26 (Internal Revenue Code).

Sure enough, modern opposition to the amendment started in the Protestant quarters.[1880]

The tragedy of the elimination of weaker Christian sects by the stronger finds its parallel in the historical record from the fourth century forward. With the Edict of Milan, Constantine the Great proclaimed religious freedom for *all* organized religions. The emperor thought that letting people worship as they pleased could foster peace in the Roman Empire.[1881]

It turned out to be the most monumental error of judgment in Roman history. He did not take the subversive power of these organizations into consideration.

Less than two centuries later, the Western Roman Empire was lost to a theocracy. A high civilization made way for filth, rot, totalitarian submission, and systemic poverty.

In Ethiopia of Luther's time, we hear that the nation was fit for producing just about anything. It was abundant in fish and game. However, in some places that were controlled by the clergy, they chose to not cultivate the land[1882] or to fish and hunt.[1883] Instead, they relied on exploiting a superstitious peasantry.[1884] *'There would be much fruit and much more tillage in the country, if the great men did not ill treat the people.'*[1885] Ethiopians never made it out of hell.

There is no hope for change as long as the root causes remain in force.

Without a currency, their economy was based on gold or salt and on bartering.[1886] Similar to Judaism and Islam, priests or friars were the merchants.[1887] Because of constant warfare with adjacent Muslim nations in the east,[1888] some of the villages in the empire were Muslim subjects to the imperial rule, segregated from Christians.[1889] The construction of mosques was prohibited.[1890]

There is no mystery.

---

[1880] Jacques Berlinerblau, Where does church end and state begin? - Georgetown/On Faith, The Washington Post, October 5, 2011.

[1881] Lactantius, *De Mortibus Persecutorum* 45.1, 48.2.

[1882] Alvarez, transl. Alderley, 1881, 35.

[1883] Ibid., 51.

[1884] Ibid., 36.

[1885] Ibid., 409.

[1886] Ibid., 62.

[1887] Ibid., 95.

[1888] Ibid., 98.

[1889] Ibid., 95.

[1890] Ibid.

Some parts of Europe, the Middle East, and Africa never recovered from Constantine's decision.

We still pay for it today.

Before Luther's Reformation, Judaism, Christianity, and later Islam were at war with each other and among their sects. Thereafter followed 500 years of religious wars.

Muslims have never stopped fighting.

Christians still fight in Africa. Sometimes in Ireland. Or in Asia.

Jews are about to sack the Temple Mount. Commanding the most modern nuclear army in the Middle East, hardly a day goes by without news about Israel's ongoing warfare under the mantle of security for the Jewish state or the biblical claims.

We are sitting at the edge of the End of the World, once more.

The future of 8 billion people, rich and poor, depends on how Judaic religions will be able to evolve toward putting priority on cooperation, prosperity, and peace. Some Judaic sect will launch more terrorist attacks, intent on unleashing a disaster if only to self-fulfil a prophecy.

A clash of civilizations will have more disastrous consequences than all the previous wars of history combined. Its justification will be found in Judaic scripture; so will its outcome. It is not a question of *if* but only a matter of *when* such a conflict will happen again. However, the cause may lie in a single man's decision to roll back safeguards that wise men introduced a long time ago.

We can no longer pretend not to know.

Survivors of the Holocaust are still alive today to tell their tragedies.

While political ideas tend to inflict their damage in the short term, religious conflicts endure for centuries. They perpetually renew themselves through scriptures and sermons. Their echoes fail to go silent even after a thousand years and even after total destruction. It is easy to inflame religious passions. Priests often do so to support their political preference – the one that supports them in return.

Once the beast is unleashed, only bleeding it out will calm it.

With our means of destruction, the consequences can be terminal for all of humanity.

The hope that some good spirit might be the protector against an evil being is a cultural myth that has been ingrained in the minds of our ancestors' childhoods. Natural disasters are neither prevented nor provoked by an evil or good spirit. Instead, humans alone hold the key to easing the pains of the unexpected and for preparing better for disasters. If global cooperation for the sake of the well-being of close and distant neighbors can be found, someone will be there to turn to should calamity strike home.

Instead, we continue to feed monsters.

Islam and Judaism are strong religions today because they are loud and militant. Christianity in the West has gone through a relatively short phase of peace since the guilt-laden Holocaust. At least in Europe – outside of Ireland – where hundreds of years of religious war devastated every corner of the continent. Or in North America, where the refugees of the European religious destruction hoped for a new beginning. This at a time when South and Central America was hit by the Inquisition. The consequences are apparent in today's economic and demographic differences. Not that the north has anything to brag about. The stories of the arriving Irish Catholics tell their own tale. They speak of the love that those with a funny English were first met after fleeing from their conflict-laden homes. They were not welcome. Treated like dogs. Snakes.

This period of relative Christian calm and increasing prosperity has brought forth a strong decline in Christian religious adherence in the industrialized West. Religious leaders will want to do something about it. They will remember that organized religion does not grow by praying silently at bedroom walls. It does so through division, militancy, extremism, and bombs.

Part of the decrease in religiosity may also lie in the widespread availability of information. Many Westerners can see through strategies of division.

Countries should turn back all bigots at their borders when they aggressively display religious symbolism or pride themselves on misogyny. Refusing to shake hands with or to talk to the opposite sex profoundly disrespects equality between men and women and the Western legal order.

Of all people on earth, Jews should be first in line to understand the consequences in all of this:

Never again.

It involves an honest oath by all Jews: never again.

The treacherous game of messianism must stop here. Never again.

The decline in Western religiosity coincided also with a dramatic drop in birthrates.

This is a global trend.

Yet, *'the fastest-growing countries are highly religious.'*[1891] They remain intent on subverting democratic processes in disregard of the damage that they cause on the entire earth.

Former President Barack Obama expressed before the United Nations in 2014 that the indoctrination must stop where violence is taught:

> *It is the task of all great religions to accommodate devout faith with a modern, multicultural world. No children – anywhere – should be educated to hate other people. There should be no more tolerance of so-called clerics who call upon people to harm innocents because they are Jewish, Christian or Muslim. It is time for a new compact among the civilized peoples of this world to eradicate war at its most fundamental source: the corruption of young minds by violent ideology.*[1892]

Obama did not seem to recognize that the problem is rooted much more deeply and that organized religion aims at binding one people together while excluding others who think differently. It is a base mechanism of ethnic hatred.

No express call to violence is needed to manipulate disciples into harming others. Religious schools do not need to explicitly teach hatred. It is embedded in the scriptural foundations that they all study and learn to believe in.

Segregation of children is a motherlode of hatred.

Britain's Prime Minister David Cameron authored an article in 2014 for the Church Times, explaining his beliefs:

> *I believe we should be more confident about our status as a Christian country, more ambitious about expanding the role of faith-based organizations, and, frankly, more evangelical about a faith that compels us to get out there and make a difference to people's lives.*[1893]

While Britain's religiosity is in a landslide, its leaders appear to be from the old guard. Of course, Mr. Cameron should not be judged by his faith.

We can no longer afford such divisiveness.

If we wish to neutralize the threat to societies, Jewish messianism and the Sharia law of Islam represent spearheads in fighting the systemic risks for humanity that they present. Their duty for conquest and jihad is excessive.

---

[1891] Pew Research Center, The Age Gap in Religion Around the World, June 13, 2018.

[1892] Barack Obama, Remarks by President Obama in Address to the United Nations General Assembly, Whitehouse, September 24, 2014.

[1893] David Cameron, My faith in the Church of England, Church Times, April 16, 2014. Copyright © 2014, reprinted by permission of Church Times.

They represent nothing less than the mass-incarceration of entire populations.

A nation can also act as a prison.

They are intellectual weapons of mass destruction. Whoever is not willing to leave them behind should be prevented from immigrating to the West.

The civilized world needs to refrain from meddling with the personal religious feelings of its people. After all, religious freedom *of the individual* is sacrosanct, indeed. Nobody should feel entitled to convert anyone to a specific religious creed or political absolutism.

Those who want to come to the West can freely choose to drop their bombastic religious baggage – or stay put. Martin Luther showed us half the way. Enter through the gates to freedom by leaving indoctrinations of unfreedom behind.

The West is free to set conditions for entry.

Nobody can pass in funny dresses, hats, or decor that identify an ethnic group.

Those who finally pass the gate are eternally free to choose within the secular laws of the West.

A landslide towards non-affiliation is reflecting these freedoms in the United States: *'about three-in-ten U.S. adults (29%) are religious "nones".*[1894] The number of the religiously unaffiliated adults in the United States is gaining about one percentage point of the total every year.[1895] Under the age of 30, the unaffiliated represent 36% of the general population. In addition, lip-service Christians number at least 70 million in the United States and 400 million in Post-Christian Europe. While they profess belonging to Christian organized churches, they neither pray daily nor go to church weekly. The numbers of those who no longer think that religion is very important in their lives are particularly strong among adults 39 years and younger.[1896]

The American religious landscape will profoundly be altered within a single generation.

This is what white nationalists are fighting against.

---

[1894] Gregory A. Smith, Pew Research Center, About Three-in-Ten U.S. Adults Are Now Religiously Unaffiliated,' December 14, 2021.

[1895] Pew Research Center, America's Changing Religious Landscape: Christians Decline Sharply as Share of Population; Unaffiliated and Other Faiths Continue to Grow, May 12, 2015.

[1896] Pew, The Age Gap, 2018.
PRII, The American Religious Landscape in 2020 (July 8, 2021): 2020 unaffiliated under 30: 36%.

A study by the researchers Jonathan Fox and Ephraim Tabory of the Bar Ilan University investigated the correlation between religiosity and economic development. It is not surprising that not only past studies have *'shown that economic development is negatively correlated with societal religiosity,'*[1897] but also that *'in all the tests, religiosity is negatively associated with economic development as measured by per-capita GDP.'*[1898]

That is so obvious that it no longer needs another study.

It reflects Christianity's *'march southward'* into developing countries.[1899] But here is what the researchers said about state coercion of organized religion:

> *In contrast, when major social institutions no longer support a single religious world-view or 'sacred canopy' (Berger 1967), the religious 'reality' is undermined at the institutional and individual levels. To the extent that people rely on others for evaluating religious beliefs, lack of consensus can undermine belief, which in turn can detrimentally affect religious participation.*[1900] *Declining state control of religion, then, entails not just freedom of religion, but also freedom from religion.*[1901]

In other words, increasing secularization and pluralism are among the keys to prosperity. They allow for freedom of religion *of the individual* and for freedom from religion. If societies are not able to balance the two, they are doomed to slide into theocracies sooner rather than later.

However, freedom of religion appears to be a sort of misnomer. Freedom of thought and conscience embraces the intention perhaps better. But individuals cannot do as they please outside of civil and criminal legal boundaries. Freedom of conscience ensures liberties for profoundly *personal* beliefs.

Laws across the world are indeed increasingly interpreted that way.

Freedom of conscience is limited to expressions and actions within reason. These originate in individuals' dependency on one another. Organized religion asserts itself not to fall under these limitations. Freedom of conscience includes the personal right to faith.

Martin Luther has defined it perfectly for us: believe or leave.

Modern France is a case study in putting the priority on humanism and secularism rather than on much abused 'religious freedom.'

---

[1897] Ibid., 257, 69:3 245-271.
[1898] Ibid., 266.
[1899] Marshall, Pew, 2018.
[1900] Fox, Tabory, Bar Ilan University, 2008, 2.
[1901] Ibid., 4.

A vision of a peaceful future was expressed by former U.S. president Jimmy Carter during a BBC table talk in 2011. Carter summed up the discrepancy between what should be and what is.

To a question of the audience what advice he would give an incoming president today, he answered:

> *I think that the main thing for the United States is to strive once more to be a genuine super power; and this is a presumptuous thing for me. I am not saying that I know more than others. I am just trying to answer the question as best as I can. The United States now has the greatest military power. Our military budget equals almost the entire budget of all the countries combined on earth; six times more than the second budget as China's. And I would like to see our country become an entity that mirrored the highest ideals of an individual human being and collectively a nation. I would hope that someday in the future, that if a person or leaders in any country on earth that was faced with a potential conflict, their natural thought would be 'let's go to Washington,' because America is a champion of peace.*

> *I think if you go around the world now and ask the people the United States' relation to peace, they would say that we are maybe one of the most warlike countries. I would hope that people throughout the world, in the future, if they had a chance for democracy or a new government, would say, 'why don't we go to Washington,' because America has evolved the finest example of democratic government on earth.*

Carter was then asked whether this hope was not precisely the promise of President Obama that could not be delivered and whether Obama might have been impeded by the limits of power or by inexperience.

> *No, I don't think he was too inexperienced. He has been in the U.S. Senate and Joe Biden has been the governor of a state, but I wouldn't say that he is inexperienced. But I am not criticizing Obama at all, but I think that those commitments that are made at the beginning should be pursued even though there are political obstacles that are almost insurmountable. I would like the United States to be looked at as a champion of addressing environmental challenges, global warming. What is our present position on global warming? I don't know. Human rights? I don't know. I would like the United States to be the champion of generosity and helping countries or people who are in need. Those are the kind of things that can be made clear, and I hope that the future presidents will do this — and also the future prime ministers of Great Britain; I am not singling out my own country. But great, powerful, secure nations that have stable democratic governments ought to be on the forefront of all these kinds of issues that relate to peace, human rights, environmental quality, the alleviation of suffering, freedom, democracy; and let that be a commitment that is sound regardless of the political accidents of*

*partisanship within a country.*[1902]

If a former president of the United States can think that way and the American people demand changes with relentless pressure on the streets, then there may indeed be hope for a world that works better for all.

To conclude, allow me to paraphrase John E. Longhurst, a little-known historian who focused on the Spanish Inquisition: I am tired of the grinding dialectic of theological dogma. I am tired of the sickening degradations visited upon men who will not accept other men's Truths. I am tired of those awful notaries who calmly recorded the agonies of heretics. And above all, I am tired of pretending to a scholarly 'objectivity' which treated atrocities as though there was a roughly equal amount of reason on both sides.

Humanity faces a global emergency.

Face the causes, not just the symptoms.

Exit!

---

[1902] Jimmy Carter, Intelligence Squared Debates with Jon Snow, BBC, October 5, 2011.

# BIBLIOGRAPHY

Isaac Aboab I, Aron ha-'Edut (The Ark of the Testimony) (ca. end of 14th century).

Francisco Alvarez, Narrative of the Portuguese embassy to Abyssinia during the years 1520-1527, translated from the Portuguese and edited by Lord Stanley of Alderley (Hakluyt Society, 1881).

Francisco Alvarez, Delle Navigationi et Viaggi, Obedienza del Prete Ianni, 1524, translated by Giovanni Baptista Ramusio, Volume 1, 3rd Edition (Giunti, 1563).

*Ante-Nicene Fathers*, Vol. 8, edited by Alexander Roberts, James Donaldson, and A. Cleveland Coxe (Christian Literature, 1886). Revised and edited for New Advent by Kevin Knight.

Augustine, *The City of God* (354–430 AD).

Augustine, *De Genesi ad Litteram* (354-430 AD).

John Aurifaber, Table-Talk of Martin Luther (Eisleben, 1566) translated by William Hazlitt (The Lutheran Publication Society).

Kathryn Babayan, Mystics, Monarchs and Messiahs: Cultural Landscapes of Early Modern Iran (Harvard University Press, 2002).

Roland Bainton, Here I Stand: A Life of Martin Luther (Pierce & Smith, 1978).

Caesaris Baronii, Annales ecclesiastici.

Norman H. Baynes, The Speeches of Adolf Hitler: April 1922-August 1939, Vol. 1, Munich, April 12, 1922 (Oxford University Press, 1942).

The Itinerary of Benjamin of Tudela (1171).

F. Bente, Historical Introductions to the Symbolical Books of the Evangelical Lutheran Church, in the Concordia Triglotta (Concordia, 2005)

Lauren Benton, Law and Colonial Cultures: Legal Regimes in World History, 1400–1900 (Cambridge, 2002).

Albrecht Beutel and Michael Beyer of the Luther-Gesellschaft, Lutherjahrbuch 78. Jahrgang 2011: Organ der internationalen Lutherforschung (Vandenhoeck, 2012).

Jean-Jacques Boissard, Leben und Kontraseiten der Türkischen und Persischen Sultanen, von Osmane an, bis auf den jetzt regierenden Sultan Mahumet II. (Dieterich von Bry Leodien, 1596)

Karl Brandi, The emperor Charles V; the growth and destiny of a man and of a world empire (Cape, 1939).

Martin Brecht, Martin Luther, translated by James L. Schaaf (Fortress Press, 1985–93).

Bukhari, ca. 864-870 AD (CMJE and the University of Southern California, 2007-2009).

Norman Cameron, R.H. Stevens, Gerhard L. Weinberg, H.R. Trevor-Roper (2007).

Eliyahu ben Elqana Capsali (c1490-c1555), Seder Eliyahu Zuta (Hebrew University, Jerusalem, 1975).

Nigel Cawthorne, Sex Lives of the Popes (Prion, 1996).

Jerome A. Chanes, Antisemitism: A Reference Handbook (ABC-CLIO, 2004).

Frederic Chase, *Fathers of the Church* (1958). Hugh Chisholm, Melchior Hofmann, Encyclopædia Britannica. 13 (11th ed.) (Cambridge University Press, 1911).

Saint Chrysostom, Homilies Against the Jews, Adversus Judaeos "Autumn 386", translated by Paul W. Harkins, The Fathers of the Church (Catholic University of America Press, 1979).

William L Cleveland, A History of the Modern Middle East (Westview Press, 2009).

Council of Constance, 1415.

Fifth Lateran Council, 1512-1517.

Forth Lateran Council, Canon 68, 1215, from H. J. Schroeder, *Disciplinary Decrees of the General Councils: Text, Translation and Commentary* (Herder, 1937).

Council of Trent, edited and translated by J. Waterworth (Dolman, 1848).

Council of Vienne (1311-1312).

Thomas Conley, The Speech of Ibrahim at the Coronation of Maximilian II (Rhetorica: A Journal of the History of Rhetoric, 2001).

C.G. Coulton, ed, *Life in the Middle Ages* (Macmillan 1910).

Roger Crowley, Empire of the sea (Faber & Faber, 2008).

Charles E. Curran, *Change in Official Catholic Moral Teaching* (1998).

Zachariā Al-Ḍāhrī, Sefer Hammusar, ed. Yehuda Ratzaby (Ben-Zvi Institute, 1965).

Dante Alighieri, *De Monarchia* (ca. 1308).

Dante Alighieri, Divine Comedy (ca. 1308) XII, Translated by Charles Eliot Norton (1999).

Ronald Daus, Die Erfindung des Kolonialismus (Hammer, 1983).

Raymond Davis, The Book of Pontiffs (Liber Pontificalis): The Ancient Biographies of the First Ninety Roman Bishops to AD 715 (Liverpool University Press, 2000).

A.J. Deus, The Jewish Serpent King in the Dome of the Rock, Primary Evidence: 'Big Daddy' of Inscriptions a Colossal Fraud (2022).

Emanuel Deutsch, Literary Remains of the Late Emanuel Deutsch (Murray, 1874).

Gotthard Deutsch, Alfred Feilchenfeld, Josel (Joselmann, Joselin) of Rosheim (Joseph Ben Gershon Loanz), in Isidore Singer, et al., Jewish Encyclopedia (Funk & Wagnalls, 1901-1906).

Thomas B. Dozeman Methods for Exodus (Cambridge University Press, 2010)

Daniel Eisenberg, Cisneros y la quema de los manuscritos granadinos (Journal of Hispanic Philology, 16, 1992) .

Marc H. Ellis, Hitler and the Holocaust, Christian Anti-Semitism (NP: Baylor University Center for American and Jewish Studies, 2004).

Abraham Eraly, Emperors Of The Peacock Throne: The Saga of the Great Moghuls (Penguin Books, 2000).

Michael Erbe, Die Habsburger 1493-1918, Eine Dynastie im Reich und in Europa (Kohlhammer, 2000).

Robert P. Ericksen (Kurt Mayer Professor of Holocaust Studies at Pacific Lutheran University) in Peter Hayes, John K. Roth, *The Oxford handbook of Holocaust studies* (Oxford University Press, 2010).

Josef van Ess, 'Abd al-Malik and the Dome of the Rock, in Bayt al-Maqdis, Part 1, eds. Julian Raby and Jeremy Johns (Oxford, 1992).

Emma Fattorini, Hitler, Mussolini and the Vatican: Pope Pius XI and the Speech That was Never Made (Polity, 2011).

Ludwig Feilchenfeld, Rabbi Josel von Rosheim (Heitz, 1898).

Israel Finkelstein and Neil Asher Silberman, The Bible Unearthed: Archaeology's New Vision of Ancient Israel and the Origin of its Sacred Texts, (Simon and Schuster, 2002).

Elizabeth Anne Finn, Home in the Holyland (Nisbet, 1866).

Maurice Finocchiaro, Defending Copernicus and Galileo: Critical Reasoning in the Two Affairs (Springer, 2010).

Catherine Fletcher, The Black Prince of Florence: The Spectacular Life and Treacherous World of Alessandro de' Medici (Bodley Head, 2016).

Jonathan Fox, Ephraim Tabory, Bar Ilan University, Contemporary Evidence Regarding the Impact of State Regulation of Religion on Religious Participation and Belief, Sociology of Religion (2008).

Francesco D'Assisi, Gli Scritti, Lettera Prima a Tutti i Fideli (1209).

Pope Francis, Apostolic Exhortation Gaudete Et Exsultate of the Holy Father Francis on the Call to Holiness in Today's World (Vatican, 2018).

Pope Francis, Laudato Si', Encyclical Letter (Vatican Press, 2015).

Sebastian Franck, Chronica Zeitbuch und Geschichtsbibel, (Beck, 1531)

Gerald Friedlander, Hellenism and Christianity (P. Vallentine, 1912).

Richard Elliott Friedman, The Exodus (HarperCollins, 2017).

Mark Galli and Ted Olsen, 131 Christians Everyone Should Know (Holman Reference, 2000).

Garcia-Martinez, Dead Sea Scrolls, [4Q396frg1col3 / 4Q397frg5-6], Transcription and translation by J. Strugnell and E. Qimron, late first century BC.

Imam Ghazali, *Deliverance from Error and Attachment to the Lord of Might and Majesty*, Introduction (1109), from Charles F. Horne, ed., *The Sacred Books and Early Literature of the East* (Parke, Austin & Lipscomb, 1917).

Sir H.A.R. Gibb, *The Encyclopaedia of Islam* (Leiden Brill, 1979).

Mary E. Giles, Women in the Inquisition: Spain and the New World (JHU Press, 1999).

Ezra Hall Gillett, The life and times of John Huss: Or, The Bohemian reformation of the fifteenth century (Gould and Lincoln, 1864).

Louis Ginzberg, Jewish Encyclopiedia (1906).

Ademar Glaber, *Annales Lemovicenses* (ad an. 1010); *Annales Beneventani* (ad an. 1010).

Joseph Goebbels, The Goebbels Diaries 1939–41, translated by Fred Taylor (Hamish Hamilton, 1982).

Peter B. Golden, Haggai Ben-Shammai, András Róna-Tas, The World of the Khazars: New Perspectives, Handbook of Oriental Studies (Brill, 2007).

Julius H. Greenstone, The Messiah Idea in Jewish History (Jewish Publication Society, 1906).

Ferdinand Gregorovius; Die Geschichte der Stadt Rom im Mittelalter (Cotta, 1872).

Ferdinand Gregorovius, History of the City of Rome in the Middle Ages (London, 1906).

Gregory the Great, *Dialogues* (ca. 600 AD).

Frederick E. Greenspahn, Jewish Mysticism and Kabbalah: New Insights and Scholarship (New York University, 2011).

Guilelmus van Gulik and Conradus Eubel, Hierarchia catholica III (Monasterii 1923).

Joseph Ha-Cohen aka Rabbi Joseph Ben Joshua Ben Meir, the Sphardi, The Chronicles, Vol. I, translated by C.H.F. Bialloblotzky (Valpy, 1836).

Joseph de Hammer, Histoire de l'Empire Ottoman (The Athenaeum, 1837).

Ernest F. Henderson, *Select Historical Documents of the Middle Ages* (London: George Bell, 1910).

Charles Herbermann, Catholic Encyclopedia (Appleton, 1912).

Herodotus, Histories.

Ze'ev Herzog, Deconstructing the walls of Jericho, 1999.

Adolf Hitler, *Mein Kampf,* official Nazi translation by James Murphy (Hurst and Blacket, 1939).

Charles A. Howe, For Faith and Freedom: A Short History of Unitarianism in Europe (Skinner House Books, 1997).

Robert Hoyland, Sebeos, The Jews And The Rise of Islam (1995).

Thomas Patrick Hughes, A Dictionary of Islam, (Allen, 1885).

William Hughes, Western Civilization: The Earliest Civilization Through the Reformation (McGraw-Hill, 1993).

David Hume, *The History Of England* (M'Creery, 1807).

John Hunwick, Jews of a Saharan Oasis: The Elimination of the Tamantit Community (Wiener, 2007).

Albert Montefiore Hyamson, A History of the Jews in England (1908).

Indiculus luminosus 854 AD.

Isidore of Seville, 560–636 AD, *Chronicon*. English translation by Kenneth B. Wolf, 2004.

Michel Jas, Braises cathares: filiation secrete a l'heure de la Réform, in Luc Racaut, The Polemical Use of the Albigensian Crusade During the French Wars of Religion (Oxford, 1999).

Paul Johnson, *A History of the Jews* (Phoenix, 1998).

Henry Kamen, The Spanish Inquisition, A Historical Revision (Yale, 2014).

Kemal H. Karpat, The Ottoman state and its place in world history (Brill, 1974).

Ian Kershaw; Hitler a Biography (Norton, 2008).

Muhammed ibn Khaldun (1332-1406 AD), The Muqaddimah (1377 AD), translated by Franz Rosenthal (Princeton University, 1958).

W. L. Kingsley, An Unnoted Martyr (New Englander and Yale Review, Volume 53, 1890).

James Kittelson, Luther The Reformer (Fortress Publishing, 1986).

Jean Lacouture, Jesuits, A Multibiography (Counterpoint, 1995).

Harold Lamb, Suleiman the Magnificent - Sultan of the East (Read Books, 2008).

Harris Lenowitz, the Jewish Messiahs (Oxford, 1998).

The Massoreth ha-massoreth of Elias Levita: being an exposition of the Massoretic notes on the Hebrew Bible: or the ancient critical apparatus of the Old Testament in Hebrew (Longmans, 1867).

Pope Leo I, Letter XIV (446 AD).

Bernard Lewis, The Jews of Islam (Greenwood, 2002).

John E. Longhurst, Luther's Ghost in Spain (1517-1546) (Coronado Press, 1964).

Steven Lowenstein, The Jewish Cultural Tapestry: International Jewish Folk Traditions (Oxford University Press, 2001).

Martin Luther, A Sermon on Keeping Children in School (1530), from Luther's Works, Vol. 46 (Fortress, 1967)

Martin Luther, *95 Theses* (1517).

Martin Luther, The Bondage of the Will (1525), translated by Henry Cole (London, 1823).

Martin Luther, Can Soldiers Be Christians, 1526, translated by Prof. W. H. Carruth (University of Kansas, 1899).

Martin Luther, The Large Catechism, Second Edition (1529).

Martin Luther, Small Catechism, 1530.

Martin Luther, That Jesus Christ was Born a Jew (1523), translated by Walter I. Brandt, in Luther's Works (Fortress, 1962).

Martin Luther, Commentary on the Sermon on the Mount, Translated by Charles A. Hay (1532).

Martin Luther, Documents Illustrative of the Continental Reformation, from B.J. Kidd, ed. (Clarendon Press, 1911).

Erlangen Edition of Luther's Works.

Martin Luther, The Letter to the Galatians, lecture 1531 (1535).

Martin Luther, *Luther's Epistle Sermons*, translated by John Nicholas Lenker (The Luther Press, 1909).

Martin Luther, *On the Jews and their Lies*, part VII (1543), translated by Martin Bertram (Fortress Press & Augsburg Fortress, 1971).

Martin Luther, On Trading and Usury (1524), translated in Works of Martin Luther (Holman, 1915).

Martin Luther, On war against Islamic reign of terror (On war against the Turk, 1528).

Martin Luther, Preface to the Prophet Ezekiel, 1532.

Select Works of Martin Luther, translated by Henry Cole (Bensley, 1824).

Martin Luther, Sermons, translated by John Nicholas Lenker.

Martin Luther, Vom Schem Hamphoras and the Lineage of Christ (Wittenberg, 1543).

Luther's Works, Edited by Jaroslav Pelikan, translated by Georg V. Schick (Concordia, 1958).

Luther's Works (Fortress, 1967).

Diarmaid MacCulloch, Reformation: Europe's House Divided, 1490–1700 (Allen Lane, 2003).

Niccolò Machiavelli, The Prince, Concerning New Principalities Which Are Acquired By One's Own Arms And Ability (1532).

Grace Magnier, Pedro de Valencia and the Catholic apologists of the expulsion of the Moriscos: visions of Christianity and kingship (Brill, 2010).

Philip Mansel, Constantinople: City of the World's Desire, 1453–1924 (St. Martin's Griffin, 1998).

Anton Margaritha, The Whole Jewish Belief / Der Ganz Jüdisch Glaub (Frankfurt, 1544).

Sean Martin, The Knights Templar: The History & Myths of the Legendary Military Order (Oldcastle, 2014).

Maximus the Confessor, The Life of the Virgin, translated by Stephen J. Shoemaker (Yale, 2012).

Michael J. McCaffrey, ČĀLDERĀN (Encyclopaedia Iranica, 1990).

Donald K McKim, The Cambridge Companion to Martin Luther (Cambridge, 2003).

Phillip Mansel, Constantinople: City of the World's Desire, 1453–1924 (St. Martin's Griffin, 1998).

Philip Melanchthon, Dass die Fürsten aus Gottes Befeh und Gebot schuldig sind/ bei ihren Untertanen Abgötterei/ unrechten Gottesdienst und falsche Lehre abzutun/ und dagegen rechten Gottesdienst und rechte Christliche Lehre auf zu richten (Wittemberg, 1540).

Philip Melanchthon, Martin Luther, Deutung der zwei greulichen Figuren Bapst-Esels zu Rom und Mönch-Kalbs zu Freiberg in Meissen funden (Johann Rhau-Grunenberg, 1523).

*The Memorial Book for the Jewish Community of Yurburg, Lithuania* (Assistance to Lithuanian Jews, 2003).

John Merriman, A History of Modern Europe, Volume One: From the Renaissance to the Age of Napoleon (Norton, 2009).

Roger Bigelow Merriman, Suleiman the Magnificent 1520-1566 (Read Books, 2007).

Robert Michael, Holy Hatred: Christianity, Antisemitism, and the Holocaust (Palgrave Macmillan, 2006).

Joseph Mieses, Die älteste gedruckte deutsche Übersetzung des jüdischen Gebetsbuches a.d. Jahre 1530 und ihr Author Anthonius Margaritha (Löwit, 1916).

Czesław Miłosz, The History of Polish Literature (University of California, 1983).

Collin P. Mitchell, The Practice of Politics in Safavid Iran: Power, Religion and Rhetoric (Tauris, 2009).

Michael Mullet, The Catholic Reformation (Routledge, 2002).

Michael A. Mullett, Luther (MacCulloch, 1986).

Sara T. Nalle, Revisiting El Encubierto: Navigating between Visions of Heaven and Hell on Earth, in Kathryn A. Edwards, Werewolves, Witches, and Wandering Spirits: Traditional Belief and Folklore in Early Modern Europe (Truman State University Press, 2002).

Gülru Necipoglu, The Dome of the Rock as Palimpsest (Harvard, 2008).

Adolph Neubauer, The Jewish Quarterly Review (Nutt, 1889).

Dorinda Outram, Panorama of the Enlightenment (Getty, 2006).

Oxford Dictionary of National Biography (2004).

Miguel Asín Palacios, *Islamic Eschatology in the Divine Comedy* (1919).

Peter Partner, The Murdered Magicians: The Templars and Their Myth (Barns & Noble, 1993) 138–144.

Naomi E. Pasachoff, Robert J. Littman, A Concise History of the Jewish People (Lanham, Rowman & Littlefield, 2005).

Ludwig von Pastor, ed. Ralph Francis Kerr, The History of the Popes, from the Close of the Middle Ages, 7 (Kegan Paul, Trench, Trübner, 1908).

James Patrick, Renaissance and Reformation (Cavendish, 2007).

Joseph Pérez, Los Comuneros (Esfera de los Libros, 2001).

Andrew Pettegree, The early Reformation in Europe (Cambridge University Press).

J. le Plat, Monumenta ad historiam Concilii Tridentini (Leuven, 1782).

Pope Paul IV, Cum Nimis Absurdum [Since it is absurd], July 17, 1555

Michael Psellus, *Chronographia*, I:29 (ca. 1078), translated by J.M Hussey (E.R.A.S., 1952).

Polycarp, The Epistle of Polycarp to the Philippians (110–140 AD).

Pratum spirituale (ca. 639 AD).

The Protestant Church in the Third Reich: Handbook of the Kirchenkampf (1956).

Jerry Rabow, 50 Jewish Messiahs: The Untold Life Stories of 50 Jewish Messiahs Since Jesus and how they Changed the Jewish, Christian, and Muslim Worlds (Gefen, 2003).

Luc Racaut, Hatred in Print: Catholic Propaganda and Protestant Identity During the French Wars of Religion (Routledge, 2017).

Raynaldus, Annales, in S.R. Maitland, tarns, *History of the Albigenses and Waldenses*, (Rivington, 1832).

Jeffrey Richards, The Popes and the Papacy in the Early Middle Ages, 476-752 (Routledge & Kegan Paul, 1979).

Michael Rocke, Forbidden Friendships: Homosexuality and Male Culture in Renaissance Florence (Oxford, 1996).

Moses Rosen, The Face of Survival, Epilogue 'The Recipe' (1987).

Elliot Rosenberg, But Were They Good for the Jews? (Birch Lane, 1997).

Joseph of Rosheim, The Historical Writings of Joseph of Rosheim: Leader of Jewry in Early Modern Germany, edited by Chava Fraenke Goldschmidt and Adam Shear, translated by Naomi Schendowich (Brill, 2006).

Erika Rummel, The Case Against Johann Reuchlin (University of Toronto, 2002).

E.G. Rupp, Benjamin Drewery, Martin Luther, Documents of Modern History (London: Edward Arnold, 1970).

Abdulaziz Sachedina, A Treatise on the Occultation of the Twelfth Imāmite Imam (Studia Islamica, 1978).

Kaya Şahin, Constantinople and the End Time: The Ottoman Conquest as a Portent of the Last Hour (Journal of Early Modern History 14, 2010).

Kaya Şahin, Empire and Power in the Reign of Süleyman: Narrating the Sixteenth-Century Ottoman World (Cambridge University Press, Kindle Edition, 2013).

Martín M. Ríos Saloma, La Reconquista. Génesis de un mito historiográfico (Historia y Grafía, 30, 2008).

H.P. Salomon, I. S. D. Sassoon, Antonio Jose in Saraiva, The Marrano Factory. The Portuguese Inquisition and Its New Christians, 1536–1765 (Brill, 2001).

António José Saraiva, The Marrano Factory: The Portuguese Inquisition and Its New Christians 1536-1765 (Brill, 2001).

Philip Schaff, History of the Christian Church, Christian Classics Ethereal Library, Bainton, Mentor edition.

Klaus Scholder, The Churches and the Third Reich. 2 vols. (Fortress Press, 1988).

Moise Schwab, The Talmud of Jerusalem, Vol. I. Berakhoth (Williams and Norgate, 1886).

Tom Scott and Robert W. Scribner, eds. The German Peasants' War: a History in Documents (Humanities Press, 1989).

R.W. Scribner: The German Reformation (London, 1986).

Sebeos' History of the seventh century, 30 (publishing ca. 660 AD), English by Robert Bedrosian (1985).

Kenneth M. Setton, The Papacy and the Levant (The American Philosophical Society, 1984).

Zaky Shalom, Ben-Gurion's Political Struggles, 1963-1967: A Lion in Winter (Routledge, 2006).

John Shearman, The Collections of the Younger Branch of the Medici (The Burlington Magazine 117 No. 862, January 1975).

Anthony Sean, The Caliph and the Heretic: Ibn Saba' and the Origins of Shi`ism (Brill, 2011).

Yehouda Shenhav, Beyond the Two-State Solution: A Jewish Political Essay (Wiley, 2013):

William L. Shirer, The Rise and Fall of the Third Reich (Secker & Warburg, 1960).

Rabbi Menachem Mendel Schneerson, Sefer Hama'amorim Melukot Al Seder Chodshei Hashana Volume 2 (Kehot Publications, 2002).

David K. Shipler, Arab and Jew: Wounded Spirits in a Promised Land (Times Books, 1986).

Rober Silverberg, The Realm of Prester John (Ohio University Press, 1996).

A.H. Silver, A History of Messianic Speculation in Israel (Beacon, 1927).

Theresia Simon, Die Augustiner-Eremiten im Spätmittelalter: Am Beispiel des Augustinerklosters in Erfurt (AV Akademikerverlag, 2014).

Shlomo Simonsohn, The Apostolic See And The Jews (Pontifical Institute of Mediaeval Studies, 1991).

Isidore Singer, Cyrus Adler, The Jewish Encyclopedia: a descriptive record of the history, religion, literature, and customs of the Jewish people from the earliest times to the present day (Funk and Wagnalls, 1912).

Isidore Singer, Phillipp Bloch (Jewish Encyclopedia, 1901-1906).

Jörg L. Spenkuch, Philipp Tillmann, Elite Influence? Religion and the Electoral Success of the Nazis (March 2017).

Federico Stefani and Guglielmo Berchet, I diarii di Marino Sanuto: (MCCCCXCVI-MDXXXIII) dall' autografo Marciano ital. cl. VII codd. CDXIX-CDLXXVII (Visentini, 1892).

Babylonian Talmud.

Julie Anne Taylor, *Muslims in Medieval Italy: The Colony at Lucera* (Lexington, 2005).

Joan Thirsk, Alternative Agriculture: A History: From the Black Death to the Present Day (Oxford, 1997)

Joe Thornton, A Cultural History of the Atlantic World, 1250-1820 (Cambridge University Press, 2012).

Brian Tierney, *The Middle Ages, Volume I, Sources of Medieval History* (McGraw-Hill, 1999).

Jean du Tillet, Sommaire de l'Histoire de la Guerre faite contre les Heretiques Albigeois, extraicte du Tresor des Chartres du Roy par feu Jehan du Tillet (1590).

Tischendorf, Novum Testamentum Graece, 8th ed (Leipzig: Giesecke and Devrient, 1869-1894).

John Victor Tolan, Gilles Veinstein, and Henry Laurens, Europe and the Islamic world: a history, translated by Jane Marie Todd (Princeton, 2013).

Aegidius Tschudi, Chronicum Helveticum, ed. Johann Rudolf Iselin, 1734.

Joseph N. Tylenda (transl.), A Pilgrim's Journey: The Autobiography of Ignatius of Loyola (Liturgical Press, 1991).

Dan Urman, Paul Virgil McCracken Flesher, Ancient Synagogues: Historical Analysis and Archaeological Data (Brill, 1995).

Ismail Safa Ustun, PhD diss. Heresy and Legitimacy in the Ottoman Empire in the Sixteenth Century (University of Manchester, 1991).

Eduard Vehse, Memoirs of the Court and Aristocracy of Austria, Volume 1 (Nichols, 1894).

J.G. Walch, Dr. Martin Luthers Sämmtliche Schriften, 23 vols. (Concordia, 1883).

Johannes Wallmann, The Reception of Luther's Writings on the Jews from the Reformation to the End of the 19th Century, n.s. 1 (Lutheran Quarterly, Spring 1987).

Donald Weinstein, Savonarola and Florence Prophecy and Patriotism in the Renaissance (Princeton, 1970).

Donald Weinstein, Savonarola: The Rise and Fall of a Renaissance Prophet (Yale, 2011).

Bat Ye'or, *The Decline of Eastern Christianity under Islam* (Associated University Presses, 1996).

Galina Yermolenko, Roxolana: The Greatest Empress of the East (DeSales University, 2005).

## *Internet Research Sites*

archive.org: Internet archive offering permanent access to digital historical collections for researchers, historians, scholars, people with disabilities, and the general public.

BBC.com

books.google.com: searchable digital library.

ccel.org: Christian Classics Ethereal Library.

cia.gov: Comparative country database. Information on the history, people, government, economy, geography, communications, transportation, military, and transnational issues of 266 world entities.

CNN.com.

earlychristianwritings.com: Peter Kirby's collection of references to the Gospel according to the Hebrews.

etymonline.com: Online Etymology Dictionary.

fordham.edu/halsall: Internet History Sourcebook Project. Extensive research site for history from Judaism through Christianity and Islam into the Renaissance and Reformation.

fourthcentury.com: Fourth-century Christian writers and timeline.

gutenberg.org: Library of thousands of historical books with lapsed copyright (access through gutenberg.org/wiki/Main_Page).

net.bible.org: searchable online Bible developed for Ministry First.

bible.catholic.net: searchable online Bible for Catholics.

JewishHistory.org.

newadvent.org: extensive digital library of Christian literature.

nytimes.com: references to articles in the *New York Times* refer to its online version.

ssrn.com: Social Sciences Research Network, an eLibrary for early research distribution in social sciences.

tertullian.org: The Tertullian Project, specialized collection of Tertullian writings

uchicago.edu: LacusCurtius, Into the Roman World, a collection of Greek and Roman authors

(access through penelope.uchicago.edu/Thayer/E/Roman/home.html).

museeprotestant.org: Virtual Protestant Museum

wikipedia.com: article collection for quick overview of a broad range of specialized topics (verifying of information is recommended for religious topics).

wikisource.org: online library of free content publications.

## Copyright Notices for the Holy Bible and the Koran

www.ingramcontent.com/pod-product-compliance
Lightning Source LLC
Chambersburg PA
CBHW070855120626
46546CB00001B/17